What Does It Mean *for the* World to Have ONE MIND?

Jerry O'Donnell

AB ASPECT Books
www.ASPECTBooks.com

World rights reserved. This book or any portion thereof may not be copied or reproduced in any form or manner whatever, except as provided by law, without the written permission of the publisher, except by a reviewer who may quote brief passages in a review.

The author assumes full responsibility for the accuracy of all facts and quotations as cited in this book. The opinions expressed in this book are the author's personal views and interpretations, and do not necessarily reflect those of the publisher.

This book is provided with the understanding that the publisher is not engaged in giving spiritual, legal, medical, or other professional advice. If authoritative advice is needed, the reader should seek the counsel of a competent professional.

Copyright © 2016 TEACH Services, Inc.

ISBN-13: 978-1-4796-0694-8 (Paperback)

ISBN-13: 978-1-4796-0695-5 (ePub)

ISBN-13: 978-1-4796-0696-2 (Mobi)

Library of Congress Control Number: 2016906006

All scripture quotations, unless otherwise indicated, are taken from the King James Version. Public domain.

Scripture quotations marked NASB are taken from the New American Standard Bible®, Copyright © 1960, 1962, 1963, 1968, 1971, 1972, 1973, 1975, 1977, 1995 by The Lockman Foundation. Used by permission.

Scripture quotations marked TLB are from The Living Bible copyright © 1971 by Tyndale House Foundation. Used by permission of Tyndale House Publishers Inc., Carol Stream, Illinois 60188. All rights reserved.

Scripture quotations marked (NIV) are taken from the Holy Bible, New International Version®, NIV®. Copyright © 1973, 1978, 1984, 2011 by Biblica, Inc.™ Used by permission of Zondervan. All rights reserved worldwide.

For more information, visit:

http://www.haveonemind.com (1ref.us/bk)

Or write the author at:

info@haveonemind.com (1ref.us/bm)

Table of Contents

Is "Having One Mind" A Good Thing Or a Bad Thing? 5

Is the World Ready For "Having One Mind"? 9
    Can't Each Side Just Have Their Own Opinion And Leave Well Enough Alone?
    How Can We Tell if We Have Reached the Time of Fulfillment?

Are Unbelievers Fairly Judging Christians? 61

Who Is Behind the Push for "One Mind"? 63
    Is There a Push for Having One Mind?
    Can We Know Who the Antichrist is?
    What Are the Identifying Marks?
    May We Have a Summary of That?
    How Does That Compare With the Futuristic Antichrist?
    What Do Historic People Say?
    Why Are There Not More People Who See This?
    How Do These Points Apply To the Real Antichrist?
    How Do These Facts and Apparent Fulfillment Affect Us?

Do People Judge Christianity Through the Wrong Eyes? 143

What Shows Which "One Mind" A Person Is On? 148

What Tools Help Enforce "One Mind"? 166

What Can People Do To Protect Themselves? 173

How Does History Repeat Itself? 202
    How Does Cain and Abel Reveal the Last Days?
    How Does Noah Point to the Last Days?
    How Does What Happened At the Tower of Babel Apply To the Last Days?
    How Does Abraham Reveal the Last Days?
    How Does Lot Parallel With the Last Days?
    How Do the Events of the Exodus Prepare Us for the Last Days?
    How Do the Feast Days Reveal the Activities of History and Especially the Second Coming?
    How Does Building An Ancient Temple Parallel the Last Day Events?
    How Does the Time of Elijah Reveal Last Day Events?
    How Does Daniel and King Nebuchadnezzar Parallel the Last Day Events?
    How Does Daniel and Belshazzar Parallel the Last Day Events?
    How Does Daniel and the Medes And Persians Parallel the Last Day Events?
    How Does John the Baptist Parallel the Last Day Events?
    How Does Jesus' First Coming Parallel the Last Day Events?
    How Does Stephen Parallel the Last Day Events?
    How Do Many More Parallels Reveal the Last Days?

What Is the Sequence of Final Events? 255
    THE FIRST PLAGUE:
    THE SECOND AND THIRD PLAGUES:
    THE FOURTH PLAGUE:
    THE FIFTH PLAGUE:
    THE SIXTH PLAGUE:
    THE SEVENTH PLAGUE:

What Is the Last Opportunity? 269

Biography 301

Is "Having One Mind" A Good Thing Or a Bad Thing?

Close up, it seems that the people of the world do their own thing. Each person has unique tastes in music, clothing, activities, and beyond. But as one steps back, there seems to be just two groups forming. Each of these groups have "one mind" or thinking alike, and depending upon which group one belongs to determines if it is a good thing, or a bad thing.

First off, what does it mean to have "one mind"? Does that mean that all of us turn into robots and think alike on everything? Must everyone have the same favorite color, same favorite food, same favorite television show, same taste in music, same clothing, same schedule, same everything? No, of course not. We do not even have to vote alike yet we can be politically the same.

To have "one mind" is to be in agreement on a broader sense. It is to act and believe in a general sense allowing for uniqueness on the level of the specifics. It is like agreeing that fruit is very important to have in the diet if one is looking to be healthy, but allowing each individual to apply that principle as they would like. Some will eat a number of the same fruit in one day and changing the fruit they eat on a daily basis. One day is a couple bananas and tomorrow is a few oranges; maybe a pear or two the next day. Others may choose to have mixed fruit each day. Others may only like apples and have one each day. Individually, the fruit eaters are expressing their individuality, but collectively, they have "one mind" when it comes to making sure they get fruit in their diet on a daily basis.

Now in regards to our subject matter, on the side of being a good thing or not, the standard of what is good and what is bad needs to be established up front. As one may know, peoples' opinions change from generation to generation, during different stages in life, even during different circumstances. So people establishing what is a good thing and what is a bad thing is probably not a good standard. So then we might turn to a moral authority, like the church, but which one? They contradict each other and change over time as well as being influenced by society instead of the church doing the influencing. Of course people are ready to point to scientific evidence as the standard. Science does declare that fruits are good for health while eating poison ivy is not a good item to use in salads. But even science is known to contradict itself and even those that do not believe in evolution have to believe in it because science has evolved over time, giving evidence at least that self-evolution is possible. As for the actual theory of evolution, that is a different story. As for science being exact, the point in the remark on evolution is was to show that science keeps evolving to the fact that science is not exact. In fact, it can even be influenced by government, government finance, political agendas, and societal opinion. Although we are referring to science to cover all aspects including medical, physics, psychology, and even mathematics, there is enough truth to science to not dismiss it wholly, but as a standard, absolutely not.

Therefore, we are going to suggest the Bible as the standard. Oh, I know that people are going to stop reading this book now because they think the Bible is a construct of human opinions, full of errors, has translation problems, was influenced by male chauvinists, and written in such a way that you can get anything you want out of it, but if we could actually prove that all of those things are lies preventing people from seeing the two "one mind" groups form and then turn around and be able to specifically point out all the dangers of the bad or dark side of "one mind" even nicknamed the dark side and point out all of the specific solutions to how to be on the good or light side of the "one mind" even nicked name as the light side, then would we not have something that we could call a standard? Of course we would.

Let us face this fact. Since people are opinionated, we definitely know that such is not the standard. Since many governments are out for world dominance, having such an agenda means that they will purposely ignore facts, hence, we cannot use them as a standard. Since we can give scientists the exact same experiments with the exact same equipment and environments and yet end up with two very different conclusions, science also cannot be trusted. But the Bible that declares "thou shalt not commit adultery" is consistent throughout the Bible and if followed would avoid unwanted marriages, unwanted babies, diseases, and other problems, it does not matter what country one is from, what the government states, nor what the person's opinion is. That is why it ought to be the standard for our investigation.

And what does the Bible say on the subject of having "one mind"? "Finally, [be ye] all of one mind, having compassion one of another, love as brethren, [be] pitiful, [be] courteous: not rendering evil for evil, or railing for railing: but contrariwise blessing; knowing that ye are thereunto called, that ye should inherit a blessing" (1 Peter 3:8-9). So, a true Christian will have compassion upon other human beings; they will have brotherly love, as well as, sisterly love; they will have pity, be courteous, not seeking to get even, and not firing off insults. In short, true Christians will be a blessing.

That alone should be interesting. With that being the description of a true Christian, one should begin to wonder if there are such in the world today, and that is going to be part of our study. For now though, tuck that thought away asking yourself, "Shouldn't all Christians be like this? And if they are not like this, could they have been influenced by the other side of the 'one mind'? And if so, are people being deceived? What does the Bible say about all of this? Has the lack of true Christianity been foretold?" Rest assure that all of these and more will be answered in due time, but we will tell you that such is the reason for this book because yes, it was prophesied, and even non-Christians are caught up in it.

Now let us take a look at the other side the dark side of having "one mind" and it being a bad thing. In fact, the Bible says, "These have one mind, and shall give their power and strength unto the beast" (Revelation 17:13). So collectively, if the world is not practicing true Christianity, it is strengthening the symbolic beast of Revelation. With "one mind" the beast of Revelation exists. That is what that verse plainly states. And that beast, as we will eventually discover, is none other than the Antichrist described fully in Revelation 13, referred by John in the smaller epistles with the title of Antichrist (1 John 2:18, 2:22; 1 John 4:3; 2 John 1:7), and foretold in the Book of Daniel as a power working against God (Daniel 7:25, 8:25), in other words, being anti God or anti Christ.

Do realize that even though people may not be religious, they are classed into one of these two groups? Obviously they are not classed in the group of true Christians, therefore they must be in the other group. And by classing into these groups, the Bible is basically is saying that we are either a true Christian or we are not. It further means that everything we hear about the Antichrist could actually be more hype than Bible fact.

As we will later investigate into who or what the Antichrist is, we will also provide you with all the information found on the subject to allow you to come to your own conclusion. And the reason you will be able to intelligently come to your own conclusion and cut through the hype is that we are not going to practice that which generated the hype in the first place.

Hype by and large is generated by picking select pieces of information and exaggerating them while burying or at least ignoring that information that provides a true but different conclusion. By revealing every single verse regarding the Antichrist, not only will you be able to identify who or what it is, you will also be able to identify the practices or activities thereof, find out the intentions, and much more. And by knowing that information, you will then be able to see how even the most devoted Christian could be deceived as well as seeing how the most anti God person that exist could actually be helping the Antichrist.

By this time, you may be thinking that for us to declare that there are but two groups is too simplistic of a way of thinking. Anyone could say there are going to be only two groups given any subject. "In the end, there's going to be people who love the color blue and everyone else!" "In the end, there's going to be people who idolize a certain sports team and everyone else!" So is it fair to say that there will be true Christians and everyone else? The answer is "Yes" because unlike those that prefer blue, they are not forcing the world to love blue. Unlike those that favor a particular sports team, they are not forcing everyone to also like that team. But in the end, those that go along with the Antichrist are going to force the rest of the world into compliance or face death.

This is brought out be continuing to read about the bad version of having "one mind" in which the Bible describes them as aligned with the Antichrist and participating in a particular act. The Bible says, "These shall make war with the Lamb" (Revelation 17:14).

So who will these forceful people be? We will see that is all those that are on the dark or ignorance side. And who will those that are considered to be forced into compliance? Those are those that have the knowledge or the light thereof.

Now one thing that you will see very quickly in this book is that we will not be telling you what the Bible means, as so many writers, preachers, religious teachers, and others try to do. The Bible calls that "private interpretation" (2 Peter 1:20), of which is condemned for "knowing this first, that no prophecy of the scripture is of any private interpretation" (2 Peter 1:20). Some that just state that a certain verse means something may be correct, but we are going to take the approach of revealing to everyone that reads this book on how we came to each conclusion and even provide room for anyone else to come to their own conclusion.

For instance, what does the "Lamb" represent in Revelation 17:14? We know it represents something or someone because it would be silly if the entire world is unified upon attacking a defenseless creature and only one particular one. Right now we could state what the word "Lamb" means symbolically, but we just got done telling you that we were not going to do that. Therefore, in searching the Bible, we find that John the Baptist reveals that answer for us. "The next day John seeth Jesus coming unto him, and saith, Behold the Lamb of God, which taketh away the sin of the world" (John 1:29). Therefore, when the world makes war with the Lamb, we conclude that they are actually making war against Jesus Christ, hence the use of the word "Antichrist".

But even the word "war" needs clarification because when people think of war, they think of weapons like guns, tanks, missiles, but that is not always true, especially from a biblical standpoint. The Bible says, "For we wrestle not against flesh and blood, but against principalities, against powers, against the rulers of the darkness of this world, against spiritual wickedness in high [places]" (Ephesians 6:12). Basically, war is not always a physical confrontation. It can be more mental like through protesting, arguing, or campaigning. And of course there are many other types of wars without a bullet or missile. There are financial wars, competitions, cyber, and more.

Now let us see how a non-religious person can align themselves to war against the Lamb in which they do not even believe in. Take for instance how evolutionists could end up warring against Jesus Christ despite not consciously believing in God. By spreading the theory of evolving from a one cell organism and descending from a common ancestor between apes and humans, it fights against the doctrine of Creation, of which Jesus taught. And later, we will see that the war between evolution and creation was predicted nearly 2,000 years ago. But for now, realize that as a description of Jesus, the Bible says, "In the beginning was the Word, and the Word was with God, and the Word was God. The same was in the beginning with God. All things were made by him; and without him was not any thing made that was made" (John 1:1-3). So evolution is a war against Jesus' part in creation.

Now look at the subject of pornography. Again, most of the people involved in pornography have little to no religious belief. How do they war against the Lamb? Well, God is all about modesty. First, he commands "Thou shalt not commit adultery" (Exodus 20:14), which is inclusive of fornication as also commanded to be avoided by Christians. "Write unto them, that they abstain from pollutions of idols, and [from] fornication" (Acts 15:20). On top of that, Jesus specifically said, "Ye have heard that it was said by them of old time, Thou shalt not commit adultery: But I say unto you, That whosoever looketh on a woman to lust after her hath committed adultery with her already in his heart" (Matthew 5:27-28). Therefore, every film, every picture, every suggestiveness including mere sounds, is a battle for not only men but women as well to stay on the side of the Lamb and avoid lusting in the heart or give in and committing adultery both mentally and eventually physically. It is a direct attack against Jesus in simply flaunting what ought not to be flaunted. Even the notion, "If you got it, show it" is very much anti Christ teaching (against Christ).

So as you should be seeing, like it or not, everyone is in one of these two groups. And when we say one of two groups, it is not just simply a classification or preference, again the second group is actively warring against Christ. And when we identify one group is Christian, automatically atheists, people from other religions, even hermits tune this subject out thinking they are not on either side since they do not believe in religion in the first place or they keep to themselves, but the Bible says differently.

What the reader also should be understanding is that the true meaning of the word "Antichrist" simply means to be against Christ. No Hollywood hype; no Christian exaggeration; nothing that makes an exciting movie script. It basically comes down to this, the Lamb, Jesus, taught doctrines; we are either living according to those doctrines or not. But what makes Antichrist exist is that there is an active effort to push a different agenda teaching the opposite of what Christ taught, so then the question comes down to, who are we going to listen to?

Evolution and pornography are but two examples of how non-religious people are involved. Imagine how involved the religious people are. Continue reading and you will find out.

Is the World Ready For "Having One Mind"?

Can't Each Side Just Have Their Own Opinion And Leave Well Enough Alone?

So, does it really matter what people think? Well, not if it would stay in the thoughts or expressed as just opinions. Though true Christians are sad to see people choosing to sin, in reality, true Christians allow people to have that freedom to choose their own opinion. Unfortunately, those on the other side having "one mind", listening to the dark side, are not satisfied in allowing others to have their opposing thoughts and opinions. Eventually, the thoughts are going to switch over into actions. And those actions will result in trying to kill the true Christians (Revelation 13:15). And please note that we are using the phrase "true Christians" because all events that have involved Christians, both in the past and even today, using force is actually examples of Christians in name only and were not true Christians.

This persecuting of the obedient by the jealousy of those that want to live in obedience is not something imaginary. The biblical record contains incident after incident of such being true, and before one quickly dismisses the biblical accounts as being Christian propaganda, ask yourself, "Why would a bunch of people that are promoting obedience to God, including not to lie (Revelation 21:8), turn around and exaggerate, lie, and misrepresent the truth in such biblical accounts?" Any of those actions perpetrated and retained on the records without making a correction would disqualify that person from entering Heaven. Unlike what unbelievers think, true Christians do not just pray to God for forgiveness but let the error stand. True Christians will attempt to correct their wrong as far as possible. A bank robber who steals money from a bank and after the heist "comes to Jesus" does not get to keep the money. True conversion means the repentant bank robber would return the money, even if that means jail time. So with that in mind, let us examine some of these biblical accounts.

First on the scene is the famous story of Cain and Abel. "Cain brought of the fruit of the ground an offering unto the LORD. And Abel, he also brought of the firstlings of his flock and of the fat thereof. And the LORD had respect unto Abel and to his offering: But unto Cain and to his offering he had not respect. And Cain was very wroth, and his countenance fell" (Genesis 4:3-5).

On the surface, it looks like God was arbitrary when He preferred Abel's offering to Cain's. For the novice reader of the Bible, that is easy to conclude, but that is where we need to follow the biblical instruction of how to correctly study the Bible. It is not to simply read and understand fully in a sequential manner. Reading the Bible through reveals the full context of the situation and that is a good start, but to understand the meaning of each of the individual pieces of the account, we must take "precept [must be] upon precept, precept upon precept; line upon line, line upon line; here a little, [and] there a little" (Isaiah 28:10). And unfortunately the lack of this practice is what has lead to the belief that anyone can get whatever they want out of the Bible. We agree that people can justify even wrong actions by the improper method of Bible study, therefore, we conclude then that there is only one true way to uncover the truth and that is by following the instructions given in Isaiah.

So, what does Isaiah mean with lines, and precepts, and little here and there? A line is equivalent to a verse in the Bible. By reading a verse that says, "Thou shalt not kill" (Exodus 20:13) would be an example of a line. Therefore, when we read in Revelation 13:15 about killing, we find that a line or verse in the Bible, specifically in the book called Exodus, that killing is a bad thing. It basically is one of the commandments. So we can conclude that being on the side of trying to kill in Revelation 13:15 is not a good thing, in fact, that is one of the activities eventually exercised by the "one mind" from the dark side.

But we may still have questions, like, "How can this world, especially the nation called the United States, turn on true Christians so much so that they would try to kill them?" Well, that is where the precepts may help. A precept is a principle in general that can be applicable but the wording is not directly identical. In fact, a precept most likely is in a form of a story, like, Cain and Abel. It is not explicitly stating a command about killing, but the principle that we will discover is applicable to the verse from Revelation describing the attempt to kill true Christians.

Now according to Isaiah, so far we are to gather lines and precepts together but this is to be done along with gathering a little here and there. What does that mean? Well, a little is taking the contents of a verse that apply but not include that which does not apply. In other words, Bible verses that contain more than one subject should not create a distraction with all of the content, and therefore we should just pull out that which applies. Be careful though, many over use this method and pull things out of context. That would not be proper Bible study then. Take for instance the verse that describes the future of these killers or murderers. The Bible says, "But the fearful, and unbelieving, and the abominable, and murderers, and whoremongers, and sorcerers, and idolaters, and all liars, shall have their part in the lake which burneth with fire and brimstone: which is the second death" (Revelation 21:8). Now do not get distracted by needing to know who are the fearful, unbelieving, abominable, etc. To apply the instructions of "here a little and there a little", look at the verse this way, "But the … murderers… shall have their part in the lake which burneth with fire and brimstone: which is the second death". By taking a little out of the verse, we conclude that those involved in the killing described in Revelation 13:15 will eventually burn with fire at the end of time, commonly referred to as hell.

In short, the argument that a person can get anything they want from the Bible is a true statement, however, that does not mean that it is obtained through proper Bible understanding. There is a right way to understand the Bible and a whole lot of wrong ways. Even the Bible says so when using the phrase "rightly dividing the word of truth" (2 Timothy 2:15). That strongly implies that there must be a wrongly way to divide the word of truth, or many "wrongly" ways.

Now notice that in trying to understand how people can move from freedom to exercise their religion to trying to kill the true Christians we have moved to the example of Cain and Abel for the precept understanding. However, this too needs further researching to understand why Cain's sacrifice was rejected. Before we do that, do notice that both Cain and Abel worshipped God through their sacrifices. One evidently is doing it according to God's expectations, the other is not and is rejected of God. This tell us that just because Christians meet together and sing nicely or even just take upon themselves the name "Christian" does not mean it is acceptable to God, even to the point that God rejects them. This basically is where we should get the idea that there is a difference between Christians and true Christians, and unfortunately the plain, uncommitted Christians are the ones that have brought a bad name upon Christianity. Were not both Cain and Abel trying to worship God? One was a true worshipper, the other in name only. Much like today, only it is not one group is correct and another is incorrect. There is among us today those that "must worship [him] in spirit and in truth" (John 4:24) and all other versions of worship that is not in spirit and in truth.

But looking at Abel's sacrifice, it was not just acceptable because an animal was used. It was acceptable because "without shedding of blood is no remission" (Hebrews 9:22). Therefore, Abel was admitting he had sinned and was properly doing the remission of sin sacrifice. Further, Abel's sacrifice was pointing to Jesus as His Savior. How? Well, Jesus declared that it was His blood that was the one to be shed to save people by saying, "For this is my blood of the new testament, which is shed for many for the remission of sins" (Matthew 26:28). Further, the Bible says, "[It is] not possible that the blood of bulls and of goats should take away sins"

(Hebrews 10:4), so do not think that all of those animal sacrifices saved anyone in the Old Testament. Those animal sacrifices were necessary to point to Jesus' true sacrifice, the shedding of His blood.

Therefore, Cain was not admitting that he was a sinner, and he was not admitting that his sins needed remitted. He was basically claiming, "I'm saved" and living carelessly with his life. He thought he could not lose salvation so it did not matter how seriously he took sin into consideration. He basically was worshipping God without claiming to need a Savior, like many Christians do today.

It seems church services are all about praising God, but is very light on dealing with sin. In fact, the motto is to make unbelievers comfortable in attending church and not make people reflect upon their sinful lives they are living. Basically, church seems to make sin acceptable. It is the Cain's form of worshipping.

So we further conclude from the Cain and Abel story that as the true Christian, Abel did what God asked, much like the true Christians that promote obedience stating that "God [is] a Spirit: and they that worship him must worship [him] in spirit and in truth" (John 4:24). However, like Cain who declares that there was no absolute truth, today's average Christian that promotes the same thing will eventually have had enough of tolerating the true Christians. They will get so irked by the constant reminder that they are not worshipping the true God and are only offering praises to Him through their unacceptable worship styles and the fact that they are not considering the seriousness of sin. More specifically, the Bible states that "sin is the transgression of the law" (1 John 3:4). Putting it together, true Christians promote the Ten Commandments to be kept, which is what Abel would promote if he were alive today, while those that just call themselves Christians are making every excuse not to be bothered by the Ten Commandments like Cain would do if he were alive today.

This pattern of those that like the concept of salvation, promise of living again after death, and having access to paradise but not wanting to live according to God's rules, is repeated over and over and over again in the Bible even to the point of one group of supposed people claiming to be on God's side attacking the true worshippers.

In addition to Cain and Abel, the Bible also tells of the story of Joseph representing the true people of God and His brothers simply claiming to be the people of God all the while plotting Joseph's death (Genesis 37:20). Then there is King Saul, the earthly king over God's people, who was later rejected of God (1 Samuel 15:23), and sought the true person of God at the time, named David, to slay him (1 Samuel 19:15). Leaping forward, there is the incident that the then King of Israel, Ahab and his wife Jezebel, tried to rid the land of God's prophets (1 Kings 18:4), specifically Elijah (1 Kings 18:17-18). And of course the ultimate example of where the bad or dark side of having "one mind" cannot tolerate the good or light side and just cannot leave them be, is with Jesus, where the Pharisees, the supposed religious leaders of God's people, gathered to make plans in eradicating Jesus (John 11:47-51), and executed those plans (Matthew 27:22).

And so it shall be repeated at the end of time. The bad or dark side of having "one mind" will no longer tolerate the good or light side and want to slay them (Revelation 13:15). And this will be on grander scale as in being globally (Revelation 13:14). In fact, everyone is so involved that "A man's foes [shall be] they of his own household" (Matthew 10:36).

But we need not worry about this today for this is the description of the events for the last generation on earth. Or do we have to worry? Are we getting close to the end of time?

How Can We Tell if We Have Reached the Time of Fulfillment?

The only concern about having "one mind" and being on the dark side is in regards to the time in which such people will try to rid the world of the good or light side. This is predicted to happen on a mass scale at the end of time. Today, there are pockets of intolerance of those claiming that they have the light and are trying to share it, but on a worldwide scale, that does not seem to be happening right now, so why the concern? Well, at some point it is going to happen, and when it does, it is going to be too late to warn anyone. Books like this will not be published. So the real question is, are we getting close to this happening causing the urgency of this material?

Oh, bring up the words "last days" to some Christians and they will tell you that we are there, and as part of the evidence, they will quote the famous references of earthquakes and wars. Just about everyone is tired of hearing those proofs, so much so that the famous rebuttal is on the tip of everyone's lips, believers and non-believers alike, and that is, "We've always had earthquakes and wars. My grandparents and great grandparents were told that Jesus would return in their lifetime and they're dead!"

This is the problem with most Christians today. They hop on some type of fluffy feeling Christianity but have no depth. And there are plenty of them out there giving Christianity a really bad name. There is a lot more to the study of end time timing than what meets the eye, definitely more than earthquakes and wars.

So let us take a moment and go beyond earthquakes and wars and see what else the Bible uses to describe the last days to be like, and before one dismisses this study by throwing Jesus' words at us saying, "But of that day and hour knoweth no [man], no, not the angels of heaven, but my Father only" (Matthew 24:36), do also recall other words like, "Now learn a parable of the fig tree; When his branch is yet tender, and putteth forth leaves, ye know that summer [is] nigh: So likewise ye, when ye shall see all these things, know that it is near, [even] at the doors" (Matthew 24:32-33). Paul even wrote, "Ye, brethren, are not in darkness, that that day should overtake you as a thief" (1 Thessalonians 5:4). From the perspective that the Bible does not contradict itself, these verses tell us that we ought not set dates, however, we should realize when we are getting closer to the end of time or not. In fact, notice the use of the word "darkness". That means ignorance and hence why we use the phrase "dark side". It is not a movie quote but rather biblical terms. We also propose that those on the wrong side of having "one mind" are the ones in ignorance on the subject of the "last day" events.

And for those that wonder why God just did not reveal the date of Jesus' return, it is easy to answer. If Jesus identified even just the year or the decade of His return, people would live very sinful lives knowing full well that they would enter the grave before the second coming. They would then take a risk of living sinful lives and only when they are nearing their own death, they would attempt to pull off a last moment conversion. Well, even those that attempt such today should realize that "God is not mocked: for whatsoever a man soweth, that shall he also reap" (Galatians 6:7).

It is true that there are deathbed conversions like the thief on the cross who uttered, "Lord, remember me when thou comest into thy kingdom" (Luke 23:42), however, God "knoweth the secrets of the heart" (Psalms 44:21). He knows the heart that thinks, "I can purposely enjoy sin, then claim forgiveness at the end, and still get into heaven." God sees through this plan and will end up rejecting such pretended conversions. Grace is not a free ticket to sin as so many Christians portray it to be, and they turn many others off from being a Christian because of their hypocrisy. Unfortunately, such Christianity seems to be so prevalent today that it is easy to judge all of Christianity as believing this wrong use of grace. How sad it is from the perspective of true Christians, but be glad as well, for that is one of the signs that many Christians do not quote as a sign of the last days and yet it is a sign! We will discuss that in detail in a bit.

So, let us take a journey through the Bible looking at as many of the references as we can find and do an honest Bible study on the subject of last day events. We will admit though that we personally do believe we are in the last days or we would not be putting any of this into print. Now do not dismiss our conclusion like we are part of the "earthquakes and wars" people. We will try to present the material in an unbiased manner as possible trying to let you come to your own conclusion. Of course it will be hard to pull such off when we have even non-biblical evidence that points to time running out.

On January 24, 2015, in Scientific American, an article appeared entitled, "Doomsday Clock Set at 3 Minutes to Midnight", in which declares that we are very close to things falling apart in this world and entering into a catastrophic doom. Although it is not as close to midnight as it was in 1953, being but 2 minutes away, it is a realization that even secular (non-religious) sense that something is going to happen.

Now, from a Biblical perspective, let us examine the verses. Instead of just taking each verse one at a time and writing up an elaborate discussion that concludes with evidence that points to the fact we are living in the last days as so many other authors do, we thought it better to provide the list of verses untainted that apply to the last day events and in an unadulterated method let you conclude your opinion before we provide any influence.

- Matthew 24:4-15 says, "And Jesus answered and said unto them, Take heed that no man deceive you. For many shall come in my name, saying, I am Christ; and shall deceive many. And ye shall hear of wars and rumours of wars: see that ye be not troubled: for all [these things] must come to pass, but the end is not yet. For nation shall rise against nation, and kingdom against kingdom: and there shall be famines, and pestilences, and earthquakes, in divers places. All these [are] the beginning of sorrows. Then shall they deliver you up to be afflicted, and shall kill you: and ye shall be hated of all nations for my name's sake. And then shall many be offended, and shall betray one another, and shall hate one another. And many false prophets shall rise, and shall deceive many. And because iniquity shall abound, the love of many shall wax cold. But he that shall endure unto the end, the same shall be saved. And this gospel of the kingdom shall be preached in all the world for a witness unto all nations; and then shall the end come. When ye therefore shall see the abomination of desolation, spoken of by Daniel the prophet, stand in the holy place, (whoso readeth, let him understand:)"

- Matthew 24:21-31 says, "For then shall be great tribulation, such as was not since the beginning of the world to this time, no, nor ever shall be. And except those days should be shortened, there should no flesh be saved: but for the elect's sake those days shall be shortened. Then if any man shall say unto you, Lo, here [is] Christ, or there; believe [it] not. For there shall arise false Christs, and false prophets, and shall shew great signs and wonders; insomuch that, if [it were] possible, they shall deceive the very elect. Behold, I have told you before. Wherefore if they shall say unto you, Behold, he is in the desert; go not forth: behold, [he is] in the secret chambers; believe [it] not. For as the lightning cometh out of the east, and shineth even unto the west; so shall also the coming of the Son of man be. For wheresoever the carcase is, there will the eagles be gathered together. Immediately after the tribulation of those days shall the sun be darkened, and the moon shall not give her light, and the stars shall fall from heaven, and the powers of the heavens shall be shaken: And then shall appear the sign of the Son of man in heaven: and then shall all the tribes of the earth mourn, and they shall see the Son of man coming in the clouds of heaven with power and great glory. And he shall send his angels with a great sound of a trumpet, and they shall gather together his elect from the four winds, from one end of heaven to the other."

- Matthew 24:37-30 says, "But as the days of Noe [were], so shall also the coming of the Son of man be. For as in the days that were before the flood they were eating and drinking, marrying and giving in marriage, until the day that Noe entered into the ark, And knew not until the flood came, and took them all away; so shall also the coming of the Son of man be."

  - Genesis 6:1-5 states, "And it came to pass, when men began to multiply on the face of the earth, and daughters were born unto them, That the sons of God saw the daughters of men that they [were] fair; and they took them wives of all which they chose. And the LORD said, My spirit shall not always strive with man, for that he also [is] flesh: yet his days shall be an hundred and twenty years. There were giants in the earth in those days; and also after that, when the sons of God came in unto the daughters of men, and they bare [children] to them, the same [became] mighty men which [were] of old, men of renown. And GOD saw that the wickedness of man [was] great in the earth, and [that] every imagination of the thoughts of his heart [was] only evil continually."

  - Genesis 6:12-13 tells us, "And God looked upon the earth, and, behold, it was corrupt; for all flesh had corrupted his way upon the earth. And God said unto Noah, The end of all flesh is come before me; for the earth is filled with violence through them; and, behold, I will destroy them with the earth."

  - 1 Peter 3:20 declares, "Which sometime were disobedient, when once the longsuffering of God waited in the days of Noah, while the ark was a preparing, wherein few, that is, eight souls were saved by water."

  - 2 Peter 2:5 says, "And spared not the old world, but saved Noah the eighth [person], a preacher of righteousness, bringing in the flood upon the world of the ungodly;"

- Matthew 24:45-51 states, "Who then is a faithful and wise servant, whom his lord hath made ruler over his household, to give them meat in due season? Blessed [is] that servant, whom his lord when he cometh shall find so doing. Verily I say unto you, That he shall make him ruler over all his goods. But and if that evil servant shall say in his heart, My lord delayeth his coming; And shall begin to smite [his] fellowservants, and to eat and drink with the drunken; The lord of that servant shall come in a day when he looketh not for [him], and in an hour that he is not aware of, And shall cut him asunder, and appoint [him] his portion with the hypocrites: there shall be weeping and gnashing of teeth."

- Luke 17:22-27 tells us, "And he said unto the

disciples, The days will come, when ye shall desire to see one of the days of the Son of man, and ye shall not see [it]. And they shall say to you, See here; or, see there: go not after [them], nor follow [them]. For as the lightning, that lighteneth out of the one [part] under heaven, shineth unto the other [part] under heaven; so shall also the Son of man be in his day. But first must he suffer many things, and be rejected of this generation. And as it was in the days of Noe, so shall it be also in the days of the Son of man. They did eat, they drank, they married wives, they were given in marriage, until the day that Noe entered into the ark, and the flood came, and destroyed them all."

- Luke 17:28-32 informs us, "Likewise also as it was in the days of Lot; they did eat, they drank, they bought, they sold, they planted, they builded; But the same day that Lot went out of Sodom it rained fire and brimstone from heaven, and destroyed [them] all. Even thus shall it be in the day when the Son of man is revealed. In that day, he which shall be upon the housetop, and his stuff in the house, let him not come down to take it away: and he that is in the field, let him likewise not return back. Remember Lot's wife."

  ◦ Genesis 13:13 mentions, "But the men of Sodom [were] wicked and sinners before the LORD exceedingly."

  ◦ Genesis 18:20 says, "And the LORD said, Because the cry of Sodom and Gomorrah is great, and because their sin is very grievous;"

  ◦ Genesis 19:4-5 records, "But before they lay down, the men of the city, [even] the men of Sodom, compassed the house round, both old and young, all the people from every quarter: And they called unto Lot, and said unto him, Where [are] the men which came in to thee this night? bring them out unto us, that we may know them."

  ◦ Genesis 19:12-14 says, "And the men said unto Lot, Hast thou here any besides? son in law, and thy sons, and thy daughters, and whatsoever thou hast in the city, bring [them] out of this place: For we will destroy this place, because the cry of them is waxen great before the face of the LORD; and the LORD hath sent us to destroy it. And Lot went out, and spake unto his sons in law, which married his daughters, and said, Up, get you out of this place; for the LORD will destroy this city. But he seemed as one that mocked unto his sons in law."

  ◦ Genesis 19:26 states, "But his wife looked back from behind him, and she became a pillar of salt."

  ◦ Isaiah 1:9-10 tells us, "Except the LORD of hosts had left unto us a very small remnant, we should have been as Sodom, [and] we should have been like unto Gomorrah. Hear the word of the LORD, ye rulers of Sodom; give ear unto the law of our God, ye people of Gomorrah."

  ◦ Isaiah 3:8-9 brings us, "For Jerusalem is ruined, and Judah is fallen: because their tongue and their doings [are] against the LORD, to provoke the eyes of his glory. The shew of their countenance doth witness against them; and they declare their sin as Sodom, they hide [it] not. Woe unto their soul! for they have rewarded evil unto themselves."

  ◦ Jeremiah 23:14 reveals, "I have seen also in the prophets of Jerusalem an horrible thing: they commit adultery, and walk in lies: they strengthen also the hands of evildoers, that none doth return from his wickedness: they are all of them unto me as Sodom, and the inhabitants thereof as Gomorrah."

  ◦ Ezekiel 16:49-50 says, "Behold, this was the iniquity of thy sister Sodom, pride, fulness of bread, and abundance of idleness was in her and in her daughters, neither did she strengthen the hand of the poor and needy. And they were haughty, and committed abomination before me: therefore I took them away as I saw [good]."

  ◦ 2 Peter 2:6 tells us, "And turning the cities of Sodom and Gomorrha into ashes condemned [them] with an overthrow, making [them] an ensample unto those that after should live ungodly;"

  ◦ Jude 1:7-8 states, "Even as Sodom and Gomorrha, and the cities about them in like manner, giving themselves over to fornication, and going after strange flesh, are set forth for an example, suffering the vengeance of eternal fire. Likewise also these [filthy] dreamers defile the flesh, despise dominion, and speak evil of dignities."

- Luke 21:8-19 mentions, "And he said, Take heed that ye be not deceived: for many shall come in my name, saying, I am [Christ]; and the time draweth near: go ye not therefore after them. But when ye shall hear of wars and commotions, be not terrified: for these things must first come to pass; but the end [is] not by and by. Then said he unto them, Nation shall rise against nation, and kingdom against kingdom: And great earthquakes shall be in divers places, and famines, and pestilences; and fearful sights and great signs shall there be from heaven. But before all these, they shall lay their hands on you, and persecute [you], delivering [you] up to the synagogues, and into prisons, being brought before kings and rulers for my name's sake. And it shall turn to you for a testimony. Settle [it] therefore in your hearts, not to meditate before what ye shall answer: For I will give you a mouth and wisdom, which all your adversaries shall not be able to gainsay nor resist. And ye shall be betrayed both by parents, and brethren, and kinsfolks, and friends; and [some] of you shall they cause to be put to death. And ye shall be hated of all [men] for my name's sake. But there shall not an hair of your head perish. In your patience possess ye your souls."

- Luke 21:26 brings us, "Men's hearts failing them for fear, and for looking after those things which are coming on the earth: for the powers of heaven shall be shaken."

- 2 Peter 3:3-7 states, "Knowing this first, that there shall come in the last days scoffers, walking after their own lusts, And saying, Where is the promise of his coming? for since the fathers fell asleep, all things continue as [they were] from the beginning of the creation. For this they willingly are ignorant of, that by the word of God the heavens were of old, and the earth standing out of the water and in the water: Whereby the world that then was, being overflowed with water, perished: But the heavens and the earth, which are now, by the same word are kept in store, reserved unto fire against the day of judgment and perdition of ungodly men."

- 2 Timothy 3:1-5 says, "This know also, that in the last days perilous times shall come. For men shall be lovers of their own selves, covetous, boasters, proud, blasphemers, disobedient to parents, unthankful, unholy, Without natural affection, trucebreakers, false accusers, incontinent, fierce, despisers of those that are good, Traitors, heady, highminded, lovers of pleasures more than lovers of God; Having a form of godliness, but denying the power thereof: from such turn away."

- 2 Timothy 4:3-4 mentions, "For the time will come when they will not endure sound doctrine; but after their own lusts shall they heap to themselves teachers, having itching ears; And they shall turn away [their] ears from the truth, and shall be turned unto fables."

- 1 Thessalonians 5:2-5 declares, "For yourselves know perfectly that the day of the Lord so cometh as a thief in the night. For when they shall say, Peace and safety; then sudden destruction cometh upon them, as travail upon a woman with child; and they shall not escape. But ye, brethren, are not in darkness, that that day should overtake you as a thief. Ye are all the children of light, and the children of the day: we are not of the night, nor of darkness."

- 2 Thessalonians 2:9-10 points out, "[Even him], whose coming is after the working of Satan with all power and signs and lying wonders, And with all deceivableness of unrighteousness in them that perish; because they received not the love of the truth, that they might be saved."

- Daniel 12:4 says, "But thou, O Daniel, shut up the words, and seal the book, [even] to the time of the end: many shall run to and fro, and knowledge shall be increased."

- 1 Corinthians 10:1-11 tells us, "Moreover, brethren, I would not that ye should be ignorant, how that all our fathers were under the cloud, and all passed through the sea; And were all baptized unto Moses in the cloud and in the sea; And did all eat the same spiritual meat; And did all drink the same spiritual drink: for they drank of that spiritual Rock that followed them: and that Rock was Christ. But with many of them God was not well pleased: for they were overthrown in the wilderness. Now these things were our examples, to the intent we should not lust after evil things, as they also lusted. Neither be ye idolaters, as [were] some of them; as it is written, The people sat down to eat and drink, and rose up to play. Neither let us commit fornication, as some of them committed, and fell in one day three and twenty thousand. Neither let us tempt Christ, as some of them also tempted, and were destroyed of serpents. Neither murmur ye, as some of them also murmured, and were destroyed of the destroyer. Now all these things happened unto them for ensamples: and they are written for our admonition, upon whom the ends of the world are come."

- James 5:3 states, "Your gold and silver is cankered; and the rust of them shall be a witness against you, and shall eat your flesh as it were fire. Ye have heaped treasure together for the last days."

  ○ Acts 2:17-21 points out, "And it shall come to pass in the last days, saith God, I will pour out of my Spirit upon all flesh: and your sons and your daughters shall prophesy, and your young men shall see visions, and your old men shall dream dreams: And on my servants and on my handmaidens I will pour out in those days of my Spirit; and they shall prophesy: And I will shew wonders in heaven above, and signs in the earth beneath; blood, and fire, and vapour of smoke: The sun shall be turned into darkness, and the moon into blood, before that great and notable day of the Lord come: And it shall come to pass, [that] whosoever shall call on the name of the Lord shall be saved."

- Proverbs 30:11-14 mentions, "[There is] a generation [that] curseth their father, and doth not bless their mother. [There is] a generation [that are] pure in their own eyes, and [yet] is not washed from their filthiness. [There is] a generation, O how lofty are their eyes! and their eyelids are lifted up. [There is] a generation, whose teeth [are as] swords, and their jaw teeth [as] knives, to devour the poor from off the earth, and the needy from [among] men."

As you see, there is more than just earthquakes and wars to be discussed. All of these verses, and probably others as well, for we do not claim to have exhausted the list of verses despite our best efforts to do so, need to be fulfilled. That means all of them together must point to a specific period in time in which when we see them all happening, we can know we are in the last days.

Individually, it is true that we always have had earthquakes. It is true, we have always had wars. But not all of these events have happened at the same time, even if they all have happened on and off. It is when the all line up that we get a more specific time period.

But before we take our first step into those verses, let us make sure we are talking the same language. You see, part of the confusion in understanding the Bible, for that matter, understanding each other, is that words have multiple meanings. I can say one word with a certain intent while you are thinking of another. Look at the word "end" for instance. What does it really mean? Some read the verse, "For Christ [is] the end of the law for righteousness to every one that believeth" (Romans 10:4) and conclude incorrectly that when Jesus came, He ushered in the time of "Just believe" with the law of the Ten Commandments needing to be obeyed coming to an end. If that is how we are to understand the word "end" to mean, then I can use the Bible to prove that God no longer exists. "Ye have heard of the patience of Job, and have seen the end of the Lord; that the Lord is very pitiful, and of tender mercy" (James 5:11). So if the word "end" means that it is over, then God ceased to exist in the time of Job, which is not true, but if one were to understand that the word "end" also means "result", then we can understand the "results of the Lord" as well as the "result of the law for righteousness." Neither God nor the law has ceased. Both have created results. The law, because we have broken it at least once, results in needing a Savior, specifically, Jesus Christ.

Now in looking at the term, "Last Days", a lot of people conclude it to mean the last couple of years or so on this planet when in fact it is a longer period of time than that. What we humans perceive with the term is that it applies to our life time when it is actually referring to the period of time as a portion of the entire world history. In other words, the Bible was written from God's perspective. We get a hint at the true meaning of "last days" being a longer period of time than just a few years by the use of the phrase, "All these [are] the beginning of sorrows" (Matthew 24:8). So, we propose that just like a movie, we know things are beginning to wrap up when all of our questions, or at least most of them, have been answered, but there are still a some loose ends to tie up. A two-hour movie may reserve the last five minutes as the ending to the movie to accomplish this. Five minutes out of two hours is about five percent of the time. If we were to apply that percentage, which is admittedly an arbitrary amount, towards the period of time from Adam and Eve to the present, we would take approximately six thousand years and find that the last days would last a period of about two hundred or so years. So yes, if Jesus is about to return, our great grandparents should have heard about the earthquakes, and it should be no surprise that today's scoffers of the second coming would say, "Where is the promise of his coming? for since the fathers fell asleep, all things continue as [they were] from the beginning of the creation" (2 Peter 3:4), or more modernly, "Where's the second coming? My parents, and their parents, and their parents, etc. are all dead and nothing much has changed since people of the 1800's claimed Jesus was returning in their day!" So, when we say "last days", we are talking about the period of time in which spans more than a person's life time. God even says, "For my thoughts [are] not your thoughts, neither [are] your ways my ways, saith the LORD" (Isaiah 55:8).

Now we will place before you the perspective we have compiled that not only identifies that we indeed are living in the last days that spans more than a century, but maybe even point to the fact that we are at the tail end of this period all the while reserving the fact that you only can make that determination for yourself. Now we are not going so supply you with a whole lot of statistics to prove our point because we know your intelligent enough to realize statistics really are in the eyes of the beholder, and depending on the source, we could end up just throwing numbers at each other. What actually matters is the perspective in which they are placed. So let us take each of the verses point by point, not necessarily in sequence, especially since some of the points are repeated.

POINT 1:
Deception

In Matthew 24:4-5, the Bible says, "And Jesus answered and said unto them, Take heed that no man deceive you. For many shall come in my name, saying, I am Christ; and shall deceive many." In Matthew 24:11, it says, "And many false prophets shall rise, and shall deceive many." Again in Matthew 24:24, it says, "For there shall arise false Christs, and false prophets, and shall shew great signs and wonders; insomuch that, if [it were] possible, they shall deceive the very elect."

Not once, not twice, but three times Jesus makes reference to deception being an issue. This is the single most important concern that Jesus had on His mind because there is no other sign of the last days that is repeated as this one is. This deception will come from people in general, from people coming claiming to be Christ, and from false prophets. The reason deception comes from multiple sources is because people, especially supposed Christians, get too smug for their own good. "Oh, I can spot a false prophet or a Christ impersonator a mile away," they say. Satan even likes that some people are gullible and do fall for the obvious because that further makes such people smug in their comfortableness, but even that is the deception. Satan knows that hardly a person would ever suspect a preacher to be a deceiver, knowingly or unknowingly, who gives all they have to the poor, is so kind, so educated in the Bible, would even give the shirt off their backs.

Now before we go any further, let us pause and make sure we are thinking the same thing when we see these words. First of all, Jesus did not say that prophets would arise in the last days. He stated that there will be false prophets. That means there are true prophets that will exist. So one aspect of deception that people, even among Christians, could be deceived upon is to believe that there are no modern day prophets. Interestingly, that contradicts the Bible for it says, "And it shall come to pass in the last days, saith God, I will pour out of my Spirit upon all flesh: and your sons and your daughters shall prophesy, and your young men shall see visions, and your old men shall dream dreams: And on my servants and on my handmaidens I will pour out in those days of my Spirit; and they shall prophesy: And I will shew wonders in heaven above, and signs in the earth beneath; blood, and fire, and vapour of smoke: The sun shall be turned into darkness, and the moon into blood, before that great and notable day of the Lord come: And it shall come to pass, [that] whosoever shall call on the name of the Lord shall be saved" (Acts 2:17-21).

Second of all, let us make sure we understand the meaning of the phrase "people coming claiming to be Christ." The Bible actually said, "For many shall come in my name, saying, I am Christ" (Matthew 24:5). To come in Jesus name is not reserved to those pretending to be Jesus Christ. Another way of saying the words "I am Christ" is to say, "I am a Christian." The word Christian was not universally recognized at the time Jesus was walking this earth in human form, in fact, the Bible says, "The disciples were called Christians first in Antioch" (Acts 11:26). So, another way the Bible makes reference to the name Christian or being of Christ is by saying, "The name of Christ." Therefore, we see fulfillment in these deceivers not only pretending to be Christ Himself, but also pretending to even be a Christian minister, for that matter, just pretending to be a Christian.

Have you ever noticed how many people start off introductions by saying, "I'm a Christian" and present themselves as able to speak in authority? That is not all wrong for I am doing it right now with this book, but when someone says, "I am a Christian" and proceeds to justify error or human theories regarding God and His ways, that is when it is wrong.

It becomes more evident that Jesus was referring to false Christians and false ministers in general when He also stated elsewhere, "Not every one that saith unto me, Lord, Lord, shall enter into the kingdom of heaven; but he that doeth the will of my Father which is in heaven. Many will say to me in that day, Lord, Lord, have we not prophesied in thy name? and in thy name have cast out devils? and in thy name done many wonderful works? And then will I profess unto them, I never knew you: depart from me, ye that work iniquity" (Matthew 7:21-23). It sure looks like a bunch of faith healers and do-gooders are going to be missing out on heaven, yet they are deceived because they think they are saved by simply taking on the title Christian. All they did was spread their iniquity or sinning around under the guise of the title Christian, hence, the deception.

Unfortunately such people outnumber the true Christians so much so that hardly a true Christian is heard or even seen. The many that are described to miss out on the Kingdom of God is contrasted by what Jesus said about the quantity that are saved. "Enter ye in at the strait gate: for wide [is] the gate, and broad [is] the way, that leadeth to destruction, and many there be which go in thereat: Because strait [is] the gate, and narrow [is] the way, which leadeth unto life, and few there be that find it" (Matthew 7:13-14). So, a further unfortunate thing about this large portion of supposed Christians is that non-believers, even atheists, get turned off from these pretentious ways. This only furthers Satan's deceptions. On one hand, he has the people thinking they are Christian and cannot be awaken to the fact that they are living in sin preparing to be lost, and then on the other, Satan pushes away all who would honestly consider studying these things out.

So, with the two premises of "last days" spanning more than just a person's life time and deceivers being more than Christ imposters, let us just look at today's preachers. Are they all of God? How could they when they contradict each other? Is God contradictory? Of course not "For God is not [the author] of confusion" (1 Corinthians 14:33). Further, the hundreds of denominations all technically separate from one another cannot all be right. The explosion of these denominations over the past two hundred years all claiming to be Christian yet contain very different practices and teachings adds to the deceptions, especially when many claim that if one does not practice them they will be lost. Further, how many of the television evangelists are really truly Christ's, and how many are just for show given into riches, fame, and other secular advantages? They all claim to come in the name of Christ, but logic dictates that they all cannot be of Christ or they would all speak the same thing and be of one denomination.

Now how this becomes a fulfillment is that up through the 1500's, there was pretty much one or two denominations, Catholic and Eastern Orthodox, maybe a few smaller groups as well. After the rise of Protestants, there has been an explosion of such denominations. According to the Center for the Study of Global Christianity at Gordon-Conwell Theological Seminary, there were approximately 1,600 denominations in the year 1900. During the following century, they grew to an estimated 34,000 denominations by 2000; and in 2012, there is an estimated 43,000 different denominations.

What is also very interesting is that there are two primary deceptions that so many Christians are caught up in. Sure, they may not be quoted exactly the same way, but there is enough evidence in the verses to conclude what Jesus meant. That means that all who believe in at least any of these two deceptions is being deceived, hence the importance of this material because we come to all not to condemn but to invite into Bible truth. Please do not be stubborn, eternal life is on the line. This is no time to be prideful. As the Bible says, "Pride [goeth] before destruction" (Proverbs 16:18), and the ultimate destruction is hell. Why someone would rather hold onto a false theory so as to avoid what they think is humiliating in accepting the fact they were deceived and give up eternal life is beyond me. Let us face it, all of us have been deceived at one point or another. Those especially who are escaping the deceptions are commissioned to go and teach (Matthew 28:19), but not just anything. Jesus said that we are to be "Teaching them to observe all things whatsoever I have commanded you" (Matthew 28:20). And keep in mind, "the truth shall make you free" (John 8:32); not truths. So yes, there is a single truth and we are being bold enough to say, "Here it is for you to examine."

And to place the seriousness upon this even further, people are not going to be lost just because they worshipped the Antichrist. They are not even going to be lost because they continued sinning. It is "with all deceivableness of unrighteousness in them that perish; because they received not the love of the truth, that they might be saved" (2 Thessalonians 2:10). People will be lost because they will not take the time to know the truth. People will be lost because they do not want to hear the truth that their sin is a sin. People will be lost because they do not want to hear who truly is the Antichrist. People will be lost because they have been deceived to thinking there is no absolute truth when it comes to the Bible, or they believe that no one can discover Bible truth. If that were so, why did Jesus say, "Search the scriptures; for in them ye think ye have eternal life: and they are they which testify of me" (John 5:39)?" That in itself declares that our preconceived ideas would be corrected if we searched the scriptures.

In fact, if no one can find the Bible truth, why even have the Bible? Now before one jumps onboard and say, "Exactly!", realize that we do have a Bible; realize it was compiled over a two thousand year period; realize that forty authors spanning those centuries did not by accident speak all the same thing when speaking on the same topic. And the Bible has not survived another two thousand years by itself despite laws banning the reading of it, attempts to burn it, and even attempts to discredit it. All of these things point to a miracle. There must be something special about this collection of books incorporated into the Bible.

And just how special is this Bible? It is special enough to have in the last days an unearthing of the Old Testament scrolls proving the accuracy of translations, recordings, and the ineffectiveness of time trying to distort the contents. God basically confirmed the majority of the Bible by having those scrolls be discovered. If almost three quarters of the Bible can be so accurate over time, I personally have faith that such is true with the remainder of the Bible, the New Testament.

So with that in mind, the first of the two primary deceptions is given as a warning regarding Jesus' return, in which it is said, "Wherefore if they shall say unto you, Behold, he is in the desert; go not forth" (Matthew 24:26). Unfortunately, there are several ministries or denominations that teach that Jesus will return and be in the desert by misquoting other scriptures. For instance, David and Zoë Sulem use Isaiah 40:3-5 that contains the word desert, but stronger still, is The Church of Jesus Christ of Latter-day Saints (also commonly referred to as Mormons) who teach the same thing, that people are to "make straight in the desert a highway for our God" (Isaiah 40:3). Now approaching the Bible as a book that does not contradict itself, and with a stark warning not to go out looking in the desert for Jesus, the use of Isaiah 40:3 must be in error.

Now again, we say this not to attack anyone or any denomination for God loves everyone, however, God has a principle. "The times of this ignorance God winked at; but now commandeth all men every where to repent" (Acts 17:30). We only mention these examples to show fulfillment of the verses.

Consider this, if you were in a building that was on fire and you knew the building would be collapsing soon, how delicate would you be treating the message regarding the destruction of the building and the fact that it is on fire? Do keep in mind that people may accuse you of hating heat, hating fires, hating even buildings. People may join forces and treat you like an outcast and say, "Why can't you just get along and let everyone enjoy their own living space?" This would especially be heard from those that do not smell smoke, see no fire, and hear no screams. People may accuse you of disturbing the peace, being obnoxious, being a "know it all", and even demand to know how you know this stuff and everyone else does not. People may demand scientific proof that the building is actually on fire or even ready to collapse. There may be people who do not believe in fire if they were never exposed to such. Some may rebut your call to get out of the building with, "What do you mean this building will collapse? It's been here all my life and it will continue as it always has!" And for those that know anything of the Bible, these are the scenarios presented at the end of time towards the people trying to help share the true gospel. And like someone concern for other's physical safety, us with the gospel are concerned about everyone's spiritual safety.

But even the first deception is not as concerning as the second deception, which seems to be catching just about every Christian. Jesus said, "Behold, [he is] in the secret chambers; believe [it] not" (Matthew 24:26). Now explicitly, I do not know a single preacher or church member that uses the words "secret chambers." So many dismiss this warning as something yet future or some other misunderstanding, however, not by coincidence, Jesus followed up His warning with "For as the lightning cometh out of the east, and shineth even unto the west; so shall also the coming of the Son of man be" (Matthew 24:27). The Book of Revelation even states, "Behold, he cometh with clouds; and every eye shall see him" (Revelation 1:7). So since every eye shall witness the second coming and since lightning that lights up the whole sky from east to west is seen by everyone, we can only conclude that the second warning deals with a message that teaches that the second coming is somehow executed in secret. More specifically, the teaching of the Secret Rapture is the massive error that so many Christians across so many denominations are buying into.

This of course is going to cause an uproar to hear that we are attacking such a prevalent, basic belief, so let us take a moment to honestly look at the evidence that the Bible in no way teaches a secret rapture, and let us not just work off of an implication as revealed thus far, even though it is a pretty strong argument.

In fact, did you know that the secret rapture theory is just that? It is an implication. It comes primarily from the Book of Revelation in which the word church is used in chapters 1, 2, 3, and at the very end of 22, the last chapter. Since Jewish references are made between chapters 3 and 22, it is assumed that there must be some type of rapture beforehand of the church leaving Jews to face the Antichrist, hence the secret rapture. You would think though, that such a subject would get more attention from the other books of the Bible, but again, only implications are used, like saying, "Well, Jesus is coming like a thief and thieves operate in secret." That may be true however, to base an entire theory on an implication is reckless. So we will look at all such verses and determine what is meant by Jesus coming as a thief.

And in regards to addressing the lack of the word "church" in chapters 4 through 21, what the supporters of the secret rapture fail to understand is that Christians are really Jews. "For he is not a Jew, which is one outwardly; neither [is that] circumcision, which is outward in the flesh: But he [is] a Jew, which is one inwardly; and circumcision [is that] of the heart, in the spirit, [and] not in the letter; whose praise [is] not of men, but of God" (Romans 2:28-29). You see, only Jews are going to heaven. Not all of them; just the ones circumcised in the heart, which means converted people. Physically, there may not be a drop of blood that is Jewish, but spiritually, they are accounted to be a Jew.

Now look at the word "thief" in relationship to Jesus, the first such reference is in Matthew 24, the famous chapter of last day events. Jesus said, "But know this, that if the goodman of the house had known in what watch the thief would come" (Matthew 24:43), however, nowhere is Jesus intending to teach secretive arrival. In full context, you will see the second description of a thief is more prevalent, and that is of time. A thief does not announce when he will arrive, and that is the only lesson to be taken from Jesus full words. "Watch therefore: for ye know not what hour your Lord doth come. But know this, that if the goodman of the house had known in what watch the thief would come, he would have watched, and would not have suffered his house to be broken up. Therefore be ye also ready: for in such an hour as ye think not the Son of man cometh" (Matthew 24:42-44). Even notice the last sentence that confirms the lesson. There is no mention whatsoever about how Jesus will arrive; it is all about when, which,

like a thief, we do not know as the opening verse stated.

The second such reference is very similar to Matthew's account and will just be shown in full context hoping you will also see that there is nothing about how (secret) Jesus is showing up, but again, it is all about not knowing when. "Blessed [are] those servants, whom the lord when he cometh shall find watching: verily I say unto you, that he shall gird himself, and make them to sit down to meat, and will come forth and serve them. And if he shall come in the second watch, or come in the third watch, and find [them] so, blessed are those servants. And this know, that if the goodman of the house had known what hour the thief would come, he would have watched, and not have suffered his house to be broken through. Be ye therefore ready also: for the Son of man cometh at an hour when ye think not" (Luke 12:37-40).

The third reference to Jesus coming as a thief is the closest opportunity to imply something more than time, but you will see it again that it falls short of declaring Jesus appearing secretly. The verse in question states, "For yourselves know perfectly that the day of the Lord so cometh as a thief in the night" (1 Thessalonians 5:2). Even the verse states the word "day", which is a time reference and not a how reference. Additionally, the surrounding verses again bring out time. Looking at the verse prior, it says, "But of the times and the seasons, brethren, ye have no need that I write unto you" (1 Thessalonians 5:1). Clearly we are in the context of time again. And the same is true with the verses after, "For when they shall say, Peace and safety; then sudden destruction cometh upon them, as travail upon a woman with child; and they shall not escape. But ye, brethren, are not in darkness, that that day should overtake you as a thief" (1 Thessalonians 5:3-4). The word "when" is about time and not about how, and it ends regarding the word "day" again.

The fourth reference that people try to pin the secretiveness of a thief instead of the timing of the thief is found in 2 Peter 3:10 in which only half the verse is ever quoted to support the secret rapture theory. "But the day of the Lord will come as a thief in the night." Why only half the verse? Well, that is because the rest of the verse clearly teaches that it is not about being secretive. "But the day of the Lord will come as a thief in the night; in the which the heavens shall pass away with a great noise, and the elements shall melt with fervent heat, the earth also and the works that are therein shall be burned up" (2 Peter 3:10). A thief making a lot of noise and commotion is not secretive at all.

The fifth reference is in the Book of Revelation. "If therefore thou shalt not watch, I will come on thee as a thief, and thou shalt not know what hour I will come upon thee" (Revelation 3:3). The word "hour" is again a reference to time.

The final reference is in Revelation 16:15, which says, "Behold, I come as a thief. Blessed [is] he that watcheth, and keepeth his garments, lest he walk naked, and they see his shame." Admittedly, there is no reference to "day" or "hour" so time is not explicitly stated, however, to imply that this is the verse that means it is a secret rapture is again just that, an implication. However, carefully reading the verse reveals two things from the one word "watch." Watch itself is a time reference while listen is a manner (secret) reference. Further, the word "watch" appears in all the four previous references and all four of those connect watch with time. Therefore, we conclude that this verse is also about time.

So that takes care of declaring the concept that there is a secret arrival of Jesus at any point because He comes as a thief. It is just nowhere in the Bible. But the same preachers of the theory also teach that the Bible states there is an escape from tribulation, therefore, a rapture prior to the tribulation must happen. Well, we looked for the common phrase of "escape tribulation" and various forms and found no such reference. Further, we looked up every verse containing tribulation only to find that the opposite was true. So let us take a look at the tribulation verses.

In Matthew 13:20-21, we see the reason why Christians need to go through tribulation. It is because anyone can claim to be a Christian. It is another thing to be one, especially enduring for a long period of time. The verses state, "But he that received the seed into stony places, the same is he that heareth the word, and anon with joy receiveth it; Yet hath he not root in himself, but dureth for a while: for when tribulation or persecution ariseth because of the word, by and by he is offended."

In Matthew 24:20-21, Jesus tells us that we would be running for our lives during the tribulation, and all we can do is hope and pray it is not in the winter or on the Sabbath day. "But pray ye that your flight be not in the winter, neither on the sabbath day: For then shall be great tribulation, such as was not since the beginning of the world to this time, no, nor ever shall be."

This is then followed up with a time reference to the tribulation of which nothing about a pre, mid, or post reference to rapturing is mentioned. "Immediately after the tribulation of those days shall the sun be darkened, and the moon shall not give her light, and the stars shall fall from heaven, and the powers of the heavens shall be shaken" (Matthew 24:29). Therefore, this verse cannot really be used to prove anything or disprove anything. A similar wording is also found in Mark 13:24.

Next, Jesus tells us specifically that we will have tribulation. "These things I have spoken unto you, that in me ye might have peace. In the world ye shall have tribulation: but be of good cheer; I have overcome the world" (John 16:33). In fact, a reinforced statement is found in the Book of Acts. "We must through much tribulation enter into the kingdom of God" (Acts 14:22).

On top of that, we should not be looking to escape from tribulation, but "We glory in tribulations also: knowing that tribulation worketh patience" (Romans 5:3), and we ought to be "exceeding joyful in all our tribulation" (2 Corinthians 7:4), which we are to also be "patient in tribulation" (Romans 12:12). And through this tribulation, the question is, "Who shall separate us from the love of Christ? [shall] tribulation, or distress, or persecution, or famine, or nakedness, or peril, or sword?" (Romans 8:35).

Then we are told not only are we to deal with tribulation but we are not alone nor should we leave others alone. "Who comforteth us in all our tribulation, that we may be able to comfort them which are in any trouble, by the comfort wherewith we ourselves are comforted of God" (2 Corinthians 1:4).

And how dare we think we shall escape tribulation when everyone in the Bible had to endure it including "John, who also am your brother, and companion in tribulation" (Revelation 1:9). Now do not think God does not realize what we will be going through for He says, "I know thy works, and tribulation" (Revelation 2:9).

Besides, the Apostle Paul "told you before that we should suffer tribulation" (1 Thessalonians 3:4). And on a broader scale, the church does not escape it for "we ourselves glory in you in the churches of God for your patience and faith in all your persecutions and tribulations that ye endure" (2 Thessalonians 1:4). And in the end, "These are they which came out of great tribulation, and have washed their robes, and made them white in the blood of the Lamb" (Revelation 7:14).

So that leaves one other stronghold, and that is the reference of one being taken and the other being left behind. This is found in Matthew 24:40-41, "Then shall two be in the field; the one shall be taken, and the other left. Two [women shall be] grinding at the mill; the one shall be taken, and the other left." Those are pretty strong verses to imply a secret rapture, but does it? You see, those words are recorded elsewhere and they bring us much understanding on the subject. "I tell you, in that night there shall be two [men] in one bed; the one shall be taken, and the other shall be left. Two [women] shall be grinding together; the one shall be taken, and the other left. Two [men] shall be in the field; the one shall be taken, and the other left"

(Luke 17:34-36). Now here is the interesting part in Luke. Jesus' disciples ask a very important question that provides us with an explanation. "And they answered and said unto him, Where, Lord?" (Luke 17:37). Now before we quote Jesus' words, ask yourself, who are we talking about in the question? Are we talking about the person left in bed? Are we talking about the woman left alone grinding at the mill? Are we even talking about the lonely person left behind in the field? No. Of course not. We know where they are at. What we want to know is where the "taken" are being taken to. So listen to Jesus' answer. "And he said unto them, Wheresoever the body [is], thither will the eagles be gathered together" (Luke 17:37).

So now we see that the destination of the taken is where the eagles are at. Does that mean the sky because eagles are birds that fly high in the air? Listen to what Jesus says elsewhere involving the eagles. "For as the lightning cometh out of the east, and shineth even unto the west; so shall also the coming of the Son of man be. For wheresoever the carcase is, there will the eagles be gathered together" (Matthew 24:27-28). Wait! Those that are taken are actually taken out of the way? They are killed? Is that not what a carcass is? A dead person? Sure enough. In other words, the opposite is true from what these false people are preaching and deceiving with. People do want to be left behind despite what movies and books claim falsely about the "left behind" people.

Further confirmation is found in other words of Jesus. Ever hear about the wheat and tares? It was a parable that Jesus taught in which the wheat were the saved and the tares were the lost. Notice what Jesus said and the sequence. "Let both grow together until the harvest: and in the time of harvest I will say to the reapers, Gather ye together first the tares, and bind them in bundles to burn them: but gather the wheat into my barn" (Matthew 13:30). The ones gathered first or taken first are burned. Is that what people want? Not me! We want to be part of the wheat that is left behind.

And then we have the final confirmation in 1 Thessalonians 4:17, which says, "Then we which are alive [and] remain shall be caught up together with them in the clouds, to meet the Lord in the air: and so shall we ever be with the Lord." Notice the word "remain". Remain means that others are gone, and that is what we have been saying. First, those that are lost are taken. They are taken out of the way. Those left behind or remain are the ones being raptured. And they are raptured after the second coming.

Sadly, the most warned about item of false teachers and preachers and prophets and other people are leading the majority of Christians away from Jesus, and so many of them think it is heretical to consider any of what we are sharing here, but all we can do is provide the information. It is up to each individual to make their own choice.

POINT 2:
Wars and Rumors of Wars

In Matthew 24:6-7, the Bible says, "And ye shall hear of wars and rumours of wars: see that ye be not troubled: for all [these things] must come to pass, but the end is not yet. For nation shall rise against nation, and kingdom against kingdom." Mark's version is, "And when ye shall hear of wars and rumours of wars, be ye not troubled: for [such things] must needs be; but the end [shall] not [be] yet. For nation shall rise against nation, and kingdom against kingdom" (Mark 13:7-8). And Luke provides, "But when ye shall hear of wars and commotions, be not terrified: for these things must first come to pass; but the end [is] not by and by. Then said he unto them, Nation shall rise against nation, and kingdom against kingdom" (Luke 21:9-10).

Now admittedly, we have always had wars and even people talking about wars to come. We have had dictators who threatened wars and nothing happened while others did carry it out. So these verses must not pertain to the general type wars. There must be something that is more surprising than the typical, "We don't like you and we're taking your land and goods." And also notice that in all the accounts, when this becomes fulfilled, it is not actually a sign of the very last days. It is more of a wakeup call.

Interestingly, comfort is also expressed . We are not to be troubled. Why would God interject this? Well, one thought is that war means a lot of death and destruction. Atheists are quick to blame God for allowing such things to happen. "If God existed, why doesn't He stop these things?" Us humans are quick to blame God for everything and not see the entire picture. We operate in a little corner and in a segment of time not seeing how fixing one little puzzle piece affects the whole puzzle.

First of all, realize that God has the ability of "declaring the end from the beginning, and from ancient times [the things] that are not [yet] done" (Isaiah 46:10). Second, "All things were made by him; and without him was not any thing made that was made" (John 1:3). So, He knows the future, and He made all things.

So with these two things (God knowing the future and everything made by Him), let us step back in time and ask the earlier version of the same question. Why did God make Satan, the devil? Is that not the first point in time accusing God of allowing evil to happen? Well, actually, God did not make the devil. He knew that the devil would exist, but God did not make a devil.

In regards to the highest positioned angel, it is said, "Thou [art] the anointed cherub that covereth; and I have set thee [so]: thou wast upon the holy mountain of God; thou hast walked up and down in the midst of the stones of fire. Thou [wast] perfect in thy ways from the day that thou wast created, till iniquity was found in thee" (Ezekiel 28:14-15). So God, despite knowing a perfect angel would become the devil, He still moved forward with creating beings. That means He even knew that Adam and Eve would sin and still created them anyways. And if one is quick to say, "Why didn't he just create everybody else but that angel and not create Adam and Eve?", well, someone would have eventually taken their place and we would have the same mess. A different angel would have turned out to be the devil. It could have been Albert and Edith instead of Adam and Eve. How do we know? Because Satan is not the only fallen angel, and Adam and Eve are not the only humans who have disobeyed God. And with Adam and Eve, "God saw every thing that he had made, and, behold, [it was] very good" (Genesis 1:31). The words "very good" is the same as saying the word "perfect" for we are to "prove what [is] that good, and acceptable, and perfect, will of God" (Romans 12:2).

Now some are quick to also say, "Why didn't God just squash out this iniquity issue right up front? Why did God not just zap the devil?" Well, once again we have to see it from a bigger picture than simply nipping the iniquity issue in the bud with a bolt of lightning or some fire and brimstone. Notice that iniquity was found in this angel. That means it was not well known. Basically, the angel was rebelling against God mentally, even planning things out in detail, and yes, the process of taking an evil thought and running with it although not physically carrying out the act is sin (James 1:14-15), while just having evil thoughts or temptations enter into our minds and expel them is not sin. Even Jesus "was in all points tempted like as [we are, yet] without sin" (Hebrews 4:15). That means when we are tempted, we are to repel it, for if we do not, that is when we commit sin. The door opens and a beautiful woman steps into the room wearing a little less clothing than she should, to turn away one's eyes from the temptation would be the wise thing to do. To stand there and fantasize undressing her the rest of the way would be sin despite not saying, not expressing, nor physically doing anything wrong. "Ye have heard that it was said by them of old time, Thou shalt not commit adultery: But I say unto you, That whosoever looketh on a woman to lust after her hath committed adultery with her already in his heart" (Matthew 5:27-28).

So, if God were to have called this angel forward and announced to the whole gathering of angels what was going on in this angel's mind and then reduced the angel to ashes, what would be the reaction of the rest of the angels? Obedience out of fear. That contradicts who God is. "God is love" (1 John 4:8), and requires the same back. Besides, all it would take is for the angel to say in front of everyone, "That's not what I was thinking!" And now there is doubt. You see such reactions by the observers all of the time as it is played out in the news. The verdict of innocent is handed down, and people disagree. That person's life is tainted no matter how far they go to prove complete innocence. Could you imagine eternity with doubt in the minds of God's subjects? That would make for an uneasy rest of eternity. It would always be present at every gathering in which some angels would be doubting that God acted correctly. And for God to wipe the memory from their minds would again not be an act of love but a type of force. God is not that type of god.

Now, what was this fallen angel really thinking? "How art thou fallen from heaven, O Lucifer, son of the morning! [how] art thou cut down to the ground, which didst weaken the nations! For thou hast said in thine heart, I will ascend into heaven, I will exalt my throne above the stars of God: I will sit also upon the mount of the congregation, in the sides of the north: I will ascend above the heights of the clouds; I will be like the most High" (Isaiah 14:12-14). So, from this we see that the identify of this angel is Lucifer, not Satan or the devil. That is what he became as he carried out his thoughts.

By the way, this activity is against one of God's commandments. The very first commandment which states, "Thou shalt have no other gods before me" (Exodus 20:3). Lucifer wanting to be like God breaks it. And for those Christians that think the Ten Commandments came into existence only through Moses, think again. If that were so, that would mean before there was even an Adam and Eve, there were no rules. But the Bible says, "where no law is, [there is] no transgression" (Romans 4:15). So that means that the opposite would also be true. Since Lucifer no longer resides in heaven, that means there must have been transgression, hence, God had a set of commandments in heaven then and still does today. Not only does He have a set of commandments, they are the same set that we have.

John, who wrote the Book of Revelation, revealed this fact. "The temple of God was opened in heaven, and there was seen in his temple the ark of his testament" (Revelation 11:19). There is an ark in heaven. That is God's throne, just like the earthly ark constructed by Moses and his team. He was told to create a temple (sanctuary) on earth, but notice what God said. "Make me a sanctuary; that I may dwell among them. According to all that I shew thee, [after] the pattern of the tabernacle, and the pattern of all the instruments thereof, even so shall ye make [it]" (Exodus 25:8-9). It was all to be developed from a pattern (original). At this point, you may be wondering why we are focusing on the pattern. It is to identify what was also placed in the ark on earth. God said, "I will write on the tables the words that were in the first tables which thou brakest, and thou shalt put them in the ark" (Deuteronomy 10:2). And God "wrote on the tables, according to the first writing, the ten commandments" (Deuteronomy 10:4). That means that Moses did not receive the Ten Commandments as the originals, break them (Exodus 32:19), and receive another set as a copy (Exodus 34:1), rather, Moses received a copy or pattern of the original in heaven, broke them (Exodus 32:19), and received a second copy (Exodus 34:1).

Therefore, the Ten Commandments is what makes up the rules of heaven and Lucifer did not like them. Through his rebellion, he was basically declaring that God's Ten Commandments were a bad idea. Unfortunately, he did not keep his thoughts to himself. He eventually shared his thoughts with other angels. Some may have rejected the thoughts while others accepted them, or Lucifer simply was selective and only discussed it with others that seemed to question God's authority or at least appeared open to listening to Lucifer. We may not know those details, but what we do know is that "there was war in heaven: Michael and his angels fought against the dragon; and the dragon fought and his angels" (Revelation 12:7). Now it was not much of a battle for they "prevailed not; neither was their place found any more in heaven" (Revelation 12:8). And just in case you do not know who the dragon is nor understand who was kicked out of heaven, the Bible says, "The great dragon was cast out, that old serpent, called the Devil, and Satan, which deceiveth the whole world: he was cast out into the earth, and his angels were cast out with him" (Revelation 12:9).

Now just how many angels went with Lucifer, which became Satan? In symbolic language, we are shown that "there appeared another wonder in heaven; and behold a great red dragon, having seven heads and ten horns, and seven crowns upon his heads. And his tail drew the third part of the stars of heaven, and did cast them to the earth" (Revelation 12:3-4). Since the dragon is Lucifer that became Satan, and Satan with his angels were cast to the earth, we can only conclude that the stars that were also cast to the earth is symbolic of those angels. So a total of one third were cast out with Satan. That means one third of all the angels that God had made ended up choosing to go with the devil.

As a result, Satan has challenged God's loving authority, which God expressed through the declaration of the Ten Commandments. God's love is on trial. Satan has been declaring that the Ten Commandments to rule lives is unnecessary while God declares that through the Ten Commandments that "no good [thing] will he withhold" (Psalms 84:11), and that His commandments are inspired out of love (1 John 5:3) for the best relationships one can experience between God and the created being as well as between created beings.

So, we have Satan and his angels verbally stating one side and God representing the other, even in written form for "the LORD delivered unto" Moses "two tables of stone written with the finger of God" (Deuteronomy 9:10). And with only two sides in the warfare, we have a stalemate. Nothing can be settled this way. What the universe needed was a demonstration, so Adam and Eve are created. God tells Adam, "Of every tree of the garden thou mayest freely eat: But of the tree of the knowledge of good and evil, thou shalt not eat of it: for in the day that thou eatest thereof thou shalt surely die" (Genesis 2:16-17). Now on the surface, one may not see that the Ten Commandments are being tested, but they are. To eat of the tree would mean that the commandment to obey one's parents would be broken. "Honour thy father and thy mother: that thy days may be long upon the land which the LORD thy God giveth thee" (Exodus 20:12). And one honors a parent through obedience (Numbers 27:20). On top of that, for Adam and Eve to do what they want instead of what God commanded breaks the first commandment, "Thou shalt have no other gods before me" (Exodus 20:3) by thinking selfishly placing themselves above God. Taking the object to gain the knowledge of good and evil, which was evidently lacking, for all they knew was good means they bowed down or gave into the inanimate object making it more valuable than obeying God, hence breaking the second commandment of bowing down to such. On top of that, the mere obsession for such knowledge that they did not have broke the tenth commandment, "Thou shalt not covet" (Exodus 20:17). The commandment "Thou shalt not take the name of the LORD thy God in vain" would also be broken because taking on the name of "Child of God" means one lives in obedience to God and not self or any other being. Although some may think certain commandments being broken may be a stretch, this one is not. Since God stated that by eating it they shall die, that means by doing so they broke the commandment "Thou shalt not kill" (Exodus 20:13). They would be killing themselves. So at the very least, three commandments were in direct jeopardy and another three indirectly. That is a total of six commandments.

So, what did Adam and Eve do? They chose Satan's side. "And when the woman saw that the tree [was] good for food, and that it [was] pleasant to the eyes, and a tree to be desired to make [one] wise, she took of the fruit thereof, and did eat, and gave also unto her husband with her; and he did eat" (Genesis 3:6). At that moment, they felt the consequence of their action for Adam said, "I was afraid, because I [was] naked; and I hid myself" (Genesis 3:10). At the same time, Satan became ruler of the planet. This is stated as such because there was a meeting one day in heaven in which representatives of each of the planets in the universe were to present themselves. Instead of Adam, Satan appeared. "Now there was a day when the sons of God came to present themselves before the LORD, and Satan came also among them. And the LORD said unto Satan, Whence comest thou? Then Satan answered the LORD, and said, From going to and fro in the earth, and from walking up and down in it" (Job 1:6-7). Now God knew the purpose of Satan appearing in Heaven after the banishment, but God had Satan state the fact because all that God does is witnessed by the universe.

Although this concept of a heavenly gathering may be unfamiliar to most despite it being in the Bible, at least realize that when Adam and Eve sinned, this planet became Satan's. In other words, this planet is playing out what it would be like if the entire universe, even heaven itself were to agree with Satan as the ruler instead of God.

Also one should realize that Adam was under the Ten Commandment law, and that the Ten Commandments did not come into existence just through Moses. The reason is that Romans 5:14 states that Adam had sinned. According to the Bible, "Whosoever committeth sin transgresseth also the law: for sin is the transgression of the law" (1 John 3:4). So, if there were no Ten Commandments at the time of Adam and Eve, then there was no sin, furthermore, no consequence to sin, but since there was a consequence to sin, made evident by the continuance thereof, that means Adam and Eve were under the Ten Commandments even though they were not written down yet.

Now God had a choice to make. He could have wiped out Satan, the fallen angels, Adam, and Eve and either make another planet to start over or just be satisfied with the two thirds of the angels that did not leave. That was one choice, however, seeing that lawlessness had just begun and the consequence to breaking the law was not fully experienced yet, if God were to have wiped all of them out, it would once again cause the remaining angels to worship God out of fear and not out of love. In other words, it was not yet settled in the remaining angel's mind that Satan's way was truly wrong. Therefore, God has to allow things to play out so as to become evident that Satan's lawlessness is the wrong choice.

Even the next incident that sin is shown as taking place was not enough. "Cain rose up against Abel his brother, and slew him" (Genesis 4:8). Besides, what was God going to do now. He loved His creation of humans on this planet. He did not create them to be a mere instrument in a play and be ready to discard them when He proved His point. He loved them so much that right after Adam and Eve had sinned, God said, "I will put enmity between thee and the woman, and between thy seed and her seed; it shall bruise thy head, and thou shalt bruise his heel" (Genesis 3:15). This was a promise of Salvation to come, in fact, God was not surprised by any of these events. He provided "hope of eternal life, which God, that cannot lie, promised before the world began" (Titus 1:2), and this "was given us in Christ Jesus before the world began" (2 Timothy 1:9). That means God knew Adam and Eve would fail but before creating them, the whole plan of how to save them was already thought of. "The Son of man is not come to destroy men's lives, but to save [them]" (Luke 9:56).

Now why could the test not end after Cain killed Abel? Just like it is today; people excuse certain sins while condemning other sins. And those that commit the really bad sins are classed as a poor example of reality. In other words, Cain sure is lost. Murder is pretty bad, but it seems that when people lose their tempers over the silliest things, all of a sudden that is not so bad and God will overlook it. In reality, Jesus said, "Ye have heard that it was said by them of old time, Thou shalt not kill; and whosoever shall kill shall be in danger of the judgment: But I say unto you, That whosoever is angry with his brother without a cause shall be in danger of the judgment" (Matthew 5:21-22). So until we see sin as absolutely evil, the test continues.

As for being a bad example of reality, Cain is classed as those that use their freedom of living without the Ten Commandments and going too far. People are not concluding that we need God's Ten Commandments but rather are saying that Cain was just a case gone too far. As long as things are kept in somewhat orderly sense, we do not need the rules. This is no different than society saying that it is alright to do whatever you want as long as it does not hurt anyone else, but God does not see it that way. Think of all the drunks at various events or lifestyles; instead of saying that alcohol use is bad, society just casts such people as poor examples. "They just cannot hold their liquor," people say.

And shame on all the churches that teach that we do not need the Ten Commandments. Is it really alright in God's eyes to murder people? Do we really think such professing Christians will go to Heaven? No right minded Christian would ever think such a person committing murder freely would be in Heaven despite how much money the murderer donates, no matter how helpful they are all other times, no matter how Christian they may practice. If they think they can commit murder at will and do so, they are not going to Heaven. So what do these churches really teach about the Ten Commandments being nailed to the cross? They teach that the really big sins have to stop, but those that they deem not so important is alright to break for we are only human. But where is that line between really big sins and allowance sins? Who gets to decide? There is nothing in the Bible making such determinations. Look at coveting! Just because it is not as bad as adultery and murder does not make it any less important. How about baring false witness? Since it too is not as serious as murder and adultery, does that make it a breakable commandment? In reality, the Ten Commandments still are binding upon each of us as evidence of our repentance and accepting the grace of Christ. It is not evidence to God as He "only knowest the hearts of the children of men" (2 Chronicles 6:30). It is for proving to ourselves if we are genuine or not. If this irks some Christians then read on and show us where our flaws may be when we revisit the subject.

So the test had to continue even beyond Cain and Abel and evidently beyond many more generations to the present time. The point is, this is not God's plan at all. Although it is said that He is in control, in reality, all of us have free will, freedom to choose, and there are consequences in which the innocent get hurt and even die. If God intervened at every moment to prevent the innocent from getting hurt, Satan would claim that his plan was interfered with and not given the allowance to fully play out, and then this war would continue on indefinitely. At the same time, God does intervene from time to time to keep things in somewhat in check because if He did not, no one would be saved. So yes, it was necessary to send the flood (Genesis 7); yes, He needed to disrupt things at the tower of Babel (Genesis 11:7-8); and yes to many other acts of God.

So some may be asking by now, "When did the excuses stop and we realized that Satan's plan is a bad choice while God's plan is good?" Well, among the universe, specifically with the angels, it only happened at the climax in which absolute evil met absolute good. Basically, "God so loved the world, that he gave his only begotten Son, that whosoever believeth in him should not perish, but have everlasting life" (John 3:16). When God, became a man and without the use of His godly powers, "was in all points tempted like as [we are, yet] without sin" (Hebrews 4:15), and suffered through the most excruciating pain and humiliating torture to die as an innocent lamb (John 1:36), that is when it happened.

Unfortunately for human beings, we have not figured that out. How do I know? Look at the world we live in; sin reigns. And so, we wait and see until enough is enough. And that happens only when the followers of Christ are treated the same way on a global basis of which is what we are studying out. When the one side that has the "one mind" of the world, of Satan, are so tired of the other side who truly have the "one mind" of Christ and worldwide tries to eradicate them like Cain did to Abel and the Jewish leaders did to Jesus, then we know the test ends even for human beings.

Think of this whole iniquity, sin, rebellion with Lucifer, the fallen angels, Adam, and Eve playing out like a picnic in which there is a large gathering all drinking merrily glasses of lemonade. It is the best lemonade going and people are just drinking it up, yet there is plenty to go around and around and around. Now imagine that one of the people drinking the lemonade discovers a black pepper flake in their drink, and they start yelling about what they found. Some may glance to see if they see any in their cup, others may just assume it was a onetime incident, yet others may perform a complete examination drinking the lemonade only after they have concluded all is fine because having pepper in lemonade just would not taste right. Now let us increase the amount of pepper from one simple flake that one person discovered into the fact that several people have discovered such a situation. Again, there would be no immediate alarm. Those discovering such would simply remove it or toss the serving and go get more lemonade, and inspecting it a bit closer before leaving the dispensing area. Continue increasing the amount of pepper and you get more and more people annoyed. Instead of one flake, there may be several, but as long as it does not affect the taste, who cares. Basically, the only thing that is going to cause everyone to wake up to the fact that the lemonade is not worth drinking is if it is unavoidable to drink the current contents of pepper in the cup, the flavor is off, and in trying to get a new glass of lemonade, the results are the same conditions. That would make all lemonade unfit for consumption. Now let us say that the person hosting the picnic wants to move everyone in doors for a more eloquent environment, even a tastier beverage, or have them leave the premise. The outdoor part of the gathering must come to an end, but people are having such a good time, and as long as the lemonade continues to flow tastefully, no one is in a hurry to leave the area for indoors or to go home. Cutting off the serving, for the purpose of this illustration, is not an option. Now the host could become appalled at any pepper in the lemonade and wanting to save their reputation, and they may do their best to not serve a single cup with pepper in it by straining every single serving through a net. However, since the lemonade seems to be the source of keeping people around, and they seem to be drinking it with pepper anyways, that would just prolong the end of the picnic indefinitely. So, the host could allow whatever is increasing the presence of the pepper to continue, which will eventually bring to everyone's attention that pepper in lemonade is awful. Now that is the message that everyone should be getting. Pepper in lemonade is awful and the kitchen staff sabotaging the picnic by adding pepper to the lemonade is not a nice thing that is happening, but it just does not seem to be sinking in the minds of those in attendance. The person in control of the kitchen staff, operating out of the large tent on the grounds, is the one ultimately responsible for sabotaging the gathering to make the host look bad and has convinced the servants to assist him. Back in the house though, there are nothing but loyal servants who have made sure that everything is absolutely perfect. Now in allowing the free flow of pepper to multiply, the host may be approached by some very sincere children with tears in their eyes asking where they could go to quench their thirst since the pepper lemonade is not an option. The host may have sympathy and intervene by screening a serving or so for those that ask with sincerity but will not just automatically do it for everyone. Finally, it has reached the climax. The gathering is starting to break up. The few people that believe that the host is not a lousy host begin to move indoors trusting that better conditions are there, while the rest have bought into the sabotage, blaming the host or maybe they even are not caring to go indoors, so they simply just go home. In either case, the picnic portion comes to an end. The end result is not too many enter the house area because of the sabotage.

Although this little story does not perfectly represent God, His servants, the fallen servants or angels, even the population on earth, or for that matter, the time on this planet, the general concept that people do not see sin for what it really is holds true. They tolerate it, like a flake or two being fine and swallowed. People put different levels on sin, as if a few flakes in lemonade is alright but too much demands a new cup. They ignore sin, like scooping it out of the glass despite the fact that the flavor of the lemonade has been affected already. It is not until so much sin gets the world to realize how awful life really is under Satan's rule that they finally say, "Enough is enough", like the large amounts of pepper that just provides no solution anywhere to deal with it. Many blame God. Many do not even believe in God. Now, we may not have arrived yet as humans to the conclusion that one flake or a bunch of flakes of sin spoils all of it, but we are getting close.

So what makes the point about wars finding fulfillment in our day? No longer does a nation attack another nation alone. It seems each clash involves many kingdoms and many nations. In the 1900's alone, we have had two world wars. Unheard of prior to the 1900's. The frequency of rumors also points to a time in which such would be easily communicated. Before the 1800's, when the rumor of a war arrived, more than likely it was already fought too. It took time to get such detail beyond the confines of one's own continent. Not today with global communications. Every hint of a disagreement is instantly reported to every nation.

POINT 3:
Famines

Matthew 24:7 and Mark 13:8 say, "There shall be famines", while Luke 21:11 just states the word "famines" in a list. Now keep in mind, that Jesus just got done referring to wars and uprisings. There just might be a connection in thought that because of the wars, we would see an increase in famines as a result of those conflicts. And before one says that such a conclusion is obvious, it was not so just a couple centuries ago. People fought, destroyed the crops, but once the war was settled, they replanted, at least the victor did. Today, because of chemical warfare, chemicals from shelling, weapons that do not just stir up the ground but completely overturns the earth, etc., famines do not just occur but are long lasting. Couple that with the water shortages and both drought and famines are increasing and the outlook points to the trend not ceasing.

POINT 4:
Pestilences

Matthew 24:7 and Luke 21:11 both mention in a list that pestilences would be prevalent. According to Webster's Dictionary, it is defined as, "A contagious or infectious epidemic disease that is virulent and devastating". In addition, the Bible also makes use in example of what it means.

Moses told Pharaoh, "For now I will stretch out my hand, that I may smite thee and thy people with pestilence; and thou shalt be cut off from the earth" (Exodus 9:15). And since Pharaoh did not cooperate, the pestilence came. What was it? Moses tells us, "Behold, to morrow about this time I will cause it to rain a very grievous hail, such as hath not been in Egypt since the foundation thereof even until now" (Exodus 9:18). So even a devastating weather occurrence can be considered a pestilence. Has such occurred? Have we seen unusual and devastating weather patterns? Have we seen a rise in infectious diseases? One would have to be stubborn not to see such happening. According to, U.S. National Institutes of Health's National Library of Medicine, they state, "Infectious diseases are spreading more rapidly than ever before, WHO warns".

Of course those that argue against this point usually declare that most of the diseases are happening because of the ease of global transportation. They continue to argue by saying, "If it were not for that, we would not see such an increase!" Well, that may be true, but Jesus did not qualify a reason for the increase or awareness. It was just going to be something noticeable towards the end of time beyond the fact that diseases and weather disasters have always existed. So again, the implication has to be that they become more noticeable as we near the end of time.

As an example of some of the diseases being of a concern, the measles outbreak in the United States at the start of 2015 is just one example. The ebola virus, aids, even TB are but the short list. Even vaccines are becoming ineffective. In fact, vaccines no longer protect individually from a diseases; it is group protection called "Herd Immunity". The more people vaccinated, the better the possibility of protection from the disease.

Now in regards to weather related devastation, Accuweather declared on November 15, 2013, "Steady Increase in Climate Related Natural Disasters." According to Live Science on October 17, 2005, they stated, "Scientists: Natural Disasters Becoming More Common." International Business Times on March 21, 2013, said, "Natural Disasters Are Hitting Harder, And Not Because Of Global Warming."

So no matter how one looks at pestilences, just as the diseases, just as the disasters, or both, it seems both diseases and disasters are steadily increasing in devastation recognized by more and more outlets.

POINT 5:
Earthquakes

In Matthew 24:7, we see just a reference to "earthquakes, in divers places", while Mark 13:8 states that "there shall be earthquakes in divers places". But notice the version in Luke 21:11 "And great earthquakes shall be in divers places". This does not mean they contradict or are in disagreement. It was simply that Matthew and Mark chose not to focus the attention on the size of the earthquakes being important. Let us face it, feeling any size tremor can be scary. But the one theme that is consistent is that they will be found in different places as if they were not being reported from such places prior to the fulfillment.

That declaration in itself can only point to a period of time in which expansion had to move beyond the then known world and communications would increase as well as testing devices, all of which point to at least the 1800's and not prior. The number of earthquakes may not have increased, but the reporting of them has greatly changed.

In fact, we believe many Christians to be nothing but alarmists when it comes to the earthquakes as well as not reading it properly. Every year for at least the past forty years of my life, some Christian has stated that earthquakes have increased in the past couple years. They are basically off in their understanding, and unfortunately they keep repeating the same message even decade after decade. No wonder unbelievers laugh and mock saying, "We've always had earthquakes!" But notice that in all three references, Jesus never predicted that the number would increase. What He predicted was the number of areas reporting earthquakes would occur. So if anyone is ready to match statistics with me, put them away because I am not going to use such. I am going to be in full agreement with those that show very little fluctuation in the numbers, even if only 5.0 earthquakes and higher were only included as is qualified by the reference of "great earthquakes" and not little ones. What we have not had though, was the different places reporting such until now, meaning since the 1800's or so.

Besides, the usual arguments from such Christians that are about numbers always try to prove that it is worse now than it was in the days of their parents and grandparents and great grandparents. Well, if they are able to prove by statistics that we have such a situation, then I would be disappointed. The reason is because in the verses, Jesus follows up with these words, "These [are] the beginning of sorrows" (Matthew 24:8, Mark 13:8). In other words, when the earthquakes are identified as being fulfilled in the last days, then realize it is the beginning of the period known as the last days. So if Christians are proving how this verse is fulfilled only in the past ten years or so, then they are preaching a long to come period of time yet before Jesus returns because they are preaching the beginning of sorrows, while I am trying to teach the end of sorrows. And if we are at the end of such activity, that means Jesus is about to return!

From what I am seeing in these verses, if one is looking forward to the second coming, let us rejoice because our great grandparents were told correctly how this was fulfilled in there day. They were at the beginning of sorrows. We must be getting close to the end of sorrows now, and I believe we are.

POINT 6:
Arrests and Killings

Matthew 24:9-10 says, "Then shall they deliver you up to be afflicted, and shall kill you: and ye shall be hated of all nations for my name's sake. And then shall many be offended, and shall betray one another, and shall hate one another."

Luke 21:12-18 says, "But before all these, they shall lay their hands on you, and persecute [you], delivering [you] up to the synagogues, and into prisons, being brought before kings and rulers for my name's sake. And it shall turn to you for a testimony. Settle [it] therefore in your hearts, not to meditate before what ye shall answer: For I will give you a mouth and wisdom, which all your adversaries shall not be able to gainsay nor resist. And ye shall be betrayed both by parents, and brethren, and kinsfolks, and friends; and [some] of you shall they cause to be put to death. And ye shall be hated of all [men] for my name's sake. But there shall not an hair of your head perish. In your patience possess ye your souls."

Many Christians who look for fulfillment in all that Jesus said will point to the atrocities that are happening to many Christians outside of the United States and Europe where many have their churches burnt to the ground, many are slain, and if there is a trial, it is usually railroaded to guilty punishable by long prison terms or death. Actually, there have even been a few church burnings in the United States as well. But we are not going to take that position. Instead, we are going to take the position that this is part of Revelation 13, which is the intent of this book, all to prove that we are on the verge of this happening and once it does, books like this will be banned, unable to be shared, and even the Bible will be brought into question. "Behold, the days come, saith the Lord GOD, that I will send a famine in the land, not a famine of bread, nor a thirst for water, but of hearing the words of the LORD: And they shall wander from sea to sea, and from the north even to the east, they shall run to and fro to seek the word of the LORD, and shall not find [it]" (Amos 8:11-12).

This does not diminish what these modern day martyrs are going through, and we praise them for their stance and willingness to die for their faith, but when Jesus mentioned that these atrocities would happen, He said that all nations would be involved. Right now, there are quite a few nations that practice freedom of religion, therefore, we are not there yet. Further, Jesus clarifies who will be doing the perpetrating. "They shall put you out of the synagogues: yea, the time cometh, that whosoever killeth you will think that he doeth God service" (John 16:2).

Christians should not be fearing that non-Christians are going to be our worst enemy at the end of time. Christians ought to be fearing the fake Christians who will unite in mass and want to remove the minority view from Christianity. Of course we do not use the word "synagogue" today to describe our places of worship, we call them churches. The ones that will be doing the killing and removing people from churches will be fellow Christians. We propose that they are the ones that are on the bad or dark side of having "one mind".

So, using what we already revealed thus far plus this point, together they point to a time in which there is a great union of Christians that are in agreement though not in agreement with the Bible teachings. Once this is accomplished, they will then turn upon all who are the true Christian having "one mind" being united with Christ who do not want to give up the Bible based doctrines, which is based upon the truth. Such false unification will then throw those staunch adherents out of the church, and if their conscience is not satisfied, such people will then turn to killing the faithful all in the name of God. The nations will accept the argument that the outcasts are nothing more than disturbing world unity and will be willing accomplices in carrying out even death decrees.

For those that cannot see such a future from the perspective of how respectful, for the most part, that the United States is towards religions today, just remember, the Bible says, "All these things happened unto them for ensamples: and they are written for our admonition, upon whom the ends of the world are come" (1 Corinthians 10:11). All through history this scenario has occurred. Why would we think at the very end that anything would be any different?

So we agree, this has not been fulfilled yet, however, when it happens, we will not need a book to point what time frame we are in. We will already be in the last days, weeks, maybe months of time.

POINT 7:
Iniquity Abounding & Love Lacking

Matthew 24:12 says, "And because iniquity shall abound, the love of many shall wax cold." This is actually two points in one. First, iniquity would increase dramatically at the end of time, and second, the love, in the context of thoughtfulness and kindness, towards each other would grow cold. In other words, people would tend to be colder towards one another as opposed to years ago. But Jesus told us that the two would follow in succession and be treated as one sign.

So, has iniquity abounded to the point that people hardly care for one another? Again, we propose yes. Iniquity comes in all forms and in all of those forms, it pretty much as greatly increased. Consider television and the movies, people joke that the television show, The Monsters, was the first program to show a single bed with both genders in bed together. This was closely followed by The Brady Bunch. Today, not only do we see married couples regularly in bed, we see unmarried couples hot and heavy with bare butts and enough exposure to body parts that hardly imagination is necessary to finish off full nudity. In the movies, they are so boarder line pornographic that they have to cut scenes just to keep it within the R-rating. Add the amount of violence and foul language, and it becomes clear that both television and movies are raunchy.

Now, look at the language as well. No, not in the movies or on television, but in conversation, on bumper stickers, and even on billboards. It used to be that if a man spoke a foul word in front of lady, well, he would ask for pardon. Today, the women out curse men sometimes.

And sex is much more freer and even expected between unmarried couples as opposed to a few decades ago. Speaking of which, sex videos used to be something purchased more in secret; now major streaming services provide it right into the homes. Robberies, embezzlements, corporate espionages, murders, etc. all statistically have greatly increased in the recent decades. It does not take much research to find that almost daily on the news is a murder, riot, theft, embezzlement, and more that is reported. Some even say that the news reporting is getting more and more depressing .

So, how about relationships between people? Consider the number of people that no longer want to get involved. They legitimately do not want to take the risk of injury, being duped, and especially losing their life. How many times do we hear the story of people stepping over a heart attack victim, women delivering a child on the sidewalk, muggings taking place in broad daylight, etc.? People have resorted to doing as much as possible electronically for fear of going out. And who wants to risk their lives on the road just to get out of the house?

POINT 8:
Gospel Going Around the World

Matthew 24:14 states, "And this gospel of the kingdom shall be preached in all the world for a witness unto all nations; and then shall the end come." Believe it or not, we are going to take the stance that we are not there yet, but that is alright. The reason is that once this happens, it is the end. That is what the verse states.

Now of course there will be people, especially end of the world zealots, that will claim that the Internet, satellites, telephone, ease of transportation, etc. all point to our time in which this is almost fulfilled, but our reply is that Jesus did not say, "A gospel shall be preached to the world." He specifically said, "This gospel."

The use of the word "this" means that there is a specific gospel that will be taken around the world. Currently, there are over 42,000 denominations of which many claim to have missionaries preaching a gospel all contradicting themselves. One says, "Just believe!" Another says, "You have to pray the rosary!" Another says, "Believe and be baptized." Another says, "Believe, be baptized, and live in obedience to the commandments." And so on. Even the idea of baptism is a confusing message. Some teach sprinkling is baptism, others teach immersion, while still others teach triple immersion. Does it matter? Should it matter? Well, Jesus answers all of this by saying, "Go ye therefore, and teach all nations, baptizing them in the name of the Father, and of the Son, and of the Holy Ghost: Teaching them to observe all things whatsoever I have commanded you" (Matthew 28:19-20). So Matthew 24:14 sounds like the declaration that Matthew 28:19-20's command to go teach has finally been completed, but Matthew 28:19-20 is our answer. Any gospel that does not teach the observation (obedience) to Jesus' teachings is a false gospel. Further, John tells us about a period of time in facing the Antichrist and states, "Whosoever transgresseth, and abideth not in the doctrine of Christ, hath not God. He that abideth in the doctrine of Christ, he hath both the Father and the Son" (2 John 1:9). Therefore, specific doctrines are important, especially in the last day gospel fulfillment. So, on that point, we see the lack of fulfillment again not as a point in which we say, "Ah hah! It's not the last days because this point hasn't been fulfilled," but rather as a point that when it is being fulfilled, it will be too late to hear a message like that contained in this book.

The understanding that Jesus expected a specific gospel to go around the world at the end of time and not just a gospel is well expressed in 1 Timothy 4:1. "Now the Spirit speaketh expressly, that in the latter times some shall depart from the faith, giving heed to seducing spirits, and doctrines of devils." Keep in mind, to leave the faith does not mean to reject Christianity; it includes being called a Christian and putting one's faith elsewhere, like away from the Bible and into "science falsely so called" (1 Timothy 6:20), turning from faith in Creation to faith in Evolution. This happens in the "latter times".

POINT 9:
Abomination of Desolation

Matthew 24:15 says, "When ye therefore shall see the abomination of desolation, spoken of by Daniel the prophet, stand in the holy place, (whoso readeth, let him understand:)".

Now keep in mind that when Jesus spoke of the end time events, He was answering two different questions for "Jesus went out, and departed from the temple: and his disciples came to [him] for to shew him the buildings of the temple. And Jesus said unto them, See ye not all these things? verily I say unto you, There shall not be left here one stone upon another, that shall not be thrown down. And as he sat upon the mount of Olives, the disciples came unto him privately, saying, Tell us, when shall these things be? and what [shall be] the sign of thy coming, and of the end of the world?" (Matthew 24:1-3)

Mixing the two answers together, some of the content has language pertaining to the overthrow of Jerusalem in 70 A.D. while the rest pertains to those living at the end of time. In this case, we have a verse with dual fulfillment. Today, we cannot stand in the Holy Place, but Daniel did speak of multiple desolations. Now, those that pertain to the end of time is what we ought to be focused upon.

One such reference is a time reference. "How long [shall be] the vision [concerning] the daily [sacrifice], and the transgression of desolation, to give both the sanctuary and the host to be trodden under foot? And he said unto me, Unto two thousand and three hundred days; then shall the sanctuary be cleansed" (Daniel 8:13-14). This particular prophecy is too large to go into detail right now, but this in fact is a desolation reference for the end of time, especially when one figures out the beginning point of the prophecy period.

However, another reference to desolation is found in Daniel 9:27, which says, "And he shall confirm the covenant with many for one week: and in the midst of the week he shall cause the sacrifice and the oblation to cease, and for the overspreading of abominations he shall make [it] desolate, even until the consummation, and that determined shall be poured upon the desolate." This one, controversially, refers to the desolation that finds its fulfillment in 70 A.D.

So after supplying an example from Daniel for both a reference to the end of the world and another for the destruction of Jerusalem, we see the intent of Jesus. He was giving a wakeup call to both groups.

But has the desolation reference in Daniel 8:13-14 been fulfilled? After personally studying out the topic in Daniel, the conclusion is yes, however, at this point in the book, you do not have enough evidence to come to the same conclusion. So, if you would be so kind as to put this point in the back of your mind, we would appreciate that as we will address this topic later in great detail.

POINT 10:
Great Tribulation

Matthew 24:21-22 says, "For then shall be great tribulation, such as was not since the beginning of the world to this time, no, nor ever shall be. And except those days should be shortened, there should no flesh be saved: but for the elect's sake those days shall be shortened."

This reminds me of Revelation 7:1-3, in which it states, "And after these things I saw four angels standing on the four corners of the earth, holding the four winds of the earth, that the wind should not blow on the earth, nor on the sea, nor on any tree. And I saw another angel ascending from the east, having the seal of the living God: and he cried with a loud voice to the four angels, to whom it was given to hurt the earth and the sea, Saying, Hurt not the earth, neither the sea, nor the trees, till we have sealed the servants of our God in their foreheads."

Also, 2 Peter 3:9 says, "The Lord is not slack concerning his promise, as some men count slackness; but is longsuffering to us-ward, not willing that any should perish, but that all should come to repentance."

Putting it all together, this point is going to rapidly be fulfilled at the very end. Every imaginable tribulation is going to be released. Right now, God, through His angels, are holding it all back by a miracle. The reason, God knows that when it starts, it will be over and He wants as many to be saved as possible. Unfortunately, the process is slow. It involves a sealing process, which we will study in another chapter. That sealing process is not an instant process, but it must be done before it all breaks loose.

But look around. Is our world on the verge of catastrophe in multiple areas? The answer is yes. The many articles that predict a world economic collapse is one area in which currently quite a few countries are bankrupt already draining the world economic resources. Speaking of resources, we are told that the natural resources are being depleted, which includes fresh water, oil, and even clean air. On top of that is the constant threat of World War III and at the very least, a rogue nation firing off a nuclear weapon. Then we have the global warming people telling us how the planet is overheating, and that we will see many more natural disasters.

These are but a few examples of tribulation as we never seen before. So which one will it be? Why do we think it is just one? How about all of it at once? Could you imagine a world economic collapse while World War III is happening with viruses spreading rampantly and natural disasters occurring in succession and having to ration the natural resources? Sounds like the perfect set up for the few in charge to control people with and even enforce their mark of authority, even the Mark of the Beast.

Needless to say, but again, a book like this would not be published under those conditions. So the lack of tribulation should not be a point in which one says, "See, we're not close to the end yet!" But are we close to the tribulation? Non-religious people print article after article saying, "Yes!"

POINT 11:
Like the Days of Noah

Matthew 24:37-39 says, "But as the days of Noe [were], so shall also the coming of the Son of man be. For as in the days that were before the flood they were eating and drinking, marrying and giving in marriage, until the day that Noe entered into the ark, And knew not until the flood came, and took them all away; so shall also the coming of the Son of man be."

Point A:
Eating and Drinking

One of the highlights that Jesus spoke of as a sign includes people eating and drinking. Wait a moment! People have always eaten and been drinking. What is the significance of that sign? Well, it must not be the act alone, it must be something more, like it being a focus, even an obsession. Are people very much obsessed about eating and drinking as compared to ages past? Of course they are. What was the American diet of the 1800's and earlier? Whatever was in the ground or in the barn is what was served up for food. Vegetables, fruits, and animals. Today, those ingredients may still all be there but the variety is sure different. In fact, most people get bored with food if it is the same meal in the same month. Look at the countless recipes for even simple things. There are dozens upon dozens of recipes just for scramble eggs. And on the menu is not just pigs, chicken, cows, and fish anymore. With refrigeration, almost anyone can sample the delicacies from around the world. And talk about drinking, there is water, sparkling water, spring water, well water, flavored water, soda water, etc. And that is just water. So an explosion of attention in the area of food and drink is definitely different from the time the prophecy was given and only in the past century or so.

Point B:
Marriages

Then Jesus said that marriage would be an issue, as in the fact that people will be marrying and giving in marriage. Again, wait a moment! Marriages have always been happening. So it is not the fact that marriages are going on; there must be something else that is significant. And there sure is. From the time of Jesus through the 1800's, for the most part, two people were joined together in a quiet manner. Yes, there may have been a number of guests attending the wedding, but today, it has become a very concentrated effort to include all kinds of elaborate celebrations, manner that service is conducted, and the debt that is associated with such a wedding.

Some claim that these words point to the high divorce rate. Well, if that were so, then let us bring to everyone's attention to the fact that although it is true that the divorce rate has skyrocketed, the rate is a distortion of the facts. The divorce rate is based upon the number of marriages recorded in a given year as compared to the number of divorces executed in the same year, but not necessarily from those marriages. The divorce could come from a marriage a decade or more ago. So from all marriages prior to the current year, anyone filing for divorce this year gets factored in. When people track all marriages and figure out which ones ended in divorced and then compared to all of those marriages continuing on, the rate is significantly lower. Instead of the popular 50% rate for divorce, it is 20% or less, as reported by Quora.com. It is still a sad statistic but it is nowhere as alarming.

Now do not dismiss the understanding of marrying and giving in marriage or remarriage as a sign of the last days, which does imply a high divorce rate. We could just state that the verse does not mean a divorce rate and focus on how elaborate marriages are today that people are more willing to throw thousands and tens of thousands of dollars at, while they leave the church collection plate quite empty. That in itself is a fulfillment today, but so is the high divorce rate. Oh, do not think we are back stepping on our words now. The marriage and divorce rate may be off, but what is also off is our understanding of how God sees marriage.

God sees marriage very differently than we see them, according to several examples including what happened between Isaac and Rebekah. The Bible says, "And Isaac brought her into his mother Sarah's tent, and took Rebekah, and she became his wife; and he loved her: and Isaac was comforted after his mother's [death]" (Genesis 24:67). Did you catch it? On one level, God says that all the couples that are living together are actually married. That should be good news to all who have felt the chastisement of Christians and churches for "shacking up". At the same time, if you think you are avoiding marriage by simply living together, you are quite mistaken. There is no such thing as "living in sin" when it comes to shacking up. Again, the account states that when two people physically join together, they are married. So by Isaac bringing Rebekah into the tent to have sex and she agreed to enter the tent and be his wife, without the presence of a minister, they were married.

Now mind you, we are not advocating such arrangements because in this society, it is too easy to walk away from the commitment and have no financial obligations to worry about. If two people are truly committed, they should go through a formal process. But with that said, go ahead and search the Bible. You will not find a single marriage ceremony anywhere conducted by a minister. Even the ministers who say that God performed the first marriage ceremony are stretching it. All the Bible says about the first union of husband and wife is, "And they were both naked, the man and his wife, and were not ashamed" (Genesis 2:25). And that statement is not that they decided to stare at each other's bodies for a certain amount of time. It means that they had sex.

So, now factor in all the couples that live together and then swap out the partner and live with someone else and so on. Now in God's eyes, that divorce rate skyrockets, but wait! We are not done yet. Both examples point to couples joining together. Although Rebekah and Eve stayed with their men, what do you think God thinks regarding long sexual relationships, though they are only boyfriend and girlfriend? Pretty much the same thing as marriage. How about all the moments that people sleep around? You see, the Bible does not teach that sex should be reserved for marriage. Sex is marriage. That is why the Bible goes into symbolic relationship between us and Jesus along the marriage lines. Paul wrote, "I have espoused you to one husband" (2 Corinthians 11:2), and to enjoy being a Christian and then enjoy a little sinning and still be thinking one is a good Christian is completely off base. James wrote, "Ye adulterers and adulteresses, know ye not that the friendship of the world is enmity with God? whosoever therefore will be a friend of the world is the enemy of God" (James 4:4), which means every sin we commit is like committing adultery against Jesus.

Now factor those things (living together, just having sex though living apart, and all the one night stands) into the statistics and we see in God's eyes that the divorce rate is well over 90% or more. Probably in less than 1 out of 10 sexual encounters stick until death does one apart. How many different sexual partners have people had? The average is well above one. This was not so before the sexual revolution. It used to be that, especially for women who slept around, it was something to be avoided and reserved for marriage. Today, virgins are avoided. It is a shame that there is that sexual inequality between men and women and that is pretty much what brought on the sexual revolution of the 1960's around. Now statistics show that women are worse than men for sleeping around.

So no matter how you look at Jesus' words regarding marriage and giving in marriage, it is out of hand today but was not so before the 1960's.

Point C:
Population Explosion

Marriage and giving in marriage along with eating and drinking are the only two points that Jesus directly stated regarding the days of Noah, however, since Jesus said that the last days would be like the days of Noe (Noah), let us investigate further to see what other parallels there are.

Genesis 6:1 starts off with, "And it came to pass, when men began to multiply on the face of the earth." So there was a population explosion happening right before the flood. Interestingly, according to the U.S. Population clock, it took all the years of this planet through 1804 to reach the first billion people. In 1927, we reached two billion. Three billion came even quicker by 1959 followed by four billion in 1974. In 1987, we reached five billion, and in 1999, the sixth billion was reached. This was followed by seven billion in 2012. Are we experiencing a population explosion? Yes.

Point D:
Unequally Yoked (Connections)

On top of that, Genesis 6:1 continues into 6:2 with, "Daughters were born unto them, That the sons of God saw the daughters of men that they [were] fair; and they took them wives of all which they chose." Now there are interesting theories regarding these verses, which are just not true, though it makes for interesting reading, however, it is nothing more than a distraction. But since angels do not marry (Matthew 22:30 and Mark 12:25), which as stated before, means that angels do not have sex as sex is what constitutes marriage, the notion that these verses apply to angels from heaven reproducing with humans is preposterous. And on top of that, how could the reference "Sons of God" apply to the angels that remained in heaven when any sinful thought caused such to be considered fallen and kicked out. And having sex with humans evidently would have been sinful because the flood destroyed the results. Besides, the "kicking out" period already had happened. That means those that stayed in heaven were the ones who committed their minds to God. They were and are pure angels. And if anyone wants to call the fallen angels by the title "Sons of God", be careful because the Bible calls them devils (James 2:19).

So on that basis, we apply the term "Sons of God" to the other biblical meaning, which is, "As many as are led by the Spirit of God, they are the sons of God" (Romans 8:14). Not only do Sons of God refer to heavenly beings but the term also applies to anyone completely converted and committed to being one of God's children. That means that the daughters that they married back in the day were from the unconverted. This ought to not have occurred and is a theme constantly appearing in the Bible, even in the New Testament. We are told, "Be ye not unequally yoked together with unbelievers: for what fellowship hath righteousness with unrighteousness? and what communion hath light with darkness?" (2 Corinthians 6:14) What greater connection is there than to be yoked up in marriage? There is none.

Now for those that would ask about being committed to God being sufficient to prevent falling into sin, the answer is no. Once we have been given free will, we do not lose it. And what happens is that even the most godly person has the free will to think that they are godly enough to have a positive influence upon a sexy young woman. "I will convert her to God!" Unfortunately, time and time again, the Bible reveals that such thinking is a trap. If one is interested in such a relationship, convert the person first, give a little bit of time to see if it is genuine, and then pursue a relationship. So yes, the possibility of a human who is a "Son of God", one day being enticed by a fair maid and take her as his wife would result in having the heart drawn away. And the continued practice thereof just degrades the relationship with God. And the reason for the offspring to be giants is that for many generations the two groups, Seth's and Cain's, were kept separate. They married within their own blood lines. But now combining such people together, who knows what combination of results could occur. So that is just the summary of things. The sons of Seth were the sons of God. The fair women of Cain were the daughters of men. Or, one could say, the godly men took worldly women as their wives.

Therefore, carelessness in marriages would be repeated at the end of time before Jesus shows up again. Men, as well as women, of God would choose marital partners based upon how one appears, like being sexy, over the biblical description of, "A virtuous woman [is] a crown to her husband" (Proverbs 12:4). Virtuous is boring. The godly people quite often think they are strong enough to not compromise with their unconverted spouses, when in fact, it is they who become converted. Such people even today ought to consider, "Wherefore let him that thinketh he standeth take heed lest he fall" (1 Corinthians 10:12).

And so, people marry across different Christian beliefs for one thing, and it is easy to do. If people do not believe in a single understanding of each doctrine and feel that it does not matter what one believes, then as long as they are Christian, it does not matter that a Catholic marries a Methodist, a Baptist marries an Episcopalian, etc. But it does not stop there. Today, supposed committed Christians allow their eyes to take them across a broader boarder including Christians marrying Jews, Christians marrying Hindus, etc. But it does not stop their either. It goes even to the level of Christians marrying atheists. The issue is not about how kind and nice they are, but God has a principle, "Neither shalt thou make marriages with them; thy daughter thou shalt not give unto his son, nor his daughter thou shalt take unto thy son. For they will turn away thy son from following me, that they may serve other gods: so will the anger of the LORD be kindled against you, and destroy thee suddenly" (Deuteronomy 7:3-4).

In this society in which Christians believe that it does not matter which type of Christian one is, as long as they believe in Jesus they are going to Heaven, well no wonder what we are about to say does not make sense to the average Christian. If one believes that there is "One Lord, one faith, one baptism" (Ephesians 4:5) and a Catholic marries a Baptists, just how shall the child be baptized? Will the child be baptized as an infant with a sprinkle of water, or will the child be baptized by immersion around the age of twelve? Doing both to cover all basis is not the solution for "Where is your faith?" (Luke 8:25). One either has a faith that believes one doctrine or the other. To do both is for both parents is to not believe in their own doctrines.

Point E:
Great Wickedness

Genesis 6:5 says, "And GOD saw that the wickedness of man [was] great in the earth, and [that] every imagination of the thoughts of his heart [was] only evil continually."

And it does not have to be adults either. Children killing children, something unheard of before the 1960's, is now regularly in the news. Even excluding terrorists, the news is filled with heinous crimes as if it is a competition. The imaginations towards evil is everywhere.

In the movies and on television, it is all about the shock factor. It used to be that a person that would get hit with a vehicle in the episode would be seen stepping into traffic, the camera would switch to the reaction of the witness as it is happening, the screeching tire noises of the driver trying to stop in time but cannot, followed by a thud noise, and then panning back to show the victim lying on the ground. Now, it is normal to see a television series include such graphical representation at one point or another thanks to computer graphic images. Even the murder content has increased from Psycho to what we see today that makes Psycho something laughable. Jaws is also found humorous today, yet both movies sent chills down everyone's back.

Cyber bullying is out of control, constant changes in how to get high, and hardly heard of before regarding parents killing their own children just for selfish reasons, all point to great wickedness.

Society was not like this decades ago. Oh sure, people claim that the crime rate has come down. Some of that is because of the newer method of calculating the crimes, and let us give credit to hospitals that are getting better at sowing people up so murder rates are down since people are not dying as much from what used to be fatal.

Wickedness does not only deal with violence, it also deals with any of the sins. That includes hardcore sexual activities with whips and chains and other unbelievable devices and instruments. It includes even simple acts of seeking and conquering just to get another notch. All the methods of cheating, adultery, and just simple fornication are all part of the wickedness, especially when even Christians see nothing wrong with uncommitted sex.

Pick any of the Ten Commandments and this world, even among Christians, finds a way to break them. And it is pretty bad when the Christians have jumped on board. It brings into question of why even become a Christian if such is powerless to stop from committing the wickedness themselves.

Point F:
Corruptness

Genesis 6:12 states, "And God looked upon the earth, and, behold, it was corrupt; for all flesh had corrupted his way upon the earth." So corruption would get out of hand.

First, we need to once again understand the meaning of the word so that we are on the same page as they say. The word "corrupt", according to Webster Dictionary, means "to cause (someone or something) to become dishonest, immoral, etc." Of all the possible definitions, this one fits the verse very well. God saw that the world was corrupt. Back then, the world influenced people to the point that "all flesh had corrupted his way". So it would be at the end of time. The world once again would influence the level of honesty, morality, right decision making, etc., according to Webster. Therefore, compare the influence over time and see if we have entered yet into a most influential time or not in that category? We are not talking small scale influence. Everyone had that friend that kept trying to talk friends into doing the wrong thing, trying the wrong thing, just downright pushing the limits. And the answer is most assuredly yes.

Up until Hollywood was born, it was pretty difficult to influence people around the world. Now with movies and television, the exposure to corruptness in morals is unprecedented. Even the early Christians who spoke out against the theatre and eventually the movies and television are silent today. They are not only silent, but they enjoy their slaughter movies, their foul language content, their nude scenes just as much as the unsaved.

But Hollywood is not the only source of corrupting influence. The music industry may actually have more influential time exposing the world to corrupting themes. It is everywhere you go, and people can be plugged in all of the time.

Then we have the filth people find on the Internet, the hordes of lust books pond off as romance novels, and the government telling even churches what is and is not acceptable despite the Bible speaking contrary.

It does not take statistics to realize that church attendance is way down; Bible believers among Christians alone are hard to come by; morality among Christians through their own surveys is continuing to slide as immorality continues to increase.

So not only are there corrupting influences in sight and sound, they have so corrupted the world that Christianity is so weak and insipid. It stands for nothing and is obnoxious about it by claiming that they are still going to Heaven. Basically, Christianity in itself in a very large portion is corrupt.

Christian churches are so corrupt that they teach their members that it is Okay to sin; God's law is no longer binding; standing for standards is legalism; paying tithe is a form of works; watching biblically what to eat was a Jewish thing; and a whole lot more is placed upon a Christian influentially all under the guise of using the term "grace" and "faith" out of context. So again, the world alone has not just become corrupt, but so many Christians who think they are Heaven bound are also given in to corrupt influences in such a way that they use a godly excuse for their ungodly actions. Such preachers and teachers are "ungodly men, turning the grace of our God into lasciviousness, and denying the only Lord God, and our Lord Jesus Christ" (Jude 1:4).

Point G:
Violence

Genesis 6:13 says, "And God said unto Noah, The end of all flesh is come before me; for the earth is filled with violence through them; and, behold, I will destroy them with the earth."

Now we are not going to try and find statistics to influence you to thinking we live in a violent society for we admit that according to the FBI statistics, the last ten to twenty years, the violent crime rate has steadily been dropping, however, do not relax. While the world identifies a violent crime as some type of force, especially that being physical, that is not the biblical definition once again.

When God says that people would be filled with violence, yes, that means murder, rape, robbery, etc., but take notice what else God says. "Violence covereth the mouth of the wicked" (Proverbs 10:6). Violence includes simply saying mean things. So, we have no statics to provide because every verbal assault that bullies perpetrate is considered a violent act in God's eyes. Every utterance that people, even in jest, say like, "I wish you were dead" or "drop dead" is a count towards violence in God's book. Such language and expressions were not found among Christians, especially of the 1800's and earlier. It is our secular society that thinks they, even Christians, can say such things, claim that it is a meaningless expression representing tremendous frustration with another person, not realizing that such is condemned of God. "Let your communication be, Yea, yea; Nay, nay: for whatsoever is more than these cometh of evil" (Matthew 5:37).

So has bullying increased? Well, the fact that schools did not worry about anti-bullying campaigns until recently should answer that. Has anger increased? The term road rage is a recent phenomenon as well, at least in the past ten or so years.

But just speaking angrily and bullying verbally is not the only definition. Ever hear of peer pressure? That was not something people worried much about in the 1800's and prior, but it sure plays a role today. Now you may be asking, "What does peer pressure have to do with violence?" The answer is that God counts such as violence. "A violent man enticeth his neighbour, and leadeth him into the way [that is] not good" (Proverbs 16:29). So every act to do evil is considered violent. That means a lot of commercials are guilty of perpetrating violence. Encouraging sex between unmarried people is violence in God's eyes, and that is just one example, but has such increased on TV? Absolutely. Condom commercials, lubricants, sexual get aways, 900 numbers, are just the commercials let alone actors and actresses promoting free sex.

There are probably other definitions in the Bible that can continue to add to this category, but we think that what we have supplied shows, hands down, it is obvious that these things are exploding in frequency today as never before in any decade, let alone the century before ours.

Point H:
Few True Christians

1 Peter 3:20 says, "Which sometime were disobedient, when once the longsuffering of God waited in the days of Noah, while the ark was a preparing, wherein few, that is, eight souls were saved by water."

The key part of this verse is about the fact that only few shall be saved. Sure, we cannot identify who is going to make it and who will be lost. In fact, we are told, "For with what judgment ye judge, ye shall be judged: and with what measure ye mete, it shall be measured to you again" (Matthew 7:2). So if we were to judge who is going to Heaven or hell, we would be working contrary to Jesus' teaching, however, Jesus also taught, "Enter ye in at the strait gate: for wide [is] the gate, and broad [is] the way, that leadeth to destruction, and many there be which go in thereat: Because strait [is] the gate, and narrow [is] the way, which leadeth unto life, and few there be that find it" (Matthew 7:13-14). Further, Peter wrote, "For the time [is come] that judgment must begin at the house of God: and if [it] first [begin] at us, what shall the end [be] of them that obey not the gospel of God?" (1 Peter 4:17) Now did you catch it? Obedience is part of the gospel message. And the verse above stated that back in Noah's day, the lost were disobedient.

Do we have some disobedient Christians today? Sure we do. In fact, the vast majority teach that obedience is not a requirement of a Christian, hence why many Christians cannot be trusted today. They state that Christians are merely saved by faith through grace without any requirement of the humans, and that is just no so. It is true that we cannot add to our salvation, however, we are to observe (Matthew 28:20) or obey what Jesus asks of us after we have accepted His free gift of salvation, which is, "Go, and sin no more" (John 8:11) and "If ye love me, keep my commandments" (John 14:15).

So, is there a minority or few that preach such a message of obedience? Yes there are, though they are so few that they are hard to find.

POINT 12:
Worldly Preachers

Matthew 24:45-51 says, "Who then is a faithful and wise servant, whom his lord hath made ruler over his household, to give them meat in due season? Blessed [is] that servant, whom his lord when he cometh shall find so doing. Verily I say unto you, That he shall make him ruler over all his goods. But and if that evil servant shall say in his heart, My lord delayeth his coming; And shall begin to smite [his] fellowservants, and to eat and drink with the drunken; The lord of that servant shall come in a day when he looketh not for [him], and in an hour that he is not aware of, And shall cut him asunder, and appoint [him] his portion with the hypocrites: there shall be weeping and gnashing of teeth."

A rise of world loving preachers will be a sign towards the end of time, and I believe we are there. Look at many of the preachers today. They are decked out with glittering objects. They speak words that keep themselves popular. They speak in a manner that encourages enjoying the world and not about sacrifice and denial. There is even the health, wealth, and prosperity gospel, when we see nothing but denial in the life of Jesus.

Many preachers incorporate sporting events, worldly holiday symbols, and much more as part of their gospel message. People are encouraged to come to Jesus as they are, but instead of becoming a better person, they are confirmed in their sins not needing to change.

Anytime obedience is mentioned, just as Jesus predicted, these worldly preachers go on the attack. They label the minority preachers that call for discipleship (discipline) as legalists despite Jesus saying, "If any [man] come to me, and hate not his father, and mother, and wife, and children, and brethren, and sisters, yea, and his own life also, he cannot be my disciple. And whosoever doth not bear his cross, and come after me, cannot be my disciple" (Luke 14:26-27). They label the minority preachers who call to give up sinning as being saved by works despite the purpose of Jesus coming, which was to "save his people from their sins" (Matthew 1:21), not in their sins. They label the minority preachers who call for obedience to the Ten Commandments as Judaizers despite the Bible teaching, "For whosoever shall keep the whole law, and yet offend in one [point], he is guilty of all" (James 2:10), and "He that saith, I know him, and keepeth not his commandments, is a liar, and the truth is not in him" (1 John 2:4).

POINT 13:
Like the Days of Lot

Luke 17:28-32 says, "Likewise also as it was in the days of Lot; they did eat, they drank, they bought, they sold, they planted, they builded; But the same day that Lot went out of Sodom it rained fire and brimstone from heaven, and destroyed [them] all. Even thus shall it be in the day when the Son of man is revealed. In that day, he which shall be upon the housetop, and his stuff in the house, let him not come down to take it away: and he that is in the field, let him likewise not return back. Remember Lot's wife." Just as we did with Noah, we are going to break things down sub point by sub point including looking at other references connected with Lot, as in, Sodom and Gomorrah.

Point A:
They Eat

One of the items that Jesus mentions in comparison in Lot's day was about eating. This is similar to the days of Noe (Noah) comparison as already addressed a while back. It is not the fact that they were eating, but it is that life revolved around the food. Instead of eating to live, people were eating for the sake of eating anything and everything they desired, to satisfy taste buds, to always push the limits with something new, etc. Again, this is pretty much describing our society today in which simple meals that meet the body's required needs is traded for something exciting and different of which is not always digestible and this is not a once in a while desire, on average, people are looking almost daily for something different to eat.

Point B:
They Drank

Again, no different than the comparison with Noe (Noah) where drinking is not the issue, but when it becomes a focus on desire instead of need, that is when this is fulfilled. And again, we have not seen drinking excess until now. And no, we are not referring to only alcoholic drinks. Just walk down the juice isle at a grocery store and see not just your basic juices but all kinds of concoctions as no generation has seen prior. People are not satisfied with just water, just grape juice, just orange juice, etc. Society thirsts for all sorts of things. The coffee isle is tremendously out of control with tons of flavors as well. Again, simple choices are gone, because people do not drink to replenish the body's liquid needs but rather to satisfy taste buds.

Point C:
Buying

Now buying is not wrong, in fact, it is almost a necessity in doing business today. People have to buy something, be it a house or even renting, be it a car or a transportation fare, be it food or what is necessary to grow one's own food. Buying is a way of life. But again, that is not what Jesus is referring to. When buying stuff reaches a point that is out of control in general, then this will be fulfilled.

So consider that up through the 1800's and even during the depression of the early 1900's, frivolous things were seldom purchased by the general public. Today, fashion rules. Impulse buying is the expected, or the checkout lanes would not be filled with such eye catching last moment purchase thoughts. Even though many donate last year's clothing to a good cause that does not justify keeping up with fashion by discarding clothing that is still in very good condition and still fits. Up through the 1800's, people were thankful for the few articles of clothing they owned while wearing them until they could not be patched anymore. Having the latest gadget despite the fact that last year's model works just fine is something unheard of even up through the 1950's. We used to repair things until they could not be repaired anymore, but today, it is more expensive to repair the item, which means that it is best to just buy a replacement, hence, in this throwaway society where we just buy, buy, buy, we have fulfilled this reference easily.

Point D:
Selling

Jesus said that people sold right up until the end before fire and brimstone came down. Again, nothing wrong with selling. It is the out of hand aspect of it. And is it out of hand? Well, when the object of the sale is solely to get the most for the item as possible without losing the sale, even if that means outright lying about the item's quality and ability, yes, we are pointing to our time again. It used to be honest dealings by a mere handshake, now we not only have contracts, but lawyers have to approve them. Lawyers review from the seller's standpoint, and other lawyers review from the buyer's standpoint. Why? Because we primarily do not trust sellers anymore. Sure, there are shady buyers that look for a loophole, purchase with the intent of exercising the loophole, only to turn around and sue the seller. Look at the driver of a camper who put the vehicle on cruise control thinking it drove as an airplane's autopilot. He sued and won. But for the most part, the handshake days are pretty much behind us because sellers have become very conniving.

Point E:
Buying and Selling

Combining the two points together pretty much describes the stock markets of today, which is nothing but buying and selling. Now the stock market is not something new. In fact, according to Investopedia, the first resemblance of the stock market occurred during the 1300's with the Venetians. The official first stock exchange, however, is actually credited to have existed only since 1531 in Belgium. But as like eating and drinking, it is not until it gets out of hand or controlling that it becomes an issue that warrants investigating it for fulfillment of prophecy or not.

Now in the 1600's, Dutch, French, and British governments working with companies in India helped bring about the expansion of the stock market concept, but it would not be until 1773 that the first official stock market in London would open, only to be followed by the famous New York Stock Exchange in 1792. And as we have already stated, we are not out to prove that the last ten years or even twenty constitutes the end of time so that we ought to be ready for Jesus to return, but rather, as a future chapter will go into detail about, the end of the 1700's and beginning of 1800's is when we are proposing as the period under investigation and 1792 definitely fits that category. Besides, just because the NYSE was born at the end of the 1700's, it would not be until the last twenty years or so that it has played the role of world influence upon buying and selling.

Even companies have bought into the stock exchange where retirement packages are not based upon the company paying out personally after a person retires, but paying into a stock market tied retirement portfolio and let the stock market pay the retirement payments.

Truly, we are in one way or another tied into the constant, worldwide buying and selling. It drives gas prices; it drives the oil markets; it drives business; it drives our personal lives.

Point F:
Planting

So the next point in Jesus' list is on planting, as in, crops. Nothing wrong with doing so, but again, when it becomes a recognized issue, that is when it is a sign. Are there any big issues when it comes to planting? Again, we would say that yes it has. Up through the 1800's, people planted with natural resources. Since the early 1900's, with ADM (Archer Daniels Midland Company) and the more recognized organization of Monsanto, planting has become a big issue, or should we say, the consumption. There is an organic and pesticide war; there is also a GMO war going on. In fact, these companies have been successful in using brute force and lawyers to wedge their way into controlling the farming around the world. Unheard of before the 1900's but now is a difficult time in which we live in, it is hard just to find just seeds called heirlooms. They are the natural seeds from the natural plants.

Point G:
Building

Again, building structures is not an issue, but when it becomes out of focus from simply providing shelter to live and even work, we have reached another point in the list of events to be fulfilled. This issue cannot be simply about building palaces and mansions today because since the time of Jesus and beforehand, there has always been the filthy rich who would build palaces or even just mansions. So there must be something else that is significant towards the end of time. May we suggests skyscrapers being an issue? Sure, there have been tall buildings before, but it seems that in our day, skyscrapers are a declaration of artistic genius. By building such, humans are being glorified for their abilities over God who provided such architectural gifts. These gifts are being misused to outdo each other, like the Burj Khalifa building in Dubai, or to make a political statement, such as the One World Trade Center, the replacement of the Twin Towers, in New York.

Skyscrapers are also a method herding people into the cities and we know what Sodom and Gomorrah were like when the cities get crowded. Sin abounds and all manner of evil is practiced.

Point H:
Remember Lot's Wife

Jesus finishes the comparison between the days of Lot and the Second Coming with those concerning words. In regards to Lot's wife, it is said that she "looked back from behind him, and she became a pillar of salt" (Genesis 19:26). They were warned, "Escape for thy life; look not behind thee, neither stay thou in all the plain; escape to the mountain, lest thou be consumed" (Genesis 19:17).

Now to figure out the significance here, we have to understand the significant meaning of the event. You see, not only do Christians not read their Bibles today, not only do they not believe in the Bible being accurate, they cannot see the deep importance of an event beyond the simple recording of it. There is spiritual meaning behind Lot's wife that is ready to be discovered.

Fleeing Sodom is representative of leaving the old sinful life behind, but if one's heart is still longing for that life, despite not physically performing such acts, God places them on the same level as Lot's wife, guilty. To say, "I wish I could have sex with as many partners as I want, but as a Christian, I'm not allowed to" is considered as guilty as doing such. To say, "I wish I could get drunk every weekend, but as a Christian, I'm supposed to set a good example" is just as guilty as getting drunk.

Jesus said, "Where your treasure is, there will your heart be also" (Matthew 6:21). So if one longs for Heaven, then their thoughts will not be on the regrets of what they had to give up in life to become a Christian. Pining for the old life while gritting one's teeth so as not to physically participate in the sin is not really a changed life, nor was Lot's wife's life changed.

So, do we have Christians today that live that way? Not only do we, but the thought of sacrificing or giving up the old life is unheard of in Christianity today. Many say, "What do you mean I'm not supposed to go to bars anymore?" "What do you mean I'm not supposed to be watching television or movies containing filth?" "What do you mean that I'm not supposed to listen to music that promotes sex, drugs, anger, etc.?" So, not only do we have a lot of Christians looking back at their old life wishing they could continue to do those things, they are actually doing those things while claiming that they cannot lose their salvation or claiming to restrict their lives from these things is legalism.

It has actually become so bad that there is a joke about Christians that goes something like this: A man was tired of his nagging wife who bugged him to go to church and on the next invitation to church he spouted off, "Let me get this straight. You and I both watch the same garbage on TV, go to the same raunchy movies, stuff ourselves at the all-you-can-eat restaurants, drink the same alcohol, smoke the same cigarettes, say the same foul words, you go to church while I stay home and watch TV. What's the difference?" And that man is right. What is the difference between a Christian and a non-Christian? Is it that one is claiming to be "saved" while the other is lost?

Point I:
General Wickedness

Genesis 13:13 says, "But the men of Sodom [were] wicked and sinners before the LORD exceedingly." Combine this with Genesis 18:20, which says, "And the LORD said, Because the cry of Sodom and Gomorrah is great, and because their sin is very grievous."

As we have done with Noe (Noah), so shall we do regarding Lot, Sodom, and Gomorrah. We are going to dig deeper into the issues surrounding them and try to learn what else Jesus may be foretelling. To start off, we see a generality of wickedness being out of control. Ask the average Christian what the sins of Sodom and Gomorrah are, and almost always at the top of the list the acts of homosexuality are mentioned. Ask them what other sins there were and hardly anyone can mention another sin. Well, we are about to see that there were a whole lot of other sins including heterosexual sex too.

But right now, let us deal with general wickedness and not only general wickedness but that which is exceeding, in other words, either extreme in the type or amount of the wickedness or intensity. Do understand that we have always had liars, thieves, adulterers, murderers, etc. In fact, we have always had periods of large quantity of mass murder, called genocide. So that cannot be it.

Therefore, we would like to propose something that has not always been until fairly recently. The first is the mass collection of the world that doubt the existence of the true God and favor some form of evolution, be it outright unbelief in God or unbelief in taking the Bible as it reads. Up through the early 1900's, even those that did not believe in God knew that anyone who did believe in God accepted the Bible as the Word of God, in other words, to be true and factual, but not so today, even among most Christians. And did you know that evolution was not a theory until the middle 1800's? It held a very minority view, but now today it rules the school educational system.

Consequently, we believe that what used to be the minority view being now the majority, and the view that the Word of God is true and a factual being the majority view has now been reduced to the minority view is considered wickedness to God. We get support from the fact that of all the sins that God could mention deserving of fire and brimstone, the unbelieving make the list. "But the fearful, and unbelieving, and the abominable, and murderers, and whoremongers, and sorcerers, and idolaters, and all liars, shall have their part in the lake which burneth with fire and brimstone: which is the second death" (Revelation 21:8). We believe that all those that hold onto any sin and refuse to give up such, be it Christian in name or not, will end up in the lake of fire. But to specifically call out these sins of all sins, this must be God's top eight list.

But this is not a surprise to the studious Bible student. It was predicted to happen and even happen in the church. In Revelation chapters 2 and 3, there are 7 churches. After careful study, it will be found that each church represents God's people during a certain period in time. Interestingly, Jesus is introduced into each period to address the most challenging point during that time. Today, we live in the seventh church period. Jesus is introduced as "the Amen, the faithful and true witness, the beginning of the creation of God" (Revelation 3:14). The fact that Jesus addresses creation in His introduction implies that such would be challenged. Seeing that this church period, after careful study, began in the mid 1800's, it is not by coincidence that evolution is the challenge of the day. Now it is one thing to be a challenge on the outside from unbelievers, but it is another thing in which it is a challenge from inside the Christian fold, where even Christians trying to comingle evolution and Bible to support evolutionary beliefs and not seem so out of touch with modern science. Basically, it is a fulfillment of prophecy.

The second item that we would like to point out that is considered wicked to God is the sanctity of marriage being made a mockery. Sex is everywhere, and even accepted among those calling themselves Christian. Even among Christians, sex is something that is expected after a few dates. For the one Bible theme that God holds sacred, society sure has reduced it to the unsacred. We call it holy matrimony. Society, well, "They have put no difference between the holy and profane" (Ezekiel 22:26).

The third and worst of all is what Christianity has turned into. Jesus said, "If ye continue in my word, [then] are ye my disciples indeed" (John 8:31), with disciples meaning that one is disciplined, but we now have the majority of Christians rejecting the Word of God as being truly the Word of God and have no will power to be disciplined, hence, it really does not exist among most nor is it preached upon. Jesus said, "If ye love me, keep my commandments" (John 14:15), but today's Christians cry, "Legalists!" Jesus said, "Ye are witnesses of these things" (Luke 24:48), while today's Christian witness for Satan all the daylong claiming to be saved while continuing in sin, and it is recognized by unbelievers as hypocrisy. Speaking of which, Jesus came to "save his people from their sins", but Christians are taught to come as you are and even stay as you are, in your sins. And the Bible teaches that "As many as received him, to them gave he power to become the sons of God, [even] to them that believe on his name" (John 1:12), when today Christians seem so powerless towards sin and Satan. They are basically the sons of Satan teaching that victory over sin and habits is not possible, when Jesus said, "All power is given unto me in heaven and in earth. Go ye therefore, and teach all nations, baptizing them in the name of the Father, and of the Son, and of the Holy Ghost: Teaching them to observe all things whatsoever I have commanded you: and, lo, I am with you alway, [even] unto the end of the world" (Matthew 28:18-20).

Point J:
Forced Sex and Homosexuality

Genesis 19:4-5 says, "But before they lay down, the men of the city, [even] the men of Sodom, compassed the house round, both old and young, all the people from every quarter: And they called unto Lot, and said unto him, Where [are] the men which came in to thee this night? bring them out unto us, that we may know them."

In the full context, this is not a good thing on two accounts. By the way, so everyone understands, "to know" someone biblically is to have sex. So, on the first account, this is forced sex. Forced anything is devil's work, let alone the sexual context presented. And yes, this would classify as an attempt at gang rape.

Now all through the centuries, rape is not new, but what is new is how it is carried out and the frequency in which it is carried out in. Sure, there is probably statistics that will declare how rape is on the decrease, along with other criminal acts, but those statistics are mostly in comparison within the past century. How about comparing over the centuries? Of course we have always had wars in which the armies raped and pillaged, but that is the same today as centuries ago. Looking strictly at societal rape, it was infrequent back centuries ago, primarily because men and women did not interact as they do today, which presents enticements and opportunities.

Swimming pools, beaches, and other places of gawking did not exist, especially in a coed environment. Additionally, women and girls in scantly clothing including gymnasts and cheerleading along with the average clothing or lack thereof that is purchased today did not exist centuries ago. Porn, which greatly sexualizes women, did not exist then. All of these things contribute to men who are not mentally stable to act upon victims. Unfortunately, rape is not limited to male offenders. Today, women are also involved in raping men as well.

Although it is not an excuse for anyone to rape someone no matter how enticing they may look, there is a responsibility on both sides as declared in the Bible. "Women adorn themselves in modest apparel" (1 Timothy 2:9). Thongs, bikinis, but crack revealing pants, see through blouses, breast revealing neckline, and even tight fitting clothing, is all condemned by God's standards. Yet, we have to remember the responsibility of not sinning still is in the beholder, or should we say to not behold. "Whosoever looketh on a woman to lust after her hath committed adultery with her already in his heart" (Matthew 5:28). So do not go to the swimming pool or beach and gawk at them. And by them, we are referring to women looking at men in banana hammocks as well. Do not buy the swimsuit editions of sporting magazines. Do not be staring at flaunting women or men for that matter. If they have it and they are flaunting it, turn away.

In addition to these things, in the same category of forcing sexual relations, is that of quid pro quo, where sexual favors are on the table, literally, not only for promotion but just to keep the job. Also, unheard of centuries ago, is the situation called date rape drugs. Even the whole dating scene is completely different as compared to centuries ago in which much pressure is put on adults that after three dates, it is time to enter into a sexual relation or the relationship is over. Even teens get caught up in the pressure.

So in the category of forced sex, have we come to a point that we are repeating Sodom and Gomorrah? We are not sure how much worse it needs to get before we finally say that it has.

But the second thing smacks against the issues of Sodom and Gomorrah from these verses is the type of relation in which God says, "Thou shalt not lie with mankind, as with womankind: it [is] abomination" (Leviticus 18:22).

Has homosexuality become prominent in society? Absolutely. So much so that laws that used to forbid such acts, in which is named after Sodom, are struck down, and replaced with legalizing marriages between these couples. We in no wise advocate gay bashing, discrimination in the work place, discrimination in commerce, or any other type of exclusionary acts. At the same time, we do not believe one ought to be forced to accommodate anyone based solely upon sexual preference either. Purposely forcing the hiring a homosexual is an example of such abuse of power by governments.

But as we also stated at the beginning of the study of Lot's time in history, it is very much unfair and even discriminatory in God's eyes to always focus upon homosexuality as being the issue in Sodom and Gomorrah. To overlook the numerous other sins, even more grievous in some cases, as we will see, is to distort the message of God.

So let us wrap up this particular point by again asking, has homosexuality greatly changed from the time of Jesus until the present? And the answer is yes. So much so that it has infiltrated Christianity to the point that gays and lesbians are made ministers in some denominations, but that was predicted to happen towards the end of time as we shall see in further investigation of end time events. And has the whole sexual activity also changed of which is condemned in the Bible? And the answer is yes.

Point K:
Mocking

Genesis 19:12-14 says, "And the men said unto Lot, Hast thou here any besides? son in law, and thy sons, and thy daughters, and whatsoever thou hast in the city, bring [them] out of this place: For we will destroy this place, because the cry of them is waxen great before the face of the LORD; and the LORD hath sent us to destroy it. And Lot went out, and spake unto his sons in law, which married his daughters, and said, Up, get you out of this place; for the LORD will destroy this city. But he seemed as one that mocked unto his sons in law."

Peter describes the mocking of the last days by recording, "Knowing this first, that there shall come in the last days scoffers, walking after their own lusts, And saying, Where is the promise of his coming? for since the fathers fell asleep, all things continue as [they were] from the beginning of the creation. For this they willingly are ignorant of, that by the word of God the heavens were of old, and the earth standing out of the water and in the water: Whereby the world that then was, being overflowed with water, perished: But the heavens and the earth, which are now, by the same word are kept in store, reserved unto fire against the day of judgment and perdition of ungodly men." (2 Peter 3:3-7). In plain language, people are going to be so caught up in the enjoyments of the world that the thought of the end of the world is going to be scoffed at, a synonym for mocked.

So, do people mock at the thought that the Second Coming could be in their life time? Absolutely. It does not help that so many Christian preachers are date setters, and when the date passes, people are made comfortable in their mocking position, even encouraged. By the mere continuance of a party-like lifestyle they re-enforce the thought that each day has passed by just as during the days of their parents, and their grandparents, and their great-grandparents, and so on. That is what is meant by multiple fathers falling asleep: father, grand-father, great-grandfather, etc. Those people heard the end was coming and then nothing happened. In fact, most have died at a good old age, and yet Jesus has not returned.

Now, no survey need be taken to provide statistics that the world mocks the idea of Jesus' soon return. How do we know? The lack of seriousness to deal with sin on a personal basis, lack of Christians telling others about Jesus' return is soon, the lack of getting serious about living a Christian life. In fact, many call Christians a bunch of hypocrites, and rightfully so. If they thought Jesus was coming anytime soon, they would be serious about getting rid of sin and be actively telling others to get ready. Instead, conversations are monopolized by sports, celebrities, fashions, and other events.

On top of that, many who are invited to hear the gospel close their ears and willfully say, "Don't tell me too much. Ignorance is bliss!" Not so of course. Jesus condemns this attitude by saying, "And this is the condemnation, that light is come into the world, and men loved darkness rather than light, because their deeds were evil. For every one that doeth evil hateth the light, neither cometh to the light, lest his deeds should be reproved" (John 3:19-20). Therefore, in the end, such people are not going to be able to claim ignorance when they did it willfully.

Point L:
Lack of Listening to the Bible and Lack of Obedience to the Law

Isaiah 1:9-10 says, "Except the LORD of hosts had left unto us a very small remnant, we should have been as Sodom, [and] we should have been like unto Gomorrah. Hear the word of the LORD, ye rulers of Sodom; give ear unto the law of our God, ye people of Gomorrah."

Another issue in Sodom and Gomorrah included not listening to the Word of God and rejecting the Ten Commandments. Admittedly, the non-Christian have always lacked listening to the Bible and definitely lived in disobedience to the Ten Commandments, but today, Christians also now reject the Bible as the Word of God and consider obedience to the Ten Commandments as acts of legalism, trying to earn Heaven. Not only is this popular opinion, but it is preached from the pulpits. This was not so a century or two ago. People used to carry their Bibles to church. The thought to mixing evolution and Bible verses was unheard of. Churches even displayed proudly the Ten Commandments.

Point M:
Blatantly Sinning

Isaiah 3:8-9 says, "For Jerusalem is ruined, and Judah is fallen: because their tongue and their doings [are] against the LORD, to provoke the eyes of his glory. The shew of their countenance doth witness against them; and they declare their sin as Sodom, they hide [it] not. Woe unto their soul! for they have rewarded evil unto themselves."

Again, unheard of even a century ago is the declaration of their sin or better known as blatant sinning. Lots of sins were done in privacy. Today, it is flaunted everywhere. Take porn for instance. What used to be something ashamed of is now regularly viewed even by Christians. In fact, it is now not normal to find someone who is not enjoying porn. On top of that, porn is reclassified to the point that it is acceptable by society to allow teenagers to view it without embarrassment and without declaring that it is corrupting minors. Take for instance certain shows on a movie network like Game of Thrones and True Blood. That is outright porn. People used to buy this stuff in alleys at night; now it is pumped into homes, even to young viewers, on demand.

Look at musicians as they keep pushing the sexual envelope further and further by each upcoming singer. Bumper stickers that include foul words show also the sin of selfishness and inconsideration for families with young children that ask their parents, "What does that word mean?" The blatant disrespect for authority even after simple sporting events with rioting and looting explained away as being something people just do. Also, look at the content being taught in schools and passed off as sex education, which would make the parents of the 1800's drop over with heart attacks.

We are evolving alright, into a sex crazed, sin blatant society. All of these acts, though nothing new from ages past, are not individually the issue but collectively an issue in the category of waving it in God's face, almost daring Him to act.

Point N:
Prophets or Preachers Committing Adultery, Lying, and Encourage Evil Doing

Jeremiah 23:14 says, "I have seen also in the prophets of Jerusalem an horrible thing: they commit adultery, and walk in lies: they strengthen also the hands of evildoers, that none doth return from his wickedness: they are all of them unto me as Sodom, and the inhabitants thereof as Gomorrah."

So again, Sodom and Gomorrah is a symbol of other sins outside of homosexuality. The ministers back then committed adultery and walked in lies.

First, realize that there is but one commandment that deals with all sinful sexual activity, and that is the one that states, "Thou shalt not commit adultery" (Exodus 20:14). That means when we see sexual issues among the ministry in general, know that it is like Sodom and Gomorrah. And have we? Sure we have. The Catholic church has been rocked with scandal after scandal these past few decades, famous ministers caught with a hooker and even child porn, and many who counsel the opposite gender get caught up in the emotions and commit adultery.

So, onto the question of, "Do ministers lie?" Absolutely and predictably as we shall see later. But for now, do recognize first that we have so many denominations all contradicting themselves, someone has to be lying. Further, I personally have gone to non-denominational Bible studies, raise a few specific truth points as the topic came up for discussion, to end up being attacked and nearly run out of the study and not be welcomed back, only to be the last one to leave with the pastor who hosted the study for them to have an opportunity to say to me, "You know you are right, but if I teach that, I would lose my congregation." So yes, they lie. They lie both in preaching untruths, but more popularly, they lie by not revealing the truth while focusing on other insignificant messages. Many ministers are accused of preaching the easy gospel, as that is considered a bad thing, which it is. Nothing what these easy gospel preachers preach may be wrong. It is what they do not preach upon that is wrong, all in the name of being popular.

And do ministers encourage evil doing or sinning? Again, absolutely. Unheard of a century ago would be any message that was light on sin, tearing down the Ten Commandments, and encouragement to stay as people are without a change and be promised to go to Heaven. All of that is absolutely wrong and that also explains why Christianity is in as poor of a condition that it is in morally. For decades the members have been told that the Ten Commandments were "nailed to the cross", that they are saved by their faith alone, that all they have to do is believe in Jesus, and that grace does away with the Ten Commandments. Believe those messages long enough and Christians see no penalty for sleeping around, losing their tempers, using foul words, watching inappropriate content, listening to filth filled songs, smoking, drinking, and doing all kinds of horrible, sinful things. Since they are saved anyways and cannot lose salvation, why would it be important to obey, for that matter, even to attend church? That's because the Ten Commandments are still relevant, and by Bible definition, "Sin is the transgression of the law" (1 John 3:4). And when it comes to grace, "For sin shall not have dominion over you: for ye are not under the law, but under grace. What then? shall we sin, because we are not under the law, but under grace? God forbid" (Romans 6:14-15). And when it comes to faith, "Do we then make void the law through faith? God forbid: yea, we establish the law" (Romans 3:31). So no, the law of the Ten Commandments have not lessened at all. Ministers have been encouraging the breaking of them, which is sin, which is evil.

Point O:
Pride, Gluttony, and Idleness

Ezekiel 16:49-50 says, "Behold, this was the iniquity of thy sister Sodom, pride, fulness of bread, and abundance of idleness was in her and in her daughters, neither did she strengthen the hand of the poor and needy. And they were haughty, and committed abomination before me: therefore I took them away as I saw [good]."

So let us start with pride. Is society out of control in this area? Absolutely! And it is unprecedented. Now surely someone will say, "We always had prideful people." That is true, but thanks to sporting events, pride has grown to an epidemic state. No longer do people just have a favorite team to watch. Vehicles are damaged, people are pummeled, and that is just little league. The major league sports players and even other celebrity type figures are more in people's faces bragging that they are the best getting worse and worse every year, so much so, that there are sporting rules to try and control such activities. Therefore, we say that since the last few decades, thanks to sports, pride is definitely out of control. Life does not matter anymore. Just look at European sporting events through the recent history. People dying because of a sporting event outcome?

Next in the list is gluttony, which if anyone says that it is not an epidemic today as compared to just a century ago, must not receive any news from the outside world. Constantly we are reminded that we are overweight. Constantly we are reminded that it continues to grow unchecked. Yes, some of the overweight statistics is based upon ideal weights that are a bit unreasonable, but it does not account for those that are obese, which way too many people are, even as compared to the 1980's and decades prior.

And then that brings us to idleness. That is basically having too much time on one's hands. Oh, we may feel like we are on the constant go, but in comparison to the 1800's and prior, children including older teens have way too much time on their hands. Up through the 1800's, all children were employed at a young age on the farm, and just about most of society were farmers. In fact, schooling was adjusted so that the children were available to be on the farms during planting and harvesting. Today, with farming more company owned and mechanically controlled, the demand for farming is not as high. Employment is reduced from sun up to sun down now to simply forty hours a week. Children spend hours watching television, playing video games, getting into trouble, etc. So when we look from the children's perspective, most definitely they are not being kept busy.

Psychologist have contributed greatly to this fulfillment of prophecy. Motivated by their own poor childhood or wishing everyone had their enjoyable one if they had one or even motivated by the ideal childhood, psychologists are down with working a lot and pushing family recreation time more and more. Parents are considered workaholics if a parent thinks quality time with children is working side by side, even if it is house chores. They teach that quality time is going to the park, playing games, and being active in non-work related ways, all of which is nowhere found in the Bible. All through the Bible, a form of work or learning is the quality time. That does not mean there cannot be a game night, a family outing time, but when recreation is pushed as the goal, that is when it is unbiblical with the danger of people growing up preferring, no, demanding the play time over getting the job done. As proof we are being influenced by society more towards idleness through these supposed experts, just look at the fruit of their work. We have a generation that procrastinates more than any generation prior. We have a generation that expects high rewards for the smallest amount of effort. We have a generation that is the most impatient, non-enduring generation of all time. We have a generation that does not even take to motivation of any sort including wealth, health, or satisfaction of completing something. We have a generation that starts many task and finishes the fewest. We have a generation that is more into gaming than worried about working to pay their bills. We have a generation that uses their parents not only as a financial safety net but as a hammock by being the generation that seems to take longer to move out on their own or being ones that come crawling back home because they cannot make ends meet.

Now all those things are stated in a general sense. Sure there are hard working older teens and young adults today but not as there were in prior generations that continue to degrade and degrade and degrade especially after the World War II generation.

Point P:
Living Ungodly

2 Peter 2:6 says, "And turning the cities of Sodom and Gomorrha into ashes condemned [them] with an overthrow, making [them] an ensample unto those that after should live ungodly."

Ungodly includes secularly, meaning that we are all about work, play, and living for the next day seeking success, recognition, and materialistic things. Again, we point out the fact that since Jesus' day, religion was an important identifier, so much so that even in the 300's AD, Christians wanted to be identified separately from Jews and chose to forgo a lot of the common connections including changing from Sabbath observance into Sunday observance and adopting pagan holidays over the optional Jewish feast days showing symbols fulfilled in Jesus.

In our society, Sunday used to be a day all stores were closed, labor was only that which was necessary, but overall, it was a family and God day, in other words, the churches were packed. As our society has grown more and more secular, church attendance even by the members on the books is down below a third or even a quarter of its membership. Truly employment and sporting events are more important than giving God any time. So even among Christians, ungodliness, not necessarily sinfulness, reigns.

Point Q:
Fornication, Strange Flesh, Defiling the Flesh, Rejecting Authority, and Speak Evil of Supernatural Beings

Jude 1:7-8 says, "Even as Sodom and Gomorrha, and the cities about them in like manner, giving themselves over to fornication, and going after strange flesh, are set forth for an example, suffering the vengeance of eternal fire. Likewise also these [filthy] dreamers defile the flesh, despise dominion, and speak evil of dignities."

Do we really have to convince anyone that fornication is running out of control? Teen pregnancy, though declining, has also seen a peak in our life time. Most teens are sexually active before they reach adulthood. Virginity is gone in 92% of people by the age of 25. Sex is all over television, movies, in the music, on billboards, in commercials, in the news, promoted in sex educational classes, is everywhere.

In referring to the strange, that is that which God did not ordain. In general, strange is like the example of a pair of brothers who were high priests. There was fire that God had kindled and was to be used for the sanctuary service. Instead of using such fire, these two drunken priests decided to use any old fire that God did not ordain. Note what God called their choice. "And Nadab and Abihu, the sons of Aaron, took either of them his censer, and put fire therein, and put incense thereon, and offered strange fire before the LORD, which he commanded them not" (Leviticus 10:1). This tells us that even though something does not appear in the Bible, instead of treating the Bible as if it is alright to do if not forbidden, we ought to look at the Bible as to say if God is silent about it, we ought not do it.

So, applying this to flesh, God uses such to mean sexual relations. "Therefore shall a man leave his father and his mother, and shall cleave unto his wife: and they shall be one flesh. And they were both naked, the man and his wife, and were not ashamed" (Genesis 2:24-25). As you see, for the union of one flesh or sex, God had made Adam and Eve, not Adam and Steve. He also made Adam and Eve; He did not make Adam and Eve and Jill and Alice and… Also, Adam got naked with Eve. Adam did not get naked with a lion, a horse, or any other creature. Adam also did not get naked before other females either, which would have been his daughters, unlike today where naked photos and movies are plentiful. The point is, any sexual activity outside of what God had set as the pattern in the beginning, without God even having to declare that this is the only way to do it, is considered strange. So yes, homosexuality, bestiality, polygamy, posing nude, and even masturbation are all strange sexual or flesh activities that should not be done as they were the sins practiced in Sodom and Gomorrah. In addition, having one committed sexual relation followed by another and another is equally considered strange. As discussed on a prior point, sex is marriage therefore it is not something to save for marriage; it is marriage and should be treated that way. That means that any activity of sex being reduced to an act of just having sex is also wrong, even in a marital relationships. It should be entered into each time as a special moment and not just a satisfaction of one's physical needs or of some type of release from built up pressure in the body. Therefore, even in marriage, sex can be considered strange to God.

In regards to defiling the flesh, we may instantly think of injections of drugs, cutting oneself not to die but for the mere rush, etc. But when we see that the Bible also states that we are not to "print any marks upon you" (Leviticus 19:28), we now see tattoos as an issue, and has such exploded with interests in recent years? Absolutely. Even Christian ministers are getting all tattooed up. On top of that, when God says, "the strange gods which [were] in their hand, and [all their] earrings which [were] in their ears" (Genesis 35:4) in the context of jewelry being condemned, then we again ask, has body piercings gotten out of control lately? And again, the answer is yes. What used to be a simple piercing in each ear of a woman has grown to be fully studded ears as well as piercing all over the body. And this also is not only an issue with women anymore, men are well studded too.

Now to be despising dominion, that is the way of saying that people don't like being ruled over even by legitimate authority, especially by some ancient book. And ever since the 1960's, rejection of authority has not ceased. It has grown so much so that individuals have no respect for each other. As stated before, parents do not appreciate inconsiderate people plastering very foul words on their bumper stickers or clothing, yet if the person was kindly asked to hide it somehow, their reaction is, "Who are you to tell me what to do?" Well, we were not telling you what to do; we were hoping to appeal to reasonableness. We definitely are living in a time where rebellion is being expressed by the majority of society because they think it to be a lack of being tough and to let anyone express authority over them. Reasonableness is dead. Humility is very much dead, as it is equated with being wimpy.

Finally we have the practice of speaking evil of supernatural beings. Thanks to evolution and atheists, God has gotten a lot of bad credit. He is blamed for every death, disaster, destruction that occurs. Sure God could stop it all, but as discussed before, that would just prolong the sinful production that Satan states is a better government than God's heavenly government. Not only that, the good angels of the Bible, especially Gabriel, are always promoted as evil in movies and television. Even among Christian preachers, they teach that the good angels had intercourse with human beings back before the flood. All of these things are a sample of evil being spoken of regarding the supernatural beings we call God and the angels.

POINT 14:
Fearful Sights

Luke 21:11 states the words "fearful sights and great signs shall there be from heaven".

In a physical sense, the heavens have been a fearful sight. Our past century saw the invention of air planes in which struck fear during the World Wars and many other wars since. Then there is always the fearful thought of nuclear annihilation.

On a combination of physical and spiritual aspect, the satellites and air waves are filled with programming that misrepresent angels and demons and end of the world scenarios, all of which strike fear into many.

And then we have the purely spiritual in which is yet to be fulfilled. John the revelator wrote, "And I saw three unclean spirits like frogs [come] out of the mouth of the dragon, and out of the mouth of the beast, and out of the mouth of the false prophet. For they are the spirits of devils, working miracles, [which] go forth unto the kings of the earth and of the whole world, to gather them to the battle of that great day of God Almighty" (Revelation 16:13-14). This is another one of those very last day events in which, when we see this happening, we know we are but days away from seeing Jesus showing up. So it will be too late to have any material like this to publish.

POINT 15:
Hearts Failing

Luke 21:26 says, "Men's hearts failing them for fear, and for looking after those things which are coming on the earth: for the powers of heaven shall be shaken."

Today, we call them heart attacks. Statistically speaking on this one, heart attacks were unheard of up through the early 1900's. Heart attacks not only became known, it became one of the leading killers of men in such a short time. And in the late 1900's heart attacks rose in women astronomically to the point that it too is now a leading killer among women.

And what is a contributor? It is all of the issues people have to be dealing with. Despite Jesus saying, "Take therefore no thought for the morrow: for the morrow shall take thought for the things of itself. Sufficient unto the day [is] the evil thereof" (Matthew 6:34), people worry more today than in ages past.

POINT 16:
Church is Full of Hypocrites

2 Timothy 3:1-5 says, "This know also, that in the last days perilous times shall come. For men shall be lovers of their own selves, covetous, boasters, proud, blasphemers, disobedient to parents, unthankful, unholy, Without natural affection, trucebreakers, false accusers, incontinent, fierce, despisers of those that are good, Traitors, heady, highminded, lovers of pleasures more than lovers of God; Having a form of godliness, but denying the power thereof: from such turn away."

How do we know this describes the condition of the church and not the world? Well, one could easily say all of this has always been practiced in the world, and they would be correct. But there is specific wording that alludes to this being the poor condition of the church before Jesus returns. People will have a form of godliness but deny the power that is to make them godly causing those that would even consider being a Christian to turn away from looking any further.

Godliness is not something the world seeks after. Godliness is a desired result of those that have an encounter with Jesus, well, at least it should be. When a true Christian has accepted salvation, they will go through various stages. The Bible describes them as, "According as his divine power hath given unto us all things that [pertain] unto life and godliness, through the knowledge of him that hath called us to glory and virtue: Whereby are given unto us exceeding great and precious promises: that by these ye might be partakers of the divine nature, having escaped the corruption that is in the world through lust. And beside this, giving all diligence, add to your faith virtue; and to virtue knowledge; And to knowledge temperance; and to temperance patience; and to patience godliness; And to godliness brotherly kindness; and to brotherly kindness charity. For if these things be in you, and abound, they make [you that ye shall] neither [be] barren nor unfruitful in the knowledge of our Lord Jesus Christ. But he that lacketh these things is blind, and cannot see afar off, and hath forgotten that he was purged from his old sins. Wherefore the rather, brethren, give diligence to make your calling and election sure: for if ye do these things, ye shall never fall" (2 Peter 1:3-10).

There are a lot of points in those words of God through the writer Peter, but notice that it starts off revealing the purpose of life, godliness. We are to form a godly character. Now, in just picking on some of the important aspects, please note how it begins. It says that divine power has been given to us to accomplish the rest of these verses. In being very direct, that power that has been granted to every new Christian that Peter wrote about is the same power that Paul wrote in his letter to Timothy describing Christians would deny. In other words, right here meets the fact of what we have been stating. There are true Christians who accept the divine power and there are pretended Christians who deny the power exists and just put on some external representation of Christianity. The pretended ones are described in the letter to Timothy while the true ones are described in Peter. In Timothy, those Christians have such an outward appearance of being a Christian but not an inward that they are the ones that go around saying, "I'm saved!", while practicing any or all of the sins that Paul listed. The true Christians are "of a meek and quiet spirit" (1 Peter 3:4), in fact, it is hard to spot them outside of the fact that that they are practicing what is described in Peter.

And please note, in Peter, true godliness is developed while in Timothy, a form of it but not heart changing godliness is present. These same pretended Christians may dress nicely for church, are helpful, donate to various causes, are wonderful people in general, but tell them to stop sinning and they are the first to yell: "Only Jesus is perfect!"; "I'm saved by grace!", as if grace gives the open freedom to be sinning; "I believe in Jesus", as if a fact of Jesus existence is all there is to salvation; etc. Peter wrote that if true Christians do what those verses state, and do it so that they are solid in the faith, they will never fall. That does not mean they will not scrape a knee or two; it means that they will not be participating in sinning and making excuses for it. Now be careful not to be taking this out of context. This does not mean true Christians have never sinned nor will they ever sin in the future, but if they do sin, they are not going to be covering it up or trying to excuse it away. In fact, another writer wrote for God, saying, "My little children, these things write I unto you, that ye sin not. And if any man sin, we have an advocate with the Father, Jesus Christ the righteous" (1 John 2:1). So, a true Christian does not make excuses for sinning; they stop sinning, but if they make a mistake and do sin, it is not like they are treated as "one strike and you're out!" The Bible says, "If we confess our sins, he is faithful and just to forgive us [our] sins, and to cleanse us from all unrighteousness" (1 John 1:9), and then Jesus is the one that "is able to keep you from falling" (Jude 1:24), not ourselves. So a true Christian who sins against another, will also provide restitution like Zacchaeus. "Zacchaeus stood, and said unto the Lord; Behold, Lord, the half of my goods I give to the poor; and if I have taken any thing from any man by false accusation, I restore [him] fourfold" (Luke 19:8). Basically, a bank robber who becomes a true Christian will give the money back and face the consequences; someone breaking something of another person's will pay for the repair or replacement. One does not just say, "I'm sorry!", or worse, one does not just say sorry to God and leave the victim in the dark.

Also notice another thing in comparing the verses of Timothy to Peter, in which he states that those who lack in godliness are unable to comprehend by being blind to the fact that Jesus purged, got rid of, removed, squashed our sinning habits. In fact, Jesus came to "save his people from their sins" (Matthew 1:21), not in their sins, as we will repeat often since this is so lacking in Christians today. Therefore, all the preachers that make it nice and comfortable to sit in their churches so that people do not have to stop sinning are false preachers, and there are tons of them.

So now, what specific sins would the pretended Christians practice? First on God's list through Paul's writing is "lovers of their own selves." Yes, people can be selfish in any generation, but when selfishness happens in the church, then one knows that we are seeing the signs of the last days. The fact that we are living in the "me" generation does not help matters, but we have moved from doing what it takes to keep a church functioning to now taking care of ourselves first and if there is anything left over, maybe we will give a portion to the church. We moved from keeping a day of rest, to at least showing up to church, to now treating church as being indifferent and unimportant. "I need to work", "I want to watch the game", "I need to get to the store", "I need to go on vacation", "I need…", "I want…" That certainly sounds like being lovers of one's self. Church statistics prove this out where less than 5% of European Christians attend church and less than one third of Christians attend church in the United States. Hardly anyone tithes, let alone provide any extra offerings.

The second item on God's list is Coveting, which is even happening between churches. One church starts a Sunday evening service, another has to. One church puts up a wavy symbol to declare they have the Holy Spirit and another church follows suit. Coveting is even among Christians individually? How do we know? They have all the impractical things just like those that are not Christian. They have the same sports cars, fashions, houses, gadgets, and much more. Granted not everything listed is wrong to possess but when it is unnecessary, then it is wrong. Christians trade their gadgets in for the latest and greatest just as often as non-Christians. Christians exploit the holidays just like non-Christians. Oh, "remember the reason for the season" while they rack up their credit cards because the recipient is expecting to get those things, which is coveting.

The third item on God's list is boasting, which is so far out of control these days, especially by all the people that go around declaring, "I'm saved" when the rest of the Bible story says, "No they are not!" Declaring the glory of God is one thing, but bragging one is saved while practicing sin is nothing short of boasting, which was not done before the 1800's. That is a new phenomenon. And the danger of believing one is saved and cannot choose in the future to give it up is that there is no motivation to act Christian. Why even go to church then? Why give tithe? Church attendance or lack thereof does not affect salvation under those circumstances despite the Bible telling us why to attend. It is "for the perfecting of the saints, for the work of the ministry, for the edifying of the body of Christ" (Ephesians 4:12).

The fourth item is Pride and is very strong among Christians today as opposed to the 1800's. In the 1800's people were more open to switching churches. Show them in the Bible where the person's church was in error and without question, they would leave their old denomination for a new one. Not today. Christians will argue every which way possible to stay right where they are or be fine all alone. Show them clear cut truth and they say, "Well, no one knows exactly the truth"; "All churches have error in their beliefs"; "Remember, no one is perfect so what does it matter?"; "Well, back in their day, they saw it differently"; "My pastor just might not know everything, but they are a good person"; etc.; etc.; and etc. The only pride God is concerned about is that of living in sin or error and refusing to give it up. "[For] the sin of their mouth

[and] the words of their lips let them even be taken in their pride: and for cursing and lying [which] they speak" (Psalms 59:12).

The fifth item is blasphemers. Taking on the names reserved for God, is one way such is done. And one very popular name used is in direct violation of a Bible principle, "holy and reverend [is] his name" (Psalms 111:9), referring to God. Our names are not reverend. Today and for some time now, even unbelievers recognize that a minster should be called Reverend. But even so, any form of disrespect towards God is blasphemous, even if it is clueless. Take for instance all the dress down appearances to attend church. People dress up for special occasions, interviews, special people, but they look like slobs at church. And what do some wear? Clothing with peace signs. The peace sign is a symbol that gives up on Christ. It is a rejection of the cross. How blasphemous is that? All the irreverence that takes place because of God accepting us as we are is out of hand. Churches used to be places that you could hear a pin drop. Today, it is a social club or circus. These things have developed only since the 1960's but prior to that, there was nothing like what we have now.

The sixth item is being disobedient to parents, which includes all forms of authority. Sure, every generation could not wait until they did not have to listen to their parents anymore, but in the 1800's and prior, without all of the socialization and distractions we have today with television and places to go, there was more respect towards parents than we have today. Being disobedient to parents does not neglect the respect either, even to other adult figures. Promoted by psychologists, today's children do not even greet adults properly anymore. In the 1970's and prior, it was Mr. or Mrs. and their last name. Today, everyone is on a first name basis. Society has contributed to the disrespect by doing such. Look at the schools and how out of control the students are where the students today challenge authority so much that they think they can get away with shooting up the place and blowing it up. Unheard of just a few decades ago. But in the Christian church, the ultimate disobedience to parents is to reach adulthood and drop out of church, which is the largest gap ever recorded. It seems that church is nice for initial education as a child and young teen, and it is good enough for the elderly, but in between, why be bogged down with all these formalities and rules?

In regards to the seventh item of being unthankful, unless we have become desensitized to living in today's world, up through the 1900's, people were very thankful for what they had. Unthankful does not mean grab and go without saying "thank you", it is also a form of being unsatisfied. A family of children in the 1950's were very thankful for one bicycle, even though all seven or so children needed to take turns. Today, not only does each child get a bicycle, but the child is not satisfied if it does not come in the color they expected. We are also a society that discard perfectly useful items just because it is not the latest version of it. We live in the most unsatisfied time in history, and it is just getting worse. We have so many choices and new choices every day and that only contributes to the problem. The Bible even says, "[Let your] conversation [be] without covetousness; [and be] content with such things as ye have" (Hebrews 13:5). Are Christians content? Most are not.

The eighth item of being unholy is basically sinning, which is the definition of breaking the Ten Commandments. The Bible says, "Sin is the transgression of the law" (1 John 3:4). And here is a list of people who do not keep the law, taking notice that the unholy is in that list. "Knowing this, that the law is not made for a righteous man, but for the lawless and disobedient, for the ungodly and for sinners, for unholy and profane, for murderers of fathers and murderers of mothers, for manslayers, For whoremongers, for them that defile themselves with mankind, for menstealers, for liars, for perjured persons, and if there be any other thing that is contrary to sound doctrine" (1 Timothy 1:9-10). So, is the church full of law or Ten Commandment breakers as opposed to generations ago and to the extreme? Absolutely. It has gotten so bad that churches are pulling down the Ten Commandments that they used to proudly display and replacing them with references to open armed Jesus to welcome a sinner to attend their church and never being encouraged to leave their sinful ways. People who openly are sinning are placed into positions, and none of this would have been thought of before the 1950's, where churches encouraged the Bible standards, including the Ten Commandments.

The ninth item of having unnatural affection is not about hugging a tree. The phrase is actually used elsewhere in the Bible. Romans 1:31 provides a list of issues back then and includes our phrase, "Without understanding, covenantbreakers, without natural affection, implacable, unmerciful" [emphasis added]. It only makes sense then to search Romans chapter 1 for the description of what is natural as opposed to unnatural. "For this cause God gave them up unto vile affections: for even their women did change the natural use into that which is against nature: And likewise also the men, leaving the natural use of the woman, burned in their lust one toward another; men with men working that which is unseemly, and receiving in themselves that recompence of their error which was meet" (Romans 1:26-27). Please note that there is a "by nature" or natural use of a woman, which these verses are stating and that it is to be satisfied by a man. And note that it is unnatural, as in, God never intended women to join sexually with another woman. We call it lesbianism. Likewise, the man has done the same thing. Instead of allowing a woman to satisfy him, men burn or lust towards other men. This is called being gay. So despite the attempt to twist away the meaning of "unnatural affection" to be applied to homosexuality, we have concluded that it does apply by looking at the context alone. So, has homosexuality infiltrated Christianity? Not only has it, they are becoming ordained preachers. Churches are removing anything that may be anti-homosexual. Even the pope is trying embrace the gay community. So yes, we always have had homosexuality but when Christianity embraces it, then it is a sign.

The tenth item is that of trucebreakers, focused once again upon Christianity, happens to be in the context of returning back to warring. A truce usually puts an end to wars, but when it comes to the Bible and Christianity, we are talking about spiritual warfare. Remember, Satan has gone "to make war with the remnant of her seed, which keep the commandments of God, and have the testimony of Jesus Christ" (Revelation 12:17). In fact, Paul wrote, "The weapons of our warfare [are] not carnal" (2 Corinthians 10:4), and Peter wrote, "Dearly beloved, I beseech [you] as strangers and pilgrims, abstain from fleshly lusts, which war against the soul" (1 Peter 2:11). Do keep in mind that fleshly lusts are not only limited to expressing sexuality or appetite. Any sinful desire that we give into works or wars against our soul. And to war against the soul means, "the soul that sinneth, it shall die" (Ezekiel 18:4). There is no eternal life for one continuing in known sin.

When a person decides to be a true Christian, one turns from all their sinful practices and is at peace with God. But these trucebreakers, who call themselves Christians, have broken that peace agreement with Christ and have returned to their indulging ways in which, as Peter wrote, "wars against our soul". Not only do today's Christians do that, but take notice regarding the title of this book. There are two groups with "one mind", as we have been saying. There are the Christians who pretend to be such, which is the bad or dark side, and then there are those that conform to the mind of Christ, the good or the light side. Please note the description of the dark side. "These have one mind, and shall give their power and strength unto the beast. These shall make war with the Lamb, and the Lamb shall overcome them: for he is Lord of lords, and King of kings: and they that are with him [are] called, and chosen, and faithful" (Revelation 17:13-14). Did you catch it? The bad or dark side not only breaks the truce, but it develops into an all out war against Jesus, the Lamb.

So back in Timothy, when it says that the there would be trucebreakers, it means that they would work against Christ; make war against Him; and just not be at peace. They basically have turned away from salvation by their own choice. Although it is true for a true Christian that God will "give unto them eternal life; and they shall never perish, neither shall any [man] pluck them out of my hand" (John 10:28), there is a constant requirement every moment of our lives. The preceding verse states, "My sheep hear my voice, and I know them, and they follow me" (John 10:27). In fact, there is a colon after verse 27 which clearly links it to verse 28 placing a condition on the relationship. Today, we read His voice; it is called the Bible. And to follow that voice means to live in obedience to all that is commanded in the Bible. So yes, no one can force us to leave God's loving protection, but no one ever gives up free will either. We can choose at any time to leave His hand. This is why Paul wrote, "I die daily" (1 Corinthians 15:31) and Jesus said, "If any [man] will come after me, let him deny himself, and take up his cross daily, and follow me" (Luke 9:23). It is a daily commitment. It is not a date of years past when someone declared they were "born again".

It stands to reason that this would be the condition of most of Christianity, truce breaking, because we cannot go from everyone believing their own thing and be right to all of a sudden getting rid of the true Christians. All that believe that they can continue in sin and try to claim Christianity and all the perks that go with it, like eternal life, cannot live in peace with those constantly reminding them that they are wrong and will be lost. You would think that they would just give up their sins, but instead they war with all kinds of unbiblical arguments justifying their unholy life. Therefore, to have that type of spirit, the false Christians must break the truce with Christ and return to their sinful ways and twist things in such a way that they think they are right and even destined for Heaven. No wonder Jesus said repeatedly to be aware of the deceptions of the last days (Matthew 24:4, 5, 11, 24).

And just how far has this truce breaking gone? Movies used to be condemned, but not only are they no longer spoken in the context of its evil influence upon society, churches hold movie night inside the church and advertise it to the public. Certain style of music, basically rock, used to be condemned, but now there are Christian rock concerts. Church used to be a place that common believers gathered to worship God, but now it is a social club and even a coffee shop. There "are given unto us exceeding great and precious promises: that by these ye might be partakers of the divine nature, having escaped the corruption that is in the world through lust" (2 Peter 1:4), and instead,

Christians have broken that truce and returned to them not only personally but collectively. It is not the fault of all the church members but the leaders who seek popularity over doing that which is right. "For when they speak great swelling [words] of vanity, they allure through the lusts of the flesh, [through much] wantonness, those that were clean escaped from them who live in error. While they promise them liberty, they themselves are the servants of corruption: for of whom a man is overcome, of the same is he brought in bondage. For if after they have escaped the pollutions of the world through the knowledge of the Lord and Saviour Jesus Christ, they are again entangled therein, and overcome, the latter end is worse with them than the beginning" (2 Peter 2:18-20).

The eleventh item to hit the Christian church at large, not just a few, is false accusing. And in the Christian world it is definitely running without control. For those that do not understand what this phrase means, this is not accusing someone of doing something wrong when they did not. This applies to all the preachers and teachers and members of the Christian body that twist scripture to make it look like those who are holding the truth are wrongly appearing to those that are honestly questioning. They even want the true Christians to appear as working evil, but the Bible says, "Woe unto them that call evil good, and good evil; that put darkness for light, and light for darkness; that put bitter for sweet, and sweet for bitter!" (Isaiah 5:20).

One example of false accusations is to accuse those that promote obedience to the Ten Commandments as being legalists. This in turn places the seed of doubt in that people will equate obedience and legalism as one in the same when that is not the proper definition of legalism at all, and it covers up the expectation that God has for His people. Legalism, by definition, is one that expects the reward of Heaven because they kept all the requirements of God to the letter. They make sure that they meet the required level, but at the same time they do not desire to go beyond because the motivation is not there. And those few that go above and beyond the level of obedience they have in their mind usually are motivated by thinking that there is extra merit in what they are doing.

An example of a legalists on the subject of tithing, which is to give ten percent of one's increase to the church being usually one's income, is an excellent illustration of legalism. That money is to be used to pay the salary of the religious staff, not for building projects or materials. Now if a wealthy person who could afford more than just ten percent sees that the staff is suffering to the point that they are considering laying off people and cutting salaries but is not moved to consider adding a bit more to their tithe amount and even states, "All I'm required is ten percent!", then we have legalism. This is why Jesus said, "Woe unto you, scribes and Pharisees, hypocrites! for ye pay tithe of mint and anise and cummin, and have omitted the weightier [matters] of the law, judgment, mercy, and faith: these ought ye to have done, and not to leave the other undone" (Matthew 23:23). They calculated to exactly ten percent, but God forbid if it was ten point one percent or higher. Legalism should not be applied to anyone that meets the expectation and goes beyond when the motivation is not for earning Heaven but simply moved to help God's church.

The biggest example of legalism is to say to oneself, "I have kept all of the commandments, all of God's statutes, have made sure I paid my ten percent, and…", and then turn around and say, "Therefore, I deserve eternal life." Legalism in this case places merit on doing the right thing. There is no merit in obedience. Unfortunately though, merit is how society works for the most part. Just ask for volunteers for anything and see how many one would get. Unless there is something in it for them, they are not interested.

Now, not meeting the expectation is outright disobedience. So those that believe in the tithing system and will bend over backwards even to the point of depriving oneself of some needs just to meet at least the ten percent are not legalists. To label such people as legalists is falsely accusing God's people of such, which fulfills this point we are making.

So why would there be false accusers in the church, let alone be the majority? The reason is because such people do not want to live up to the standards of the Bible, and they think that if they can diffuse the rule on tithing here on earth, they will be alright for Heaven still, as if earthly rules matter. They do not understand that it is the heavenly perspective, where the rules do not bend. And for some reason if these false accusers can convince a larger number of people to live in disobedience, that too somehow brings comfort, as if numbers matter. You would think that Noah and Lot would both stand out as examples against the numbers game, especially since Jesus Himself brought this to the attention as a sign of the last days. So numbers do not matter to God; quality does. Sure God would like to see everyone in Heaven, but the reality is that only a handful of people at any point in time are willing to live according to the rules that even Satan rejected before Adam and Eve ever sinned.

The false accusers not only twist verses on the subject of tithing, but they also twist it on a list of other things. Pulling one verse out of the Bible and saying, "Just believe!" in the context of disregarding all other verses containing rules, is what is currently happening today, and on top of that, calling all others that say, "There is more to it than just believe" as being workers of salvation is another example of falsely accusing. Calling those that state anything about the Bible diet or Sabbath observance as Judaizers, calling those that believe in baptism by immersion as being all wet, calling those that speak out against homosexual practices wrong as being homophobes, etc. are all further examples of the many, and we could quote more, false accusations. Basically, arguing against the righteous in the world so as to feel good in one's own sins is the motivation of the false accusers. These are the people that are running the churches today, including twisting the message of, "God loves everyone!" Sure, God does love everyone, but love does not mean everyone gets to go to Heaven. He expects us to love Him back. And Jesus said, "If ye love me, keep my commandments" (John 14:15).

And there you have it. False accusers are the people that want to go to Heaven without any rules to follow or have any restrictions on one's life. These are the same arguments Satan used before getting kicked out of Heaven. These are the same lies that he inspires into the rebellious humans. The worst part is that these false Christians have taken on the name Christian and are bringing a bad name to Christianity.

The twelfth item is Incontinent and is used only once in the Bible, which means "without self control". As Webster would say, it is lacking self-restraint. Again, we have always had people that have no self control, but our focus is upon the members of the church, supposed Christians. Is self-control lacking among Christians, and is that a recent discovery? Yes! Everyone knew that Christians were teetotalers even into the 1900's. Those that drank were consider drunkards by the Christians no matter how little or how much they drank. Several denominations still practice the forbiddance of such today, but the vast majority of Christians do drink and many get just as drunk as the non-Christian. Today, many Christians in name only pig out just like the non-Christian. Supposed Christians waste so much time with video games as well as with expensive, wasteful hobbies as the non-Christian. [Not all hobbies are wasteful, but a lot are.] Christians have the same buying impulses, same excuse of "I couldn't help myself", same giving into curiosities, pretty much the same everything when it comes to self control or the lack thereof. In fact, up through the 1800's, there was much talk about holy living, but then something changed. Since apparently no one can be perfect, imperfections of sinning were permitted; sins were relabeled as habits; and more and more emphasis on what Jesus has done for the Christian believer while downgrading the requirements of Christian character was being preached. And the end result is that we have so many Christians that all have the same disease: they cannot stop sinning no matter how hard they try. And they use that to reinforce the fact that "no one is perfect!" There is a solution to that, but that is not our point right now. We will state though that part of the issue is that they alone are trying so hard, when they need to partner up with God, which is more than seeing the rules.

The thirteenth item is being fierce or savage like, which is the result of lost self-control in the area of losing their tempers, and is, by observation, practiced among most Christians today. They get into a fit of rage just like non-Christians. Bring the fact that Christians ought not act a certain way and that just makes them rage even the more. Now keep in mind, anger is not a sin. If it were, God would be guilty (Zephaniah 2:2). We may get angry at a rapists, at a thief, at a bully, at a cheat, at… any sinful situation you can name. Someone accidently spilling milk, on the other hand, is something we may not get angry over. Someone does anything that is by accident, we may not get angry with them. A sports team or celebrity competition not having the expected outcome, we may not get angry over. And many other related situations that have nothing to do with righteousness being under attack, are all things that we are not to get angry over and yet, there is no difference between many Christians and non-Christians. And even in the anger over righteous things being under attack, we still need to be in self-control and not let the anger become fierce. Just like God when He sees a person that "humbled himself, the wrath of the LORD turned from him, that he would not destroy [him] altogether" (2 Chronicles 12:12). If righteous anger cannot be turned off, it then has crossed the line and is now sinful.

As for the church being made up of "despisers of those that are good", which is the fourteenth item, need we really address this? It has been addressed in almost all of the other points in the list. That is what prompts the false accusations to fly. That is what prompts a lot of the uncontrolled fierceness, people to be proud and let others know it through the boasting, starting with being trucebreakers towards God. How far will they carry it? Well, that is our study. That is what this book is about. There are those that are pretended Christians, and there are the few true Christians. How far it will go is eventually an attempt to get rid of the truth filled Christians, but more on that later.

The fifteenth item of traitors are those who appear to be supportive of the group they belong to while all the while working for the enemy. It is even when people switch sides, as in, being on one side in a war and then choosing to defect and fight for the other side. When a person becomes a Christian, they agree to fight against sin and Satan by representing righteousness, teaching righteousness, and worshipping the Commander, Jesus. Do keep in mind that to whom one obeys is a form of worship. In fact, God says, "My little children, let us not love in word, neither in tongue; but in deed and in truth" (1 John 3:18). So going to church to worship God and yet, the deeds or actions of the person all week long are like that of the devil means that the person is really worshipping the devil.

Keeping that in mind, the Bible says of these people, "For [it is] impossible for those who were once enlightened, and have tasted of the heavenly gift, and were made partakers of the Holy Ghost, And have tasted the good word of God, and the powers of the world to come, If they shall fall away, to renew them again unto repentance; seeing they crucify to themselves the Son of God afresh, and put [him] to an open shame" (Hebrews 6:4-7). The sad thing is, we have Christians that not only have left Christianity to write books, speak on radio and television programs, proclaiming to be an expert in the religion of Christianity only to tear it down, but we have Christians that claim to remain as Christians while replying to those that call them on their practicing of sin, "Oh, well, I don't follow that rule." Could you imagine a person in the military saying that? They would be tossed in the stockade. Others in the military depend upon everyone doing exactly as ordered. Unfortunately we have moved from always having a handful of people in the church being traitors to today where the majority of the members are living sinful lives excusing them away. Worse yet, we have officers in God's army who teach insubordination towards our Commander by teaching from the pulpits and in Bible study that we do not have to follow the rules, the Ten Commandments.

The sixteenth item of being heady is to be rash or reckless. Getting behind the wheel of a vehicle without taking proper education is reckless. To toss away the instructions to take on a task prompted only by what one thinks is the right thing to do is reckless. Before the 1950's, the Bible was taken as the Word of God not as an object but for what instruction it contained and the education it provided. Today, according to many secular (non-religious) surveys, hardly a Christian opens the Bible; hardly a Christian can quote the Bible; hardly a Christian seeks its guidance at all. Today's Christians have tossed the instructions away. They go on an imaginary concept thinking they know what Jesus would do if He were there when in reality they are mixing up kindness and true love. In addition, by tossing the Bible aside, they think they know Jesus when in fact the only are getting the gossip of Jesus from their preachers, who typically preach one sided. Preachers do not show how Jesus dealt with the traitors, even those in leadership, calling them hypocrites (Matthew 23:13-15). They do not show how Jesus continuously stated that eternal life involves obedience to the commandments (Matthew 19:16-19). They do not show how Jesus told that only a few people are going to Heaven (Matthew 7:14). They do not show a lot of things that would disturb their popularity. Many think kindness is the mark of a Christian when numerous times loving the soul is more important in which one must disappoint the soul or person. For example, the Bible is not fond of smoking at all (1 Corinthians 6:19). To see a person struggling to open up a pack of cigarettes only to be kind and say, "Here, let me open that for you", would be wrong for the Christian to do. Yet it is done for numerous sins. It is estimated by one set of statistics from ABC News that 94% of Christians basically have thrown the instruction guide, the Bible, away, maybe not physically but mentally.

The seventeenth item of being high minded is a form of being proud, but proud was already in the list. So instead of pointing again to how many Christians go around claiming proudly, "I'm saved", while still openly sinning and do not even care to try and stop sinning, let us look at this from the perspective of the placement of the word in the list. If one has become reckless and thrown away the instruction book, could it be possible then to develop and unchangeable attitude that is actually prideful in knowing how a Christian ought to behave? Not only is it possible, but that pretty much describes most Christians and Christian preachers today. Show them what the Bible says in which contradicts their belief or message and they are too proud to admit their form of Christianity that they have is wrong. It used to be that people were like a group from the days of the Apostle Paul called the Bereans. "And the brethren immediately sent away Paul and Silas by night unto Berea: who coming [thither] went into the synagogue of the Jews. These were more noble than those in Thessalonica, in that they received the word with all readiness of mind, and searched the scriptures daily, whether those things were so. Therefore many of them believed; also of honourable women which were Greeks, and of men, not a few" (Acts 17:10-12). Christians used to spend hours discussing what the Bible said. Christians used to go to the Bible to see if something were right or wrong. Not today. As the motto is, "If it feels right, do it." So, when one is told that drinking (Proverbs 20:1) and smoking are wrong according to the Bible, those Christians that advocate the use of them will argue the medical benefits, and we know that God is all for medical benefits. There is no convincing these people otherwise. The concept of "Submit yourselves therefore to God, resist the devil, and he will flee from you" (James 4:7) is lost upon many of today's Christians.

Need we say anything about the eighteenth item where today's Christians being "lovers of pleasure more than lovers of God"? Our comments thus far proves that where people donate for every other cause all kinds of money, they even blow money for mere excitement, but when it comes to the collection plate, a mere twenty dollar bill is dropped in and they think they have done great at giving. On top of that, we already stated that Christians are so into sports games that they would rather attend the sporting event over a godly event, like church. Many Christians enjoy their Friday or Saturday nights out and have a hard time waking up for church the next day. And as stated before, there is no difference between a Christian and a non-Christian except the one may attend church service. They both are entertained by not only sports, but the same R-rated movies, garbage television, celebrity magazines, loose moral clothing, same foul language, same brands of tobacco products, same alcoholic drinks, same party atmosphere, despite God saying to be careful what the eyes (Psalms 101:3) and ears (Judges 5:3) are exposed to, to dress modestly (1 Timothy 2:9), watch the conversation (Philippians 1:27), not to drink (Proverbs 20:1), not to put poison into the body (Deuteronomy 29:18, 20), and even warns about not partying (Matthew 24:48-51). Today's Christians are all on board criticizing the Bible as some old fuddy duddy set of rules that ended in the 1800's, especially when it comes to modern dating. Even whole churches have been given over to such pleasure by offering movie nights, instead of just doing what God say, "Teach" (Matthew 28:20). Jesus didn't say, "Get their attention first."

Now the problem is that these false Christians that have made one excuse after another for not stopping these disgusting behaviors turn around and put some outward show of being a Christian that they "have a form of godliness", so that means they are not really godly. Well, obviously they are not if they are doing some or all of those things in the list.

To accomplish the feeling of all is well, they have to deny the power that is given to a Christian. That power, once again, is the "power of God unto salvation" (Romans 1:16), "Who are kept by the power of God through faith unto salvation" (1 Peter 1:5), which is to mean that Jesus "is able to keep you from falling" (Jude 1:24), but more directly, it is "His divine power hath given unto us all things that [pertain] unto life and godliness" (2 Peter 1:3). Godliness is not like clothing we wear, but more like a soaking rain that penetrates deep down, even to the "converting the soul" (Psalms 19:7). You see, that is what the problem is. There are way too many people claiming to be Christian, but all of them are unconverted. Now, in regards to a true Christian, "if any man [be] in Christ, [he is] a new creature: old things are passed away; behold, all things are become new" (2 Corinthians 5:17), and that is what is missing from these fake Christians. They have not left off their old ways. This why even in their so called evangelism they are using the methods of the world, like movies, sport outings, Christian rock bands, and more.

There is even a warning given to these Christians who do not make the Word of God their solid basis for all their beliefs, actions, and life in general. "If any man teach otherwise, and consent not to wholesome words, [even] the words of our Lord Jesus Christ, and to the doctrine which is according to godliness; He is proud, knowing nothing, but doting about questions and strifes of words, whereof cometh envy, strife, railings, evil surmisings, perverse disputings of men of corrupt minds, and destitute of the truth, supposing that gain is godliness: from such withdraw thyself" (1 Timothy 6:3-5). And note that we are to withdraw from these people, not just give them credit by focusing upon their good. If a Christian, a preacher, a teacher speaks contrary to the fully supported Word of God, mark them and avoid them. They may call themselves Christians, but out of their own ignorance of the Word of God because they do not think it is relevant today, they are false teachers, false prophets, false godly people. And just because they use the Bible does not make the doctrine sound. In fact, most avoid actual doctrine despite having a really good message. That alone should be a red flag, but alas, many rather risk having eternal life with the easy gospel than strive for the true one, hence why Jesus says, "Few there be that find it" (Matthew 7:14). Have you found it?

But the end result is that the rest of the world sees it and from such a poor display of what a Christian is, the world turns away from Christianity and seeks other things. Could that even be the reason why those opposing any form of Christianity in public schools seem to warm up to the Muslim religion?

POINT 17:
Unsound Doctrine Prevalent

2 Timothy 4:3-4 says, "For the time will come when they will not endure sound doctrine; but after their own lusts shall they heap to themselves teachers, having itching ears; And they shall turn away [their] ears from the truth, and shall be turned unto fables."

Even with the many denominations of the 1800's, people frequently changed churches, but not for the reasons today. They changed churches because they found out that their doctrine was not biblically sound. Today, people change churches because the carpet is not the right color, a better children's program; more entertaining, younger or older crowd, active, helpful, etc. But what we do not hear today is the doctrine. In fact, if a preacher gets up and preachers a biblically sound doctrine against a particular sin and the guilty parties are in the pews, instead of either disproving the preacher with the Bible or submitting to the words of truth, those people leave for someone else that will preach pleasant words to the ear even outright lies or fables, hence why so many Christians are still sinning. It is because they will find some teacher or preacher out there that will make them feel comfortable in their sin using whatever unbiblical excuse they can find all to be popular. Why do mega churches become mega? Because the preacher preaches only positive and uplifting messages and does not touch controversial subjects, especially popular sins. Even Christian radio stations do the same thing. It is all to stay popular. Let us face it, a preacher or radio station condemning movies, television, smoking, drinking, sex outside of marriage, the lack of tithe paying, etc. is not going to have much of an audience. So it should be a sign that mega churches are drawing away from many churches not because the doctrine is sound but because they are preaching fables, and the worst one being, "You are saved in your sins!"

POINT 18:
Peace and Safety Message

1 Thessalonians 5:2-5 says, "For yourselves know perfectly that the day of the Lord so cometh as a thief in the night. For when they shall say, Peace and safety; then sudden destruction cometh upon them, as travail upon a woman with child; and they shall not escape. But ye, brethren, are not in darkness, that that day should overtake you as a thief. Ye are all the children of light, and the children of the day: we are not of the night, nor of darkness."

By the way, this is where we get the dark side versus the left side from. Those that are unstudied, not searching, not taking God as His Word are in darkness or on the dark side. Those seeking truth as defined by God's Word are on the light side. This peace and safety is not necessarily a physical thing because even today, peace is allusive. We live under the threat of terrorism every day; some having it worse than others. When it comes to messages being given, usually the Bible is referring to spiritual messages, right or wrong. In this case, the message of "peace and safety" is a false reliance. And the only reliance regarding "peace and safety" is with God.

In fact, Jesus is described as, "For unto us a child is born, unto us a son is given: and the government shall be upon his shoulder: and his name shall be called Wonderful, Counsellor, The mighty God, The everlasting Father, The Prince of Peace" (Isaiah 9:6). Why Prince of Peace as a title? When Jesus was born, it was proclaimed, "Glory to God in the highest, and on earth peace, good will toward men" (Luke 2:14). That peace could not be world peace, yet the earth, not just Israel, was to receive that peace. How so? Jesus is the one that brought peace to the relationship of humans towards God the Father.

You see, "The wages of sin [is] death; but the gift of God [is] eternal life through Jesus Christ our Lord" (Romans 6:23). Knowing full well that we shall die is not very peaceful, but Jesus told us that it does not have to be so. He brought a way to bring us back to right standing with God to be able to stand in Heaven. How? Through the death and resurrection of Jesus, our Peace, who was perfect throughout His life, so much so that He was "without sin" (Hebrews 4:15). That is what is meant by, "For to be carnally minded [is] death; but to be spiritually minded [is] life and peace" (Romans 8:6). That life is the gift of eternal life being offered to everyone but not forced. So if people rather enjoy sin, well, it will end in death.

This is also what is meant by the popular verse in John 3:16. "For God so loved the world, that he gave his only begotten Son, that whosoever believeth in him should not perish, but have everlasting life." We do not have to perish. We can have everlasting life, as long as we accept Jesus as our Peace offering.

POINT 19:
Have Not the Love of the Truth

2 Thessalonians 2:9-10 [Even him], whose coming is after the working of Satan with all power and signs and lying wonders, And with all deceivableness of unrighteousness in them that perish; because they received not the love of the truth, that they might be saved.

In a future chapter, we will discuss signs and lying wonders, but for now, let us focus upon the truth or the lack of belief in it. We live in a society that promotes what is truth for one person may not be truth for another, however, we are told that we ought to accept both as being true. This false philosophy is very prevalent in the Christian world that it has fueled the ecumenical movement started in the 1960's. If each denomination is accepting of the fact that another denomination, though different, honestly believe that what they have as truth, then the conclusion would be that there is no such thing as absolute truth, which is wrong. But further, that means since it has been accepted that there is no absolute truth and everyone should accept as truth to whatever someone else believes to be true, then when it comes to God and then Bible, why even discuss doctrines, hence, the ecumenical movement is all about believing in one God, even if it is not the Christian perspective. So, the fact that for fifty years the ecumenical movement has been spreading and is acceptable more and more is evidence that this is true in our day, in that people do not love the truth. And it has grown so much so that it has now crossed into other religions outside of Christianity. For instance, we are told that all of us serve the same God, despite Allah telling their followers to go and kill the infidel Christians and Jews for reward of seventy virgins. Prior to the 1960's, every denomination believed that they were God's true church and used to, as they call it, steal the sheep.

The fact of the matter is that there are absolute truths in the world as well as in the Bible. Tell a brain surgeon that their calculations do not have to be absolutely true and we have a difference between a successful operation and one that leads to the person being a vegetable or dead. Tell NASA that precise calculations are not necessary and we would have more explosions on the launching pad than we have experienced.

The Bible is the same way. Either baptism is by full immersion just once at an age that a person recognizes accountability or it is not. Either we commit adultery by simple thought let alone activity or it is not. Either we reject the notion of Lent as being pagan or we do not. And so on and so on. There are tons of absolutes that we will eventually get to, but people, according to this verse that we are expanding upon, either accepts and follows that absolute set of truths or they will be lost. And because the majority are indifferent and think they are fine as is, they could actually live a conscious sinless life and still be lost. Why? "Because they received not the love of the truth."

POINT 20:
Running Freely and Knowledge Increasing

Daniel 12:4 says, "But thou, O Daniel, shut up the words, and seal the book, [even] to the time of the end: many shall run to and fro, and knowledge shall be increased."

Before we address this point, realize that there are two school of thoughts on this, though interestingly, both do fulfill at the same time, so it does not matter which one you choose, or choose both.

One thought is that it is a physical reference, while the other is spiritual. Those who focus on the physical take notice of the mode of transportation, which helps one move to and fro at ease. Up through the 1700's, it was the same method with different appearances. It was walking, boat, riding on animal, or an animal pulling a buggy, be it a chariot, stagecoach, or other version of a buggy. But into the 1800's and beyond, especially today, we have automobiles, submarines, cruise ships, airplanes, even space craft. Truly we are able to move about the planet with ease. Likewise, the knowledge on this planet astronomically has increased once we had gotten out of the Dark Ages. It has increased so much that to write down some of the knowledge in books and publish it, that knowledge would be considered old. Therefore, we turn to the computer age as evidence of this increased knowledge, which decade after decade just seems to astonish people with the technology at our disposal. Truly knowledge has greatly increased from the time of Daniel.

Speaking of him, that is the spiritual application. Daniel himself did not even have the knowledge to understand what he wrote. "And I Daniel fainted, and was sick [certain] days; afterward I rose up, and did the king's business; and I was astonished at the vision, but none understood [it]" (Daniel 8:27). And we also see that no one of the elite, highly educated of the time, could lend any help. Even at the time of Jesus, they were clueless. Jesus said, "When ye therefore shall see the abomination of desolation, spoken of by Daniel the prophet, stand in the holy place" (Matthew 24:15), but even so, they did not understand. In fact, it was not until the 1800's when people became so aware of the Book of Daniel. With Bible societies springing up and the printing presses and concordances (books that identify where in the Bible certain words appear) along with the Bible being printed very plentifully, people began searching Daniel as well as the other books, and the knowledge contained therein has also exploded in quantity. People are more educated in the Bible as never before. And today, with the ability of electronic word searches, it is even easier to do Bible studies running to and fro through the Word.

So with both the physical and spiritual getting there starts in the 1800's, this is pretty much an absolute, without question, sign that we are in the end times.

Now when we say that, do keep in mind that it is from God's perspective. God sees several generations living in the last days. To us, having our great grandparents or great, great grandparents starting the time of the end, it is hard to imagine we are still in it or that it is lasting so long. Look at it from a clock perspective though. If we were to trace

Adam and Eve to the time of Jesus on a twelve hour clock, Jesus would have showed up at 8:00. Continuing further, the 1800's would not have started until 24 minutes before 12:00. If I were to ask you to wait 12 hours and it was now 11 hours and 36 minutes later, you could say, "Well, we're at the end of our waiting time." That does not mean it is 12:00. It surely is not the beginning nor the middle of our waiting time. That only leaves the end.

POINT 21:
Practices of the Israelites Repeated Spiritually

1 Corinthians 10:1-11 says, "Moreover, brethren, I would not that ye should be ignorant, how that all our fathers were under the cloud, and all passed through the sea; And were all baptized unto Moses in the cloud and in the sea; And did all eat the same spiritual meat; And did all drink the same spiritual drink: for they drank of that spiritual Rock that followed them: and that Rock was Christ. But with many of them God was not well pleased: for they were overthrown in the wilderness. Now these things were our examples, to the intent we should not lust after evil things, as they also lusted. Neither be ye idolaters, as [were] some of them; as it is written, The people sat down to eat and drink, and rose up to play. Neither let us commit fornication, as some of them committed, and fell in one day three and twenty thousand. Neither let us tempt Christ, as some of them also tempted, and were destroyed of serpents. Neither murmur ye, as some of them also murmured, and were destroyed of the destroyer. Now all these things happened unto them for ensamples: and they are written for our admonition, upon whom the ends of the world are come."

Although we are encouraged to read the entire account of the Exodus, as covered by the books Exodus, Leviticus, Numbers, and Deuteronomy, we will simply allow the summary in Corinthians to be our focus. To investigate how the account back then applies to those upon whom the end of the world is come by detailing every incident could of itself be a book. That includes the parallel with the plagues, leaving the world or Egypt behind, being a unique people, being tempted to return to the world or Egypt, specific murmuring and complaining accounts, facing sexual distractions, and more.

What we see listed here begins with unbelief, which resulted in being overthrown in the wilderness; lusted after evil things; were idolaters; were interested in play; committed fornication; tempted God; and murmured. So let us address each one of these individually, keeping in mind, we are not talking about worldly, unconverted people. These were supposedly God's people back then, and so we are looking at the supposed people of God today, called Christians. We have always had unbelievers, which we call atheists. We always have people that are into things of the world instead of being religious. Sex is pretty much an activity abused in all generations. And we have always had people who challenge God by saying, "If you really exist…!" And as for murmuring, that goes without saying. The unconverted always complain about something, so our focus is not upon those of the world, but upon those that call themselves Christian.

Do we have unbelief in the church? Consider that most Christians do not believe in a literal creation; most Christians do not believe Jesus was sinless; most Christians do not believe God's rules are necessary to be obeyed, especially as they read; most Christians do not believe in an unchanging God; most Christians believe that we need to update the rules because society has changed, so they do not believe in the Bible as it reads; yes, we have unbelief in the majority of Christianity along with church leaders.

Do we have Christians lusting after evil things? Well, if we are the ones to evaluate the evil, then we still can say yes. Do Christians participate in adultery, illicit sexual activity, get angry to get their own way, want the latest gadgets, are as much of a glutton as the unconverted, etc.? Absolutely. Some times worse. But if one can handle this intended focus and one can honestly look at all of the references in Exodus, Numbers, Leviticus, and Deuteronomy for any form of the word "lust", all the verses appear with this scenario: "And the mixt multitude that [was] among them fell a lusting: and the children of Israel also wept again, and said, Who shall give us flesh to eat?" (Numbers 11:4) Eating flesh is the only thing such people lusted after. Believe it or not, the word lust does not appear in the sin of false worship, sexual activity with Moabite women, arguing over who shall be the leader, arguing over the direction to go, complaining about the lack of water, etc. When God was providing only a manna diet, which is a type of bread (Exodus 16:15), the people refused and lusted after the flesh (Numbers 11:6). Although, for the hardness of their hearts, God outlined what flesh was and was not be eaten (Leviticus 11), it was not God's intent, so even though God did hand over to them their desires, notice the result. "And there went forth a wind from the LORD, and brought quails from the sea, and let [them] fall by the camp, as it were a day's journey on this side, and as it were a day's journey on the other side, round about the camp, and as it were two cubits [high] upon the face of the earth. And the people stood up all that day, and all [that] night, and all the next day, and they gathered the quails: he that gathered least gathered ten homers: and they spread [them] all abroad for themselves round about the camp. And while the flesh [was] yet between their teeth, ere it was chewed, the wrath of the LORD was kindled against the people, and the LORD smote the people with a very great plague. And he called the name of that place Kibrothhattaavah: because there they buried the people that lusted" (Numbers 11:31-34). Quail, according to God's list, is an allowable creature to be eaten, yet, in the end, those that ate ended up dying. Who were these people? Not just Israelites, they were the ones who "lusted", just as Corinthians warned against. Is the same happening today? Absolutely! Mention that it is healthier to cut back on the meat eating and people, both in Christianity and outside of Christianity throw an adult size fit. They even use the excuse that is over 2,500 years old.

What is that aged old excuse? At the time of Daniel, who "purposed in his heart that he would not defile himself with the portion of the king's meat, nor with the wine which he drank: therefore he requested of the prince of the eunuchs that he might not defile himself" (Daniel 1:8), the person in charge, "the prince of the eunuchs said unto Daniel, I fear my lord the king, who hath appointed your meat and your drink: for why should he see your faces worse liking than the children which [are] of your sort? then shall ye make [me] endanger my head to the king" (Daniel 1:10). Did you catch it? People who are convinced that a heavy meat diet is required for good health think that those who cut out meat eating are going to wither away, be weak. It stated that people's faces are going to look thin and droopy and have other ill effects, all of which is nothing but a 2,500 year old lie.

Next, do we have Christians given into idolatry? Now, we will not stretch the concept of pointing out how the majority of Christians idolize actors, actresses, sports figures, and celebrities in general as evidence, although that is a pretty good start. We also will not use as evidence of how Christians have a form of worship for money, position, vehicles, popularity, etc., although that does give further evidence of such happening today, when in times past, none of those things were desired among the majority of Christians. Again, we are looking at the majority and acceptability of idolatry. Just about every church preaches against such, but there is a form of idolatry that used to be unique to the Catholic Church that is gaining momentum among non-Catholic Christians. We cannot call them Protestants anymore because they have ceased protesting against the idolatry. It seems that a growing number of non-Catholics are being infatuated in worshipping Mary as well as participating in a completely pagan ritual of Lent. Now, there are additional idolatry practices that we could list, but let us save them for a future chapter.

So in moving on, do we have Christians given into play? It is not the playing that is the problem, it is the fact that people are more interested in such as opposed to godly things. In the 1950's and prior, there was a reverence towards God if one were a Christian. People rested from their labors on Sunday. They attended church in the morning, and then enjoyed a family outing in the afternoon. It eventually evolved into more and more fun in which people after the 1950's saw nothing wrong with going to the movies right after church and further evolved into skipping church entirely. Christians are more interested in sports statistics, celebrity activities, and other worldly things as opposed to Bible study, church attendance, or even giving to God financially. Further, for those that do go to church, what do they expect? Prior to the 1960's, it was serious business. People went to church quietly, sung some songs, did some praying, listened to a sermon, examined their lives, and discussed the sermon content with the family so that the family were obedient Christians. Now people attend church to see a play, listen to a rock band, feel good even if they are sinning, and overall, having a good time. Yes, Christianity has indeed changed from the Moses style of reverently worshipping God and receiving messages through His Word into Aaron's form of dancing, shouting, and partying.

But do we have Christians committing fornication? We already addressed this before but we shall address this again, although only briefly. Many Christians see nothing wrong with sexual activity in a serious relationship without the full intent of being married, despite God stating that a sexual union is marriage. In fact, many Christians feel that the Bible needs updating to fit with today's social interaction and such carefulness between dating couples as described in the Bible is outdated not realizing that the very thing they struggle with is the thing that was predicted to be an issue at the end of time among Christians. As the example stands, in Numbers 25:1, on the verge of entering into the "Promised Land", "The people began to commit whoredom with the daughters of Moab" (Numbers 25:1). Sexual distractions would repeat at the end of time and they certainly are. Easy access to porn, easy access to sex, constant sexualizing the clothing, sexually suggestive content, improper sex is everywhere, even in the conversations of supposed Christians.

Do Christians tempt God? Well, what Christians do not? Every Christians that asks, "Is God really going to strike me dead over a little sin?" is tempting God. The answer is, "Yes He will." As it is written, "Thou shalt love the Lord thy God with all thy heart, and with all thy soul, and with all thy strength, and with all thy mind" (Luke 10:27). "And the very God of peace sanctify you wholly; and [I pray God] your whole spirit and soul and body be preserved blameless unto the coming of our Lord Jesus Christ" (1 Thessalonians 5:23). One cannot be giving ALL of one's heart to God if they refuse to hand over even the smallest sin. One cannot be blameless while excusing the so-called little sins. All of these actions and statements are but taunting God to see what He shall do. Even ministers preach such imperfection to their congregations, so yes, Christianity tempts or taunts God on a regular basis and by the vast majority unlike the days of just a century ago.

And do Christians murmur or complain? Well, according to the Bible, when things go wrong, "My brethren, count it all joy when ye fall into divers temptations; Knowing [this], that the trying of your faith worketh patience." (James 1:2-13). But instead, most Christians are as impatient as non-Christians. Further, Jude foresaw this being an issue: "These are murmurers, complainers, walking after their own lusts" (Jude 1:16).

POINT 22:
Heaping Treasures

James 5:3 says, "Your gold and silver is cankered; and the rust of them shall be a witness against you, and shall eat your flesh as it were fire. Ye have heaped treasure together for the last days."

Now this verse in context or intent would apply to the general public instead of just the Christian community, however, Christians ought to know better, but instead are just as guilty. So, have we had people only recently that are heaping treasures or has been heaping treasures? Well, if one takes any percentage of people as being guilty of such, then the answer is that we have always had people doing this, but that is just it. These signs are not just the exercise of it here or there; it is what the general public practices and finds acceptable.

In general, people used to practice meeting only the needs. Up through the 1800's, a family was content with food on the table, togetherness, roof over their head, clothes on their backs. Today, the general attitude is "give me", "give me", "give me". Today, people collect the latest gadget instead of using the gadget until it can be used no longer. Only recently have some of those gadgets been considered worthy of donating. Most did not consider donating, hence, the junk drawer was born.

People trade in cars every three years because their treasure has become less valuable, and even the industry is on board with this and pushing the general public into leasing programs. Just about every vehicle commercial is about leasing it, and not purchasing it. It used to be that people bought the car and kept it until the wheels fell off. Leasing was mostly a business concept, but now people that want to own the car need to ask for that price as if purchasing is no longer the normal method of acquiring.

But let us go further. Up through the 1800's, people were content with a house that provided for an eating and sleeping area. Not that having separate bedrooms is a bad idea, but there is the study room, play room, living room, family room, dining room, breakfast room, sun room, etc.

People heap all kinds of treasures today that the two car garage no longer holds the two cars. The cars are parked outside so that the garage can be used for storage of the treasures people have accumulated. People have large basements to provide for more storage areas, and closets are full of treasures. Dresser drawers are even inefficient in holding all of the treasures. It has gotten so bad that it has created a boom for the storage industry. People can rent monthly space in various sizes to store their treasures or junk.

So in both hanging on to stuff as well as always trading in for the latest and greatest, it is quite obvious that we have reached fulfillment as a general public.

POINT 23:
Rise of Prophets

Acts 2:17-21 says, "And it shall come to pass in the last days, saith God, I will pour out of my Spirit upon all flesh: and your sons and your daughters shall prophesy, and your young men shall see visions, and your old men shall dream dreams: And on my servants and on my handmaidens I will pour out in those days of my Spirit; and they shall prophesy: And I will shew wonders in heaven above, and signs in the earth beneath; blood, and fire, and vapour of smoke: The sun shall be turned into darkness, and the moon into blood, before that great and notable day of the Lord come: And it shall come to pass, [that] whosoever shall call on the name of the Lord shall be saved."

Now we are not going to address the sun, moon, blood, fire, vapor, etc., because if we see those things happening, it will be very doubtful that anyone would be reading the book, however, what we will focus on is the rise of dreamers and visionaries, usually referred to as prophets.

All along we have been providing thought provoking insight to point to a period of time referred to in the Bible as the "end of time", which is not necessarily the year or decade that Jesus is going to return but a period of time spanning a hundred or two hundred years. And being so long of a period as compared to human life, it in turn does point to the fact that this period of a couple hundred years is coming to an end very soon. That period we are suggesting started around the 1800's and is not going to last forever.

Now looking over the past two hundred years, have we seen more prophets appearing as opposed to prior to the 1800's? And the answer we believe is, "Yes". The 1800's especially have some famous names, not necessarily true, but several denominations were born and even continue today. Joseph Smith and the Latter Day Saints, Mary Baker Eddy and the Christian Science, Ellen White and the Seventh Day Adventists, Charles Taze Russell and the Jehovah Witness, and many other lesser known names. Some even include Herbert Armstrong and the Church of God. But even today, one can call up a predictor or visionary to get a reading. Palm, tarot card, and crystal ball readers are plentiful. Tabloids reveal such prophets as well. Some even have articles in newspapers, magazines, and online content. Society is full of these people as never before.

But that is not the fulfillment of the verses. God says that He will raise up dreamers and visionaries for His purpose. The reason we have pointed out all the prophets that we did is to show, the fact that if Satan is so active since the 1800's that has to mean that he knows there must be true ones among us that have risen up in that time frame. Sure, Satan popped up one here or there outside of the 1800's, like Nostradamus of the 1500's, but there is no use of creating all these distractions during the 1800's if God was also not being active. And Satan has become so intent on distracting away from God's activity that basically even Christians today do not believe in modern day prophets despite the Bible stating that He would send true prophets.

POINT 24:
Evil Generation

Proverbs 30:11-14 says, "[There is] a generation [that] curseth their father, and doth not bless their mother. [There is] a generation [that are] pure in their own eyes, and [yet] is not washed from their filthiness. [There is] a generation, O how lofty are their eyes! and their eyelids are lifted up. [There is] a generation, whose teeth [are as] swords, and their jaw teeth [as] knives, to devour the poor from off the earth, and the needy from [among] men."

Here is a long list of a generation of people who are so self-centered that nothing else matters, and so we are going to provide a perspective to let you evaluate these for yourself. Do teenagers and young adults fully respect authority, including their parents, or do they disrespect their parents and authority? Keep in mind, we are not talking just these teens. We are talking about teens going back in each of the generations. Although the Bible says a specific generation, we propose that each generation is just getting worse and worse from the point in which it started. We once again propose that teens were respectful up through the 1800's and even into the 1900's, mostly because they really did not have time to be such rebellious youth. They went to school and worked on the farm or even were homeschooled. But we believe God is stating that there would be a time that these youth would socialize more, think largely of themselves, be very self-centered and demanding to the point of being rebellious. Look at each of the teens during these decades. The 1950's rock rebellion generation; the 1960's burning of the draft cards and bras generation, also known as the hippie generation, who did not trust anyone over 30, which included their own parents; the 1970's drug generation; the 1980's the me generation; the 1990's the naughty generation; the 2000's laziness and taking advantage of their parents generation. And with the last generation, it is quite fitting because they demand that they be taken care of by their parents. Could it be that the more socialization that is happening, the more of a problem rebellion has become? Could it be that the criticism of protective parents and even of homeschoolers as being unsocialized is nothing more than an attempt to fuel the continuous rebellions?

As for the self proclaimed "pure" generation when in fact they are in their "filthiness", we only have to remind everyone about the theme of things. These are the people who declare to be saved yet have not practiced the "putting away of the filth of the flesh" (1 Peter 3:21). They refuse to "lay apart all filthiness and superfluity of naughtiness" (James 1:21). They refuse to "cleanse ourselves from all filthiness of the flesh and spirit, perfecting holiness in the fear of God" (2 Corinthians 7:1), and do not get us started on "perfecting holiness". There is not an angrier bunch of people than Christians who hear the word "perfection". Basically, unlike other generations before the 1900's, it seems this last generation really thinks they are going to Heaven while being the most excusing of sin generation ever. As stated in other points, they are no different than non-Christians and have turned everything respectful of religion into disrespect. Churches turned into coffee houses, church services into parties, meeting rooms into movie rooms, reverent hymns into rock music, anti-doctrine, anti-obedience, etc. Even the title non-denominational is wrong. What makes a group of people denominated is adhering to what they believe the doctrines of the Bible are. To be non-denominational means that they allow all kinds of doctrines, do not stand for anything specific, and permit compromise of which God hates. Truth cannot compromise with evil.

Now when we say that there is a generation, we are not talking about the people born from one period to another, we are talking about the attitudes of teens and young adults in each period of time, so is there a generation that have lofty ideas, even high expectations that are set so unrealistically that they are out of reality? Again, we would point such to now. Prior to the 1800's, sure people dreamed about being king or a wealthy ruler, but they did not have the realistic idea of achieving it. Most knew their lot in life happened to be and that was being a farmer or peasant. Today, youth graduate and expect as their first job interview not only being successful but beyond successful. Not only do they expect to get the job, they expect to be put in a management role. Not only do they expect to be in a management role without any real experience, they also expect to have one of the best offices the company can provide, especially one with a window. When on their first few attempts at such, they cannot understanding why they are not getting what they thought they deserved; they cannot understand why they cannot be an under 30 something achieving such high goals; they cannot understand why they cannot be one of these under 30 billionaires with just an idea; they then turn around being nothing more than a deflated balloon and are unmotivated. Even in school, these same students expect to have an "A" as a grade without doing the work. And that is just it; the key is that none are willing to go to work.

And how in the world do these youthful people get these ideas of loftiness? Television shows that show the countless successful people in sitcoms just hanging around at the bars running up huge tabs, some walking into a restaurant and picking up everyone's tabs, and overall living an unrealistic life. The news constantly worship the few young successes, even when reporting negatively about them, does not help matters much either. Basically, the youth are more bombarded with unrealistic, lofty ideas as no generation prior.

As for the generation that devour the poor, it is a metaphor for stating that the weaker people of society would be taken advantage of and ridiculed more. Teeth as swords and jaws of knives are representative of evil being spoken of. Although even in Jesus' day it was said, "Ye have the poor always with you" (Matthew 26:11), up through the 1800's and into the 1900's, people were not taken advantage of as they are today. Today, and back a few decades, people are daily being taken advantage of. The poor is not always on a scale with money, but knowledge as well. And like never before, all the products that are promised to do something but do not, they far outweigh the occasional snake oil sales person that would wonder into town centuries ago. There are more scandals to swindle funds from the elderly than never before. In a crisis situation, governments have been prompted recently to enact all kinds of restrictions. In Florida, for instance, that is one state that requires every contractor to be licensed. This was prompted by the numerous incidences of crisis victims being taken advantage of after a tornado or hurricane. That is how bad it has gotten of the generation taking advantage of others that we need laws of protection. Sure, one could argue that we have always had laws on the books to protect the person lacking knowledge, but those laws were not written specifically towards "the poor". They are written for all parties.

So, the generation that God foresaw is equivalent to the generation in which would see more socialization than other generations from its teens. And such only continues to get worse with every passing generation. Therefore, not only are we suggesting that it has been recently fulfilled, it is being fulfilled over and over.

Are Unbelievers Fairly Judging Christians?

Dear Unbeliever…

Yes, think of this like the first of several open letters to unbelievers, especially atheists, but even those of other religions who look upon the mess called Christianity and turn away. Remember, Christianity was predicted to have that affect upon the world. The Bible says that Christians would be "Having a form of godliness, but denying the power thereof: from such turn away" (2 Timothy 3:5). Christians would be annoying because they claim to have God-blessing upon them while denying the power to actually be godly people. So it is saying that most Christians would actually be ungodly people. And because they are obnoxious with the, "I'm saved" and can't be lost attitude, they are not open to hearing what the Bible really says, and they just compound their ungodliness. All the while, people like yourself (an unbeliever) look upon this so-called example of Christianity, and as predicted, such people like yourself turn away from Christianity. And quite frankly, I would too if I were in that situation.

Now, after reading the topic, which can be summarized by calling it the "signs of the times" or "last day events" or something like that, you should at least come away with the understanding that what Jesus started the Christian Church (Matthew 16:18) and what it has become today are two different things pointing to the fact that today's vast number of denominations cannot all be right.

Unfortunately by making such a statement, many unbelievers get turned off from all the bickering and the claims that "we're right" and another saying, "No! We're right", and so on. And we too could be lumped into that category because anyone who even has listened to the views of multiple denominational teachings will see what we have here as just another version of the same old story. Yes, I do believe we have the right understanding of everything, but that does not convince anyone. Even when I say that this has been assembled by using the only God given method of studying the Bible outlined in Isaiah 28:9-10 and that all others are simply picking verses at random does not seem to convince any skeptic. So I am just going to ask that you hear the whole story, use a bit of logic, and come hopefully to the right conclusion.

Simply put, we did not list out or criticize Christianity in the last chapter just to dig at Christianity, but to say, "Before you throw Christianity and the Bible away, wait! Exactly as you see Christianity being all messed up was actually predicted to happen. Therefore, since it is happening that means there must be something to that book called the Bible. On top of that, if there is something, that means God does exist; Jesus did come; and Jesus is coming again, so therefore, there are true Christians in the world today. You just have to be willing to search long and hard for them."

Do keep in mind that if you did believe in a spiritual being called Satan, would this not be part of his game plan in which he confuses everyone with such splintering of Christianity into over 42,000 forms of it? To hide the true teachings, would he not have many voices pretending to be the true representatives? And then on top of that, would he not then work on discrediting the only instrument that could actually identify the true teachings so much so that the average Christian does not even believe in it either, referring to the Bible? And would it not also be a smart move to actually drum up lies to discredit the true representatives of Christianity, so not only to distract from the truth but to attack the truth? The fact that not only are these in existence today, but they are so prevalent that they are everywhere one turns. That should point to the fact that indeed Satan does exist. On top of that, would it not be right up Satan's ally to take extremists and exploit Christianity to the point of it being a laughing stock? Of course He would.

So believe it or not, we are going to, for the most part, agree with you on the crazy aspects. There has been enough evidence and more to come that completely discredits so many denominations, not that we are attacking them, but if they are declaring they are a representation of Christianity, then we want them representing Christianity properly. So yes, all those faith healers that scam people for their money are a bunch of phonies. All the preachers teaching that people can live in sin and be saved are a bunch of phonies. All the Christian that get these warm fuzzy feelings and claim they are being filled with the Holy Spirit are a bunch of phonies. All the people that attribute every hiccup to an act of God are a bunch of phonies. All the people who see a sign under a rock, on toast, on a tree, in a window, or anywhere, are phonies because they are experiencing the deception of Satan. All the Christians who drop catch phrases but are logically not right in the mind are a bunch of phonies.

And you know who they are. They are the ones that encounter a problem, declare they will pray about it, and go on their merry way. The Bible even criticizes such actions as being un-Christian. "Say not unto thy neighbour, Go, and come again, and to morrow I will give; when thou hast it by thee" (Proverbs 3:28). Although it may sound like it is a promise to deliver the next day at least, in reality, the Bible teaches that the phrase tomorrow can be taken as just meaning another time. It is no different than saying to someone, "Wait a minute" when you know it will be longer than sixty seconds. So to come to a situation in which a Christian can physically help, but simply offers up some lofty catch phrase or prayer, and not lend a helping hand today, is actually un-Christian, especially if tomorrow does not ever come.

Again, although we just called a whole bunch of people phony Christians, it is actually phony Christianity. To the individuals, they are but deceived, victims, and we feel for them.

Now , there are many, many misrepresentations of Christianity that to find true Christianity might be harder than finding a needle in a twenty haystacks. What we also have noticed is that most unbelievers have expectations of what a Christian ought to be like, which is actually better than what most Christians think that Christians should be. So we do agree that in general, Christians are a bunch of hypocrites, but instead of condemning them, we simply consider them also unbelievers and are hoping that something will wake them up and are hoping by becoming aware of these things, such as through this book, such can put on real Christianity.

Like we said, this is but the beginning. There is more to reveal, and it is our hope that you will continue reading to see the beautiful truth to be revealed because it is our desire and God's that all shall be saved.

May God bless you on your journey.

Who Is Behind the Push for "One Mind"?

Is There a Push for Having One Mind?

According to Revelation 17:13, the Bible says, "These have one mind, and shall give their power and strength unto the beast." Now let us face it, there is not an animal that the world is going to strengthen to be a leader. The word "beast" is symbolic. The Book of Revelations is a "signified" (Revelation 1:1) book. It is full of symbolism, which we could tell you what it all means, but that would make us no different from all the other authors, preachers, and teachers that just make up stuff. So we shall let the Bible provide the definitions, but before we get there, let us address the question using the symbolism provided and by placing the verse of Revelation 17:13 in more context.

"And the beast that was, and is not, even he is the eighth, and is of the seven, and goeth into perdition. And the ten horns which thou sawest are ten kings, which have received no kingdom as yet; but receive power as kings one hour with the beast. These have one mind, and shall give their power and strength unto the beast." (Revelation 17:11-13). All we want to point out is that the people who have "one mind" do not create the beast; the beast already has power and authority. Evidently while exercising such power and authority, it gets further support along the way, which in turn strengthens the beast even further. This is no different than a popular governor exercising their authority in their state, having other states appreciate the accomplishments, encouraging them to run for president, and becoming such. So the beast has the power and authority and is going to gain in strength over time.

This is evident in a larger description of the beast from Revelation 13. "And I stood upon the sand of the sea, and saw a beast rise up out of the sea, having seven heads and ten horns, and upon his horns ten crowns, and upon his heads the name of blasphemy. And the beast which I saw was like unto a leopard, and his feet were as [the feet] of a bear, and his mouth as the mouth of a lion: and the dragon gave him his power, and his seat, and great authority. And I saw one of his heads as it were wounded to death; and his deadly wound was healed: and all the world wondered after the beast. And they worshipped the dragon which gave power unto the beast: and they worshipped the beast, saying, Who [is] like unto the beast? who is able to make war with him?" (Revelation 13:1-4) And as stated, take note that the beast has power, has a seat, and great authority. By Revelation 17, the beast gets additional strengthening.

As we also see just with these verses provided, the world is going to be behind the beast because it states, "all the world wondered after the beast" (Revelation 13:3). And with worship involved, even though it is being directed towards the dragon, there is some type of great authoritative respect, possibly a religious connection because of the use of "worship". Then again, people do idolize celebrities, and some celebrities do seem to say something and the masses just adore and follow.

So now, let us decode one of the symbols that we have received so far. It is in regards to the dragon for the Bible says, "And the great dragon was cast out, that old serpent, called the Devil, and Satan, which deceiveth the whole world" (Revelation 12:9). So the beast receives the authority, the power, the seat to rule from all from Satan. You could say that this beast is a child of Satan. In the Christian world, we use the Bible term of "Antichrist" (1 John 2:18, 1 John 2:22, 1 John 4:3, 2 John 1:7).

So the answer to the question for this chapter is that the Antichrist is the one behind the movement to form a "one mind" agreement that is not in agreement with the "one mind" that we should have, which is with Jesus Christ. This could be a very short chapter because you have the answer, however, it is going to be greatly extended because we now have a follow up question. Who or what is the Antichrist? Just knowing that the Antichrist is forming the wrong side of "one mind" should not be satisfactorily acceptable. We ought to want to know who or what is the mysterious entity that it happens to be because the fact is that according to the Bible, it is not a matter of avoiding the Antichrist as it is important to be part of Jesus Christ. We will see the details of this later, but for now, realize that there are only two sides.

Jesus said, "He that is not with me is against me; and he that gathereth not with me scattereth abroad" (Matthew 12:30). That means that even if we decide to not get caught up in all these religious arguments, all these religious rituals, and just go off living a peaceful life, we would automatically be classed as being on the wrong side of the "one mind" group. There is no neutral ground even if keep to ourselves. One can be actively involved on both sides, but to be inactively involved on either side simply places the person on the wrong side. So one could conclude that if they do not choose a side, the choice of not being on Jesus side classes such a person on the wrong side.

And let us take this one step further stating that there are two groups of "one mind" people. One is for Jesus Christ. That means that the wrong side is for Antichrist. Even if one is not religious and refuses to participate, they are part of Antichrist. Once again, there is no neutral ground. But by such a declaration, people may declare that it is unfair. It almost sounds childish. "If you are not on my side, you are my enemy!" But is it childish? As Jesus said, "He that gathereth not with me scattereth abroad" (Matthew 12:30). A non-religious person, an unbeliever is going to scatter other people away from Jesus Christ by their actions and by their speech.

God commands "Thou shalt not kill" (Exodus 20:13), and Jesus said, "Ye have heard that it was said by them of old time, Thou shalt not kill; and whosoever shall kill shall be in danger of the judgment: But I say unto you, That whosoever is angry with his brother without a cause shall be in danger of the judgment" (Matthew 5:21-22). So as an unbeliever, such a person would see no problem in supporting a sporting event called boxing. That clearly falls into the category described as being angry with another without a moral cause. No one can enter a boxing ring without getting all psyched up thinking their opponent is the enemy. All kinds of taunting happens prior just to get them angry at each other. As the sporting event goes, this is acceptable practice. Now, as an unbelievers, such a person may encourage others to support the sport. They are then, in effect, working anti or against Christ. They are scattering away people from having "obeyed the gospel" (Romans 10:16) of kindness, and promoted unacceptable allowances. And the question one must ask then is, "What shall the end [be] of them that obey not the gospel of God?" (1 Peter 4:17).

God also commands "Thou shalt not commit adultery" (Exodus 20:14), and Jesus said, "Ye have heard that it was said by them of old time, Thou shalt not commit adultery: But I say unto you, That whosoever looketh on a woman to lust after her hath committed adultery with her already in his heart" (Matthew 5:27-28). So any unbeliever who says that they do not believe in this religious stuff yet supports porn or even the lesser objectionable content of swimsuit calendars and swimsuit magazines and sexy commercials, are all working anti or against Jesus Christ.

So in just these two examples, we see two things. First, when we speak of Antichrist, it is not only reference to an entity but it is the harboring of the "[spirit] of Antichrist" (1 John 4:3). Second, to be Antichrist is simply to work against Christ. Therefore, even the person that is against swimsuit models because it exploits women, and who is against all forms of anger, and is actually a peaceful person, somewhere along the line is going to be working against Christ if they are not committed to Jesus Christ. So this is how God can say that one is either part of the group of having "one mind" towards Jesus Christ or one is automatically classed as being of "one mind" against Christ or Antichrist.

Basically, Jesus has this home called Heaven. Everything is perfect in which there are no problems in Heaven; there are no clicks among people; everyone is everyone's friend; there is no sin; "there shall be no more death, neither sorrow, nor crying, neither shall there be any more pain" (Revelation 21:4), and He is inviting us to be part of it. To enter, Jesus paid the admission price, which is too broad of a topic to go into detail right now, but at the same time, He did not pay the price for someone that does not want to go and live that lifestyle. Like any trip that anyone is invited to go on, Jesus is taking a head count. We get counted or not counted respectively when "He that believeth and is baptized shall be saved; but he that believeth not shall be damned" (Mark 16:16). In addition, the price He paid are for those that appreciate it. He's not going to admit into Heaven a bunch of grumps, which are the ones that complain about all of the rules and look for ways to avoid as many of them as possible because Heaven is full of rules. At the same time, He is not going to allow people to exercise the free admittance pass while still holding onto what Jesus had freed them from because there is no dragging those things into Heaven, and no, there is no magic brainwashing at the "gate". So if we enjoy the gluttony, the fibbing, the porn, the smoking, the partying, the sinning, etc., we will not be going. And those that do not want to find out about this place because they do not believe in any of it, well, they are not going either. But there is one more catch. He is the only one that provides life (Job 33:4). He created life (Genesis 2:7); He sustains life (Ezekiel 37:5); He is life (John 14:6). And so when it is all over, all the unbelievers do not get to continue on in their own little worlds while the ones on the side of Jesus Christ get to enjoy Heaven. No! The plug will be pulled. The breath of life will be cut off. Only those that pay the electric bill get to enjoy the electricity of life, so only those that have paid or "obeyed the gospel" (Romans 10:16) of "have crucified the flesh with the affections and lusts" (Galatians 5:24) get to enjoy life, while everyone else perishes. "That whosoever believeth in him should not perish, but have eternal life. For God so loved the world, that he gave his only begotten Son, that whosoever believeth in him should not perish, but have everlasting life. For God sent not his Son into the world to condemn the world; but that the world through him might be saved" (John 3:15-17). Now there is a solution for all the unbelievers so they get to live eternally if they want to without God. All they have to do is find a way to generate their own electricity called the "breath of life" (Genesis 2:7). Interestingly, despite how brilliant we as a people think we are with all of the scientific breakthroughs, we have yet to be able to create life out of nothing. God is the only one that has that claim.

And above when we compared the paying of an electric bill and paying for life, do not cancel out what we have said over and over. In fact, I could say one thousand times that we cannot earn Heaven, add to the gift of eternal life, and make it clear that Jesus pays the whole price, but there will always be those with that have a kneejerk reaction to a word out of context and twist the meaning of the sentence and all of those thousand statements are ignored no matter what. I will be accused of earning Heaven, teaching that one has to earn Heaven, and who knows what else, all of which cannot be done. However, by ceasing from sin we do pay "a" price but not "the" price. Declaring oneself to be a Christian at the wrong time and the wrong place may have one pay for that decision with their life. Declaring that one does not get drunk pays for that decision with the loss of their drunken friends, none of which earns any piece of Heaven, but at the same time, the Christian that lies to save their life so they will not be shot in a staunch Muslim country would lose that entrance into Heaven. That person that does not want to lose their friends and so continues to drink with them will lose Heaven as well. That is the only context we place the word "pay" into. It is the earthly reference and not the salvation reference in which Jesus has paid fully the salvation one. It is up to the people around us that will cause us to pay the earthly price.

So now we should be able to see clearly why this is not unfair. We are either are on the side of Jesus Christ to receive of His promises, including "eternal life, which God, that cannot lie, promised before the world began" (Titus 1:2), or we are not and we receive nothing, in fact, we perish (John 3:16). Those that will perish are on the side of working against Christ or being part of the "Spirit of Antichrist" (1 John 4:3).

Interestingly, the Bible definition of Antichrist is that of working against Christ. In Daniel 7:25, it is said with the words: "Against the most High". That is the definition to John's coined term of Antichrist. How else could John make the statement, "Ye have heard that Antichrist shall come" (1 John 2:18)? In carefully searching the Bible, the term "Antichrist", it only appears in John's writings, but when one searches for activity against God, against the Most High, and other like phrases, then we see plenty of references in the Book of Daniel and elsewhere, hence it can truly be said that the people have heard of the subject already. In our search, for instance, Belshazzar being on the throne after the passing of King Nebuchadnezzar, is referenced as, "But hast lifted up thyself against the Lord of heaven" (Daniel 5:23). Therefore, Belshazzar was a type of Antichrist.

Of course when Daniel wrote the prophecies about a power being against the Most High, the name Christ was not stated as of that moment. It was John who later realized that to work against the Most High was to also work against all that Jesus Christ taught, lived, and said, "Go ye therefore, and teach all nations" (Matthew 28:19). So, as Jesus said, "He that is not with me is against me" (Matthew 12:30) and to be against Christ is to be Antichrist.

Can We Know Who the Antichrist is?

Now, with all of that background, it is time now to investigate who or what is the Antichrist. In similar manner practiced earlier, we are going to provide you with a list of all known verses describing the Antichrist, the followers, and the affects thereof, without comment so you may draw your own conclusions. Then we will repeat the content doing a Bible study to reveal the full meaning of the identifying marks followed by the answer. So here is the list of verses:

- Daniel 7:3-8 And four great beasts came up from the sea, diverse one from another. The first [was] like a lion, and had eagle's wings: I beheld till the wings thereof were plucked, and it was lifted up from the earth, and made stand upon the feet as a man, and a man's heart was given to it. And behold another beast, a second, like to a bear, and it raised up itself on one side, and [it had] three ribs in the mouth of it between the teeth of it: and they said thus unto it, Arise, devour much flesh. After this I beheld, and lo another, like a leopard, which had upon the back of it four wings of a fowl; the beast had also four heads; and dominion was given to it. After this I saw in the night visions, and behold a fourth beast, dreadful and terrible, and strong exceedingly; and it had great iron teeth: it devoured and brake in pieces, and stamped the residue with the feet of it: and it [was] diverse from all the beasts that [were] before it; and it had ten horns. I considered the horns, and, behold, there came up among them another little horn, before whom there were three of the first horns plucked up by the roots: and, behold, in this horn [were] eyes like the eyes of man, and a mouth speaking great things.

- Daniel 7:20-21 And of the ten horns that [were] in his head, and [of] the other which came up, and before whom three fell; even [of] that horn that had eyes, and a mouth that spake very great things, whose look [was] more stout than his fellows. I beheld, and the same horn made war with the saints, and prevailed against them;

- Daniel 7:24-25 And the ten horns out of this kingdom [are] ten kings [that] shall arise: and another shall rise after them; and he shall be diverse from the first, and he shall subdue three kings. And he shall speak [great] words against the most High, and shall wear out the saints of the most High, and think to change times and laws: and they shall be given into his hand until a time and times and the dividing of time.

- Daniel 8:8-12 Therefore the he goat waxed very great: and when he was strong, the great horn was broken; and for it came up four notable ones toward the four winds of heaven. And out of one of them came forth a little horn, which waxed exceeding great, toward the south, and toward the east, and toward the pleasant [land]. And it waxed great, [even] to the host of heaven; and it cast down [some] of the host and of the stars to the ground, and stamped upon them. Yea, he magnified [himself] even to the prince of the host, and by him the daily [sacrifice] was taken away, and the place of his sanctuary was cast down. And an host was given [him] against the daily [sacrifice] by reason of transgression, and it cast down the truth to the ground; and it practised, and prospered.

- Daniel 11:45 And he shall plant the tabernacles of his palace between the seas in the glorious holy mountain; yet he shall come to his end, and none shall help him.

- 2 Thessalonians 2:3-4 Let no man deceive you by any means: for [that day shall not come], except there come a falling away first, and that man of sin be revealed, the son of perdition; Who opposeth and exalteth himself above all that is called God, or that is worshipped; so that he as God sitteth in the temple of God, shewing himself that he is God.

- 2 Thessalonians 2:7-10 For the mystery of iniquity doth already work: only he who now letteth [will let], until he be taken out of the way. And then shall that Wicked be revealed, whom the Lord shall consume with the spirit of his mouth, and shall destroy with the brightness of his coming: [Even him], whose coming is after the working of Satan with all power and signs and lying wonders, And with all deceivableness of unrighteousness in them that perish; because they received not the love of the truth, that they might be saved.

- 1 Timothy 4:1-3 Now the Spirit speaketh expressly, that in the latter times some shall depart from the faith, giving heed to seducing spirits, and doctrines of devils; Speaking lies in hypocrisy; having their conscience seared with a hot iron; Forbidding to marry, [and commanding] to abstain from meats, which God hath created to be received with thanksgiving of them which believe and know the truth.

- 1 John 2:22-23 Who is a liar but he that denieth that Jesus is the Christ? He is Antichrist, that denieth the Father and the Son. Whosoever denieth the Son, the same hath not the Father: [(but) he that acknowledgeth the Son hath the Father also].

- 1 John 4:1-6 Beloved, believe not every spirit, but try the spirits whether they are of God: because many false prophets are gone out into the world. Hereby know ye the Spirit of God: Every spirit that confesseth that Jesus Christ is come in the flesh is of God: And every spirit that confesseth not that Jesus Christ is come in the flesh is not of God: and this is that [spirit] of Antichrist, whereof ye have heard that it should come; and even now already is it in the world. Ye are of God, little children, and have overcome them: because greater is he that is in you, than he that is in the world. They are of the world: therefore speak they of the world, and the world heareth them. We are of God: he that knoweth God heareth us; he that is not of God heareth not us. Hereby know we the spirit of truth, and the spirit of error.

- 2 John 1:7-9 For many deceivers are entered into the world, who confess not that Jesus Christ is come in the flesh. This is a deceiver and an Antichrist. Look to yourselves, that we lose not those things which we have wrought, but that we receive a full reward. Whosoever transgresseth, and abideth not in the doctrine of Christ, hath not God. He that abideth in the doctrine of Christ, he hath both the Father and the Son.

- Revelation 13:1-10 And I stood upon the sand of the sea, and saw a beast rise up out of the sea, having seven heads and ten horns, and upon his horns ten crowns, and upon his heads the name of blasphemy. And the beast which I saw was like unto a leopard, and his feet were as [the feet] of a bear, and his mouth as the mouth of a lion: and the dragon gave him his power, and his seat, and great authority. And I saw one of his heads as it were wounded to death; and his deadly wound was healed: and all the world wondered after the beast. And they worshipped the dragon which gave power unto the beast: and they worshipped the beast, saying, Who [is] like unto the beast? who is able to make war with him? And there was given unto him a mouth speaking great things and blasphemies; and power was given unto him to continue forty [and] two months. And he opened his mouth in blasphemy against God, to blaspheme his name, and his tabernacle, and them that dwell in heaven. And it was given unto him to make war with the saints, and to overcome them: and power was given him over all kindreds, and tongues, and nations. And all that dwell upon the earth shall worship him, whose names are not written in the book of life of the Lamb slain from the foundation of the world. If any man have an ear, let him hear. He that leadeth into captivity shall go into captivity: he that killeth with the sword must be killed with the sword. Here is the patience and the faith of the saints.

- Revelation 13:18 Here is wisdom. Let him that hath understanding count the number of the beast: for it is the number of a man; and his number [is] Six hundred threescore [and] six.

- Revelation 14:9 And the third angel followed them, saying with a loud voice, If any man worship the beast and his image, and receive [his] mark in his forehead, or in his hand,

- Revelation 17:1-11 And there came one of the seven angels which had the seven vials, and talked with me, saying unto me, Come hither; I will shew unto thee the judgment of the great whore that sitteth upon many waters: With whom the kings of the earth have committed fornication, and the inhabitants of the earth have been made drunk with the wine of her fornication. So he carried me away in the spirit into the wilderness: and I saw a woman sit upon a scarlet coloured beast, full of names of blasphemy, having seven heads and ten horns. And the woman was arrayed in purple and scarlet colour, and decked with gold and precious stones and pearls, having a golden cup in her hand full of abominations and filthiness of her fornication: And upon her forehead [was] a name written, MYSTERY, BABYLON THE GREAT, THE MOTHER OF HARLOTS AND ABOMINATIONS OF THE EARTH. And I saw the woman drunken with the blood of the saints, and with the blood of the martyrs of Jesus: and when I saw her, I wondered with great admiration. And the angel said unto me, Wherefore didst thou marvel? I will tell thee the mystery of the woman, and of the beast that carrieth her, which hath the seven heads and ten horns. The beast that thou sawest was, and is not; and shall ascend out of the bottomless pit, and go into perdition: and they that dwell on the earth shall wonder, whose names were not written in the book of life from the foundation of the world, when they behold the beast that was, and is not, and yet is. And here [is] the mind which hath wisdom. The seven heads are seven mountains, on which the woman sitteth. And there are seven kings: five are fallen, and one is, [and] the other is not yet come; and when he cometh, he must continue a short space. And the beast that was, and is not, even he is the eighth, and is of the seven, and goeth into perdition.

- Revelation 18:1-9 And after these things I saw another angel come down from heaven, having great power; and the earth was lightened with his glory. And he cried mightily with a strong voice, saying, Babylon the great is fallen, is fallen, and is become the habitation of devils, and the hold of every foul spirit, and a cage of every unclean and hateful bird. For all nations have drunk of the wine of the wrath of her fornication, and the kings of the earth have committed fornication with her, and the merchants of the earth are waxed rich through the abundance of her delicacies. And I heard another voice from heaven, saying, Come out of her, my people, that ye be not partakers of her sins, and that ye receive not of her plagues. For her sins have reached unto heaven, and God hath remembered her iniquities. Reward her even as she rewarded you, and double unto her double according to her works: in the cup which she hath filled fill to her double. How much she hath glorified herself, and lived deliciously, so much torment and sorrow give her: for she saith in her heart, I sit a queen, and am no widow, and shall see no sorrow. Therefore shall her plagues come in one day, death, and mourning, and famine; and she shall be utterly burned with fire: for strong [is] the Lord God who judgeth her. And the kings of the earth, who have committed fornication and lived deliciously with her, shall bewail her, and lament for her, when they shall see the smoke of her burning.

Believe it or not, there are well over fifty points to identify the Antichrist with. Many skeptics may be able to argue a point or two or even several away, but we are not talking about dismissing six out of eight points. If someone were able to argue even eight of them away, that is still over forty-two points that point the finger, and those eight points of contention would then just be that skeptic's opinion. Our point is that the Bible clearly reveals who or what the Antichrist is, and it is up to us to accept it, reject not only the Antichrist but all the false teachings, or we are on the side of Antichrist even if we do not believe it or even in God Himself.

What we are going to do now is collect the similar content into the various points and do a Bible study to reveal the detailed meaning of certain words to clarify certain points. We are not going to just repeat the verses above in sequence because so many identifying marks would be repeated. Numerous times the word "blasphemy" is used, therefore let us collect them and use the Bible to define it further.

Now we do have one word of caution before we begin, and that is, remember that "God is love" (1 John 4:8). God is not providing these verses to be ignored, nor is He providing these verses to hurt anyone, and this is not a game of just "who done it" either. This is not a game! This also not a test to see if you agree or if we agree with you. God provides these verses to save people. This is serious business. It is no different than telling a young child not to touch a hot stove. Is it because a parent does not want the child to have fun? Of course not. Is it because the parent wants to make the child feel bad? Of course not. Is it because the parent just likes to make up silly rules just because they can? Of course not. A good parent does not want the child to get burned is the bottom line. Likewise, we have pulled out all the verses that we are aware of not to condemn anyone, make anyone hate us, cause problems, make people feel bad, or any such thing like that. These words are being provided so the person who did not know they were associated with the Antichrist or the way of thinking along with working against Christ would realize now before it is too late that they need to stop doing that and follow God's way creating a great distance between their old way of thinking and now God's way.

What Are the Identifying Marks?

So, without any further delay, let us approach this subject open and honestly.

IDENTIFYING MARK #1: ANTICHRIST IS NOT FUTURE

1 John 2:18 says, "Ye have heard that Antichrist shall come, even now are there many Antichrists", where we shall focus upon the part that says, "even now".

2 Thessalonians 2:7 says, "For the mystery of iniquity doth already work: only he who now letteth [will let], until he be taken out of the way."

Many people and many Christians are taught that the Antichrist is some person that is going to dominate the world with a massive army and be part of bringing on a world war. There are many variants of that understanding, but the bottom line is that the world is being prepared to expect the Antichrist in the future. This allows the true Antichrist to continue unobserved, be unexpected, and to mass together for the final conflict of which even professed Christians that think they are saved will be enlisted into the service of Antichrist of which we will see more on that in another topic. But with these verses, one could say that the Antichrist will claim to have its roots from the time of the apostles.

However, both John and Paul contradict the modern understanding of Antichrist by stating the words "even now" as well as "who now" respectively. Thankfully there are other verses that will support what is being stated so if you are concerned about drawing this conclusion, in a little while, we will even provide dates.

IDENTIFYING MARK #2: ANTICHRIST IS NOT A SINGLE PERSON

1 John 2:18 says, "Ye have heard that Antichrist shall come, even now are there many Antichrists", where we shall focus upon the part that says, "even now".

Yes, we are repeating the verse but now with the Antichrist being declared to already be in existence at the time of John, that means the Antichrist cannot be a person, as no one has ever lived since the time of Jesus more than two hundred years let alone two thousand years, but more on that later.

IDENTIFYING MARK #3: ANTICHRIST IS AGAINST CHRIST, NOT AGAINST JEWS

Daniel 7:25 says, "And he shall speak [great] words against the most High, and shall wear out the saints of the most High.

We could approach this point by simply referring to the name "Antichrist". It does not say "anti-Jew", yet, as the modern story of Antichrist goes, Antichrist will come to power, mass an army, attack Israel with at least three or four major world powers and with the support of at least ten smaller powers. Obviously from that story, if Antichrist is attacking Israel, that means the Antichrist would be anti-Jews and not Antichrist. Remember, Christ said, "I will build my church" (Matthew 16:18). That declaration means that Jews had their opportunity and failed. They were cut off basically. There is even a time prophecy that we shall examine that specifies exactly when the Jews stopped being God's special people. So the Antichrist attacking Israel is completely meaningless if the Antichrist thinks they are getting back at God.

So, to be Antichrist means to work against Christ by definition. The Antichrist would be against Christ's church and what it stands for. In fact, the Bible says that to work against the Most High is to have "rebelled against the words of God, and contemned the counsel of the most High" (Psalms 107:11). "Yet they tempted and provoked the most high God, and kept not his testimonies" (Psalms 78:56).

Even in this discussion, we can see many more obvious contradictions between the Bible version of the Antichrist and modern Christianity's version, but we will try to refrain from combining all the points into one long discussion.

IDENTIFYING MARK #4: WAR AGAINST THE DOCTRINES OF JESUS CHRIST

2 John 1:9 says, "Whosoever transgresseth, and abideth not in the doctrine of Christ, hath not God. He that abideth in the doctrine of Christ, he hath both the Father and the Son." And in 2 John 1:7, John connects this to the Antichrist. So we pick up right where the previous point left off.

And again we will make reference to the modern version of the Antichrist to show yet another contradiction in the modern story and hopefully you are sensing that the popular perpetrating of spreading this false story, despite claiming to be Christian and despite claiming to be saved, are actually fueling the progression of the true Antichrist activity, as we stated would happen. In the modern story, Antichrist is a military leader that will use the modern warfare to attempt to crush Israel. So, all eyes are on people who have risen and fallen, rebellious countries who have tried and failed, which have a background in being a threat to the world, especially the towards the nation of Israel. For the longest time, eyes were upon Saddam Hussein, even Mahmoud Ahmadinejad. Countries like Iraq, Iran, and even North Korea, since they have ties to either Russia or China or both who are to be part of the union of the anti-Israeli force.

In reality, the Bible reveals that the Antichrist is a war on words, as stated in the previous point and here in this point's verse. Not only is the war on just any words but those against the Most High, against the testimonies or better known as the books of the Bible, and now we see from this verse that the words are against the doctrines and not only doctrines but specifically those that Christ established. So one can see that by taking everyone's eyes off of the doctrines and onto weapons of destruction is just an effort to allow everyone to believe what they want and still be considered fine in God's eyes. By placing the attention upon physical warfare is helping the Antichrist to continue to change the doctrines and pass on those erroneous doctrines. The activity of the Antichrist therefore is a focus upon undoing Jesus' teachings, even declaring the Bible to be in error and even denying the fact that "All scripture [is] given by inspiration of God, and [is] profitable for doctrine, for reproof, for correction, for instruction in righteousness" (2 Timothy 3:16). Today however, the war of Antichrist being upon words and not military activities is unheard of because the teaching of today among Christians is that we ought to all just believe in the existence of Jesus and get along despite the doctrines. In fact, "doctrines divide," they say, and therefore should not be focused upon at all. Interestingly, there is a warning against such thinking. "When they shall say, Peace and safety; then sudden destruction cometh upon them" (1 Thessalonians 5:3). That peace incorporates the spiritual peace between all supposed Christian brothers and sisters.

So, for Christians to continue to think that doctrines do not matter, they are actually not filled with the Holy Spirit as they claim but are filled with the "Spirit of Antichrist" (1 John 4:3). This is but one example of how those that claim to be on the side of Jesus Christ are actually and unknowingly on the side of Antichrist and furthering the activity of Antichrist. On top of that, even unbelievers that accept or even repeat these phrases in any manner are continuing Antichrist's lie. This even how governments that claim to be neutral on the subject actually are continuing the promotion of this lie. In fact, there are some laws in place that restrict the belief of there being one true doctrine in the Christian religion as opposed to accepting every doctrine. Even some antidiscrimination laws make it challenging to not cross the line or have to choose between the Bible and the government.

The Bible says, "Be ye not unequally yoked together with unbelievers" (2 Corinthians 6:14). That is in every aspect including marriage, close friendship, even employment. Now take employment laws into consideration. Though the example we are about to use does not matter the particular denomination, in several other denominations it does. Let us say that a Methodist organization is trying to put together a staff. Not only do they need religious staff, but they would need the non-religious positions to be filled as well including a secretary, computer person, and others. Would they want a Baptist or Hindu or atheist answering the phone in which potentially one of the callers may be interested in becoming a Methodist or have a Methodist question? Sure, all calls could be redirected to a proper religious person, but even in first contact, there is something that could be concerning. So, if the Methodist post on a job board such a position hoping a Methodist will respond and instead a Lutheran wants the position, by law, if that Lutheran is the most qualified for the position on ability and not belief, the Methodist must hire that person. Now like I said, typically the Methodist do not have such a problem, but take a denomination that is not considered mainstream and the story is different. Much hiring in such denominations is usually done behind the scenes. But this is how even a neutral governments can be part of the problem.

IDENTIFYING MARK #5: TRADITION ABOVE THE BIBLE

Daniel 7:8 says, "... and, behold, in this horn [were] eyes like the eyes of man...".

To have eyes like the eyes of a man is to see things from a humans perspective instead of God's perspective. In fact, the Bible makes a contrast with Daniel's description of the Antichrist and with God's position on things. Psalms 32:8 says, "I will instruct thee and teach thee in the way which thou shalt go: I will guide thee with mine eye." So there is God's eyes and there are man's eyes. And in regards to the last identifying mark, there are God's doctrines and there are man's doctrines. And Jesus had a thing or two to say about that stating, "Making the word of God of none effect through your tradition, which ye have delivered: and many such like things do ye" (Mark 7:13). So instead of getting the doctrines out of the Bible, people create traditions to be followed instead. The truest definition of a cult is when one discards the Bible and relies on human beings to define the beliefs. Sounds like there ought to be some serious investigation then upon what one's denomination teaches.

So that means once again that all Christians who do not believe that doctrines matter and that it is no big deal if they are not solidly found from scripture, they are not only simply mistaken but are on the side of the Antichrist. God just said, "Whosoever transgresseth, and abideth not in the doctrine of Christ, hath not God" (2 John 1:9). Even plainer said is that if one is not obeying the doctrines outlined in the Bible and the Bible alone, they are NOT saved, and having opportunity to cease that transgression and yet pass over it as if it is no big deal is not something that God is just going to allow. Therefore, the logical conclusion would be to make sure what one beliefs are solidly based on the Bible and not the traditions set forth by humans. Additionally, if that means the church that one is attending is full of doctrines not supported by the Bible then they must be in one of those churches that the Antichrist has greatly influenced and should consider departing quickly.

IDENTIFYING MARK #6: RELIGIOUS POWER

2 Thessalonians 2:4 says, "He as God sitteth in the emple of God, shewing himself that he is God".

By the Antichrist pretending to play God and even be seated in a religious place makes the Antichrist a religious power.

IDENTIFYING MARK #7: IS A KINGDOM OR NATION

Revelation 13:1 says, "And I stood upon the sand of the sea, and saw a beast rise up out of the sea." Daniel 7:3 says, "And four great beasts came up from the sea, diverse one from another." Daniel 7:17 says "These great beasts, which are four, [are] four kings, [which] shall arise out of the earth." Daniel 7:23 says "Thus he said, The fourth beast shall be the fourth kingdom upon earth, which shall be diverse from all kingdoms, and shall devour the whole earth, and shall tread it down, and break it in pieces."

Putting it altogether, both John and Daniel see beasts rise from the sea. Daniel is told specifically that these beasts represent kings or kingdoms. Seeing that "Jesus Christ the same yesterday, and to day, and for ever" (Hebrews 13:8), that means that John's beast is also a kingdom, which is equivalent to a nation. Therefore, let us get our eyes off of people being the Antichrist and start looking on a map for a nation instead.

IDENTIFYING MARK #8: LOCATED IN A POPULATED AREA SPEAKING MANY LANGUAGES

According to Revelation 13:1, the Bible says, "And I stood upon the sand of the sea, and saw a beast rise up out of the sea".

Many people do not study the Bible as detailed as they ought. For instance, many people look at these words and start speculating things about the Antichrist beast. They say, "It will arise to power through the United Nations" or "It will come to power from the desert locations like the Middle East" or some other speculation. Well, we do not have to guess where the beast power arises from. The Bible tells us that it arises from the sea. Of course we refer to Revelation 1:1 to realize that it is not literally the sea but is "signified". So, do not be looking for a city under the sea or some Antichrist character to step out of a submarine. Now, the question to ask is, "What does the sea or water mean in this case?"

In Revelation 17:15, the Bible says, "And he saith unto me, The waters which thou sawest, where the whore sitteth, are peoples, and multitudes, and nations, and tongues." Now we do not need to worry about the whore or the fact that she is sitting, the focus is upon the definition of water, which makes up the sea. God does not define water for the whore and water for the beast; God is consistent. If we know the water definition for the whore, we will know it for all prophetic use. The answer is, the water represents "peoples, and multitudes, and nations, and tongues" or languages. So the Antichrist is not in a country that speaks just one language; many different languages are spoken. Also, it is populated as well, and on top of that, there are many nations in close proximity, according to the description. Therefore, the Antichrist will not rise up from Hawaii, being isolated. The Antichrist will not rise up in any country where the official language is but one language.

IDENTIFYING MARK #9: DENIES THAT JESUS IS THE CHRIST

1 John 2:22, says, "Who is a liar but he that denieth that Jesus is the Christ? He is Antichrist, that denieth the Father and the Son."

So at first glance, it looks like we are looking at a non-Christian nation, but that would be an incorrect conclusion. This is thought of because of focusing upon the words stating that the Antichrist "denieth that Jesus is the Christ." Now, who in their right mind would be a Christian let alone a nation of Christians denying that Jesus is the Christ? It does not make sense. But it does make sense when we investigate what is meant by denying that Jesus is the Christ.

The Bible says, "For there are certain men crept in unawares, who were before of old ordained to this condemnation, ungodly men, turning the grace of our God into lasciviousness, and denying the only Lord God, and our Lord Jesus Christ" (Jude 1:4). So we have people who joined the Christian community back in Jude's day, John's day, and even Paul's day, which cover about the same time frame, that have exploited the grace of God making it into some lascivious thing. By doing that, the verse states that they are denying Jesus Christ. So they were calling themselves Christian but teaching a different form of grace is the bottom line.

The Bible definitions to lasciviousness is filthy, unbridled lust, wantonness, and being in excess. Looking at another verse in the Bible to clarify it further, it says that "lasciviousness, to work all uncleanness with greediness" (Ephesians 4:19). So any preacher that teaches that grace allows for filthiness or uncleanness, lusts, lack of limitation, or permitting excesses, is changing the intent of grace into something that it was not intended, which will cause people to be lost. Now such teachers and preachers have a huge following because the natural inclination of people, including Christians is to "not endure sound doctrine; but after their own lusts shall they heap to themselves teachers, having itching ears" (2 Timothy 4:3). In other words, a preacher or teacher that allows people to live in sin is going to have a greater following than a preacher that lists all of the things a person is to give up to be a true Christian.

That means that the Spirit of Antichrist continues the original Antichrist teaching that lightens up on the restrictions claiming that grace makes such allowance. This is the opposite of what Jesus taught. "If any [man] will come after me, let him deny himself, and take up his cross, and follow me" (Matthew 16:24). This truly reveals how Antichrist is working against Jesus Christ on the teaching level. You see, being nuked by a rogue nation that hates Jews is not going to change the status of salvation, but seeing that the devil does not want people going to heaven, he is going to create an entity that draws people away from Christ's teaching into error so people do lose salvation over wrong beliefs, hence the name Antichrist.

So again, all of today's preachers who preach that there are no limits in a Christian's life because of grace, they are teaching the original Antichrist message. And again, you can see how the vast majority of Christians are being lead to the slaughter of hell by just about every Christian preacher today. However, not all teach grace that does away with the restrictions; not all teach that grace replaces the Ten Commandments; but there are a few that adhere to "Preach the word; be instant in season, out of season; reprove, rebuke, exhort with all longsuffering and doctrine" (2 Timothy 4:2). It is a matter of finding them. This is why the Bible can describe the following aspect of the Antichrist as being "all the world wondered after the beast" (Revelation 13:3). People do not have to be directly associated with the Antichrist to wonder after the beast. They can be listening to preachers who are teaching the same errors as the Antichrist purported starting in John, Paul, and Jude's day. And this is not to say that just a few or even half of the Christians are deceived. There are so many that have repeated the Antichrist lies that from God's perspective, He says, "all the world wondered"! That is serious. Too bad so many Christians are blinded by the twisted grace definition, and think they are happily are headed to heaven while outright sinning. This is why Jesus declares "strait [is] the gate, and narrow [is] the way, which leadeth unto life, and few there be that find it" (Matthew 7:14), not the majority, but "few". This also is how Jesus can say of the last generation on earth that "if [it were] possible, they shall deceive the very elect" (Matthew 24:24). So only the "very elect", the most Bible studious person that has the love for Jesus' in their hearts along with keeping to Jesus' doctrines only are going to "endureth to the end shall be saved" (Matthew 10:22).

And there is not just one lie on this subject. The devil has many. Some Christians believe the Ten Commandments are not just the Ten Suggestions and ought to be obeyed, but then when reviewing the commandments, they are not as restrictive as printed. There are some denominations that teach a certain amount of rules but they are not that disruptive to one's life version, in fact, they can change as society changes, as if society dictates religion instead of the other way around.

So, to continue as a Christian and call obedient Christians who live with restrictions as legalists is to not have the true gospel, therefore, we invite all to come over to the true gospel that teaches the true meaning of grace. The only Bible definition of grace is found with the writer associated with the Ten Commandments. Moses wrote, "If now I have found grace in thy sight, O Lord, let my Lord, I pray thee, go among us; for it [is] a stiffnecked people; and pardon our iniquity and our sin, and take us for thine inheritance" (Exodus 34:9). Grace is forgiveness or pardon for the sins we have committed and offers us eternal life. It does not permit us to continue sinning. The Bible says about grace being used to keep us from sinning with the words, "And now, brethren, I commend you to God, and to the word of his grace, which is able to build you up, and to give you an inheritance among all them which are sanctified" (Acts 20:32). Sanctification is holy living, not sinning living! Even Paul, the great grace writer wrote, "What shall we say then? Shall we continue in sin, that grace may abound? God forbid. How shall we, that are dead to sin, live any longer therein? " (Romans 6:1-2). And those that think Paul wrote about replacing the obedience to the Ten Commandments with grace, he wrote, "For sin shall not have dominion over you: for ye are not under the law, but under grace. What then? shall we sin, because we are not under the law, but under grace? God forbid. Know ye not, that to whom ye yield yourselves servants to obey, his servants ye are to whom ye obey; whether of sin unto death, or of obedience unto righteousness?" (Romans 6:14-16) And "Do we then make void the law through faith? God forbid: yea, we establish the law" (Romans 3:31).

IDENTIFYING MARK #10: DENIES THAT JESUS CAME IN THE FLESH

1 John 4:3 says, "And every spirit that confesseth not that Jesus Christ is come in the flesh is not of God: and this is that [spirit] of Antichrist, whereof ye have heard that it should come; and even now already is it in the world."

So in the previous point, the Antichrist denies that Jesus is the Christ and we saw how that it worked out to be a false gospel of grace that makes grace a lascivious thing, basically sinful. We also saw that one can actually be a Christian while accomplishing that. Now the question is about a similar statement that just looks way to obvious to believe in the existence of Jesus yet not believe that He came in the flesh. It sounds contradictory; it sounds impossible. Does the Antichrist just refer to Jesus as a spirit or ghost or some other non-human entity?

Again, to answer this, we must not apply the first thing that comes to mind when we read these words. We must allow the Bible to provide the definition even when we are very sure of ourselves. The word "flesh" seems natural to conclude that it means skin, bones, blood pumping, a physical being, but that is not the only definition. Besides, to be a believer of Jesus must mean somehow one believes in a literal existence of Jesus. So flesh cannot just refer to a physical body.

Looking at various Bible definitions of the word "flesh", we find that Jesus warned us, "Watch and pray, that ye enter not into temptation: the spirit indeed [is] willing, but the flesh [is] weak" (Matthew 26:41). The "flesh" in this context does not refer to the physical description of a being. It refers to thinking and feeling with our senses. Spiritually, we know that gluttony is wrong, but if we think about what our taste buds like and what our stomachs want, we may eat beyond being comfortable. Why? Because it is part of the flesh that is weak. Why do so many people become determined to give up things only to find out hours, days, weeks later they are enjoying what they wanted to stop? It is not because they are flesh or a physical being. It is because the flesh or desires of the body are stronger, which we need to resist and put into self control, which is to be "temperate in all things" (1 Corinthians 9:25).

So, "For what the law could not do, in that it was weak through the flesh, God sending his own Son in the likeness of sinful flesh, and for sin, condemned sin in the flesh" (Romans 8:3). Did you catch it? Jesus came not as a God to walk among humans, sacrifice Himself, and rise again, but Jesus came to set an example to live by. In other words, Jesus "was in all points tempted like as [we are, yet] without sin" (Hebrews 4:15). If Jesus was mere God walking on earth, there would be no temptation. But "verily he took not on [him the nature of] angels; but he took on [him] the seed of Abraham" (Hebrews 2:16). Did you also catch that? He was not like an angel either, but more importantly, He was not made like Adam before Adam fell into sin. Jesus was made like a child of Abraham. He took on the nature that Abraham had. That is the human nature. Jesus sensed hunger and controlled His appetite. He sensed sleepless nights and yet did not lose His temper. He saw women throughout the day and yet did not have a fantasy about having sex with any of them, despite what the movies portray. Jesus probably hit His thumb with a hammer in the carpenter shop during the years before public ministry and yet did not utter a foul word. Jesus was teased, was shoved, was even spat upon (Matthew 26:67), and finally crucified (Mark 15:15), yet He did not lash out angrily at anyone.

There is no other way around the fact that Jesus took upon Himself our nature because if we believe that Jesus was somehow superior to us, then how could He be tempted in all points like we are? If Jesus took on Adam's nature before the fall, then Jesus would have been tempted in all points like Adam was and not us. Further, how could the Bible say, "He that saith he abideth in him ought himself also so to walk, even as he walked" (1 John 2:6)? If Jesus was made like Adam before he sinned, then there is no way we could ever live the rest of our lives like Jesus yet we are told to do so. To complicate matters, Jesus says, "To him that overcometh will I grant to sit with me in my throne, even as I also overcame, and am set down with my Father in his throne" (Revelation 3:21). So if Jesus was like Adam before sin, then how can we overcome temptation as Jesus overcame temptation? We would not be able to do so. Therefore, the only conclusion is that Jesus was born with the same nature as we are. That nature is the meaning of the word "flesh". Of course, most Christians and preachers ignore all of that so they can teach the allowance of sinning.

You see, until we become converted, the Bible describes us by stating, "Among whom also we all had our conversation in times past in the lusts of our flesh, fulfilling the desires of the flesh and of the mind; and were by nature the children of wrath, even as others" (Ephesians 2:3). Please note the equating of flesh and nature in that verse, but before one jumps to the conclusion that we are saying that Jesus had sinful feelings and lusts, that is not what we are saying. Remember, the Bible said that Jesus was without sin (Hebrews 4:15). Those that have a kneejerk reaction to what we say do so because of the confusion in their minds in which people think temptation is sin, and that is not true.

If temptation were sin, then the verse we quoted would not make sense. Jesus was "in all points tempted like as [we are, yet] without sin" (Hebrews 4:15). In fact, the same is promised to us for "The Lord knoweth how to deliver the godly out of temptations" (2 Peter 2:9). Even keep in mind that "Blessed [is] the man that endureth temptation: for when he is tried, he shall receive the crown of life, which the Lord hath promised to them that love him" (James 1:12). And in conclusion of the topic of temptation, Jesus "himself hath suffered being tempted, he is able to succour them that are tempted" (Hebrews 2:18). So just as we are tempted, He was tempted. Jesus could have sinned but did not. We too can choose not to sin.

The bottom line is that the Antichrist would perpetrate the lie that Jesus was either only God walking among us or was made human but only like Adam before he sinned. Not much thought is usually given to this matter among Christians, but the end result of hearing that "Only Jesus was perfect" is the concerning factor. Although it is true that "all have sinned, and come short of the glory of God" (Romans 3:23), we can live the rest of our days walking as He walked, overcoming as He overcame. In fact, it is God's expectation that we cease sinning. "Forasmuch then as Christ hath suffered for us in the flesh, arm yourselves likewise with the same mind: for he that hath suffered in the flesh hath ceased from sin" (1 Peter 4:1). And there is the verse that is plainly written in black and white that we are equally able to overcome every single temptation like Jesus and not give into sin. In fact, the only reason we do give into temptation is this, "every man is tempted, when he is drawn away of his own lust, and enticed" (James 1:14). It is because we want to give in. And to all the "born again" Christians that continue sinning, the Bible says that if one is truly born again, then "Whosoever is born of God doth not commit sin; for his seed remaineth in him: and he cannot sin, because he is born of God" (1 John 3:9).

So, we would be supporting the Antichrist lie by thinking that we are going to, as Christians, continue sinning until our death or second coming. By continuing to utter, "Only Jesus is perfect!" Those are some of the lies of Antichrist and to do so is to have the Spirit of Antichrist.

IDENTIFYING MARK #11: KILLS GOD'S SAINTS

Revelation 13:7 says, "And it was given unto him to make war with the saints, and to overcome them". Revelation 17:6 says, "And I saw the woman drunken with the blood of the saints, and with the blood of the martyrs of Jesus." Daniel 7:21 says, "I beheld, and the same horn made war with the saints, and prevailed against them." Daniel 7:25 says, "And shall wear out the saints of the most High."

First, the word saint as used in the Bible is a reference to a godly person on earth and not what many religions have turned it into, beings in Heaven that have earned a special title. As an example, the Bible says, "Peter passed throughout all [quarters], he came down also to the saints which dwelt at Lydda" (Acts 9:32), so Peter visited real people in a town called Lydda. Additionally, Paul, in writing to the Christians in Rome, wrote, "To all that be in Rome, beloved of God, called [to be] saints" (Romans 1:7). A calling to be a saint is a calling to be godly, a true Christian. In fact, Paul even stated a stark warning against Christians sinning, "But fornication, and all uncleanness, or covetousness, let it not be once named among you, as becometh saints" (Ephesians 5:3). If one wants to be a saint, do not be doing those sinful things.

So the Antichrist will wage war against them both in the physical as well as in other means like, printing up lies and publically speaking wrongful condemnations, among other things. The Antichrist will create martyrs, in which killing a saint is killing a true Christian.

IDENTIFYING MARK #12: COMES TO FULL POWER AFTER 476 A.D.

Revelation 13:1-2 says, "And I stood upon the sand of the sea, and saw a beast rise up out of the sea, having seven heads and ten horns, and upon his horns ten crowns, and upon his heads the name of blasphemy. And the beast which I saw was like unto a leopard, and his feet were as [the feet] of a bear, and his mouth as the mouth of a lion: and the dragon gave him his power, and his seat, and great authority." Not by coincidence, the individual body parts are referenced in Daniel 7:1-8, which says, "In the first year of Belshazzar king of Babylon Daniel had a dream and visions of his head upon his bed: then he wrote the dream, [and] told the sum of the matters. Daniel spake and said, I saw in my vision by night, and, behold, the four winds of the heaven strove upon the great sea. And four great beasts came up from the sea, diverse one from another. The first [was] like a lion, and had eagle's wings: I beheld till the wings thereof were plucked, and it was lifted up from the earth, and made stand upon the feet as a man, and a man's heart was given to it. And behold another beast, a second, like to a bear, and it raised up itself on one side, and [it had] three ribs in the mouth of it between the teeth of it: and they said thus unto it, Arise, devour much flesh. After this I beheld, and lo another, like a leopard, which had upon the back of it four wings of a fowl; the beast had also four heads; and dominion was given to it. After this I saw in the night visions, and behold a fourth beast, dreadful and terrible, and strong exceedingly; and it had great iron teeth: it devoured and brake in pieces, and stamped the residue with the feet of it: and it [was] diverse from all the beasts that [were] before it; and it had ten horns. I considered the horns, and, behold, there came up among them another little horn, before whom there were three of the first horns plucked up by the roots: and, behold, in this horn [were] eyes like the eyes of man, and a mouth speaking great things."

It is the sequence of representations in the Book of Daniel that eventually leads to the date provided. As the beast in Revelation 13 contains all of the animal parts of Daniel 7, one must logically conclude that this is not a coincidence, therefore, the notion to take the parts of the beasts and compare it with the animal symbols of today's nations is but a distraction from connecting many of the Antichrist identifying marks, for if one declares that the lion represents today's England, the bear represents Russia, the leopard represents maybe a middle eastern country, and the dragon represents China, then all of the descriptive verses in Daniel is thrown away. Further, we also lose much of the activity that is described by Daniel as well. So if I were the devil, sure I would want to redirect the attention from the Bible symbols and get people anticipating some union of powerful nations, but to the "very elect" or well studied Christian, that would not suffice.

We are not talking that the beast in Revelation matches just one beast in Daniel. We are not even saying that it is just two beasts or three, but four beasts plus ten parts making five objects in detail to match up. This is not a coincidence. So to modernize the meaning of the animals is to go against John's intention in Revelation 13. This is further supported by the numerous references John makes to Daniel's period like equating Babylon, a physical kingdom in Daniel's day, to the Antichrist spiritually.

Now, as John sees a single beast arising to power, please realize that Daniel sees them individually. There is a significance to this that we shall discuss later, but for now, please recall that a beast represents a kingdom, therefore, as we enter into the Book of Daniel, apply the fact that each beast is a kingdom, one in succession after another. This is obtained by the verse that says, "And four great beasts came up from the sea, diverse one from another" (Daniel 7:3).

So, "The first [was] like a lion, and had eagle's wings: I beheld till the wings thereof were plucked, and it was lifted up from the earth, and made stand upon the feet as a man, and a man's heart was given to it" (Daniel 7:4).

Looking at the first beast, do recognize another parallel here. Daniel 2 revealed a dream of King Nebuchadnezzar in which he saw "a great image. This great image, whose brightness [was] excellent, stood before thee; and the form thereof [was] terrible. This image's head [was] of fine gold, his breast and his arms of silver, his belly and his thighs of brass, His legs of iron, his feet part of iron and part of clay" (Daniel 2:31-34). On top of that, it is further explained in Daniel 2:41 by saying, "And whereas thou sawest the feet and toes, part of potters' clay, and part of iron, the kingdom shall be divided; but there shall be in it of the strength of the iron, forasmuch as thou sawest the iron mixed with miry clay." So, what we are seeing is that in Daniel 2, there are four metals with the last metal divided into ten. Each item described to Daniel represents a kingdom, like in Daniel 2:39, "And after thee shall arise another kingdom inferior to thee, and another third kingdom of brass, which shall bear rule over all the earth." Not by chance, there are four beasts with the last beast having ten horns and also representing kingdoms as stated in Daniel 7:23, "The fourth beast shall be the fourth kingdom upon earth, which shall be diverse from all kingdoms." Therefore, we are going to rely upon Daniel 2 to help us understand Daniel 7.

So since we are examining the first beast of Daniel 7, which is the Lion, if we know what the first metal represents, being the head of gold, we should get our answer to who represents the first kingdom. So, when Daniel tells King Nebuchadnezzar of the dream, he is the king of the first then known world empire called Babylon. Daniel did say to him, "Thou [art] this head of gold" (this head of gold). So King Nebuchadnezzar and Babylon are the head of gold as well as being represented by a Lion.

And according to the Bible, it says, "[as swift] as the eagle flieth" (Deuteronomy 28:49) and "They are passed away as the swift ships: as the eagle [that] hasteth to the prey" (Job 9:26). So therefore, Babylon comes to power in haste or swiftness.

In regards to the heart, the Bible says that King Nebuchadnezzar had a change of heart. He was very prideful, so God had punished him. "Let his heart be changed from man's, and let a beast's heart be given unto him; and let seven times pass over him" (Daniel 4:16). Although Daniel 7:4 states that a man's heart is to be given to the Lion, do keep in mind that if King Nebuchadnezzar's heart, which in Daniel 4:16 was a man's heart, was removed and turned into the heart of a beast, by the time King Nebuchadnezzar could state, "my reason returned unto me; and for the glory of my kingdom, mine honour and brightness returned unto me; and my counsellors and my lords sought unto me; and I was established in my kingdom, and excellent majesty was added unto me" (Daniel 4:36). So after the event, his man heart was returned to him. Basically, Daniel 7:4 is identifying King Nebuchadnezzar's conversion for "Now I Nebuchadnezzar praise and extol and honour the King of heaven, all whose works [are] truth, and his ways judgment: and those that walk in pride he is able to abase" (Daniel 4:37).

All of this detail is being provided in Daniel 7:4 so that we can know for certainty that we are on the right track. If Daniel 7:4 simply said that there was just a Lion, we might be able to argue what that represents, but when you add the swiftness that happened and especially that this is the only beast that has a heart transplant, we can begin our dating with surety. Even Jeremiah associated lions with Babylon, also known as Assyria. "Israel [is] a scattered sheep; the lions have driven [him] away: first the king of Assyria hath devoured him; and last this Nebuchadrezzar king of Babylon hath broken his bones", (Jeremiah 50:17). Speaking of which, Babylon came to power in 606 B.C. and lasted until 538 B.C.

Now moving on to the second beast, it is described as "Another beast, a second, like to a bear, and it raised up itself on one side, and [it had] three ribs in the mouth of it between the teeth of it: and they said thus unto it, Arise, devour much flesh" (Daniel 7:5). Not by coincidence, the second metal of Daniel 2 also describes the second beast. Daniel 2:32 says, "His breast and his arms of silver". And while Daniel is speaking to King Nebuchadnezzar, Daniel describes this metal with the words, "After thee shall arise another kingdom inferior to thee" (Daniel 2:39).

So the bear and the silver body part both represent a world empire that follows Babylon. The body part explicitly state a focus upon the arms because the second power to arise and rule the then known world was not a single power. Although Daniel does not name that power at this moment, he does refer to it elsewhere.

In Daniel 5, there is a wild party going on in Babylon. "Belshazzar the king made a great feast to a thousand of his lords, and drank wine before the thousand. Belshazzar, whiles he tasted the wine, commanded to bring the golden and silver vessels which his father Nebuchadnezzar had taken out of the temple which [was] in Jerusalem; that the king, and his princes, his wives, and his concubines, might drink therein" (Daniel 5:1-2). During this party, a chin dropping, knee knocking experience occurs. "In the same hour came forth fingers of a man's hand, and wrote over against the candlestick upon the plaister of the wall of the king's palace: and the king saw the part of the hand that wrote. Then the king's countenance was changed, and his thoughts troubled him, so that the joints of his loins were loosed, and his knees smote one against another" (Daniel 5:5-6). After looking for answers through pagan means, "they could not read the writing, nor make known to the king the interpretation thereof" (Daniel 5:8), "Then was Daniel brought in before the king" (Daniel 5:13). Daniel then said, "I will read the writing unto the king, and make known to him the interpretation" (Daniel 5:17). "And this [is] the writing that was written, MENE, MENE, TEKEL, UPHARSIN. This [is] the interpretation of the thing: MENE; God hath numbered thy kingdom, and finished it. TEKEL; Thou art weighed in the balances, and art found wanting. PERES; Thy kingdom is divided, and given to the Medes and Persians. Then commanded Belshazzar, and they clothed Daniel with scarlet, and [put] a chain of gold about his neck, and made a proclamation concerning him, that he should be the third ruler in the kingdom. In that night was Belshazzar the king of the Chaldeans slain. And Darius the Median took the kingdom, [being] about threescore and two years old" (Daniel 5:25-31).

So the answer is the joint efforts of the Medes and Persians, hence the two arms of agreement, and hence why the bear lifts up on one side and then the other. The reference to the breast matches the strength of the bear for when one looks upon a body for muscles, it is usually in the arms and chest. The three ribs in the bear's mouth as well as the reference to devouring much flesh is the expansion of the Medes and Persian territory by conquering three areas known as Lydia, Egypt, as well as Babylon. The reference to being inferior is a reference to wealth. As gold is more valuable than silver, so the wealth will also be inferior.

Looking back at our time line, we now have moved from 538 B.C. to 331 B.C., which was the ruling period of the Medes and Persians. So that leaves two more beasts to look at.

Our third beast is identified as, "After this I beheld, and lo another, like a leopard, which had upon the back of it four wings of a fowl; the beast had also four heads; and dominion was given to it" (Daniel 7:6). The matching metal is described as "his belly and his thighs of brass" (Daniel 2:32), which is explained as "another third kingdom of brass, which shall bear rule over all the earth" (Daniel 2:39). So, we have a doubly swift conquering kingdom in addition to being a fast animal. We also have a kingdom that eventually has four heads or leaders. The belly representing appetite while thighs appeal to appearance.

Now Daniel did not tell King Nebuchadnezzar who that third kingdom would be, neither did he experience the third kingdom to appear, however, he did have a vision that named the third kingdom. "And I saw in a vision; and it came to pass, when I saw, that I [was] at Shushan [in] the palace, which [is] in the province of Elam; and I saw in a vision, and I was by the river of Ulai. Then I lifted up mine eyes, and saw, and, behold, there stood before the river a ram which had [two] horns: and the [two] horns [were] high; but one [was] higher than the other, and the higher came up last. I saw the ram pushing westward, and northward, and southward; so that no beasts might stand before him, neither [was there any] that could deliver out of his hand; but he did according to his will, and became great. And as I was considering, behold, an he goat came from the west on the face of the whole earth, and touched not the ground: and the goat [had] a notable horn between his eyes. And he came to the ram that had [two] horns, which I had seen standing before the river, and ran unto him in the fury of his power. And I saw him come close unto the ram, and he was moved with choler against him, and smote the ram, and brake his two horns: and there was no power in the ram to stand before him, but he cast him down to the ground, and stamped upon him: and there was none that could deliver the ram out of his hand. Therefore the he goat waxed very great: and when he was strong, the great horn was broken; and for it came up four notable ones toward the four winds of heaven" (Daniel 8:2-8).

As for highlights in the vision, we have two different beasts, representing kingdoms once again. One is a ram that extended the territory beyond the original area, which can only match the representative activity of the bear from Daniel 7. So it is the Medes and Persian kingdom. It is the he goat that we are more interested in though. Please note that it is so swift that it does not touch the ground, just as described by a double set of wings on the leopard as well as it being a fast animal. On top of that, the he goat had one single horn that breaks followed by four horns in its place matching the four heads of the leopard.

But now for the answer to the question, who is this kingdom? For confirmation of the first animal symbol, the Bible says, "The ram which thou sawest having [two] horns [are] the kings of Media and Persia" (Daniel 8:20). And now the second animal, the Bible says, "And the rough goat [is] the king of Grecia: and the great horn that [is] between his eyes [is] the first king. Now that being broken, whereas four stood up for it, four kingdoms shall stand up out of the nation, but not in his power" (Daniel 8:21-22). So the answer is Greece.

Greece was definitely one of the fastest kingdoms to be set up. At the head of the kingdom was King Alexander, who, by the age of 30 conquered everything he knew to conquer, gave into the desires of the belly through alcohol, ending up drinking himself to death. Leaving no will or testament, no mention to succession, the four top generals split the kingdom into four sections. Cassander took the west, Lysimachus took the north, Ptolemy took the south, and Seleucus took the east. This gave way of course to what is well known in history as the Ptolemaic wars. Even today ancient Greece is known more for the art or appearance of the kingdom as opposed to other things, fulfilling the prophetic description. But God is not done. There is still another beast that arises, but at this point in our time line, we have moved from 331 B.C. to 168 B.C.

The fourth beast is described in Daniel 7:7 as, "After this I saw in the night visions, and behold a fourth beast, dreadful and terrible, and strong exceedingly; and it had great iron teeth: it devoured and brake in pieces, and stamped the residue with the feet of it: and it [was] diverse from all the beasts that [were] before it; and it had ten horns." Not by coincidence, iron is involved in Daniel 2:33 as well. "His legs of iron, his feet part of iron and part of clay." Further description is "And the fourth kingdom shall be strong as iron: forasmuch as iron breaketh in pieces and subdueth all [things]: and as iron that breaketh all these, shall it break in pieces and bruise. And whereas thou sawest the feet and toes, part of potters' clay, and part of iron, the kingdom shall be divided; but there shall be in it of the strength of the iron, forasmuch as thou sawest the iron mixed with miry clay" (Daniel 2:40-41).

So this world empire would be known for the use of iron. Now when we think of iron, people think of current nations and immediately think Russia, but that is not what the Bible states. Now Daniel did not tell King Nebuchadnezzar who the fourth kingdom was, nor does Daniel live through it. On top of that, we do not even have a vision. So Daniel is not going to be our resource in this matter. All we can go on is the fact that this kingdom arises around 168 B.C. From that, we could check the history books, encyclopedias, and other resources and I am sure they could reveal this fearful kingdom to us. We know it is fearful because not only are they noted for their use of iron, they are also noted for just moving in and destroying things. So there you go! Can we find in the Bible a reference to a fearful kingdom bent on destroying?

It seems that in the time of Jesus, He was performing miracles, speaking contrary to the church leaders of His day, and just considered a troublemaker. Please take note of the reaction from those church leaders. "But some of them went their ways to the Pharisees, and told them what things Jesus had done. Then gathered the chief priests and the Pharisees a council, and said, What do we? for this man doeth many miracles. If we let him thus alone, all [men] will believe on him: and the Romans shall come and take away both our place and nation" (John 11:46-48). The answer is, it is the Roman Empire who indeed began reigning from 168 B.C. up through 476 A.D. And now we have reached our date that we were looking for, but before we mention anything about the Antichrist, we still have the ten horns or ten toes to deal with.

As a side note, if you consider yourself a Christian and wonder if this information is in agreement with what you have been taught, the answer is yes. Just about all Christians believe in exactly what was stated, however, especially with the Antichrist, there are some variant teachings that place all of these kingdoms more on just rulers, even of the same kingdom, and everything is in B.C. times having no application in Jesus' day, let alone, our day. That of course does not make sense one bit because Daniel told King Nebuchadnezzar that the statue represents "what should come to pass hereafter: and he that revealeth secrets maketh known to thee what shall come to pass" (Daniel 2:29). "The great God hath made known to the king what shall come to pass hereafter: and the dream [is] certain, and the interpretation thereof sure" (Daniel 2:45). And the last event being "in the days of these kings shall the God of heaven set up a kingdom, which shall never be destroyed: and the kingdom shall not be left to other people, [but] it shall break in pieces and consume all these kingdoms, and it shall stand for ever" (Daniel 2:44). So from the time of Babylon, through the Medes and Persians, through Greece, through Rome, and through the ten toes or horns, all the way until the second coming, God just revealed all the major players in world history without skipping any time frame. So the notion that everything was taken care of in B.C. time is only a distraction from the true fact as expressed.

So now, let us look at the ten horns and the ten toes where Daniel 7:7 says that in regards to the fourth beast, "it had ten horns." Looking at the statue of Daniel 2, the Bible says, "And whereas thou sawest the feet and toes, part of potters' clay, and part of iron, the kingdom shall be divided; but there shall be in it of the strength of the iron, forasmuch as thou sawest the iron mixed with miry clay. And [as] the toes of the feet [were] part of iron, and part of clay, [so] the kingdom shall be partly strong, and partly broken" (Daniel 2:41-42).

Now this is where we are going to differ from the modern version, unbiblical take on all of this. Since hardly anyone is fooled into thinking that all of these events happened only in B.C. times, the lies of Antichrist then throw the rest of the events into the future, which disembodies the timeline. In other words, the ten toes and the ten horns are lifted out of 476 A.D., thrown into some ambiguous future, and the item at stake, doctrines, is changed into a physical military warfare. And on top of that, the focus of attack is lifted of what Christ established, the Christian Church, and put on an object that God no longer embraces as a special people, the Jews.

As we are about to state, these ten horns and ten toes begin in 476 A.D. and continue forward. So, now as an objective reader you may be asking, "who is right?" By us stating, "We're right" would be meaningless, although we are. So let us examine the evidence.

First, since Daniel says that God revealed what would come to pass from the time of Babylon until the second coming, does it make sense to pause the timeline and then pick up some time after the year 2,000? We say no. A timeline is a timeline. There was no indication of a breakage. In fact, the identification of Babylon being immediately replaced by the Medes and Persians, which was immediately replaced by Greece, which was immediately replaced by Rome, only indicates that the next phase of the ten horns and toes would immediately follow.

Second, even the wording of the appearance of the ten toes and horns leads one to conclude that it immediately follows. This is found in the fact that the head was connected to the breast and arms of silver, connected to the belly and thighs of brass, connected to the legs of iron, which the ten toes are connected to. Likewise, the fourth beast has ten horns is what is stated, meaning, somehow it is connected to the original fourth beast. Just as the leopard had four heads in which the single king of Alexander the Great left the kingdom divide into four and yet were part of Greece, likewise, Rome would divide into ten parts. Daniel 2 even says, "The kingdom shall be divided" (Daniel 2:41). A kingdom cannot divide if it were not originally one. And the only kingdom to divide would be the one prior to the divisions.

So, the one Kingdom of Rome, we are proposing, would divide into ten parts. The interesting thing about our presentation being different from the popularly accepted theory is that we are the ones with the strong Bible evidence while they have nothing, but why is it that we need to prove ourselves or justify ourselves to explain that everyone's head is attached to their bodies, attached to their thighs, attached to their legs, attached to their feet and toes showing logical progression without a break. No one's toes are disconnected. Further, God did not tell Daniel to tell King Nebuchadnezzar that God would show the king everything to transpire from his kingdom to the second coming with an exception of an unknown period of time lasting over 1,500 years (476 A.D. to present). Daniel said that it would be from this moment in time, Babylon, until the end when Jesus sets up His kingdom. No exceptions! No blank periods! No vagueness! So if you happen to be part of the group that believes in a future joint effort with ten kingdoms, we invite you to undo that thinking right now because as we shall show later in this chapter, that theory was actually born out of the Antichrist to distract away from the finger pointing.

Yes, we believe in the verse that says, "The ten horns which thou sawest are ten kings, which have received no kingdom as yet; but receive power as kings one hour with the beast" (Revelation 17:12). In fact, that is our study because the next verse says, "These have one mind, and shall give their power and strength unto the beast" (Revelation 17:13), and that is not a good thing. But what is happening here is that we read it today as if those kingdoms do not exist yet but when they do, they exist with the Antichrist beast for a prophetic hour in some type of union, hence all the hype among Christians when the European Union was formed in 1993. Christians were counting the number of countries that were joining and predicting that when it reaches ten, then they would unite with the yet to be revealed Antichrist and we shall have World War III. Today, we are up to twenty-eight member nations, well past the ten mark. Shortly after eleven, twelve, and thirteen nations joined, among those that still believed this union would usher in the Antichrist, they started reporting that at some point certain countries will back out and eventually be left with but ten. And it would be those ten that we need to keep an eye. Since then, such a message has been squashed and they are looking for another symbol of ten countries to make another false prediction, but it all centers around some type of union, even though that also contradicts the Bible.

Here is what the Bible says about the ten toes, "And whereas thou sawest iron mixed with miry clay, they shall mingle themselves with the seed of men: but they shall not cleave one to another, even as iron is not mixed with clay" (Daniel 2:43). So even with the attempt of intermarrying that went on leading up to World War I, the ten would not be able to be united. They shall NOT cleave one to another. There will never be a union formed. What they will do is each agree to think alike with the Antichrist but that does not make a union. If I were to ask ten people for permission and each of them were indifferent to my request, but they all gave me permission does the fact that they all thought alike in granting me permission cause a union? Of course not.

So, to properly understand Revelation 17:12, which again says, "The ten horns which thou sawest are ten kings, which have received no kingdom as yet; but receive power as kings one hour with the beast", one must take into consideration that from the writer's perspective in the first century, 476 A.D. had not happened yet. Therefore, while living under the Roman Empire, John sees in the near future that they will exist, like in 476 A.D., and at some point later, they will work with the Antichrist for a prophetic hour that we will study out later.

By now, and you can check your history books, Rome did not fall to another empire. Instead a bunch of Germanic tribes broke apart the weakened empire, and when the dust settled, ten nations existed. Now since then, three of those nations no longer exist, and there is a prophecy that we shall investigate in this chapter explaining that, but for now, here are the ten nations that followed Rome, which by the way points out that only God could have known such detail. Let us face the fact that if a human was trying to make predictions, it would seem that a fifth single empire would be the logical choice. On top of that, to hit the number ten precisely is a pretty good long shot for such human efforts, in other words, it was not human devising, it was God.

1. The Alamani, which are today's Germans.
2. The Burgundians are today's Swiss.
3. The Franks are today's French.
4. Lombards are today's Italians.
5. Saxons or Anglo Saxons are the English.
6. Suevi are the Portuguese.
7. Visigoths are the Spanish.
8. Heruli no longer exist.
9. Vandals no longer exist.
10. Ostrogoths no longer exist.

Now although Daniel 7 is pretty much in line with Daniel 2, especially when both predict that God's kingdom is next, Daniel 7 offers a bit more information. Primarily the rise of the Antichrist. In Daniel 2:44-45, it is said, "And in the days of these kings shall the God of heaven set up a kingdom, which shall never be destroyed: and the kingdom shall not be left to other people, [but] it shall break in pieces and consume all these kingdoms, and it shall stand for ever. Forasmuch as thou sawest that the stone was cut out of the mountain without hands, and that it brake in pieces the iron, the brass, the clay, the silver, and the gold; the great God hath made known to the king what shall come to pass hereafter: and the dream [is] certain, and the interpretation thereof sure." To have these nations break in pieces means that there is no way this prophecy refers to all the B.C. time leaders and Jesus' spiritual kingdom that He established at His first coming as the application of the prophecy since there is a total consumption of the nations.

The parallel to Daniel 2:44-45 is in Daniel 7:13-14 that states, "I saw in the night visions, and, behold, [one] like the Son of man came with the clouds of heaven, and came to the Ancient of days, and they brought him near before him. And there was given him dominion, and glory, and a kingdom, that all people, nations, and languages, should serve him: his dominion [is] an everlasting dominion, which shall not pass away, and his kingdom [that] which shall not be destroyed."

So, what is the extra detail? "I considered the horns, and, behold, there came up among them another little horn, before whom there were three of the first horns plucked up by the roots: and, behold, in this horn [were] eyes like the eyes of man, and a mouth speaking great things" (Daniel 7:8). There is the rise of the Antichrist power. Now keep in mind, the Antichrist system started in Jude, John, and Paul's day. We already covered that, but what is going to yet happen is that we will eventually reach a time that it is officially recognized as having the final author- ity like Revelation 13 says it would have. "And the dragon gave him his power, and his seat, and great authority" (Revelation 13:2).

Therefore, the Antichrist power rises to power after 476 A.D. is our conclusion.

IDENTIFYING MARK #13: IS LOCATED IN EUROPE

Daniel 7:8 says, ""I considered the horns, and, behold, there came up among them another little horn."

Another way to say this using the previous point as explanation, "I considered Europe, and, behold, there came up among them another little country." So, to consider the ten horns or Europe is to focus one's eyes on a map of Europe and nowhere else. So that is the location of the Antichrist. Not the Middle East; not the United States; not even the United Nations.

IDENTIFYING MARK #14: IS A SMALL NATION

Daniel 7:8 says, ""I considered the horns, and, behold, there came up among them another little horn."

The word little in comparison to the other nations is a small country. Keep in mind Switzerland is already one of the other ten horns. So this nation is smaller than Switzerland!!!!

IDENTIFYING MARK #15: LOCATED ON SEVEN MOUNTAINS OR HILLS

Revelation 17:9 says, "The seven heads are seven mountains, on which the woman sitteth" and couple that with Revelation 13:1, which says, "And I stood upon the sand of the sea, and saw a beast rise up out of the sea, having seven heads and ten horns."

So the seven heads of the beast represents seven mountains. That means if you want to know who or what is the Antichrist right now by name, look at a map of Europe and look for where the seven mountains are.

IDENTIFYING MARK #16: NOT JUST A POLITICAL KINGDOM

Daniel 7:24 says that the Antichrist, well, "he shall be diverse from the first", that is, different from the first ten.

So this nation is not an ordinary nation. It would be different. Although a country having a king and queen was typical in those days, not every nation was created the same. As we see even in the title, a simple political kingdom declaring blasphemies against God would not be as seriously taken as one who would work against Christ while appearing to be working for Christ. In other words, to be a different kingdom from all the other political kingdoms would involve some form of religion to be associated with it, and in a strong way.

Again, as long as we are looking for a kingdom that is not just political, and combining that with a previous point, that being a religious power, we have as an identifying mark a nation that is both political and religious.

IDENTIFYING MARK #17: APPEAR TO BE CHRISTIAN

2 Thessalonians 2:3 says, "Let no man deceive you by any means: for [that day shall not come], except there come a falling away first, and that man of sin be revealed, the son of perdition."

When Christians think of the Antichrist, they usually look outside of Christianity, mostly towards a Muslim nation, and pick a notorious character. Well, it is not by coincidence that the Bible describes the Antichrist as the son of perdition, which is only used twice in the entire Bible. The other time it is used is in John 17:12, which says, "While I was with them in the world, I kept them in thy name: those that thou gavest me I have kept, and none of them is lost, but the son of perdition; that the scripture might be fulfilled." This is in reference to Judas. He was a follower of Jesus, one of His disciples. In fact, one could say that Judas was a type of Antichrist, an example. So since Judas was pretending to be a follower while really being a betrayer (Matthew 26:25), traitor (Luke 6:16), and was a thief (John 12:6), likewise, the Antichrist will operate inside Christianity by betraying Christ through undermining activities in the doctrines (2 John 1:9), by being a traitor working for Satan (Revelation 13:2), and being a thief stealing souls (Revelation 13:3).

So do not be fooled into thinking the Antichrist means Antichristian. Antichrist simply means to work against Christ, but that can be done while being wearing the name Christian.

IDENTIFYING MARK #18: REMOVES THREE OF THE ORIGINAL TEN KINGDOMS

Daniel 7:8 says, "I considered the horns, and, behold, there came up among them another little horn, before whom there were three of the first horns plucked up by the roots." And Daniel 7:20 says, "And of the ten horns that [were] in his head, and [of] the other which came up, and before whom three fell."

So this explains why the Heruli, Vandals, and the Ostrogoths no longer exist. As the Antichrist power was coming to full strength and in exercise of its "great authority" (Revelation 13:2), three of the kingdoms must first fall. The understanding of "before" could imply at the hand of the Antichrist or simply stating that before the Antichrist has the recognized authority, they must fall, but they can fall at the hands of others.

IDENTIFYING MARK #19: APPEARS POMPOUS

Daniel 7:20 says, "Whose look [was] more stout than his fellows."

In looking up the word "stout", the Bible says in another situation, "I will punish the fruit of the stout heart of the king of Assyria, and the glory of his high looks." Ignore that the topic is the king of Assyria, but focus on the use of the word "stout". In this context, it means to have "high looks", like one sticking their nose in the air thinking they are better than everyone else. Also, in Malachi 3:13-15, it gives another explanation by saying, "Your words have been stout against me, saith the LORD. Yet ye say, What have we spoken [so much] against thee? Ye have said, It [is] vain to serve God: and what profit [is it] that we have kept his ordinance, and that we have walked mournfully before the LORD of hosts? And now we call the proud happy; yea, they that work wickedness are set up; yea, [they that] tempt God are even delivered." So in this context, the word "stout" also means being proud. So the Antichrist will appear to be better than others and have that acceptably recognized characteristic because we remind everyone again, "All the world wondered after the beast" (Revelation 13:3).

It is no different than a celebrity bragging how great they are and a whole bunch of people agreeing being their followers. Never mind the sin of pride; people like that person and that is it. So the Antichrist will get away with making bragging claims therefore to go along with the crowd and speak favorably of the Antichrist, even if not wholly convinced with all of the Antichrist's actions, is to align oneself with the Antichrist.

IDENTIFYING MARK #20: WOULD TAKE ON GOD'S TITLES

Revelation 13:6 opens up with, "And he opened his mouth in blasphemy against God, to blaspheme his name." Now couple that with 2 Thessalonians 2:4, which says, "Who opposeth and exalteth himself above all that is called God, or that is worshipped; so that he as God sitteth in the temple of God, shewing himself that he is God. "

Now how many people are going to be fooled into thinking that when a kingdom or representative of that nation goes around saying, "I'm God" are going to be fooled? Well, even if a large quantity of people are fooled, even more will be deceived when taking on other titles reserved for God. In fact, the Spirit of Antichrist is quite prevalent among many denominations. For instance, "holy and reverend [is] his name" (Psalms 111:9), referring to God. Therefore, to be claiming to be recognized as Reverend, they are blaspheming God. They are showing themselves to be God. Therefore, to continue to acknowledge such people as "reverend" or as "holy" in the context of authority is to be also having the Spirit of Antichrist.

Jesus also provided a list of titles that were not to be applied to humans in a spiritual manner. "But be not ye called Rabbi: for one is your Master, [even] Christ; and all ye are brethren. And call no [man] your father upon the earth: for one is your Father, which is in heaven. Neither be ye called masters: for one is your Master, [even] Christ" (Matthew 23:8-10). Now just as the Bible also makes references to relatives of father, grandfather, great-grandfather, etc., all as the term "father", so we may call our male parent father without going against Christ, but Antichrist would use such titles for themselves in a spiritually authoritative position. That is when it is wrong.

IDENTIFYING MARK #21: SPEAKS BLASPHEMOUSLY

Revelation 13:5-6 says, "And there was given unto him a mouth speaking great things and blasphemies; and power was given unto him to continue forty [and] two months. And he opened his mouth in blasphemy against God, to blaspheme his name, and his tabernacle, and them that dwell in heaven." Daniel uses a different wording to mean blasphemy. Daniel 7:8 says, "I considered the horns, and, behold, there came up among them another little horn, before whom there were three of the first horns plucked up by the roots: and, behold, in this horn [were] eyes like the eyes of man, and a mouth speaking great things." Daniel 7:20 says, "And of the ten horns that [were] in his head, and [of] the other which came up, and before whom three fell; even [of] that horn that had eyes, and a mouth that spake very great things, whose look [was] more stout than his fellows." Daniel 7:25 says, "And he shall speak [great] words against the most High, and shall wear out the saints of the most High, and think to change times and laws: and they shall be given into his hand until a time and times and the dividing of time."

So the Antichrist would speak in such a manner that is blasphemous towards God, and in a moment, we will see two specific ways, but the concerning thing here is not that the Antichrist does this; it is the fact that "all the world" (Revelation 13:3) does not care, does not see the seriousness, and just consider the whole matter trivial. So all those that continue to promote the speeches of the Antichrist without flinching is serving the Antichrist.

IDENTIFYING MARK #22: CLAIMS TO BE GOD

2 Thessalonians 2:4 says, "Shewing himself that he is God." On top of that Daniel 8:11 says, "Yea, he magnified [himself] even to the prince of the host."

To be magnified of himself is to escalate that pompous description to the highest level. Not only will the Antichrist think to be better than everyone else but will also make themselves into being God on earth.

Even one of the two Bible definitions of blasphemy states that this would be so. Jesus was accused of blasphemy. The reason is that the Pharisees applied a particular definition of blaspheme to Jesus, though incorrectly applied as "Jesus is the Son of God" (1 John 5:5). John 10:32-33 says, "Jesus answered them, Many good works have I shewed you from my Father; for which of those works do ye stone me? The Jews answered him, saying, For a good work we stone thee not; but for blasphemy; and because that thou, being a man, makest thyself God."

So one definition of blasphemy is when one makes themselves God, as in replacement thereof. But also mentioned before, not everyone shall be fooled by that, so titles that belong to God will be used by the Antichrist to try and fool more people. However, that is not the point. The point is that we should be able to uncover evidence that would be in Antichrist's possession where the Antichrist actually claims to be God.

IDENTIFYING MARK #23: CLAIMS TO BE ABLE TO FORGIVE SINS

A second definition of blasphemy is found in Mark 2:7, "Why doth this [man] thus speak blasphemies? who can forgive sins but God only?"

Now Jesus was able to do that being the Son of God, but the Antichrist claiming to have that ability is blasphemy. So to seek forgiveness for a personal sin from another human being is actually contributing to the blasphemy in action. Now do "Confess [your] faults one to another, and pray one for another" (James 5:16), but only those faults or sins that involve that person. Private sins are to be kept private, in fact, "if thy brother shall trespass against thee, go and tell him his fault between thee and him alone: if he shall hear thee, thou hast gained thy brother" (Matthew 18:15). Even public sins that only involve certain witnesses and those involved should be the only ones that confession should be made to, otherwise, towards Jesus, "If we confess our sins, he is faithful and just to forgive us [our] sins, and to cleanse us from all unrighteousness" (1 John 1:9), and no one else needs to be involved.

IDENTIFYING MARK #24: SHALL REIGN A PROPHETIC 1,260 DAYS, 3½ YEARS, OR 42 MONTHS

Revelation 13:5 says, "Power was given unto him to continue forty [and] two months." Daniel 7:25 says, "They shall be given into his hand until a time and times and the dividing of time."

It is all the same amount of time, where 42 months times 30 days in a month is 1,260 days. Likewise, 3 years of 360 days is 1,080 days plus a ½ year of 180 days is 1,260 days.

Now, in Daniel, the phrase used is "a time", meaning a year, "times", meaning more than a year being plural but since there is no specific number attached, two is used, and then dividing of a single time is to cut a year in half being a total of three and a half years. The Bible even does this math for us. During the power of the Antichrist, when it is at the height of exercising such unmatched authority, a symbolic woman seeks protection during that time. Notice two different verses covering the same time. One will use Daniel's phrase, and the other will use our calculation with definitions. Revelation 12:14 says, "And to the woman were given two wings of a great eagle, that she might fly into the wilderness, into her place, where she is nourished for a time, and times, and half a time, from the face of the serpent." Revelation 12:6 says, "And the woman fled into the wilderness, where she hath a place prepared of God, that they should feed her there a thousand two hundred [and] threescore days." So biblically, a time, times, and a half or dividing of a time is equivalent to the twelve hundred and sixty years.

Now, unfortunately many Christians are looking to the future for some magical 3½ year literal reign of the Antichrist, however, that's part of the popular false theory that we believe we have already well discredited, so this future reign should also be held in suspect, especially when God has a principle that needs to be applied. It is called the "day for a year" principle.

This principle is found in two places in the Bible. Numbers 14:34 says, "After the number of the days in which ye searched the land, [even] forty days, each day for a year, shall ye bear your iniquities, [even] forty years, and ye shall know my breach of promise." Ezekiel 4:6 says, "And when thou hast accomplished them, lie again on thy right side, and thou shalt bear the iniquity of the house of Judah forty days: I have appointed thee each day for a year." Ignoring the specific circumstances involved in both verses, the point presented is that God has an "each day for a year" principle.

Now how do we apply the principle? Evidently when Jesus said, "Destroy this temple, and in three days I will raise it up" (John 2:19), referring to the fact that He was going to be tortured and crucified, He did not mean that three years later He would be raised up. He meant three literal days.

So when it comes to Bible prophecy, which is mostly contained in Daniel and Revelation but not restricted to only those books, when we encounter time as mentioned among the symbolism, then there is a probability of applying the day for a year principle. But the question comes in as to knowing when to apply it and when not to apply it. Most Christians read the seventy weeks time prophecy as four hundred and ninety years instead of days, which is correctly applied, but then they turn around and say that the time among similar symbolism is to be literal.

Looking at Daniel 9:24, it says, "Seventy weeks are determined upon thy people and upon thy holy city, to finish the transgression, and to make an end of sins, and to make reconciliation for iniquity, and to bring in everlasting righteousness, and to seal up the vision and prophecy, and to anoint the most Holy." To anoint the Most Holy is to anoint Jesus. In other words, it is a time prophecy predicting when Jesus would show up the first time. If taken literally as seventy weeks, from the time of Daniel, we would end up in four hundred something B.C. Surely Jesus did not arrive then, but if we apply the principle of each day for a year, we arrive from Daniel's time to exactly the year Jesus was baptized or anointed in 27 A.D. So, Jesus confirms that such a principle is to be applied. However, most of these same people then look at the above time provided of twelve hundred and sixty days as literal days. In other words, there is an inconsistent application all to suit the Antichrist.

If the period of ruling is in years and not in literal days and the Antichrist is spreading the story that it is in the future when the time of rule has already arrived, the Antichrist gets to rule unnoticed.

Therefore, we will consistently apply the day for a year principle, otherwise, only the elite would know when and when not to apply it. And since the Bible states that "God is not [the author] of confusion" (1 Corinthians 14:33), we think we are better off understanding it this way. So that means that the Antichrist is going to have a twelve hundred and sixty year reign. That also means there must be a definite event that begins and ends the period for us to be able to tell if it happened or not. Our understanding also fits along the lines of being told that the Antichrist is not future but started in the days of the apostles and comes to full power at some point after 476 A.D., when it rises in Europe.

IDENTIFYING MARK #25: RECEIVES A DEADLY WOUND

Revelation 13:3 says, "And I saw one of his heads as it were wounded to death."

So the Antichrist will die, and we are going to table any further discussion on this point until we cover the next identifying mark of the Antichrist.

IDENTIFYING MARK #26: THE DEADLY WOUND IS HEALED

Revelation 13:3 says, "And his deadly wound was healed."

So the Antichrist comes back to life.

Now, as the story goes with the futuristic theory, after the literal 3½ years of the Antichrist ruling, the Antichrist dies, however, he, being a person, comes back to life. Now that just does not sit well even with me, a believer in miracles. We know science and the Bible do not always agree, but this is just ridiculous. How many people do you know that have been absolutely dead and come back to life to resume their life as normal? Not too many. There's Jesus Christ, as atheists would say, "Supposedly", while it is an accepted belief among true Christians. In addition, there are all the people that Jesus affected, like Lazarus, which shows what dead means; the body begins to decay. Now that is dead. There are times that a prophet was used to call upon God to restore the person's life, like in the case of Elisha (2 Kings 8:1) and even Peter (Acts 9:40). Now people who are quick to speak about all of those near death experiences, well, they do not count because they were near death and not dead. Even the stories of people being pronounced dead do not count because even though humans declare the person to be dead, they may not really have been dead. Basically, when the Bible says that the Antichrist receives a deadly wound, the Antichrist is dead. Period. No mistakes. It is God's perspective and not the human perspective that matters. God declares a time when the Antichrist is dead, but God also says that the Antichrist comes back to life as well, and we are saying that this further discredits the futurists theory of a single person being the Antichrist.

So, if we say, "Oh, there must be a mistake in the future regarding the Antichrist. He just will appear dead", then we are contradicting the Bible. However, if one takes the perspective of really, truly staying with the Bible realizing that beasts represents kingdoms or nations and not a person, one can see how a country can die and be reborn without the need of a miracle or to defy science. Look at Israel as an example. In 70 A.D., it ceased to be a country, but it came back to life in 1948 when it was recognized again as a nation. Israel is not the only nation to die and come back to life; evidently at the end of the twelve hundred and sixty year reign, the Antichrist nation dies.

Again, throwing away futurism of Antichrist and choosing to follow only Bible consistency method of understanding, it has all the pieces fitting together, without jumping through hoops, defying science, and twisting the meaning of things. Those that have come up with such a theory for the future are also going against the Bible principle, "Knowing this first, that no prophecy of the scripture is of any private interpretation" (2 Peter 1:20). That means, we ought not have to run to these teachers and ask, "I see time is used in Daniel, is this when the day for a year principle is applied?" Instead, we say apply it always in symbolic prophecy. We do not have to run to these teachers to help work out inconsistencies, like, "How can someone who is not Jesus Christ come back to life without the power of God? And if God gives the Antichrist that life back, couldn't we claim God is out of His mind?" God would be out of His mind to resurrect from the dead such a dreaded being as the Antichrist, if it were a person. Again, Satan cannot provide life or he would claim to be able to offer eternal life to all of his followers. He cannot, therefore he cannot bring from the dead the real person that died. Oh, Satan and the devils can appear as them, called personating, which is different from impersonating. The Bible says, "Satan himself is transformed into an angel of light" (2 Corinthians 11:14), so if he can do that, he certainly can appear as a dead human come back to life. They can actually appear to be that person. These futurist teachers have a private interpretation that they become the source of knowledge and not the Bible.

Credibility to the Bible is only established in letting the Bible explain everything for us. We are looking for the Antichrist kingdom that is going to cease for a period of time and come back to life. That is a very simple way to understand it and well supported by the Bible.

IDENTIFYING MARK #27: WILL SURVIVE UNTIL THE SECOND COMING

Daniel 7:21-22 says, "I beheld, and the same horn made war with the saints, and prevailed against them; Until the Ancient of days came, and judgment was given to the saints of the most High; and the time came that the saints possessed the kingdom." Also, 2 Thessalonians 2:8-9 says, "And then shall that Wicked be revealed, whom the Lord shall consume with the spirit of his mouth, and shall destroy with the brightness of his coming: [Even him], whose coming is after the working of Satan with all power and signs and lying wonders."

So after the Antichrist's wound is healed, it will survive until the second coming when it will be destroyed finally, which fits in with other descriptions about kingdoms at the second coming. Daniel 2:44 describes the future of all other kingdoms outside of Jesus' Kingdom, "And in the days of these kings shall the God of heaven set up a kingdom, which shall never be destroyed: and the kingdom shall not be left to other people, [but] it shall break in pieces and consume all these kingdoms, and it shall stand for ever." Daniel 7:26 says, "But the judgment shall sit, and they shall take away his dominion, to consume and to destroy [it] unto the end."

Now do not fall back away from associating the Antichrist with a nation because you see the word "his" in Daniel 7:26, referring to a person. Antichrist cannot be just a person as many of the identifying marks refer to inanimate objects. Remember also, there is an authoritative figure at the head of this nation described as "eyes like the eyes of man" (Daniel 7:8). Unlike all other kingdoms in the Bible that are simply referred to as beasts or horns even with crowns, this nation's representative is all about the furtherance of the nations dominance in the world in a specific area, that of leading people away from the "eyes of God" and onto the "eyes of man". Besides, all other nations have rulers that when they switch leadership, so does the agenda. For instance, no longer is France trying to make a united Europe or world because Napoleon is dead, and they have a different outlook. No longer is Germany attempting to take over the world since Hitler is dead and they also have a different outlook. Even in the United States and England, the same is true. Change out the president or minister and a new agenda is in place. In the United States, it is more of a party's agenda and the president is but a figurehead, but not so with the Antichrist.

In the succession of leaders, the "mouth speaking great things" pretty much continues the original agenda of being against Christ, hence the term Antichrist. And that is specifically in reworking of Christ's doctrines as we are about to see, leading people away from searching the God given scriptures into accepting the teachings of humans.

IDENTIFYING MARK #28: THINK TO CHANGE THE TEN COMMANDMENTS

Daniel 7:25 says, "And think to change times and laws."

To think one does something does not mean that it is actually done, therefore, God's laws still exists despite popular Christian belief. If the Antichrist is going to make an appearance towards changing God's laws, that means from God's perspective, the original laws are still in effect. If the Ten Commandments were done away with, then the description in this verse would read more like, "And would implement times and laws", but it does not say that. The description is to make one to "think" that they can "change" the existing laws but really do not have such authority.

This is why Revelation 13:2 says, "the dragon gave him his power, and his seat, and great authority." The dragon (Satan according to Revelation 12:9) thought to change or do away with the commandments when he rebelled in Heaven. That same satanic thinking and false power is past onto the Antichrist thinking they can do the same thing. But the only authority they have comes from all the minds that Satan has been successfully creating rebellion in. And each of us can test to see if we are prepared to give that authority to the Antichrist or Jesus Christ. Just check to see if you are happy in keeping all Ten Commandments without exception. If not, then Satan has been successful in making you a loyal subject of Antichrist, against Christ, rebellious.

Antichrist is not a new controlling power. It goes back to the original intent of Satan, which was to rebel against the commandments of God. Either we obey God's laws or listen to Satan. On this point, the Bible says, "Know ye not, that to whom ye yield yourselves servants to obey, his servants ye are to whom ye obey; whether of sin unto death, or of obedience unto righteousness?" (Romans 6:16) Sure, none of us have lived perfectly obedient lives using the Ten Commandments as the standard, but look at the expectations. "But God be thanked, that ye were the servants of sin, but ye have obeyed from the heart that form of doctrine which was delivered you" (Romans 6:17). The Bible acknowledges that, yes, we did live our lives breaking God's laws by living in sin, but we, by the grace of God that offers an erasure of the penalty associated with all of our sinning that we confessed and ask forgiveness for (1 John 1:9) as well as the power to live obediently (John 1:12, Jude 1:24) causes us now from the heart to live according to God's laws, His doctrines.

And did you catch that? Reading the verses together, the laws and doctrine go hand and hand. The instrument of the devil, called the Antichrist, is to get people to break God's laws, hence why the activity of appearing to change the laws as well as implement different doctrines is so prevalent. If people obey the changed version of God's laws, then Satan has that soul!

So that is one of the doctrinal changes where the Ten Commandments will appear to be altered by the Antichrist, but as usual, Satan has both sides covered. There is the "Spirit of Antichrist" (1 John 4:3) that also works against the doctrines. So when Jesus said, "If ye love me, keep my commandments" (John 14:15) being a direct quote out of the Ten Commandments (Exodus 20:6), and when Jesus said, "Thou shalt love the Lord thy God with all thy heart, and with all thy soul, and with all thy mind. This is the first and great commandment. And the second [is] like unto it, Thou shalt love thy neighbour as thyself" (Matthew 22:37-39), which looks like the replacement of the Ten Commandments with but two and followed up quickly to say that it is a summary of them by stating, "On these two commandments hang all the law and the prophets" (Matthew 22:40), the Spirit of Antichrist would not just provide a different set of alterations, but would actually do away with them.

Speaking of doctrinal teachings and the alteration of the Ten Commandments, the Bible describes the Antichrist in this manner: "She made all nations drink of the wine of the wrath of her fornication" (Revelation 14:8), "the inhabitants of the earth have been made drunk with the wine of her fornication" (Revelation 17:2), and "all nations have drunk of the wine of the wrath of her fornication" (Revelation 18:3). What is that wine? The Bible says, "[It is] not for kings, O Lemuel, [it is] not for kings to drink wine; nor for princes strong drink: Lest they drink, and forget the law, and pervert the judgment of any of the afflicted" (Proverbs 31:4-5). Alcoholic wine and strong drink help people forget the law, also known as the Ten Commandments. So the Antichrist church system would have teachings or doctrines that alter and even do away with God's Ten Commandments. And altering them is sufficient in the devil's mind because "whosoever shall keep the whole law, and yet offend in one [point], he is guilty of all" (James 2:10).

Ask an average Christian if the Ten Commandments are required for salvation sake and the answer will probably be, "No." Other answers could be more intensely expressed by saying, "Absolutely not! That would be working one's way to Heaven!"; "Oh no way. Jesus nailed them to the cross when He died!"; "Of course not. We're under grace!"

In reality, God says, "Blessed [are] they that do his commandments, that they may have right to the tree of life, and may enter in through the gates into the city" (Revelation 22:14). "By this we know that we love the children of God, when we love God, and keep his commandments. And hereby we do know that we know him, if we keep his commandments. He that saith, I know him, and keepeth not his commandments, is a liar, and the truth is not in him" (1 John 2:2-4). "Here is the patience of the saints: here [are] they that keep the commandments of God, and the faith of Jesus" (Revelation 14:12). "If ye keep my commandments, ye shall abide in my love; even as I have kept my Father's commandments, and abide in his love" (John 15:10). "If thou wilt enter into life, keep the commandments" (Matthew 19:17). And that is but a small sampling of the many places where the Ten Commandments are still identified as being required, not to earn Heaven but to live as citizens now of Heaven being ambassadors today.

Therefore, to live by an altered set of commandments or to do away with the commandments is to be on the wrong side of Christ. They would be part of Antichrist despite how much the Christian says that they have a relationship with Jesus. The lack of keeping the Ten Commandments could be one of the reasons why Jesus describes a whole bunch of disappointed Christians in this way when the second coming occurs: "Many will say to me in that day, Lord, Lord, have we not prophesied in thy name? and in thy name have cast out devils? and in thy name done many wonderful works? And then will I profess unto them, I never knew you: depart from me, ye that work iniquity" (Matthew 7:22). You know they are Christian because of all the things done in Christ's name, yet they shall be cast away into hell. Why? Because of working or doing iniquity, which is another name for sin (Revelation 18:5). The Bible definition for sin is, "Whosoever committeth sin transgresseth also the law: for sin is the transgression of the law" (1 John 3:4).

So, only complete obedience to the original Ten Commandments will provide a safeguard against the Antichrist and the Spirit of Antichrist.

IDENTIFYING MARK #29: ACCEPTS A DIFFERENT CYCLE OF TIME

Daniel 7:25 says, "And think to change times and laws." Now couple that with the fact that with Genesis 1:14, which says, "And God said, Let there be lights in the firmament of the heaven to divide the day from the night; and let them be for signs, and for seasons, and for days, and years."

Before we show the importance of these two verses, we must address people's attitudes towards God's Word, the Bible. People read the Bible and think that as long as the Bible does not say the words "must", "only", "have to", etc., that they are free to change God's intention. They treat God as a human being that though things are plainly stated, as humans, we think that the other person will be impressed with our input, and that is just not so. When looking at cars and one spouse says, "I really want it in red" only to turn around to buy a blue one instead, explaining, "I really thought you would rather save money than to special order it," well that might not go over very well. Claiming, "Well, you didn't really say that it was the only color you wanted", is not going to be an impressive excuse. But when it comes to God, not only do we not give back to God exactly what He expects, but it is called sin, disobedience, even rebellion.

This is why we have examples in the Bible, like King Saul who acted much like the average person acts today when it comes to God's intention. He was told, "Now go and smite Amalek, and utterly destroy all that they have, and spare them not" (1 Samuel 15:3). So in general, King Saul was to slaughter their enemies and not give into any "please let us go" cries or attempts to make peace or any such thing, however, nowhere did God explicitly state that every single person had to be slaughtered. So, "Saul and the people spared Agag, and the best of the sheep, and of the oxen, and of the fatlings, and the lambs, and all [that was] good, and would not utterly destroy them: but every thing [that was] vile and refuse, that they destroyed utterly" (1 Samuel 15:9). Now did King Saul do exactly as God said? Well, Saul thought so. "Yea, I have obeyed the voice of the LORD, and have gone the way which the LORD sent me, and have brought Agag the king of Amalek, and have utterly destroyed the Amalekites" (1 Samuel 15:20). But the prophet Samuel, speaking for God, said, "Because thou hast rejected the word of the LORD, he hath also rejected thee from [being] king" (1 Samuel 15:23).

So this shows that God does not have to explicitly detail and be careful with every word. God tries to treat us with a little intelligence in the area of obedience to Him. Despite what people think, God is not a dictator. So in the Bible, we will frequently see simple statements that people treat as not important or not a command, when in fact, it is a kind way of expressing His will without coming across dictatorially. What type of relationship would spouses have if they spoke always in a commanding way? "Get me a drink!" instead of saying, "Honey, could you get me something to drink please?" It would not be a very good relationship if every person's will was spoken as a demand. Just as a spouse wants to fulfill the wishes to whom they are married to, we should do the same thing. In fact, for those that pray the "Lord's prayer", right inside it are the words "Thy will be done" (Matthew 6:10). "So God, if it is your will that we track time according to the lights of the sky, so be it. Thy will be done!" That should be our attitude for everything we encounter in the Bible, "Thy will be done", and be looking for "Alright God, I will do your demand!"

Now when it comes to interacting with the world, using the world's time schedule is not what we are referring to as being disobedient upon. What is a disobedience is when we change God's schedule of events, but more on that later. And this understanding of using the non-God given time to interact with nonbelievers is permitted out of necessity to interact with them. Even looking at Jesus, He never tried to correct the matter. It was not even brought to anyone's attention, despite the world empire having created the cycle of time based upon paganism and enforcing it upon the nations under her jurisdiction. Jesus still, "as his custom was, he went into the synagogue on the sabbath day" (Luke 4:16). "The Master saith, My time is at hand; I will keep the passover at thy house with my disciples" (Matthew 26:18). He knew when the Sabbath was and when the feast days were.

So back on the verse in discussion, the Antichrist will be instrumental in changing from God's schedule of time to something different. Do recall though, according to Daniel 7:25, the Antichrist will "think to change times." That is plural. That means at least two of God's appointed times are going to be affected. One of them is to abandon for religious purposes, God's day of reckoning. Remember, in Genesis 1:14, we are to use the lights of the sky to track even the days. As God's will on that matter, the Bible says, "And the evening and the morning were the first day" (Genesis 1:5); "And the evening and the morning were the second day" (Genesis 1:8); "And the evening and the morning were the third day" (Genesis 1:13); "And the evening and the morning were the fourth day" (Genesis 1:19); "And the evening and the morning were the fifth day" (Genesis 1:23); "And the evening and the morning were the sixth day" (Genesis 1:31). Now all of these references are not in place just because that is how they kept time back then. No! It is a pattern being set for us to follow God's will of time reckoning. And as a Christian, "ye ought to walk and to please God" (1 Thessalonians 4:1).

Directly speaking and reminding everyone that the matter has nothing to do with interacting with people in keeping appointments, marking dates on a calendar, etc. This only applies to religious observances, but the Antichrist will instill religious reckoning, not based upon God's days of sunset to sunset but from the Roman pagan system of midnight to midnight. Instead of observing days one, two, three, four, five, preparation, and Sabbath, the Antichrist will use Sunday, Monday, Tuesday, Wednesday, Thursday, Friday, and Saturday instead.

And to reinforce the war between Jesus Christ and Antichrist, remember that it is said of Jesus, "All things were made by him; and without him was not any thing made that was made" (John 1:3). That includes the sunset to sunset schedule being made through Jesus, who saw (eyes of God) what was best for humans to live by being sunset to sunset while the Antichrist saw fit (eyes of a man) to use the midnight to midnight schedule instead.

IDENTIFYING MARK #30: CHANGE GOD'S WORSHIP TIME

Daniel 7:25 says, "And think to change times and laws." Couple that with Exodus 20:8-11, "Remember the sabbath day, to keep it holy. Six days shalt thou labour, and do all thy work: But the seventh day [is] the sabbath of the LORD thy God: [in it] thou shalt not do any work, thou, nor thy son, nor thy daughter, thy manservant, nor thy maidservant, nor thy cattle, nor thy stranger that [is] within thy gates: For [in] six days the LORD made heaven and earth, the sea, and all that in them [is], and rested the seventh day: wherefore the LORD blessed the sabbath day, and hallowed it."

As Daniel states, at least more than one "time" would be affected by the Antichrist. Search the scriptures and one does not find many reckonings of time. We already addressed one of God's times, which is the beginning and ending of a day. In fact, it is the whole calendar recognition. The names of the weekly cycle have been changed. The measurement of the yearly cycle along with the names of the months have also be altered. But do keep in mind, even Jesus did not speak up against the Roman institution of the new calendar system as long as people still kept the proper worship days according to God's cycle of time.

Now one could argue that the calendar acceptance would count as another alteration of time, except, that has no religious consequence. In fact, the yearly cycle today is based on what God said it should be: the lights of the heavens. It takes 365.25 days for earth to circle the sun. Sure, the 360 day cycle God mapped out for the Jews has been replaced, of which every so often a thirteenth month was added to compensate for being short by 5.25 days each year, but it is still was based upon the lights of the heavens. Sure, the 30 days per month in all months has been replaced and it used to be recognized as "new moon" celebrations, but again, that does not affect Christians today.

But how about the month change? Why does that not affect Christians? The Bible says, "Let no man therefore judge you in meat, or in drink, or in respect of an holyday, or of the new moon, or of the sabbath [days]: Which are a shadow of things to come; but the body [is] of Christ" (Colossians 2:16-17). What this is saying is that all the feast days and new moons pointed to Jesus, and when He showed up, there is no requirement to keep them anymore. Of course if you want to recognize those days, do not let anyone judge you differently.

So how do these things point to Jesus? Paul wrote, "Christ our passover is sacrificed for us" (1 Corinthians 5:7), which Passover was the first feast day. "Purge out therefore the old leaven, that ye may be a new lump, as ye are unleavened" (1 Corinthians 5:7), which the feast of unleavened bread was the second feast day. "Christ the firstfruits" (1 Corinthians 15:23), which First Fruits was the third feast day. "The day of Pentecost" (Acts 2:1), "they were all filled with the Holy Ghost, and began to speak with other tongues, as the Spirit gave them utterance" (Acts 2:4). Pentecost was the fourth feast day. "Let both grow together until the harvest" (Matthew 13:30) or second coming, which is the seventh feast day. The feast of trumpets (fifth feast) and atonement (sixth feast) are also representative of Christ as well, but that is beyond our study here. Do take note though, that the feast days had another name. They were called Sabbath days (Leviticus 23:24, 32, 39). Therefore, Colossians 2:16-17 does not do away with the Sabbath of the Ten Commandments; it refers to the Sabbaths of feast days. Which brings us to the only other time that God has specifically outlined that the Antichrist would change.

We are proposing that since God stated that at least two of His times would appear to be changed by the Antichrist, the Antichrist would be instrumental by the devil to change the weekly worship time called the Sabbath. According to the commandment, "the seventh day [is] the sabbath" (Exodus 20:10); not the first day. And besides, the Sabbath is at sunset, not at midnight. So the first day of the week God set up is not even equivalent to the day called Sunday. Not only has the Sabbath been changed from sunset Friday until sunset Saturday into another day, but it is also on a different cycle of time no longer being on a counting day. The supposed Christian Sabbath starts part way in on the first day of God's week at midnight and continues into the second day of the week until midnight, hours past God's cycle of sunsets. God's first day is sundown on Saturday, and God's second day is at sundown on Sunday.

For those that think the day was changed by Jesus or somewhere in the New Testament, just read Hebrews 4. It answers all the arguments.

- Does it still exist? "There remaineth therefore a rest to the people of God" (Hebrews 4:9).

- Was it changed to another day? "He limiteth a certain day" (Hebrews 4:7).

- Did Jesus change it? "For if Jesus had given them rest, then would he not afterward have spoken of another day" (Hebrews 4:8). In other words, Jesus never mentioned another day as the Sabbath day. In fact, no one ever got that impression from Jesus that He was trying to change the day. Even up to Jesus' death, "The women also, which came with him from Galilee, followed after, and beheld the sepulchre, and how his body was laid. And they returned, and prepared spices and ointments; and rested the sabbath day according to the commandment" (Luke 23:55-56).

- Is keeping the Sabbath an act against the gospel? "Unto us was the gospel preached" (Hebrews 4:2).

- Is salvation not just a matter of belief, therefore we do not need to keep the commandments, let alone, the Sabbath? "We which have believed do enter into rest" (Hebrews 4:3).

- Which day are we really supposed to keep? "For he spake in a certain place of the seventh [day] on this wise, And God did rest the seventh day from all his works" (Hebrews 4:4). In fact, "God blessed the seventh day, and sanctified it" (Genesis 2:3). Nowhere in the New Testament is a day explicitly blessed or sanctified nor is the blessing or sanctification removed from the seventh day.

- Does the Sabbath subject irk people and resist keeping it? "To day if ye will hear his voice, harden not your hearts" (Hebrews 4:7).

- What are we supposed to do or not do on the Sabbath? "For he that is entered into his rest, he also hath ceased from his own works, as God [did] from his" (Hebrews 4:10).

- Is the Sabbath easy at first to keep? "Let us labour therefore to enter into that rest, lest any man fall after the same example of unbelief" (Hebrews 4:11).

- Is it a salvation issue? "For the word of God [is] quick, and powerful, and sharper than any twoedged sword, piercing even to the dividing asunder of soul and spirit, and of the joints and marrow, and [is] a discerner of the thoughts and intents of the heart" (Hebrews 4:12).

And changing the day of worship is not out of Satan's realm of ideas, in fact, worship is His ultimate goal. "Again, the devil taketh him up into an exceeding high mountain, and sheweth him all the kingdoms of the world, and the glory of them; And saith unto him, All these things will I give thee, if thou wilt fall down and worship me. Then saith Jesus unto him, Get thee hence, Satan: for it is written, Thou shalt worship the Lord thy God, and him only shalt thou serve" (Matthew 4:8-10).

Besides, in keeping a day as commanded by a being recognizes them to be God, hence why it is said of the Antichrist, "Who opposeth and exalteth himself above all that is called God, or that is worshipped; so that he as God sitteth in the temple of God, shewing himself that he is God" (2 Thessalonians 2:4). The further description of the Antichrist is that "all that dwell upon the earth shall worship him" (Revelation 13:8). That does not mean everyone is going to be bowing on hands and knees, but they will accept Antichrist's new day of worship that they created instead of God. They may not keep it holy but ask an atheist which day the Christian Sabbath is and they will state it as fact that it is Sunday. It is still a form of homage not to correct the error even if one does not believe in the practice thereof.

Further, those Christians that keep the Sabbath are not doing it to be saved. They keep it to recognize who saved them. The Bible says, "Moreover also I gave them my sabbaths, to be a sign between me and them, that they might know that I [am] the LORD that sanctify them" (Ezekiel 20:12).

So one may claim to be a Christian and worship Jesus every Sunday, but in reality, by keeping Sunday as God's holy day is actually in veneration of the day the Antichrist acknowledged as the new Christian Sabbath even when they use the excuse, "Jesus rose from the tomb on that day." It is even a form of pagan or sun worship. To truly keep the first day of the week, one would have to begin at sundown on Saturday and not wait until midnight.

Again, since God says that the Antichrist will attempt to change God's times, which means more than one, and we find that there are only two commands of God that deal with time, and both have been affected by the Antichrist, it should bring to mind that the original command is still in effect. The seventh day Sabbath is still to be regarded.

But if you are like the average Christian or even atheist, you probably do not even keep the day holy. Treating it like a yard work day, a day of recreation, a day to go shopping or to the movies, etc. is not keeping it holy. Now, since the Bible says that when one keeps the Sabbath of the seventh day we acknowledge God as our Savior that means keeping Sunday acknowledges Antichrist to be our savior, and keeping no day means that we do not need a savior, which a common phrase comes to mind of, "Good luck with that!"

IDENTIFYING MARK #31: JESUS' SACRIFICE WOULD BE REPLACED

Daniel 8:11 says, "By him the daily [sacrifice] was taken away."

Now in the Bible system of sacrifices, each day there were sacrifices offered for the sins of the people known as "the daily burnt offering" (Numbers 29:6). Now keep in mind that the sins were not removed because of the animal sacrifices, "For [it is] not possible that the blood of bulls and of goats should take away sins" (Hebrews 10:4). In fact, "In burnt offerings and [sacrifices] for sin thou hast had no pleasure" (Hebrews 10:6). "Then said he, Lo, I come to do thy will, O God. He taketh away the first, that he may establish the second. By the which will we are sanctified through the offering of the body of Jesus Christ once [for all]" (Hebrews 10:9-10). So, Jesus replaced the symbolism of the Old Testament by the sacrifice of Himself. Daily then refers to the daily pleading of Jesus blood from the one sacrifice of Himself. It is that in which would be taken away by the Antichrist and in its place a new daily sacrifice instituted.

IDENTIFYING MARK #32: GOD'S SANCTUARY SERVICE WOULD BE REPLACED

In Daniel 8:11, we also read, "The place of his sanctuary was cast down." Couple that with the fact that God "hath looked down from the height of his sanctuary; from heaven did the LORD behold the earth" (Psalms 102:19).

Did you know that there is a real sanctuary in Heaven? "Christ being come an high priest of good things to come, by a greater and more perfect tabernacle, not made with hands, that is to say, not of this building" (Hebrews 9:11). In fact, what Moses and the Israelites built was not an original. But God told Moses to build it "According to all that I shew thee, [after] the pattern of the tabernacle, and the pattern of all the instruments thereof, even so shall ye make [it]" (Exodus 25:9). That means Heaven, the original, has a courtyard, a holy place, and a most holy place, where God dwells. Just as the high priest went into the most holy place to appear before God, so Jesus has done the same thing before the Father. In fact, Daniel reveals exactly this. "I saw in the night visions, and, behold, [one] like the Son of man came with the clouds of heaven, and came to the Ancient of days, and they brought him near before him" (Daniel 7:13).

On top of that, Jesus, upon his resurrection, entered into the holy place, not the most holy place though. John said, "I was in the Spirit on the Lord's day, and heard behind me a great voice, as of a trumpet, Saying, I am Alpha and Omega, the first and the last: and, What thou seest, write in a book, and send [it] unto the seven churches which are in Asia; unto Ephesus, and unto Smyrna, and unto Pergamos, and unto Thyatira, and unto Sardis, and unto Philadelphia, and unto Laodicea. And I turned to see the voice that spake with me. And being turned, I saw seven golden candlesticks; And in the midst of the seven candlesticks [one] like unto the Son of man" (Revelation 1:10-13). How we know this is just the holy place is because of the seven candlesticks, which are found in the first compartment known as the holy place (Hebrews 9:2).

So, the Antichrist would replace the heavenly sanctuary.

IDENTIFYING MARK #33: CAST DOWN THE TRUTH

Daniel 8:12 says, "It cast down the truth to the ground; and it practised, and prospered."

Now as usual, we are not going to be satisfied with the generic phrase and leave it at that. Let us dig deeper into what the Bible considers truth to be. First, "Jesus saith unto him, I am the way, the truth, and the life: no man cometh unto the Father, but by me" (John 14:6). Therefore, the Antichrist will, despite using the name of Jesus, will attack Jesus, as already referenced in previous points.

Second, God's "law [is] the truth" (Psalms 119:142), better known as the Ten Commandments. This goes along with a previous point in which the Antichrist would "think to change times and laws" (Daniel 7:25). Therefore, look for the Antichrist to change not one but at least two of God's commandments. The sad part is that the Antichrist is getting away with it since it continues to practice and prosper.

Third, God's "word is truth" (John 17:17), so the Antichrist will criticize the Bible, make non-authoritative, even to the point of trying to get rid of it. Again, even atheists are on board assisting with such through evolution, "science falsely so called" (1 Timothy 6:20), and human reasoning. We are to "Beware lest any man spoil you through philosophy and vain deceit, after the tradition of men, after the rudiments of the world, and not after Christ" (Colossians 2:8). And yet today, philosophy seems to rule. People trust to all forms of philosophy, even disguised as therapists and psychologists who do nothing more than experiment on society.

And that also makes sense from the identifying mark that says that the Antichrist would place tradition above the Word of God.

IDENTIFYING MARK #34: CAUSES CHRISTIANS TO FALL AWAY, ESPECIALLY FROM KEEPING THE COMMANDMENTS

2 Thessalonians 2:3 says, "Let no man deceive you by any means: for [that day shall not come], except there come a falling away first, and that man of sin be revealed, the son of perdition."

Keep in mind again that this is equivalent to the reference in Daniel, which says, "In this horn [were] eyes like the eyes of man, and a mouth speaking great things" (Daniel 7:8). We are not to equate 2 Thessalonians as a reference to a single human Antichrist, but that the leader that is replaced each time the previous one leaves office would continue to speak great things against the things Jesus Christ established. And to speak great things from a nation's perspective is to do so through legislation. In other words, when a country enacts laws, it speaks; the law is then announced by the leader of the country. These laws that God is bringing out here are not about the speed limits, curfews, currency, or any such things. Explicitly, they are laws that contradict God's laws.

Following the chain of identifying marks thus far, it should be making sense. Since the Antichrist shall think to change God's laws, since it is going to attack the truth of God's law, it only makes sense that it would enact laws and pronounce them to the world. As the world accepts them as law over God's Ten Commandments, this will cause people to fall away from God, even without them knowing it.

And we know that it is involving the Ten Commandments because of the title given to the Antichrist while it causes the falling away. The title is "man of sin". Sin, according to 1 John 3:4, is "the transgression of the law." So to be the man of sin is to be the man to cause the transgression of the law, the Ten Commandments.

Therefore, those that accept the Antichrist's new version of the Ten Commandments, including the one about the Sabbath, God considers those people as fallen away despite how great of a Christian they happen to be.

Now you may ask how we know the Christians and not the Jews are the focus. That is answered by reading the 2 Thessalonians reference in context. 2 Thessalonians 2:1-2 says, "Now we beseech you, brethren, by the coming of our Lord Jesus Christ, and [by] our gathering together unto him, That ye be not soon shaken in mind, or be troubled, neither by spirit, nor by word, nor by letter as from us, as that the day of Christ is at hand." Please note that Paul is addressing the brethren, as in, brothers and sisters in Christ or Christians. Further, only Christians look forward to the second coming of Christ. Jews definitely are not. Atheists do not believe it will ever happen. And the other religions do not support the theology regarding Christ coming again.

So, it is Christians, and seeing Paul states that the Antichrist causes people to fall away from the faith, that means the notion of "once saved, always saved", meaning one cannot lose salvation, is a lie.

IDENTIFYING MARK #35: RULES FROM WHAT IS CONSIDERED GOD'S TEMPLE

2 Thessalonians 2:4 says, "He as God sitteth in the temple of God" (2 Thessalonians 2:4).

Now physically, there is no temple that God has ordained to be built that exists today, or for that matter, will ever exist. God did ordain Moses and the Israelites to build such, when He said, "And let them make me a sanctuary; that I may dwell among them" (Exodus 25:8). He did commission Solomon to do so as well, when Solomon wrote in remembering the conversation between God and his father David, "And, behold, I purpose to build an house unto the name of the LORD my God, as the LORD spake unto David my father, saying, Thy son, whom I will set upon thy throne in thy room, he shall build an house unto my name" (1 Kings 5:5). And then there was the rebuilding of the temple along with Jerusalem because Babylon had destroyed all of it, "Know therefore and understand, [that] from the going forth of the commandment to restore and to build Jerusalem unto the Messiah the Prince [shall be] seven weeks, and threescore and two weeks: the street shall be built again, and the wall, even in troublous times" (Daniel 9:25).

Unfortunately, futurists throw this event into the future and state that the Antichrist will help rebuild the temple, removing the Dome of the Rock, and then rule from there. At the completion of such, Antichrist will break his agreement with the Jews, that will cause World War III, and the rest of the story. Interestingly, the futurists properly understand that the time prophecy in Daniel covering verses 24 through 26, which includes the questionable verse 25, was all done between 456 B.C. and 27 A.D. They agree that Jesus was the anointed one from verse 24 ("anoint the most Holy"); the command to rebuild Jerusalem and specifically the temple was given by King Artaxerxes (Ezra 7:12-19) and even financed the operation (Ezra 7:20); and Jesus was baptized on time. But the futurists take the last seven years in the prophecy, throws them into an ambiguous future where the Antichrist "plays nice" for three and a half years with the Jews, breaks the covenant, and tries to slaughter the Jews making Antichrist more anti-Jew than anti-Christ or anti-Christian. Futurists claim that when the temple was destroyed in 70 A.D., the foundation, such as known today by the name "Wailing Wall", was not completely destroyed. In reality, they ignore the fact that the purpose of the temple, of holding services, has not been able to be exercised in that manner since the destruction. In all essence, the temple has been destroyed. Besides, the rebuilding of the temple was only in regards to the start of the seventy weeks. There is absolutely no reference to any rebuilding of yet another temple just to mark the last seven years.

When Jesus said, "See ye not all these things? verily I say unto you, There shall not be left here one stone upon another, that shall not be thrown down" (Matthew 24:2), He was not referring to that which was under the earth, the foundation. It was quite common in those days to have armies destroy buildings, leaving the foundations, and build a new building from the left over foundation. The context of Jesus' statement also proves this to be so. "And Jesus went out, and departed from the temple: and his disciples came to [him] for to shew him the buildings of the temple" (Matthew 24:1). Another account says, "And as he went out of the temple, one of his disciples saith unto him, Master, see what manner of stones and what buildings [are here]!" (Mark 13:1) Again, it is said, "And as some spake of the temple, how it was adorned with goodly stones and gifts" (Luke 21:5). Did you catch it? The reference to one stone not on top of another is in reference to the "goodly stones". One does not use "goodly stones" in the foundation. One uses strong stones no matter how ugly they are because for the most part, they will be buried. Further, as the disciples admired the stones of the temple, no one dug up the foundation and said to Jesus, "Look how pretty they are." And even in the use of the word "buildings" points to the fact that indeed, all stones used in the sanctuary buildings were destroyed leaving nothing more than foundation stones in which they are a foundation and not a building.

So accepting that the temple was destroyed in 70 A.D. being the temple that Daniel saw would be rebuilt, there is absolutely no reference to a command to go forth and build yet another temple in which the Antichrist will rule. However, there are temples, church buildings, cathedrals, and many other structures around the world that are considered holy structures or temples of God. In other words, the Antichrist will not be ruling from the White House. That is not a temple or holy structure. Neither is the Kremlin, United Nations building, the Sears Tower, the new World Trade Center, the Eifel Tower, or any other structure that is just an ordinary building. But from a religious building, the Antichrist shall show himself to be God.

While we are on the subject and to put one more death nail into the futurist theory of Antichrist, the questionable last verse that is applied to the Antichrist is very much amazing. Daniel 9:27 says, "And he shall confirm the covenant with many for one week: and in the midst of the week he shall cause the sacrifice and the oblation to cease, and for the overspreading of abominations he shall make [it] desolate, even until the consummation, and that determined shall be poured upon the desolate." Nowhere in the Bible does the words "the covenant" ever refer to a generic agreement between human beings; it is always between God and humans. Sure, the phrase "they covenanted" and "made a covenant" as a generic covenant is used between human beings. But all 102 verses of the words "the covenant" referring to a specific covenant is always between God and humans.

Further, Daniel just had prayed concerning "the covenant". In Daniel 9:4, it says, "And I prayed unto the LORD my God, and made my confession, and said, O Lord, the great and dreadful God, keeping the covenant and mercy to them that love him, and to them that keep his commandments." So when verse 27 says that "the covenant" would cease, one of the covenants made with human beings was that of the sin sacrificial system, also known to be oblations. "And every oblation of thy meat offering shalt thou season with salt; neither shalt thou suffer the salt of the covenant of thy God to be lacking from thy meat offering: with all thine offerings thou shalt offer salt" (Leviticus 2:13). Why do Christians not sacrifice animals for sin offerings like the Jews did? Colossians 2:16-17 says, "Let no man therefore judge you in meat, or in drink, or in respect of an holyday, or of the new moon, or of the sabbath [days]: Which are a shadow of things to come; but the body [is] of Christ." Those meat offerings pointed to Jesus Christ. Jesus caused the sacrifices or the ceremonial covenant to cease because they were no longer necessary.

Interestingly, Jesus was baptize in autumn of 27 A.D. and exactly three and a half years later was crucified making the temple sacrifices null and void. To make sure of such was understood, "Jesus, when he had cried again with a loud voice, yielded up the ghost. And, behold, the veil of the temple was rent in twain from the top to the bottom" (Matthew 27:50-51). And not by coincidence, another three and a half years later, the Jews "stoned Stephen" (Acts 7:59) ending the Christian message to be contained within Israel only, "Therefore they that were scattered abroad went every where preaching the word" (Acts 8:4).

So a verse (Daniel 9:27) that is supposed to reveal what Jesus Christ had done for humans has been twisted by futurists to point it to the Antichrist all by implication. Again, it is only a cover up by those multitude of teachers and preachers that have the "Spirit of Antichrist" serving the actual Antichrist.

And so, to recognize that the Antichrist has authority sitting in a holy place dedicated to God showing himself to be God, even if not in agreement with the Antichrist, is to be on the side of the Antichrist.

IDENTIFYING MARK #36: EXALTS ABOVE THAT WHICH IS CALLED GOD

2 Thessalonians 2:4 says, "Who opposeth and exalteth himself above all that is called God."

Before we can make an application of this verse, we need to understand the phrase "called God." In other words, is the verse saying that a particular object, like a tree, is now called God? Is a particular building now called God? Is a particular statue now called God? Of course not. The Bible says, "People, which are called by my name" (2 Chronicles 7:14) applies to the fact that the Israelites would be considered to fit this category. Today, true Christians are called by God's name, meaning, the basic definition of a Christian is to be a follower of Christ. We are called by His name. So when we see the phrase "called God", it actually means, "called by His name".

Look at another example that applies His name, this time, to a building, but the building itself is not God. Jeremiah 7:10 says, "Come and stand before me in this house, which is called by my name." In fact, that phrase is repeated in Jeremiah 7:11, 14, 30, and elsewhere. Jeremiah 25:29 says, "City which is called by my name", applying it to a city. Daniel uses it two different ways, by praying, "O my God: for thy city and thy people are called by thy name" (Daniel 9:19). So people and a city are called God or called by His name. Neither is replacing God, and people are not God walking around either, but they are called by His name.

Now in proper Bible study manner, one would scourer the Bible for the phrase "called God" exactly as stated. In all of the Bible, the phrase "called God" or "called …" is nowhere else found to be explicitly told the meaning thereof. So we see the name "God" is indeed one of God's names. So searching the Bible, "Called by My name" is the only connection left.

A better phrase in plain human language is to just simply say, "Who opposeth and exalteth himself above all that God puts His name on." The reason we suggest this is because it is easy to see from previous points how it fits together. God says that these things are mine while the Antichrist thinks to have exalted power to take over ownership. God has His Ten Commandments; Antichrist thinks to change them. God has His Sabbath day to be kept holy; Antichrist commands his day to be kept holy. God has His Word; Antichrist places their traditions above the Bible. So all that is called God's, Antichrist thinks they are above it all. They even exalt themselves above God's people, the Christians, and even gets irked when true Christian do not obey their declarations, which is exactly what Antichrist has done and will do. Daniel saw, "I beheld, and the same horn made war with the saints, and prevailed against them" (Daniel 7:21), and John wrote, "I saw the woman drunken with the blood of the saints, and with the blood of the martyrs of Jesus" (Revelation 17:6).

Now do not be so quick to point fingers at the Antichrist and all those that wonder after it because we could actually have the Spirit of Antichrist in ourselves when we think we know better than what is provided by what is called God. When we think we know what is and is not the inspired Word, when we think we know what is and is not a fable in the Bible, when we think to try and suit the commandments of God to fit our lifestyle, whenever we place ourselves above what God calls His, we have the Spirit of Antichrist. Yes, the Antichrist reinterprets scripture, changes the commandments, and makes up rules to be dictated to Christians, but it can even be worse to do it ourselves and live by our own belief and call it God's will. The prayer is "Thy will be done" (Matthew 6:10); not "Our will be done!"

We hope you are seeing that Antichrist is dangerous enough, but the Spirit of Antichrist is even worse.

IDENTIFYING MARK #37: USES SIGNS AND WONDERS

2 Thessalonians 2:9 states, "[Even him], whose coming is after the working of Satan with all power and signs and lying wonders."

May we ask why Christians automatically associate miracles with God? If something supernatural happens, automatically it must be from God, especially if it is religious in nature. Take for instance the report of statues crying or oozing human blood, healings, and much more. Why do so many Christians think the devil cannot pull off the same thing? There is nowhere in the Bible that says the devil is restricted from doing miracles. Unfortunately Christians also get so narrow minded and focused upon the event and not even see the big picture. They ask, "This person just got healed. Are you saying the devil did that? Why would he do that?" The Bible says of the devil, "no marvel; for Satan himself is transformed into an angel of light" (2 Corinthians 11:14). If Satan can appear as an angel of light, he surely can pull off a miracle. Even Jesus warned, "For there shall arise false Christs, and false prophets, and shall shew great signs and wonders; insomuch that, if [it were] possible, they shall deceive the very elect" (Matthew 24:24). In fact, the purpose of working even good miracles is "For they are the spirits of devils, working miracles, [which] go forth unto the kings of the earth and of the whole world, to gather them to the battle of that great day of God Almighty" (Revelation 16:14).

So many times Christians get all excited about this sign or that miracle, and then when brought to the Word of God, it is like rain on their celebration. Of course they retort with, "How can you be so sure?" It is because of knowing the Bible. It needs to be studied daily over and over, reinforced, no matter how much one knows or thinks they know. We are to "Study to shew thyself approved unto God, a workman that needeth not to be ashamed, rightly dividing the word of truth" (2 Timothy 2:15). And the lack of knowledge is what is contributing to the Christians flocking to one sign after another.

This is why we are saying that it is one thing to identify the Antichrist and avoid the direct relationship but it is another thing to be subject to the "Spirit of Antichrist". Any Christian that does not use the Bible as the source of belief, does not know the Bible to be able to answer even the simplest of beliefs, criticizes the Bible in any manner, are all examples of having the "Spirit of Antichrist". And if the "very elect" could get to the point of nearly believing and being deceived, how easy is it for those that are not "very elect".

And the "very elect" are not people God randomly chooses. The "very elect" are the studious ones. Like the training given to bank tellers, they study the original currency, so likewise, Christians ought to be studying God's original teaching and be able to reject these deceptions.

The Bible says in this matter, "If there arise among you a prophet, or a dreamer of dreams, and giveth thee a sign or a wonder, And the sign or the wonder come to pass, whereof he spake unto thee, saying, Let us go after other gods, which thou hast not known, and let us serve them; Thou shalt not hearken unto the words of that prophet, or that dreamer of dreams: for the LORD your God proveth you, to know whether ye love the LORD your God with all your heart and with all your soul. Ye shall walk after the LORD your God, and fear him, and keep his commandments, and obey his voice, and ye shall serve him, and cleave unto him" (Deuteronomy 13:1-4). In other words, signs and wonders will happen, and the ministers of them will teach other doctrine than is outlined in the Bible, and if people choose to listen to those ministers because of the sign or wonder, God just proved that those people are unworthy to take to Heaven.

Today, a sign or wonder is not to lead people to believe in the god called Baal or even the Greek or Roman gods, but to make Jesus out to be someone He is not. "We must be of God because I just healed this person of their ailment!" "We must be of God because I made this statue cry blood!" "Now listen to me when I say, …" The "very elect" will say back, "That's not what the Bible says!"

So to avoid being on the side of Antichrist, directly or by the spirit thereof, know the Word and continue to study to know even more. Accept the fact that there are miracles, but also be cautious because the devil is willing to heal thousands, work signs that seem to glorify God, etc. all to achieve the snaring of Christians, which is to cause them to be in disobedience to God. Remember, that is Satan's goal for "Whosoever transgresseth, and abideth not in the doctrine of Christ, hath not God" (2 John 1:9). It is only "He that abideth in the doctrine of Christ, he hath both the Father and the Son" (2 John 1:9).

IDENTIFYING MARK #38: FORBID MARRIAGES

1 Timothy 4:1-3, "Now the Spirit speaketh expressly, that in the latter times some shall depart from the faith, giving heed to seducing spirits, and doctrines of devils; Speaking lies in hypocrisy; having their conscience seared with a hot iron; Forbidding to marry."

Although this verse does not specifically associate with the Antichrist but speaks generally about people leaving the faith, we are including it as a description because of the many indirect references. For instance, in the last days, there will be doctrines of devils. Well, the Antichrist is working on teaching doctrines that are different from those of Jesus Christ all in the name of causing Christians to live in disobedience (2 John 1:9). If it is not Jesus' doctrines, that means it must be the doctrines of devils. The speaking of lies and hypocrisies matches the speaking "blasphemes" and "great things" that both Daniel and John note. And overall, causing people to depart from the faith is a reference to an outside source that is not teaching true Christianity and all along we have been examining that source. It is called Antichrist or the "Spirit of Antichrist." This is what is meant by "falling away" (2 Thessalonians 2:3), which is a direct reference to Antichrist.

So with that established, is the Antichrist is going to tell everyone to stop getting married? No, of course not, but it will have the practice of forbidding certain people from marrying.

IDENTIFYING MARK #39: COMMANDS CHRISTIANS TO ABSTAIN FROM EATING MEAT

1 Timothy 4:1-3 continues with "… [and commanding] to abstain from meats, which God hath created to be received with thanksgiving of them which believe and know the truth."

Using the same reasoning, it states that an outside source is going to command with a godly reason to stop eating meat, maybe not entirely, but definitely would put on a restriction, even if it is periodically. That influential power can be none other than the Antichrist or Spirit of Antichrist. It is not a coincidence of timing that in these days we have to deal with the Antichrist and there is a departing of Christians from the faith.

Please note that on these subjects of marriage and meat eating being forbidden, the minds of these followers are so hotly stubborn that they cannot accept anything that speaks contrary to their practice and belief. People are convinced that if it is for a godly reason, what can it hurt? Well, if the Antichrist is making up the rules, then it hurts a lot because we are obeying Antichrist instead of Jesus Christ. In fact, God says, "Behold, to obey [is] better than sacrifice" (1 Samuel 15:22). So doing something against the Word of God in the name of God for a godly reason is not acceptable to God because He wants obedience, something that is very lacking among Christians today.

For those that cannot see the seriousness of the matter, would you think it is acceptable for a complete stranger with good intentions to take your child for the afternoon to some proper and enjoyable event giving you the break to get things done without a little one underfoot? Of course not! We could argue, "What is the harm?" And saying, "Well, we don't know their intent" does not hold because we just told you that there is no harm, no risk, no issue, and all safety precautions in place. Bottom line is that things do matter.

That is why the urgency of this material. Not only have we declared Antichrist being active even today, but the Spirit of Antichrist is so prevalent that it is acceptable among Christians to live in disobedience to God and still think one is going to Heaven. This alone, in fulfilling the verse of "all the world wondered after the beast" (Revelation 13:3), tells us that we are nearing the second coming.

We also want to keep in balance though because the profession of belief based solely upon the excitement is evaluated by God in regards to the sincerity. God sees through all those that are facing a crisis but take away the crisis and the old life returns. "God is not mocked" (Galatians 6:7). So, though we want people to quickly move into action and study these things out and make decisions for Christ before it is too late, we also do not want just quick decisions based upon the feelings of urgency alone. This is a logical decision initiated by feelings. The motivation for any of our actions should be love, but our decision to live according to God's will is based upon the truth revealed in His Word, the logic.

IDENTIFYING MARK #40: BASED UPON SATAN INSPIRED RELIGION (PAGANISM)

Revelation 13:1-2 says, "And I stood upon the sand of the sea, and saw a beast rise up out of the sea, having seven heads and ten horns, and upon his horns ten crowns, and upon his heads the name of blasphemy. And the beast which I saw was like unto a leopard, and his feet were as [the feet] of a bear, and his mouth as the mouth of a lion: and the dragon gave him his power, and his seat, and great authority." And Revelation 13:4 says, "And they worshipped the dragon which gave power unto the beast."

Now whenever worship is involved, either we are worshipping the true God of Heaven or we are not. In the loose use of the word, "paganism" is the term applied to any worship that is not towards the true God. Usually when people think of paganism, they think of the "stone god", "the gods of the universe", "the gods of the elements", etc. That is not what we are referring to alone. Hardly anyone believes or would worship Jupiter or Zeus or Baal or any other man made god today. Although it is blatant paganism, what we are referring to is the fact that despite believing in God, believing in Jesus, singing songs and praying to them, one can actually be worshipping and performing acts that are not biblical but Satan inspired. In other words, there is a true form of Christianity and many pagan forms disguised as being Christian.

Not that we are going to tell you to throw away the Christmas holiday, but there are all kinds of Christian excuses of why certain things are done today, which is not really Christian but pagan yet a Christian reason is given for doing such. Putting lights on the house and lights on the tree is to remind us that we are the light to the world. Well, in reality the lights have a pagan root connected to fairies. It is one thing to decorate, but it is another thing to worship in a pagan way. That is what is dangerous.

By participating knowingly or unknowingly in the unbiblical worship practices, especially instituted by the Antichrist and continued by the "Spirit of Antichrist", constitutes not the worship of Jesus Christ but, as the verse states, worship of the dragon. According to Revelation 12:9, "The great dragon was cast out, that old serpent, called the Devil, and Satan, which deceiveth the whole world." So Satan inspired doctrines and practices, especially involving worship, will be brought in by the Antichrist.

On top of the verses explicitly stating that people would be worshipping Satan while thinking they are worshipping God, notice the Antichrist appearance as described in Revelation 13:1-2. It is made up of the body parts that Daniel described separately. We already covered those definitions found in Daniel 7:4-8, where the lion represents Babylon, the bear represents Medo-Persia, the leopard represents Greece, and the ten horns represent Europe. Both Daniel and John in Revelation do not identify the fourth one by name, but it is Rome. What do all of them have in common? They are truly pagan empires, where they did indeed command the public to worship idols and manmade gods. Well, it is not by chance that the Antichrist is described with those body parts. It is because, despite appearing to be a Christian nation, mentioned in our earlier points, the Antichrist's true source of doctrines is found in the pagan rituals and practices, many of which are superstitions.

Therefore, to avoid both the Antichrist and the "Spirit of Antichrist", it would be a very good idea to put away all practices and beliefs that are pagan and not supported by the Bible.

IDENTIFYING MARK #41: BLASPHEME THE BEINGS OF HEAVEN

Revelation 13:6 says, "And he opened his mouth in blasphemy against God, to blaspheme his name, and his tabernacle, and them that dwell in heaven."

The phrase "them that dwell in heaven" can be taken two ways. One way is to say that there are beings in Heaven and the Antichrist blasphemes them. God is not included as one of them as He is individually identified as being blasphemed against. The other way to understand the verse is to state beliefs of placing people into Heaven, which really are not there, and that is counted as blaspheme. In either case, it is our belief that the Antichrist would do both.

One way to blaspheme beings already in Heaven, like the angels, is to have doctrines that wrongly describe the angels. One of those, carried mostly by the "Spirit of Antichrist" is to have such beings intermarry with humans by misinterpreting Genesis chapter 6. The bottom line is that angels do not have sex! (Matthew 22:30) Also, another doctrine is to have these baby angels, known as cherubs, flittering around like bumble bees. Cherubs are special angels, but in nowise are they little babies. That is just wrong.

As for doctrines related to beings not in heaven and yet placing them there is the definition of the word "saint". According to the Bible, the word "saint" refers to human beings like "All the saints salute you, chiefly they that are of Caesar's household" (Philippians 4:22). A saint is not someone that has to go through a rigorous investigation and be declared to be one who then is allowed to be prayed to. In fact, that in itself is just wrong. "[There is] one God, and one mediator between God and men, the man Christ Jesus" (1 Timothy 2:5). We do not need to be praying to saints, which goes against the Bible.

A third way this verse is being fulfilled and by both the Antichrist and especially the "Spirit of Antichrist" is the understanding of death. The Bible says nearly seventy times that death is a sleep. "For if we believe that Jesus died and rose again, even so them also which sleep in Jesus will God bring with him" (1 Thessalonians 4:14). In fact, none of us get to go to Heaven until the second coming. "For as in Adam all die, even so in Christ shall all be made alive. But every man in his own order: Christ the firstfruits; afterward they that are Christ's at his coming" (1 Corinthians 15:22-23). And what an event that shall be! "Behold, I shew you a mystery; We shall not all sleep, but we shall all be changed, In a moment, in the twinkling of an eye, at the last trump: for the trumpet shall sound, and the dead shall be raised incorruptible, and we shall be changed. For this corruptible must put on incorruption, and this mortal [must] put on immortality. So when this corruptible shall have put on incorruption, and this mortal shall have put on immortality, then shall be brought to pass the saying that is written, Death is swallowed up in victory. O death, where [is] thy sting? O grave, where [is] thy victory?" (1 Corinthians 15:51-55) Further, that is what the coming resurrection is all about: to wake the people out of their graves to be alive again but until then, they are asleep. "Marvel not at this: for the hour is coming, in the which all that are in the graves shall hear his voice, And shall come forth; they that have done good, unto the resurrection of life; and they that have done evil, unto the resurrection of damnation" (John 5:28-29). Peter even gave a speech regarding David, who is not in Heaven right now. "Men [and] brethren, let me freely speak unto you of the patriarch David, that he is both dead and buried, and his sepulchre is with us unto this day" (Acts 2:29). So by teaching that people go to Heaven and Hell right away is blaspheme towards those that dwell in Heaven because they are not there. There are some exceptions, such as Enoch (Genesis 5:24), Elijah (2 Kings 2:11), and Moses (Jude 1:9), along with probably those at the time of Jesus' death and resurrection in which, "the graves were opened; and many bodies of the saints which slept arose, And came out of the graves after his resurrection, and went into the holy city, and appeared unto many" (Matthew 27:52-53).

So, to believe angels have sex or there are baby angels is blasphemous. On top of that, to reserve the term "saint" only to special dead people is also blasphemous, especially when praying to such people, but even the belief of immediate life after death in a spirit world is blasphemous. And all three are well entrenched in the entity called Antichrist and perpetrated to the mass of uneducated Christians who are easily impressed by signs and wonders, especially resembling dead loved ones.

IDENTIFYING MARK #42: THE NUMBER OF THE NAME BEING 666

Revelation 13:18 says, "Here is wisdom. Let him that hath understanding count the number of the beast: for it is the number of a man; and his number [is] Six hundred threescore [and] six."

Please note the number is part of the description of the beast while remembering that a beast in prophecy represents a king and their kingdom. Also, the reference to the phrase "a man" does not mean the human's name adds up to 666, but as Daniel described "behold, in this horn [were] eyes like the eyes of man" (Daniel 7:8), yet, so many people do that. They take a person's actual name and try to run the numbers on their name. Ronald Wilson Reagan was thought of as being the Antichrist because of 6 characters in each of his three part name. Of course he was not the Antichrist being dead now. The number has been applied to a number of people in this manner, or worse, taking a name in a different language, compare it to Roman numerals, and claiming that they are the Antichrist.

For instance, an American name of John Smith adds up to 0 despite people claiming that at least the letter "i" has a value of 1. The letter may indeed represent 1 if the name were Roman, but it is not. Basically, some languages attach a value to their letters, like the Roman numerals of I, V, X, C, etc. In America, we do not have such a numbering system. Our alphabet is separate from our numbering system. So when the name adds up to 666, it is only in a language that contains a numbering system that is also their alphabet. Nowhere in the verse does the Bible say that the name, used in the Roman numbering system, is the number 666. The Bible never intended for the Roman numeric system to be the world's standard for checking everyone's name. There is more than one language that overlap numbers and letters. So let us not assume something that is not there.

The other point we are making about the reference of "a man" that we are suggesting is not to look at individual names, as such come and go as leaders do, but more of a man's title. Ronald Reagan, George Bush, Sr., William Clinton, George Bush, Jr., and Barrack Obama all are or were different names of the man in office in the White House, however, the name given to represent the position held is the name "president". So when "a man" is elected, the name used is "president". Therefore, the name or title of "a man" in office for the Antichrist is going to add up to 666, but not the person's name specifically, especially since the number applies to the kingdom that the man speaks for. And when that man is replaced, the name for that man stays the same because it is not a personal name, it is a title. By the way, the name "King" does not add up to 666 in any language with or without numbers associated with it.

Now recently it has been said that there was a misinterpretation in the verse and the number is really 616 and not 666. The interesting part is that for so long we have believed it to be 666, and now we are told it is in error? We believe it is the effort of the Antichrist once again to undermine the identification. In the next chapter, we will see that there is absolutely no doubt that the number is 666.

IDENTIFYING MARK #43: THE ANTICHRIST USES A SYMBOLIC WOMAN

Revelation 17:3-6 says, "So he carried me away in the spirit into the wilderness: and I saw a woman sit upon a scarlet coloured beast, full of names of blasphemy, having seven heads and ten horns. And the woman was arrayed in purple and scarlet colour, and decked with gold and precious stones and pearls, having a golden cup in her hand full of abominations and filthiness of her fornication: And upon her forehead [was] a name written, MYSTERY, BABYLON THE GREAT, THE MOTHER OF HARLOTS AND ABOMINATIONS OF THE EARTH. And I saw the woman drunken with the blood of the saints, and with the blood of the martyrs of Jesus: and when I saw her, I wondered with great admiration."

Sitting on the beast is a woman. As Revelation states, the woman is not literal but symbolic. In fact, Revelation 17:18 says, "And the woman which thou sawest is that great city, which reigneth over the kings of the earth." The woman represents a great city that rules over all of the nations of the earth. Also noteworthy is the fact that there is another symbolic use of a woman, for there is "a woman clothed with the sun, and the moon under her feet, and upon her head a crown of twelve stars" (Revelation 12:1). This too is symbolic but it is not the same woman. The reason she is not the same woman is because instead of being on the side of the dragon, "when the dragon saw that he was cast unto the earth, he persecuted the woman which brought forth the man [child]. And to the woman were given two wings of a great eagle, that she might fly into the wilderness, into her place, where she is nourished for a time, and times, and half a time, from the face of the serpent. And the serpent cast out of his mouth water as a flood after the woman, that he might cause her to be carried away of the flood" (Revelation 12:13-15).

At this moment, we have two different women. One woman sits on top of the beast that received power form Satan to begin with, therefore, she is in cooperation with the dragon and the beast. The other woman is attacked by the dragon, both directly and indirectly.

So, what does a woman also represent? Well, God says, "I have likened the daughter of Zion to a comely and delicate [woman]" (Jeremiah 6:2). So when a woman is delicate or comely in appearance, think the name Zion. When the woman is not such a delicate woman, more specifically, a whore, God equates that with disobedience. "And I saw, when for all the causes whereby backsliding Israel committed adultery I had put her away, and given her a bill of divorce; yet her treacherous sister Judah feared not, but went and played the harlot also" (Jeremiah 3:8).

Please note that God was speaking to the territories known as Israel and Judah during their civil war saying that when they, as in, the people backslid, committed spiritual adultery, they were being a harlot. Please also recognize that spiritual adultery is equivalent to incorporating worldly practices as being part of the service that is supposed to be dedicated to God. The Bible says, "Ye adulterers and adulteresses, know ye not that the friendship of the world is enmity with God? whosoever therefore will be a friend of the world is the enemy of God" (James 4:4).

Therefore, even today when Christians are enjoying the same raunchy television programs, listening to the same sinful music, hanging out at the bar, being greedy like non-Christians, and basically being worldly, they are actually committing spiritual adultery towards God. The sad part is, such Christians still think they are going to go Heaven. Do you really think that a groom that is about to get married to his bride would be willing to get married and go on a honeymoon with her when she had been sleeping around up through the day of the wedding? How dare Christians think they can enjoy the world being spiritually adulterous and still thinking they are saved!

On top of that, what makes spiritual adultery even worse is the fact that it is incorporated into the worship and church services. Rock bands are nowhere found in the Bible but rather, simple hymns are, which was sung in all churches up through the middle of the 1900's. The Bible says, "There shall not be found among you [any one] that maketh his son or his daughter to pass through the fire, [or] that useth divination, [or] an observer of times, or an enchanter, or a witch, Or a charmer, or a consulter with familiar spirits, or a wizard, or a necromancer" (Deuteronomy 18:10-11), and yet, numerous churches thought nothing of conducting movie night at the church featuring the beloved witches and wizards in the Harry Potter series. And God "gave some, apostles; and some, prophets; and some, evangelists; and some, pastors and teachers; For the perfecting of the saints" (Ephesians 4:11-12), yet churches avoid talking about sin and turn to social reasons for gathering. They offer coffee and snacks between study time and the worship hour as if they are running some coffee shop. They perform dramas instead of listening to soul convicting sermons that call sin by its right name, a sin. And many other worldly activities have found themselves incorporated into the churches replacing biblical practices. Even Christian radio makes no difference with the worldly radio. They both have the same contests; same style of music, despite Jesus being mentioned in the lyrics, but then again many religious songs are so close to the worldly music without mentioning Jesus that even the world accepts the songs; have the same jovial conversations; report the same news about sports and celebrities; etc.

It is all so poisonous because of having a religious connection as the theme, Christians think it is godly when in fact, it is no different than the adultery of Israel and the playing a harlot like Judah.

Again, in case you have forgotten, the Bible thus far distinguishes between two women. One woman symbolizes Zion; the other woman represents worldliness and backsliding being incorporated into the practices. Now let us further define the nice woman, Zion. The Bible says, "Zion, Thou [art] my people" (Isaiah 51:16). So the nice woman is truly God's people. The harlot, like Judah and Israel, which were in name only, actually at the time, just pretended to be God's people. Therefore, the woman that rides the beast will pretend to be Christian, but really are not. They are filled with worldly practices. The woman from Revelation 12 that the dragon persecutes represents the true people of God.

Now, let us take this one step further by saying that the delicate woman represents God's true people or true Christians and the harlot as fake Christians or pretended people of God is a mouthful. There are Bible terms that are associated with God's people. Here are two of them: "Unto the church of God which is at Corinth, with all the saints which are in all Achaia: Grace [be] to you and peace from God our Father, and [from] the Lord Jesus Christ" (2 Corinthians 1:1-2). The first term is easily recognized; it is the word "saints". But that term only applies to true Christians, in God's eyes. The other term, "church", is not so easily picked out of the verse but is appropriately used because the word church simply means "gathering of people".

So, what we are declaring is that there is God's true church and there is a false church, each represented by a woman. The harlot is the backslidden or worldly church, which is riding the beast. Therefore, the Antichrist uses a false church system to promote its Christianized beliefs, worldly practices given a Christian reason, which is nothing more than backslidden or worldly practices. This is not off base at all, for the Bible does speak of Satan using a church or the synonym word of synagogue (Revelation 2:9, 3:9).

To avoid both the Spirit of Antichrist as well as the Antichrist, one should align oneself with Biblical reason for every religious practice as well as shun all non-biblical practices that are simply from the world.

IDENTIFYING MARK #44: OFFICIAL COLORS ARE PURPLE AND SCARLET

Revelation 17:4 says, "And the woman was arrayed in purple and scarlet colour."

Nations have colors associated with them. Many fly a flag of colors, while others may have a uniform. This nation makes use of the colors purple and scarlet.

IDENTIFYING MARK #45: RICH

Revelation 17:4 says, "And the woman was arrayed in purple and scarlet colour, and decked with gold and precious stones and pearls."

With all that adorning, the Antichrist kingdom would be rich.

IDENTIFYING MARK #46: ASSISTED BY ANOTHER KINGDOM

Revelation 13:11-12 says, "And I beheld another beast coming up out of the earth; and he had two horns like a lamb, and he spake as a dragon. And he exerciseth all the power of the first beast before him, and causeth the earth and them which dwell therein to worship the first beast, whose deadly wound was healed."

As noted before, a beast represents a kingdom or a country. This one comes up from the earth instead of the water. Remember, according to Revelation 17:15, the Bible says, "The waters which thou sawest, where the whore sitteth, are peoples, and multitudes, and nations, and tongue." So the earth being the opposite of water must mean not so many people, not so many multitudes, not so many nations, and not so many languages.

The important thing to note, though, is that a kingdom or nation will arise from a sparsely populated area of the planet, which will then assist in promoting the Antichrist. The country starts out with horns like a lamb, which is a description of being peaceful (Numbers 6:14), but eventually turns into speaking like a dragon, which means that this young nation gets a bit full of themselves and starts forcing people to go against the free exercise of their religious and civil rights.

It is not by coincidence, that Revelation 12 describes some activity regarding the use of the word "earth", which will help us understand who this second nation is.

- Revelation 12:1-2 says, "And there appeared a great wonder in heaven; a woman clothed with the sun, and the moon under her feet, and upon her head a crown of twelve stars: And she being with child cried, travailing in birth, and pained to be delivered."

What does this mean? Remember, a delicate and comely woman represents God's people, the church (Jeremiah 6:2, Isaiah 51:16). In searching for the symbolic use of the sun, Psalms 84:11 says, "For the LORD God [is] a sun and shield: the LORD will give grace and glory: no good [thing] will he withhold from them that walk uprightly." God is with His people is the answer.

In looking at the symbolic use of the moon, Psalms 81:3 says, "Blow up the trumpet in the new moon, in the time appointed, on our solemn feast day." It is the tracking of feast days, which pointed to Jesus Christ.

In searching out the twelve stars, Genesis 37:5-9 says, "And Joseph dreamed a dream, and he told [it] his brethren: and they hated him yet the more. And he said unto them, Hear, I pray you, this dream which I have dreamed: For, behold, we [were] binding sheaves in the field, and, lo, my sheaf arose, and also stood upright; and, behold, your sheaves stood round about, and made obeisance to my sheaf. And his brethren said to him, Shalt thou indeed reign over us? or shalt thou indeed have dominion over us? And they hated him yet the more for his dreams, and for his words. And he dreamed yet another dream, and told it his brethren, and said, Behold, I have dreamed a dream more; and, behold, the sun and the moon and the eleven stars made obeisance to me." In short, Joseph dreamed about stars representing his eleven brothers, which would later be tribes. Joseph is the twelfth one of course. And Genesis 49:28 confirms with the word, "All these [are] the twelve tribes of Israel: and this [is it] that their father spake unto them, and blessed them; every one according to his blessing he blessed them." In the New Testament, it is the twelve Apostles that lay the foundation, keeping in mind that Judas was replaced with Matthias (Acts 1:23).

- Now Revelation 12:3-5, says, "And there appeared another wonder in heaven; and behold a great red dragon, having seven heads and ten horns, and seven crowns upon his heads. And his tail drew the third part of the stars of heaven, and did cast them to the earth: and the dragon stood before the woman which was ready to be delivered, for to devour her child as soon as it was born. And she brought forth a man child, who was to rule all nations with a rod of iron: and her child was caught up unto God, and [to] his throne."

The dragon, of course is none other than Satan, as previously reviewed and will be stated again. The drawing of one third of the stars are the fallen angels, also reviewed and will see again. The rest of the verse clearly describes Jesus Christ, and what vehicle did Satan use to try to devour the Child, Jesus, at His birth? Rome with Herod decreeing to kill all children two years and younger is the answer. Matthew 2:13,16 says, "And when they were departed, behold, the angel of the Lord appeareth to Joseph in a dream, saying, Arise, and take the young child and his mother, and flee into Egypt, and be thou there until I bring thee word: for Herod will seek the young child to destroy him. Then Herod, when he saw that he was mocked of the wise men, was exceeding wroth, and sent forth, and slew all the children that were in Bethlehem, and in all the coasts thereof, from two years old and under, according to the time which he had diligently enquired of the wise men." But praise God the Child came forth who was destined to rule all nations! Matthew 2:6 says, "And thou Bethlehem, [in] the land of Juda, art not the least among the princes of Juda: for out of thee shall come a Governor, that shall rule my people Israel." And He ascended to the Father, according to John 20:17, which says, "Jesus saith unto her, Touch me not; for I am not yet ascended to my Father: but go to my brethren, and say unto them, I ascend unto my Father, and your Father; and [to] my God, and your God." And His throne, from which He serves on our behalf is in heaven, is described in Hebrews 9:11 which says, "But Christ being come an high priest of good things to come, by a greater and more perfect tabernacle, not made with hands, that is to say, not of this building".

This of course infuriated Satan because now he is a defeated foe (Hebrews 2:14). When Jesus comes back, He is coming for His faithful followers (John 14:2-3). And ever since the resurrection, Satan has been trying to mislead as many followers of Christ as possible to get them to use the freedom of choice to leave. At the same time, Satan has been doing a marvelous job at confounding what it means to be saved so as to discourage the average person even from finding it.

Why does God allow this and just does not show up to prove He is God? It is because God wants to be loved completely without doubt. Would a woman accept a marriage proposal from a stranger? No. The man has to prove worthiness. At the very least, she needs to ask questions. Now in the case of God, we do not have inform God, it is us that need to be proved. We need to prove to ourselves just how much we love God. It is easy to say, "I love God", but it is much harder when it involves having "forsaken all" (Matthew 19:27). It is easy for a man to say, "I love you dear", but when around all of his guy friends, "It's not so easy." A woman even appreciates a bit of fighting for her. So to wrestle through all the lies of Satan is to prove our love to ourselves towards Jesus. He does not want lukewarm Christians. He wants red hot Christians! "So then because thou art lukewarm, and neither cold nor hot, I will spue thee out of my mouth" (Revelation 3:16).

The reason for this is because there has been an awful lot of lies said of God. If we are going to spend eternity with Him, there cannot be a single doubt towards God's character, or the relationship will eventually fall apart. Seeing that "affliction shall not rise up the second time" (Nahum 1:9), all seed of sin, which is through doubt, must not exist. That will be the ones ready for Heaven.

Just as a woman has to know her man so that when the man is falsely accused of adultery, she then needs to believe him without a doubt at all, otherwise, the marriage will eventually fall apart. Eternity is a long time. Doubt is hard to push aside when all the evidence seems to point differently than what the husband or God is saying.

That is why the Bible says, "The just shall live by faith" (Romans 1:17). Despite the fact that science says we evolved, it takes faith to believe God is the Creator. Despite the fact that a certain sin is just too hard to resist, it takes faith to believe that God will help us become an overcomer. Despite even Christians cutting up the Word of God, it takes faith to take it as it reads.

- Revelation 12:6 "And the woman fled into the wilderness, where she hath a place prepared of God, that they should feed her there a thousand two hundred [and] threescore days."

It is not by chance that the woman, or church is in hiding during the 1,260 prophetic day period, which is the 1,260 year period (Numbers 14:34, Ezekiel 4:6). That matches the Antichrist rule for the same amount of time. In fact, you could say that God's people are shown fleeing from the Antichrist.

- Revelation 12:7-9 says, "And there was war in heaven: Michael and his angels fought against the dragon; and the dragon fought and his angels, And prevailed not; neither was their place found any more in heaven. And the great dragon was cast out, that old serpent, called the Devil, and Satan, which deceiveth the whole world: he was cast out into the earth, and his angels were cast out with him."

So, now we get to look at a more detailed representation of the same message of Revelation 12:1-6 in which before the church on earth was formed, there was a war in Heaven. The war included Satan and his angels being cast out of Heaven. The war continues on earth in which the whole world (Adam and Eve) was deceived, and it will continue until Jesus returns.

- Revelation 12:10-11 says, "And I heard a loud voice saying in heaven, Now is come salvation, and strength, and the kingdom of our God, and the power of his Christ: for the accuser of our brethren is cast down, which accused them before our God day and night. And they overcame him by the blood of the Lamb, and by the word of their testimony; and they loved not their lives unto the death."

Salvation and strength came at the cross. That is a reference to Jesus. The kingdom of grace was established with the realization of the power we can tap into to defeat and resist every temptation and sin that Satan dangles before humans. Well, some Christians believe in that power at least, which is our point.

Satan is a defeated foe, especially when all people that believe in being able to overcome every sin are claiming the blood of the Lamb being sufficient in power to defeat Satan at every temptation. They are part of the "glorious church, not having spot, or wrinkle, or any such thing; but that it should be holy and without blemish" (Ephesians 5:27). Members of this church, which is not a denomination as we understand denominations, believe that "God of peace sanctify you wholly; and [I pray God] your whole spirit and soul and body be preserved blameless unto the coming of our Lord Jesus Christ" (1 Thessalonians 5:23).

These things were promised to Israel as the sacrificial system pointed forward to Jesus and the cross. Today, as Christians, we look back at the cross to claim the blood.

- Revelation 12:12 says, "Therefore rejoice, [ye] heavens, and ye that dwell in them. Woe to the inhabiters of the earth and of the sea! for the devil is come down unto you, having great wrath, because he knoweth that he hath but a short time."

Now, after the cross, the early apostolic persecutions, occurred. Satan sensed that he was a defeated being though he still holds out hope for victory. His current objective is to deceive as many as possible, knowing that it is just a short time.

- Revelation 12:13-14 says, "And when the dragon saw that he was cast unto the earth, he persecuted the woman which brought forth the man [child]. And to the woman were given two wings of a great eagle, that she might fly into the wilderness, into her place, where she is nourished for a time, and times, and half a time, from the face of the serpent."

So, the persecution of the true people of God picks up, not by coincidence, the Antichrist is also ruling for 1,260 prophetic days as well. Please note that the persecution time is for a prophetic period of time that matches the 1,260 days a moment ago in verse 6. In other words, it is the same story with added detail. As a reminder, a time is one year; times being plural means more than 1 year but since there is no number associated with it, it is 2 years; and a half a time is 6 months. Remember, it is prophetic using the consistent Bible prophecy rule of "each day for a year" (Numbers 14:34, Ezekiel 4:6). Therefore, the time period is actually in years.

- Revelation 12:15 says, "And the serpent cast out of his mouth water as a flood after the woman, that he might cause her to be carried away of ∆109

- Here we see lots of water, a flood of water, which is representative of "peoples, and multitudes, and nations, and tongues" (Revelation 17:15) who assist in persecuting God's true people.

- Revelation 12:16 says, "And the earth helped the woman, and the earth opened her mouth, and swallowed up the flood which the dragon cast out of his mouth."

So some nation rises up that is not very populated. It appears after Jesus brings us salvation. That means, since 31 A.D., look all over the earth for a new nation that was formed that is initially without a whole lot of people not speaking a whole lot of languages. Now that could refer to a lot of countries, so let us read on with more of what we know. The nation that arises is after the early church series of persecutions in which the Apostle John was exiled to the island of Patmos (Revelation 1:9) over. So now our time frame is sometime after 100 A.D. But this nation that rises up also is after a long period of running away from the Antichrist that spanned a 1,260 year period in which renders the persecution powerless. Now using some points about the Antichrist that we already know, that period of 1,260 years does not begin until after 476 A.D. What year specifically, well, we did not pinpoint yet, but we will. So, let us do some math. At the very least, add 476 to 1,260 and you end up in 1736. Therefore, the new nation that helps the true Christians flee from persecutions appears on the scene after the year 1736. That should greatly narrow down the field of possible choices. In fact, when we find out the exact starting time of the 1,260 years, we find out it is even a bit later.

But from what dates we do have, it should be sufficient to answer the question, what nation formed after 1736 helped Christians practice their beliefs freely without persecution? There is but one country that fits this description. It is none other than the United States.

Therefore, do not be surprised that the United States is involved in helping the Antichrist around the world. Not by coincidence, one of our national symbols that has small horns like a lamb and yet is as mean as anything is none other than the buffalo. That is not by coincidence.

But we are not done….

- Revelation 12:17 says, "And the dragon was wroth with the woman, and went to make war with the remnant of her seed, which keep the commandments of God, and have the testimony of Jesus Christ."

So, Satan is angry at the Christian church in general, however, he tolerates the compromised Christians and focuses his main attacks upon a smaller group of people. They are identified as keeping all of God's commandments and holding onto the testimony of Jesus Christ. This fits in with the rest of Revelation 13 in which the United States will even assist in the enforcement of the beast's mark.

On top of that, it all fits into the bigger picture that we have been describing and well supported by tons of verses. The vast majority of Christians are not God's true Christians and are irked by those living the true Christian lifestyle. Such irked, pretended Christians, will form an allegiance, having "one mind" to attack those that have the "one mind" of Christ.

Now, we are not anti-government. We believe in being "subject to principalities and powers, to obey magistrates, to be ready to every good work" (Titus 3:1), but when the United States enforces laws contrary to the Bible, as Peter said, "We ought to obey God rather than men" (Acts 5:29).

And if one dares quote the separation of church and state in the context that such religious intolerance is not possible and would never happen, wake up! It already has been happening. Catholic and other religious organizations are forced into support abortions in one form or another at the threat of losing funding, Boy Scouts needing to change their policies on homosexuals, health care requiring support of contraceptives even among many Catholic organizations, Christian businesses not allowed to turn away service based upon religious beliefs, Mormon religious rights to polygamy has been prevented for a couple centuries, Jehovah Witnesses have not always been successful in rejecting blood transfusions, and many other things. Even the religious exemption of vaccines is in the process of being revoked, homeschooling being challenged, and much more. Agree or not, biblical or not, it does not matter. This country is forcing compliance despite one's religious beliefs is fulfilling that description of starting off with lamb like horns as by expressing freedom of religion and is now speaking, through laws, like a dragon.

IDENTIFYING MARK #47: HAS A MARK (OF ALLEGIANCE)

Revelation 13:17 says, "And that no man might buy or sell, save he that had the mark, or the name of the beast." Revelation 14:9-10 says, "If any man worship the beast and his image, and receive [his] mark in his forehead, or in his hand, The same shall drink of the wine of the wrath of God." Revelation 14:11 says, "They have no rest day nor night, who worship the beast and his image, and whosoever receiveth the mark of his name." Revelation 16:2 says, "There fell a noisome and grievous sore upon the men which had the mark of the beast."

Putting these verses together, it seems that the Mark belongs to the beast, as in, the Antichrist. Without it, one will not be able to buy or sell. It also seems that worship is involved heavily. Most people, without consulting the Bible, focus on the physical worship and immediately think of bowing down or praying to the beast, when in fact, that is not the only way to show worship.

God expects to be worshipped as well, especially as Jesus said, "But the hour cometh, and now is, when the true worshippers shall worship the Father in spirit and in truth: for the Father seeketh such to worship him" (John 4:23). From this verse, we see that truth is involved. Well, truth to be used in worship is not about acknowledging something as true or not, but living it. Peter wrote, "Seeing ye have purified your souls in obeying the truth through the Spirit unto unfeigned love of the brethren, [see that ye] love one another with a pure heart fervently" (1 Peter 1:22), which matches the verse that says, "What shall the end [be] of them that obey not the gospel of God?" (1 Peter 4:17). On top of that, the lost is not about the sins and unbelief alone, for as Paul wrote, "And with all deceivableness of unrighteousness in them that perish; because they received not the love of the truth, that they might be saved" (2 Thessalonians 2:10).

So, worship or acceptance of the Mark is about obedience, of which that is what the Antichrist seeks. Antichrist wants to be obeyed and God disobeyed. Now it is not in all things, but evidently in one particular area of disobeying God, the Antichrist gains the allegiance of exclusive obedience, which is a form of allegiance. In fact, the Antichrist may have a Mark, God has a Seal (Revelation 7:2); Antichrist has a Mark, God has a sign (Exodus 31:17).

Therefore, it is not enough to reject the Mark of the

Beast (Revelation 16:2) as it is to have the Seal of the Living God (Revelation 7:2).

IDENTIFYING MARK #48: MOTHER OF HARLOTS

Revelation 17:5 says, "THE MOTHER OF HARLOTS".

Let us remind everyone that we are looking at two women and that women represent groups of people, either professing to be of God or they are really of God (Jeremiah 6:2, Isaiah 51:16). Judah stands as our example of falling into this category. It was a nation that was supposed to be of God, dedicated to God, even carried the name of God, yet while backsliding into the world, was referred to as, "Judah feared not, but went and played the harlot also" (Jeremiah 3:8). That is alright; Israel did not do much better since "backsliding Israel committed adultery" (Jeremiah 3:8). Translated into today's application, since the Antichrist is in the Christian community, as noted previously, to be the mother church would naturally be the mother of other Christian churches. This does not mean that the Antichrist controls the other churches; it can mean that the other churches recognize the Antichrist as the mother church while independently operating.

This is much like real life, in which a mother may raise a number of daughters, but once they are out on their own, they can independently operate recognizing mother in name only. Usually they go forth doing something that connects them back to mother, like it or not. Obviously it is not the name, as female last names usually change upon marriage, but there is usually some practice that such women, if they would pause and reflect, might say, "Oh my, I'm like my mother!"

IDENTIFYING MARK #49: IS INVOLVED WITH SPIRITUALISM

Revelation 18:2 says "And he cried mightily with a strong voice, saying, Babylon the great is fallen, is fallen, and is become the habitation of devils, and the hold of every foul spirit, and a cage of every unclean and hateful bird."

Notice what foul spirits do, as recorded in Mark 9:25, "When Jesus saw that the people came running together, he rebuked the foul spirit, saying unto him, [Thou] dumb and deaf spirit, I charge thee, come out of him, and enter no more into him." Foul spirits possess people. That alone is a form of spiritualism.

Also, a synonym to "foul spirits" is the phrase "familiar spirits", which we are given council in Leviticus 19:31, "Regard not them that have familiar spirits, neither seek after wizards, to be defiled by them: I [am] the LORD your God." Now how do we get spiritualism from this verse is by looking at a situation involving "foul" or "familiar spirits": "And Saul disguised himself, and put on other raiment, and he went, and two men with him, and they came to the woman by night: and he said, I pray thee, divine unto me by the familiar spirit, and bring me [him] up, whom I shall name unto thee" (1 Samuel 28:8). This woman that Saul sought out practiced "familiar spirits", which seems to bring people back from the dead. That again is spiritualism.

IDENTIFYING MARK #50: ACCEPTS ALL KINDS OF BELIEFS EXCEPT FOR GOD'S

Revelation 18:2 says "And he cried mightily with a strong voice, saying, Babylon the great is fallen, is fallen, and is become the habitation of devils, and the hold of every foul spirit, and a cage of every unclean and hateful bird."

On top of the previous understanding of these words, the phrase "foul spirit" is in the context of something to be avoided, we see another synonym in 1 Timothy 4:1, "Now the Spirit speaketh expressly, that in the latter times some shall depart from the faith, giving heed to seducing spirits, and doctrines of devils." So "foul spirit" or a "seducing spirit" is connected to different doctrines. Different doctrines is not limited to one person believing in sprinkling for baptism while another believes in immersion. Different doctrines can mean the acceptance of other religions. That should sound familiar as the world seems to be chanting, "We all serve the same God!" Really? The same God has conflicting doctrines? The same God treats people differently depending upon which religion it is? And some of them are quite hateful.

Despite the fact that it looks like we are pointing fingers at all the error accepted by many, many Christians, we are "speaking the truth in love" (Ephesians 4:15). Truth has to be revealed because "the truth shall make you free" (John 8:32) and not the acceptance of your belief and other people's beliefs so as to be at peace with one another. We love everyone too much to see anyone burn in hell.

This expanded understanding of "foul spirit" is further encouraged to be correctly understood in this manner, especially as we listen to the words of Jesus, "For false Christs and false prophets shall rise, and shall shew signs and wonders, to seduce, if [it were] possible, even the elect" (Mark 13:22). In the last generation, even the well educated, if it were possible, could be seduced by people falsely representing Christ as well as false preachers or prophets. What could the elect be seduced by? Seductive spirits or doctrines of course.

Paul also wrote in concern of seduction in the last

days, "But evil men and seducers shall wax worse and worse, deceiving, and being deceived" (2 Timothy 3:13), along with John, "These [things] have I written unto you concerning them that seduce you" (1 John 2:26).

Now in searching for the reference of a "cage of every unclean and hateful bird", we come across the verse in Jeremiah 5:27, which says, "As a cage is full of birds, so [are] their houses full of deceit." So the Antichrist would be a cage of all kinds of deception. Keep in mind that the deception is not a human source for "the dragon gave him his power" (Revelation 13:2).

Many people can see through deceptions of entertainment magicians. Many people can see through April Fool's Day pranks. Many people pride themselves on not being able to be deceived by easily by other humans. But that is just it. These doctrinal deceptions are not humanly created. We are up against the devil. Why people think they can go up against these deceptions without consulting God's insight through His Word, the Bible, is beyond me.

We are warned that "Because strait [is] the gate, and narrow [is] the way, which leadeth unto life, and few there be that find it" (Matthew 7:14), and "For there shall arise false Christs, and false prophets, and shall shew great signs and wonders; insomuch that, if [it were] possible, they shall deceive the very elect" (Matthew 24:24). We are even told that "all the world wondered after the beast" (Revelation 13:3), and yet, so many people still fall back on asking, "How can any of this be true? Hardly anyone else sees it this way about the Antichrist!" Exactly our point. That in itself is the fulfillment of the deception. That is how broad these seducing spirits, false doctrines, unclean birds, etc. happens to be. And the deceptions are only getting more and more tougher to see through, especially as non-religious (secular) activity, like the United States happens to be getting involved not only in our country but policing it around the world, as predicted.

So therefore, even this world wide push for unification of all world religions can only be made possible if the Antichrist is first open to being a habitation of these devilish doctrines and foul teachings. Having spirits coming back from the dead, as noted in the previous point, to reinforce these actions also aids in the deception. And as we saw, the only way not to be seduced is to be of the elect, which we already studied out, happens to be Bible believing studious Christians (2 Peter 1:2-11).

Now when we say "worldwide push", again, the United States, as predicted, is well involved policing this unification. Completely unreligious, through laws that even forbid preachers from saying certain references that would cause disunity are on the books incurring jail time.

And the United States is using the United Nations, not by coincidence being located within the United States, to create international laws as well. All of these laws may not be fully enforced, but they will one day, according to the Bible. This is why laws do matter and this current attitude of "What does it matter if a disagreeable law is enacted? it's not like they will really enforce it" in reality does matter.

IDENTIFYING MARK #51: MINISTERS WOULD BE VERY RELIGIOUS

2 Corinthians 11:13 says, "For such [are] false apostles, deceitful workers, transforming themselves into the apostles of Christ."

We can easily tie this verse to the ministers of the Antichrist by looking at the verse very closely. They appear to be apostles of Christ, but the verse states that they are not. Therefore, they are not working for Christ, they are working against Christ. They are Antichrist, just as John wrote, "Ye have heard that Antichrist shall come, even now are there many Antichrists" (1 John 2:18). "For many deceivers are entered into the world, who confess not that Jesus Christ is come in the flesh. This is a deceiver and an Antichrist" (2 John 1:7).

Once again, people have a knee jerk reaction being full of pride. Admittedly, no one wants to be considered having been deceived. We pride ourselves in spotting fakes all through life, not realizing that they are but decoys for the real deception.

The concern is the type of deception that is going on. These are not people who claim to be God or Jesus. Those are too obvious to spot, despite the number of people following them. These are not the ones that even speak contrary to the Bible, although there are plenty of those. These are the most deceptive ones. They have infiltrated denominations so high up that they are considered apostles. That is equivalent to missionaries, but it is also equivalent to the boards at the headquarters of any denomination. That includes conference and parish leaders. In some organizations, there are overseers called bishops.

These deceivers have transformed in all appearances to be as godly or as religious as possible. They can be the church theologians. And the sad part is, we are not looking for the handful that are corrupt in their methods; we are looking for a handful of those that are not corrupt. In fact, it is safe to say that in every denomination, there are more serving Antichrist or the Spirit of Antichrist as there are serving God through His Word. Unfortunately the church members, parishioners, the laity, or whatever name one wants to give to those that listen to these ministers, they simply do not know the standard, the Word of God, well enough to spot any of this, hence why whole congregations are deceived.

These ministers may use the Bible like no others do and can argue every single point they present. They do wonderful works, even giving the shirt right off of their backs. They are the kindest, most helpful ministers anyone would ever meet. Everything they teach is right on target. So what makes them deceptive? It is what they do not teach. They preach justification by faith so much so but leave off living a sanctified life. They will harp and preach and be hardnosed about the commandments between human beings, but ignore the commandments dealing with God, even the one about the Sabbath day. These are the preachers that will sadly fulfill prophecy but it will be too late once they are exposed. "Many will say to me in that day, Lord, Lord, have we not prophesied in thy name? and in thy name have cast out devils? and in thy name done many wonderful works? And then will I profess unto them, I never knew you: depart from me, ye that work iniquity" (Matthew 7:22-23). These are the ministers that we are warned about who are preaching such a comfortable message that tickle the ears and people flock to "for the time will come when they will not endure sound doctrine; but after their own lusts shall they heap to themselves teachers, having itching ears" (2 Timothy 4:3).

This point about the Antichrist appeals to all the Christians out there that see nothing wrong with their denomination, with their minister, even with the unification for the sake of the movement that is just for uniting. To avoid being influenced by the ministers of Antichrist or the ministers not associated with Antichrist but have the "Spirit of Antichrist", we need to stop evaluating ministers on their kindness and patience and only on the words they preach. We need to start digging deeper and find out what they are ignoring, covering up, even twisting a little bit but in a manner that is not detected.

It is no different than a politician that promises all kinds of things that sound so good while ignoring the real issues that once they are elected are unable then to deliver upon their promises and are unable to handle the problems. This is how politicians usually get elected. No one wants to hear about having to fix problems that involve people tightening their belts. The ones that get elected are the ones that promise the world: better education, cuts in taxes, better health care, free college, easier to get the giveaways, etc. Instead, the ones that lose are the ones that run on dealing with crime, dealing with social security falling apart, dealing with road reconstruction, etc.

Unfortunately, when it comes to religion, we only get one vote. If we vote and stick with that decision, the day we realize it was the wrong choice is the day that it will be too late. Eternity shall pass us by. So if the message is too good to be true, it probably is.

The minister that promises eternal life while enjoying the world, while not having to forsake every sin, while not having to contribute financially through the tithing system, that allows any doctrine, should be a wakeup call that Antichrist is involved. Jesus taught obedience is required, but only by a motivation of love (John 14:15). And tithing should not be left undone (Matthew 23:23).

So do not be looking for Antichrist ministers that steal children, secretly rapes and steals, and are full of lies. Rather, they shall be very godly.

IDENTIFYING MARK #52: FOLLOWERS WILL APPEAR RELIGIOUS

Revelation 13:4 says, "And they worshipped the dragon which gave power unto the beast: and they worshipped the beast, saying, Who [is] like unto the beast? who is able to make war with him?" Matthew 7:21-23 says, "Not every one that saith unto me, Lord, Lord, shall enter into the kingdom of heaven; but he that doeth the will of my Father which is in heaven. Many will say to me in that day, Lord, Lord, have we not prophesied in thy name? and in thy name have cast out devils? and in thy name done many wonderful works? And then will I profess unto them, I never knew you: depart from me, ye that work iniquity."

Although we saw the verses in Matthew just a point ago, please note that it also applies to the Antichrist followers. So all the wonderful helpful projects Christians are involved with that appear to be religious, in reality, it is a cover up to the fact that people are still doing iniquity, sinning in other words. So while they are willing to share the gospel, they have not controlled their foul language. While they are part of the committee to fix up houses, they are cracking dirty jokes. While they help around the church, they cannot wait to get home and look at porn.

Now of course these religious people know no better. They have been told that obedience to the Ten Commandments is not necessary and that they may stay as long as they keep coming to church, in other words, they can keep their sins.

And again, Worship is not only attending church or treating a human as being God, it also includes giving unnecessary praise to people. "Oh, what a marvelous man he is…" "Oh, can you believe what he just did…?" "Who else can do something like that?" "We should be more like them!"

IDENTIFYING MARK #53: ESTABLISHES THEIR PRESENCE IN ISRAEL

Daniel 11:45 says, "And he shall plant the tabernacles of his palace between the seas in the glorious holy mountain; yet he shall come to his end, and none shall help him."

What is meant by this reference? The Bible says, "Jerusalem shall be called a city of truth; and the mountain of the LORD of hosts the holy mountain" (Zechariah 8:3). Therefore, the seas in which the land sits between is the Mediterranean Sea and the Dead Sea. Therefore, do not be surprised that the Antichrist establishes a presence in Jerusalem or at least in Israel.

IDENTIFYING MARK #54: WOULD BE A WORLD INFLUENCER

The Bible says, "All the world wondered after the beast".

Now keep in mind that when the Bible says that "All the world", it is figuratively speaking because if it is truly every single soul actually obeying the Antichrist, then Jesus' words would be contradicted. "Upon this rock I will build my church; and the gates of hell shall not prevail against it" (Matthew 16:18). The church is made up of people, and if all people are wondering after the Antichrist then truly Jesus' church would be prevailed over.

So what we have is that like or dislike the Antichrist, the Antichrist will receive world recognition, what is taught will be partially or wholly accepted, and there would be a sufficient number that do wonder after the beast that the number of true Christians would be so hidden that it would be easier to find a needle or a handful of needles in a haystack. At a distance, it would look like nothing more than a hay stack. Only through individual examination of each piece of hay would one eventually start finding needles here or there.

May We Have a Summary of That?

For over fifty pages, we have been elaborating on each point. We have not given our opinion, but we have used the Bible to define the terms that are often assumed to be one thing in the modern language when in fact they mean something else when compared with other verses in the Bible. And although all of us may have known certain definitions without the use of the Bible clarifying it, we also saw the extra detail and categories in which certain points were made. So it is very easy to lose track of all of them and so we are going to just show the conclusion of each of the points for your review purposes.

ID MARK #1:
Antichrist Is NOT Future

ID MARK #2:
Antichrist Is NOT a Single Person

ID MARK #3:
Antichrist Is AGAINST CHRIST, NOT Against Jews

ID MARK #4:
War Against the Doctrines of Jesus Christ

ID MARK #5:
Tradition Above the Bible

ID MARK #6:
Religious Power

ID MARK #7:
Is a Kingdom or Nation

ID MARK #8:
Located In a Populated Area Speaking Many Languages

ID MARK #9:
Denies That Jesus Is the Christ

ID MARK #10:
Denies That Jesus Came In the Flesh

ID MARK #11:
Kills God's Saints

ID MARK #12:
Comes To Full Power After 476 A.D.

ID MARK #13:
Is Located In Europe

ID MARK #14:
Is a Small Nation

ID MARK #15:
Located on Seven Mountains or Hills

ID MARK #16:
Not Just a Political Kingdom

ID MARK #17:
Appear To Be Christian

ID MARK #18:
Removes Three of the Original Ten Kingdoms

ID MARK #19:
Appears Pompous

ID MARK #20:
Would Take On God's Titles

ID MARK #21:
Speaks Blasphemously

ID MARK #22:
Claims To Be God

ID MARK #23:
Claims to Be Able to Forgive Sins

ID MARK #24:
Shall Reign a Prophetic 1,260 Days, 3½ years, or 42 Months

ID MARK #25:
Receives A Deadly Wound

ID MARK #26:
The Deadly Wound is Healed

ID MARK #27:
Will Survive Until the Second Coming

ID MARK #28:
Think to Change the Ten Commandments

ID MARK #29:
Accepts a DifferenT Cycle of Time

ID MARK #30:
Change God's Worship Time

ID MARK #31:
Jesus' Sacrifice Would Be Replaced

ID MARK #32:
God's Sanctuary Service Would Be Replaced

ID MARK #33:
Cast Down the Truth

ID MARK #34:
Causes Christians to Fall Away, Especially From Keeping the Commandments

ID MARK #35:
Rules From What is Considered God's Temple

ID MARK #36:
Exalts Above That Which is Called God

ID MARK #37:
Uses Signs and Wonders

ID MARK #38:
Forbid Marriages

ID MARK #39:
Commands Christians to Abstain from Eating Meat

ID MARK #40:
Based Upon Satan Inspired Religion (Paganism)

ID MARK #41:
Blasphemes the Beings of Heaven

ID MARK #42:
The Number of the Name Being 666

ID MARK #43:
The Antichrist Uses a Symbolic Woman

ID MARK #44:
Colors Used Are Purple and Scarlet

ID MARK #45:
Rich

ID MARK #46:
Assisted by Another Kingdom

ID MARK #47:
Has a Mark (of Allegiance)

ID MARK #48:
Mother of Harlots

ID MARK #49:
Is Involved With Spiritualism

ID MARK #50:
Accepts All Kinds of Beliefs Except for God's

ID MARK #51:
Ministers Would Be Very Religious

ID MARK #52:
Followers Will Appear Religious

ID MARK #53:
Establishes Their Presence in Israel

ID MARK #54:
Would Be a World Influencer

How Does That Compare With the Futuristic Antichrist?

Now, before you dismiss these points and say, "This is not what I have been taught", let us consider what many have been taught and what impact it has on this list. To continue to believe the futuristic theory about the Antichrist,

11. The notion that beasts represent nations must be thrown out because the Antichrist of the future is portrayed as a single mastermind person.

12. The future Antichrist is not so much against Christ or even Christians as his focus is upon the Jews negating all the verses that say otherwise.

13. All the marks that point to the Antichrist being Christian in appearance have to be dismissed because, as the story goes, we are told that the Antichrist is either an atheist or Muslim leader, primarily someone hating Jews.

14. Most importantly, all the verses that speak of Antichrist beginning back in the days of the apostles have to be thrown out because that does not fit the future picture. That also includes the reference that Antichrist is not a single person but many people.

15. On top of that, all the warring and bloodshed references to the saints that stand up for the true doctrines needs to be reinterpreted as massing physical armies to attack the nation of Israel, which inadvertently cancels out the many verses that speak of a doctrinal battle.

16. All the verses related to the Antichrist must be kept on the surface because any secondary or even third level understanding of Bible words reveals way too much that the futuristic Antichrist is nothing but a lie or distraction. For example, keeping "blaspheme" to simply meaning making of crass and arrogant statements against God is keeping it on the surface, while getting the Bible definition of what blasphemy really is happens to reveal that is anyone claiming to forgive sins is also blasphemy.

17. All of the verses describing the activity of the world pretty much has to be ignored, otherwise, it would reveal how much of a Christian focus for the Antichrist and not so much focused upon Israel. Working of miracles and doing wonderful works in the name of Christ just does not fit the picture since Jews do not believe in Jesus Christ.

18. Complete prophecies have to be disjoined so as to fit all the futuristic theories in place, like removing the ten toes from the statue that shows immediate succession of every body part; the removing of the ten horns that come up immediately from the fourth beast in Daniel; and separating the final week of the seventy week time prophecy in Daniel. Without precedence, these objects are detached and thrown into some undefined period of time that has not started yet.

19. The blatant activity of the Antichrist has to be ignored or that reveals again a different focus of attention such as changing times and laws, having not the doctrine of Jesus Christ, casting down the truth, etc.

20. Verses that apply to the activity of Jesus Christ at His first coming must be reinterpreted for the second coming and those of the second coming need to be made to appear as if they apply to the first coming. For example, taking the quiet and meek way of the first coming is described for the

second coming with the belief in the false theory of the secret rapture while the verses stating that Jesus will not keep silent being applied to the time He cleansed the temple.

21. Time prophecies have to become inconsistent in which the final week of prophetic time of the seventy week prophecy is properly interpreted in years using the "day for a year" principle, but when it comes to the forty-two month long reign, it is interpreted incorrectly as literal time.

22. Even unscientific methods are supernaturally applied to the Antichrist person of the future, such as being declared dead and then coming back to life when all supernatural, life giving properties are only God provided, of which the devil cannot mimic.

23. An incorrect standard of counting people's names to add up to 666 has to be implemented to distract from the real person.

24. The interpretation of the second beast, which obviously represents the United States when compared with all the references to the prophetic word "earth" in Revelation, also is made out to appear to be a human of the future.

25. The understanding of women in prophecy has to remain vague, otherwise, seeing it applied to either God's true people or those who claim to be of God's people but are actually backslidden or an apostate group of people begins to point the finger at themselves.

As you can see, it takes a lot of effort to pull off the futuristic theory, but it is easily accepted today by the vast majority of Christians since hardly any Christian reads and studies their Bibles. This is but a small list of the twisting of what we studied to be historically accurate but a futuristically impossible. Interesting enough, as we shall see, the belief of the future Antichrist is based upon a theory that was put forth by the Antichrist power to counteract the finger pointing in the first place. So argue all one wants to in favor of a future Antichrist keeping in mind that we see it as none other than taking marching orders from the Antichrist indirectly being known as the "Spirit of Antichrist".

The Bible even predicts that all of the purposeful twisting of scripture to hide the truth and keep people in darkness would take place. "But of the times and the seasons, brethren, ye have no need that I write unto you. For yourselves know perfectly that the day of the Lord so cometh as a thief in the night. For when they shall say, Peace and safety; then sudden destruction cometh upon them, as travail upon a woman with child; and they shall not escape. But ye, brethren, are not in darkness, that that day should overtake you as a thief. Ye are all the children of light, and the children of the day: we are not of the night, nor of darkness" (1 Thessalonians 5:1-5). Even now do we hear very strongly of creating peace between all religions to have worldwide safety, but it is through keeping people in the dark that once the final events spring upon the world, it takes those in darkness easily captive who will attack those that see these things coming and are trying to make people aware of the truth while there is still opportunity. Basically, those in darkness will eventually think alike, which they are doing more and more each day, and see dissidents working against the world peace movement, the world unity movement, the one acceptable way of practicing religion, stirring up problems like Abel, Joseph, Moses, Joshua, Daniel, even Jesus Himself, and want to put to death those annoying people claiming they have the light of truth and refuse to go along with all of it.

What Do Historic People Say?

Martin Luther, founder of the Lutheran denomination, declared, "We here are of the conviction that the papacy is the seat of the true and real Antichrist", *Faith of Our Fathers*, Vol. 2., pg. 121.

John Calvin, founder of the Presbyterian denomination, declared, "Some persons think us too severe and censorious, when we call the Roman pontiff Antichrist. But those who are of this opinion do not consider that they bring the same charge of presumption against Paul himself, after whom we speak, and whose language we adopt. And lest anyone should object, that we improperly pervert to the Roman pontiff those words of Paul, which belong to a different subject, I shall briefly show that they are not capable of any other interpretation than that which implies them to the papacy", *Institutes of the Christian Religion*.

John Knox, a Scottish Presbyterian, said, "That tyranny which the pope himself has for so many ages exercised over the church. The very Antichrist, and son of perdition, of whom Paul speaks." *The Zurich Letters*, page 199.

Thomas Cranmer, an Anglicans, "Whereof it followeth Rome to be the seat of Antichrist, and the pope to be very Antichrist himself. I could prove the same by many other scriptures, old writers, and strong reasons." *Works by Cranmer,* Vol. 1, pp. 6-7.

Roger Williams, the first Baptist Pastor in America, said, "The pretended Vicar of Christ on earth, who sits as God over the Temple of God, exalting himself not only above all that is called God, but over the souls and consciences of all his vassals, yea over the Spirit of Christ, over the Holy Spirit, yea, and God himself...speaking against the God of heaven, thinking to change times and laws; but he is the son of perdition (II Thess. 2)." *The Prophetic Faith of Our Fathers,* Vol. 3, pg. 52.

The Westminster Confession of Faith contains, "There is no other head of the church but the Lord Jesus Christ. Nor can the pope of Rome in any sense be head thereof; but is that Antichrist, that man of sin and son of perdition that exalteth himself in the church against Christ and all that is called God." *The Creeds of Christendom,* With a History and Critical Notes, III, p. 658, 659, ch. 25, sec. 6.

Cotton Mather, a Congregational Theologian, wrote "The oracles of God foretold the rising of an Antichrist in the Christian Church: and in the Pope of Rome, all the characteristics of that Antichrist are so marvelously answered that if any who read the Scriptures do not see it, there is a marvelous blindness upon them." *The Prophetic Faith of Our Fathers,* Vol. 3, pg. 113.

John Wesley, founder of the Methodist denomination, wrote, "He is in an emphatical sense, the Man of Sin, as he increases all manner of sin above measure. And he is, too, properly styled the Son of Perdition, as he has caused the death of numberless multitudes, both of his opposers and followers... He it is...that exalteth himself above all that is called God, or that is worshipped...claiming the highest power, and highest honour...claiming the prerogatives which belong to God alone." *Antichrist and His Ten Kingdoms,* pg. 110.

But each denomination today hardly refers to such statements. That is because most denominations have been infiltrated by those that do not hold onto the basic premise: "Sola scriptura", Latin for "by Scripture alone". It is the true Protestant Christian doctrine that the Bible is the supreme authority in all matters of doctrine and practice.

How do we know that the denominations are infiltrated? Less than 6% of Christians believe in "Sola scriptura". Among Christians, they declare that the Bible is an old and impractical book, full of fables, good lessons to learn from but not very practical overall, written by male dominated opinions, and just erroneous in general.

Basically, the Bible declares that an entity would arise who will cause "a falling away first" (2 Thessalonians 2:3) from God's ways through His Word, "abideth not in the doctrine of Christ" (2 John 1:9), "think to change times and laws" (Daniel 7:25), having "all the world wondered after" (Revelation 13:3) it in thought or to "have one mind, and shall give their power and strength unto" (Revelation 17:13) them by thinking the same way, so as to "opposeth and exalteth himself above all that is called God, or that is worshipped; so that he as God sitteth in the temple of God, shewing himself that he is God" (2 Thessalonians 2:4). And all those that declare, "I'm not a Catholic!" are actually worse because they have the "[spirit] of Antichrist" (1 John 4:3), which is to be against what Christ taught on a more individual basis. To call oneself a Christian while rejecting the teachings of Christ as contained in the Bible, is basically working against Christ. In fact, the very thing that Protestants fought against, making up beliefs outside of the Bible teachings, is the very thing most Christians do today. Therefore, they may say they are a Methodist, a Lutheran, an Episcopalian, or other denomination, but to reject the full authority of the Bible is to be Catholic.

Now as it is, God nor we are against Catholics. We are against Catholic teachings and especially supposed Protestant teachings that are not supported by the Bible. A Protestant by definition is one who Protests against the fact that beliefs are not found in the Bible or are even directly opposed to the Bible teaching. Further, we are against anyone's thought that they can stay with such organizations, being fed week after week the contradictory messages and are calling as God calls, "Come out of her, my people, that ye be not partakers of her sins" (Revelation 18:4). Today, one cannot remain a true Christian by staying in these Antichrist denominations or many of the Protestant ones either. It is time to have "one mind [and] one mouth glorify God, even the Father of our Lord Jesus Christ" (Romans 15:6).

To dismiss this book and especially all the founders quotations as just some simple misunderstanding is not only a wrong opinion, it is a conscious effort to reject the requirements of the true gospel. It is to have "received not the love of the truth, that they might be saved" (2 Thessalonians 2:10). It is to "profess that they know God; but in works they deny [him], being abominable, and disobedient, and unto every good work reprobate" (Titus 1:16). "He that saith, I know him, and keepeth not his commandments, is a liar, and the truth is not in him" (1 John 2:4).

On the contrary, "If ye abide in me, and my words abide in you, ye shall ask what ye will, and it shall be done unto you" (John 15:7). "Therefore whosoever heareth these sayings of mine, and doeth them, I will liken him unto a wise man, which built his house upon a rock" (Matthew 7:24). "If a man love me, he will keep my words: and my Father will love him, and we will come unto him, and make our abode with him" (John 14:23). "Blessed [are] they which are called unto the marriage supper of the Lamb. And he saith unto me, These are the true sayings of God" (Revelation 19:9).

So, now how has the Protestants moved from knowing who the Antichrist was to holding a position in which they are uncertain but they know the Antichrist is not here and now but points to a future Antichrist? That is what is meant by the infiltration. With the heat of the early 1500's from Martin Luther successfully pointing the finger at the true Antichrist and going as far as gaining many in Germany to also see it, so much so that even Germany's King Fredrick III protected Martin Luther from the papists, with purposeful intent, the papacy sat out to counteract the Lutheran message. Therefore, to dismiss these events as a mere accident in thinking is to resist the working of the Holy Spirit. This is not a simple misunderstanding. This was truly purposeful intent by the Antichrist to be able to continue working against Christ because the system is not really Christian. They are "false prophets, which come to you in sheep's clothing, but inwardly they are ravening wolves" (Matthew 7:15).

Therefore, the papists tried to figure out how they can continue when such evidence was so strongly pointing the finger drawing a guilty verdict. Instead of honestly sitting down with Martin Luther and other reformers, not by coincidence, the papacy or Vatican set forth a series of meetings creating what is known as the counter reformation theology. If the papists were in favor of souls, they would have had a big Bible study, but instead, the Bible was treated as if it had no authority; Martin Luther was a heretic; and the papists wanted him dead. So with intent of making the Bible fit a different picture of Antichrist, a new theology was being created counter to the Protestant reformation of getting back to the Bible. They knew that to give in a this point would mean that everything would go. All power would be lost.

Take for instance the many characteristics and contrasts. There is the pope who has been carried around, lives in an expensive facility, has people waiting on him, decked out in expensive garb including different forms of jewelry, having his hand kissed by rulers of nations. Then there is Jesus, who washed people's feet (John 13:5), had no place to lay His head (Matthew 8:20), was of the working class or a peasant (Mark 6:3), and submitted to the rulers of the day (John 18:33, Acts 8:32). The pope rules an earthly kingdom, so much so that he could send many into the crusades, when Jesus said, "My kingdom is not of this world" (John 18:36), and it still is not. His earthly kingdom comes after the second coming.

And so, just like the leaders in Jesus' day, which said, "If we let him thus alone, all [men] will believe on him" (John 11:48), and "it is expedient for us, that one man should die for the people" (John 11:50). Therefore, they resisted negotiating their position and accept the Bible doctrines. They did not want anyone trying to discover all the biblical truths that for over a thousand years were covered up by tradition. From 1545 through 1563, the cardinals, special groups, and the pope met in what is called the Council of Trent to hammer out the process of diffusing the reformation. Agreed upon was to charge the newly formed order, called the Jesuits, which were founded in 1540, to act as spies and infiltrators. Their priority was and is the preservation of the papacy, no matter what it takes. Under the disguise of being a religious body, the Jesuit order was and is also a political arm of the Vatican. They are not only minister's in the church, not only teachers in the schools, but they are also political operatives.

An example of such activity is found in this reference at *Wikipedia*. "On 12 March 1977, Rutilio Grande, a Jesuit priest and personal friend of Romero who had been creating self-reliance groups among the poor, was assassinated." It is not uncommon that many of the assassinated priests over the years, around the world, are because of retaliations for the undermining that goes on. That is because the Jesuit order is a political machine, who are also not above carrying out their own assassinations.

According to the Bible, we need to stop looking at the papacy, the Vatican, the Jesuits as just another religious organization no different than another denomination or other world religion. According to the Bible, as we already have been exposed to in the points above, it is a political and religious body. Further, most Catholics are unaware that they are part of such a religious-political system and are just thinking that they are loving Jesus with all of their hearts. That is because it is not the congregation of people that is the issue. They were just commandeered. The Vatican is using the Catholic Church as a disguise for it is hard to keep out such from any country or that country would be accused of not supporting religious freedom. Well, some countries do go that far but are even feeling the pressure, especially, not by chance, by the United States. Why else do you think there is a lightening up of religious beliefs in China, for example? Pressure from the United States and those behind the United States.

As all political powers are concerned, the goal is to take over the world, to capture all power, and wealth. It is hard to believe that such a system like the Vatican is interested in power, control, and wealth over souls, but that is what the Bible describes. The Vatican is not by accident.

It is a purposeful intent to further the system, but overall, the very religious appearance once again, is an identifying mark. Basically, it is part of the grand deception. How can such a sweet looking person who appears to honestly be concerned in the welfare of humans be part of the Antichrist? This is especially true of the current pope who seems to be working against the wishes of the Cardinals, but it is all a disguise. Well, congratulations to those that cannot see past the disguise, sarcastically speaking. That is how deceptive all of this is. Remember, the deception is marvelously masterminded because it is not human. The power is of the devil (Revelation 13:2).

So, out of the Council of Trent was born two ideas. One idea was called preterism. This is the belief that all of the prophecies regarding the Antichrist were fulfilled by ancient Rome with the ultimate Antichrist being Nero.

The other theory that was rejected as a Catholic belief but was sent out into the Protestant world to create confusion was the theory of futurism. "The futurist view was first proposed by two Catholic Jesuit writers, Manuel Lacunza and Francisco Ribera. Lacunza wrote under the pen name 'Ben-Ezra.'" Take a moment and find a copy of Ribera's writings on futurism and see what similarities there are with modern futurism that most Protestants believe. One will find it remarkably too much like a game plan to undo the reformation. Interestingly though, it would actually not be accepted by Protestants until around the 1900's, of which would become the current theology of most Protestants, or should we say, Evangelicals. So in other words, all the people who dismiss the historic representation of these prophecies that were acknowledge by most of the original church denominational founders is actually believing the interpretation the Antichrist released. And the Antichrist does not care if you believe in preterism, which is what a good Catholic is to believe in, or if you believe in futurism. All they want to have happen is that people would stop seeing historicism, and the world pretty much has, so much so that to be a believer in historicism is to be anti-Catholic, a bigot, a peace breaker, or one "that troubleth Israel" (1 Kings 18:17), like Elijah who faced the harlot of his day known as Israel's wife of King Ahab, Jezebel.

In fact, studying the events of Elijah dealing with backslidden Israel is pretty much a spiritual fulfillment with true Christians being against the Antichrist or erroneous doctrines.

But overall, this is why God can say, "all the world wondered after the beast" (Revelation 13:3). Instead of allowing the Bible to be the interpreter of prophecy, like we have shared, the world follows the marching orders of the Antichrist. On top of that, most denominations actually are being influenced by Jesuits without even knowing it. On top of that, many in congress and even in the White House have attended Jesuit run schools, like George Town, though the attendees being Protestant, have been influenced by the Jesuit way.

And why do theologians from other denominations not see this? As stated a moment ago, since the Bible is not the standard and are playing the "Spirit of Antichrist", such denominations are actually infiltrated, not by a few, but by many of the Jesuit order. Everything that Martin Luther and early reformers protested about is practiced in just about every non-Catholic denomination. Truly the "Spirit of Antichrist" has taken over. The beliefs are not wholly supported by the Bible; improper study happens on a regular basis where people pit one verse against another instead of looking for the harmony of all scriptures; outright lies are perpetrated by twisting the scriptures; and there is plenty of power struggle and greed to fuel it all. So again, "Come out of her, my people, that ye be not partakers of her sins, and that ye receive not of her plagues" (Revelation 18:4).

Why Are There Not More People Who See This?

The bottom line is selfishness. What we are experiencing among Christians is the fulfillment of 2 Timothy 4:3-4, "For the time will come when they will not endure sound doctrine; but after their own lusts shall they heap to themselves teachers, having itching ears; And they shall turn away [their] ears from the truth, and shall be turned unto fables." Most Christians, if they follow any rules, obey them grudgingly. We hear it in the conversations: "I'm not allowed to do that anymore." "I can't go there anymore." "I..." and fill in the blank of what they are missing out on. Instead of realizing that they have been saved from sin disguised as entertainment and fun, they look at all the things they cannot do anymore. So when a preacher comes along quoting only a certain imbalanced view of the Bible offering a little allowance in certain things, then the listeners, without consulting the Bible through deep study, latch onto it, especially where a good covering through carefully constructed wording ends up calling "evil good, and good evil; that put darkness for light, and light for darkness; that put bitter for sweet, and sweet for bitter" (Isaiah 5:20). They say that it is evil to stand for the truth or believe in a single truth and it is good to compromise because Jesus loves everyone, which is intentionally mixing up love and ignoring judgment. It is evil to stay strict to one's beliefs while avoiding unholy family gatherings by saying, "No religion is right if it puts religion above the family." It is evil to stay true to God's Word while it is good to make associations with the forbidden, opening the door to go to questionable events, do questionable things, all to stay being friends with people.

God clearly says, "The LORD [is] longsuffering, and of great mercy, forgiving iniquity and transgression, and by no means clearing [the guilty], visiting the iniquity of the fathers upon the children unto the third and fourth [generation]" (Numbers 14:18). So, although God is loving and is willing to forgive and forget all the sins a person has committed upon sincere repentance and confession, He will not clear those that choose to stay sinning, "will by no means clear [the guilty]" (Exodus 34:7), and therefore "whosoever was not found written in the book of life was cast into the lake of fire" (Revelation 20:15). It may sound religiously good that God's love for everyone prevents Him from destroying a single person, but God is balanced. And "God cannot be tempted with evil" (James 1:13) meaning, we cannot trick Him with a false confession. This is where God has an advantage over human beings. "Search me, O God, and know my heart: try me, and know my thoughts: And see if [there be any] wicked way in me, and lead me in the way everlasting" (Psalms 139:23-24). He can read the heart, the intent; humans cannot.

So, if people are promised eternal life and do not have to follow the rules, why not? These preachers then start becoming popular and trusted simply because they claim to be a Christian preacher, but we are told, "Beware of false prophets, which come to you in sheep's clothing, but inwardly they are ravening wolves" (Matthew 7:15). However, it does not stop there. To outdo one another in popularity, other preachers relax the rules and so people flock to them now. And before one knows it, Christianity becomes a pit of sin, a disgrace, as was predicted. "This know also, that in the last days perilous times shall come. For men shall be lovers of their own selves, covetous, boasters, proud, blasphemers, disobedient to parents, unthankful, unholy, Without natural affection, trucebreakers, false accusers, incontinent, fierce, despisers of those that are good, Traitors, heady, highminded, lovers of pleasures more than lovers of God; Having a form of godliness, but denying the power thereof: from such turn away" (2 Timothy 3:1-5).

Since Jesus said, "Wherefore by their fruits ye shall know them" (Matthew 7:20), just look at what "once saved, always saved" has lead to. The belief that a person on a certain day claims to be saved and cannot be lost by any future choices leads easily to the fruit of carelessness. No one has to be serious about lifestyle if they are going to Heaven anyways. So Christians then begin to enjoy more and more of what the world offers and less and less true godliness is practiced. More and more focus is on kindness and less and less is on true love, which may not be the kind thing to do. For instance, it may not be kind to grab a person by the arm and yank them backwards, but it may be the loving thing to do if they were unconsciously stepping off a curb right in the path of an oncoming vehicle.

The sad part of this corrupting theology is that each subsequent generation takes it a step further and further into sin, so much so that, as stated before, the Christian radio stations pretty much are the same as non-Christian radio stations. The church service is one big entertainment mess. The activities between Christians and non-Christians are the same, including illicit sexual activity. And much more.

Therefore, to believe in the fact that the papacy is the historical, present, and future Antichrist means that all of the anti Christ or anti Christian activity needs to cease. Specifically, when Antichrist throws the scriptures down in favor of tradition, that means that Christ expects us to "Search the scriptures; for in them ye think ye have eternal life" (John 5:39), but hardly any Christians wants to do a Bible study, let alone stand up against scientifically proven evolution, which is not scientifically proven for it is only a theory. That means that the rules spoken of in the Bible still apply, and many of those rules interfere with the enjoyment of the average Christian. For instance, in the strictest sense, all exposure to evil visually and audibly ought to be avoided as far as possible. That means televisions, movies, and most music should be discarded from the home, just as preached in the early 1900's, but the average Christian not only allows it, they don't stop at the appropriate point and even go all the way claiming, "I'm adult enough to view porn!" So an ambiguous future Antichrist is more pleasant because the future one is all about physical wars instead of spiritual battles against sin.

Now let us go a step further. To accept the correct understanding of the Antichrist, who has thought to change the Ten Commandments, means that Christ's Ten Commandments are still required despite being saved by grace. As predicted, preachers today have been fulfilling another prophecy. "For there are certain men crept in unawares, who were before of old ordained to this condemnation, ungodly men, turning the grace of our God into lasciviousness, and denying the only Lord God, and our Lord Jesus Christ" (Jude 1:4). And nothing turns grace upside down from the original intent by teaching that grace wipes out all your past sins and allows people to continue sinning. That surely sounds good to the unconverted.

Let us go even further. Another anti Christ activity is to think that it has changed Christ's times. We say that it is Christ's time, because "All things were made by him; and without him was not any thing made that was made" (John 1:3). And Him refers to Christ.

As stated before, there are only two "times" that is set in motion that, not by coincidence, the papacy has altered and will be shown in a moment. That includes God's reckoning of the days from sundown to sundown as well as the fourth commandment identifying specifically an entire day being kept holy from sundown on Friday to sundown on Saturday, which is God's Sabbath day, established before a single Jew walked the earth (Genesis 2:1-3). It was not only established before sin entered the world, but when all of this is over, "It shall come to pass, [that] from one new moon to another, and from one sabbath to another, shall all flesh come to worship before me, saith the LORD" (Isaiah 66:23). So who in their right mind wants to keep an entire day to God when we live in a society that is twenty-four hours a day and seven days a week? Football games would be affected, yard sales would be missed, weekend partying would be interfered with, and much more.

So in naming but three of the many activities of the Antichrist, that if the Antichrist is so busy trying to make it appear as things have changed, in itself establishes the fact that they have not changed. Therefore, all true Christians unaffected by Antichrist or the "Spirit of Antichrist" ought to be into their Bibles, into keeping the commandments, and into keeping the Sabbath. If they are not doing such and care not to change, they are affected by the Antichrist or the "Spirit of Antichrist" and will be lost, hence our plea again, "Come out of her, my people, that ye be not partakers of her sins, and that ye receive not of her plagues" (Revelation 18:4). And, "turn ye, turn ye from your evil ways; for why will ye die?" (Ezekiel 33:11).

Therefore, it is not a matter of not believing what has been presented thus far, it is about the selfish heart that needs to be circumcised (Romans 2:29). "Then said Jesus unto his disciples, If any [man] will come after me, let him deny himself, and take up his cross, and follow me" (Matthew 16:24). And denial is something unheard of today in Christianity because of the fear of being works oriented. To that, James wrote, "Yea, a man may say, Thou hast faith, and I have works: shew me thy faith without thy works, and I will shew thee my faith by my works" (James 2:18). We need to "Submit yourselves therefore to God. Resist the devil, and he will flee from you" (James 4:7). And how much effort does it take to be in submission? Paul wrote, "Ye have not yet resisted unto blood, striving against sin" (Hebrews 12:4). "Enter ye in at the strait gate: for wide [is] the gate, and broad [is] the way, that leadeth to destruction, and many there be which go in thereat: Because strait [is] the gate, and narrow [is] the way, which leadeth unto life, and few there be that find it" (Matthew 7:13-14.

In short, self is in the way, which brings up one final point. This entire book is not about pointing out the Antichrist or even the Spirit of Antichrist happens to be. It is not about revealing the Mark of the Beast nor showing how the United States is assisting the beast. All of it is about the influence upon people and is ultimately dying to self. As Paul wrote, "I protest by your rejoicing which I have in Christ Jesus our Lord, I die daily" (1 Corinthians 15:31). All the knowledge is not going to save anyone. It is dealing with what we want to do, when we want, and however we want. All of that needs to die, and as long as self is alive, then none of this is believable. When self is dead, then all of it is not only believable, but the eyes shall see a whole lot more.

How Do These Points Apply To the Real Antichrist?

First, let us begin with addressing the possible shock. If you are like, even myself, it becomes both surprising and overwhelming. It was very surprising since my goal in life was to become a Catholic priest, being born and raised very much Catholic and even was more devout than anyone I knew, including the priests and nuns. When I was exposed to this truth, I chose the way of submission realizing that my entire world was turned upside down. Everything I thought that was being devout to Christ was actually devout to Antichrist and against Christ. There was going to be a lot of changes required to become a devout Christian instead of a devout Catholic, a devout Christ follower of what Christ commanded and taught as opposed to the teachings and commands from the Antichrist. And believe me, there are obvious choices that satisfy only one and not the other.

Now others take a different approach to dealing with what was just exposed. They think that if they are successful at undoing just one of the fifty plus points that somehow it removes the guilty verdict of being the Antichrist away from the Vatican and puts it upon something yet unrevealed. Such people may be successful in undoing a point or two, but that is only in their own minds. They are exercising the same power that the Antichrist is using: "think to change" and not "actually change". These points are quite clearly using the Bible as the definitions and not human logic. Further, we are not talking about removing one peg from the list of five; we are talking about a list of over fifty. The astronomical calculation for any entity to satisfy forty-nice out of fifty is proof that only twisting of God's meaning on that fiftieth point is off in the human mind. Not only would forty-nine out of fifty be hard to stand up in a courtroom to allow the defender, the Vatican, off the hook, it would be equally difficult to dismiss the Vatican from being guilty even if only forty-eight points match, forty-seven, forty-six, or even forty-five. Anyone that tries to argue the innocence of the Vatican is just purposefully rejecting the Bible and God Himself.

God specifically states timelines, appearances, activities, influences, assistance, and more in detail that all match the Vatican. What people have unfortunately done is wave around only about three or four known items to describe the Antichrist, declared that they are the only items, and since they are so vague, they could apply to any entity. They look for the name being 666, powerful person that hates Israel and can mass an army against them, but first makes a covenant and then breaks it after the temple has been rebuilt in which he sits in and plays God. Therefore, the public, including atheistic movies, all focus upon 666, when in fact, that is just an ancillary reference. It is important but not as important as to what is portrayed. All of "This is a deceiver and an Antichrist" (2 John 1:7) or at least the "Spirit of Antichrist" (1 John 4:3). So please do not let pride get in the way. Please do not even allow unbelief and feelings get in the way. Treat this like a court case where at the very least, certain points may have not been as clear as you may have wanted them, but the weight of the evidence demands a guilty verdict on well over ninety percent of the counts.

There is absolutely no way that a future Antichrist could get, shall we say, this lucky to hit so many points. Take any ten points and you will probably will never discover in history any nation to have come so close to just ten. Again, we have shown over fifty points of which a reasonable person cannot argue them all away.

And for those that say, "Well, I'm not going to worry about all of this. I'm a good person and I am just going to keep to myself" or just continue as is with a personal relationship with God, be careful. Do you know who is actually going to hell? "But the fearful, and unbelieving, and the abominable, and murderers, and whoremongers, and sorcerers, and idolaters, and all liars, shall have their part in the lake which burneth with fire and brimstone: which is the second death" (Revelation 21:8). Do you see the second item? The unbelieving is in the list! That is not just one who does not believe in Jesus, for He said, "If ye continue in my word, [then] are ye my disciples indeed" (John 8:31). Also listen to Jesus parable of how believing the Word is just as important as believing in Jesus, "Now the parable is this: The seed is the word of God. Those by the way side are they that hear; then cometh the devil, and taketh away the word out of their hearts, lest they should believe and be saved. They on the rock [are they], which, when they hear, receive the word with joy; and these have no root, which for a while believe, and in time of temptation fall away" (Luke 8:11-13). So thinking one is alright in remaining neutral is not an option. Part of the reason is that we then ignore the fact that there is a code of conduct that the Antichrist has hidden or made appear as a change that is to be in our own lives. Continuing to go to church on Sunday, for instance, is still supporting the Antichrist even if you are not caught up in all of this Antichrist stuff or not even Catholic.

If it sounds like we are pressing the same appeal over and over, if it appears that we are being very strong in declaring that it is time to come out of the association with most Protestant/Evangelical churches as well as the Catholic Church itself, it is because we, or more specially, I do not want to see you lost. There is no way one should be lost. "God sent not his Son into the world to condemn the world; but that the world through him might be saved" (John 3:17), but realize something, though He has not been sent to condemn, He does follow up with, "This is the condemnation, that light is come into the world, and men loved darkness rather than light, because their deeds were evil" (John 3:19). Therefore, to stay in darkness on purpose, not to acknowledge that this is the truth and obey it, God does not condemn, we condemn ourselves. His hand will be forced to condemn the people remaining in darkness on purpose to hell in the end, but right now, neither I nor God is condemning anyone. We are inviting people to escape into salvation. So I have not written this to condemn Catholics. I have not written this to condemn Protestants who have given up the protest. I have written this for the saving of souls! Not only that, but it is with the urgency because already the Vatican, through the pope, is making the final moves. It is very likely that we may actually live to see the true Christ put Antichrist in its place. "The fifth angel poured out his vial upon the seat of the beast; and his kingdom was full of darkness; and they gnawed their tongues for pain, And blasphemed the God of heaven because of their pains and their sores, and repented not of their deeds" (Revelation 16:10-11).

So now, let us look at each of the points and weigh the evidence, which they even admit to, so as to see for ourselves that truly the Vatican is guilty of being a political machine seeking power and recognition while using the Catholic Church as a religious disguise allowing them to establish outposts in every country along with deceiving innocent people to continue to repeat the lies and untruths as compared to all the truths that Christ established. In other words, we are going to reveal how the Vatican is truly against Christ being Antichrist.

IDENTIFYING MARK #1: ANTICHRIST IS NOT FUTURE

This point can apply to just about any historical entity, but keep in mind, we are just applying identifying marks to whom it has been concluded as the Vatican and though it is broad, we have to ask, does it apply? Did the Vatican ever exist in history or does it exist today? Though they are silly questions, the answer is yes to both. The Vatican also identified as the papacy and even popery is a historical institution and a present one at that. Further, according to the Catholic Encyclopedia, New Advent, they claim to trace the papacy, series of popes, all the way back to the Apostle Peter.

IDENTIFYING MARK #2: ANTICHRIST IS NOT A SINGLE PERSON

Using the same reference, Peter was not the only pope, according to the Catholic Church. Including Peter, there have been 266 popes to present Pope Francis. Truly that is not a single person. Further, the Antichrist is not made up of just the line of popes, remember, the Antichrist is a nation. The Vatican is the Antichrist with the pope speaking for it. So the real question is, in regards to the Vatican, is it made up of just the pope, or are their others involved? Of course the answer is the latter one.

From the Catholic weekly publication called, The Sothern Cross, it is stated that the Pope has a cabinet made up of Cardinals and other staff that comprises the Vatican.

IDENTIFYING MARK #3: ANTICHRIST IS AGAINST CHRIST, NOT AGAINST JEWS

Although the Vatican and the Jews have not always had a favorable relationship, Jews are not the focus of the Vatican. As an example, Christ established the church upon Himself, where the Vatican twists a verse in the Bible to make Peter the first Pope. When Jesus said, "That thou art Peter, and upon this rock I will build my church; and the gates of hell shall not prevail against it" (Matthew 16:18), Jesus established that Peter, seated away from Christ with the use of the word "Thou", is but a mere pebble, which is the meaning of the name Peter. Peter is but a human. So, Jesus is doing a comparison here. "Peter, your name is pebble, but I am going to build my church upon the Rock." Christ, with the word "this" referred to Himself, the speaker, to declare that He was the Rock, not Peter.

Besides, the gates of hell prevailed against Peter on a number of occasions. There was the whole denying being associated with Christ not once or twice but three times (Matthew 26:75), although some would argue that the words were for after Peter was converted (Luke 22:32). However, then there was Peter's prejudice (Galatians 2:11-13), which was well after His conversion. Any time a person sins, Satan has prevailed, even temporarily, because through confession, we are restored.

And no sooner did Jesus finish the famous verse of Matthew 16:18 that then Jesus "turned, and said unto Peter, Get thee behind me, Satan: thou art an offence unto me: for thou savourest not the things that be of God, but those that be of men" (Matthew 16:23). So the gates of hell prevailed right at the same discussion setting.

Therefore, by declaring the beginning of popery from Peter on forward, the Vatican already has gone against Christ on this point, and other points, and is attempting to have, not just the Jews, but all Christians, and in fact, all the world to accept the pope as head of all religious matters is the focus. For that matter, even political issues should get the blessing of the Vatican.

And just to settle the confusion about that verse on building the church upon Jesus, the Bible says, "That Rock was Christ" (1 Corinthians 10:4). In fact, when it comes to such a relationship, no human being has ever been given that much responsibility. "The LORD [is] my rock, and my fortress, and my deliverer" (2 Samuel 22:2, Psalms 18:2), and not human beings. "He only [is] my rock and my salvation" (Psalms 62:2, 6). And directly stated, "Now therefore ye are no more strangers and foreigners, but fellowcitizens with the saints, and of the household of God; And are built upon the foundation of the apostles and prophets, Jesus Christ himself being the chief corner [stone]" (Ephesians 2:19-20). The cornerstone or rock is what the house of God or church is built upon while the apostles make up the mere foundation, and over the generations, others have built upwards.

Now how the foundation was laid and how we continue even today to build up the church that is built upon Christ, the Bible says, "The spirits of the prophets are subject to the prophets" (1 Corinthians 14:32). All the writers were prophets. If anyone is impressed to speak in the name of God or write something in the name of God, even though not a prophet, like this book, the Bible says, "To the law and to the testimony: if they speak not according to this word, [it is] because [there is] no light in them" (Isaiah 8:20). Therefore, all teachings have to be in harmony with the Bible. They first have to be in harmony with Christ and then in harmony with the foundation through the writings of Matthew, Mark, Luke, John, Paul, and Jude, the New Testament writers for the New Testament Church, but since "Jesus Christ the same yesterday, and to day, and for ever" (Hebrews 13:8), the Old Testament should not be ignored either. If the teachings are not in harmony, it is to be rejected.

So truly, the Vatican is not after Jews, it is after the world, working against what Christ has established.

IDENTIFYING MARK #4: WAR AGAINST THE DOCTRINES OF JESUS CHRIST

This point asks the question, "Are their doctrines of the Catholic Church as published by the Vatican and the pope contradictory to those in the Bible? Of course there are a number of doctrines that fit this, but one could argue that other denominations also have the same issue. That may be true, but no other denomination is a country. So let us examine just a handful to see if they have at least one doctrine contrary to the Bible.

Jesus Christ said, "Call no [man] your father upon the earth: for one is your Father, which is in heaven" (Matthew 23:9). Although the Bible also uses the word "father" and "fathers" to refer to relatives in a parental view point here on earth, that is not what Jesus was referring to. By stating that only God the Father is Our Father, that puts it in a religious context. And so, the doctrine of labeling priests as fathers and the pope as the "holy father" is one doctrinal example. These titles are found via the Catholic organization known as Catholic Answers.

Jesus Christ said, "When ye pray, use not vain repetitions, as the heathen [do]: for they think that they shall be heard for their much speaking" (Matthew 6:7), yet the Vatican teaches that Catholics ought to be literally repeating the prayer called the "Our Father" as well as a prayer called the "Hail Mary". In fact, after confessing one's sins to a priest, another doctrine that is most definitely against Christ, it is common to be told to go and perform an act of penance by praying ten Hail Mary's or even an entire rosary containing over fifty of them. God does not listen to such prayers. He wants regular conversations. He even labels such people as heathens, hence why we are trying to inform everyone that is just as guilty as I was to cease such prayers and pray real communicative prayers from the heart.

The Bible says, "Then Joseph being raised from sleep did as the angel of the Lord had bidden him, and took unto him his wife: And knew her not till she had brought forth her firstborn son: and he called his name JESUS" (Matthew 1:24-25). Read carefully the words about Joseph "knowing" Mary. In other words, Jesus was born and afterwards, Joseph and Mary had as much sex as any other couple would have, although many couples have sex during pregnancy, Joseph refrained. Yet the Vatican doctrine states that Mary was always a virgin, hence the reference "Virgin Mary" when referred to her.

The Bible says, "[There is] one God, and one mediator between God and men, the man Christ Jesus" (1 Timothy 2:5), yet the Vatican's doctrine states that we ought to be praying to Mary and the saints. The direct line through Jesus Christ is supposedly being intercepted first by another level, and that is wrong. We have a direct line to Jesus without Mary or the saints getting involved.

The Bible teaches in numerous places, as already stated in another point, that the word "saints" refers to living and breathing true believers, yet the Vatican's doctrine is that the a person has to go through them and their process of canonization after they are dead and must have done recognizable saint quality activities and be voted into this small membership.

The Bible teaches "Thou shalt not make unto thee any graven image, or any likeness [of any thing] that [is] in heaven above, or that [is] in the earth beneath, or that [is] in the water under the earth: Thou shalt not bow down thyself to them, nor serve them: for I the LORD thy God [am] a jealous God, visiting the iniquity of the fathers upon the children unto the third and fourth [generation] of them that hate me; And shewing mercy unto thousands of them that love me, and keep my commandments" (Exodus 20:4-6). On the other side, the Vatican has promoted the use of statues and other objects claiming that it is no different than the Ark of the Covenant. First, it was only several objects, unlike the numerous objects blessed by the Vatican or the church system it uses, assuming one includes the tables and the candle holders from the temple where the ark was, but do keep in mind that God Himself commanded them to be made. God has not commanded objects to be made since then. Further, none of the objects were ever prayed to as is different in the Catholic Church. Even the use of the excuse that they are but a reminder and not actually being prayed to does not hold up because many statues are kissed, being a form of worship, and many carry an object that treating it like a "good luck" charm, like a Christopher's metal for safe travel. Without such in the car, hanging from the rearview mirror, hanging around someone's neck, or sitting on the dashboard, it is believed that people are taking a risk when they hit the road. That is worship of an object instead of God.

Now this small list is not being nitpicky. Without going into detail on more of the major doctrines brought out below, this should suffice to see truly that the Vatican does promote doctrines different than what Jesus taught and what is contained in the Bible fulfilling this point.

IDENTIFYING MARK #5: TRADITION ABOVE THE BIBLE

Jesus said, "If ye continue in my word, [then] are ye my disciples indeed" (John 8:31) while the Vatican declares, according to Catholic Answers, entitled Scripture and Tradition, it states "To the successors of the apostles, sacred Tradition hands on in its full purity God's word, which was entrusted to the apostles by Christ the Lord and the Holy Spirit." In other words, traditions that the Vatican makes up that are in conflict with the Bible supersede the Bible's authority. So the teachings of Jesus can be and have been undone by "sacred tradition".

IDENTIFYING MARK #6: RELIGIOUS POWER

The question of the Antichrist being a religious power is a bit obvious that no research has to be done, however, officially from the Vatican according to the Encyclical Of Pope Leo XIII, point 13 declares that the Church, referring to themselves, holds to "the principle of civil and religious power is one and the same".

IDENTIFYING MARK #7: IS A KINGDOM OR NATION

According to Catholic Answers, the question, "Is the Vatican really a country?" is answered as "Yes". All of the things that make it a nation are also in place, according to the details in their answer. "It operates, among other things, a mint, a post office, an astronomical observatory, and a world-class radio station, and it administers a legal system, although in criminal matters (such as the assassination attempt against the pope) Italian courts have jurisdiction."

IDENTIFYING MARK #8: LOCATED IN A POPULATED AREA SPEAKING MANY LANGUAGES

Again, we need to rely on observance. So, is the Vatican located in the middle of the desert, in the middle of an ice continent, or in the great forests of many different nations? No, of course not. It is located inside of the city of Rome, a very populated location in the world, which is inside of a country called Italy, also very populated, which is inside the continent of Europe, also very populated.

In regards to the languages, the Vatican uses Italian, English, French, German, and Spanish, Latin, Portuguese, Chinese, and Arabic. Further, being surrounded by so many nations, there are definitely a multitude of languages around, unlike Australia, Canada, even the United States, though there is more than one language spoken in each of them.

IDENTIFYING MARK #9: DENIES THAT JESUS IS THE CHRIST

As discussed prior and only summarized here, this point is not about denying the physical presence of Jesus. This is not even denying that He was "God with us" (Matthew 1:23). This is "turning the grace of our God into lasciviousness, and denying the only Lord God, and our Lord Jesus Christ." (Jude 1:4).

So, what doctrine goes against the Bible teaching of grace that permits people to continue to sin? According to the outlet called Catholic Answers, they have an article called, What is it and What It Does. In the article, we are told that there are two categories of grace: sanctifying and actual. The teaching compares a person on land being instantly transported to the bottom of the sea. Without the necessary equipment, that person would die trying to reach the surface. While on land, that person could naturally breath. So actual grace is what is necessary to live on earth, but when we get to Heaven, we cannot be sinning anymore, therefore, upon death, we receive the sanctifying one. In other words, just the actual or realistic version of grace is stating, "Come on, we're always going to be enjoying sin, so God knows this and He tolerates us with one version of grace, but when we die and He has to live with us, He changes us." That second type of grace they call it sanctifying grace, and quoting, "Sanctifying grace implies a real transformation of the soul."

Interestingly, the Bible teaches, "And the very God of peace sanctify you wholly; and [I pray God] your whole spirit and soul and body be preserved blameless unto the coming of our Lord Jesus Christ" (1 Thessalonians 5:23). Sanctification happens before the second coming, not after. Therefore, the teaching is definitely allowing people to continue to sin, despite some very strong language against such. Confusion reigns is all I can say.

IDENTIFYING MARK #10: DENIES THAT JESUS CAME IN THE FLESH

Again, according to Catholic Answers, on the question, "Could Jesus have sinned?", the answer is "Absolutely not". This then means that they deny that Jesus came in the flesh. Again, the reference to flesh is that of being subject to the possibility of sinning. The Bible clearly teaches, "We have not an high priest which cannot be touched with the feeling of our infirmities; but was in all points tempted like as [we are, yet] without sin" (Hebrews 4:15). If Jesus could not have sinned then the verse should say, "We have not an high priest which cannot be touched with the feeling of our infirmities; but was without sin." Keep in mind, temptation is not sin. Even right after baptism, "Jesus led up of the Spirit into the wilderness to be tempted of the devil" (Matthew 4:1).

As is the error in most denominations, it is taught that whatever humanity that Jesus took on, it was simply the feeling of pain, hunger, sadness, gladness, tiredness, seriousness, stress, suffering, etc. But as for the internal, especially the mind, it was not human, it was God. In other words, Jesus had a shell of humanity to cover up the fact that He was God. This is not true. Some go as far as to say that, Jesus did take on the human nature, but it was the same nature that Adam had before the fall into sin. Again, this is not true either.

As a reminder, the Bible says, "For verily he took not on [him the nature of] angels; but he took on [him] the seed of Abraham" (Hebrews 2:16). Abraham was a fallen man, therefore, Jesus took on a nature that was fallen as well. No, He did not have rebellion in His heart and had to be converted, He was like Enoch, who "walked with God" so much so that "God took him" (Genesis 5:24), as in, Enoch went to Heaven without seeing death.

If Jesus could not be tempted to sin, then the devil wasted his time in the desert, and Jesus has absolutely no clue what it feels like to wrestle with temptation, yet we are told that "He that saith he abideth in him ought himself also so to walk, even as he walked" (1 John 2:6). So, how can we live a life like Jesus, after we are converted, with the natures we have if they are different than Jesus' nature? Not only that, but the Bible is quite clear that salvation is for those that truly do walk like Jesus walked. "To him that overcometh will I grant to sit with me in my throne, even as I also overcame, and am set down with my Father in his throne" (Revelation 3:21). Jesus overcame every temptation to sin and only those that consciously do the same go to Heaven. Jesus is not only our substitute that wipes away every penalty of our past sins, He is also our example of how we ought to live the rest of our lives. Sure, we may not know all the correct things and ways to obey, but at "the times of this ignorance God winked at; but now commandeth all men every where to repent" (Acts 17:30). So honest ignorance is excused, but even when we are enlightened, we are to repent, change, stop doing what we did not know was a sin at the time but now we do.

So again, those that believe "only Jesus is perfect", implies that we will never be able to stop sinning is repeating the Antichrist lie that Jesus did not come in the flesh. And even without being directly associated with the Antichrist, the "Spirit of Antichrist" seems to be repeating the same lie in one form or another.

IDENTIFYING MARK #11: KILLS GOD'S SAINTS

Although it may be reported that Catholics have suffered for their beliefs as well, the focus is upon the Vatican being the ones to be the persecutors. Below is but a few examples of the atrocities carried out:

- Waldensians from 1215 and hundreds of years later were declared heretics for belief in living a life of poverty and sticking more true to the original doctrines

- John Wycliffe in 1384 was burned for translating the Bible into English.

- Jan Hus in 1415 burned for questioning Catholic doctrine.

- William Tyndale in 1536 was convicted of heresy for translating the Bible into English and executed by strangulation, but after, his body was dug up and burnt at the stake.

- John Rogers in 1555 was burned at the stake for also being a Bible translator.

- Spanish Inquisition from 1478 through 1834, where no fewer than 3,000 protestors died.

- Huguenots massacre at St. Bartholomew's in 1572, where no fewer than 5,000 and as many as 30,000 were slaughtered for not agreeing with the Vatican.

Overall, the slaughter of Protestants by the hands of the Vatican, directly and indirectly, numbers in the millions.

IDENTIFYING MARK #12: COMES TO FULL POWER AFTER 476 A.D.

In 533 A.D., Emperor Justinian wrote the following decree:

"With honor to the Apostolic See, and to Your Holiness, which is, and always has been remembered in Our prayers, both now and formerly, and honoring your happiness, as is proper in the case of one who is considered as a father, We hasten to bring to the knowledge of Your Holiness everything relating to the condition of the Church, as We have always had the greatest desire to preserve the unity of your Apostolic See, and the condition of the Holy Churches of God, as they exist at the present time, that they may remain without disturbance or opposition. Therefore, We have exerted Ourselves to unite all the priests of the East and subject them to the See of Your Holiness, and hence the questions which have at present arisen, although they are manifest and free from doubt, and, according to the doctrine of your Apostolic See, are constantly firmly observed and preached by all priests, We have still considered it necessary that they should be brought to the attention of Your Holiness. For we do not suffer anything which has reference to the state of the Church, even though what causes the difficulty may be clear and free from doubt, to be discussed without being brought to the notice of Your Holiness, because you are the head of all the Holy Churches, for We shall exert Ourselves in every way (as has already been stated), to increase the honor and authority of your See."

In essence, the Roman Emperor Justinian had handed the kingdom over to the See or Papacy by this decree. This is reminiscent of the verse that says, "The dragon gave him his power, and his seat, and great authority" (Revelation 13:2). And 533 is after the year 476 A.D.

IDENTIFYING MARK #13: IS LOCATED IN EUROPE

Here is another one of those points that anyone with a map would be able to get the answer. The Vatican is located in the city of Rome, which is in the country of Italy, which is part of Europe satisfying this point.

Interestingly, the Bible said, "I considered the horns, and, behold, there came up among them another little horn" (Daniel 7:8). It did not say that it would come up in addition to, like a separate nation requesting to be voted in as the eleventh nation to Europe. It did not use the word "besides", which would have also implied a request to join the European nations. The Bible used the word "among". That means the ten countries would be established and within the borders of those ten nations, the Antichrist would come up to power, and that is exactly the case. Right inside one of the ten countries, Italy, the papacy came up.

IDENTIFYING MARK #14: IS A SMALL NATION

According to Catholic Answers, the question, "Is the Vatican really a country?" It is stated that it is "the world's smallest country, at just 109 acres, it has a population of roughly one thousand, with citizenship being largely restricted to those employed by the Vatican."

IDENTIFYING MARK #15: LOCATED ON SEVEN MOUNTAINS OR HILLS

Nearly one hundred cities are located on seven hills or mountains around the world, however, since the Bible clearly teaches that Europe is our focus, that brings the number down to about forty. Although there are many cities on the list, keep in mind that a woman sits upon them. As a reminder, a woman is representative of a church. A harlot is an apostate church while a delicate woman is representative of the true church. It is the harlot that sits on the seven hills or mountains, and there is but one apostate church that rules from such a position and is on the list: Rome. And inside Rome is the Vatican who runs the apostate church system known as the Catholic Church.

From Vatican.com, "The seven hills are, The Quirinal Hill, The Aventine Hill, The Caelian Hill, The Viminal Hill, The Capitoline Hill, The Esquiline Hill, and The Palatine Hill."

IDENTIFYING MARK #16: NOT JUST A POLITICAL KINGDOM

According to *Wikipedia*, one and only one system stands as both a Christian religious power and a political power combined. This is called a Theocracy and is held by none other than the Vatican.

IDENTIFYING MARK #17: APPEAR TO BE CHRISTIAN

According to the *Catholic League,* "the Catholic Church is the world's longest living institutional testimony to Christianity."

IDENTIFYING MARK #18: REMOVES THREE OF THE ORIGINAL TEN KINGDOMS

The first of the three kingdoms addressed here are the

Heruli. According to *Wikipedia,* "In 508 they were defeated by the Lombards and are reported to have migrated back to Scandinavia."

The second of the three kingdoms addressed here are the Vandals. According to *Wikipedia,* "Their kingdom collapsed in the Vandalic War of 533–4, in which Justinian I managed to conquer again the province for the Eastern Roman Empire.

The third of the three kingdoms addressed here are the Ostrogoths. According to *Wikipedia,* there was a "Siege of Rome" from "537-538" of which was unsuccessful, which weakened them, and were no longer found part of Europe.

So, all three horns were plucked up one way or another before the Vatican or papacy could exercise full authority. Was it at the hands of the Vatican that the armies were commanded? Evidently the last group, the Ostrogoths, were defeated by someone defending the Vatican, located in Rome. In either case, all three were removed by the interesting year of 538 A.D., as we shall shortly see.

IDENTIFYING MARK #19: APPEARS POMPOUS

According to *EWTN,* Global Catholic Network, "The most powerful man on earth is the Pope, that is the message contained in the language of these citations. This is Catholic Truth, there is no man on earth greater than Peter's successor, the Head of the Catholic Church."

Other quotes include:

- "The pope is the supreme judge of the law of the land....He is the vicegerent of Christ, and is not only a priest forever, but also King of kings and Lord of lords." La Civilta Cattolica, March 18, 1871. [Vicar or vicegerent means 'replacement.'"]

- Pope Innocent III (1198-1216) wrote: "For the Pope holdeth place on earth, not simply of a man but of the true God." (1 Book of Gregory 9 Decret. c.3)

IDENTIFYING MARK #20: WOULD TAKE ON GOD'S TITLES

Jesus is "KING OF KINGS, AND LORD OF LORDS" (Revelation 19:16). The pope is declared to be "Our Lord God the pope; another God upon earth, king of kings, and lord of lords." (*Dissertations on the Prophecies,* London: B. Blake, Bell-Yard, Temple-Bar, 1831, p. 456).

God is referred to as "Holy Father" (John 17:11). The pope, according to the official Vatican website Vatican.va, is declared to be "THE HOLY FATHER, The Roman Pontiff, as the successor of Peter, is the perpetual and visible principle and foundation of unity of both the bishops and of the faithful."

In all nine Bible references (Psalms 30:4, 47:8, 48:1, 60:6, 97:12, 108:7; Jeremiah 23:9; Amos 4:2; Hebrews 12:10), "His holiness" applies to God and never once to a human. The pope, according to the Catholic outlet known as *EWTN,* the head of the Catholic Church is known as "His Holiness The Pope."

IDENTIFYING MARK #21: SPEAKS BLASPHEMOUSLY

According to Catholic Answers, the question, "What's Your Authority?" was raised. By the time one reads the entire lengthy article, it basically removes the premise of "sola scriptura" or "the Bible alone" so much so that it makes it look like no one can ever figure out the Bible. Then steps in the authority of the Pope or the Vatican.

"The Church is the only divinely constituted teacher of Revelation. Now, the Scripture is the great depository of the Word of God. Therefore, the Church is the divinely appointed Custodian and Interpreter of the Bible. For, her office of infallible Guide were superfluous if each individual could interpret the Bible for himself...God never intended the Bible to be the Christians' rule of faith independently of the living authority of the Church." (*The Faith of* Our Fathers, p. 77).

The Bible clearly teaches that the scriptures interpret themselves. "Whom shall he teach knowledge? and whom shall he make to understand doctrine? [them that are] weaned from the milk, [and] drawn from the breasts. For precept [must be] upon precept, precept upon precept; line upon line, line upon line; here a little, [and] there a little" (Isaiah 28:9-10). Also, "Knowing this first, that no prophecy of the scripture is of any private interpretation" (2 Peter 1:20). And, "All scripture [is] given by inspiration of God, and [is] profitable for doctrine, for reproof, for correction, for instruction in righteousness: That the man of God may be perfect, throughly furnished unto all good works" (2 Timothy 3:16-17).

It is blasphemy to think only the Pope and the Vatican can understand and interpret scripture, as is claimed. Adding blasphemy to blasphemy, the notion that we are to provide a verse that states that we are to use only the Bible, implying that the lack of such a verse means outside practices are permitted, is preposterous. It is not in there, but God hardly states anything with the word "only", although He does so from time to time.

But if we were to treat the Bible as providing requirements just when the word "only" is used, then a whole lot of rules would not exist.

- Nowhere does the Bible say, "only baptism by immersion is to be practiced", yet, by example, that is the expectation despite all those that practice sprinkling and other forms of baptism.

- Nowhere does the Bible say, "only pray to God", but all Christians know that praying to Satan is a bad thing to do.

- Nowhere does the Bible say, "only obey God's commandments", but everyone one ought to know that obeying any other command in contradiction thereof is wrong.

- Nowhere does the Bible say, "have sex only with your spouse", but we know through much strong language about adultery and fornication that sex outside of marriage is wrong.

And there is a list of many other "lack of only" items, yet we know for a fact that it is to be the "only" way or we are going against God.

That is but two examples of speaking blasphemy, though on the same subject. There are many others as we shall see, but what has been provided is sufficient.

In essence, the papacy claims to be the sole authority for the interpretation of the scriptures allowing them to add additional rules and practices, alter the Bible teachings (example: baptism by sprinkling instead of immersion), and start and stop practices at will, where recently Limbo theology was discarded, which is a theology about the location of dead but unbaptized babies go. It is not only a misguided thought to have such authority, but it becomes blasphemous to step into the place of the interpreter, which is the Bible itself (Isaiah 28:9-10) through the Holy Spirit (John 16:8).

So, by claiming in addition to Bible teachings that there are other practices to be performed for salvation sake is equally blasphemous. Nowhere is Lent referenced in the Bible, yet, to be a "good Catholic", it is expected to be practiced. Nowhere is penance, works performed after confessing one's sins, ever referenced in the Bible, though where restitution can be made, it is to be done for sincere repentance sake. Nowhere in the Bible is it required to keep the "holy days" that the Vatican have created over the years and are different in each country, but if one misses those days, it is a confessable sin. And the list of blasphemes continue in further points.

IDENTIFYING MARK #22: CLAIMS TO BE GOD

"The Pope is of so great dignity and so exalted that he is not a mere man, but as it were God, and the vicar of God." *Ferraris Ecclesiastical Dictionary.*

"The Pope is not only the representative of Jesus Christ, but he is Jesus Christ himself, hidden under the veil of flesh." *The Catholic National,* July, 1895.

"We hold upon this earth the place of God Almighty." Pope Leo XIII.

"The Pope takes the place of Jesus Christ on earth... by divine right the Pope has supreme and full power in faith, in morals over each and every pastor and his flock. He is the true vicar, the head of the entire church, the father and teacher of all Christians. He is the infallible ruler, the founder of dogmas, the author of and the judge of councils; the universal ruler of truth, the arbiter of the world, the supreme judge of heaven and earth, the judge of all, being judged by no one, God himself on earth." Quoted in the New York Catechism.

These words are written in the Roman Canon Law 1685: "To believe that our Lord God the Pope has not the power to decree as he is decreed, is to be deemed heretical."

Father A. Pereira says: "It is quite certain that Popes have never approved or rejected this title 'Lord God the Pope,' for the passage in the gloss referred to appears in the edition of the Canon Law published in Rome in 1580 by Gregory XIII."

Writers on the Canon Law say, "The Pope and God are the same, so he has all power in heaven and earth." Barclay Cap. XXVII, p. 218. Cities Petrus Bertrandus, Pius V. - Cardinal Cusa supports his statement.

Pope Nicholas I declared: "the appellation of God had been confirmed by Constantine on the Pope, who, being God, cannot be judged by man." Labb IX Dist.: 96 Can. 7, Satis evidentur, Decret Gratian Primer Para

Roman Catholic Canon Law stipulates through Pope Innocent III that the Roman pontiff is "the vicegerent upon earth, not a mere man, but of a very God;" and in a gloss on the passage it is explained that this is because he is the vicegerent of Christ, who is "very God and very man." Decretales Domini Gregorii translatione Episcoporum, (on the transference of Bishops), title 7, chapter 3; Corpus Juris Canonice (2nd Leipzig ed., 1881), col. 99; (Paris, 1612), tom. 2, Devretales, col. 205

As we see, it is not an arbitrary claim of being God by just one pope, but all of these quotes cover more than 300 years and some go back even further. To say that no modern pope believes this would be to put words into the Vatican's mouth. The fact is, there has never been a renunciation of these statements.

IDENTIFYING MARK #23: CLAIMS TO BE ABLE TO FORGIVE SINS

"Seek where you will, through heaven and earth, and you will find one created being who can forgive the sinner, who can free him from the chains of hell. That extraordinary being is the priest, the Roman Catholic priest." *The Catholic Priest,* p. 78.

"To pardon a single sin requires all the OMNIPOTENCE OF GOD ... But what only God can do by His omnipotence, the priest also can do." *Dignity and Duties of the priests,* Vol. 12 p. 34.

Catholic Encyclopedia says, "Absolution proper is that act of the priest whereby, in the Sacrament of Penance, he frees man from sin."

"The minister to whom confession is made is the delegate of Christ, Who is the Judge of the living and the dead." St. Thomas Aquinas (Catholic Bible 101).

"The priest has the power to forgive all sins in the Sacrament of Penance", Catholic News Agency.

IDENTIFYING MARK #24: SHALL REIGN A PROPHETIC 1,260 DAYS, 3½ YEARS, OR 42 MONTHS

Recognized at the Catholic Encyclopedia highlights Justinian I, who wrote a decree in 533 A.D. (full decree is online at http://www.constitution.org/sps/sps12.htm) stating:

"Justinian: victor, pius, fortunate, ever Augustus, to John, the most holy Archbishop and patriarch of the noble city of Rome. Paying honor to the Apostolic See and to Your Holiness, as always has been and is our desire, and honoring your Blessedness as a father, we hasten to bring to the knowledge of Your Holiness all that pertains to the condition of the churches , since it has always been our great aim to safeguard the unity of your Apostolic See and the position of the holy churches of God which now prevails and abides securely without any disturbing trouble. Therefore we have been sedulous to subject and unite all the priests of the Orient throughout its whole extent to the See of Your Holiness. Whatever questions happen to be mooted at present , we have thought necessary to be brought to Your Holiness' knowledge, however clear and unquestionable they might be, and though firmly held and taught by all the clergy in accordance with the doctrine of Your Apostolic See; for we do not suffer that anything which is moored to Your Holiness, however clear and unquestionable, pertaining to the state of the churches, should fail to be known to Your Holiness, as being the head of all the churches. For as we have said before, we are zealous for the increase of the honor and authority of your See in all respects." Croly quotes a letter of March 25, 533 from Justinian to Epiphanius where Justinian repeats the parts of the statement above, which had been sent earlier in March, that the Bishop of Rome is: "head of all Bishops and the true and effective corrector of heretics."

This decree, when executed is what actually provides the authority to lead all other churches, which at the time, pretty much worked independently using a gathering council from time to time to establish solutions to critical issues, however, there was no recognized physical head.

Being offered supreme authority, the papacy then responded in 534 A.D.:

"One shines as a star, his reverence for the Apostolic chair, to which he has subjected and united all the churches, it being truly the Head of all; as was testified by the rules of the Fathers, the laws of the Princes, and the declarations of the Emperor's piety."

Now just because a decree exists, that does not make it so. Look at our own history. Just because some states in a united fashion seceded from the union did not make it so. If the south would have won the civil war, then it would have been so.

As a prior point stated, according to Daniel's writings, three horns or kingdoms of Europe needed to be removed before the recognition of the little horn's authority, therefore, even at 534 A.D., the 1260 year clock did not begin. It is not by chance that the Ostrogoths attacked Rome and waged a war upon Rome. It was not Rome that they were after. Implied strongly is that they opposed the authority of the Vatican. How can we make that connection? Quoting from *Wikipedia*, it is not by chance someone connected with granting authority to the papacy was involved. From the Siege of Rome, " Justinian took advantage of this to intervene in the affairs of the Ostrogoth state."

Not only was the war to depose the papacy unsuccessful in 538 A.D., it weakened the Ostrogoths so much so that they retreated out of Europe because it was not the Ostrogoths that became Italy, it was the Lombards. Upon withdrawal of the Ostrogoths from Rome and eventually to the point of not having a presence in Europe, all the churches united under the papacy. But the significant date of 538 A.D. had been established, the beginningof exercising that decree.

Adding 1260 years to 538 A.D. brings us to 1798. Did anything significant happen to the papacy in 1798?

According to *Wikipedia*, "General Berthier marched to Rome, entered it unopposed on 10 February 1798, and, proclaiming a Roman Republic, demanded of the pope the renunciation of his temporal authority. Upon his refusal he was taken prisoner, and on 20 February was escorted from the Vatican to Siena, and thence to the Certosa near Florence."

What happen to the Papal State? Again according to *Wikipedia*, "The Roman Republic (Italian: Repubblica Romana) was proclaimed on 15 February 1798 after Louis Alexandre Berthier, a general of Napoleon, had invaded the city of Rome on 10 February. The Roman Republic was a client republic under the French Directory composed of territory conquered from the Papal States. Pope Pius VI was exiled to France and died there in 1799. It immediately took the control of the other two former-papal revolutionary administrations, the Tiberina Republic and the Anconine Republic."

So the papacy came to exercise full, unchallenged authority in 538 A.D. and in 1798 lost even their land.

IDENTIFYING MARK #25: RECEIVES A DEADLY WOUND

As already stated, according to *Wikipedia*, "The Roman Republic (Italian: Repubblica Romana) was proclaimed on 15 February 1798 after Louis Alexandre Berthier, a general of Napoleon, had invaded the city of Rome on 10 February. The Roman Republic was a client republic under the French Directory composed of territory conquered from the Papal States. Pope Pius VI was exiled to France and died there in 1799. It immediately took the control of the other two former-papal revolutionary administrations, the Tiberina Republic and the Anconine Republic."

The Vatican being no longer recognized as a nation and the land being annexed as part of Rome marks the deadly wound.

IDENTIFYING MARK #26: THE DEADLY WOUND IS HEALED

According to *Wikipedia*, "The Lateran Treaty (Italian: Patti Lateranensi; Latin: Pacta Lateranensia) was one of the Lateran Pacts of 1929 or Lateran Accords, agreements made in 1929 between the Kingdom of Italy and the Holy See, settling the "Roman Question". They are named after the Lateran Palace, where they were signed on February 11, 1929. The Italian parliament ratified them on June 7, 1929. Italy was then under a Fascist government, but the succeeding democratic governments have all upheld the treaty. In 1947, the Lateran Pacts were incorporated into the democratic Constitution of Italy.[1] It recognized the Vatican as an independent state, with Mussolini agreeing to give the church financial support in return for public support from the pope at the time."

Also from *Wikipedia*, "The independent city-state, on the other hand, came into existence in 1929 by the Lateran Treaty between the Holy See and Italy, which spoke of it as a new creation."

From The Grolier Multimedia Encyclopedia, 1995, "... not until 1929 with the LATERAN TREATY was the 'Roman Question' – the problem of nonnational status for the pope - solved. The treaty, which created in the heart of Rome a tiny, sovereign Vatican state, restored to the papacy a measure of temporal independence but left it with political influence rather than actual political power."

"In affixing the autographs to the memorable document, healing the wound which has festered since 1870,extreme cordiality was displayed on both sides." *Los Angeles Times*, February 12, 1929.

Please note that the Los Angeles Times is not a religious organization and yet they inadvertently used the biblical wording in the article.

Even from secular magazine, Time, on the cover of September 28, 2015 issue had the title Pope Francis and the New Roman Empire.

IDENTIFYING MARK #27: WILL SURVIVE UNTIL THE SECOND COMING

This point will only be verified at the Second Coming, but let us face it, it will be doubtful that anyone will be holding out on a decision for Christ until that time making sure that all the points match. If all the other points match but a person is waiting to see if this one comes true, the person has a bigger problem than counting identifying marks. Besides, if a person does not make a decision prior to the second coming, it will be too late anyways.

That does bring up an interesting point though that needs addressed. First, even if one has already accepted Christ as Lord and Savior, this information is very pivotal in a continued relationship. To claim John 10:28, which says, "And I give unto them eternal life; and they shall never perish, neither shall any [man] pluck them out of my hand", without accepting John 10:27, which says, "My sheep hear my voice, and I know them, and they follow me", is an imbalanced Christian. Many of the "once saved, always saved" Christians love to point to John 10:28 alone and say, "See! I can't be lost." But the reality is that John 10:27 places a condition on that verse. As long as we are, every moment, hearing the voice of Jesus, and today we read it in the Bible, will get to know Him, and if we know Him, then we will follow or obey no matter the cost. To think we are permanently saved and it does not matter that one takes this book seriously by altering one's life in full accordance to what has been revealed is in for a rude awakening come the second coming, and we are trying to avoid that for as many people as possible. How do I know this to be so? Well, here in John, we see that we get to "know" Jesus through continual hearing and reading with obedience to what we hear and read. We know this to be a continual relationship because the Bible says, "He that saith, I know him, and keepeth not his commandments, is a liar, and the truth is not in him" (1 John 2:4). That is pure Bible right there. If anyone is breaking the commandments, at any time, especially when enlightened to the fact that the Antichrist and the "Spirit of Antichrist" are working against the commandments and yet one continues to disregard the true commandments, Jesus is going to say, "I never knew you: depart from me, ye that work iniquity" (Matthew 7:23). And that is despite the fact that so "Many will say to me in that day, Lord, Lord, have we not prophesied in thy name? and in thy name have cast out devils? and in thy name done many wonderful works?" (Matthew 7:22). Therefore, a whole lot of Christians are going to have a rude awakening.

Now the purpose of this book again is not to point out the Antichrist but seeing ignorance is not something that is going to be able to be claimed in the last generation, we make the appeal reminding everyone, at "the times of this ignorance God winked at; but now commandeth all men every where to repent" (Acts 17:30). God does not want us in ignorance. It is all about saving. So this is not a hate book but a saving book. So please, if this all seems quite different than what you have known, set those things aside, check to see if these things are so, and come on out all that deception. Jesus is waiting for your decision.

But back to the point, we see that this identifying mark is simply providing the explanation of why the Vatican exists today and seems to be getting strong and stronger. That is because it once again will become the world influencer to go up against Christ.

IDENTIFYING MARK #28: THINK TO CHANGE THE TEN COMMANDMENTS

According to the official Vatican website, the Catholic version of the Ten Commandments are:

ONE   I, the Lord, am your God: you shall not have strange Gods before me.

TWO   You shall not take the name of the Lord your God in vain.

THREE   Remember to keep holy the Lord's Day.

FOUR   Honor your father and your mother.

FIVE   You shall not kill.

SIX   You shall not commit adultery.

SEVEN   You shall not steal.

EIGHT   You shall not bear false witness against your neighbor.

NINE   You shall not covet your neighbor's wife.

TEN   You shall not covet your neighbor's goods.

But the Bible teaches, using Vatican's reference of Deuteronomy 5:6-21 and not Exodus 20:3-17:

1. I [am] the LORD thy God, which brought thee out of the land of Egypt, from the house of bondage. Thou shalt have none other gods before me. (Deuteronomy 5:6-7, which matches the Vatican first commandment)

2. Thou shalt not make thee [any] graven image, [or] any likeness [of any thing] that [is] in heaven above, or that [is] in the earth beneath, or that [is] in the waters beneath the earth: Thou shalt not bow down thyself unto them, nor serve them: for I the LORD thy God [am] a jealous God, visiting the iniquity of the fathers upon the children unto the third and fourth [generation] of them that hate me, And shewing mercy unto thousands of them that love me and keep my commandments. (Deuteronomy 5:8-10, which is missing from the Vatican list allowing for the use of the prolific amount of statues)

3. Thou shalt not take the name of the LORD thy God in vain: for the LORD will not hold [him] guiltless that taketh his name in vain. (Deuteronomy 5:11, which matches the Vatican's second commandment)

4. Keep the sabbath day to sanctify it, as the LORD thy God hath commanded thee. Six days thou shalt labour, and do all thy work: But the seventh day [is] the sabbath of the LORD thy God: [in it] thou shalt not do any work, thou, nor thy son, nor thy daughter, nor thy manservant, nor thy maidservant, nor thine ox, nor thine ass, nor any of thy cattle, nor thy stranger that [is] within thy gates; that thy manservant and thy maidservant may rest as well as thou. And remember that thou wast a servant in the land of Egypt, and [that] the LORD thy God brought thee out thence through a mighty hand and by a stretched out arm: therefore the LORD thy God commanded thee to keep the sabbath day.

(Deuteronomy 5:12-15, which in a sense matches the Vatican's third commandment)

5. Honour thy father and thy mother, as the LORD thy God hath commanded thee; that thy days may be prolonged, and that it may go well with thee, in the land which the LORD thy God giveth thee. (Deuteronomy 5:16, which matches the Vatican's fourth commandment)

6. Thou shalt not kill. (Deuteronomy 5:17, which matches the Vatican's fifth commandment)

7. Neither shalt thou commit adultery. (Deuteronomy 5:18, which matches the Vatican's sixth commandment)

8. Neither shalt thou steal. (Deuteronomy 5:19, which matches the Vatican's seventh commandment)

9. Neither shalt thou bear false witness against thy neighbour. (Deuteronomy 5:20, which matches the Vatican's eighth commandment)

10. Neither shalt thou desire thy neighbour's wife, neither shalt thou covet thy neighbour's house, his field, or his manservant, or his maidservant, his ox, or his ass, or any [thing] that [is] thy neighbour's. (Deuteronomy 5:21, which matches the Vatican's ninth and tenth commandments)

As you see, there is a different list, not only different from how we see it, but ask a good Jew and they, if they know their commandments, will also have the same list as shown with the Bible verses. The Vatican disguises the second commandment under the first but does not worry about the details as they pass it off to mean simply that there is to be no other gods before God, be it human or manmade. But God says that there is a difference between the two. The first guards against the recognition of a human or someone imaginary although not an object required, like Jupiter, Zeus, Dagon, pharaohs, etc. to be a god. The second is against using stone, wood, and other material to be a god. The commandment about the graven images even begins with a clear distinction of being another commandment by the use of "Thou shalt not". True, there is another "thou shalt not" in the middle of the second commandment, which in following our rule, would create yet a third commandment, but it does not by the context. It says in the second use of the phrase, "Thou shalt not bow down thyself unto them", which implies connection to the prior declaration on the basis of "them" having to refer to something prior. So again, we see a natural separation between the two commandments as one regarding humans taking the place of God and the other of objects taking the place of God.

On top of that, to retain the number ten, a single verse regarding coveting is broken into two under the Vatican version, when it is the act of coveting that is wrong and not the item or items to be coveted. If that were the case, we could easily create many more commandments by identifying each object that ought not to be coveted. In short, the last commandment is "Thou shalt not covet."

And take a look at this bold statement: "What power has claimed authority to change God's law? The Papacy in Rome. The Pope is of so great authority and power that he can modify, explain, or interpret even Divine Laws...The Pope can modify divine law, since his power is not of man, but of God, and he acts as vicegerent of God upon earth." Translated from Lucius Ferraris, Prompta Bibliotheca (Ready Library), Papa, art. 2.

IDENTIFYING MARK #29: ACCEPTS A DIFFERENT CYCLE OF TIME

So Julius Caesar in Rome comes up with a calendar system to honor many of the pagan gods as well as the Caesars, which were treated like gods anyways. It included having different day names of the week, where one, two, three, four, five, preparation, and Sabbath were now Sunday, Monday, Tuesday, Wednesday, Thursday, Friday, and Saturday. But it also changed from God's sunset to sunset of reckoning of a day (Genesis 1:14) to the midnight to midnight scale, according to the Hermetic Systems website. God's months were an even thirty days long, but now some had thirty-one and of course February was cut short.

So how does the Vatican get involved? At the height of the Vatican power in the Dark Ages, Pope Gregory XIII instituted a revised calendar system in 1582. One would think that with so much power, the supposed love of God, and a strong enough influence over all the world, well, at least in the West, and people ready to be receptive of such a new institution as a new calendar system having the subjects being mostly religious in nature on top of that, seeing evolution was not even a thought yet, that one would set the record straight for God. Instead, as quoted from the Hermetic Systems website, "The Gregorian Calendar begins days at midnight, but not all calendars do (for example, the Jewish Calendar has nychthemerons which begin at sunset)."

So, in all honesty, it was not just a matter of the Vatican using something Julius Caesar set in motion, but rather, in producing a new calendar system, which is quite brilliant in its calculations, midnight to midnight schedule of time was embraced. It is clear that the Vatican, as predicted, got involved in passing on to all the world a replacement to one of God's instituted times: when a day begins and ends.

IDENTIFYING MARK #30: CHANGE GOD'S WORSHIP TIME

Now if Daniel would have wrote of the Antichrist that it would think to change God's time, then the previous mark would have been sufficient, but instead Daniel wrote the word "times". Evidently God had instituted things based upon time and at least two of those things would be under attack by the Antichrist. In looking at everything involving time from God, there are not many items, especially when we see that Daniel wrote it would be connected with thinking to change God's laws or commandments.

The fact that God established a certain timeframe of feast and holy days is not a target of the Antichrist for "the law having a shadow of good things to come" (Hebrews 10:1). The law referenced here is in the context of the ceremonial law. They all pointed to Jesus Christ.

- The Passover (Leviticus 23:4) pointed to Jesus being the Lamb to be sacrificed for all that use the blood of Jesus properly to pass over into Heaven (Matthew 26:2).

- The Feast of Unleavened Bread (Leviticus 6-8) pointed to Jesus purging our sins (1 Corinthians 5:7).

- The Feast of First Fruits (Leviticus 23:9-14), where a small sampling of the gathering is represented, it pointed to Jesus' Resurrection (1 Corinthians 15:20).

- The Feast of Pentecost (Leviticus 23:15-22) pointed to Jesus sending His Holy Spirit (Acts 2:1-4).

- The Feast of Trumpets (Leviticus 23:23-25) pointed to Jesus waking people up in the predicted Great Awakening (Revelation 10:5-7).

- The Feast of Atonement (Leviticus 23:26-32) pointed to Jesus' Judgment time (Revelation 14:7).

- The Feast of Ingathering (Leviticus 23:33-44) points to Jesus' Second Coming (Revelation 14:14-16).

All of these feasts days were treated like floating Sabbath days. But the Vatican moving such days around is insignificant since the shadow is no longer needed.

The only other time that God has set in motion, outside of the calendar, and is also connected with the Ten Commandments is the commandment regarding the Sabbath day, which is to be observed from sunset Friday until sunset Saturday.

Interestingly, the single commandment that deals with time is attacked from two different directions and both instituted before sin ever entered the world as well as there ever being a Jew, which many equate the Sabbath being a Jewish thing, when it is not. The day was established to be sunset to sunset (Genesis 1:14), and the seventh day Sabbath day was set in place (Genesis 2:1-3).

So, has the Vatican tampered with the seventh day Sabbath day? Not only have the sunset times been changed, but the whole day itself, and boldly too.

From the Question and Answer Catechism:

Question--How do you prove that the (Catholic) Church has power to command Feasts and Holy days?

Answer--By this very act of changing the Sabbath into Sunday, which is admitted by Protestants, and therefore they contradict themselves by keeping Sunday so strictly, and breaking most other Feasts commanded by the same church.

The Sabbath is God's period of time, which begins sundown Friday and ends sundown Saturday. Their substitution is not just simply adopting the first day of the week but rather the acceptance of a time period that begins and ends at midnight named Sunday.

Other quotations from the Vatican or representative of include:

- "Have you not any other way of proving that the Church has power to institute festivals of precept? Had she not such power, she could not have done that in which all modern religionists agree with her, she could not have substituted the observance of Sunday, the first day of the week, for the observance of Saturday, the Seventh day, a change for which there is no Scriptural authority." Stephen Keenan, A Doctrinal Catechism, 3rd ed. p. 174

- "The Catholic Church,... by virtue of her divine mission, changed the day from Saturday to Sunday." official organ of Cardinal Gibbons, Sept. 23, 1893.

- "Is Saturday the 7th day according to the Bible and the 10 Commandments? I answer yes". "Is

Sunday the first day of the week and did the Church change the 7th day, Saturday, for Sunday, the 1st day? I answer yes". "Did Christ change the day? I answer no!" "Faithfully yours, J. Cardinal Gibbons" Gibbons' autograph letter.

- "Which is the Sabbath day? Saturday is the Sabbath day. Why do we observe Sunday instead of Saturday? We observe Sunday instead of Saturday because the Catholic Church transferred the solemnity from Saturday to Sunday." Peter Geiermann, (1946 ed.), p.50. Geiermann received the "apostolic blessing" of Pope Pius X on his labors, January 25, 1910.

IDENTIFYING MARK #31: JESUS' SACRIFICE WOULD BE REPLACED

Jesus "died unto sin once" (Romans 6:10), the Vatican instead instituted the mass. During the mass, called the "Liturgy of the Eucharist", this is what is said:

Priest: Pray, brethren that our sacrifice may be acceptable to God, the almighty Father.

Congregation: May the Lord accept the sacrifice at your hands for the praise and glory of his name, for our good, and the good of all his church.

And then the priest takes the bread, which to them is Christ's body and breaks it (sacrifices it). (Today' Missal, Sept. 6 – Nov. 28, 1992, page 48, 53, 55, 57, 58)

The Vatican also dictates to the churches to celebrate the Eucharist, which, according to Catholic Answers, states: "The Eucharist is a true sacrifice".

Further information from Catholic Answers, "At every Catholic Mass, following the command of Jesus himself, the celebrant raises the host and says, "Take this, all of you, and eat it: This is my body, which will be given up for you." Then he lifts the cup and says, "Take this, all of you, and drink from it: This is the cup of my blood, the blood of the new and everlasting covenant. It will be shed for you and for all so that sins may be forgiven. Do this in memory of me." The doctrine of transubstantiation, the teaching that bread and wine are converted into the actual flesh and blood of Jesus Christ."

"So the institution of the Eucharist, especially the subject of transubstantiation, where the priest takes the flesh and blood of Jesus and sacrifices Him again replaces the single sacrifice of Jesus, hence, they are the only nation to concentrate on doing anything with the replacement of the single sacrifice of Jesus. On top of that, it is the only service involving the sacrificial replacement on a daily basis as the mass is said every day and even several times a day, where it is boasted that somewhere in the world at any given moment in time, Jesus is being sacrificed again in the form of the Eucharist."

IDENTIFYING MARK #32: GOD'S SANCTUARY SERVICE WOULD BE REPLACED

According to The Catholic Encyclopedia, "Sanctuary signified in the Middle Ages sometimes a ciborium-altar, a structure resting on pillars and covered with a baldachino that was set over an altar, sometimes an ostensory or monstrance, a tower-shaped vessel for preserving and exhibiting relics and the Blessed Sacrament, sometimes, lastly, like to-day, it was the name of the vessel holding the pyx. That is, at the present time in ecclesiastical usage it is only the name for the receptacle or case placed upon the table of the high altar or of another altar in which the vessels containing the Blessed Sacrament, as the ciborium, monstrance, custodia, are kept."

In plain language, in each Catholic Church, usually towards the front, there is a place known as the holy place where is stored the unused communion wafers but more important to them is a larger wafer contained in a special casing. This is taken out at special times of the year and placed on the altar, which is also a counterfeit sanctuary item seeing altars were done away with at the cross.

On top of that, the act of a priest washing his hands symbolically, lifting up the bread and wine, breaking of the bread, and much more during the Eucharist period of the church service is all in accordance to replacing the sanctuary service in Heaven with an earthly one.

IDENTIFYING MARK #33: CAST DOWN THE TRUTH

As a reminder, truth is found in the Word (John 17:17), in Jesus (John 14:6), and in the Ten Commandments (Psalms 119:142). Therefore, the fact that the Vatican has a different set of commandments, has doctrines that are not found in the Bible and not exercising other doctrines that are in the Bible, plus contradicting Jesus' direct words, the truth indeed has been cast down. Specific examples include:

- The second commandment is ignored.

- The tenth commandment is broken into two commandments.

- The Sabbath commandment is used to refer to a different day on a different cycle of time.

- The doctrine of purgatory is nowhere found in the Bible, nor is the doctrine regarding indulgences, the Vatican instituted process of purchasing time to get out of purgatory early in a manner of paying ahead or paying for someone else already there.

- The Bible doctrine of baptism by immersion has been replaced with sprinkling.

- Jesus said to call no man spiritually your father yet the Vatican places such titles upon their ministers and emphasizes "Holy Father" for the pope.

IDENTIFYING MARK #34: CAUSES CHRISTIANS TO FALL AWAY, ESPECIALLY FROM KEEPING THE COMMANDMENTS

Making Catholics recite a different version of the Ten Commandments as well as be in compliance with them in which many cling to their idols of statues and metals as well as religious jewelry, is evidence of compliance with this identifying mark.

IDENTIFYING MARK #35: RULES FROM WHAT IS CONSIDERED GOD'S TEMPLE

The reference to God's Temple is not a reference to the temple that Moses made in the desert for that was replaced with Solomon's temple. It is also not a reference to Solomon's temple, as it was destroyed during the Babylonian raid. It is also not in reference to the rebuilt temple of 457 B.C., for it was destroyed in 70 A.D. by the Romans. And to date, there is no specific temple of God on this planet, nor does the Bible predict such, despite what people may hear.

The rumors through much of Christianity about another temple in the future is the misapplication to the prophecy of Daniel referring to the rebuilt one in 457 B.C. but destroyed in 70 A.D. after the Messiah was welcomed (Daniel 9:27). Most Christians that are clinging to a future Antichrist dismiss the application to the rebuilt temple of 457 B.C. because one foundation wall still remained after 70 A.D. Why is that important? Jesus said, "There shall not be left here one stone upon another, that shall not be thrown down" (Matthew 24:2). The futurists purposely ignore that the actual temple that was built upon the foundation was built upon an existing foundation. They ignore the fact that Daniel said, "Know therefore and understand, [that] from the going forth of the commandment to restore and to build Jerusalem unto the Messiah the Prince [shall be] seven weeks, and threescore and two weeks: the street shall be built again, and the wall, even in troublous times" (Daniel 9:25) happened perfectly. The command was given to rebuild, including a bonus of being financed by a pagan kingdom in 457 B.C. (Ezra chapter 7) and the Messiah was baptized right on time in 27 A.D. (Luke 3:1-22). But because the foundation stones still remained on top of each other after 70 AD, it is all dismissed for yet another supposed rebuilding. But the actual temple stones themselves that were used during the rebuilding process of 476 B.C. were all removed during that raid of 70 A.D., thus Jesus' words were indeed fulfilled.

So the futurists either try to make the Daniel prophecy predict two rebuilding events or they ignore the one that was rebuilt. Having two rebuilding events does not fit the single tense of Daniel 26 and so that would actually result in such as being error. To completely ignore the rebuilding in 457 B.C. would not fit the logical intent of the Daniel prophecies. Why would anyone say, "There's going to be a rebuilding", a rebuilding event happens, and then turn around and say, "No, I didn't mean that one"? It does not make sense no matter how one tries to put it into the future.

Also, look at Jesus' words again. Jesus said, "See ye not all these things?" That means He is referring to the temple right before their eyes. In fact, the verse prior said, "And Jesus went out, and departed from the temple: and his disciples came to [him] for to shew him the buildings of the temple" (Matthew 24:1). Then the next verse says, "And Jesus said unto them, See ye not all these things? verily I say unto you, There shall not be left here one stone upon another, that shall not be thrown down." So the temple that the disciples were looking at, the temple that Jesus just left, the temple that the disciples came from, the temple that Jesus said, "See ye not all these things?" in regards to, that is the temple that will not have a stone left upon itself. In other words, it is the temple built in 457 B.C. and not a future one!

Therefore, since God no longer dwells in a temple on earth, God's temple must be a reference to a recognized religious place on earth in connection to the Christian God. It would not be just a church, but it would act like the temple in Jerusalem. There were plenty of synagogues and temples for daily sacrifices throughout Israel but there was one recognized main temple for the holiest of all sacrifices and gatherings. So, does such a place exist today in which above all other religious buildings and locations one stands as the main one?

"Bishop of Rome, or the pope, gave her a new lease on life, and made her again the capital - this time the religious capital - of the civilized world." *Abbot's Roman History*, p. 236.

IDENTIFYING MARK #36: EXALTS ABOVE THAT WHICH IS CALLED GOD

"The Pope is of so great dignity and so exalted that he is not a mere man, but as it were God, and the vicar of God." Ferraris Ecclesiastical Dictionary.

"The Pope is not only the representative of Jesus Christ, but he is Jesus Christ, hidden under a veil of flesh." The Catholic National July 1895.

Lucius Ferraris, in his 'Prompta Bibliotheca': "The pope is as it were God on earth, sole sovereign of the faithful of Christ, chief king of kings, having plenitude of power, to whom has been intrusted by the omnipotent God direction not only of the earthly but also of the heavenly kingdom. . . . The pope is of so great authority and power that he can modify, explain, or interpret even divine laws."

"We hold upon this earth the place of God Almighty." Pope Leo XIII, in an Encyclical Letter June 20, 1894.

Pope Innocent III (1198-1216) wrote: "For the Pope holdeth place on earth, not simply of a man but of the true God." (1 Book of Gregory 9 Decret. c.3)

These quotes come from EWTN, a Catholic Q&A website. The question, by a sincere Catholic is, how should we understand these things? The answer reveals that first, these items are not centuries old only, but the position of the Catholic Church as of December 21, 2003 is:

Dear Joe, One should first of all examine the authenticity of each of these laudatory statement, their authors, the circumstances under which they appeared. That should be done first and properly. However, the most powerful man on earth is the Pope, that is the message contained in the language of these citations. This is Catholic Truth, there is no man on earth greater than Peter's successor, the Head of the Catholic Church. I would simply read these texts analogically, taking that which is true out of them, by analogy. We all know the Pope is not divine, not God, not the Holy Spirit. He is a man like you and I physically, he eats and he sleeps, but look at the supreme powers Christ has bestowed on his Office as Pope. What power and authority he can and does use. He pronounces Truth, dogmatic truth, which we have to accept with divine Faith. This is the focus I would use in understanding these texts. God bless you. Fr. Bob Levis

IDENTIFYING MARK #37: USES SIGNS AND WONDERS

One of the greatest signs and wonders approved by the Vatican is that of the dead appearing in apparitions, with the most noted one being Mary, the mother of Jesus. The dead speaking to the living is known as spiritualism. And nowhere in the Bible, other than Jesus, has anyone died and come back to the living to speak with them. Sure, Moses and Elijah appeared on what is called the mount of transfiguration (Matthew 17:3) and talked with a living person, Jesus (Mark 9:4), but Jesus "was transfigured before them: and his face did shine as the sun, and his raiment was white as the light" (Matthew 17:2). So there was a little bit of a special circumstance happening at the time. Do keep in mind, Moses and Elijah did not speak to the disciples, only to Jesus.

Also, many that teach that spiritualism is taught in the Bible will point to the incident between King Saul and the dead prophet Samuel. With the use of "a woman that hath a familiar spirit at Endor" (1 Samuel 28:7) and King Saul only "perceived that it [was] Samuel" (1 Samuel 28:14), this is nothing more than witchcraft at its best. If Samuel truly was brought back to life, why would "An old man cometh up" (1 Samuel 28:14) when he should have been coming down from Heaven. This situation that allowed something called Samuel to speak to King Saul was not orchestrated by God, but by Satan.

Outside of that, "the dead know not any thing, neither have they any more a reward; for the memory of them is forgotten" (Ecclesiastes 9:5). "If a man die, shall he live [again]? all the days of my appointed time will I wait, till my change come" (Job 14:14). "For now shall I sleep in the dust; and thou shalt seek me in the morning, but I [shall] not [be]" (Job 7:21). "And many of them that sleep in the dust of the earth shall awake, some to everlasting life, and some to shame [and] everlasting contempt" (Daniel 12:2).

In plainly stating the fact, when one dies, they are dead. There is no immediate Heaven or Hell. There is no walking the earth. All of the apparitions or the dead coming back is nothing more than each person's evil angel that followed them throughout life now simply personating them. This is not an impersonation where someone tries to sound like someone else. This is a personating of the person. An evil angel can look, talk, act, and even smell like the departed love one. They know that deceased person better than their own mother did.

Remember, especially in the last days, "the spirits of devils, working miracles, [which] go forth unto the kings of the earth and of the whole world" (Revelation 16:14). So a loved one coming back to speak to the living is sadly nothing more than a personating from the spirits of devils. The dead loved one is unconsciously waiting "For the Lord himself shall descend from heaven with a shout, with the voice of the archangel, and with the trump of God: and the dead in Christ shall rise first: Then we which are alive [and] remain shall be caught up together with them in the clouds, to meet the Lord in the air: and so shall we ever be with the Lord" (1 Thessalonians 4:16-17). It is at that time, "We shall not all sleep, but we shall all be changed, In a moment, in the twinkling of an eye, at the last trump: for the trumpet shall sound, and the dead shall be raised incorruptible, and we shall be changed" (1 Corinthians 15:51-52). You see, "in Christ shall all be made alive. But every man in his own order: Christ the firstfruits; afterward they that are Christ's at his coming" (1 Corinthians 15:22-23). And "Marvel not at this: for the hour is coming, in the which all that are in the graves shall hear his voice, And shall come forth; they that have done good, unto the resurrection of life; and they that have done evil, unto the resurrection of damnation" (John 5:28-29).

To believe in an immediate spirit rewarded Heaven and Hell is to do away with the purpose of the resurrection. Those that teach the resurrection is just a reconnection of the spirit and body forget that the bodies have become dust as well as not being the bodies we will have anyways. We are getting new bodies and not taking on the ones that went down into the grave. God is not resurrecting old bodies.

Therefore, the fact that the Vatican is heavily into Marian apparitions in itself is fulfillment of this identifying mark, but even bleeding statues, humans bleeding where Jesus had nails, rosaries turning colors, the sun dancing, and much more has the world in its grip. Signs and Wonders is a Catholic right arm magazine focusing on the signs and wonders associated with the Catholic Church. (Signs and Wonders Online).

Although this is supposed to be an investigation to see if the Vatican fulfills the identifying mark, which it does, non-Catholics need to be very careful. This fascination with television and movies portraying people going to Heaven and coming back to tell their story is the same spiritualism in a different form, hence why the "Spirit of Antichrist" is sometimes more dangerous than the Antichrist himself.

Those that cannot see the purpose of Satan bringing dead people back to life and speaking in a manner that directs people to God are not seeing the end goal. We get a lot of people who say, "I'm visited by my dead (fill in the blank), and I learned a lot about God and Heaven. What use does Satan have by telling me the truth? I'm more closer to God than I ever was." My dear friends, Satan is the greatest false preacher of all time. He is not forbidden from telling the truth. He is even most affective in using mostly truth to get the final point in, and that is disobedience to any of the Ten Commandments. So Satan will personate a departed loved one and come off as confirming the person in their faith for the soul reason that their faith is in error. What they believe is not all of the truth, and then when the truth comes along, it is rejected. Why? "Well, my dead loved once told me I am right just where I am."

Remember, "To the law and to the testimony: if they speak not according to this word, [it is] because [there is] no light in them" (Isaiah 8:20). "And no marvel; for Satan himself is transformed into an angel of light" (2 Corinthians 11:14).

IDENTIFYING MARK #38: FORBID MARRIAGES

From the website Vatican.va, "In the patristic era, clerical celibacy, strictly speaking meant the inability to enter marriage once a higher Order had been received."

According to Catholic Answers, "The tradition in the Western or Latin-Rite Church has been for priests as well as bishops to take vows of celibacy, a rule that has been firmly in place since the early Middle Ages."

The Vatican does not have to ban all marriages for the Bible did not declare that. As long as there is some forbiddance, which there is, the identifying mark is satisfied.

IDENTIFYING MARK #39: COMMANDS CHRISTIANS TO ABSTAIN FROM EATING MEAT

According to Catholic Answers, "Abstinence from eating meat or some other food according to the prescripts of the conference of bishops is to be observed on all Fridays, unless a solemnity should fall on a Friday. Abstinence and fasting are to be observed on Ash Wednesday and Good Friday."

From *EWTN*, "The law of abstinence requires a Catholic 14 years of age until death to abstain from eating meat on Fridays in honor of the Passion of Jesus on Good Friday."

IDENTIFYING MARK #40: BASED UPON SATAN INSPIRED RELIGION (PAGANISM)

Paganism does not mean the worship of Satan. Paganism is any practice or worship of a human creation passed off as a requirement of God.

Do keep in mind, although the Bible does not forbid the use of the items listed below that are given a Christian meaning, the fact that the Bible is specific in how we are to remember Jesus, communion (1 Corinthians 11:24-25, John 13:14) and baptism (Romans 6:3-4), means that anything beyond those items is of a human invention. Those human inventions being made part of the worship service is no different than God's reaction when ordinary fire was used in the service by Nadab and Abihu. "And Nadab and Abihu, the sons of Aaron, took either of them his censer, and put fire therein, and put incense thereon, and offered strange fire before the LORD, which he commanded them not. And there went out fire from the LORD, and devoured them, and they died before the LORD" (Leviticus 10:1-2).

It is no different than taking a blue teddy bear to a red team's sporting event finding out that even though the blue teddy bear was just a simple purchase at a store, if it has ties back to the opposing team wearing blue, well, there is going to be an uproar.

The fact that pagan religions incorporated many religious symbols, performed many religious acts, and offered certain prayers, just because now they are being used in a religious manner for Christ does not make it acceptable to God.

To drive this point home, things sometimes need to be looked at in the extreme because when we only look at the innocent intent of things, everything seems acceptable when it is not. If during the church service we asked all parents of kids in diapers to bring forth their child's soiled diapers collected all week long and lay them up front where the minister is, there would be an awful stench to the service, both physically and spiritually. It becomes obvious that it is inappropriate to do that even if we claim a Christian reason, such as, "These diapers represent the days when Jesus was a young child." Yet, we see the practices of Babylon, Medo-Persia, Greece, and Pagan Rome, where they have become Christianized with a Christian reason, and then it is passed to the world as acceptable when it stinks to God just as much as those soiled diapers do.

Here is a small list of paganism that is found in the Vatican but not something practiced in the Bible.

26. According to *Wikipedia,* Christmas is the celebration of the rebirth of the sun for the Roman sun god, Sol Invictus.

27. According to Ancient Origins' website, Easter is really the celebration of the goddess Ishtar, who stood for fertility, love, war, and sex, which explains why bunnies, chicks, and eggs are all part of the Easter celebration.

28. Lent is the renamed time period that God foresaw as "women weeping for Tammuz" (Ezekiel 8:14). And now the "Spirit of Antichrist" has expanded Lent to include non-Catholic denominations.

29. Sunday is the veneration of the sun, replacing God's Sabbath day.

30. The wafer used during the communion service, being much different from the unleavened bread that Jesus used, finds a connection to the "Egyptian priests practiced 'transubstantiation', claiming to be able to transfer the sun god Osiris into a circular wafer. In rituals prefiguring Catholic Mass, the faithful then ate the 'body' of their god to nourish their souls. The letters IHS on the sun-shaped wafers stood for Isis, Horus, and Seb (later, Roman Catholics claimed they were the first three letters of Jesus' name in Greek)."

31. Speaking of the letters IHS that are inscribed on many garments in the Catholic Church, it has no meaning from the Bible. Although many defenders of the Catholic Church try to dismiss any mention of it as being reference to Isis, Horus, Seb, which are three Egyptian pagan references, and somehow tied to anti-Catholic people, do keep in mind that we are not against Catholics. We are no more against them as we are against atheists, other Christians denominations, Muslims, Jews, Hindus, or other groups. But the fact remains that though they claim no scientific evidence and it is just Catholic bashing, at the same time, why is it there in the first place since it has no biblical connection.

32. The miter on popes, cardinals, and even bishops very much match the Babylonian head garb of wearing a fish in worship of the fish god called Dagon.

33. Wedding rings of priests and nuns is the same practice of Babylon's priests and priestesses who wore them demonstrating that they were married to the temple.

34. The skull cap, worn by popes, cardinals, and bishops is the same type worn by the sun priests of Egypt.

35. The obelisk standing in the center of Vatican Square came from Egypt and is a sun worshipping symbol.

36. The cross like item that appears to be four triangles connected at the point, called the Maltese Cross, is connected to Shamash, another god of the sun as well as justice.

37. The pinecone staff is a symbol for worship of the solar god Osiris.

38. The P and X combined symbol, known as Chi-Rho, was brought into Catholicism through Constantine, who supposedly received a vision and ordered to put the symbol on the shields of his forces (*Wikipedia*). This is the same Constantine that brought us Sunday as the Christian day of worship, along with Ishtar or Easter, Christmas, Lent, and much more.

39. The old pagan statues were renamed, where Catholic Answers state, "As far as I know, it seems that it is true. The Apostles were aparently applied to various gods. Matthew was Mithras, Thomas - Tammuz, Mark - Mars, John - Oannes, Peter - Jupiter, Paul - Apollo".

40. Sun symbols are frequently part of many displays including the largest sun dial in the world being called Saint Peter's square.

These are but fifteen questionable items that have some type of connection to pagan origins. Dismiss a few and we still have more than a half dozen. Also realize that this is just a partial list. So no doubt that there is some type of paganism involved, again, not just as in ignorance but actually and explicitly incorporated.

So it may be that instead of celebrating the rebirth of the sun, we are celebrating the birth of Jesus. Although Jesus rose on a Sunday does not make the day honoring the rising sun the new Sabbath. Although there are Christian names to the old Roman statues does not mean we ought to skip the commandment that forbids them in the first place. Though the obelisk is just a pillar and though Saint Peter's square is a sundial, in the name of not offending God and the fact they can easily be removed, why are they not removed?

The bottom line is this, what is in the heart? If wanting to please God is in the heart, then anything hinting at paganism would be removed much like the golden calf was removed in the time of Moses (Exodus 32:20) and the prophets of Baal in the time of Elijah (1 Kings 18:40). Both were instituted as a different form of worship, but it was not the true form. God even rejected Cain's offering, so yes, God is picky.

And we are not just talking a symbol or two or three. The entire church service is wrong. What are we doing with the altar of sacrifice, a most holy place, sun symbols, incense, layered garb, the reference to calling the priest "father", use of wafers for communion, use of actual alcohol, the washing of the hands, the mystical words uttered by the priest, the fact they are called priests, the canned prayers, the symbols worn and displayed, the holy waters used, the genuflecting, the sacrifice of Christ again both body and blood, and much more. This is all incorporated into just a one hour church service. Where is the simplicity of the reason for gathering? It is distracted with all that was mentioned. It certainly is not Bible based, and if it is not Bible based, then it is considered pagan.

IDENTIFYING MARK #41: BLASPHEME THE BEINGS OF HEAVEN

The first mentioned blaspheme of beings in Heaven is the notion that angels having sex with humans. According to *Wikipedia*, " Vatican Library, connect the origin of the nephilim with the fallen angels." As also mentioned before, this is not a correct understanding. When Jesus said that angels do not marry, which is to have sex, (Matthew 22:30), that is not just the heavenly angels, but it includes all angels. Angels were not created to have such an ability and evidently we will lose that ability upon being resurrected, "For in the resurrection they neither marry, nor are given in marriage, but are as the angels of God in heaven" (Matthew 22:30).

The second blasphemous notion is having the ability to create saints that can be prayed to. According to Catholic Online, a saint is a canonized or recognized holy individual who has died and is now in Heaven. As mentioned before, the Bible states that a saint is a person living a holy life here and now.

The third blasphemous act is the placement of people in Heaven in the first place. According to the Catholic Herald, "As Catholics, we believe that when a person dies, the soul separates from the body. He then stands before God in judgment." The Bible teaches that we do not go to Heaven until the second coming (1 Corinthians 15:23).

So all three unbiblical activities of Heavenly beings are under attack through the Vatican dispersing its theology through the Catholic Church.

IDENTIFYING MARK #42: THE NUMBER OF THE NAME BEING 666

So how does one add up a name? As mentioned, in various languages, the alphabet and numerical systems are intertwined, such as Latin, Greek, etc. Other languages separate the two such as English, German, etc. The significance is that all American names are thrown out along with names in British, German, Spanish, etc. because the value of those names are zero unlike Latin where the letters of one's name matches values from the associated numeric system which is Roman. Letters include I, V, X, etc. The point that is being made is that one cannot take an American name and use Roman Numerals. An American name using the English alphabet must use the English numerals. The languages are not interchangeable. God never said that the number of a man would add up to 666 using the Roman numeric system. He said that the name would simply add up to 666. So look at languages that use alphabet letters to represent numbers. Below is a list of various languages that do incorporate the numerical system inside their alphabet and using the titles of the papacy, let us see the results.

According to the Catholic magazine, Our Sunday Visitor, April 18, 1915, there was a question asked: "What are the letters inscribed on the Pope's crown, and what do they signify if anything? The letters inscribed in the Pope's mitre are these: VICARIUS FILII DEI, which is the Latin for Vicar of the Son of God."

Now in Latin the letters have numerical value which is better known as Roman numerals. An example is that an "I" means 1; a "V" means 5; and an "X" means 10. What does a "U" equate to? "U" is the same as "V" because the original Latin did not distinguish between vowels and constants. With that background, let us look at the value of the entire name:

V - 5,
I - 1,
C - 100,
A - 0,
R - 0,
I - 1,
U - 5,
S - 0 = 112.
F - 0,
I - 1,
L - 50,
I - 1,
I - 1 = 53.
D - 500,
E - 0,
I - 1 = 501.

Add the numbers 112, 53, 501 together and one gets 666. That is not by chance or coincidence.

But wait, there is more. If it was just one title that added up to 666, then there would be some wiggle room to try and discredit this point, but notice some other titles:

- Other official titles of the Pope in various languages include: Greek, the name Lateinos means Latin Man or Church

  L - 30,
  A - 1,
  T - 300,
  E - 5,
  I - 10,
  N - 50,
  O - 70,
  S - 200 = 666.

- In Hebron, the name is Romiith which means Roman Kingdom

  R - 200,
  O - 6,
  M - 40,
  I - 10,
  I - 10,
  T - 400,
  H - 0 = 666.

- The Roman names of Duxcleri and Ludo Vicus mean Captain of the Clergy and Chief Vicar of the Court of Rome respectively.

  D - 500,
  U - 5,
  X - 10,
  C - 100,
  L - 50,
  E - 0,
  R - 0,
  I - 1 = 666

L - 50,
U - 5,
D - 500,
O - 0,
V - 5,
I - 1,
C - 100,
U - 5,
S - 0 = 666

As we see, not just one title adds up to such, but several. Sure, there are other names of other entities that probably add up to 666, but remember, we are just making sure that that Vatican at least adds up to such, and it does.

IDENTIFYING MARK #43: THE ANTICHRIST USES A SYMBOLIC WOMAN

The symbolic woman is a church. The church that is pure, like Revelation 12, is the true church, while the harlot women of Revelation 17 represents a church that pretends to be of God when in fact it does not listen to God's commandments, His Word, or even Jesus. We call this apostate or a church in apostasy, where the rules are not from the Bible but from other sources.

So is there a church system that the Vatican uses that fits that description? The answer is yes. It is called the Catholic Church, made up of many wonderful people who love God just as much as anyone else does. Unfortunately, the Vatican has caused "a falling away" from the truth as it is found in Jesus, the Word, and in the Commandments. Before it is too late, it is our desire to help such souls to reject the deceptions and choose to be in full obedience. In fact, God, through the use of humans, is "saying, Come out of her, my people, that ye be not partakers of her sins, and that ye receive not of her plagues" (Revelation 18:4). Unfortunately, direct connection with the Vatican through remaining a Catholic is not something that can be maintained and still be in perfect relationship with Jesus. I know personally as I initially tried to do that.

So again, the Vatican indeed fulfills this identifying mark by using the congregations knows as the Catholic Church.

IDENTIFYING MARK #44: OFFICIAL COLORS ARE PURPLE AND SCARLET

Wikipedia reports on the Catholic Cardinals as, "When in choir dress, a Latin-rite cardinal wears scarlet garments — the blood-like red symbolizes a cardinal's willingness to die for his faith."

"The Bishops wear the color purple to symbolize royalty, because of their position within the Church."

According to the National Catholic Reporterd, "When worn by bishops and cardinals, the cassock traditionally has a colored trim, with purple for bishops and red for cardinals."

Cappa Magna, "A cloak with a long train and a hooded shoulder cape...[it] was purple wool for bishops; for cardinals, it was scarlet watered silk (for Advent, Lent, Good Friday, and the conclave, purple wool); and rose watered silk for Gaudete and Laetare Sundays; and for the pope, it was red velvet for Christmas Matins, red serge at other times." Cassock (also Soutand): "The close-fitting, ankle-length robe worn by the Catholic clergy as their official garb. ...The color for bishops and other prelates is purple, for cardinals scarlet" (Ibid., pp. 175, 178).

IDENTIFYING MARK #45: RICH

According to Slate, a daily web magazine since 1996, printed on March 14, 2013, "How Rich Is the Catholic Church? Pope Francis is not just the spiritual leader of one of the world's major religions: He's also the head of what's probably the wealthiest institution in the entire world."

According to *CNBC,* the Vatican Bank "has about 33,000 accounts, a distribution network in more than 100 countries, and an estimated $8 billion in assets. "

According to *NY Mag,* the Pope "will also oversee a massive religious business whose holdings are worth billions of dollars."

IDENTIFYING MARK #46: ASSISTED BY ANOTHER KINGDOM

Does the United States assist the Vatican agenda? The most memorable event is of course is Ronald Reagan with John Paul II known as the Holy Alliance.

According to *PBS*, the United States President, since President Dwight D. Eisenhower in 1959, has been the most represented country to the Vatican with no other country being a close second. In fact, "President George W. Bush traveled to the Vatican more than any other

American president." Further, papal visits to outside countries always includes the United States.

According to *LA Times,* Pope John Paul II and President Bill Clinton worked together globally with climate change stance.

According to *Huffington Post,* President Obama and Pope Francis continue to work together globally on climate change.

And before one dismisses climate change stance between the United States and the Vatican as something insignificant, do realize that it is the single agreed upon political movement that has invaded every country in which one can pose sanctions, forced compliance, and even control monetary exchanges.

And in 2015, joint houses of Congress permitted the pope to address them as if the pontiff had more influence upon the members than what was lead to believe.

IDENTIFYING MARK #47: HAS A MARK (OF ALLEGIANCE)

"Of course the Catholic Church claims that the change was her act. And the act is the MARK of her ecclesiastical power and authority in religious matters." Faith of Our Fathers, p. 14, C.F. Thomas, Chancellor of Cardinal Gibbons. The change is in reference to the following conversation between a curious Catholic and Cardinal Gibbons.

One day a man picked up Peter Geiermann's Convert's Catechism of Catholic Doctrine and read the following on page 50:

Q. Which is the Sabbath day?

A. Saturday is the Sabbath day.

Q. Why do we observe Sunday instead of Saturday?

A. We observe Sunday instead of Saturday because the Catholic Church transferred the solemnity from Saturday to Sunday.

The man was dumbfounded and supposed there must be some mistake so he wrote a letter to the then famous James Cardinal Gibbons of Baltimore, and asked if the Catholic church did, indeed, change the day of worship from Saturday to Sunday. The Cardinal replied, "Of course, the Catholic church claims that the change was her act. And the act is a MARK of her ecclesiastical power and authority in religious matters."

Also, notice the following words from The Catholic Record of London, Ontario, Canada, September 1, 1923: "Sunday is our MARK of authority...the church is above the Bible, and this transference of Sabbath observance is proof of that fact."

IDENTIFYING MARK #48: MOTHER OF HARLOTS

According to *Presentation Ministries,* a Catholic outlet, October 2014, "The Church without frontiers, Mother to all, spreads throughout the world a culture of acceptance and solidarity, in which no one is seen as useless, out of place or disposable. When living out this motherhood effectively, the Christian community nourishes, guides and indicates the way, accompanying all with patience, and drawing close to them through prayer and works of mercy."

According to *Catholic News Agency,* September 3, 2014, "This is the Church: a mother who has at heart the good of her children."

According to *Wikipedia,* "The Roman Catholic Church is thought by some to be the mother church of the Protestant and other churches that broke away from it over time. Prominent among these are Lutheran, Reformed, Anglican churches and other Christian faith communities formed over time from these."

Basically, we have the Catholic Church as the recognized mother. It is well established throughout Catholic literature. Protestants are daughters who broke away and are considered harlot daughters because they claim to be Christian while they "transgresseth, and abideth not in the doctrine of Christ" (2 John 1:9) and for that "hath not God" (2 John 1:9). "He that abideth in the doctrine of Christ, he hath both the Father and the Son" (2 John 1:9).

The Protestants originally brought to the attention of the Vatican the lack of using the Bible to establish all beliefs and doctrine, but over time, Protestants had stopped looking for their beliefs from the Bible and resorted to the same false teachings while claiming to be nothing like their mother. They believe they are still protesting because of minor differences between the Vatican and Protestants.

Most Protestant denominations have renamed themselves to Evangelicals and still hold onto Sunday worship without a single verse that clearly establishes it as such while Jesus' custom was to keep the Sabbath (Luke 4:16); His followers understood to continue it even at the point of burying Jesus (Luke 23:56) as recorded by a Gentile writer decades after the resurrection not as a fact of it happening but stressing how important the Sabbath still was regarded; His followers practiced it regularly through the apostles (Acts 18:4, 11); and we will continue to keep the Sabbath in Heaven (Isaiah 66:23). The Vatican even knows this to be true and taunt Protestants that continue to hold to Sunday:

"You may read the Bible from Genesis to Revelation, and you will not find a single line authorizing the sanctification of Sunday. The scriptures enforce the religious observance of Saturday." James Cardinal Gibbons, *The Faith of Our Fathers*, p. 89.

Question--How do you prove that the (Catholic) Church has power to command Feasts and Holy-days?

Answer--By this very act of changing the Sabbath into the Sunday, which is admitted by Protestants, and therefore they contradict themselves by keeping Sunday so strictly, and breaking most other Feasts commanded by the same church.

Question--How do you prove that?

Answer--Because by keeping Sunday they acknowledge the power of the (Catholic) Church to ordain Feasts and to command them under sin, and by not keeping the remainder, equally commanded by her, they deny in fact the same power. Daniel Ferris, Manual of Christian Doctrine: or, Catholic Belief and Practice, pp. 67-68.

"It is well to remind the Presbyterians, Baptists, Methodists, and all other Christians, that the Bible does not support them anywhere in their observance of Sunday. Sunday is an institution of the Roman Catholic Church, and those who observe the day observe a commandment of the Catholic Church." Priest Brady, in an address, reported in the Elizabeth, NJ 'News' on March 18, 1903.

"Protestants ... accept Sunday rather than Saturday as the day for public worship after the Catholic Church made the change... But the Protestant mind does not seem to realize that ... in observing Sunday, they are accepting the authority of the spokesman for the Church, the pope." *Our Sunday Visitor*, February 5th, 1950

"There is but one church on the face of the earth which has the power, or claims power, to make laws binding on the conscience, binding before God, binding under penalty of hell-fire. For instance, the institution of Sunday. What right has any other church to keep this day? You answer by virtue of the third commandment (the papacy did away with the 2nd regarding the worship of graven images, and called the 4th the 3rd), which says 'Remember that thou keep holy the Sabbath day.' But Sunday is not the Sabbath. Any schoolboy knows that Sunday is the first day of the week. I have repeatedly offered one thousand dollars to anyone who will prove by the Bible alone that Sunday is the day we are bound to keep, and no one has called for the money. It was the holy Catholic Church that changed the day of rest from Saturday, the seventh day, to Sunday, the first day of the week." - T. Enright, C.SS.R., in a lecture delivered in 1893.

Protestants may claim that Catholics are about works for salvation while Protestants have grace, but they continue to ignore the Bible doctrine on not eating God's garbage disposals that is unfit for food called unclean (Leviticus 11). They ignore the call to tithe paying (Matthew 23:23). Many accept infant baptism and the incorrect form of it with sprinkling. And the whole notion of spirits or souls floating off into another realm; be it Purgatory, Hell, or Heaven; is also a common error held by the Protestant daughters. There are many more beliefs that are in error and when one adheres to these errors refusing to correct them, that is when they are a harlot, a harlot daughter that is.

IDENTIFYING MARK #49: IS INVOLVED WITH SPIRITUALISM

As a reminder, listen to what the Bible teaches of people who died and rose again or simply were taken alive to Heaven. Jesus "that liveth, and was dead; and, behold, I am alive for evermore, Amen; and have the keys of hell and of death" (Revelation 1:18). "Enoch walked with God: and he [was] not; for God took him" (Genesis 5:24). "And it came to pass, as they still went on, and talked, that, behold, [there appeared] a chariot of fire, and horses of fire, and parted them both asunder; and Elijah went up by a whirlwind into heaven" (2 Kings 2:11). "Yet Michael the archangel, when contending with the devil he disputed about the body of Moses, durst not bring against him a railing accusation, but said, The Lord rebuke thee" (Jude 1:9). "And the graves were opened; and many bodies of the saints which slept arose, And came out of the graves after his resurrection, and went into the holy city, and appeared unto many" (Matthew 27:52-53).

Outside of those listed above, none others are mentioned to be in Heaven, by body, by spirit, or by soul. The Bible clearly teaches, "Dust thou [art], and unto dust shalt thou return" (Genesis 3:19). And a soul is not what a person has, but it is the combination of two things: a body and breath of life. "And the LORD God formed man [of] the dust of the ground, and breathed into his nostrils the breath of life; and man became a living soul" (Genesis 2:7). So, "Thou takest away their breath, they die, and return to their dust"

(Psalms 104:29). We do not float off to Heaven or Hell. Just like Job, "If a man die, shall he live [again]? all the days of my appointed time will I wait, till my change come" (Job 14:14). We wait unconsciously in the grave until the time of the change. When is that? "Behold, I shew you a mystery; We shall not all sleep, but we shall all be changed, In a moment, in the twinkling of an eye, at the last trump: for the trumpet shall sound, and the dead shall be raised incorruptible, and we shall be changed" (1 Corinthians 15:51-52). And just in case one is not connecting these verses to the second coming, "For as in Adam all die, even so in Christ shall all be made alive. But every man in his own order: Christ the firstfruits; afterward they that are Christ's at his coming" (1 Corinthians 15:22-23). And further, Jesus tells us when Heaven and Hell happens. "Marvel not at this: for the hour is coming, in the which all that are in the graves shall hear his voice, And shall come forth; they that have done good, unto the resurrection of life; and they that have done evil, unto the resurrection of damnation" (John 5:28-29).

So that means that if anyone comes back from the dead in ghost, spirit, or whatever form and starts speaking to the living, that is spiritualism, of which is well practiced and recognized from the Vatican.

According to *Catholic Doors,* a Catholic website tracing apparitions approved of by the church:

1061: OUR LADY OF WALSINGHAM, ENGLAND, Lady Richeldis de Faverches, a widow who lived in a manor in Walsingham, experienced three visions by Mary.

1170-1221: ST. DOMINIC, received the Rosary from the Virgin Mary as the greatest weapon against heresies.

1265: ST. SIMON STOCK, received the Brown Scapular from the Virgin Mary with the promise that those who die while wearing it, they will be saved.

1531: OUR LADY OF GUADALUPE, Our Lady appeared to Juan Diego in Mexico City, imprinting her image on the Holy Tilma.

1594: OUR LADY OF GOOD SUCCESS IN QUITO, ECUADOR, Our Lady of Good Success began to appear in Spain to Saint Mariana de Jesus, also known as "The Lily of Quito."

1830: THE MIRACULOUS MEDAL, Our Lady appeared to Catherine Laboure in Paris, France when she was a novice with the St. Vincent de Paul's Daughters of Charity. This is where the origin of the Miraculous Medal comes from, its devotion supporting the Immaculate Conception of Mary as the dispenser of graces.

1846: OUR LADY OF LA SALETTE, Our Lady appeared to two children, Melanie and Maximin. In tears, she warned of a coming chastisement if the people did not do penance for their sins.

1858: OUR LADY OF LOURDES, Appearing to Bernadette Soubirous, Our lady introduced herself as the Immaculate Conception.

1859: ST. JOHN VIANNEY, was blessed with countless visions of Jesus, Mary and demons. He also prophesied the coming chastisement and the final triumph of Mary.

1859: OUR LADY OF GOOD HELP, appeared to Adele Brise in the Diocese of Green Bay, Wisconsin, USA. The Holy Mother did not appear in a crowded city or to people of wealth and power. Instead, she appeared to an unlikely person in an unlikely place.

1871: PONTMAIN, FRANCE, Our Lady appeared to four young children during the time of the Franco-Prussian War.

1879: KNOCK, IRELAND, Our Lady appeared to a group of villagers of mixed ages. This fortified the Irish in their struggle against religious and social oppression.

1917: OUR LADY OF FATIMA, PORTUGAL, Our Lady of Fatima appeared once a month in the Cova da Iria to the 3 children of Fatima, Lucia, Jacinta and Francisco from May 13, 1917 to October 13, 1917.

1922: CHARLES VON HAPSBURG, enjoyed many apparitions from Mary while living in a convent in Switzerland.

1923: SISTER JOSEFA MENENDEZ, received apparitions of Jesus and Mary related to Divine Love and understanding the Sacred Heart.

1930: BANNEUX, BELGIUM, Our Lady appeared to Mariette Beco, just as Hitler was coming to power in Germany.

1932: BEAURAING, BELGIUM, 33 times, Our Lady appeared to 5 children ages 9 to 15 years old.

1976: BETANIA, VENEZUALA, Our Lady appeared to hundreds of persons.

1980: OUR LADY OF NICARAGUA, appeared to Bernardo Martinez and gave him some prophesies, some having passed already.

1981 to 1989, KIBEHO, RWANDA, AFRICA, Six girls and one boy received apparitions and private messages from Our Lady.

1982: OUR LADY OF SOUFANIEH, Since November 27, 1982, Our Lady has been appearing to Mirna Nazzour in Damascus, Syria.

IDENTIFYING MARK #50: ACCEPTS ALL KINDS OF BELIEFS EXCEPT FOR GOD'S

According to *News Now,* November 3, 2014, "Pope backs evolution, Vatican calls creation 'blasphemous.'" "Pope Francis made his staunch support of Darwinian evolution over the Genesis account of creation very clear, backing the Roman Catholic Church's long-established endorsement of the controversial theory."

According to *Catholic Culture,* April 29, 2015, "The Vatican's dangerous embrace of climate-change theory."

According to *Western Journalism,* June 6, 2014, "The pope just invited Islam into the Vatican, Christians aghast."

According to *New York Post,* June 8, 2014, "First ever Jewish, Muslim, Christian prayers at Vatican."

So while putting traditions above the Bible, changing the Ten Commandments, and going directly against the teachings of Jesus, the Vatican accepts and embraces those things listed above and others. Though we ought not mistreat others not of our faith, we in no wise are to join together in worship, even prayer with them. That theme is throughout the Bible and summed up with, "Be ye not unequally yoked together with unbelievers" (2 Corinthians 6:14).

IDENTIFYING MARK #51: MINISTERS WOULD BE VERY RELIGIOUS

This one is fulfilled by observation answering the question, do they appear to be religious? Absolutely. In fact, many do not just appear religious, they are sincerely devoted to religious activities because of their love of God. Mother Theresa could not have done what she did if she was not devoted honestly to serving God. Many priests, bishops, cardinals, and even popes are in many ways, motivated to perform religious activities because of their devotion to God.

So the mark is satisfied as it would be by any religious organization, but the focus is on the Vatican, being at the right place at the right time frame as prophesied, to make sure it satisfies this mark and it does. Unfortunately, their sincere religious activity does not negate the fact that their teaching is erroneous.

What we need to do though is separate in thought that to fulfill this mark does not mean that everyone is faking it. Somehow when we think of Antichrist or even the "Spirit of Antichrist" we think that all involved can do no good for the right reason and only use the good as a purposeful disguise knowing full well that they are the deceivers, and that is not the case. No one ever said that everyone in the Vatican or even the Catholic Church is aware of these things. Be taught a lie long enough and people cannot see the truth right before their eyes. So, the ministers and other officials may sincerely be performing these acts while teaching error, and we should not hold that against them. However, we ought to make such people are aware before it is too late so that they too can choose to escape the deception.

IDENTIFYING MARK #52: FOLLOWERS WILL APPEAR RELIGIOUS

Again, by observation, we see that many Catholics are truly devoted religiously. Most are not aware of these accusations, have been brainwashed to thinking all of this is just anti-Catholic rhetoric without any real basis, etc. And again, the description of the last days among the followers of Antichrist is that they would do real outreach in helping the poor, feeding the hungry, providing shelter to the widows and homeless, and much more. They would even go so far as to see manifestations like prophesying, casting out demons, healing the seriously sick, and even speaking in tongues (Matthew 7:22). But in the end, Jesus will say, "I never knew you: depart from me, ye that work iniquity" (Matthew 7:23). And that is just it, because such people remain in the deception, they do not get a free exemption card. Jesus warned plenty to "Take heed that no man deceive you" (Matthew 24:4). So as they give an answer to their faith, they are uttering nothing but lies without knowing it.

These too, for the love of God, are not to be treated harshly, "But speaking the truth in love" (Ephesians 4:15). The appeal is not to dismiss this as an agenda to attack the Catholic Church. It is simply taking a look at over fifty points that the Bible says identifies who the Antichrist is and what the false doctrines are because, and this proves that we are not anti-Catholic, one does not have to be Catholic to fall for the deception of the "Spirit of Antichrist". Many anti-Catholic Protestants are being deceived by the original Antichrist teaching for not giving them up, especially that one on keeping Sunday instead of the Sabbath. So we are no more anti-Catholic as we would be anti-Protestant. What we are is anti-error having a love for souls in this spiritual warfare.

IDENTIFYING MARK #53: ESTABLISHES THEIR PRESENCE IN ISRAEL

According to *Voice of America,* June 5, 2014, "Pope Francis Gets Involved In Middle East Peace Process."

That is the significant point so far, but we await and see what more fulfills this point, but in the mean time, this is significant in fulfilling this mark.

IDENTIFYING MARK #54: WOULD BE A WORLD INFLUENCER

No other leader gets as much world attention as does the pope. No other leader draws as much in numbers at gatherings as does the pope. And when it comes to religious competition, Hindus, all Christian denominations, Jews, and even Muslims have some type of respect and recognition. The pope is considered the world religious leader.

According to the *Huffington Post,* October 5, 2015, "Pope Francis is officially the leader of the Catholic Church -- however in giving his best to the world, Catholics and non-Catholics alike, he is a leader for us all."

According to *Market Watch,* July 21, 2015, "Pope Francis is not just leading a 'Second American Revolution,' he is rallying people across the Earth, middle class as well as poor, inciting billions to rise up in a global economic revolution, one that could suddenly sweep the planet, like the 1789 French storming the Bastille."

According to *News.va,* the official Vatican Network, December 2, 2014, "Religious leaders gathered in the Vatican".

According to *The New York Times,* March 20, 2013, "Pope Meets Other Religious Leaders, Pledging Respect".

According to *Climate Progress,* a publication of Think Progress, on June 23, 2015, stated, "On Tuesday, a group of religious leaders took out a full-page advertisement on the back page of Politico to offer resounding support for Pope Francis and his recently-released encyclical on the environment."

According to *Time,* June 17, 2015, "On social media and in formal statements, Protestant, Jewish, Buddhist and Muslim leaders have backed the pope's call for strong action to address climate change."

According to *US News,* on July 3, 2015, "Pope urges Christian unity: 'When they kill a Christian they don't ask, Are you Catholic?'"

According to *The Washington Examiner,* November 28, 2014, "Pope Francis: Christians, Muslims must unite to fight Islamic State".

According to *The Huffington Post,* June 4, 2014, "Pope Francis' Influence In World Politics Has Made Vatican Globally Relevant Again".

According to *The New Statesman,* April 2, 2015, "Beloved of the people: how the Pope has again become a leader for our times".

According to *Newsweek,* April 28, 2015, "Pope is the Most Influential World Leader on Twitter".

According to *NBC News, Today News,* March 20, 2014, "Pope Francis tops Fortune's 'World's Greatest Leaders' list, but no Obama".

According to *Esquire,* September 12, 2013, "Leading Atheist: Pope Francis 'Is the Kind of World Leader We Need'".

However widely accepted the pope and the Vatican seem to be enjoying, not all will bow down to the papacy and the Vatican. According to prophecy, "He shall enter also into the glorious land, and many [countries] shall be overthrown: but these shall escape out of his hand, [even] Edom, and Moab, and the chief of the children of Ammon" (Daniel 11:41). The named areas are all Muslim areas. So if one thinks that the Vatican will never gain the respect of all of the Muslims, they are correct. But the papacy will gain enough world influence that it will not be needful to have every single person pay homage to the papacy, and yet God is able to say, "All the world wondered after the beast" (Revelation 13:3).

How Do These Facts and Apparent Fulfillment Affect Us?

No doubt we have angered a few. Many will discredit through unbelief what has been shared, based upon past experience, what we see published on the internet, etc. And that is a shame.

Many try to pick off a few of the marks and say, "Ah ha! The Vatican does not fulfill this" or "I don't see the verse quite the way as explained." But like we said before, it is not by coincidence that so many of these marks are right on target, and significant ones at that. So to disagree with a few minor ones, even though it may not appear to the beholder to be on target, is to be wrestling with God and not the mark identified.

Who can argue about location, time frames, activities, etc.? Yet, many are ready to dismiss all of these points because of one thing and one thing only, selfishness. No one wants to change their lives. They are comfortable in their beliefs and feel that they are in a saving relationship as they are, but remember, Jesus said, "Because thou art lukewarm, and neither cold nor hot, I will spue thee out of my mouth" (Revelation 3:16). Lukewarm, complacency, self justification, etc., God hates all of that. And remember also, it is "with all deceivableness of unrighteousness in them that perish;

because they received not the love of the truth, that they might be saved" (2 Thessalonians 2:10). So it is not enough to just discard a few points in order to dismiss this entire book, but if one really loves the truth but does not think this is the truth, they need to prove the true meaning of these things. To go on to say that one is not smart enough but they know this is not the truth is just another way to lie to oneself.

If God's way was beyond understanding, He would not have bent over backwards in trying to convey it to us. For instance, "Thy way, O God, [is] in the sanctuary: who [is so] great a God as [our] God?" (Psalms 77:13) So pictorially, look at the sanctuary and tell us how we are wrong. The sanctuary even identifies that people are not taken unto Heaven until the symbolic last feast day, which is far separated from the time Jesus rose to present Himself as the first fruits, all of which matches the words in the Bible, "Christ the firstfruits; afterward they that are Christ's at his coming" (1 Corinthians 15:23). So who started the doctrine of going to Heaven or Hell right after death? The Vatican.

God would not have tried to preserve His Word and provide us with a picture representation if He was going to just say, "You fools! You can't see this stuff because I am beyond figuring out."

Do People Judge Christianity Through the Wrong Eyes?

Dear Unbeliever:

Yes, this is our second letter to hopefully an audience that is beyond just the professed Christian, although many professed Christians do need to read this so that you are not just professing but actually living Christianity. We are hoping to appeal to unbelievers who have dismissed Christianity thanks to the activities of the Antichrist, even the "Spirit of Antichrist".

What is called Christianity today and what has been called Christianity in the past, is not Christianity. In fact, true Christianity is "the hidden man of the heart" (1 Peter 3:4), meaning it is done in quietness and most of what is done openly is for show by the pretended Christian. Jesus even said, "That thine alms may be in secret: and thy Father which seeth in secret himself shall reward thee openly" (Matthew 6:4); "But thou, when thou prayest, enter into thy closet, and when thou hast shut thy door, pray to thy Father which is in secret; and thy Father which seeth in secret shall reward thee openly" (Matthew 6:6); and "That thou appear not unto men to fast, but unto thy Father which is in secret: and thy Father, which seeth in secret, shall reward thee openly" (Matthew 6:18). Yet, what has been and is demonstrated to the world as Christianity is nothing but being done in the open to be seen. Some of it is annoying, but other parts are downright dangerous.

Now we do not dismiss that Christians ought to be "the light of the world. A city that is set on an hill cannot be hid. Neither do men light a candle, and put it under a bushel, but on a candlestick; and it giveth light unto all that are in the house. Let your light so shine before men, that they may see your good works, and glorify your Father which is in heaven" (Matthew 5:14-16). This reference is to the Christian that is living it, not to be seen on purpose, but is who they are. And when they are around friends or in public, they do not hide who they are. But this is different from the Christian that brags about their good deeds or do deeds in such a way that comes across as wearing a bumper sticker "look at what I did in the name of Jesus". Those that hide their Christianity are the ones putting Christianity under a bushel basket, and that is wrong also.

Basically, Christianity is balanced. It excuses itself from participating in sin or those things that will probably lead to sin, while at the same time does not compromise upon principle. Christianity is ready with an answer when asked directly or indirectly. Christianity does not go out of its way to purposely cause problems, but will not participate where compromise is required. True Christianity does not condemn to hell or even to the world anyone, but is always willing to reach out to help people up out of sin, despite falsely being accused of judging. Yes, true Christianity does judge but in a way to save. In fact, for how much the world is against judging, every day it judges. The difference is the action is what is to be judged. Yes, those attached to sinful actions, if continued therein, will end up in hell, but the purpose of judging the action is to seek and save the lost as Jesus did. "For God sent not his Son into the world to condemn the world; but that the world through him might be saved" (John 3:17), but He added, "And this is the condemnation, that light is come into the world, and men loved darkness rather than light, because their deeds were evil" (John 3:19). So all those that claim, "Don't judge me", especially from Christian lips, are speaking erroneously. To judge and gossip or to judge and dismiss the person from the gospel is wrong. To become aware that a practicing sinner needs help overcoming is the balanced form of judging.

So we would like everyone to dismiss the false Christianity and look at the true form of it. Again, for those that wonder how we can tell what is true and what is false Christianity, the answer is again, the practice of "rightly dividing the word of truth" (2 Timothy 2:15), which is being "weaned from the milk, [and] drawn from the breasts. For precept [must be] upon precept, precept upon precept; line upon line, line upon line; here a little, [and] there a little" (Isaiah 28:9). Also, accepting "God is not [the author] of confusion" (1 Corinthians 14:33), therefore, the Bible must be understood in a manner that does not contradict itself.

This is easily demonstrated by the fact in the New Testament, we have verses that put down the use of the law with regards to salvation and other places the law is explicitly commanded to be obeyed if we are a true Christian. Many that interpret the Bible incorrectly dismiss the Ten Commandments. That would contradict all the verse like "If thou wilt enter into life, keep the commandments" (Matthew 19:17). On the other hand, if we think we ought to be keeping the Passover still, then certain verses do not make sense like, "For the law having a shadow of good things to come, [and] not the very image of the things, can never with those sacrifices which they offered year by year continually make the comers thereunto perfect" (Hebrews 10:1). The conclusion is that when we see verses commanding to keep the law, it refers to the Ten Commandments, which have not been nailed to the cross, not been replaced by grace, and are not used to work one's way to Heaven, but is the conduct of a person saved by grace. Likewise, when the verses in context speak of not having to keep the law, they then, without contradiction, speak of the ceremonial law that directed a visual representation towards Jesus. Since Jesus has already come, there is no need to be pointing to Jesus to come with the practice of such anymore.

Although it may appear arrogant to think only a few people are the only ones on this planet that have the right understanding of the Bible, it is the truth, "because strait [is] the gate, and narrow [is] the way, which leadeth unto life, and few there be that find it" (Matthew 7:14), and "all the world wondered after the beast" (Revelation 13:3), meaning, almost every Christian is listening and obeying the lies of the Antichrist or even the "Spirit of Antichrist". They do not have to obey all of what is commanded through them, but any of it that is accepted is poison enough. Satan does not care if 100% of poison is swallowed or 5%. In the end, it kills.

With that in mind, if one is turned off from Christianity because of the scientific rejections of the past, like Galileo discovering that the earth was not the center of the universe and the world was not flat as Columbus proved, we agree. The Vatican or papacy at that time had no right to condemn such people as heretics because of their discoveries. However, there is "science falsely so called" (1 Timothy 6:20), but one still does not try to silence such. We as Christians ought to just not believe it, unlike the practice of old, in which stake burning was much desired.

If one is turned off from Christianity because of the crusades, again, we are in total agreement. "Jesus answered, My kingdom is not of this world: if my kingdom were of this world, then would my servants fight, that I should not be delivered to the Jews: but now is my kingdom not from hence" (John 18:36). True Christianity has no physical army, so all of those attempts to conquer in the name of the papacy, was all wrong. It also condemns the atrocities of Catholics slaughtering Protestants and Protestants slaughtering Catholics. Have not such people learned a lesson from the time Jesus was snubbed? He did not destroy them. In fact, "it came to pass, when the time was come that he should be received up, he stedfastly set his face to go to Jerusalem, And sent messengers before his face: and they went, and entered into a village of the Samaritans, to make ready for him. And they did not receive him, because his face was as though he would go to Jerusalem. And when his disciples James and John saw [this], they said, Lord, wilt thou that we command fire to come down from heaven, and consume them, even as Elias did? But he turned, and rebuked them, and said, Ye know not what manner of spirit ye are of. For the Son of man is not come to destroy men's lives, but to save [them]. And they went to another village" (Luke 9:51-56).

If one is turned off from Christianity because of its practice both inside the Catholic Church as well as most Protestant denominations of putting people in Heaven or Hell right now, we agree. Despite Jesus teaching a parable that involved the subject of apparent Heaven and Hell by saying, "Father Abraham, have mercy on me, and send

Lazarus, that he may dip the tip of his finger in water, and cool my tongue; for I am tormented in this flame" (Luke 16:24), it was not to be taken literally. It was a parable, a story to teach a particular point, for "All these things spake Jesus unto the multitude in parables; and without a parable spake he not unto them" (Matthew 13:34). That point was to demonstrate that we may not know who is destined for Heaven and Hell by outward appearance. Our reality of who we think goes to Heaven and Hell is a bit off. Besides, if one did believe in immediate Heaven and Hell by spirit form, just how can the rich man have a tongue? Dig up any grave and their tongue, unless decomposed, will be there. So again, if you are turned off by such teachings of people being in Heaven, we are on your side. The Bible teaches that we go to Heaven and burn in Hell with physical bodies. Again, dig up any grave, those bodies will be uncovered in what is known as a state of unconscious sleep. Yes, when God "takest away their breath, they die, and return to their dust" (Psalms 104:29), so they will decompose, but upon the second coming, "all that are in the graves shall hear his voice, And shall come forth; they that have done good, unto the resurrection of life; and they that have done evil, unto the resurrection of damnation" (John 5:28-29). Those bodies will be reconstructed. Those headed to Heaven, God "shall change our vile body, that it may be fashioned like unto his glorious body" (Philippians 3:21), and those headed to Hell, will come up pretty much the way they entered.

If one is turned off by Christianity with the excuses for being allowed to sin, you are not alone. That is nothing more than pretended Christians that well outnumber the true Christians. In the world, we use the phrase, "a few bad apples", well, the opposite is true in Christianity. There are only "a few good apples." Even the Bible says, "He that saith, I know him, and keepeth not his commandments, is a liar, and the truth is not in him" (1 John 2:4), and just about every Christian is carelessly breaking the commandments, and this is beside the obvious one, which is the disregarding of the Sabbath day. Christians pull practical jokes, lie on contracts, are lazy, commit adultery, are not careful in what they listen to or watch, all of which is a small list of what constitutes breaking the commandments.

If one is turned off by Christianity with the speaking of tongues, especially from the perspective of it being a bunch of gibberish, we agree. The speaking in tongues should have the result "that every man heard them speak in his own language" (Acts 2:6), and not some unknown unproductive usage. Basically, where there is no interpreter, the Holy Spirit steps in. And "wherefore tongues are for a sign, not to them that believe, but to them that believe not" (1 Corinthians 14:22). So all of those church services where people gather to speak in tongues or when Christian believers come together for worship and someone breaks out in tongues, know full well that it is not of God.

If one is turned off by Christianity where people just pray and let God handle things, realize we also are turned off because God is not some genie. He also does not do for us what we can do for ourselves. In fact, Jesus told a parable on this subject. "A certain [man] went down from Jerusalem to Jericho, and fell among thieves, which stripped him of his raiment, and wounded [him], and departed, leaving [him] half dead. And by chance there came down a certain priest that way: and when he saw him, he passed by on the other side. And likewise a Levite, when he was at the place, came and looked [on him], and passed by on the other side. But a certain Samaritan, as he journeyed, came where he was: and when he saw him, he had compassion [on him], And went to [him], and bound up his wounds, pouring in oil and wine, and set him on his own beast, and brought him to an inn, and took care of him. And on the morrow when he departed, he took out two pence, and gave [them] to the host, and said unto him, Take care of him; and whatsoever thou spendest more, when I come again, I will repay thee. Which now of these three, thinkest thou, was neighbour unto him that fell among the thieves?" (Luke 10:30-36) Was it the ones that may have offered up a prayer, referring to the Levite and priest? Of course not. It is the one that got his hands dirty. So all those Christians that approach a crisis, offers up a prayer or says, "I'll go pray about it", are not true Christians.

If one is turned off by Christianity because of declaring once to have been saved and anything that seems to be any effort is dismissed as salvation by works, again, are not true Christians. One Christian says that they do not go to the movies because Jesus would not want them seeing and hearing certain things, is easily obeyed by a person who never cared for movies anyways, while another Christian that claims to be saved as well, will sit through full on naked women, foul words flying around so much that it comes across as the primary language, along with super intense violence, etc. And yet another supposed Christian will have no problem in watching porn claiming that it is acceptable today. It all depends on a person's tolerance of putting any effort into walking like Christ walked (1 John 2:6) or conducted His life. To the porn viewer, to have those urges is too much to have to deal with and therefore, since they are "saved" anyways, why put so much effort into resisting? Well, the Bible would say, "Ye have not yet resisted unto blood, striving against sin" (Hebrews 12:4), and "the soul that sinneth, it shall die" (Ezekiel 18:4). To those that do not want to stand out from their worldly friends and will sit through trashy movies, God says, "He that taketh not his cross, and followeth after me, is not worthy of me" (Matthew 10:38). All such Christians have been deceived by an easy gospel and are no representation of Christianity whatsoever.

Now on the other hand, if one is looking for such allowance and are turned off by all the do's and don'ts, well, true Christianity would not be for such a person. Basically, we live in a world that everything is tainted by sin, and where we can resist such, we are to do so, because the rule is, "Whatsoever things are true, whatsoever things [are] honest, whatsoever things [are] just, whatsoever things [are] pure, whatsoever things [are] lovely, whatsoever things [are] of good report; if [there be] any virtue, and if [there be] any praise, think on these things" (Philippians 4:8). Although it is pretty hard to conduct one's shopping without being exposed to sexual songs, it is our responsibility to not have it on in our cars or at home. Although it is pretty hard to interact with people who use foul language, we are not to be paying good money to be entertained by such nor adding such words to our conversation. Although there is nothing wrong with having a little fun, the world's version of fun involves sin mostly and we are not to be part of that for we "are not of the world" (John 17:16). In fact, true Christians "Love not the world, neither the things [that are] in the world. If any man love the world, the love of the Father is not in him" (1 John 2:15). So true Christians are not sports fanatics, cannot careless what Hollywood produces or promotes, and are very much family oriented protecting from what society considers to be normal and acceptable all the while criticizing parents who shelter their children.

If one is turned off by Christianity because of the superstitions, especially through prayer, we agree. We already covered "vain repetitions" (Matthew 6:7), but all of those notes that fly around on the Internet that say, "Repeat this prayer and something will happen" is all the work of the devil. All those prayers said at a certain hour each day in hopes of something happening is also superstition. Again, God is not magic.

If one is turned off by Christianity because of scientifically proven fact that transubstantiation is a hoax, we agree. We also agree on the Shroud of Turin being a fake. Constantine putting an emblem on all of his soldiers shields created trust in an emblem and not looking to God. Although science tries to explain away all miracles, all miracles are not to be attributed to God, and especially worshipped.

If one is turned off by Christianity because you cannot serve a God that gets His jollies out of tormenting people throughout eternity, well, you are not alone. The Bible does not teach that, although there is a burning: "behold, the day cometh, that shall burn as an oven; and all the proud, yea, and all that do wickedly, shall be stubble: and the day that cometh shall burn them up, saith the LORD of hosts, that it shall leave them neither root nor branch" (Malachi 4:1). "And ye shall tread down the wicked; for they shall be ashes under the soles of your feet in the day that I shall do [this], saith the LORD of hosts" (Malachi 4:3). It is a little hard to live in hell throughout eternity when one is reduced to ashes. In fact, to Satan, "Thou hast defiled thy sanctuaries by the multitude of thine iniquities, by the iniquity of thy traffick; therefore will I bring forth a fire from the midst of thee, it shall devour thee, and I will bring thee to ashes upon the earth in the sight of all them that behold thee. All they that know thee among the people shall be astonished at thee: thou shalt be a terror, and never [shalt] thou [be] any more" (Ezekiel 28:18-19). Even Satan will be no more. Although God cannot allow everyone into Heaven because the whole point is to eradicate sin, He is merciful to those that refuse to surrender their sins and will in a very short period of time, burn them up and reduce them to ashes. Besides, the most famous verse quoted among Christians reveals that God is not a tortuous god. "For God so loved the world, that he gave his only begotten Son, that whosoever believeth in him should not perish, but have everlasting life" (John 3:16). What are the choices? Either perish or have eternal life. It does not say that the lost will suffer everlasting perishing. Also, it is only to the saved that everlasting life is promised, but if one were to burn in hell, that too would be a form of everlasting life, now would that not be so? Of course it would. So no, God is not going to torture people throughout eternity. The lost will perish, be devoured (Revelation 20:9), and "the soul that sinneth, it shall die" (Ezekiel 18:4). Nowhere in the Bible is there a hint at an immortal soul, so even the notion that the soul will continue on is false. Eternity is only for those that choose to live according to God's commandments, while the rest are put out of their misery. "if thou wilt enter into life, keep the commandments" (Matthew 19:17), while those that do not, perish.

Basically, there is much of what is called Christian that is not Christian at all. It is Christianized paganism for the most part and acts of Satan to encourage the continuation thereof. True Christianity is practical, not forceful, and is not based primarily upon emotions and feelings. True Christianity makes all around them better. As it is said, "Charity suffereth long, [and] is kind; charity envieth not; charity vaunteth not itself, is not puffed up, Doth not behave itself unseemly, seeketh not her own, is not easily provoked, thinketh no evil; Rejoiceth not in iniquity, but rejoiceth in the truth; Beareth all things, believeth all things, hopeth all things, endureth all things" (1 Corinthians 13:4-7). True Christianity will suffer loss if it especially means a proper witness for God.

So, we ask the unbeliever to reevaluate Christianity upon its true merits and not by observation by the so many pretended ones that do not use the guidebook, the Bible, as their rule of faith, are taught by preachers who also do not accept the Bible in its authoritative position, and everyone blaming the Holy Spirit for leading them to being who they are.

What Shows Which "One Mind" A Person Is On?

There are two groups of people that basically have "one mind", as exposed so far. One is either having the mind of Christ, or they have the mind of Antichrist, through even the "Spirit of Antichrist". Those that are of Christ are to be "with one mind [and] one mouth glorify God, even the Father of our Lord Jesus Christ" (Romans 15:6). Those influenced by the Antichrist, they "receive power as kings one hour with the beast. These have one mind, and shall give their power and strength unto the beast" (Revelation 17:12-13).

As we have revealed from the Bible, the war, the battle, the conflict is all about the mind, so how does that understanding apply to the interesting topic about the mark of the beast? Before we answer that, as our practice has always been, we will provide you with all the Bible verses uninfluenced so you can come to your own conclusion first. Just as Isaiah 28:9-10 tells us, we have to the best of our ability gathered all of the verses dealing with the mark of the beast. The Bible verses on the subject are these:

- Revelation 13:17 And that no man might buy or sell, save he that had the mark, or the name of the beast, or the number of his name.

- Revelation 14:9-10 And the third angel followed them, saying with a loud voice, If any man worship the beast and his image, and receive [his] mark in his forehead, or in his hand, the same shall drink of the wine of the wrath of God, which is poured out without mixture into the cup of his indignation; and he shall be tormented with fire and brimstone in the presence of the holy angels, and in the presence of the Lamb.

- Revelation 14:11 And the smoke of their torment ascendeth up for ever and ever: and they have no rest day nor night, who worship the beast and his image, and whosoever receiveth the mark of his name.

- Revelation 15:2 And I saw as it were a sea of glass mingled with fire: and them that had gotten the victory over the beast, and over his image, and over his mark, [and] over the number of his name, stand on the sea of glass, having the harps of God.

- Revelation 16:2 And the first went, and poured out his vial upon the earth; and there fell a noisome and grievous sore upon the men which had the mark of the beast, and [upon] them which worshipped his image.

- Revelation 19:20 And the beast was taken, and with him the false prophet that wrought miracles before him, with which he deceived them that had received the mark of the beast, and them that worshipped his image. These both were cast alive into a lake of fire burning with brimstone.

- Revelation 20:4 And I saw thrones, and they sat upon them, and judgment was given unto them: and [I saw] the souls of them that were beheaded for the witness of Jesus, and for the word of God, and which had not worshipped the beast, neither his image, neither had received [his] mark upon their foreheads, or in their hands; and they lived and reigned with Christ a thousand years.

Now nowhere in these verses does the Bible explain what the mark of the beast happens to be explicitly, however, because money appears to be involved in the buying and selling, all attention is given to mechanisms of purchase or identification for purchase. But consider this, if the battle is for the mind, why would the mark of the beast be a physical object? Have we not learned the lesson from the Corinthians? "Howbeit [there is] not in every man that knowledge: for some with conscience of the idol unto this hour eat [it] as a thing offered unto an idol; and their conscience being weak is defiled. But meat commendeth us not to God: for neither, if we eat, are we the better; neither, if we eat not, are we the worse. But take heed lest by any means this liberty of yours become a stumblingblock to them that are weak. For if any man see thee which hast knowledge sit at meat in the idol's temple, shall not the conscience of him which is weak be emboldened to eat those things which are offered to idols; And through thy knowledge shall the weak brother perish, for whom Christ died? But when ye sin so against the brethren, and wound their weak conscience, ye sin against Christ. Wherefore, if meat make my brother to offend, I will eat no flesh while the world standeth, lest I make my brother to offend" (1 Corinthians 8:7-13). Basically, meat offered to idols means nothing to God. They had the freedom to consume it, however, Paul would choose not to eat such in front of those weaker Christians that thought it did mean something. By eating the meant, that may cause them to sin, at least in the mind, but nonetheless, the sin would be upon Paul for causing such and not taking the precaution. The point is, a credit card, an identification number, laser beamed code on foreheads, chips in our hands, all mean nothing to God. God is not about objects, in fact, getting pinned down by a mob and being chipped against one's will does not make that person lost, nor does the forced laser beam across one's forehead.

Besides, in addition to the mark of the beast, God has His own marking. Here are the verses on the subject in which now you have two markings in the Bible: one for God and one for Antichrist.

- Revelation 7:2-3 And I saw another angel ascending from the east, having the seal of the living God: and he cried with a loud voice to the four angels, to whom it was given to hurt the earth and the sea, Saying, Hurt not the earth, neither the sea, nor the trees, till we have sealed the servants of our God in their foreheads.

- Revelation 7:4-8 And I heard the number of them which were sealed: [and there were] sealed an hundred [and] forty [and] four thousand of all the tribes of the children of Israel. Of the tribe of Juda [were] sealed twelve thousand. Of the tribe of Reuben [were] sealed twelve thousand. Of the tribe of Gad [were] sealed twelve thousand. Of the tribe of Aser [were] sealed twelve thousand. Of the tribe of Nepthalim [were] sealed twelve thousand. Of the tribe of Manasses [were] sealed twelve thousand. Of the tribe of Simeon [were] sealed twelve thousand. Of the tribe of Levi [were] sealed twelve thousand. Of the tribe of Issachar [were] sealed twelve thousand. Of the tribe of Zabulon [were] sealed twelve thousand. Of the tribe of Joseph [were] sealed twelve thousand. Of the tribe of Benjamin [were] sealed twelve thousand.

- Revelation 9:4 And it was commanded them that they should not hurt the grass of the earth, neither any green thing, neither any tree; but only those men which have not the seal of God in their foreheads.

- Revelation 14:1 And I looked, and, lo, a Lamb stood on the mount Sion, and with him an hundred forty [and] four thousand, having his Father's name written in their foreheads.

- Revelation 22:4 And they shall see his face; and his name [shall be] in their foreheads.

So God has a seal and the Antichrist has a mark. The Seal of God identifies that we have "one mind" of Jesus Christ, while the mark of the beast identifies that we have "one mind" with the Antichrist. How much more do we believe then that the Seal of God is a literal seal? Do we really think an angel is going to brand our foreheads with a seal that everyone else can see, therefore, preventing such people from getting the mark of the beast? It is just not so, and further study on the subject will reveal this.

Although we do not negate the fact that an electronic tracking system will be in place, possibly including a certain credit card, even a chip, the card or the chip is not the mark of the beast. Again, further study shall prove this out, but before we do, let us make some observations between the mark of the beast and the seal of God.

1. God has a seal while the Antichrist has a mark.

2. God's seal may only be received in the forehead, while the Antichrist accepts either the forehead or the hand.

3. God's seal is applied before some world crisis or combination of more than one strikes, while the mark of the beast is brought in during a period of time where buying and selling is controlled globally, probably following the crisis for typically, with good intention, governments usually assert such controls during periods of crisis so that things are rationed properly.

4. God's seal is placed upon but a few people, while the mark of the beast is, with all the world wondering after it (Revelation 13:3), open to numerous people to receive it.

5. God's seal is protective from the end result of the crisis with the final result being gathered into Heaven along the sea of glass, while the mark of the beast will end with being unprotected and eventually suffering the future plagues (Revelation 16:2) and the fires of hell.

6. God's seal makes it difficult to survive the controls placed upon the world, while the mark of the beast allows one to freely enjoy commerce.

7. The battle between the seal of God and the mark of the beast involves worship, witnessing, and the Word of God, which really begins to point to the fact that the mark of the beast is not a literal object but a spiritual one.

8. God's seal has his name imprinted, while the mark of the beast is either the number or the name of the Antichrist beast.

These are but some of the conclusions we see in those verses, but here is something that is interesting. There is a whole lot of talk about the mark of the beast, but not so much on the seal of God. Did you know that if one is successful in avoiding the mark of the beast, they do not automatically receive the seal of God and will still be lost? In fact, it is safe to say that to have the seal of God is to be able to successfully avoid the mark of the beast. So since the seal of God is actually more important than avoiding the mark of the beast, let us study both subjects giving precedence towards God's seal.

Now let us make sure we all understand the subject matter of seals and marks. We are not talking about an arbitrary mark or symbol. The word "seal" means different things to people. But in the political or official realm of things there is a specific description to it. We say political because God's seal is representing that He is the ruler ruling from Heaven as opposed to any earthly ruler, which have their own political seals. A seal contains three parts. There is the person's name, what office they hold, and what territory they rule over. In a president's seal, there is the name of the president, the title of president, and the territory they can command over. Putting a seal on a document declaring all Canadians are now obligated to pay a tax to the United States would be worthless because of missing an important part: the appropriate territory. Likewise, if I were to declare that United States citizens no longer have to pay taxes, my name may carry some weight, but my title as citizen does not, even though I am of the United States. So all three pieces are required.

Now on this planet, there are many that fight for authority, and we are not talking human beings. In the past, there were the pagan gods; today there are the atheists with evolution; multiple religions that some even have multiple gods; and other competition. So we need to find a title that is connected not to just a god, but that declares the true God, and find out what territory He claims. The Bible says, "But the LORD [is] the true God, he [is] the living God, and an everlasting king: at his wrath the earth shall tremble, and the nations shall not be able to abide his indignation. Thus shall ye say unto them, The gods that have not made the heavens and the earth, [even] they shall perish from the earth, and from under these heavens. He hath made the earth by his power, he hath established the world by his wisdom, and hath stretched out the heavens by his discretion" (Jeremiah 10:10-12). Inside these verses we see the true God is identified along with His unique title of Maker or Creator and the territory being all nations. In reality, His territory is the universe, but all nations is sufficient.

Let us start with comparing God's people to the beast's people.

1. God's people "worship Him that made heaven, earth, sea, and fountains of water" (Revelation 14:7), while those that are deceived by the Antichrist "worship the beast and his image, and receive [his] mark in his forehead, or in his hand" (Revelation 14:9). So again, think of some mark that reveals worship. A credit card, a chip, etc. does not do that.

2. God's people as "true worshippers shall worship the Father in spirit and in truth" because

"God [is] a Spirit: and they that worship him must worship [him] in spirit and in truth" (John 4:23-24), while on the beast side, the people "received not the love of the truth, that they might be saved" (2 Thessalonians 2:10). So the mark of the beast is involved with truth versus a lie. Interestingly, the Bible clearly says that this conclusion is so. "I have not written unto you because ye know not the truth, but because ye know it, and that no lie is of the truth. Who is a liar but he that denieth that Jesus is the Christ? He is Antichrist, that denieth the Father and the Son" (1 John 2:21-22). "We are of God: he that knoweth God heareth us; he that is not of God heareth not us. Hereby know we the spirit of truth, and the spirit of error" (1 John 4:6). Can a credit card or chip reflect truth or error, truth or lies? No, of course not. It tracks. Chips can track location, track activity, and state facts, but it cannot declare the truth.

3. God's people "keep the commandments of God, and the faith of Jesus" (Revelation 14:12), while the people influenced by the beast have given into the notion that the Antichrist was able to "change times and laws" (Daniel 7:25). In fact, "We do know that we know him, if we keep his commandments. He that saith, I know him, and keepeth not his commandments, is a liar, and the truth is not in him"(1 John 2:3-4).

4. God's people will, as He says, "love me, he will keep my words: and my Father will love him, and we will come unto him, and make our abode with him" (Revelation 14:12), while the deceived people will be part of "a falling away" (2 Thessalonians 2:3) and "shall depart from the faith, giving heed to seducing spirits, and doctrines of devils" (1 Timothy 4:1).

Again, we remind everyone that the issues appear to be all spiritual, and we ought not get caught up in the hype about credit cards, chips, laser beams, electronic tracking, etc. We ought to be considering that the mark shows that the Antichrist has usurped worship, cast down the truth, changed the commandments, and rejected the word. So the mark should be worship related over a lie regarding the commandments that are not substantiated by the Word of God. Further investigation will indeed reveal exactly this, and thinking along the lines that if we understand how one is sealed, then we ought to see exactly how one is marked.

So in regards to receiving the seal of God, realize that first, the Holy Spirit is involved in the sealing process for "He which stablisheth us with you in Christ, and hath anointed us, [is] God; Who hath also sealed us, and given the earnest of the Spirit in our hearts" (2 Corinthians 1:21-22).

Second, notice when people are sealed. "In whom ye also [trusted], after that ye heard the word of truth, the gospel of your salvation: in whom also after that ye believed, ye were sealed with that holy Spirit of promise" (Ephesians 1:13). We are sealed by the Holy Spirit when we hear the truth and believe it. Remember, truth is found in three locations, the Word (John 17:17), Jesus (John 14:6), and the Ten Commandments (Psalm 119:142).

Third, "when he, the Spirit of truth, is come, he will guide you into all truth" (John 16:13), so the Holy Spirit will guide us to the Word of God, keep the commandments, and follow the teachings of Jesus.

Fourth, of the three locations of the truth (Jesus, the Word, and the Law), the Holy Spirit concentrates particularly on one of them. "Bind up the testimony, seal the law among my disciples" (Isaiah 8:16). A disciple of God is sealed with the law.

Fifth, and since we have narrowed down the seal to the point that it is contained within the Ten Commandment law, which one is specifically containing God's name, title, and territory? The answer is in Exodus 20:8-11, which says, "Remember the sabbath day, to keep it holy. Six days shalt thou labour, and do all thy work: But the seventh day [is] the sabbath of the LORD thy God (1): [in it] thou shalt not do any work, thou, nor thy son, nor thy daughter, thy manservant, nor thy maidservant, nor thy cattle, nor thy stranger that [is] within thy gates: For [in] six days the LORD made (2) heaven and earth (3), the sea, and all that in them [is], and rested the seventh day: wherefore the LORD blessed the sabbath day, and hallowed it." As numbered in the verse, the three components of the Seal of God are found right in the middle of the Sabbath Commandment, where He is referenced as "Lord thy God", carrying the title that He "made", and identifying the territory of "heaven and earth".

Now let us see if it truly is declared in the Bible to be such. Is the Sabbath really the Seal of God? According to Exodus 31:13, it says, "Speak thou also unto the children of Israel, saying, Verily my sabbaths ye shall keep: for it [is] a sign between me and you throughout your generations; that [ye] may know that I [am] the LORD that doth sanctify you." Ezekiel 20:12 says, "Moreover also I gave them my sabbaths, to be a sign between me and them, that they might know that I [am] the LORD that sanctify them."

Ezekiel 20:20 says, "And hallow my sabbaths; and they shall be a sign between me and you, that ye may know that I [am] the LORD your God."

Now in each of those verses, the word "seal" does not appear but the word "sign" does. Are they one in the same? What does the Bible have to say about that? According to Romans 4:11, the words are used as synonyms. "And he received the sign of circumcision, a seal of the righteousness of the faith which [he had yet] being uncircumcised: that he might be the father of all them that believe, though they be not circumcised; that righteousness might be imputed unto them also." And according to Webster's Dictionary, a "seal" is an indication; sign; token. Therefore, not once but several times, God has told us plainly what His seal is. And it should make sense. The Sabbath shows who the creator is as opposed to evolution because nowhere in science can they explain the seven day week of time for even a month contains thirty days and not twenty-eight. It shows dependency upon Him because during that time that His followers observe the Sabbath, others are out doing work or making money to get ahead. Do we really trust that God will provide or do we trust ourselves instead?

What is interesting about the Bible, not only does it declare things, but it also demonstrates things. Let us look at the sealing process in action. "And thou shalt love the LORD thy God with all thine heart, and with all thy soul, and with all thy might. And these words, which I command thee this day, shall be in thine heart: And thou shalt teach them diligently unto thy children, and shalt talk of them when thou sittest in thine house, and when thou walkest by the way, and when thou liest down, and when thou risest up. And thou shalt bind them for a sign upon thine hand, and they shall be as frontlets between thine eyes" (Deuteronomy 6:5 8). The frontlets between the eyes represent the forehead.

Now let us examine a New Testament example. "[Whereof] the Holy Ghost also is a witness to us: for after that he had said before, This [is] the covenant that I will make with them after those days, saith the Lord, I will put my laws into their hearts, and in their minds will I write them" (Hebrews 10:15-16). The forehead, in prophecy, is symbolic of the mind.

So, as we have seen, the Seal of God is not some outward sign physically on our foreheads declaring the name of God, but rather, the Holy Spirit is involved in convicting us "of sin, and of righteousness, and of judgment" (John 16:8), with the true meaning of being filled with the Holy Spirit, whereas, the speaking of tongues movement is a false representation of being filled by the Spirit, even a counterfeit perpetrated by the "Spirit of Antichrist" just to confuse things. Then, we saw that the Holy Spirit moved further by impressing upon us to want to learn and obey the truth, which is found in the law, the Word, and Jesus. But even as Jesus invites, one of these becomes the seal of God, for He had even said, "If ye love me, keep my commandments" (John 14:15). But not just any of them would be the sign between God and man of who is actually providing salvation, but the Sabbath day is that sign. Therefore, we ought to see the same progression away from the Sabbath as revealed by the Antichrist to show who is in allegiance to them. We know this to be true instead of some outward mark because the Bible clearly teaches what the Antichrist battle is all about.

- 1 John 2:18-22, "Little children, it is the last time: and as ye have heard that Antichrist shall come, even now are there many Antichrists; whereby we know that it is the last time. They went out from us, but they were not of us; for if they had been of us, they would [no doubt] have continued with us: but [they went out], that they might be made manifest that they were not all of us. But ye have an unction from the Holy One, and ye know all things. I have not written unto you because ye know not the truth, but because ye know it, and that no lie is of the truth. Who is a liar but he that denieth that Jesus is the Christ? He is Antichrist, that denieth the Father and the Son."

- 1 John 4:3-6, "And every spirit that confesseth not that Jesus Christ is come in the flesh is not of God: and this is that [spirit] of Antichrist, whereof ye have heard that it should come; and even now already is it in the world. Ye are of God, little children, and have overcome them: because greater is he that is in you, than he that is in the world. They are of the world: therefore speak they of the world, and the world heareth them. We are of God: he that knoweth God heareth us; he that is not of God heareth not us. Hereby know we the spirit of truth, and the spirit of error."

- 2 John 1:7-9, "For many deceivers are entered into the world, who confess not that Jesus Christ is come in the flesh. This is a deceiver and an Antichrist. Look to yourselves, that we lose not those things which we have wrought, but that we receive a full reward. Whosoever transgresseth, and abideth not in the doctrine of Christ, hath not God. He that abideth in the doctrine of Christ, he hath both the Father and the Son."

- Daniel 8:9-12, "And out of one of them came forth a little horn, which waxed exceeding great, toward the south, and toward the east, and toward the pleasant [land]. And it waxed great, [even] to the host of heaven; and it cast down [some] of the host and of the stars to the ground, and stamped upon them. Yea, he magnified [himself] even to the prince of the host, and by him the daily [sacrifice] was taken away, and the place of his sanctuary was cast down. And an host was given [him] against the daily [sacrifice] by reason of transgression, and it cast down the truth to the ground; and it practised, and prospered.

In all four references to the word "Antichrist" along with Daniel's description of the Antichrist in action, it is all the same with different wording. It is the true verses the false. It is the spirit of truth verses the spirit of error. It is having the true doctrines of Jesus Christ or the false doctrines of the Antichrist. And it is having the truth uplifted or cast down to the ground. Nowhere is there a hint of financial greed, political control, numbering the people, or any such thing that is being perpetrated as the mark of the beast, especially in books of fiction and the movies.

We know it is hard to undo the multitudinous voices that claim the mark is a chip, a card, a laser imprint, a physical object visible to everyone, however, that just shows how far both the Antichrist, through a Jesuit priest named Ribera, and the "Spirit of Antichrist" that latched onto this work of fiction has passed it off as truth in a sensationalized manner using books and movies. In other words, it is fulfilling the description of "all the world wondered after the beast" (Revelation 13:3). The Left Behind content is a nearly five hundred year old work of fiction direct from the Antichrist to cover up true spirituality and all the world, especially the Christian world, is accepting it as Bible doctrine.

With that said, let us address the step by step progress that parallels the opposite of God's seal.

First, as already stated, the Bible says, "And an host was given [him] against the daily [sacrifice] by reason of transgression, and it cast down the truth to the ground; and it practised, and prospered" (Daniel 8:12). So the truth that the Holy Spirit impresses upon hearts of desired followers and begins the process of being sealed is cast down by the Antichrist and of course, the "Spirit of Antichrist". So the first step was to undermine the truth, where well over ninety percent of Christians no longer treat the Bible as anything different than worldly authors.

Second, regarding the Antichrist, "He shall speak [great] words against the most High, and shall wear out the saints of the most High, and think to change times and laws: and they shall be given into his hand until a time and times and the dividing of time" (Daniel 7:25). So where the Holy Spirit selects the commandments to be a sealing of character and conduct among Christians, the Antichrist and the "Spirit of Antichrist" think they can change them. In actuality, the "Spirit of Antichrist" is very prominent among Protestants and is actually worse than dealing with the Antichrist directly. At least the Vatican still has a set of commandments to be adhered to. Protestants, despite some churches still displaying the Ten Commandments, claim that the commandments were "nailed to the cross", done away with by grace, no longer necessary as our schoolmaster, and many more arguments against obeying the commandments.

And the third step, using the same verse, "He shall speak [great] words against the most High, and shall wear out the saints of the most High, and think to change times and laws: and they shall be given into his hand until a time and times and the dividing of time" (Daniel 7:25). As the Holy Spirit presses the Sabbath as a sign or seal among true believers, the Antichrist gets the nerve to pass off a different Sabbath day that even Protestants arguments are much stronger than the Vatican's. At least the Vatican comes right out and states in a question and answer format that they simply changed the day. According to the Catholic Catechism:

Q. What is the Third Commandment?

A. The Third Commandment is: Remember that thou keep holy the Sabbath day.

Q. Which is the Sabbath day?

A. Saturday is the Sabbath day.

Q. Why do we observe Sunday instead of Saturday?

A. We observe Sunday instead of Saturday because the Catholic Church transferred the solemnity from Saturday to Sunday.

Q. Why did the Catholic Church substitute Sunday for Saturday?

A. The Church substituted Sunday for Saturday, because Christ rose from the dead on a Sunday, and the Holy Ghost descended upon the Apostles on a Sunday.

On top of that, the Vatican then goes and makes an obvious declaration that they have performed such an act without a command from the Bible: "The church is above the Bible and this transference of Sabbath to Sunday is proof of that fact." The Catholic Record.

Protestants on the other hand use Catholic arguments and then some. As noted, the Vatican simply pointed to two events as justification to pick up the day and move it: the resurrection and the day of Pentecost. That is not a command though, to allow the papacy to do it; they simply did it. Their argument for being able to do this comes from Matthew 16:19, which says, "And I will give unto thee the keys of the kingdom of heaven: and whatsoever thou shalt bind on earth shall be bound in heaven: and whatsoever thou shalt loose on earth shall be loosed in heaven." There are two problems with the way the Vatican uses this verse. First, the verse is not just for the papacy despite the claim that the preceding verse refers to the first pope. "And I say also unto thee, That thou art Peter, and upon this rock I will build my church; and the gates of hell shall not prevail against it" (Matthew 16:18). The keys are given to the church, the people, to go forth spreading the gospel "Teaching them to observe all things" (Matthew 28:20).

And the second way the Vatican uses the verse is also not supported by the Bible in which it is not an allowance to go and make up church rules, change Bible rules, or totally discard Bible rules. We are to use the keys, the scriptures, as described earlier, to teach obedience to all that Jesus has commanded. In fact, the Bible says that "the key of knowledge" is what is being referred to, and not keys to make allowance for modification. We are to share the gospel's grace message which includes both justification (forgiveness) and sanctification (obedience) by the power of God. If people reject any part of the message, their sins shall remain bound. If people accept and implement the message, their sins shall be loosed.

Protestants then try to twist the Bible to justify keeping Sunday. They basically become strong allies with the Vatican in supporting the mark of the beast. There is only one day and one day only that the Bible declares is the Sabbath day, and it is not the midnight to midnight day called Sunday.

Not only do Protestants claim that the events of Jesus rising and the Holy Spirit being poured out on Pentecost being both Sunday events,

1. Protestants dismiss so easily the fact that the Sabbath day is not only on a different day but is on a different cycle of time, when God declared that the sunsets determined a period called a day (Genesis 1:14). Also, God explicitly commands in the Sabbath commandment to recognize "the seventh day [is] the sabbath of the LORD thy God" (Exodus 20:10). Further, in the command, God states to "Remember the sabbath day" (Exodus 20:8), while everyone seems to have forgotten it. Additionally, He tells us "to keep it holy" (Exodus 20:8) instead of trying to make another day holy.

2. Protestants declare that the "Lord's Day" is Sunday when the verse they quote does not identify what day the Lord's day actually is. John simply stated, "I was in the Spirit on the Lord's day, and heard behind me a great voice, as of a trumpet" (Revelation 1:10). We will tell you that the Lord's day is not Sunday though, for Jesus declared, "For the Son of man is Lord even of the sabbath day" (Matthew 12:8). Although Jesus is Lord of all days, He specifically declared that if there is a specific Lord's day, it is the Sabbath day. Now to settle the argument, all one would have to do is look up all the references of the phrase "The Lord's Day" throughout the Bible, just as Isaiah 28:9-10 tells us, but unfortunately the phrase is nowhere else found in the Bible. So at the very least, we should all agree that the reference to "The Lord's Day" is non-specific making the declaration of Sunday as such nothing more than simply an assumption, and a poor one at that.

3. Protestants declare that they practice "One man esteemeth one day above another: another esteemeth every day [alike]. Let every man be fully persuaded in his own mind" (Romans 14:5). Not only is the verse being taken out of context, but why would one use it, and then criticize true Sabbath keepers for keeping the Sabbath day holy? On top of that, why do Protestants then hold on to Sunday so strongly if all days may be esteemed? Worse yet, why would one use it to justify keeping their day of choice when it matches that of the Antichrist? It also matches the day of the original pagan worship of the sun. Why not pick a different day entirely if that is the attitude? The truth of the matter though is that after reading all of Romans 14, one sees that the Sabbath, which is never mentioned directly at all in the Book of Romans nor is there reference to the "seventh day", is not even under discussion. What is under discussion is the feast days, seeing that in the same chapter, discussion of the proper preparation of food for these days is also addressed: "For one believeth that he may eat all things: another, who is weak, eateth herbs" (Romans 14:2). Since when is the Sabbath day of the Ten Commandments involving food requirements? It clearly is teaching that if a person wants to keep the feasts days, outlined in Leviticus 23, go ahead, but do not make it a requirement to be obeyed by Christians. If one wants to esteem Passover, Unleavened Bread,

Wave Sheaf, Pentecost, Trumpets, Atonement, and Ingathering, go right ahead, but anyone that does not esteem those days, do not get on their case for treating it like any ordinary working day.

4. Protestants declare that we ought not have arguments about the Sabbath because we are to "Let no man therefore judge you in meat, or in drink, or in respect of an holyday, or of the new moon, or of the sabbath [days]" (Colossians 2:16). Interestingly, Protestants are all about getting off their backs about the Sabbath day, but where does the New Testament actually uplift a new Sabbath day. In other words, they are quick to find a verse, out of context, that puts down the keeping of the Sabbath without having a verse that supports their adherence to keeping Sunday. There is no verse in the New Testament that replaces the Sabbath commandment. Looking alone at this verse though, this has nothing to do with the Sabbath of the Ten Commandments. The mention of the word "meat" is a reference to foods prepared for the feast days once again. The mention of the word "drink" is a reference to the drink prepared for the feast days. The reference to the word "holyday" is what the feast days were treated as… holy days. The reference to the "new moons" is reference to the "new moon" feast day that was held in addition to those outlined in Leviticus 23. And then we get to the "Sabbath days" reference. Why would anyone think that after four references to the feast days we would think the "Sabbath days" refers to the Ten Commandments? If that were so, why not just say, "or of the Ten Commandments"? Think about it, what is essentially being argued is that God arbitrarily has reduced the Ten Commandments down to nine. Sunday as the new Sabbath is nowhere established in the New Testament, so that is what we have. It does not make sense. Therefore, and as defended by reading Leviticus 23, the "Sabbath days" are in reference to the special days or the holy days. There were days of holy periods that were marked by floating days called Sabbath days carrying the same requirements as the Sabbath commandment. In fact, to start Leviticus 23 off, there is an open understanding to set the pattern for the rest of the chapter. In other words, before all of Leviticus 23 is revealed, the word "Sabbath" is going to appear and the writer wants everyone, using the vernacular of today, on the same page when it comes to the observance. The verse is not stated to include the Sabbath commandment as part of the feasts. It simply states, "Six days shall work be done: but the seventh day [is] the sabbath of rest, an holy convocation; ye shall do no work [therein]: it [is] the sabbath of the LORD in all your dwellings" (Leviticus 23:3). How do we know that this is so? Because the next verse states, "These [are] the feasts of the LORD, [even] holy convocations, which ye shall proclaim in their seasons," referring to the remaining verses, therefore, when a mention of a floating Sabbath day appears, one should know how to keep it. "Speak unto the children of Israel, saying, In the seventh month, in the first [day] of the month, shall ye have a sabbath, a memorial of blowing of trumpets, an holy convocation" (Leviticus 23:24). "It [shall be] unto you a sabbath of rest, and ye shall afflict your souls: in the ninth [day] of the month at even, from even unto even, shall ye celebrate your sabbath" (Leviticus 23:32). "Also in the fifteenth day of the seventh month, when ye have gathered in the fruit of the land, ye shall keep a feast unto the LORD seven days: on the first day [shall be] a sabbath, and on the eighth day [shall be] a sabbath" (Leviticus 23:39). And as a person's birthday changes every year, never falling on the same day of the week, so these Sabbath days also floated, and are no longer to be judged as requirements.

5. Protestants argue incorrectly that there was a church offering on Sunday according to 1 Corinthians 16:2, establishing that it was the normal practice to assemble upon Sundays for church and a collection, like passing around a collection plate, was being done. The verse states, "Upon the first [day] of the week let every one of you lay by him in store, as [God] hath prospered him, that there be no gatherings when I come" (1 Corinthians 16:2). Now, nowhere in that verse is it a collection or offering taking place. What is actually commanded is to go to work in gathering for the collection because it states that we do not want any gatherings when Paul arrives, so on the first day of the week, which is the first working day after the Sabbath, go gather from the fields and place it in easily accessible storage. Why? Because the day before the first day of the

week, being the Sabbath, there is to be no work done, which gathering would constitute. Further, to "lay by him in store" is not a collection handed over to Paul but rather is a command to go out and get stuff and store it up. Again, it is a command to work. The verse doubly states that gathering, which is work, is to happen on the first day. Think of the verse more like a church service announcement. One might hear the following if they were sitting in church on the Sabbath day, "My brothers and sisters, as you know, our fellow brothers and sisters in Christ living in Jerusalem are experiencing tough times. The apostle Paul will be passing through collecting donations. Now we do not want to hold up our dear brother by gathering stuff when he arrives, so upon the first day of the week, go out and gather all that you are willing to contribute and store it safe somewhere so that there is no gathering when Paul arrives."

6. Protestants argue about the first day of the week being God's new Sabbath day because Jesus rose from the dead on a Sunday also falls short in the Bible because the Christians at that moment observed the Sabbath and not the first day of the week. The full account states, "And, behold, [there was] a man named Joseph, a counsellor; [and he was] a good man, and a just: (The same had not consented to the counsel and deed of them;) [he was] of Arimathaea, a city of the Jews: who also himself waited for the kingdom of God. This [man] went unto Pilate, and begged the body of Jesus. And he took it down, and wrapped it in linen, and laid it in a sepulchre that was hewn in stone, wherein never man before was laid. And that day was the preparation, and the sabbath drew on. And the women also, which came with him from Galilee, followed after, and beheld the sepulchre, and how his body was laid. And they returned, and prepared spices and ointments; and rested the sabbath day according to the commandment" (Luke 23:50-56). Clearly if Jesus taught that there was going to be a new Sabbath, these people did not hear it, and they were one of the closest people to Jesus. Now those that argue that Jesus had not risen yet so that it was not yet taught falls as a lame excuse because care and detail is being provided here to make sure we see the Sabbath observance as it is being penned by a Gentile. If the Sabbath were not important, Luke would not have given it such attention. He even made sure that we knew what Jesus regular practice was. "And he came to Nazareth, where he had been brought up: and, as his custom was, he went into the synagogue on the sabbath day, and stood up for to read" (Luke 4:16). In fact, Luke, the only Gentile writer of the four gospels, makes references almost double the number of Matthew, Mark, or John. In fact, Matthew, Mark, and John mention it a total of twenty-eight times while Luke alone mentions it twenty-seven times between the Gospel of Luke and the Book of Acts. For a Gentile writer to give that much attention to the Sabbath day can only mean that it still was taught to be observed. And if the Sabbath were to become Sunday by Jesus' further teaching after the resurrection, a significant event in itself, then why is there silence in the Bible of such teachings? Why are we left to a mere implied hint? Think about it. If thunder and lightning and even death to anyone touching mount Sinai (Exodus 20:18), except those that God had chosen being Joshua and Moses primarily (Exodus 24:13), was used to reveal the Ten Commandments that existed from the beginning of time, does not anyone see that at least a one liner in the Bible should appear somewhere about the change? The notion that every Christian knew of the change and so there was no need to mention it is preposterous! That still does not cancel out the numerous references to the old Sabbath day then, and in detail. The fact of the matter is, as scripturally stated soon, Jesus did not teach such.

7. And then we have Protestants who detest the Book of Hebrews trying to convince all that it was just for the Hebrews, when in fact it is for everyone. Hebrews is no more just for the Jews as the Books of Timothy is just for Timothy or the sections of Revelation referring to seven churches was only for those seven churches. Now why do Protestants hate Hebrews? Because Hebrews chapter 4 refutes every argument against doing away with the Sabbath, in fact, it well establishes the fact that the Sabbath still exists. And do recognize that the Sabbath topic is in the New Testament despite the many lies from Protestants teaching that the Sabbath is not taught in the New Testament.

- In the opening verse, Hebrews 4:1, we are encouraged to enter into the Sabbath rest instead of discouraging from following it. "Let us therefore fear, lest, a promise being left [us] of entering into his rest, any of you should seem to come short of it."

- In Hebrews 4:2, the argument that if one is keeping the Sabbath commandment means that such people do not have the gospel or such people lack faith, as if faith and the gospel does away with the Sabbath, is not true. "For unto us was the gospel preached, as well as unto them: but the word preached did not profit them, not being mixed with faith in them that heard [it]."

- In Hebrews 4:4, multiple arguments are settled. First, which day is to be observed? The seventh. What is and is not allowed to be done on the Sabbath? Rest is allowed while work is not. Of course rest does not mean sleeping away the Sabbath nor ceasing from work means nothing gets done. Jesus clarifies that which cannot be avoided still continues including, rescuing an animal, feeding, emergency healing, preaching and all that goes with it. So, we are allowed to make our beds, clear the table after eating, put away our pajamas, and so on. What we are not to do is work that earns income, that is considered avoidable chores (feeding animals is unavoidable), that distracts greatly from keeping the Sabbath holy like watching sporting events, that uses money like shopping, etc.

- In Hebrews 4:6, the argument that the Sabbath has been done away with is also silenced along with the notion that all we have to do is "believe in Jesus" and that does away with the commandment. "Seeing therefore it remaineth that some must enter therein, and they to whom it was first preached entered not in because of unbelief."

- In Hebrews 4:7, the argument about treating all days alike or allowing people to pick their own Sabbath day is refuted. "Again, he limiteth a certain day, saying in David, To day, after so long a time; as it is said, To day if ye will hear his voice, harden not your hearts."

- In Hebrews 4:8, the notion that Jesus taught a different day is completely muted. "For if Jesus had given them rest, then would he not afterward have spoken of another day."

- In Hebrews 4:9, the argument that the Sabbath has been done away with receives a second refuting. "There remaineth therefore a rest to the people of God."

- In Hebrews 4:10, the notion of not knowing how to keep the Sabbath is addressed, where God is our example. Did God cease all of His work on the Sabbath? No, of course not. His sustaining life continued on, while His creative work ceased. "For he that is entered into his rest, he also hath ceased from his own works, as God [did] from his." That tells us that feeding animals, once again, is fine, while pulling weeds, building a shed, planting, and other creative work is not. Again, if one can postpone any labor to another day, it should be postponed.

- In Hebrews 4:11, the notion that if anyone has to put effort into keeping the Sabbath, somehow it constitutes working one's way to Heaven, is addressed. "Let us labour therefore to enter into that rest, lest any man fall after the same example of unbelief."

- In Hebrews 4:12, the notion that the Sabbath has nothing to do with salvation is completely rebuked. "For the word of God [is] quick, and powerful, and sharper than any twoedged sword, piercing even to the dividing asunder of soul and spirit, and of the joints and marrow, and [is] a discerner of the thoughts and intents of the heart."

8. Protestants argue that the apostles did not continue it despite the fact that Paul sought out a synagogue in a gentile land of Antioch. "But when they departed from Perga, they came to Antioch in Pisidia, and went into the synagogue on the sabbath day, and sat down" (Acts 13:14). Even "the Gentiles besought that these words might be preached to them the next sabbath" (Acts 13:42), which "The next sabbath day came almost the whole city together to hear the word of God" (Acts 13:44). And preaching can happen any day of the week and people will gather, so the notion that Paul tried winning Jews primarily is off when the vast majority were Gentiles. And when Paul was in a place

where there was not a Jew or synagogue, "On the sabbath we went out of the city by a river side, where prayer was wont to be made" (Acts 16:13), meaning, Paul personally kept it. And "Paul, as his manner was, went in unto them, and three sabbath days reasoned with them out of the scriptures" (Acts 17:2), which a manner means that it was the regular practice. First day observance was not his manner, nor was Sunday. Again, Paul "reasoned in the synagogue every sabbath, and persuaded the Jews and the Greeks" (Acts 18:4), in which amounted to seventy-eight Sabbaths, for "he continued [there] a year and six months, teaching the word of God among them" (Acts 18:11).

9. Protestants claim that the mere appearing of Jesus after the resurrection on the first day of the week constitutes as the new Sabbath. There are several problems with that theory. The Bible says, "Then the same day at evening, being the first [day] of the week, when the doors were shut where the disciples were assembled for fear of the Jews, came Jesus and stood in the midst, and saith unto them, Peace [be] unto you" (John 20:19). The first problem is that the "first day of the week" is not Sunday. Remember, God's day is "evening and the morning" (Genesis 1:5, 8, 13, 19, 23, 31), which He tells us, "Let there be lights in the firmament of the heaven to divide the day from the night; and let them be for signs, and for seasons, and for days, and years" (Genesis 1:14). Basically, God's day is sunset to sunset. So, when it was evening on the first day of the week, Jesus actually showed up at the beginning of the first day, which is shortly after sunset on Saturday night. In other words, Jesus showed up Saturday evening and not at any point on Sunday. And no, Jesus did not wake them up after midnight. But here is the second problem, Jesus shows up a second time, but on a different day. "And after eight days again his disciples were within, and Thomas with them: [then] came Jesus, the doors being shut, and stood in the midst, and said, Peace [be] unto you" (John 20:26). If the mere showing up constitutes a new Sabbath or holy day of the week, then sunset Sunday to sunset Monday should be the Sabbath day for that is the last recorded day of His appearing. And if we go with the midnight to midnight schedule and we go with the first appearance as declarative of the new Sabbath, then the new Sabbath would be Saturday. So three problems with that implied theory, make it four, as we lead off with it. So here are the four problems in summary: First, anyone can get anything out of implications, so why not be direct and state that the Sabbath changed, but since no such statement exists in the Bible, it did not happen. Second, the first day of the week is not Sunday, it is sundown Saturday to sundown Sunday. Third, with Jesus appearing Saturday night and not on Sunday itself in nowise confirms Sunday from midnight to midnight, but with Jesus showing up Saturday night, at best, would confirm Saturday instead of Sunday, however, God's time is not midnight to midnight. Fourth, Jesus' inconsistency of showing up unannounced on different days of the week demonstrates no favoritism to a new day of worship.

By the way, the Vatican is not afraid of Hebrews chapter 4. Again, they boast of taking the established Sabbath day and arbitrarily changing it, which is a demonstration of their power and authority, and because all believe it was done, and so many Protestants defend it, they treat it as their allegiance mark. Ask an atheist when the Christian Sabbath is, and they will mostly respond with Sunday. Ask a Protestant the same question, and obviously Sunday is the reply. Ask a Catholic, and they will say Sunday. In fact, ask anybody from other religions, and they will say Sunday. In fact, if a Sabbath keeping Christian were to request off Friday from sundown to Saturday sundown or tell friends and family that they cannot join in certain activities during that time, the usual remark is, "Are you Jewish?" So, it is well accepted by all the world that Sunday is their mark of authority.

The real definition of Protestant is one that objects to any doctrine that is not solidly taught in the Bible. That doctrine includes those things commanded to be observed as well as those things commanded to stop observing. So we are commanded to keep holy the Sabbath day (Exodus 20:8-11), while it is the invention of the Vatican to promote observing holy days as well as the period called Lent. Many Protestants have given up protesting that they are renaming themselves, primarily to Evangelical or some other smooth sounding name. Has the Vatican aligned their doctrines with the Bible that the protest is over? Of course not. So no matter how anti-Catholic so many Protestants are, they are still wondering after the beast, as predicted.

Besides, logical conclusion to the above listed items and many sub items that show the fallacy of all of the lame arguments against the keeping of the weekly Sabbath day that is made by Protestants reveals what is truly among the non-Catholics. They may even call the mother church, the Vatican, names including the Antichrist and harlot woman like some do, especially The Lutheran Church Missouri Synod, but holding onto the notion that Sunday is the Christian Sabbath means only one thing: the "Spirit of Antichrist" is alive and well. Again, it is not enough to see who the Antichrist really is, but to also reject the "Spirit of Antichrist."

Even the Vatican taunts Protestants:

- "From this same Catholic Church you have accepted your Sunday, and that Sunday, as the Lord's day, she has handed down as a tradition; and the entire Protestant world has accepted it as tradition, for you have not an iota of Scripture to establish it. Therefore that which you have accepted as your rule of faith, inadequate as it of course is, as well as your Sunday, you have accepted on the authority of the Roman Catholic Church." D.B. Ray, *The Papal Controversy,* 1892, p. 179.

- "You may read the Bible from Genesis to Revelation, and you will not find a single line authorizing the sanctification of Sunday. The scriptures enforce the religious observance of Saturday." James Cardinal Gibbons, *The Faith of Our Fathers,* p. 89.

- "Of course the Catholic Church claims that the change was her act. And the act is the MARK of her ecclesiastical power and authority in religious matters." *Faith of Our Fathers,* p. 14, C.F. Thomas, Chancellor of Cardinal Gibbons.

- Question--How do you prove that the (Catholic) Church has power to command Feasts and Holy-days? Answer--By this very act of changing the Sabbath into the Sunday, which is admitted by Protestants, and therefore they contradict themselves by keeping Sunday so strictly, and breaking most other Feasts commanded by the same church. Question--How do you prove that? Answer--Because by keeping Sunday they acknowledge the power of the (Catholic) Church to ordain Feasts and to command them under sin, and by not keeping the remainder, equally commanded by her, they deny in fact the same power. Daniel Ferris, *Manual of Christian Doctrine: or, Catholic Belief and Practice,* pp. 67-68.

- "There is but one church on the face of the earth which has the power, or claims power, to make laws binding on the conscience, binding before God, binding under penalty of hell-fire. For instance, the institution of Sunday. What right has any other church to keep this day? You answer by virtue of the third commandment (the papacy did away with the 2nd regarding the worship of graven images, and called the 4th the 3rd), which says 'Remember that thou keep holy the Sabbath day.' But Sunday is not the Sabbath. Any schoolboy knows that Sunday is the first day of the week. I have repeatedly offered one thousand dollars to anyone who will prove by the Bible alone that Sunday is the day we are bound to keep, and no one has called for the money. It was the holy Catholic Church that changed the day of rest from Saturday, the seventh day, to Sunday, the first day of the week." - T. Enright, C.S.S.R., in a lecture delivered in 1893.

Now for those that are all worked up claiming that the mark of the beast is a physical object, especially since one can receive the mark "in their right hand, or in their foreheads" (Revelation 13:16), we remind everyone that to be looking for a literal mark is to go against the intent of the verse. First, "The Revelation of Jesus Christ, which God gave unto him, to shew unto his servants things which must shortly come to pass; and he sent and signified [it] by his angel unto his servant John" (Revelation 1:1). To signify something, as a reminder, is to be symbolic, not literal. So the mark of the beast is not literally inserted into the hand or into their foreheads, but rather the mark of the beast is symbolically inserted into their actions and into their minds.

Second, the object name is quite symbolic. It is called the "mark of the beast". It is not called the "mark of the Antichrist" or "mark of the Vatican". In other words, if we think the mark is literal, then the word "beast" is to be literal too, and we better be checking some zoos for such a beast that has ten horns, seven heads, body parts of a lion, leopard, bear, and another animal, along with wearing crowns.

Third, the entire chapter is full of symbolism. In verse 11 is a dragon speaking type of an animal with lamblike horns resembling pretty much the buffalo, symbolic of the United States. Then in verse 14, it constructs an image, which in modern times, is not going to deceive people into thinking the object is a god, so it too is a symbolic image, especially when the image begins to speak. An image of something is a likeness. Just as the Vatican crushes personal freedom, the United States will become more oppressive of its people, even to the point of taking away religious freedom. In fact, it is well under way as we speak.

So that means, as we already revealed, the forehead represents the mind. What we think determines which side we are on. Unfortunately, only God can read our minds. So there has to be an outward sign associated with it as well. That is where the right hand comes in at.

For those that are still stuck on literal interpretation, does that mean all people who have their right arms and hands amputated are unable to receive the mark of the beast? For those that say, "That's where the forehead comes into play", we then further ask, "If I were to be chipped in my right hand, and Jesus says, 'And if thy right hand offend thee, cut it off, and cast [it] from thee" (Matthew 5:30), does that free me then from the mark of the beast?" Basically, the arguments get quite silly when taken literally.

So let us see how the Bible references the hand and the forehead by reading Exodus 13:16, which says, "And it shall be for a token upon thine hand, and for frontlets between thine eyes: for by strength of hand the LORD brought us forth out of Egypt." So the hand and the frontlets or forehead are in the context of tokens, something that is not literal. In fact, when it comes to the hand, Ecclesiastes 9:10 says, "Whatsoever thy hand findeth to do, do [it] with thy might; for [there is] no work, nor device, nor knowledge, nor wisdom, in the grave, whither thou goest."

The forehead being symbolic of how we think, the hand is symbolic of what we do. Therefore, the outward sign to let the Antichrist know that the subject is in compliance or not with the mark of the beast is the action of obedience to it. In other words, one can think all they want about Sunday not being the Sabbath, but by continually arguing in favor of it as well as keeping it through obedience, one is considered aligned with the beast.

The reference to it being the right hand and not just the hand is symbolic of approval. Jesus did not just sit next to the Father, He "sat down on the right hand of God" (Hebrews 10:12). The sheep and the goats are not simply separated, "He shall set the sheep on his right hand, but the goats on the left" (Matthew 25:33). Stephen, in is dying breath while facing a stoning looked up and "saw the glory of God, and Jesus standing on the right hand of God" (Acts 7:55), which is approving of Stephen's actions. Peter and John did not just take the lame person by the hand, Peter "took him by the right hand, and lifted [him] up: and immediately his feet and ankle bones received strength" (Acts 3:7).

Therefore, it is not just actions, but approving actions that shows the acceptance of the mark of the beast. This is opposed to the forced actions, as we mentioned before. If it were a literal mark and some mob were to force us to the ground and use a laser to burn in 666 in our right hand or across our forehead, are we doomed? The answer is no because we did not approve of it.

And again, "We wrestle not against flesh and blood, but against principalities, against powers, against the rulers of the darkness of this world, against spiritual wickedness in high [places]" (Ephesians 6:12).

Look at it from a different and very simple perspective. All of us agree that we are to have the Father's name in our foreheads. "And I looked, and, lo, a Lamb stood on the mount Sion, and with him an hundred forty [and] four thousand, having his Father's name written in their foreheads" (Revelation 14:1). All of us agree in regards to the Father that the Bible says, "Abba, Father" (Galatians 4:6). Is it by coincidence that right in the middle of the word "Sabbath" is "Abba"?

So now let us look at it simply from the beast perspective. Revelation 14:11 tells us to avoid worshipping the beast by saying, "They have no rest day nor night, who worship the beast." In reality, "They worshipped the dragon which gave power unto the beast" (Revelation 14:11). Revelation 12:9 tells us "the great dragon was cast out, that old serpent, called the Devil, and Satan." Other names for Satan include, "O Lucifer, son of the morning" (Isaiah 14:12). And God foresaw, "the inner court of the LORD'S house, and, behold, at the door of the temple of the LORD, between the porch and the altar, [were] about five and twenty men, with their backs toward the temple of the LORD, and their faces toward the east; and they worshipped the sun toward the east" (Ezekiel 8:16). God sees sun worshippers of the future in His house. In other words, He foresaw a time that Christians would worship the sun or Sunday instead of having His name by honoring the Sabbath day, keeping it holy.

The Bible says that one could receive "the number of his name" (Revelation 13:17). In fact, those that get to go to Heaven and "stand on the sea of glass, having the harps of God" are those that "had gotten the victory over the beast, and over his image, and over his mark, [and] over the number of his name" (Revelation 15:2). So, how does the number of the Antichrist, "the number of the beast", "the number of a man" (Revelation 13:18) fit into all of this?

To receive the number of a man or of the beast is to accept the authority. This is different from acknowledging the existence of it. I can acknowledge that the number of the official title assigned to the pontiff is 666, which by having the pontiff as the controlling voice, makes it the beast number as well. To accept the authority of the pontiff, papacy, Vatican, whatever name you want to use, we already discovered that their only claim of power is by changing the Sabbath day into Sunday of which the world in one form or another accepts. Christians and non-Christians plainly state that the Christian Sabbath is Sunday. That's accepting it. On everything else, people are oblivious to or ignore widely.

How is the change of the Sabbath the single authoritative acknowledgement of the papacy? The Catholic way to be baptized is sprinkling as a baby, while it is pretty much rejected widely by the world, where the average person, Christian or not, believes it is full immersion. The Catholic declaration of putting people in purgatory is pretty much rejected by another false teaching where people are placed directly in Heaven or Hell. Indulgences, which is the purchase to get someone out of purgatory sooner or to be freely able to indulge in sin without it affecting the record in Heaven, is fully rejected by everyone else. And we can go down the list of all the beliefs dictated to Catholics through the Vatican that are rejected by both non-Christians and most of the Protestant world. True, some Protestants believe in sprinkling and in other false doctrines but none receives as much attention as does the change from Sabbath to Sunday.

So then, to accept Sunday is by default the way to accept the number of the beast or pontiff, but with that said, we will dig deeper regarding the number being involved.

Let us provide supporting evidence from various sources, including *Wikipedia* that basically state the following:

- First, in pagan days, wearing of amulets or medallions with magic squares on the back of them was quite common.
- These magic squares represented heavenly objects made up of numbers, where the numbers between 1 and the number assigned to the heavenly object.
- The numbers were laid out in columns and rows.
- Each row and each column summed up to the same number.
- All rows summed had to match the sum of all the columns.
- The arrangement of the numbers required the use of all of the numbers, such as 1 through 9 in equal rows required 3 rows and 3 columns, without duplicating a single number nor letting off a number.

According to *Wikipedia's* topic "Magic Square", here are a few examples, where all rows and all columns individually are set:

- Saturn used the numbers 1 through 9 and added up to 15 on each row and each column with a sum total of all the rows or columns being 45.

Saturn=15		
4	9	2
3	5	7
8	1	6

- Jupiter, using the numbers 1 to 16 in a 4 by 4 square had rows and columns each adding up to 34 with a sum total of all rows or columns being 136.

Jupiter=34			
4	14	15	1
9	7	6	12
5	11	10	8
16	2	3	13

- Mars, using the numbers 1 through 25 in a 5 by 5 layout, had the sum of each column or row being 65 and a total of all columns or all rows of 325.

- Venus, using the numbers 1 through 49 in a 7 by 7 square, had 175 for each row or column and a total of all the columns or all of the rows of 1225.

Mars=65

11	24	7	20	3
4	12	25	8	16
17	5	13	21	9
10	18	1	14	22
23	6	19	2	15

Venus=175

22	47	16	41	10	35	4
5	23	48	17	42	11	29
30	6	24	49	18	36	12
13	31	7	25	43	19	37
38	14	32	1	26	44	20
21	39	8	33	2	27	45
46	15	40	9	34	3	28

- Sol or sun, using the numbers 1 through 36 in a 6 by 6 square, had 111 on each row or each column with a sum of the rows or columns being 666.

- Mercury, using the numbers 1 through 64 in an 8 by 8 layout, was 260 on each row or each column and a total of the rows or columns of 2080.

Sol=111

6	32	3	34	35	1
7	11	27	28	8	30
19	14	16	15	23	24
18	20	22	21	17	13
25	29	10	9	26	12
36	5	33	4	2	31

Mercury=260

8	58	59	5	4	62	63	1
49	15	14	52	53	11	10	56
41	23	22	44	45	19	18	48
32	34	35	29	28	38	39	25
40	26	27	37	36	30	31	33
17	47	46	20	21	43	42	24
9	55	54	12	13	51	50	16
64	2	3	61	60	6	7	57

- Luna or the moon, using the numbers 1 through 81 in a 9 by 9 layout, had 369 on each row or each column and had a total of all the rows or columns equal to 3321.

Luna=369								
37	78	29	70	21	62	13	54	5
6	38	79	30	71	22	63	14	46
47	7	39	80	31	72	23	55	15
16	48	8	40	81	32	64	24	56
57	17	49	9	41	73	33	65	25
26	58	18	50	1	42	74	34	66
67	27	59	10	51	2	43	75	35
36	68	19	60	11	52	3	44	76
77	28	69	20	61	12	53	4	45

Our focus is on the magic amulet of Sol, which is another name for the sun. It is not by coincidence that numbers match the beast and the man to be avoided, hence, to avoid receiving the number is to avoid the reference to sun or Sunday worship.

And the significance of the amulet for Sol or the sun involving the numbers totaling 666 is the reason why we greatly downplay the notion that there is a misunderstanding in the number. The number in nowise in Revelation 13:18 is 616. To promote such a potential correction is the undermining of none other than the Antichrist regarding the truth. The number 666 refers to the sun, to the person, to the beast.

Now before we finish this topic, let us address the reservation that many may have because so long have people been told through preachers, teachers, movies, books, etc. that the mark of the beast is some physical object, in fact, it is a purchasing card and physical markings on the skin, even implanting of a chip. But it is our "desire that ye might be filled with the knowledge of his will in all wisdom and spiritual understanding" (Colossians 1:9). Again, "we wrestle not against flesh and blood, but against principalities, against powers, against the rulers of the darkness of this world, against spiritual wickedness in high [places]" (Ephesians 6:12). And this is what we have been trying to do, which is to move people off of looking at the physical things because "we have sown unto you spiritual things" (1 Corinthians 9:11), "Which things also we speak, not in the words which man's wisdom teacheth, but which the Holy Ghost teacheth; comparing spiritual things with spiritual" (1 Corinthians 2:13). If you need us to say it point blank, here it is. God is not concerned about the physical objects. God is concerned about our spiritual stance. For "the hour cometh, and now is, when the true worshippers shall worship the Father in spirit and in truth: for the Father seeketh such to worship him. God [is] a Spirit: and they that worship him must worship [him] in spirit and in truth" (John 4:23-24). On top of that, not once in Matthew 24, the great predictions of Jesus, does Jesus ever mention to avoid some physical object. What does say is, "Take heed that no man deceive you" (Matthew 24:4), "For many shall come in my name, saying, I am Christ; and shall deceive many" (Matthew 24:5), "And many false prophets shall rise, and shall deceive many" (Matthew 24:11), "For there shall arise false Christs, and false prophets, and shall shew great signs and wonders; insomuch that, if [it were] possible, they shall deceive the very elect" (Matthew 24:24). Again, it is to be aware of and avoid the false teachings. And Sunday as the Christian Sabbath is definitely a false teaching.

So, if that does not convince anyone that God is more interested in the day of worship as compared to some credit card, here is not just one point, but several points that say that we need to be thinking more on the spiritual level.

1. Look at the end time warning messages comparing the first angel's message to the third angel's message. The first, identifies the true worship, while the third warns away from the false worship.

What we are referring to is that in Revelation 14:14, there is a symbolic representation of the second coming. "And I looked, and behold a white cloud, and upon the cloud [one] sat like unto the Son of man, having on his head a golden crown, and in his hand a sharp sickle." Prior to that are messages beginning in verse 7 represented by angels that must be used to warn the people to get ready for the second coming. Three angels are providing messages in which the first one says, "Saying with a loud voice, Fear God, and give glory to him; for the hour of his judgment is come: and worship him that made heaven, and earth, and the sea, and the fountains of waters." Now why would God send a message to fear Him if we already are doing it correctly along with an awareness of judgment and specifically a call to worship Him, who is the Creator. The answer is that the world, especially Christians do not fear God, are careless about the judgment, and are not worshipping the Creator, at least properly.

To fear God, the Bible says, "Fear God, and keep his commandments: for this [is] the whole [duty] of man" (Ecclesiastes 12:13). With denominations teaching that the commandments have been nailed to the cross, evidently they are not fearing God, nor are their parishioners.

In regards to the judgment, the next verse says, "For God shall bring every work into judgment, with every secret thing, whether [it be] good, or whether [it be] evil" (Ecclesiastes 12:14). James even wrote, "For whosoever shall keep the whole law, and yet offend in one [point], he is guilty of all. For he that said, Do not commit adultery, said also, Do not kill. Now if thou commit no adultery, yet if thou kill, thou art become a transgressor of the law. So speak ye, and so do, as they that shall be judged by the law of liberty" (James 2:10-12). Again, the Ten Commandments play a role. Are Christians keeping the Ten Commandments or not. If not, they go to hell, if so, is it because they are trying to be saved, then they too shall go to hell. The commandments are to be kept revealing that we have been saved, and not to be saved. And do keep in mind, "He that saith, I know him, and keepeth not his commandments, is a liar, and the truth is not in him" (1 John 2:4).

Finally, worshipping the Creator is not simply saying that one worships God. Tracing the words of Revelation 14:7 through the Bible, one will encounter two verses that simply acknowledge God as the Creator and the remaining verse actually using those words in the context of worship, and it is in Exocdus 20:8-11, which is all about the Sabbath commandment.

So the first angel identifies those that "worship the Father in spirit and in truth: for the Father seeketh such to worship him" (John 4:23). Now contrast that with the third angel's message, "And the third angel followed them, saying with a loud voice, If any man worship the beast and his image, and receive [his] mark in his forehead, or in his hand, The same shall drink of the wine of the wrath of God, which is poured out without mixture into the cup of his indignation; and he shall be tormented with fire and brimstone in the presence of the holy angels, and in the presence of the Lamb: And the smoke of their torment ascendeth up for ever and ever: and they have no rest day nor night, who worship the beast and his image, and whosoever receiveth the mark of his name" (Revelation 14:9-11).

As revealed, it is a message about those being lost who worship the beast, like refusing to give up Catholicism and refuse to give up acknowledging the papacy or Vatican as the head of Christianity dictating beliefs; who worship the image, which is mostly the same teaching via the "Spirit of Antichrist" as passed on from the Protestants of the United States; and receiving or accepting of the mark of his name, which in the context of worship, is to accept Sunday in one form or another as the Christian Sabbath.

2. Revelation 12 shows the result of listening to the three angels' messages. If one does worship God properly and keep His commandments, they will be able to avoid the beast, the image, and the mark. What does it take? "Here is the patience of the saints: here [are] they that keep the commandments of God, and the faith of Jesus" (Revelation 14:12). It does not say, "Here are they that refused to accept the credit cards, the chip, the laser marking." No, it says that the saved were successful in rejecting the mark because they kept the Ten Commandments. How can that be? Well, if one in heart and mind keep all Ten Commandments including the Sabbath commandment, then they will have rejected the Sunday Sabbath mark of authority. But that is just one piece because in action, one could do such, but it is having the faith of Jesus along with it. That means "The just shall live by faith" (Romans 1:17), which refers to the justified, the forgiven, the free gift of eternal life. It is accepting salvation and by such an effect, these people keep the Commandments. They realize that God said, "I gave them my sabbaths, to be a sign between me and them, that they might know that I [am] the LORD that sanctify them" (Ezekiel 20:12). And as a result, they avoid the mark of the beast, the beast, and the image of the beast.

3. The fact that the Antichrist "think to change times and laws" (Daniel 7:25) means that the Antichrist knows where the Seal of God is and is try-

ing to replace God's seal with his own mark. Changing the commandments, specifically the one on time to a different cycle of time (midnight to midnight) as well as a different day (Sunday is not the same as God's first day of the week), means that the Antichrist knows that God says, "Moreover also I gave them my sabbaths, to be a sign between me and them, that they might know that I [am] the LORD that sanctify them" (Ezekiel 20:12) and that we are to "hallow my sabbaths; and they shall be a sign between me and you, that ye may know that I [am] the LORD your God" (Ezekiel 20:20).

4. And look at the Antichrist focus. The people of the world, "They worshipped the beast" (Revelation 13:4). Antichrist "opposeth and exalteth himself above all that is called God, or that is worshipped; so that he as God sitteth in the temple of God, shewing himself that he is God" (2 Thessalonians 2:4). A credit card, a chip, etc. has nothing to do with worship. Recognizing Sunday as the Christian Sabbath on the other hand does.

There are two declarative statements being made. Again we remind everyone of the Vatican's declarative statement from The Catholic Record of London, Ontario, Canada, September 1, 1923: "Sunday is our MARK of authority...the church is above the Bible, and this transference of Sabbath observance is proof of that fact."

And may we remind you of God's declarative statement: "Hallow my sabbaths; and they shall be a sign between me and you, that ye may know that I [am] the LORD your God" (Ezekiel 20:20).

What Tools Help Enforce "One Mind"?

Before we delve into this chapter, a word of caution to those that are not reading this book in proper sequence or are simply skipping sections because they think they know everything contained therein. Even if one is familiar with many of these topics, there are always important view points on other aspects of the topic that should be considered and not glossed over. This book is not a mystery novel; it is not a love novel; it is a study. And a study is a building process, where if enough smaller objects are ignored, the whole building can collapse. It is not just the supporting beams that hold things up, and it will become evident that a person has skipped sections and even chapters if a knee jerk reaction of simply dismissing the contents of this chapter because it does not fit the way one was taught from their youth up.

As stated before, yes, the focus is upon avoiding the Antichrist, but as previous chapters have demonstrated, there is something even worse than facing the Antichrist; it is called the "Spirit of Antichrist" (1 John 4:3). Facing the errors blatantly held by the Vatican as the early reformers had done is one thing, but to be lulled into thinking, "I'm not Catholic so I have nothing to worry about" while practicing the same errors is very dangerous and deceptive. The theology in most Protestant denominations or Evangelical churches happen to encourage one to be lulled into a false security. One does not have to worry about the false doctrines of the Vatican when doctrines do not matter anyways. One does not have to worry about the false doctrines of the Vatican when one just has to say once in their life time, "I believe in Jesus" because from that moment on, they cannot be lost anyways. One does not have to worry about the false doctrines of the Vatican when they are going to be secretly raptured away any day now. These and many other false theories are lulling people to sleep.

So, we are appealing to all the saints who have read each page thoughtfully and prayerfully and looking things up in their own Bibles. The appeal is to your "patience and longsuffering" (Colossians 1:11). I would like to summarize real quickly some important points for the careless reader before entering into this chapter.

First off, through many, many verses and allowing the Bible to explain itself, even when we thought the modern definition of a term was sufficient, we found over fifty points that identify the Antichrist. As the reformers were correct, it is the Vatican or papacy, in which have commandeered the Catholic Church. And trying to deny a handful of points as well as undermining other understandings of points is not sufficient to dismiss all of them or even half of them. Therefore, we conclude that anyone that tries to deny where the finger points is just willfully being ignorant.

Second, through another dozen or more verses, including a timeline, it seems that the second beast of

Revelation 13 points to none other than the United States who would be in position to influence the world on behalf of the Antichrist. Even despite how anti-Catholic or anti-Christian the current president appears to be, the fact is that the United States has been put into such a position of influence in the world, has since 1965 been working quite well together reaching a most revealing togetherness during the Regan administration.

Third, looking up the definition of Antichrist in the epistles of John and also confirming from the Book of Daniel, the key issues at stake are all about the doctrines. This is summarized in 2 John 1:7-11, which says, "For many deceivers are entered into the world, who confess not that Jesus Christ is come in the flesh. This is a deceiver and an Antichrist. Look to yourselves, that we lose not those things which we have wrought, but that we receive a full reward. Whosoever transgresseth, and abideth not in the doctrine of Christ, hath not God. He that abideth in the doctrine of Christ, he hath both the Father and the Son. If there come any unto you, and bring not this doctrine, receive him not into [your] house, neither bid him God speed: For he that biddeth him God speed is partaker of his evil deeds." The notion that doctrines do not matter is the work of the "Spirit of Antichrist".

Fourth, It has also been well demonstrated that the mark of the beast is not a physical object like a credit card, chip, or laser beam numbers. Though such may be used in tracking, the object of the beast is worship. After showing clearly that God's seal or sign is none other than the Sabbath, we showed clearly that the mark of the beast is the recognition of the day he declared to be holy, being Sunday. This was clearly laid out in the form that the Holy Spirit seals us (Ephesians 4:30); He seals us with the truth (Ephesians 1:13); He seals us specifically with the Ten Commandments (Isaiah 8:16); and finally in the middle of the Sabbath commandment is laid out God's name, title, and territory (Exodus 20:8-11), the ingredients of a seal, specifically, the Seal of God. We then showed how the Antichrist great accomplishments is to have cast down the truth (Daniel 8:12), changed the Ten Commandments (Daniel 7:25), and specifically changed the timing cycle as well as the day itself (Daniel 7:25) passing off to all Christians their "Mark of Authority" that they so blatantly brag about. They even taunt Protestants for holding the position about Sunday as they do.

It is with these four great truths that if anyone disagrees with or have not thoroughly understood them then such people will also find this chapter to be difficult to accept. Where most of the difficulty comes in at is the media blitz, including all the Sunday sermons, that tell of a completely different story. Further, one begins to question the contents here because so many believe it another way. One could then say there is a fifth item to the list, and that is about quantity. As already covered, the vast majority of Christianity will be lost (Matthew 7:13); only a few will be saved (Matthew 7:14). Of course this too is not what is being preached, but who are they? Jesus said, "Strait [is] the gate, and narrow [is] the way, which leadeth unto life, and few there be that find it" (Matthew 7:14). And just to confirm that the majority will be lost, Jesus said, "Many will say to me in that day, Lord, Lord, have we not prophesied in thy name? and in thy name have cast out devils? and in thy name done many wonderful works? And then will I profess unto them, I never knew you: depart from me, ye that work iniquity" (Matthew 7:22-23). And "wide [is] the gate, and broad [is] the way, that leadeth to destruction, and many there be which go in threat" (Matthew 7:13).

As a sixth important item to understand before entering into this chapter, one must not be looking for a physical image, like in the days of Babylon, to be erected and worshipped. Pulling from the physical, John in Revelation is applying it spiritually. To "make an image to the beast" (Revelation 13:14) is to turn this country into a reflective resemblance pleasing the beast or Antichrist, as we will reveal is currently happening.

So now let us see what tools will be used to enforce the "One Mind". With the United States in the forefront of the issuance of the mark of the beast (Revelation 13:16) as well as raising up a faithful people (Revelation 12:17), it should be no mystery why we will be concentrating upon the tools used in the United States.

As the Bible describes the activity of the United States in Revelation 13:11, "Another beast coming up out of the earth; and he had two horns like a lamb, and he spake as a dragon", it should be no wonder to what is going on politically in this country. Do we really think it is by accident that this country is so dynamically opposed towards each other in what appears to be a different type of civil war? Every political issue is a war. It is not simply one side trying to tax and spend while the other is opposed to it. It is not simply one group wanting bigger government while the other wants a smaller government. It is not simply one cares so much for the underprivileged that they think the government should be everyone's mother and the other side seems to be cold towards the idea of a helping hand. Though some of these descriptions may be a stretch, the point is that the topics of today are very much tearing the fabric of this country apart. The sad reality is that both major parties are not innocent. There is an obvious progression to an end goal that one party seems to be against while the other is going full steam ahead, however, upon closer examination, both major parties are actually progressively moving forward towards the end game and the appearance of opposition is more of a disguise instead of an accomplishment. What the opposing party usually is against seems to be for it just about twenty years later.

But now let us get more specific. The United States has been morally and politically bankrupt for years now moving away from the initial lamb like horns in which is contained Jesus like strengths or principles and more towards Satanic like force. Horns, according to the Bible in Psalms 89:17, is associated with strength. This country was founded upon two great and strong principles that Christ would approve. One is called Republicanism in which the people hold the power, also referred to as civil liberties. The other is called Protestantism, in which a person may have the freedom to live according to the morals defined in the Bible as a person understands them, also referred to as religious liberties. In other words, we were founded upon the power by the people and for the people while exercising the freedom of religion.

And just look at where we have come since our founding, in which there is no longer protection towards individuals wanting to practicing freedom of religion. In fact, recent Supreme Court rulings have made it more difficult to do so. Other court cases have also taken the power away from the people and strengthen the government.

One of the tools that is influencing people to have "One Mind" for the wrong side is the obvious one, media. One can only be blind to the fact that media does shape the thoughts. Television, music, and news outlets have been brainwashing people more and more away from Christian truths to point that if anyone actually adheres to the Christian truth, they are looked upon as peculiar, out of touch, weird folk, and just a joke. The media uplifts the abnormal and presents it as normal. The media twists the opposing view and couches any exposure in such a way that makes it appear that they do not have the facts correct. They attack the messenger hoping the message will fall as well, and it does appear to be successful. When the media finally have to succumb to the acknowledgment of the truth, they purposely delay admitting it so that it is considered ancient history, in fact, it is presented that way because they have now moved on to the next step to further their agenda, and to now discuss how wrong they are makes the people who were right all along as unforgiving, even though it was never addressed, and as living in the past.

In one example of the success the media has had is in the area of sex. We have moved from the time in which a married couple were not allowed to be filmed in the same bed together to now in which can only be classed as soft core porn, even during the family hour. There used to be a 10:00 pm rule in which the FCC would not allow explicit sexual scenes, foul words, explicit sexual innuendos, or anything deemed inappropriate for minors to be exposed to prior to that time. Speaking of soft core porn, or porn in general, it was something that used to be difficult to obtain. Now it is one of the best selling channels without the shame that used to go along with it. Many of today's music stars are nothing but whores dancing on stage, and yet, they are placed before the children as something to look up to. By the time the average teenager reaches adulthood, the indoctrination of having uncommitted sexual relationships is so brainwashed into the youth that even committed Christians have a hard time remaining celibate until marriage. And when we say uncommitted, we are not endorsing hopping from one committed relationship to another, as is portrayed in the media, including the music.

But free expression of sexuality is actually not the point; that is just the distraction. The media has convinced even Christian homes that their children need to be on birth control as early as thirteen, maybe even younger. To recommend abstinence, not only is it lacking in the entertainment world, but the constant bombardment by the news media reporting how it does not work, that ot is old fashion thinking, and it is out of touch thinking, makes it quite difficult to raise teens in a manner that they do not experiment with sexual intercourse. The entertainment constantly dangling more than the carrot of sexual expression does not help matters at all. Further, it does not help that so called unbiased programming where studies have been supposedly conducted ends up undermining the Bible principles. They do so by referring to the concept of abstinence only being related to necessity during cavemen days, but in this day, we do not need to account for the hunting and gathering aspect. The local grocery store provides easy access to food, therefore, have sex with as many people as they want.

Now we hope you were not seeing the above material as related to being pro abstinence and anti freedom of sexual activity among youth, although that is the Bible stance. Again, that was not the focus. The focus is on media reshaping society's thoughts of sexual expression. The media has been so successful that regular conversations usually include sexual connotations to them; people are not shocked by explicit acts anymore; and public display is acceptable.

Change the topic from sex to something else and it is the same thing. How do you think the homosexual agenda has gotten as far as it has. All the positives were pumped into brains through television, music, and print. All opposing views were greatly exaggerated to the point that Bible believers on this matter were made to be a bunch of homosexual haters. They basically gave two options. One is either for the homosexual agenda or such people hate homosexuals, when that is not the case at all. True Christians can oppose homosexuality and still be friends, treat everyone equally, and work together. They do not seek the death of any homosexuals. They do not seek loss of employment either. Homosexuals should get equal medical treatment, able to sit anywhere they want on public transportation, able to buy houses and cars, have a driver's license, and much more. But if a baker refuses to put two brides or two grooms on the same wedding cake, yet knowingly serve homosexuals just like every other customer outside of that request, they should not be sued and have their business foreclosed. The abomination declared in the Bible is superseded by the media. And where is the sympathetic media when book publishers are now being targeted for lawsuits simply for printing the Bible? On top of that, we do not need the brainwashing infomercials, since the Supreme Court ruling regarding marriages for homosexuals, telling us that love comes in all forms and if one disagrees, they need to go to an indoctrinating website to stop the hateful feelings. True Christians do not hate homosexuals!

Again, did you get distracted by the topic of homosexuality, or did you follow the media trail in which the media has convinced everyone that the abnormal practices are acceptable and that to stand with God and His Word is unacceptable? The Bible says, "Woe unto them that call evil good, and good evil; that put darkness for light, and light for darkness; that put bitter for sweet, and sweet for bitter!" (Isaiah 5:20)

Change the topics of sex and homosexuality into yet another topic, like marijuana use, and the same media brainwashing techniques are employed. The Bible is clear that no such substance should enter the temple of God. "If any man defile the temple of God, him shall God destroy; for the temple of God is holy, which [temple] ye are" (1 Corinthians 3:17). Yet, the media shows all of the heart tugging cases where medical marijuana just seems to be the only solution to situations, while they silence and squash the number of stories reporting how it is a gateway drug. The entertainment business continues the agenda along with the news outlets.

The same is true for every single subject. Why do we have forced health care participation? The media is the answer once again. And for those that think this is a political topic in the middle of a religious book, it is not. Forget the fact it is health care for a moment. The issue at hand is the fact that forced participation in something is definitely not lamb like horns guiding the United States, but rather, it is the dragon speaking. The media convinced everyone that people should be tired of welfare people going to the hospital for a headache when they should just see a doctor. These abuses were brought across the television, in print, and all over the Internet. They even appealed to the wallet declaring how inexpensive health care would be, when it is not. It is actually more expensive now. Any positive message about people being better off taking care of themselves was reported as abusers of the system, undermining the betterment of the country, and just uncooperative. Many examples of people not having insurance and being a drain on the system was reported. The media did everything they could to bolster the support of the people demanding the health care enforcement.

The media controlling public opinion is especially true when it comes to vaccinations. Although the science on both sides of the issue actually allows people to freely choose if they want their children vaccinated or not, the media, celebrities, and other outlets have created the opinion that those that do not vaccinate their children are causing other children to be at a serious health risk. The non-vaccinated children could eventually cause the death of thousands upon thousands of children, including the vaccinated ones. They are reporting it in such a way that the freedom to not vaccinate is being taken away, and the fear that has been created has everyone against those that choose not to. Again, the issue is not vaccination as it is the freedom to choose.

So, the first primary tool at the hand of the United States is the media in all of its forms: print, Internet, television, music, movies, etc.

The second tool used are the scientists, which includes psychiatrists, psychologists, doctors, health nutritionists, etc. Although the media is involved primarily, the idea is that with media quoting scientist after scientist who claim the scientific evidence for climate change, requirements for vaccinations and that there are no harmful side effects, how homeschooling damages children, how a vegetarian diet is harmful, how masturbation is healthy, how multiple sexual partners is necessary, how abortions have no consequences upon a woman's body, how eating many meals through the day is healthier than three square meals despite the increase in obesity, how this planet is at least billions of years old, and so on, they are convincing the recipients to believing things one way and taking away the freedom of the other. Any opposing scientists are made to look like goons. Reasonable evidence that speak to the contrary is squashed. In reality, there are some times more scientists on the opposing side than there are those that promote the false beliefs. It is just that they are not part of the agenda. In other words, a scientist can be bought. All the evidence can have a bias to it.

Look at carbon dating for instance, which takes the world wide flood out the equation. The same object can be tested in multiple labs around the world and be dated hundreds, thousands, even tens of thousands years difference. A simple experiment with carbon is the amount of time it takes to make a diamond verses a fake diamond, which is one made in a lab through much pressure instead of waiting the many years for the process to occur naturally.

Besides, who wants to work themselves out of a job? If the scientists promoting global warming were to honestly declare there is nothing humans are doing to bring it on, and that is all a cycle of the earth, there would be no need for such scientists. But through global warming, an entire industry has been created. Governments can control the people more, all in the name of "saving the planet". And power corrupts those in authority, of which global warming belief has very much contributed to such abuse.

The next tool used is education. By employing mostly people that agree with the agenda and place them in positions of teachers, our children are being brainwashed into many ways of the agenda and definitely against God. The few teachers that do stand up against the agenda are disrespected by other teachers, even in front of students, which removes much of their authority as a teacher needs to exercise so as to conduct a class. In our schools, sympathy is created for whatever agenda is at hand. Theories, such as evolution, is passed off as fact, while the opposing view is not permissible. While recommending children avoid pregnancy and sexually transmitted diseases, they are handed condoms, allowed to be escorted off campus for birth control and abortions without a parent's consent, and more. Abstinence topics are either not permitted or is so briefly permitted while teaching students how to put a condom on a piece of fruit takes high priority. While the Bible takes a stance against the practices of homosexuals, just as it takes a stance against any sin while calling the sinner to repentance, sympathy and twisted political unfairness are exposed to our children while the opposing view is looked upon as bigoted. The same is true with the transgender topic, sexual changes, and more. Look at climate change, or when it was called global warming when young elementary kids would come home crying because their parents drove cars causing penguins and polar bears to lose their homes due to the melting ice caps. The emotional perspective is always wheeled out to create a divide between the stubborn parents who do not agree with the agenda and the young minds who believe their teachers would never lie to them.

By the time a child graduates into adulthood, they have been taught to be more than sympathetic to the planet to the point that they ought to feel guilty for living and contributing to the problem. They are taught to hate those that use the Bible, that hold a different view, and only be kind to those that are all inclusive, which is an oxymoron since they exclude those that have an opposing opinion. So much for inclusiveness. They graduate not only simply being accepting of the homosexual lifestyle but staunch defenders of it. Basically, everything that the agendas stands for is well indoctrinated among the math, English, physical education, and supposedly other non-political agendadized courses. Even the history class rewrites history to help promote the agenda or the party most supportive of the agenda.

The next tool is legislation. If the government deems a rule should be made, without consulting the religious leaders, it becomes law. In fact, the more that the preachers declare their beliefs, the more the notion of separation of church and state is claimed. In other words, their arguments for or against something based upon the Bible actually hurts the possibility of preventing the law from being enacted.

This is not only true with homosexual laws, but more and more, religious liberties are being undermined. Homeschooling, vaccinations, marriage and divorce, tithing and other donations, homeschooling, and many other things are all controlled through legislation.

One sly trick of the government, which takes away rights from religious organizations is the concept of 501c3, charitable corporations. Unless registered as such with the government, all donations are taxable. So in wanting a tax deduction, religious organizations sign up to be a 501c3. In exchange, technically they are not allowed to attack other 501c3's as each are actually an extension of the government. When ministers state, "By the power invested in me by the…", they are acting as a government representative. Now when we say attack, it means that any activity to undermine a fellow 501c3 is prohibited. The Department of Energy does not start building nuclear weapons to compete with the Department of Defense and say how incompetent the Defense is. So, Lutherans ought not point out what Methodists are doing wrong according to Bible practices and Methodists should not do the same to Lutherans. Likewise, none of the denominations truly should be pointing out the errors of the Vatican, hence, we have government sponsored ecumenicalism. In addition to diffusing the truth and different doctrines, the government also dictates what is and what is not allowed to be practiced. For instance, the passage of redefining marriage will prohibit the denominations from standing against homosexuality. Those that do continue to voice their opposition can face revoking of their 501c3 status, which carries a penalty of paying back years of tax exemptions they had enjoyed. This is true for everything that the United States deems is acceptable but preachers are to preach against. So the 501c3 is a diffusing of the Bible stance.

Now once we have the media, scientists, public education, and the government combined, next is the populace. The populace does not think for themselves, even though we supposedly have independent voters. They easily quote, "Well, it's a government rule", "It's legal", "It's…" and fill in whatever dependency upon the government there is. People who take advantage of the government through loopholes ought to think that just because one can does not make it right before God. Another example is the number of Christians that drink. They quote the fact that at age 21 it is legal. And just because one becomes the age of consent, an adult, does not mean one has to be sleeping around.

But beyond personal choices, there is the notion that if the media says it is so and the government has rules enforcing that, then it is alright to pressure the noncompliant people into compliance. Today it is putting pressure on non-vaccinating parents to vaccinate including a willingness to have laws to take away the freedom of choice. The pressure has already come down upon those that oppose the homosexual agenda. Although the arguments continue, pro choice has a much stronger voice than those that are anti-abortion.

So, going beyond the media, scientists, public education, and government legislation, the next tool is the so-called grassroots movements. This is where carefully selected catch phrases are propagated at talking levels among the citizens to bolster support and squeeze out the opposition. It is done in subtle ways and eventually becomes the norm for thought processes.

Look at the homosexual agenda. They carefully constructed argument is that if one is against the agenda, then such people are homophobes. There is no other option presented despite the fact that it is not true. One does not have to fear homosexuals or even be anti-homosexual to simply be against certain aspects. In fact, people can have friends, co-workers, and other encounters on a regular basis without discrimination towards such people and yet be against making homosexuality a protected minority class based upon sexual preference.

Look at the pro-vaccination movement, which will eventually be the law of the land. There was an incident at Disney where a measles breakout occurred. The only reason it occurred was because someone was not vaccinated. And the public bought into such arguments hook, line, and sinker. It became the talking point at family gatherings, but no one is using their own thought processes. How did the non-vaccinated person get the measles? It is not just in the air like a common cold. One does not get it from a plant. It is transmitted from person to person. So either someone was a carrier from an outside country that was kept silent, or more than likely, someone was recently vaccinated and during the incubation period for the child's immunity to kick in, as vaccines are to do, it was transmitted to the non-vaccinated person. In other words, vaccinated children are carriers of the disease. Doctors do not tell anyone to keep their child out of the public after being vaccinated, and no one wants to be told to keep a child away from others for any length of time until the vaccination runs its course. Parents think they can leave the doctor's office and come in contact with the disease and be protected. That is not true, but the medical community does a poor job in informing the public of such.

And if one were to use their minds for a moment and realize the arguments on the "militant" side of things is at the level of grasping at straws, one would see through the never before heard of argument of "Group Effectiveness". In "Group Effectiveness", a fairly recent term to lessen the concern of vaccine ineffectiveness, a vaccine is only as good as the number of people vaccinated. The lower the percentage, the likelihood that the vaccine will not work. So if we have ten kids and two are not vaccinated, it is likely that the vaccinated children are at risk. That makes no sense. When a child is injected with the measles vaccine, it is to build up a resistance to the measles virus in the body. This is called antibodies. So then when a vaccinated child encounters the measles virus, the virus is not affective because the body knows what that virus is, has already dealt with that virus, and has rejected it now. The body is immune to it.

Tell the argument about "group effectiveness" to all the missionaries with children who enter countries with all kinds of diseases that no one there is vaccinated against although the missionaries and their family members are vaccinated. While there, the odds are one in a hundred, maybe even a thousand against the vaccinated person. If group vaccination is the only way vaccines work, then no one would take children on mission trips. The odds of contacting a deadly virus then is extremely high, and no mission trip is worth playing Russian roulette.

But again, this is not about vaccinating or not vaccinating. It is about stirring up the masses to be against the minority viewpoint to the point that people are intolerable towards the non-conformists. As the saying goes, "Everyone has freedom of speech as long as they agree with the agenda." One of these agendas is eventually going to be the mark of the beast being enforced. We will have been so conditioned as a society that no verse, no study is going to undo the brainwashing, so now is the time to know and be established on the truth.

As this is not a document trying to convince one to not vaccinate and as this is not a document that is trying to stop the homosexual agenda and as this is not a document trying to convince people that global warming or climate change is hoax, likewise, our next example is not about supporting the rich. Our point, like the other topics is about making people aware of the creation of these social catch phrases that people utter not really realizing the true meaning and in which creates animosity towards another group. There is animosity towards those that disagree about calling a homosexual union a marriage. There is animosity towards those that choose to home school. There is animosity towards those that choose not to vaccinate. And there is animosity towards the rich.

The catch phrase that is creating the animosity is "fair share". We hear a lot about corporations and the rich needing to pay their fair share, when in reality, corporations and the rich pay more than their fair share. How is it that one class owes, as an example, 10% of their income in taxes and another class having to pay 50% in taxes fair? What is fair is that we all pay the same rate, just like God's tithing system is. It is called a flat tax in which everyone pays the same percentage. Now that is fair.

For those that do not understand, let us say that 20% is the flat tax rate. If I make only $1.00 as a poorer person, I owe 20 cents of that dollar to taxes, and as a rich person making $1.00 I should also only have to pay 20 cents. That is fair. Instead, we have the poorer class paying 10 cents and the richer class paying 50 cents for every dollar earned. Again, God's tithing system is based on 10% of one's increase, which also means that God believes in deductions. The class warfare, created through the grass root efforts, generates animosity towards the rich to keep raising their percentage rate for taxes. The evil corporations are also not paying enough, they say. And speaking of which, how is it fair that the corporation is hit with a corporate tax before they distribute what is called dividends to shareholders and then those shareholders receiving those dividends have to pay taxes again? In other words, the money is double taxed.

But as a reminder, this is not about class warfare as it is about the creating of controlled animosity towards certain groups of people as chosen targets.

So, between the media, scientists, public schools, government legislation, and these grass root efforts of creating animosity towards certain groups of people, and it being so successful, it is just a matter of time to turn it towards God's people. Before all of these devices, people pretty much kept to themselves and just dealt with life. Today, it is hard enough to deal with the issues of the day personally, let alone having to deal with the animosity that has been falsely created.

Even one avenue that the mark of the beast can come in is creating such momentum. It is the religious approach to the green movement. We say religious because it is a type of worship. And those that do not believe in global warming, climate change, or whatever else they call it, are looked upon as polluters, unconcerned for the environment, and downright disrespectful towards the planet. The true stance is that we ought to do what is respectful, not be wasteful, but at the same time, not send us to live in caves and without automobiles and other conveniences. Legislation is out of control trying to experiment with all kinds of ways to conserve energy, even to the destruction of car engines through the use of corn for gasoline. Even the light bulb was not safe, forcing people to use unhealthy fluorescents. Of course that was repealed, but destruction of progress and even of people's health is of no concern for the agenda, and to raise questions and deal rationally is considered being anti-earth making those in favor of the green movement to resent those that oppose. Eventually, they will realize that the best thing to do is shutdown as much of society once a week to conserve energy. It is not by chance that the pope is quite involved with the climate change group. He too sees an avenue for bringing in laws uplifting the mark of authority they had established.

Now we are not predicting that the mark of the beast will come in that way, but the possibility is there, especially in the pope's encyclical called "Care For Our Common Home", there is a section suggesting a day of rest being on Sunday. It states, "Sunday, like the Jewish Sabbath, is meant to be a day which heals our relationships with God, with ourselves, with others and with the world. Sunday is the day of the Resurrection, the "first day" of the new creation, whose first fruits are the Lord's risen humanity, the pledge of the final transfiguration of all created reality."

Now, looking past all the implied political positions that are also moral ones, what you should take away from this chapter is that it is no longer the freedom to disagree. The media tells people what to believe; scientists provides the proof of that belief; the public schools educate generation after generation in that belief; the government legislates the belief; and the grass roots create out right hatred to all that oppose.

What Can People Do To Protect Themselves?

We already gave the answer away to this question, but for those that have missed it or need to have it expanded, we will do so now. First, let us answer the question directly by setting the scene. Jesus is pictured in Revelation 14:14 as returning to earth, known as the second coming. "And I looked, and behold a white cloud, and upon the cloud [one] sat like unto the Son of man, having on his head a golden crown, and in his hand a sharp sickle."

Prior to this verse, specifically starting with verse 6 is the warnings that cover the entire earth. They are represented by angels. "And I saw another angel fly in the midst of heaven, having the everlasting gospel to preach unto them that dwell on the earth, and to every nation, and kindred, and tongue, and people, Saying with a loud voice, Fear God, and give glory to him; for the hour of his judgment is come: and worship him that made heaven, and earth, and the sea, and the fountains of waters. And there followed another angel, saying, Babylon is fallen, is fallen, that great city, because she made all nations drink of the wine of the wrath of her fornication. And the third angel followed them, saying with a loud voice, If any man worship the beast and his image, and receive [his] mark in his forehead, or in his hand, The same shall drink of the wine of the wrath of God, which is poured out without mixture into the cup of his indignation; and he shall be tormented with fire and brimstone in the presence of the holy angels, and in the presence of the Lamb: And the smoke of their torment ascendeth up for ever and ever: and they have no rest day nor night, who worship the beast and his image, and whosoever receiveth the mark of his name" (Revelation 14:6-11).

So who is giving the messages? Who listens to the messages and complying with the warnings given to conform one's life? The answer to these questions and the chapter's question is found in Revelation 14:12. "Here is the patience of the saints: here [are] they that keep the commandments of God, and the faith of Jesus." Not just faith in Jesus will save; obeying the Ten Commandments alone is legalistic; but obeying the Ten Commandments through faith is the answer. That means that those that do not reject the Mark of the Beast, end up worshipping the Beast, or end up worshipping the Image of the Beast are breaking the Ten Commandments.

How will obeying the Ten Commandments feed families when "no man might buy or sell, save he that had the mark, or the name of the beast, or the number of his name" (Revelation 13:17)? How will the Ten Commandments prevent people from becoming subject to "the woman drunken with the blood of the saints, and with the blood of the martyrs of Jesus" (Revelation 17:6)? The answer to any of the physical questions regarding the Ten Commandments is, it does not protect. In fact, it is what angers the Beast and the Image of the Beast as well as their followers for "he had power to give life unto the image of the beast, that the image of the beast should both speak, and cause that as many as would not worship the image of the beast should be killed" (Revelation 13:15). But remember, those that think in the physical realm, despite how much of a Christian they had been practicing, will be lost, for "God [is] a Spirit: and they that worship him must worship [him] in spirit and in truth" (John 4:24). Besides, "whosoever will save his life shall lose it: and whosoever will lose his life for my sake shall find it" (Matthew 16:25). So those that try to save their skins will lose eternal life, but those that lose their physical life for God's sake "shall come forth; they that have done good, unto the resurrection of life" (John 5:29).

But the Ten Commandments is the answer, including the one that says, "Remember the sabbath day, to keep it holy" (Exodus 20:8), where "the seventh day [is] the sabbath of the LORD thy God" (Exodus 20:10) and none other day while treating Sunday as a work day instead.

This also explains why Satan is ignoring most of Christianity and is warring with only a few. "And the dragon was wroth with the woman, and went to make war with the remnant of her seed, which keep the commandments of God, and have the testimony of Jesus Christ" (Revelation 12:17). Remember, the woman represents a collection of people called church (compare Jeremiah 6:2 to Isaiah 51:16). If the Ten Commandments do not matter, why is the dragon warring only with those that keep them? I mean, if Christians think it is up to everyone to choose but overall we are saved without obedience to them, then why be warring only against those that keep them? The reality is, even the dragon, Satan, knows that it is the key to avoiding the Beast, the Image of the Beast, and the Mark of the Beast. It is key to retaining eternal life. When we choose to sin instead of obedience, we choose to reject the gift of God. Sure, the dragon is wroth with the woman, Christianity at large, but it is only because of the constant reference to Jesus. The dragon does not care if one sings, prays, and talks of Jesus as long as they are not obeying God's Word and especially those Ten Commandments. When one does obey, only then does he war against them.

On top of that, why is the Antichrist targeting the Ten Commandments as well? If the Ten Commandments mean nothing, why do they "think to change times and laws" (Daniel 7:25)? That's because of the principle of "whosoever shall keep the whole law, and yet offend in one [point], he is guilty of all. For he that said, Do not commit adultery, said also, Do not kill. Now if thou commit no adultery, yet if thou kill, thou art become a transgressor of the law" (James 2:10-11)

But for those that insist that obedience to the Ten Commandments is not necessary, let us search as commanded by Isaiah 28:9-10. "Whom shall he teach knowledge? and whom shall he make to understand doctrine? [them that are] weaned from the milk, [and] drawn from the breasts. For precept [must be] upon precept, precept upon precept; line upon line, line upon line; here a little, [and] there a little." Do keep in mind, we will be looking primarily at the New Testament references as that is where the controversy happens. Everyone agrees that the commandments were necessary in the Old Testament.

Now this is why we say the "Spirit of Antichrist" is worse than the Antichrist themselves when it comes to doctrine. Like the Sabbath, the Antichrist admits that the Ten Commandments are required in the equation for salvation, again, not to be saved but is the fruit of a saved person, and they just offer a different version. Who shall we be loyal to is the question. Will we be loyal in obeying God's Ten Commandments or the Vatican's version? Protestants, mostly Evangelicals, teach that the Ten Commandments have nothing to do with salvation and on top of that, once a person is saved, there is no such thing as losing eternal life, as if when we come to Jesus, somehow we give up our free will.

Paul knew he had to wrestle with free will. There are all kinds of temptations trying to pull us away from God. This is why he said, "I protest by your rejoicing which I have in Christ Jesus our Lord, I die daily" (1 Corinthians 15:31). And do take note that if he were alive today, he would say, "I protest that you claim to be saved, which is in Christ Jesus, I die daily." Saving is a daily process "because iniquity shall abound, the love of many shall wax cold. But he that shall endure unto the end, the same shall be saved" (Matthew 24:12-13).

Now fitting once again is the topic of temptation. For salvation sake towards those that have been poisoned with "once saved, always saved" and "as long as I'm mostly good" beliefs, temptation is not for the thief, murderer, prostitute, liar, adulterer. Temptation carries a guilt when given into. These practicing sinners do not have such guilt. Now if one were "once saved, always saved" or even lived with allowance of sin here or there thinking that because as long as they are mostly good they will be going to Heaven, well, temptation then is meaningless in the Bible. There would be no such thing, yet it is in the example prayer, "Lead us not into temptation, but deliver us from evil" (Matthew 6:13). Do keep in mind, only Christians pray this prayer, so even Jesus is telling us directly that Christians are the ones that are to be struggling with temptation, not worldly people. Worldly people already threw away salvation, at least for the present time. Temptation is only for those that have the risk of losing eternal life. That is why Satan tempts us because he knows there is no such thing as guaranteed salvation. He knows that up until our last breath, he has a chance to draw us away from God.

But the next question is, temptation for what? Yes, to sin or do evil. But what is the consequence? Well, following the logic, temptation comes at the cost of losing something. Is it losing house, land, spouse, children? Ask a gambler who has lost all of those things, and they will agree, but ask a professional gambler that is living off their winnings and they would disagree. Besides, if we lost those things in the right way, God actually encourages it. "And every one that hath forsaken houses, or brethren, or sisters, or father, or mother, or wife, or children, or lands, for my name's sake, shall receive an hundredfold, and shall inherit everlasting life" (Matthew 19:29). So then, what is temptation's goal? There is only one thing we can lose that the devil would spend so much time and effort, especially towards those that keep those pesky Ten Commandments. It is called eternal life.

So, just how dangerous is the "Spirit of Antichrist" regarding the Ten Commandments? Well, the failure begins with the pretended Christian. We call them the pretended Christian because these people look for easier and easier ways to ignore Jesus' words, "Ye cannot serve God and mammon" (Matthew 6:24). And for those that do not understand mammon, maybe these words will help. "Ye adulterers and adulteresses, know ye not that the friendship of the world is enmity with God? whosoever therefore will be a friend of the world is the enemy of God" (James 4:4). These are the Christians who want to live a bit like the world and yet claim to go to Heaven. They like their TV, their music, their unconverted friends, their drinking a bit, their gluttony a little, their smoking, their lifestyle, or any combination of this list and then some. So, these people "will not endure sound doctrine; but after their own lusts shall they heap to themselves teachers, having itching ears" (2 Timothy 4:3). And this book is very sound compared to all the false easy gospels going around. Teachers who address peoples itching their ears are like those that scratch behind a dog's ears. It is pleasant. They could sit there and take it all the day long, like many sermons full of allowances towards sin. So, these supposed Christians look towards "men, turning the grace of our God into lasciviousness, and denying the only Lord God, and our Lord Jesus Christ" (Jude 1:4). These men teach grace in manner that is considered lasciviousness and they deny Jesus Christ, at least the part of making true Christians holy in reality.

Paul directly addressed these people who go around preaching, "We're not saved by the Commandments; we're saved by grace!" Although such people even quote the Bible, saying, "For sin shall not have dominion over you: for ye are not under the law, but under grace" (Romans 6:14), they fail to read the follow up verse so that there is no misunderstanding, "What then? shall we sin, because we are not under the law, but under grace? God forbid" (Romans 6:15). So no, grace does not do away with the obedience to the Ten Commandments, but in nowise can we ever say, "Because I have obeyed the commandments now, it makes up for all the times I did not." God forbid if we ever thought that. But grace is not freedom to continue on sinning. Grace is the free removal of our past sins, and to allow Jesus to be "able to keep you from falling" (Jude 1:24).

Those that read just Romans 6:14 also misunderstand Galatians 5:4, which says, "Christ is become of no effect unto you, whosoever of you are justified by the law; ye are fallen from grace." And so the answer is no, we are not saved by the Ten Commandments for we are saved by grace, however, once we are saved by grace, we do not continue to live in sin, but rather we now live in obedience to the commandments.

For those that say, "All you have to do is believe and you are saved without the Ten Commandments" because they see the one verse that says, "Believe on the Lord Jesus Christ, and thou shalt be saved" (Acts 16:31), they fail at the fact that the Bible is not written in a manner that one can take a single verse or even just a handful and build a belief. God gave us the Bible, not just a verse. And then He even tells us how to study it, which as a reminder, it is "precept [must be] upon precept, precept upon precept; line upon line, line upon line; here a little, [and] there a little" (Isaiah 28:10). Even Paul wrote, "In the mouth of two or three witnesses shall every word be established" (2 Corinthians 13:1). So we need more than the one liner of Luke to establish God's intent. And when one does that, one finds out that there is indeed more than just an acknowledgement of belief to be saved, for instance, "He that believeth and is baptized shall be saved" (Mark 16:16). So now we see believing and being baptized is required. We are also told, "Believe on the name of the Son of God" (1 John 5:13), so now we have that we need to believe on Jesus specifically and be baptized, not just believe whatever we want. The Bible further goes and says, "The devils also believe, and tremble" (James 2:19), so if the devils have a reaction, that means we should too. So, believe, believe on Jesus, be baptized, and react to being saved. But by further searching on the word "believe", we find out what our reaction ought to be. "For therefore we both labour and suffer reproach, because we trust in the living God, who is the Saviour of all men, specially of those that believe" (1 Timothy 4:10). The reaction we ought to have is to labor, as in work, which encompasses both the work that is necessary to resist sin as well as the work to winning souls all along the way enduring the reproach or ridicule. To simply believe is a resistance to this work because no one wants to be accused of working their way to Heaven, however, if one truly believes, then just as if a building were on fire and one believes that it really is on fire, they will work to the point of avoiding getting burnt and work towards saving others. Of course, there is more to it than what we have demonstrated through this mini study, but one should understand to simply quote a verse and ignore all of these other verses is to do as Bible believers are accused of doing: getting anything you want from the Bible. And that is simply not so. There is only one correct way to gather knowledge and doctrine from the Bible (Isaiah 28:9-10) and all the rest are wrong.

Now let us address those that believe all that one needs for salvation is faith. As James wrote under the inspiration of God, who is "the author and finisher of [our] faith" (Hebrews 12:2), "Yea, a man may say, Thou hast faith, and I have works: shew me thy faith without thy works, and I will shew thee my faith by my works" (James 2:18). He goes on to write, "Even so faith, if it hath not works, is dead, being alone" (James 2:17), but notice the sequence. If one has faith, then the works that they do will reveal that faith. If I have faith in God, I will, by my works pray to God. Praying to God is a form of effort or work, even if you love God. If I have faith that God has forgiven me of my sins, I will, by my works, not be walking around continuing to condemn myself. Sure, I will feel sad for the results and may seek ways to ease the situation that I created and will not pretend it did not happen, but that is different from thinking God is going to reject me from Heaven, which He will not, if we have honestly confessed it. If I faith that God is all powerful, greater than Satan, then I will, by my works, cease from sinning because when I commit sin, that is my works that reveal Satan is greater. But all in all, at no point will I ever say to God, "God, because I pray, because I have faith that I am forgiven, because I keep your commandments and do not sin, I deserve Heaven. See how perfect I am God?" That is completely wrong. We are saved only by the blood of Jesus. Period. But it is our works that show what our faith is like. Even the apostle Paul wrote, "Do we then make void the law through faith? God forbid: yea, we establish the law" (Romans 3:31). To establish the law is to obey it, be walking examples of it, be the ruling part of our life.

And somehow, Christians are convinced that the Ten Commandments were required before the cross but after the cross, we are saved by grace. Keep in mind, Catholics do not believe that, hence the continued push for obedience. Although the wrong motivation and wrong set of commandments are in use, we agree that the commandments did not end at the cross. This is how much more dangerous is the "Spirit of Antichrist". Besides, the people of the Old Testament were no more saved by commandment keeping as we are today. The Commandments or the Law does not save us. And in addition, the only Bible definition of the word "grace" is not found in the New Testament, as one would expect for how much we are taught that it is a New Testament concept, but rather, it is found in the Old Testament. Moses, of all people, in conversation with God said, "If now I have found grace in thy sight, O Lord, let my Lord, I pray thee, go among us; for it [is] a stiffnecked people; and pardon our iniquity and our sin, and take us for thine inheritance" (Exodus 34:9). Grace is a pardon of our iniquities, our sins, and provides entrance into the inheritance of eternal life. That is Bible definition, which is found written by the one who people credit as the Commandment keeping requirement giver. People today who hear the call to keep the Ten commandments will say, "That's Moses' law, which has been done away with!" Actually, it is God's laws for they are on "tables of stone, written with the finger of God" (Exodus 31:18). Since God was the one to take over the writing of them, they must be pretty important.

But even logically the argument does not make sense. If people of the Old Testament were saved by the obedience to the commandments but now we are under grace, that means either breaking a single commandment just once condemns a person to hell, for only grace forgives and is being taught as only those of the New Testament, or we bring in the theology of being mostly good is what counted, which is fallacy. Just what percentage is considered mostly good? Is it 51%, 60%, 75%, 90%? But if the one strike and a person is out of Heaven rule would apply, then no one in the Old Testament will be in Heaven. Moses sinned at least twice. Once for killing an Egyptian in the name of leading his people (Exodus 2:12) and the other is for striking a rock that God said to speak to so as to reveal some symbolism that Moses messed up (Numbers 20:8-10). David murdered (2 Samuel 11:14-17), committed adultery (2 Samuel 11:4), and disobediently counted the people when he was not to do so (2 Samuel 24:1, 10). However, according to the Bible, both are saved. Moses was resurrected (Jude 1:9), and David is awaiting in the grave for the resurrection (Acts 2:29-36).

Looking at even what Jesus said, "Think not that I am come to destroy the law, or the prophets: I am not come to destroy, but to fulfil. For verily I say unto you, Till heaven and earth pass, one jot or one tittle shall in no wise pass from the law, till all be fulfilled. Whosoever therefore shall break one of these least commandments, and shall teach men so, he shall be called the least in the kingdom of heaven: but whosoever shall do and teach [them], the same shall be called great in the kingdom of heaven" (Matthew 5:17-19). Some Christians have been taught that Jesus came to fulfill the obedience to the Ten Commandments so we do not have to worry about keeping them as strictly as those of the Old Testament, but that does not make sense. In short, they are saying that the words of Jesus are, "I have not come to destroy the law but to destroy it." When He made reference to not destroying it, that is inclusive of not removing any obligation on our part. Besides, in the context of things, Jesus even said that not even the smallest mark of the commandments would be removed. But for those that argue to say, "Yes, but Jesus fulfilled everything at the cross", well, that is not so. Jesus still had to rise. Jesus still had to ascend into Heaven. Jesus still has to come again. In fact, there is the judgment and hell yet to deal with after that. So no, everything has not been fulfilled. And anyone teaching that the commandments are not so required today, they are considered least. That is not that they will go to Heaven and be treated like a lower class while the other class is considered great. The least, from Heaven's perspective, means that they will not be there. The least people of earth are equivalent to the lost people of earth.

And the "Spirit of Antichrist" really looks for excuses in the Bible to get people to break the commandments by claiming, "Wherefore the law was our schoolmaster [to bring us] unto Christ, that we might be justified by faith. But after that faith is come, we are no longer under a schoolmaster" (Galatians 3:24-25). Does that mean keeping the commandments is no longer necessary? Well, the "Spirit of Antichrist" would want you to think that way, but in reality all this is referring to is the fact that "the deeds of the law there shall no flesh be justified in his sight: for by the law [is] the knowledge of sin" (Romans 3:20). The law or commandments cannot save us. The purpose of the law is to make us realize that we need a Savior. Again, keeping all of the Ten Commandments perfectly for the rest of our lives after committing one sin will not save us. The only way to be saved is by Jesus. Further, the law tells us that "whosoever shall keep the whole law, and yet offend in one [point], he is guilty of all" (James 2:10). And guilty means death "for the wages of sin [is] death" (Romans 6:23). So we are basically under the condemnation by the schoolmaster, the law. In fact, Galatians 3:24-25 could be best understood in this manner: The breaking of the law condemns us to death, but by faith, we are justified, forgiven of breaking them and are no longer under the condemnation of the law. This is exactly what Romans 6:14 also tells us, where it says, "Ye are not under the law, but under grace" or "You are not under the condemnation of the law, which is death, but now you are under grace that you may live eternally." Grace is the only reason we get to go to Heaven. The whole of Romans 6:23 says, "For the wages of sin [is] death; but the gift of God [is] eternal life through Jesus Christ our Lord." None of us deserves Heaven. It is a free gift from God through Jesus Christ, however, in none of this wording is permission given to then go forward and continue sinning or breaking the commandments. So the theme regarding of the Ten Commandments throughout the Bible, as we compare scripture with scripture in a manner that does not contradict itself, we find that the word "under" means only in regards to the penalty. It does not mean what popular preachers teach, which is, we are no longer under the obligation to keep the law then, which contradicts many other verses in the Bible saying that we are still under obligation.

Take a look at a non-literal rendition of the second coming. We say non-literal because when Jesus shows up the second time, there will be no communication going on. There will be no pleading our cases. Jesus says, "I come quickly; and my reward [is] with me, to give every man according as his work shall be" (Revelation 22:12). So when Jesus shows up, there will be only the lost who will cry unto "to the mountains and rocks, Fall on us, and hide us from the face of him that sitteth on the throne, and from the wrath of the Lamb: For the great day of his wrath is come; and who shall be able to stand?" (Revelation 6:16-17) Or, there will be those that are saved yelling, "Lo, this [is] our God; we have waited for him, and he will save us: this [is] the LORD; we have waited for him, we will be glad and rejoice in his salvation" (Isaiah 25:9). So let us learn the meaning of the event as described by Jesus when He said, "Many will say to me in that day, Lord, Lord, have we not prophesied in thy name? and in thy name have cast out devils? and in thy name done many wonderful works? And then will I profess unto them, I never knew you: depart from me, ye that work iniquity" (Matthew 7:22-23). Their activities are commendable, but here is an example of Heaven calling these people least. They are working iniquity. These people both do and teach people that iniquity, and that is the condemnation. Iniquity or "sin is the transgression of the law" (1 John 3:4), so not to obey the commandments and teach others also that the law is not important, well, that is to be the workers of iniquity.

On top of all the excuses that the "Spirit of Antichrist" looks for, the motivation is so they can live carelessly regarding sinning, carelessly regarding the Sabbath, and overall, able to enjoy what the world has to offer without stressing out regarding salvation. To accomplish this, they allow the single word "law" to apply towards the Ten Commandments or all laws of the Old Testament when in fact the single word "law" may apply to the Ten Commandments and then again, may actually apply only to the ceremonial laws used in pointing to Jesus. Now that Jesus has come, died, and rose, we do not need the reminder of Him coming to do those things described in the ceremonial law, so the ceremonial law has been taken "out of the way, nailed to the cross" (Colossians 2:14). Unfortunately, wherever in the New Testament there is a reference to doing away with the law, such people are quick to apply it to the Ten Commandments. That is where their selfish desires come in at. To accomplish this however, requires a bit of work on their part because there are numerous places, as already mentioned, that are so strong in pointing out that the Ten Commandments still exist.

Looking at the verse mentioned about "nailing it to his cross" (Colossians 2:14) as an example of this attitude, many Christians will utter the phrase, "Jesus nailed the Ten Commandments to the cross!" That is not what is in the Bible. The Bible actually says, "Blotting out the handwriting of ordinances that was against us, which was contrary to us, and took it out of the way, nailing it to his cross" (Colossians 2:14). First, if this verse were referring to the Ten Commandments, then how does one nail stone to the cross? It cannot be done without first carefully drilling a hole and hanging them by a nail, otherwise, the stone would shatter. And if one were to take such care, they are not nailing the stone tablets to the cross, they are hanging them on the cross, which is fitting because it was our breaking of them that put Jesus on the cross to begin with. But look at the context of the verse. Does any of it sound like it is the Ten Commandments? The law that was handwritten is being referred to. Remember, "tables of stone" were "written with the finger of God" (Exodus 31:18), while it was "Moses" who "had made an end of writing the words of this law in a book" (Deuteronomy 31:24). The law that was nailed was the one referred to as ordinances, in which are separate from the Ten Commandments. Even Zacharias and Elisabeth "were both righteous before God, walking in all the commandments and ordinances of the Lord blameless" (Luke 1:6). So Luke, a Gentile, even recognized that ordinances are not the Ten Commandments. Further examination of the Colossian verse includes an obscure reference to the law being against and contrary towards the people. The law that was against people was not the Ten Commandments but "this book of the law, and put it in the side of the ark of the covenant of the LORD your God, that it may be there for a witness against thee" (Deuteronomy 31:26). The Ten Commandments are on stone tablets, not a book. Besides, if the Ten Commandments were nailed to the cross, which was upon Jesus' death, then why did the women, who were at the cross, go home "and prepared spices and ointments; and rested the sabbath day according to the commandment" (Luke 23:56)? The reason is because the Ten Commandments were not nailed to the cross. Just as prophesied, Jesus would "cause the sacrifice and the oblation to cease" (Daniel 9:27).

Now let us look at the hypocrisy that the "Spirit of Antichrist" is perpetrating in that Protestantism started because the early church fathers in each century, gathered together to make what were considered little concessions, which eventually created a situation in which the papacy or Vatican was so far off from the Bible that it took Martin Luther to call them back to the Bible of which they had been too stubborn to do so. So beginning with the requirement of doctrines being substantiated by the Bible, Protestants moved into the same position as the Catholic Church teaches. Church councils, church leaders, church organizations are above the Bible. To all of them, listen to Jesus' words, "Why do ye also transgress the commandment of God by your tradition? For God commanded, saying, Honour thy father and mother: and, He that curseth father or mother, let him die the death. But ye say, Whosoever shall say to [his] father or [his] mother, [It is] a gift, by whatsoever thou mightest be profited by me; And honour not his father or his mother, [he shall be free]. Thus have ye made the commandment of God of none effect by your tradition. [Ye] hypocrites, well did Esaias prophesy of you, saying, This people draweth nigh unto me with their mouth, and honoureth me with [their] lips; but their heart is far from me. But in vain they do worship me, teaching [for] doctrines the commandments of men" (Matthew 15:3-9). Church traditions and practices is considered hypocritical in God's eyes, especially when it comes to the collection of commandments known as the Ten Commandments. That is what Jesus is talking about here. Notice the reference to honoring mother and father. That is one of the commandments. So to alter it, even in good reasoning, is condemned. So by saying that the Sabbath commandment has been changed because Jesus rose on that day may be good reasoning but it is wrong in God's eyes. To lighten up the commandments is also equally wrong.

Speaking of lightening up the Ten Commandments, no phrase is more hypocritical than the one that states, "I don't keep the letter of the law, I keep the spirit of the law." What is that to mean? This is based upon the verse that says, "we should serve in newness of spirit, and not [in] the oldness of the letter" (Romans 7:6). They take the words to mean that the letter of the law has ceased, are not required, have been replaced with the spirit, as if the two are opposites when in fact they are not. It is a continuation of the letter to serve in spirit. Jesus explained it best. "Ye have heard that it was said by them of old time, Thou shalt not commit adultery: But I say unto you, That whosoever looketh on a woman to lust after her hath committed adultery with her already in his heart" (Matthew 5:27-28). The spirit of the law is not to lust at the opposite gender simply by using our minds. The letter of the law is to not sleep with that person physically. So if the two are opposites, then that means as long as one does not lust after another's body, it is alright to have sex with whoever one wants and even while married? Faithfulness is no longer required. That would be the letter of the law. Is that what Jesus meant? Of course not. To live according to the letter of the law is to fully comply physically only with the commandment, but in the mind and even a little out of the mind, a bit of "excitement" would be allowed. As long as no intercourse was occurring, it would be considered fine to lust after another, which is where whistling comes in, but even further. It would be alright to attend strip clubs as long as one does not physically touch or go to bed with any of the nude people. Porn movies, porn magazines, and even sexy women not nude, like the swimsuit annual magazine, would be fine. But Jesus says that it is not so! Looking upon another and thinking sexual thoughts is also wrong. Going to strip clubs, looking those magazines, watching the porn, even enjoying the swimsuit issues, are all condemned in the spirit of the law. So the spirit of the law does not replace the letter of the law; it extends it. It moves the law from logic only into also our hearts, exactly where the new covenant writes them. "This [is] the covenant that I will make with them after those days, saith the Lord, I will put my laws into their hearts, and in their minds will I write them" (Hebrews 10:16).

Here is another spirit versus letter example, again by Jesus. "Ye have heard that it was said by them of old time, Thou shalt not kill; and whosoever shall kill shall be in danger of the judgment: But I say unto you, That whosoever is angry with his brother without a cause shall be in danger of the judgment" (Matthew 5:21-22). The letter of the law guards against killing someone while the spirit of the law is against getting angry without, according to the context, a religious cause. Getting angry with someone because your favorite sports team lost is wrong. Getting angry with someone for being caught in sin, being hurtful, and otherwise being ungodly, is not wrong, though guided by the principle, "[he that is] slow to anger appeaseth strife" (Proverbs 15:18). So, according to Jesus, do not get angry unnecessarily with people, but if one is not to follow the letter of the law and only the spirit, then it is alright to kill them; just kill them without being angry with them. That is not what Jesus meant at all.

So as one should see, one cannot just keep the spirit of the law; it is necessary to keep the letter as well. Besides, everyone seems to agree that the letter of the law needs to be kept when it comes to things like adultery, killing, honoring parents, lying, and stealing, but when it comes to the Sabbath, then many Christians become hypocrites listening to the "Spirit of Antichrist". Keeping Sunday is keeping the spirit of the Sabbath," is what they say.

As for the "Spirit of Antichrist" goes though, in regards to working against Christ's words and really stretching it, Jesus once said, "If thou wilt enter into life, keep the commandments. He saith unto him, Which? Jesus said, Thou shalt do no murder, Thou shalt not commit adultery, Thou shalt not steal, Thou shalt not bear false witness, Honour thy father and [thy] mother: and, Thou shalt love thy neighbour as thyself" (Matthew 19:17-19). The "Spirit of Antichrist" says, "Jesus never mentions the Sabbath in the list and was only following the theme of the New Testament teaching, 'For all the law is fulfilled in one word, [even] in this; Thou shalt love thy neighbour as thyself' (Galatians 5:14)" and "Love worketh no ill to his neighbour: therefore love [is] the fulfilling of the law" (Romans 13:10). This is to suggest that the first four commandments are not important, primarily, the one on the Sabbath. As long as we love each other here on earth, that means we love God. However, that cannot be more further from the truth. Who knows how far Jesus would have gone with the list of commandments. In the context, it looks like Jesus was cut off. "The young man saith unto him, All these things have I kept from my youth up: what lack I yet?" (Matthew 19:20) The logic would then dictate that since the Sabbath was not mentioned, nor were the first three commandments; referring to not allowing others before God, making objects to be God, and forbidding taking His name in vain; that means God would not mind if we start worshipping other human beings as God, worshipping objects as God, and using His name as a foul word. Obviously that is not the case, and if those three still exists, so does the one on the Sabbath.

Besides, Jesus never taught that love for our other humans would supersede our love to God. In fact, just the opposite is true. "He that loveth father or mother more than me is not worthy of me: and he that loveth son or daughter more than me is not worthy of me" (Matthew 10:37). Here, the actual teaching of Jesus was, "Thou shalt love the Lord thy God with all thy heart, and with all thy soul, and with all thy mind. This is the first and great commandment. And the second [is] like unto it, Thou shalt love thy neighbour as thyself. On these two commandments hang all the law and the prophets" (Matthew 22:37-40). So if there is an importance, it certainly is not the second set of commandments governing our actions between people. Basically the first four commandments are more private, and it appeared the young man was in well standing with the local synagogue, so it was not necessary for Jesus to start the list off with the first four commandments.

And here is another little unknown fact that the "Spirit of Antichrist" is spreading. The notion that "thou shalt love thy neighbour as thyself" is a New Testament teaching is not true. The full context of the quoted words are found in the Old Testament, specifically in Leviticus 19:18. It says, "Thou shalt not avenge, nor bear any grudge against the children of thy people, but thou shalt love thy neighbour as thyself: I [am] the LORD" (Leviticus 19:18). Interestingly, that goes along with Jesus' teaching of "whosoever shall smite thee on thy right cheek, turn to him the other also" (Matthew 5:39).

And speaking of Matthew 22:40, where Jesus said, "On these two commandments hang all the law and the prophets", that means the concept of just loving God and loving people are only summaries statements. It is only through the first four commandments that we know how to love God. It is through the last six commandments that we know how to love our neighbors. If we love God, then we will not be placing human beings above God, yet, Christians do. Show such Christians from God's Word where the "Spirit of Antichrist" has infiltrated their denomination with false doctrines and they stay loyal to their denomination. Show where the "Spirit of Antichrist" knowingly or unknowingly has entered into their pastors and teachers and they excuse it away by saying that they may be a little mistaken, as if to say, "Everyone is mistaken, just on different points." Whatever happened to the notion that regarding Jesus' church, "The gates of hell shall not prevail against it" (Matthew 16:18)? Now, this is different from attending a church, commonly referred to a denomination, where the doctrines are correct, but the people are not following them and even the pastors and teachers are teaching differently. Still, such pastors and teachers ought to be avoided, but it is what is on the books. This is what is known, regarding wheat and tares being allowed to "both grow together until the harvest" (Matthew 13:30). We will have the obedient and disciplined disciples of Christ as well as the unconverted in the same denomination.

Many Christians also do not know how to keep the second commandment of not bowing down to idols, nor even making them, because they trust to their objects, even if they do not pray to them. As the joke goes, but is so true of most Christians, is that a car full of Christians symbols on the trunk lid and bumper was pulled over and the woman, who was acting out of control over a simple pedestrian taking too long to cross the road tying up traffic, was arrested for stealing the vehicle because the officer did not think that such a Christian person would act in that manner. Today's Christians seem to be more interested in putting on Christian jewelry, hanging pictures of Jesus, putting slogans on shirts and bumper stickers, to show that they are a Christian, but Peter wrote, "let it not be that outward [adorning], but [let it be] the hidden man of the heart, in that which is not corruptible, [even the ornament] of a meek and quiet spirit, which is in the sight of God of great price" (1 Peter 3:3-4).

Of course the commandment of taking the Lord's name in vain is done quite frequently, especially if one includes reputation in that category. By purposefully misquoting Jesus, including not verifying the accuracy, is to discredit Jesus' reputation. All though "God is love" (1 John 4:8), He is also "The just LORD" (Zephaniah 3:5). God is the balance between the requirement of justice and the acts of love. God "will by no means clear [the guilty]" (Exodus 34:7). If we continue to sin unrepentantly, we will remain guilty and die in our sins. It is only "If we confess our sins, he is faithful and just to forgive us [our] sins, and to cleanse us from all unrighteousness" (1 John 1:9). And to make sure one understands that this qualifies as taking the Lord's name in vain, Jesus said, "But in vain they do worship me, teaching [for] doctrines the commandments of men" (Matthew 15:9). So any doctrine that is by tradition of people, not soundly found in the Bible, is basically breaking the third commandment.

And we do not have to really mention how many Christians are breaking the fourth commandment. It used to be about keeping a day, then it was reduced to a church service, and now all seven days are treated alike. So the argument of Sunday versus Sabbath is pretty much an argument of keeping the Sabbath or not.

Now that takes care of the first four, but how about our love to our neighbors? Again, many Christians struggle with these as well because they mix up love and kindness. Love is to be true while showing compassion. Kindness is more worried about not hurting feelings. So if we truly love our neighbors, then we will respect authority, yet even Christians disrespect authority beyond, mom and dad, all of the time. Finding humor in television programming that shows teachers and parents being idiots and rebellious kids as the smart ones, even fits that category. Purposely breaking the laws because one knows how to do so is a spirit of disrespect also.

Next, as already referenced, many Christians do not have the "do not kill" commandment under control. As Jesus said, "That whosoever is angry with his brother without a cause shall be in danger of the judgment" (Matthew 5:22), one must consider how many times a day one loses their temper over the silliest things. The only anger permitted is on a religious matter. Outside of that, all other type of anger is but breaking the commandment.

And in regards to the commandment on adultery, of course many Christians are as much into wearing nearly nothing at the beach and swimming pools as non-Christians, all of which is considered nudity towards God. Many Christian men enjoy their nearly nude magazine issues. And dating among couples is even worse when it comes to the physical aspects as compared to non-Christians, according to surveys.

Stealing comes in all forms including stealing time from employers, taking from the office objects that are to remain at the office, and more. Even the disrespect of having people always waiting for one's arrival is form of stealing.

And when it comes to the whole lying bit, where do we begin this huge transgression among many Christians. Santa Clause, Easter Bunny, Tooth Fairy are lies, and to encourage a child to believe in such is contributing to lying. The whole notion of teasing and joking is based on nothing but lies. The Bible even says, "It not be once named among you, as becometh saints" (Ephesians 5:3), of which it is actually a list of things not in a Christians character in which one of them is "jesting" (Ephesians 5:4). So-called "white" lies and situational lies are taught as acceptable among Christian, but nowhere in the Bible are exceptions stated. It simply says, "Thou shalt not bear false witness against thy neighbour" (Exodus 20:16).

And coveting when we should be simply happy for the success and purchases of our neighbors ought to be practiced, but instead, even if one cannot afford it, the keeping up with the Jones is prevalent among many Christians. Even if one can afford it, the need to have the latest model is not of a Christian character; practicality should be the rule. Be satisfied that the car still works. Be satisfied that last year's smart phone is still in very good condition. Be satisfied that the clothing still fits. The Bible says, "[Let your] conversation [be] without covetousness; [and be] content with such things as ye have" (Hebrews 13:5).

Of course the "Spirit of Antichrist" works against Jesus Christ when teaching that eternal life has no relationship with the Ten Commandments. This is contrary to what Jesus taught. "And, behold, a certain lawyer stood up, and tempted him, saying, Master, what shall I do to inherit eternal life? He said unto him, What is written in the law? how readest thou? And he answering said, Thou shalt love the Lord thy God with all thy heart, and with all thy soul, and with all thy strength, and with all thy mind; and thy neighbour as thyself. And he said unto him, Thou hast answered right: this do, and thou shalt live" (Luke 10:25-28). To live is to live eternally, and what did Jesus say or confirm? "Thou shalt love the Lord thy God with all thy heart, and with all thy soul, and with all thy strength, and with all thy mind; and thy neighbour as thyself" (Luke 10:27). And we know from above that these two loves is a summary of the Ten Commandments. Now the confusion from the "Spirit of Antichrist" is in the cart and the horse relationship. The "Spirit of Antichrist" simply gets rid of both, but true Christianity has the proper order. The horse pulls the cart, therefore, Christ saves us empowering us to live in obedience to the commandments. We do not put the cart first by keeping the commandments to be saved.

Then the "Spirit of Antichrist" among the unbiblical denominations also exaggerate Luke 16:16, which says, "The law and the prophets [were] until John: since that time the kingdom of God is preached, and every man presseth into it." At a quick glance, it looks like Jesus just did away with the whole Old Testament, but that would contradict where Jesus also said, "Search the scriptures; for in them ye think ye have eternal life: and they are they which testify of me" (John 5:39). So He cannot mean to do away with the Ten Commandments and even all that the prophets wrote. So looking in a non-contradictory method, Jesus was simply stating that Moses' writings, the law, and the rest of the Old Testament, which are the prophets, taught of the event to come in which "the kingdom of God is preached". Even the Ten Commandments point to Jesus, not in a way to be done away with, but just a fact. How so? "The law [is] holy, and the commandment holy, and just, and good" (Romans 7:12), but then is not God also holy, just, and good? Sure He is.

But look at the commandments, where it says, "And shewing mercy unto thousands of them that love me, and keep my commandments" (Exodus 20:6). How is mercy or pardon for sin provided? Through grace, for the Bible says, "Let us therefore come boldly unto the throne of grace, that we may obtain mercy, and find grace to help in time of need" (Hebrews 4:16). So, where does grace come from? "For if by one man's offence death reigned by one; much more they which receive abundance of grace and of the gift of righteousness shall reign in life by one, Jesus Christ" (Romans 5:17).

Now while the "Spirit of Antichrist" attempts to toss out the law of Ten Commandments, Jesus Christ taught "It is easier for heaven and earth to pass, than one tittle of the law to fail" (Luke 16:17). As you can see, this is truly the battle ground, disguised as the gospel, disguised as Christianity. True Christianity listens to Jesus Christ declaring that the sky and this planet would be easier to pass away than a mere declaration that grace covers it all, including willful disobedience. One ought to figure that after all this is said and done, as in this life where the devil remains active is passed away, are we not going to follow the rules in Heaven? Think about it. Is stealing all of a sudden allowed in Heaven? How about murder and lying? Of course not. When God declares, "For as the new heavens and the new earth, which I will make, shall remain before me, saith the LORD, so shall your seed and your name remain. And it shall come to pass, [that] from one new moon to another, and from one sabbath to another, shall all flesh come to worship before me, saith the LORD" (Isaiah 66:22-23), so when we gather weekly in the New Jerusalem to worship on the Sabbath day, will some come on the actual Sabbath day or will that be Sunday or will they not participate at all declaring that we do not need to observe any day now? And do not be listening to the "Spirit of Antichrist" trying to say, "In Heaven, there will be no time!" because God just said there will be new moons and Sabbaths to gather together, so evidently some type of time is going to transpire. You see, the rest of the week is going to be spent fulfilling another heavenly prophecy. "And they shall build houses, and inhabit [them]; and they shall plant vineyards, and eat the fruit of them. They shall not build, and another inhabit; they shall not plant, and another eat: for as the days of a tree [are] the days of my people, and mine elect shall long enjoy the work of their hands. They shall not labour in vain, nor bring forth for trouble; for they [are] the seed of the blessed of the LORD, and their offspring with them. And it shall come to pass, that before they call, I will answer; and while they are yet speaking, I will hear. The wolf and the lamb shall feed together, and the lion shall eat straw like the bullock: and dust [shall be] the serpent's meat. They shall not hurt nor destroy in all my holy mountain, saith the LORD" (Isaiah 65:21-25). So, it will be six days at our country estate and the seventh worshipping in the New Jerusalem on the Sabbath day. What a glorious thought!

Now those that think grace does away with obedience, which again is the "Spirit of Antichrist" working, many quote, "For the law was given by Moses, [but] grace and truth came by Jesus Christ" (John 1:17). They declare that the Ten Commandments came by Moses and Jesus took them away replacing them with grace and truth. Then does that mean Cain was alright in killing Abel (Genesis 4:8)? Was it alright for Joseph's brothers to covet (Genesis 37:4)? Would it have been alright for Abram to have not left the idolatry country and even worshipped idols? Let us put it this way, there must have been some serious idol worship going on in the homeland to forbid Isaac, his son, from ever returning even for a visit (Genesis 24:6-7). It was not alright that the Israelites were breaking the Sabbath, established in Eden and before written on stone as they die according to Exodus 16:27. It was not alright for Adam and Eve to disobey their parent, God, and were banished from the garden and losing immortality (Genesis 3:24). Of course choosing the serpent's words over God's words meant choosing Satan as God, which had the same consequence (Genesis 3:6). Even not committing adultery was well understood among a pagan king (Genesis 12:17-20). Joseph's brothers knew what stealing was (Genesis 44:8). And if one were to search honestly, one would probably find the other two of the Ten Commandments of taking God's name in vain and baring false witness as being wrong even before they were written down on stone. Besides, we already covered the fact that Moses' law was in a book, therefore, all of those feast days and offerings are not necessary since Jesus made His appearance. So yes, the law of Moses was necessary to point to Jesus as the "Lamb of God" (John 1:29), but now we are under grace and truth. In other words, we do not have to sacrifice animals anymore. Praise the Lord!

Now for those influenced by the "Spirit of Antichrist" to have a reaction to hearing about obedience to the Ten Commandments and still try to claim it is Moses' law, then when "Philip findeth Nathanael, and saith unto him, We have found him, of whom Moses in the law, and the prophets, did write, Jesus of Nazareth, the son of Joseph" (John 1:45), what part of the Ten Commandments point to Jesus to come? The answer is, there is not one commandment that predicts anything about Jesus. It is strictly the rules that a follower of God, Old or New Testament, would obey. However, the laws written by Moses in a book depicting Jesus indeed foretells of Jesus. So no, the Ten Commandments and Moses' law are not one in the same.

Continuing with that theme, sure Jesus said, "Did not Moses give you the law, and [yet] none of you keepeth the law? Why go ye about to kill me?" (John 7:19) Truly this refers to the Ten Commandments. But just because Moses gave them the law, as in, presented the two tables of stone does not make it Moses' law to be done away with. If a person buys you a gift, hands it to me to deliver to you, does that make it my gift to you? Of course not. But I did give you the gift, right? Of course I did. Likewise, God's Ten Commandments were not handed by God directly to the people. They were given to Moses who gave them to the people. He was just the delivery person, unlike the Book of the Law in which Moses wrote out, even though inspired by God.

Now be careful also of the next thing Jesus said. "If a man on the sabbath day receive circumcision, that the law of Moses should not be broken; are ye angry at me, because I have made a man every whit whole on the sabbath day?" (John 7:23) The "Spirit of Antichrist" would have you believe the Sabbath is part of Moses' law, however, closer examination actually shows that Jesus is distinguishing a separation. There is the Ten Commandments of God and the law of Moses to circumcise. In the Old Testament, circumcision was required to be done, even on the Sabbath day, which God ordained. Certain everyday practices are permitted, like "on the sabbath days the priests in the temple profane the sabbath, and are blameless" (Matthew 12:5). That is because the Sabbath day is the hardest day for a priest and much work is involved. Even feeding and watering animals is permitted work on the Sabbath (Luke 13:15). Rescuing an animal as well is permitted on the Sabbath (Luke 14:5). The point is, the law of Moses referred to by Jesus is about practicing circumcision and not about the fourth commandment.

Again, the "Spirit of Antichrist" twists the words of Jesus, when He said, "A new commandment I give unto you, That ye love one another; as I have loved you, that ye also love one another. By this shall all [men] know that ye are my disciples, if ye have love one to another" (John 13:34-35). It is implied by the "Spirit of Antichrist" that this "new commandment" replaces the Ten Commandments. This apparently is reinforced by Paul's words, "For all the law is fulfilled in one word, [even] in this; Thou shalt love thy neighbour as thyself" (Galatians 5:14). First, nowhere does either account make mention that the Ten Commandments are being replaced. If you were to have received ten gifts and some time has passed, and then I present you with a "new gift" unrelated to the other gifts, does it replace those other ten? Of course not. Besides, just as Paul said, if a person respects authority, respects life, respects sexually each other and commitments made like marriage, respects other people's belongings, respect people's thoughts, and respects the fact that people generally will have cool things that would be nice to have but other people have instead, is how we show our love to one another as well as fulfilling the law by love. So there is no contradiction with both Jesus' and Paul's statements with still obeying the Ten Commandments.

The "Spirit of Antichrist" is always active and ever looking for ways to twist the words of Christ and in a manner even worse than Antichrist, where even Antichrist says, "Keep my Ten Commandments" as opposed to Jesus, who said, "If ye love me, keep my commandments" (John 14:15). Quickly the "Spirit of Antichrist" speaks up and says, "That's the replacement commandments of loving God and loving our neighbors", especially when Jesus says, "This is my commandment, That ye love one another, as I have loved you" (John 15:12). Well, that is not so. First, we know from earlier that both of those commands are but summary of the first four showing how we love God and the last six showing how we love our neighbors. But in addition to this is the realization that when Jesus said to keep His commandments, it is declaring that those Ten Commandments were not written by God the Father but by Himself. Too many Christians believe that the God of the Old Testament is God the Father and the time Jesus walked was the time for God the Son but now it is the Holy Spirit time. In actuality, all three are and were and will be present, however, there is a bit of distance between us and God the Father. When the human race sinned and we continued to sin, just one sin cuts us off. In fact, "The LORD thy God [is] a consuming fire" (Deuteronomy 4:24). That means, even if God the Father wanted to, He could never speak directly to Adam or Eve after the fall because of the transgression. This is why, as symbolism goes, the Israelites were commanded to have "fire without the camp: it [is] a sin offering" (Exodus 29:14). Sin is consumed. So the only reason the human race has not been consumed is because "grace, which was given us in Christ Jesus before the world began" (2 Timothy 1:9). Jesus was ready to step in before sin even entered this world, and when it did, then "[there is] one God, and one mediator between God and men, the man Christ Jesus" (1 Timothy 2:5). So from the beginning, Jesus has always been playing the role of Mediator. That means all direct communication as noted in the Old Testament is between humans and the Mediator. The God of the Old Testament is Jesus, which means, He wrote the Ten Commandments, and they are His. Jesus even confirmed this by the conversation, "Your father Abraham rejoiced to see my day: and he saw [it], and was glad. Then said the Jews unto him, Thou art not yet fifty years old, and hast thou seen Abraham? Jesus said unto them, Verily, verily, I say unto you, Before Abraham was, I am" (John 8:56-58). So if we love Jesus, we will obey His Ten Commandments.

Then we have the "Spirit of Antichrist" which states that there is no condition to God's love. Although God even still loves the devil, that does not equate to allowance to have eternal life. Besides that, nowhere in the Bible does the word "unconditional" appear. And then Jesus even explicitly states, "He that hath my commandments, and keepeth them, he it is that loveth me: and he that loveth me shall be loved of my Father, and I will love him, and will manifest myself to him" (John 14:21). Jesus also said, "If ye keep my commandments, ye shall abide in my love; even as I have kept my Father's commandments, and abide in his love" (John 15:10). It looks like there are conditions for the manifestation of God to a person as well as expressing His love back. That does not mean God is unloving to those that do not keep the commandments; He just does not express it as He would like because sin is in the way. And if sin remains in the way, such people will eternally be cut off. "For the LORD loveth judgment, and forsaketh not his saints; they are preserved for ever: but the seed of the wicked shall be cut off" (Psalms 37:28).

Now here is a subject that the "Spirit of Antichrist" really likes to twist. It is called justification. Justification, in the simplest forms, is forgiveness of our sins and "to present [you] faultless before the presence of his glory" (Jude 1:24). That is something we cannot earn; it is not something we can repay; in fact, it is something that cost the life of Jesus. This is summarized in Romans 3:20 by stating, "Therefore by the deeds of the law there shall no flesh be justified in his sight: for by the law [is] the knowledge of sin." On top of that, "We conclude that a man is justified by faith without the deeds of the law" (Romans 3:28). And it is on these two verses as well as others that appear to exploit the forgiveness to the point that people may continue sinning as they will. It appears such people that believe this error are just automatically guaranteed Heaven, but such is a false teaching of the "Spirit of Antichrist" for Romans 2:13 states, "For not the hearers of the law [are] just before God, but the doers of the law shall be justified." At a quick glance, it looks like the Bible is contradictory, but those exercising patience with understanding the Bible, the truth is revealed. Although keeping the Ten Commandments does not justify us and allow us to go to Heaven, the keeping of them is the expectation of life in Heaven and even now. Seeing that sin or "affliction shall not rise up the second time" (Nahum 1:9), God cannot take practicing sinners to Heaven. So to balance these verses out in the spirit of not contradicting each other, the only conclusion is that a true Christian will be obedient to the Ten Commandments after being justified or forgiven. Only such people who are obeying the commandments and commit a sin are, upon confession of that sin, forgiven and then justified. As has been stated all along, we do not keep the Ten Commandments to be justified or saved. We keep them because we are justified. Think of it this way, in which if I were handing out money to cover one's college education to anyone who believes that I would do such a thing, would it not make sense that only college bound students get the college money? Do keep in mind though, that college is hard work but that has no bearing on my willingness to pay freely the education. The gift is still there. Likewise, if a further restriction is in place requiring a student to maintain at least a "C" grade, does that change my gift towards such students? Of course not. The money is still free. Only the recipients change. So likewise, Heaven is free. The price has been paid for only those that want to live there. One may say, "Well, everyone wants to live there. Who wouldn't?" Be careful. Heaven has rules. Will people really want to not steal for all eternity? Well, we need to demonstrate that here then. The same is true with all of the commandments. Those are the rules. So, only those bound to live by those rules in Heaven by living such now will receive the free gift of justification "For all have sinned, and come short of the glory of God" (Romans 3:23), but the goal is "that ye sin not. And if any man sin, we have an advocate with the Father, Jesus Christ the righteous" (1 John 2:1), so "If we confess our sins, he is faithful and just to forgive us [our] sins, and to cleanse us from all unrighteousness" (1 John 1:9) placing us back in a justified state. And for those that teach otherwise are simply guilty of being "ungodly men, turning the grace of our God into lasciviousness" (Jude 1:4).

Of course the "Spirit of Antichrist" takes a simple concept of faith and twists that as well. Over the pulpits, the Ten Commandments appear as being the opposite of living by faith. If one obeys the commandments, then they must be lacking in faith, as they say. They get this thought by ripping a verse out of context and making it appear as faith and commandment keeping being opposites. "if they which are of the law [be] heirs, faith is made void" (Romans 4:14). This appears to be reinforced when Paul wrote, "But Israel, which followed after the law of righteousness, hath not attained to the law of righteousness. Wherefore? Because [they sought it] not by faith, but as it were by the works of the law" (Romans 9:31-32). And a similar theme is found in the Galatians 2:16, which states, "Knowing that a man is not justified by the works of the law, but by the faith of Jesus Christ, even we have believed in Jesus Christ, that we might be justified by the faith of Christ, and not by the works of the law: for by the works of the law shall no flesh be justified. " But one should know the solution because of the previous discussions. And here appears another antagonistic question: "Received ye the Spirit by the works of the law, or by the hearing of faith?" (Galatians 3:2) And we would do disservice to the argument of the "Spirit of Antichrist" if we were to ignore "the law is not of faith" (Galatians 3:12). Paul appears to continue such a strong argument that faith is the opposite of the law when he wrote, "And be found in him, not having mine own righteousness, which is of the law, but that which is through the faith of Christ, the righteousness which is of God by faith" (Philippians 3:9). Those are all of the verses that appear to have the obedience to the law of Ten Commandments being the opposite of living by faith, however, it is how people read into it, or the lack of knowledge of the rest of the Bible verses. First, to think these verses do away with keeping the Ten Commandments, then in the understanding that the Bible does not contradict itself, one has to explain all of the positive verses that declare we need to be obeying the commandments, and such cannot be done, especially when some are very, very strong. For instance, "He that saith, I know him, and keepeth not his commandments, is a liar, and the truth is not in him" (1 John 2:4). So what is the answer? The answer is in the placement of the keeping of the commandments once again. If we are keeping the commandments to be saved, then we are undoing our faith in a Savior. There is absolutely no disagreement whatsoever from that perspective. We agree that keeping the Ten Commandments to be saved makes void faith, as was stated. However, none of those verses that seem to put down keeping the Ten Commandments ever mention that if we live by faith that it means we can now purposefully live our lives by sinning. That is the answer. The Bible teaches we are to keep the commandments after, through faith, we have accepted Jesus as our Savior. Even Paul, who wrote all that confusion, comes out and clears up the misunderstanding by saying, "Do we then make void the law through faith? God forbid: yea, we establish the law" (Romans 3:31). Besides, faith and commandment keeping are not opposites. They are the best of friends for "Here is the patience of the saints: here [are] they that keep the commandments of God, and the faith of Jesus" (Revelation 14:12). These are the true saved Christians. Those that have faith in Jesus to save us, and the respect towards His saving grace to live in obedience. And we have faith that we can, by His grace, obey them.

Now here is the motivation of the "Spirit of Antichrist" in which, "Because the law worketh wrath: for where no law is, [there is] no transgression" (Romans 4:15). If there is no Ten Commandments, then there is no such thing known as transgressing or breaking them, and we would be free to keep or break them at will without consequence. Although keeping the Ten Commandments to be saved works up God's wrath, this verse, taking to be understood, as the "Spirit of Antichrist" tries to convey, would ultimately mean that Satan should be allowed back into Heaven. As a reminder, this concept of not having the law is based upon the notion that prior to the cross, they had to keep the Ten Commandments to be saved, but afterwards, it is all by grace. Seeing grace is forgiveness when a person breaks a commandment, that means those before the cross were also under grace, including Satan. And if we were to further say that grace did not exist before the cross, then there is not a single person that was perfect for one sin cancels out the salvation by works plan. Again, all of that is the "Spirit of Antichrist" confusing things. In reality, the Ten Commandments were never for saving but because people were saved. Grace is both before and after the cross and we even showed that "grace, which was given us in Christ Jesus before the world began" (2 Timothy 1:9). Besides, we all know sinning is happening in the world, so that means "Whosoever committeth sin transgresseth also the law: for sin is the transgression of the law" (1 John 3:4). So by such an activity of sin, it establishes the fact that the law is still in place.

Another apparent contrast that the "Spirit of Antichrist" pulls off is to imply that because the law is powerless, it is not necessary to be kept since Jesus is all powerful. "For what the law could not do, in that it was weak through the flesh, God sending his own Son in the likeness of sinful flesh, and for sin, condemned sin in the flesh: That the righteousness of the law might be fulfilled in us, who walk not after the flesh, but after the Spirit" (Romans 8:3-4). Just reading verse 3, one gets that apparent contrast but by also reading verse 4, a different application is explained. First, the "Spirit of Antichrist" still tries to stretch it by saying that the righteousness being fulfilled in us permits us to not worry about our sins, however, that does not fit with the rest of the verse. If we are not walking by the flesh, but by the spirit, of which only those that walk by the Spirit get to have Christ's righteousness, the Bible just got done saying "that the law is spiritual" (Romans 7:14). So for those that walk after the spirit, the law, receive Christ's righteousness as being fulfilled, otherwise, that would mean those that do not walk after the spirit, they do not obey the Ten Commandments, do not get Christ's righteousness. In other words, the ungodly preachers who are "turning the grace of our God into lasciviousness" (Jude 1:4) are claiming one can be indifferent about the Ten Commandments and still receive Christ's righteousness when such is not so. Further, for the context to also state that we are "not to walk after the flesh but after the Spirit" tells us that it is even more serious. All Christians who are into the latest movies, watch a bunch of television, reading non-religious material that exploits the things of the world, listening to all of the unreligious type music, following celebrities and sports teams, dressing like the world, etc., are all walking according to the flesh. To walk according to the Spirit is to give up all that leads back to the world and increase the amount of religious content as possible. Sure, people have to have secular jobs, but we do not need to be watching movies that is full of violence, sex, and foul language. We do not need to be listening to music that encourages worldly activity. Yes, it is a boring life compared to the fun the devil has in mind but if people want to enjoy eternity, this boredom for 70, 80, even 90 years is nothing in comparison. You see, when we feed on all of that carnal stuff, "the carnal mind [is] enmity against God: for it is not subject to the law of God, neither indeed can be" (Romans 8:7). There is a principle in the Bible in which, what we behold, by seeing and hearing mostly, we are changed towards that even if we cannot sense that, for by "beholding as in a glass the glory of the Lord, are changed into the same image from glory to glory" (2 Corinthians 3:18).

And the activity of the "Spirit of Antichrist" continues to blind people by taking the words "But Israel, which followed after the law of righteousness, hath not attained to the law of righteousness. Wherefore? Because [they sought it] not by faith, but as it were by the works of the law" (Romans 9:31-32) and saying, "See, Israel was under the Ten Commandments to be saved but we are under faith!" Remember, Paul already stated, "Do we then make void the law through faith? God forbid: yea, we establish the law" (Romans 3:31). So that already negates that thought, however, let us reveal what is going on with this verse in chapter 9. The problem is not the law. The problem is with the motivation of Israel. The Ten Commandments, through Israel, moved from being the result of a saving relationship into the erroneous thought of being saved by the keeping of the Ten Commandments. Doing so eliminates faith in Jesus and that is what is condemned.

The "Spirit of Antichrist" constantly tries to equate the ceremonial and ritualistic laws of the Book of Moses as being inclusive of the Ten Commandments when Paul even identifies that there is a difference. "Circumcision is nothing, and uncircumcision is nothing, but the keeping of the commandments of God" (1 Corinthians 7:19). We see that in the Book of Moses the requirement of circumcision that is no longer required while we also see that Paul, in the same verse, makes claim that the commandments of God is something, something to be obeyed that is.

Then the "Spirit of Antichrist" goes way too far with Paul's activity in winning people to Christ. It is written "And unto the Jews I became as a Jew, that I might gain the Jews; to them that are under the law, as under the law, that I might gain them that are under the law; To them that are without law, as without law, (being not without law to God, but under the law to Christ,) that I might gain them that are without law" (1 Corinthians 9:20-21). What the "Spirit of Antichrist" would have one think is that Paul kept the Ten Commandments when trying to reach those that feel it necessary to keep them, but to another group who were not keeping the Ten Commandments, he became like one of them and did not keep them either, as if, it really does not matter if one keeps the commandments or not, but that logic is so far off that only those who are not studying upon the Word of God are so easily brainwashed and with a heart wanting the ways of the world while claiming to be saved, it sounds so good. Looking at it from that perspective then, that would mean that when he was trying to win the Gentiles to Christ, he slept with the women he studied with, killed those that disagreed with him, took whatever he needed for his own personal use without feeling guilty, but when studying with the Jews, he did not sleep around, kill any Jew, or take any possessions that were not his. What nonsense! Simply put, the law in the verses is the ceremonial law. To the Jews, Paul kept the feast days including Passover, Pentecost, and the rest of them, but when he was with the Gentiles, he did not practice those things as it really does not matter if one does or does not. That is what was nailed to the cross and no longer under obligation to be kept.

In continuous twisting of scripture, the "Spirit of Antichrist" in the spirit of doing away with the Ten Commandments takes us to 1 Corinthians 15:56-57, which says, "The sting of death [is] sin; and the strength of sin [is] the law. But thanks [be] to God, which giveth us the victory through our Lord Jesus Christ" and tries to make it appear that as long as we promote the Ten Commandments, we are actually promoting sin since sin is strongest with the law. That same evil spirit turns around and makes it appear that victory is a type of credit given to an individual just because they believe in Jesus without having actual victory over sin. This again fulfills prophecy in which most Christians are "Having a form of godliness, but denying the power thereof" (2 Timothy 3:5). In other words, to believe the spirit who is working against the commandment promoting Jesus Christ also strips the gospel message of any power. It basically is declaring that sin is more powerful than God's "power to become the sons of God" (John 1:12). And by continuing to break the Ten Commandments, which "sin is the transgression of the law" (1 John 3:4), we are sons of Satan instead. So the truth of the matter is, that once we have become aware of God's will, which we ought to "delight to do thy will, O my God: yea, thy law [is] within my heart" (Psalms 40:8), sin becomes stronger. This is because when we do not come to Christ, we think whatever the world finds acceptable is, well, acceptable. So watching women topless in movies is no big deal. Listening to foul words in song and in other things called entertainment is no big deal. But when we come to Christ, we realize there is a whole list of things that is sinful just in one commandment, like not committing adultery. As Jesus said, "Whosoever looketh on a woman to lust after her hath committed adultery with her already in his heart" (Matthew 5:28), so not only is the nude magazines and movies gone, so should the desire to look at the opposite gender in sexy outfits including skimpy bathing suits. Gone from our mouths should be sexual innuendos especially towards people we are not married to and even those we just pal around with. Sexual content should be private and God should be public, not the other way around. But from that perspective, it may seem like such an impossibility. Well, not only "With men this is impossible; but with God all things are possible" (Matthew 19:26), but Jesus, according to the verse in question, has already given us the power of victory. We just need to accept that gift. That is basically what those verses are stating. It is real victory over real sin because the Ten Commandments have become more enlightened to us through our commitment to be disciples of Christ.

Exploiting the word "dead" in this next verse, the "Spirit of Antichrist" would equate that as ignoring the Ten Commandments. The Bible says, "For I through the law am dead to the law, that I might live unto God" (Galatians 2:19), and is made more complicated by misunderstanding the follow up verse, "I do not frustrate the grace of God: for if righteousness [come] by the law, then Christ is dead in vain" (Galatians 2:21). So it appears that if we keep the Ten Commandments then Christ is dead to us and we frustrate grace, so for that not to happen, we ought to be dead to the law instead. Well, we get the insight by bringing up an old argument over the verse of "Knowing that a man is not justified by the works of the law, but by the faith of Jesus Christ" (Galatians 2:16). Now recalling the answer to this misunderstanding, in which we ought to know by now, that all Ten Commandments, as they are written without alteration, is to be kept. However, it is the sequence of events that is twisted. If anyone tries to keep the commandments to be saved, they are then making Christ dead, frustrating the gospel, and all of His efforts of dying on the cross are in vain. But none of these verses negate the fact that we ought to be dead to the thought we are saved by the commandments, yet, after being saved, now obeying them.

The solution of sequence of events, in that we keep the commandments because we are saved, answers every single question and statement in the rest of Galatians. "This only would I learn of you, Received ye the Spirit by the works of the law, or by the hearing of faith?" (Galatians 3:2) "He therefore that ministereth to you the Spirit, and worketh miracles among you, [doeth he it] by the works of the law, or by the hearing of faith?" (Galatians 3:5) "For as many as are of the works of the law are under the curse: for it is written, Cursed [is] every one that continueth not in all things which are written in the book of the law to do them. But that no man is justified by the law in the sight of God, [it is] evident: for, The just shall live by faith. And the law is not of faith: but, The man that doeth them shall live in them. Christ hath redeemed us from the curse of the law, being made a curse for us: for it is written, Cursed [is] every one that hangeth on a tree." (Galatians 3:10-13). And all of that is correct. We are not saved by keeping the commandments. We are not justified by the commandments. It is all by faith that we are saved because there is no messenger sent from Heaven to acknowledge such, however, God is more powerful than Satan and so to be witnesses for the kingdom of God and the gospel message, we are empowered then to keep the commandments. And besides, what truly are we free from? Obedience or the curse? The curse of the law is the answer. It is the consequences of the law we are freed from. "For the wages of sin [is] death; but the gift of God [is] eternal life through Jesus Christ our Lord" (Romans 6:23). It does not say, "For the obedience of the commandments is death; but the gift of God [is] eternal life through Jesus Christ our Lord."

Now in regards to being given our mansion and country estate in Heaven as an inheritance, the "Spirit of Antichrist" would have you believe that any doing of the Ten Commandments voids that. "For if the inheritance [be] of the law, [it is] no more of promise" (Galatians 3:18). This is further complicated by the statement, "Wherefore then [serveth] the law? It was added because of transgressions, till the seed should come to whom the promise was made; [and it was] ordained by angels in the hand of a mediator" (Galatians 3:19). Well, in continuing in the context, we already addressed the summary verse of "Wherefore the law was our schoolmaster [to bring us] unto Christ, that we might be justified by faith" (Galatians 3:24). But now addressing those verses prior, though there is a combination of Ten Commandments and Moses' Book of the Law being referenced, it was straight in Paul's mind when he wrote these verses when he referred to the Commandments, the Book of the Law, or both. However, to us, it is quite confusing. Yes, there was a law that ended at the cross but not both laws. Paul even states such by saying, "[Is] the law then against the promises of God? God forbid" (Galatians 3:21). But wait! He also said above that there was a law in place "till the seed should come", referring to Jesus. Sounds contradictory! And many weak Bible students do see the Bible that way and so they walk away thinking the Bible is irrelevant because it contradicts itself. The reality is that the verses should read, "Wherefore then [serveth] the Book of the Law, which is the ceremonial laws of sacrifices? It was added because of transgressions, till the seed should come to whom the promise was made" and "[Is] the law of Ten Commandments then against the promises of God? God forbid."

And here is a favorite of the "Spirit of Antichrist" that promotes worldly feelings over keeping the Ten Commandments. "But if ye be led of the Spirit, ye are not under the law" (Galatians 5:18). The statement is true that if we are listening to the Holy Spirit, whose job it is to "reprove the world of sin, and of righteousness, and of judgment" (John 16:8) and allowing Him to "guide you into all truth" (John 16:13), then there is no concern about being under the condemnation for breaking the Ten Commandments, the law. That phrase of not being "under the law" does not negate obedience to it. It simply stating that if we break one commandment, we are under the condemnation of the law, which is death. But if we are listening to the Spirit leading us into truth, which "all thy commandments [are] truth" (Psalms 119:151), listening to His prompting away from sin, which "sin is the transgression of the law" (1 John 3:4), listening to His prompting of being judged, which means that we will be "judged by the law of liberty" (James 2:12) referring to the Ten Commandments (James 2:10-11), and listening to His promptings on righteousness, which "all thy commandments [are] righteousness" (Psalms 119:172), then we will be living in obedience not worrying about the condemnation. We will not even have to be reviewing the Ten Commandments because they will be natural to us to keep.

Another trick of the "Spirit of Antichrist" against people following Jesus command to keep the commandments is fast reads. Read Ephesians 2:15 quickly and see if it does not initially seem like the Ten Commandments have been abolished. "Having abolished in his flesh the enmity, [even] the law of commandments [contained] in ordinances; for to make in himself of twain one new man, [so] making peace." So, did you fall for it? Does it sound like the Ten Commandments have been abolished? Some may even still be thinking that way while others have found the key word that makes the subject of the commandments not the Ten Commandments. The word is "ordinances". An ordinance is in reference to specifying the guidelines of conducting a feast or holy day. There is not one single ordinance in the Ten Commandments. So the verse does not even apply to the Ten Commandments.

Now if the "Spirit of Antichrist" is trying to convince everyone that the Ten Commandments have been done away with, then why would Paul clarify one of them to children? "Children, obey your parents in the Lord: for this is right. Honour thy father and mother; (which is the first commandment with promise;) That it may be well with thee, and thou mayest live long on the earth" (Ephesians 6:1-3). Here is the answer. The "Spirit of Antichrist" is wrong; it is lying; it is hoping people will listen to it, live in disobedience to the commandments or at least one of them because it only takes one commandment not to be kept that prevents the lawbreaker from going to Heaven, which then gives God no choice but to reject them from Heaven, which means hell.

And here is another favorite of the "Spirit of Antichrist" to get people thinking that the commandment keeping is against faith. Now we already addressed this earlier where even Paul stated, "Do we then make void the law through faith? God forbid: yea, we establish the law" (Romans 3:31). So here is the verse in question. "And be found in him, not having mine own righteousness, which is of the law, but that which is through the faith of Christ, the righteousness which is of God by faith" (Philippians 3:9). Now carefully approaching the verse, it appears if we keep the Ten Commandments, we are claiming our own righteousness for Heaven, but if we rely upon Jesus' perfect life of righteousness, not worrying about our obedience or disobedience, then we are saved by faith. As stated, that is not what the Bible teaches, even by the apostle Paul. But we cannot just ignore this verse. There has to be a non-contradictory understanding of this verse, and there is. First, "Little children, let no man deceive you: he that doeth righteousness is righteous, even as he is righteous. He that committeth sin is of the devil; for the devil sinneth from the beginning. For this purpose the Son of God was manifested, that he might destroy the works of the devil" (1 John 3:7-8). So we see that us doing our own righteous act of keeping the law is credited as being righteous, which really is the opposite of the verse in Philippians. And on top of that, anyone committing a sin, which we should have memorized now, "Whosoever committeth sin transgresseth also the law: for sin is the transgression of the law" (1 John 3:4), is therefore of the devil. So the verse in Phillipians cannot mean for us to disregard the Ten Commandments. Well, here is the solution to understanding the verse without contradiction. If anyone keeps the Ten Commandments and points to their life and says, "See, I have kept the commandments. I deserve Heaven!" is totally off in their theology. That is a legalist. Again, we do not keep the commandments to claim our righteousness to enter Heaven, but rather after accepting through faith, Christ's righteousness, we are then empowered to live in obedience to them. In fact, that is the only way it can happen. Without faith, our keeping of the

Ten Commandments is futile "Because the carnal mind [is] enmity against God: for it is not subject to the law of God, neither indeed can be" (Romans 8:7), so it is only after conversion when we lose the carnal mind "That the righteousness of the law might be fulfilled in us, who walk not after the flesh, but after the Spirit" (Romans 8:4). Further, "we beseech you, brethren, and exhort [you] by the Lord Jesus, that as ye have received of us how ye ought to walk and to please God, [so] ye would abound more and more. For ye know what commandments we gave you by the Lord Jesus. For this is the will of God, [even] your sanctification, that ye should abstain from fornication: That every one of you should know how to possess his vessel in sanctification and honour" (1 Thessalonians 4:1-4).

Yet another trick up the sleeve of the "Spirit of Antichrist" is using modern or specific incorrect defined words from the Bible when there is a different intended meaning. Take for instance where it says, "Now the end of the commandment is charity out of a pure heart, and [of] a good conscience, and [of] faith unfeigned" (1 Timothy 1:5). One can easily conclude that the law is over and finished, using one particular definition of the word "end". The word "end" indeed means it is done. If one runs a race and crosses the finish line, they have reached the end and ended the race. But there are other definitions of the word "end", such as meaning "result". Putting that in the proper place of the verse, it would read, "Now the result of the commandment is charity out of a pure heart, and [of] a good conscience, and [of] faith unfeigned." And truly that is the result of keeping the Ten Commandments, as stated in a follow up verse, "But we know that the law [is] good, if a man use it lawfully" (1 Timothy 1:8). If a person properly keeps the Ten Commandments, loving one's neighbors would be the result. In fact, that is exactly what Jesus said. "Thou shalt love the Lord thy God with all thy heart, and with all thy soul, and with all thy mind. This is the first and great commandment. And the second [is] like unto it, Thou shalt love thy neighbour as thyself. On these two commandments hang all the law and the prophets" (Matthew 22:37-40). So on those two love commandments is summarized what happens when one keeps the first four towards God and the last six towards our fellow human beings, our neighbors. Besides, if the word "result" is not the proper substitution for the word "end", then what do we do about God being dead? The Bible says, "Ye have heard of the patience of Job, and have seen the end of the Lord; that the Lord is very pitiful, and of tender mercy" (James 5:11). So evidently in the time of Job, God ended. There was and is no more God. Well, we know that that is not true, but if we put the word "result" into the verse instead, we get "Ye have heard of the patience of Job, and have seen the result of the Lord; that the Lord is very pitiful, and of tender mercy", which makes perfect sense. So, in rephrasing what was said, the word "end" can mean both "finality" as well as "result". The context should support it. In either case, the result of the law is love to the neighbor is further confirmed by James, "If ye fulfil the royal law according to the scripture, Thou shalt love thy neighbour as thyself, ye do well" (James 2:8).

In 1 Timothy 1:9-10, we have another speed reading situation perpetrated by the "Spirit of Antichrist". It says, "Knowing this, that the law is not made for a righteous man, but for the lawless and disobedient, for the ungodly and for sinners, for unholy and profane, for murderers of fathers and murderers of mothers, for manslayers, For whoremongers, for them that defile themselves with mankind, for menstealers, for liars, for perjured persons, and if there be any other thing that is contrary to sound doctrine." The "Spirit of Antichrist" would have Christians believe that since they are covered by Christ's righteousness, the Ten Commandments are not for them, but that is not what it says. It says that the commandments are not for a righteous man, and we agree. A righteous man, by definition, is one that is already obeying the commandments. In other words, a righteous man does not struggle in keeping the commandments. A righteous man just does, so they do not have to be reviewing the commandments to see if they are out of line or not. But those that are not well studied and living a sinning life, the commandments are for them. They stand as a reminder that they need a Savior. The righteous man has already met the Savior and will "walk, even as he walked" (1 John 2:6), "He" as in Jesus. Jesus kept the commandments and so will a righteous person. Besides, "he that doeth righteousness is righteous, even as he is righteous" (1 John 3:7), "And they were both righteous before God, walking in all the commandments and ordinances of the Lord blameless" (Luke 1:6).

The "Spirit of Antichrist" will also bring to mind that there are two covenants mentioned in the Bible. It is taught that there is a covenant based on the Ten Commandments and there is a covenant of grace. The covenant based upon the Ten Commandments supposedly ended at the cross and was replaced by the covenant of grace. We also agree that there are two covenants, but those are not the two found in the Bible. The Bible says, "This [is] the covenant that I will make with them after those days, saith the Lord, I will put my laws into their hearts, and in their minds will I write them; And their sins and iniquities will I remember no more" (Hebrews 10:16-17). The New Covenant did not replace the Ten Commandments with that of forgiveness through grace, but rather the New Covenant relocates the commandments from the stony tablets unto our hearts. And when we are motivated "to walk and to please God" (1 Thessalonians 4:1), we have the right motivation and God is willing to forgive us. Those that simply want to live free from the Ten Commandments restrictions, well, "they that are in the flesh cannot please God" (Romans 8:8). Specifically, Jesus invites the right motivation when He stated, "If ye love me, keep my commandments" (John 14:15), but understand this, the invitation is not new with Jesus when He walked this earth, rather, being the same God of the Old Testament, right in the middle of the Ten Commandments are the words that Jesus spoke. "And shewing mercy unto thousands of them that love me, and keep my commandments" (Exodus 20:6). And Jesus was not merely quoting the words, but rather by saying the same words in essence, Jesus declared, "I wrote the Ten Commandments and I invite everyone, if they love Me, keep my commandments."

So, the "Spirit of Antichrist" usually is not satisfied with just freely discussing what the Bible actually says; they turn to criticism, in which is declared, all that do the Ten Commandments are legalists, perverts of the gospel, and other nasty names. Interestingly, Christ, through His writers, wrote the opposite view by stating, "But whoso looketh into the perfect law of liberty, and continueth [therein], he being not a forgetful hearer, but a doer of the work, this man shall be blessed in his deed" (James 1:25).

Now if the Ten Commandments were done away with at the cross, then it is very unfair of God to be using them to judge with, for "Whosoever shall keep the whole law, and yet offend in one [point], he is guilty of all. For he that said, Do not commit adultery, said also, Do not kill. Now if thou commit no adultery, yet if thou kill, thou art become a transgressor of the law. So speak ye, and so do, as they that shall be judged by the law of liberty" (James 2:10-12). So somebody would have to inform God that it is unfair to judge people with the high standard that supposedly was done away with. Well, if God is still using the standard to judge with, then His actions speak to the positive that the Ten Commandments still exist and are to be obeyed.

You see, God, through Christ says, "Behold, all souls are mine; as the soul of the father, so also the soul of the son is mine: the soul that sinneth, it shall die" (Ezekiel 18:4), but the "Spirit of Antichrist" would have one think that they can live in sin, especially when one feels they are missing out on so much. Well, the "Spirit of Antichrist" removes that guilt by removing the Ten Commandments, however, Christ is who we ought to be listening too instead. And He says, "For when they speak great swelling [words] of vanity, they allure through the lusts of the flesh, [through much] wantonness, those that were clean escaped from them who live in error. While they promise them liberty, they themselves are the servants of corruption: for of whom a man is overcome, of the same is he brought in bondage. For if after they have escaped the pollutions of the world through the knowledge of the Lord and Saviour Jesus Christ, they are again entangled therein, and overcome, the latter end is worse with them than the beginning. For it had been better for them not to have known the way of righteousness, than, after they have known [it], to turn from the holy commandment delivered unto them. But it is happened unto them according to the true proverb, The dog [is] turned to his own vomit again; and the sow that was washed to her wallowing in the mire" (2 Peter 2:18-22). Please note, that under the inspiration of Christ, Peter just told us that worldly preachers would preach the wrong message even encouraging people to return to the vomit they had escaped.

In addition to doing away with the commandments, the "Spirit of Antichrist" is good on creating catchy phrases. For instance, one of them is declaring that someone who does not study the Bible, let alone read it, is somehow able to say, "I know my Savior!" Well, Christ speaks to that through His writer John by having him state, "And hereby we do know that we know him, if we keep his commandments. He that saith, I know him, and keepeth not his commandments, is a liar, and the truth is not in him" (1 John 2:3-4).

And with the catch phrases comes a list of material wealth that such people claim as evidence that Christ is with them, when in actuality, the "Spirit of Antichrist" resides. That is because "whatsoever we ask, we receive of him, because we keep his commandments, and do those things that are pleasing in his sight. And this is his commandment, That we should believe on the name of his Son Jesus Christ, and love one another, as he gave us commandment. And he that keepeth his commandments dwelleth in him, and he in him. And hereby we know that he abideth in us, by the Spirit which he hath given us" (1 John 3:22-24).

The "Spirit of Antichrist" is not above lying either. In fact, it is through the "Spirit of Antichrist" that declares the Ten Commandments are too hard to keep. Christ tells us through John, "By this we know that we love the children of God, when we love God, and keep his commandments. For this is the love of God, that we keep his commandments: and his commandments are not grievous" (1 John 5:2-3).

And as a reminder, the "Spirit of Antichrist" does not want people knowing how to survive the end time events, yet inspired by Jesus Christ, the Bible says, "And the dragon was wroth with the woman, and went to make war with the remnant of her seed, which keep the commandments of God, and have the testimony of Jesus Christ" (Revelation 12:17). "Here is the patience of the saints: here [are] they that keep the commandments of God, and the faith of Jesus" (Revelation 14:12). "Blessed [are] they that do his commandments, that they may have right to the tree of life, and may enter in through the gates into the city" (Revelation 22:14).

So, it comes down to four groups, of which only one is correct. The Antichrist is all for keeping the Ten Commandments, however, there are a couple alterations as the devil also knows that breaking just one of the ten without repentance is guilt that condemns one to hell (James 2:10). Then there at the protestors that brought back the second commandment criticizing those that follow knowingly or blindly the commandments put forth by the Antichrist. They condemn Catholics for the use of statues and rosaries when praying, all the while they cling to an altered version of the fourth commandment regarding the Sabbath day. These Protestants are a decoy because while they disagree with the Antichrist, they are still just as guilty for not returning completely to the Ten Commandments unaltered. This spirit among them is one form of the "Spirit of Antichrist", as they work against Jesus Christ, since "the Son of man is Lord even of the sabbath day" (Matthew 12:8). In addition to those two groups, there is the second form of the "Spirit of Antichrist" which simply gets rid of the Ten Commandments. This is why the "Spirit of Antichrist" is so much more concerning. Finally, we have Jesus Christ who simply asks, "If ye love me, keep my commandments" (John 14:15)

The ultimate goal of Antichrist and the Spirit of Antichrist is to continue breaking the commandments, even in the name of Jesus, all to steal souls from God. Working in conjunction, Christians are either keeping the wrong set of commandments or they are keeping none of them.

And what we have just done is to have completed a pretty long exercise according to Isaiah 28:9-10. We have taken precepts upon precepts, line upon line, and even used a little here and a little there. And nowhere in the Bible, specifically the New Testament, if studied in a manner that removes all apparent contradictions, is there a teaching that the commandments are done away with. In fact, we are still open to seeing such a verse, but after looking at every verse with "law" or "commandment", we find no such teaching as to nullify the required obedience to the Law of Ten Commandments.

So after showing in no uncertain terms that all the arguments against the Ten Commandments fall short, including those against the seventh day Sabbath, we now turn our attention towards another area that influences our survival. Between the Antichrist offering an altered version of the Ten Commandments, which deceives people into still breaking them, and having the "Spirit of Antichrist" so active in just dismissing them completely from regarding them as being part of the salvation equation, there are still a significant number of people that do keep the Ten Commandments. If this were not the case, then Revelation 12:17 would have no significance. Remember, Satan does not care about the Christian community at large, Catholics or the majority of Protestants. Satan's focus is upon "the remnant of her seed, which keep the commandments of God, and have the testimony of Jesus Christ" (Revelation 12:17). His focus is upon those that do keep the commandments and keep true to the testimony of Jesus Christ, which "the testimony of Jesus is the spirit of prophecy" (Revelation 19:10). These are the people that are true Bible believers and even believe in the fulfillment of what God said, "I will pour out my spirit upon all flesh; and your sons and your daughters shall prophesy, your old men shall dream dreams, your young men shall see visions" (Joel 2:28). If there were only five people in the entire world, they would pretty much be ignored as being insignificant like Noah and his family or more would have gotten on the ark. If fifty were found obedient, still they would not register an excitement from Satan especially if they were spread out in each of the fifty states of the United States. Even five hundred people spread around the world means nothing to stir up Satan. Five thousand may seem like a lot but compared to over seven billion, not so much. Fifty thousand today and finally these would be getting some attention in the form of animosity, but having "hundred forty [and] four thousand, having his Father's name written in their foreheads" (Revelation 14:1), now that is worth Satan's efforts. Now Satan has to get involved. He knows full well that this constitutes a might army even though it is so small still in comparison to the rest of the world. That is because he knows history. "The same day there were added [unto them] about three thousand souls" (Acts 2:41) and eventually it grew to the point that they were recognized as having "turned the world upside down" (Acts 17:6).

So when Jesus Christ says, "If ye love me, keep my commandments" (John 14:15) and Antichrist agrees but throws out the second commandment, allowing idol worship, changing the day of the fourth commandment both in the cycle of time different from sunset as well as the number of the day being the first day, and splitting the last commandment into two coveting commandments, we have a direct conflict that fooled so many people for many hundreds of years. Then in protest, Protestants restored the second commandment and rejoined the commandment on coveting back to one commandment but still adhered to the altered Sabbath commandment, so all Christians who are not caught up in the commandments being falsely assumed to have been nailed to the cross are still guilty of breaking God's commandments. It is very deceptive because while being against the Antichrist they are actually still working with the Antichrist, where they accused the Antichrist of "abideth not in the doctrine of Christ, hath not God" (2 John 1:9) while thinking they "abideth in the doctrine of Christ, he hath both the Father and the Son" (2 John 1:9) when it is not so. Then comes along in the past century or so, a group that has greatly influenced the non-Catholic Christians to the point of believing the commandment are insignificant teaching "once saved, always saved", justification is all that matters, and the impossibility of complete obedience. No matter how one looks at it, it is all against what Christ commanded when He said, "Teaching them to observe all things whatsoever I have commanded you" (Matthew 28:20), which is more than just "believe and be saved" (Luke 8:12). Keeping in mind that Jesus "In flaming fire taking vengeance on them that know not God, and that obey not the gospel of our Lord Jesus Christ" (2 Thessalonians 1:8). So the gospel includes obedience.

Therefore, Satan has to be even more subtle in his ways to undermine those that would make up the hundred and forty four thousand, literally or symbolically, who will be used at the end of time to bring into the fold multitudes (Revelation 7:9), which still will be few in comparison to the lost for Jesus said, "Strait [is] the gate, and narrow [is] the way, which leadeth unto life, and few there be that find it" (Matthew 7:14). Hardly a Christian wants to hear that there are rules to follow because somehow it conflicts in their mind of grace being free when both actually coincide without conflict as discussed in full length many different ways already.

Now this subtleness goes beyond the Ten Commandments even though it is an extension thereof. It is called influence. We already looked at the fact, a number of times, that true Christians will avoid much of what is called entertainment because of its influence, even if the contents are not sinful. When applying the principle, "Whatsoever things are true, whatsoever things [are] honest, whatsoever things [are] just, whatsoever things [are] pure, whatsoever things [are] lovely, whatsoever things [are] of good report; if [there be] any virtue, and if [there be] any praise, think on these things" (Philippians 4:8), one is basically ready to toss the television and stop going to the movies. Even leisure reading books are tossed along with video games, concerts, sporting events, and most music, including much of what is called Christian music. The prophet Ezekiel wrote, "Then said I unto them, Cast ye away every man the abominations of his eyes, and defile not yourselves with the idols of Egypt: I [am] the LORD your God" (Ezekiel 20:7). Today, this verse could be stated as, "Then said I unto them, Cast ye away every man the abominations of his eyes, and defile not yourselves with the idols of Hollywood: I [am] the LORD your God." This is also inclusive of following celebrities, including sports teams and players. Who cares that such a person or group of people have come down with a cold? Most people do, but to waste time in reading and following of these celebrities is nothing more than a waste of time and a temptation to covet.

And to those that just have to watch that latest television show, David wrote, "I will behave myself wisely in a perfect way. O when wilt thou come unto me? I will walk within my house with a perfect heart. I will set no wicked thing before mine eyes: I hate the work of them that turn aside; [it] shall not cleave to me" (Psalms 101:2-3). So, if we are serious about Heaven and surviving the coming Mark of the Beast, then we should stop setting that wicked thing, called the television, before our eyes. When it comes down to it, what is television in relationship to the Bible? "Turn away mine eyes from beholding vanity; [and] quicken thou me in thy way. Stablish thy word unto thy servant, who [is devoted] to thy fear" (Psalms 119:37-38). "He that walketh righteously, and speaketh uprightly; he that despiseth the gain of oppressions, that shaketh his hands from holding of bribes, that stoppeth his ears from hearing of blood, and shutteth his eyes from seeing evil; He shall dwell on high: his place of defence [shall be] the munitions of rocks: bread shall be given him; his waters [shall be] sure. Thine eyes shall see the king in his beauty: they shall behold the land that is very far off" (Isaiah 33:15-17). Television is vanity, bloodshed in many cases, and evil. Why submit ourselves even to what we consider "good programming"? Is the loss of Heaven worth it?

But there is one more area that will influence our survival during the coming crisis and end up in the Kingdom of God. Adam and Eve gave into it, John the Baptist rebuked it, Jesus Christ showed us the way, and Paul taught it. "know ye not that your body is the temple of the Holy Ghost [which is] in you, which ye have of God, and ye are not your own?" (1 Corinthians 6:19) It is called appetite. What we eat and drink greatly affects our spiritual stance. And if we do not think God is serious then that means we are ignoring the fact that God says, "I wish above all things that thou mayest prosper and be in health, even as thy soul prospereth" (3 John 1:2). He wants us in the best health possible.

Eating and drinking is very serious with God,

for Jesus had us to take note regarding end times, of all things to list out, He states, "they were eating and drinking" (Matthew 24:38), and "they did eat, they drank" (Luke 17:28). And in both cases, Jesus says, "Even thus shall it be in the day when the Son of man is revealed" (Luke 17:30).

Appetite is so serious that not only did Adam and Eve fall over the issue, "when the woman saw that the tree [was] good for food, and that it [was] pleasant to the eyes, and a tree to be desired to make [one] wise, she took of the fruit thereof, and did eat, and gave also unto her husband with her; and he did eat" (Genesis 3:6), but even before Jesus started His ministry, Jesus "fasted forty days and forty nights" (Matthew 4:2). And what was the first temptation? "And when the tempter came to him, he said, If thou be the Son of God, command that these stones be made bread." This was serious because after the fast, Jesus "was afterward an hungred" (Matthew 4:2). May we say starving? Adam and Eve probably ate earlier that day or the day before and failed on the temptation of appetite. Here is Jesus who is about to end His fast facing the temptation of appetite. What a disadvantage! Well, we have good news, Jesus "answered and said, It is written, Man shall not live by bread alone, but by every word that proceedeth out of the mouth of God" (Matthew 4:4).

Now everyone ought to know gluttony is just wrong. Parents of old even turned their children over to the authorities saying, "This our son [is] stubborn and rebellious, he will not obey our voice; [he is] a glutton, and a drunkard" (Deuteronomy 21:20). Then "All the men of his city shall stone him with stones, that he die: so shalt thou put evil away from among you; and all Israel shall hear, and fear" (Deuteronomy 21:21). There is also a Proverb that says, "For the drunkard and the glutton shall come to poverty" (Proverbs 23:21), and spiritual poverty is to lose eternal life.

But what about the specifics of what we eat and drink. We are told, "But the end of all things is at hand: be ye therefore sober, and watch unto prayer" (1 Peter 4:7). Sober, though encompassing more than alcohol in this verse, indeed does include it for one cannot be properly praying and watching themselves in avoiding sin and deceptions by partaking of alcohol, but what does the Bible say? "Wine [is] a mocker, strong drink [is] raging: and whosoever is deceived thereby is not wise" (Proverbs 20:1).

That is a very strong statement that appears to be very much against the use of alcohol. As a true Bible student, if we take the position that the Bible does not condemn the use of alcohol, then we need to explain this verse away using the Bible and the Bible alone. And no matter how one looks at it, it just cannot be done. This verse does not allow wiggle room at all. If we use it or believe the reports of the benefits of alcohol, then we are not wise unto God and are even deceived. To say, that this was for a recovering alcoholic, as scholars try to imply is the case with Solomon, discredits the purpose of the verse being in the Bible in the first place. Besides, what does one then do with the verse in Isaiah 5:11? "Woe unto them that rise up early in the morning, [that] they may follow strong drink; that continue until night, [till] wine inflame them!" And then there is Isaiah 5:22-23, "Woe unto [them that are] mighty to drink wine, and men of strength to mingle strong drink: Which justify the wicked for reward, and take away the righteousness of the righteous from him!" So a declaration that people are foolish to think alcohol is for healthy living, even a woe is placed upon them.

In regards to the purpose of the verse being in the Bible, the Bible is not a book written about events that have no implication upon us today. Instead, "All these things happened unto them for ensamples: and they are written for our admonition, upon whom the ends of the world are come" (1 Corinthians 10:11). Many other prophets wrote much content that is not found in the Bible. There is the "book of Jasher" (Joshua 10:13) that Joshua encouraged reading, but it is not found in the Bible. There is also the "book of Nathan" (1 Chronicles 29:29) also not part of the Bible. Even the prophets themselves with their followers should have recorded something, like the words of John the Baptist, but they are not found in the Bible. Where are those writings? Someone should have written something. Maybe they did, but it is not part of the Bible because those writings were more of a specific event that would have little application for us, and that is probably the case. So to dismiss the verse in Proverbs arbitrarily by being for Solomon, is to go against the intent of God. Besides, if we then are the ones to identify which verses are applicable and which are not, would that not make us superior to the Bible? Of course it would. That makes us above the Bible when it ought to be the other way around.

Now by stating that alcohol should not be part of a Christian's life if they are serious about resisting the devil, avoiding the Antichrist teachings, seeing through the deceptions of the "Spirit of Antichrist", and avoiding the Mark of the Beast, there is certainly going to be a number of arguments contrary to this position against the use of alcohol. And so, to be an honest student of the Bible, let us examine the verses on "strong drink" and "wine".

To start off with, we need to address one thing right up front. The Bible says, "Thus saith the LORD, As the new wine is found in the cluster, and [one] saith, Destroy it not; for a blessing [is] in it" (Isaiah 65:8). The point here is that when we use the word "wine", we automatically think that it is alcoholic wine, but that is not how the Bible uses the word. The word "wine" in the Bible refers to the liquid of the grape. Left to rot over time, sure, it becomes alcohol. But this verse just stated that it is not to be destroyed through the rotting process. Just as the wine is growing in the cluster, it ought to be consumed right away for the blessings of it. In fact, by now one should have heard that a glass of wine is good for health. That is not wholly true, well, it is if one uses that biblical definition of wine. The thought that a glass of alcoholic wine is good for health is actually incorrect. A glass of grape juice is what is healthy. It is not the alcohol, it's the antioxidants of the grape, but people have been trained that grape juice is for kids and alcoholic wine is for adults. Many are uncomfortable in serving grape juice at a dinner instead of alcoholic wine, as if grape juice does not go with a meal.

And interestingly, there was a loud spreading of the news when it was declared a glass of alcoholic wine a day was good for health. People who did not even drink wine were spreading the word, but now, many years later, it is being reported in the news that the biblical stance of the grape juice is the blessing and not the alcoholic version. However, many people are not hearing that to be so. News outlets will report if from time to time, but we do not hear people spreading that news as they did before. Why? Because people like their alcohol, and that is a shame, for rest assure that those who continue in the practice of consuming alcohol will end up missing out on Heaven. They will have drank their way out of Heaven.

So when the Bible uses the word wine, we have to leave the context explain itself of which it is. For instance, wine connected with strong drink and is condemned is obviously the alcoholic version. Someone getting drunk, again, is the alcoholic version. The use of wine in reference to an offering to God makes no mention of it being alcoholic or non-alcoholic, therefore, we rely upon other Bible verses to find out that it is the non-alcoholic version being offered to God for if God commanded a bit of yeast or leaven to be removed during certain feast days (Exodus 12:15) being a symbolism of the removal of sin, then surely alcohol would be looked upon that same way as well. Therefore, the numerous verses that state "wine [for] a drink offering" (Exodus 29:40) is going to be treated as non-alcoholic.

Now both the Antichrist and the "Spirit of Antichrist" are active in promoting alcohol for one reason or another. More than likely, it is being instigated by Satan for he knows perfectly well that although we have a lot of brain cells, it is not by coincidence that each sip of alcohol kills the cells used in our thought process never to regenerate. It is said that humans use only ten percent of their brains, but it is that ten percent that alcohol also kills off. And if Satan can dumb down our thought processes any, well, he is all but too happy to do so. This contributes to the reason why many are not as smart or comprehend things in their older age as opposed to their younger age.

For instance, it is stated that people of God drank wine and even point to Noah as such a person. The Bible says, "Noah found grace in the eyes of the LORD" (Genesis 6:8). So when the Bible says, "He drank of the wine, and was drunken" (Genesis 9:21), it is taught that somehow God was alright with this. First off, God's righteous people are not automatically without freewill to sin. Although we do not have any further account on Noah regarding his attempt to deal with pressure nor the repentance thereof, the incident that followed this should have woken him up to the fact that he ought not get drunk again. Although serious depression is no excuse in God's eyes, we do see that Noah attempted to drink himself to a better state. This actually should be a lesson to all those that try to drink their sorrows away. It usually complicates matters instead of improving them.

And for those that wonder why Noah would be so depressed, do realize that for "an hundred and twenty years" (Genesis 6:3) Noah had invited everyone and anyone into the ark, but no one took Noah seriously. So feeling like a failure would be depressing enough, but add on to that the fact that everyone he knew, worked with, grew up with, were instantly wiped out, it is a heavy burden despite trusting in God. There are no more neighbors. The neighborhood and much more had been destroyed beyond recognition. Life as they knew it was forever changed. That would definitely cause much anguish and depression, but again, it is not a justification for drinking.

Secondly, regarding God's people and their representation, the rule is, like Paul stated, "be ye followers of me" (1 Corinthians 4:16) but only "in the Lord" (Ephesians 6:1). We are not to follow David into murder (2 Samuel 11:14-17) and adultery (2 Samuel 11:4). We are not to follow Samson in his example of sleeping around (Judges 16:1) and becoming full of himself (Judges 16:3) being disrespectful to parents (Judges 14:3). We are not to follow Joseph in his bragging (Genesis 37:10). We are not to follow Moses in taking matters into his own hands (Exodus 2:12). We are to follow the example as they are in the lord. So Noah's drinking is not "in the Lord" therefore should not be followed.

What Antichrist and the "Spirit of Antichrist" would have one believe is that wine, in moderation, is acceptable, yet, there is not one good Bible account of drinking wine in which does not contain drunkenness. Take for instance, Lot's daughters who got their father drunk twice so that he would not know he was having sex with them to produce offspring (Genesis 19:32-36). They quote Ephesians 5:18 for justification of this though, which says, "And be not drunk with wine, wherein is excess; but be filled with the Spirit" (Ephesians 5:18). The argument is that it is alright to drink, just do not get drunk. But that is not quite what this verse is saying. Instead of feeling good from a buzz or drunkenness, be filled with the Holy Spirit. That has eternal feelings. A buzz or drunkenness will eventually wear off.

And what is considered being drunk? When one is lying in their own vomit? When one cannot stand up without falling? When one simply cannot hold their head up anymore and have to lay it down on a bar or table? Is it when then speech is slurred? Is it when the thoughts get mixed up? Is it when the head starts feeling tingly? Is it when the extra energy seems to pulse in the body? There is all sorts of levels of being considered drunk that even governments have measurements for what is considered legally drunk. On top of that, a single glass may not have an apparent affect but if one waits until they think they are at the limit, the body is quite delayed in processing of that, which means, one is actually across the drunk line when it is fully absorbed. The point being is that it is quite silly to try and set measurements. It is clear that God does not want His people drinking it, so do not do it is the bottom line.

Antichrist and the "Spirit of Antichrist" would have one think that if there is a forbidding or practice of avoiding alcohol use with the words like, "I pray thee, and drink not wine nor strong drink" (Judges 13:4), then that means that they were not to be doing like others that were permitted to drink it. These people were being called for a special purpose, otherwise, there is an implied permission. This includes the Levites, "Do not drink wine nor strong drink, thou, nor thy sons with thee" (Leviticus 10:9); Nazarites, "He shall separate [himself] from wine and strong drink, and shall drink no vinegar of wine, or vinegar of strong drink" (Numbers 6:3); Manoah's wife, "Behold, thou shalt conceive, and bear a son; and now drink no wine nor strong drink" (Judges 13:7); Hannah, "I have drunk neither wine nor strong drink" (1 Samuel 1:15); Lemeul, "[It is] not for kings, O Lemuel, [it is] not for kings to drink wine; nor for princes strong drink" (Proverbs 31:4); sons of the house of the Rechabites, "We will drink no wine: for Jonadab the son of Rechab our father commanded us, saying, Ye shall drink no wine, [neither ye], nor your sons for ever" (Jeremiah 35:6); and John the Baptist, "he shall be great in the sight of the Lord, and shall drink neither wine nor strong drink" (Luke 1:15). But this is not so, for in several of those verses, it states in full context, "She may not eat of any [thing] that cometh of the vine, neither let her drink wine or strong drink, nor eat any unclean [thing]: all that I commanded her let her observe" (Judges 13:140). Using the logic that people were permitted to practice something unless called out on it means, like in this case, Manoah's wife was not only to stop drinking, she was also not to eat anything unclean. Does that mean all the other Israelites were allowed to eat unclean things? Of course not. None of them were allowed to eat unclean things either. What the truth of these twenty or so verses happens to be is that, as usual, the so-called believers were mixed with those that obey the commands and a bunch of liberals who make excuses to break the rules. In other words, it may have been very popular among the Israelites to drink wine and strong drink, even in the day of John the Baptist, but that does not make it right. These statements are all about making sure these people were obeying the original commands. All those that liberalized away the drinking restrictions, will probably end up in hell. Even churches today experience the same thing when it comes to the rules in that, we must ask, "How many know the rules and yet break them despite claiming to be right with God?" Usually it is the majority of the church. That includes all the people who gossip, who are greedy, who are uninvolved with church activities, and other such things that give evidence of saving relationship with Jesus. So to imply that a special call out means everyone else was permitted to drink alcohol is more than a stretch.

Besides, what does one get out of alcohol? "Who hath woe? who hath sorrow? who hath contentions? who hath babbling? who hath wounds without cause? who hath redness of eyes? They that tarry long at the wine; they that go to seek mixed wine. Look not thou upon the wine when it is red, when it giveth his colour in the cup, [when] it moveth itself aright. At the last it biteth like a serpent, and stingeth like an adder. Thine eyes shall behold strange women, and thine heart shall utter perverse things. Yea, thou shalt be as he that lieth down in the midst of the sea, or as he that lieth upon the top of a mast. They have stricken me, [shalt thou say, and] I was not sick; they have beaten me, [and] I felt [it] not: when shall I awake? I will seek it yet again" (Proverbs 23:29-35). "But they also have erred through wine, and through strong drink are out of the way; the priest and the prophet have erred through strong drink, they are swallowed up of wine, they are out of the way through strong drink; they err in vision, they stumble [in] judgment. For all tables are full of vomit [and] filthiness, [so that there is] no place [clean]" (Isaiah 28:7-8).

If there is any permission given to drinking strong drink or alcoholic wine, it is to those bent on hell or those that are so far gone in their self inflicted depression. "Give strong drink unto him that is ready to perish, and wine unto those that be of heavy hearts. Let him drink, and forget his poverty, and remember his misery no more" (Proverbs 31:6). Now that does not mean alcohol is a cure for depression. As stated before, alcohol makes such problems worse. What is happening here is that they are not trusting in God; they may even be blaming God for their woes. They may be rejecting God's way of dealing with the issues, nonetheless, the lack of trust in God shows the need of salvation in their life, but God has a rule, He will not force Himself on anyone. So, if they are in this state, let them have the alcohol for their comfort. This is more of a sarcastic statement. "You don't trust in God, might as well trust in the bottle then."

Now in many churches there is a song that the youth have sung quite often. It is called, "Dare to Be a Daniel". Well, this is what Daniel did when sitting at the king's table noticing all of the unclean meats and the alcohol. Despite the high probability of being executed, Daniel made a request, "Prove thy servants, I beseech thee, ten days; and let them give us pulse to eat, and water to drink" (Daniel 1:12). And, "Thus Melzar took away the portion of their meat, and the wine that they should drink; and gave them pulse" (Daniel 1:16). Daniel rejected the wine, among other things.

So when we hear doctors and specialists and even scholars tout the fact that alcohol is perfectly fine, do realize that all those that are eager to take the things that Christ said we were not to do and replace them with what these people tell us is allowed to be done is a fulfillment of a prophecy. "If a man walking in the spirit and falsehood do lie, [saying], I will prophesy unto thee of wine and of strong drink; he shall even be the prophet of this people" (Micah 2:11). Notice that it is a falsehood, so do not believe all the supposed evidence. As stated before, pure grape juice provides the same or better health effects than alcoholic wine.

Now according to the Bible, we are told, "He that saith he abideth in him ought himself also so to walk, even as he walked" (1 John 2:6). So what was Jesus' practice? "And they bring him unto the place Golgotha, which is, being interpreted, The place of a skull. And they gave him to drink wine mingled with myrrh: but he received [it] not. And when they had crucified him, they parted his garments, casting lots upon them, what every man should take" (Mark 15:22-24). Even facing sure death along with being in horrific pain, Jesus refused the alcohol.

But Antichrist and the "Spirit of Antichrist" would have everyone believe that Jesus drunk wine. And the famous quote is the wedding feast. "And the third day there was a marriage in Cana of Galilee; and the mother of Jesus was there: And both Jesus was called, and his disciples, to the marriage. And when they wanted wine, the mother of Jesus saith unto him, They have no wine. Jesus saith unto her, Woman, what have I to do with thee? mine hour is not yet come. His mother saith unto the servants, Whatsoever he saith unto you, do [it]. And there were set there six waterpots of stone, after the manner of the purifying of the Jews, containing two or three firkins apiece. Jesus saith unto them, Fill the waterpots with water. And they filled them up to the brim. And he saith unto them, Draw out now, and bear unto the governor of the feast. And they bare [it]. When the ruler of the feast had tasted the water that was made wine, and knew not whence it was: (but the servants which drew the water knew;) the governor of the feast called the bridegroom, And saith unto him, Every man at the beginning doth set forth good wine; and when men have well drunk, then that which is worse: [but] thou hast kept the good wine until now. This beginning of miracles did Jesus in Cana of Galilee, and manifested forth his glory; and his disciples believed on him" (John 2:1-11). Reread all these verses and point out where alcohol is being served? The word "wine", remember, is nothing more than the liquid of a grape. It can be alcoholic or non-alcoholic. It is the context that determines which is being referred to. And just because most wedding feasts today are with alcohol, we cannot simply apply that practice to this reference of almost two thousand years ago. Think of it this way, in which, if this were a court case and the prosecutors are looking to pin a guilty verdict upon Jesus for turning water into alcohol and avoiding paying taxes on that alcohol and this is all the evidence being submitted, what is the likelihood of the prosecutor winning without a reasonable doubt? Not likely. They have not proven without a reasonable doubt that what transpired was anything else but Jesus simply turning water into grape juice, non-alcoholic wine. And if one disagrees with this conclusion, remember, a true Bible student knows that "God is not [the author] of confusion" (1 Corinthians 14:33). He would not condemn alcohol so strongly in other books of the Bible and then turn around and make it appear in a miracle to now allow it. That is confusion. That means if we were to believe this was an alcoholic miracle, then we have an equal obligation to know what those condemning verses really mean. One cannot just ignore them. That is exactly how we are in this mess and how both Christians and non-Christians can say, "You can get anything you want out of the Bible!" Sure people can when they are pulling verses out and leaving the opposing verses unexplained. That is not proper Bible study as directed in Isaiah 28:9-10.

Besides, think of things in this manner. "Jesus began to preach, and to say, Repent: for the kingdom of heaven is at hand" (Matthew 4:17). So one could say that Jesus was representing the Kingdom of Heaven or God here on earth. Is there alcohol in Heaven? No, of course not. And most people know that. There is even a Polka song titled In Heaven There Is No Beer. So, with Jesus representing the Kingdom of God, why would He perform a miracle that goes against the principles of Heaven? He would not. From that perspective then, the wedding feast was not an alcoholic miracle.

Now Antichrist and the "Spirit of Antichrist" state that He was labeled as a drinker of wine. Well, that is not quite the story. The Bible says, "For John came neither eating nor drinking, and they say, He hath a devil. The Son of man came eating and drinking, and they say, Behold a man gluttonous, and a winebibber, a friend of publicans and sinners. But wisdom is justified of her children" (Matthew 11:18-19). Basically, just because one is labeled as doing such does not make it so. In plain speak, this is nothing more than gossip. So, to believe the gossip is to believe a lie.

But of course Antichrist and the "Spirit of Antichrist" would have people believe that the ministers are fine with a little alcohol. They quote, "Likewise [must] the deacons [be] grave, not doubletongued, not given to much wine, not greedy of filthy lucre" (1 Timothy 3:8). Even an aged woman was told the same thing. "The aged women likewise, that [they be] in behaviour as becometh holiness, not false accusers, not given to much wine, teachers of good things" (Titus 2:3). "Much wine" implies that some is alright. Well, not so fast. A higher up person, a bishop, has this description that they are to follow: "A bishop then must be blameless, the husband of one wife, vigilant, sober, of good behaviour, given to hospitality, apt to teach; Not given to wine, no striker, not greedy of filthy lucre; but patient, not a brawler, not covetous" (1 Timothy 3:2-3). So deacons are allowed a little while bishops are not to be given into any? That does not make sense, especially, since Levites were explicitly forbidden and then we have the whole list of verses that tell us very strongly, even with woe's attached, not to drink the alcohol. First, there is only an implication that alcohol is involved. It could mean that, in the context with greedy and double tongued, that there is a normal consumption amount and an abnormal amount of drinking grape juice. In other words, this may be a warning against the glutton intake of the liquid. That is one understanding. The second may involve alcohol in which to combat sterilization issues, especially when polluted water is the only other option to drink. This verse may be a reference to people who tend to make excuses for medicinal purposes when in reality it is just an excuse to drink. That is a stretch, but in either case, if one were to think this is permission, then there is a whole lot of very strong verses that need explaining. And to build a doctrine on one verse is always dangerous and unbiblical for "In the mouth of two or three witnesses shall every word be established" (2 Corinthians 13:1).

Now Antichrist and the "Spirit of Antichrist" would exploit medicinal needs of Timothy as an excuse of using alcohol on a regular basis. The Bible says, "Drink no longer water, but use a little wine for thy stomach's sake and thine often infirmities" (1 Timothy 5:23), however, there is no context that places this in an alcoholic perspective. It is all assumption again, and that is never a good thing to use to establish doctrine. Timothy was simply told to stop drinking the water. That it is the source of causing the stomach issues. What other choice does he have? Probably goat's milk or grape juice, but if Timothy is having such reactions from water, there is a good possibility the same would happen with goat's milk since the goats were drinking the water too. So, for Timothy's sake, I hope he drank the grape juice.

To weaken our minds, Antichrist and the "Spirit of Antichrist" would have one believe that alcohol consumption is fine when it is not. No matter how much or how little one drinks, the moral stronghold begins to weaken right away. That is part of the "good feeling" one gets just on the onset. Drink until one is feeling a little tingling and a lot more morals struggle to stay intact. Overall though, Christ says not to drink it, even in moderation, while Antichrist and the "Spirit of Antichrist" says the opposite.

People even use the excuse that it helps them to relax. Folks, that is called dependency. It is no different than taking any other drug since alcohol is just that, a drug. And the devil fully knows that if one is relaxed, that means they are not going to worry too much about being serious with God's word, wanting to know the absolute truth, or even commit to wholly living in obedience, let alone wanting to share it with others.

Now with drinking out of the way, what about solid foods? The Antichrist and the "Spirit of Antichrist" would have people believe that there is no restriction upon this area of our life, yet, even in the New Testament, there are restrictions. Christians are not to eat any meat that still has the blood in it. Yes, an Old Testament restriction that is referenced from the New Testament, in which God said, "But flesh with the life thereof, [which is] the blood thereof, shall ye not eat" (Genesis 9:4), but notice who God is speaking to. "God blessed Noah and his sons, and said unto them, Be fruitful, and multiply, and replenish the earth" (Genesis 9:1). Before there was ever a Jew, before even Abraham, the father of the Jews (Matthew 3:9), was even born, God spoke this to be something followed by everyone, especially since all of us are related to Noah. A lot of people believing in creation credit that Adam and Eve populated the world with their children, of which married each other, but do not stop to think that it all started over again with Noah and his wife, along with his children.

But setting that aside, realize that the blood restriction was in place from at least Noah forward, and we see that a church council expressed that point by stating, "But that we write unto them, that they abstain from pollutions of idols, and [from] fornication, and [from] things strangled, and [from] blood" (Acts 15:20). Just so we do not miss it, the abstinence from blood is repeated a few verses later. "That ye abstain from meats offered to idols, and from blood, and from things strangled, and from fornication: from which if ye keep yourselves, ye shall do well. Fare ye well" (Acts 15:29). And then it is repeated even a few chapters later. "As touching the Gentiles which believe, we have written [and] concluded that they observe no such thing, save only that they keep themselves from [things] offered to idols, and from blood, and from strangled, and from fornication" (Acts 21:25). Yet, hardly a Christian church mentions such to their members, for they themselves think nothing of grabbing some bloody stakes and cooking them to rare, medium, well done, and all points in between. This was not something to be done away with for the physical law put into place thousands of years ago is still standing today. When God said that the life was in the blood, He basically is telling us that what diseases an animal had at the time of slaughter is passed on to those that eat the animal with the blood in it, despite what modern science tries to tell us. Who are we going to believe, "science falsely so called" (1 Timothy 6:20) or God?

However, it is more than just removing the blood from the animal. God did not have Noah just haphazardly bring the animals onto the ark, and no, Noah did not take the animals by female and male only. God specifically said, "Of every clean beast thou shalt take to thee by sevens, the male and his female: and of beasts that [are] not clean by two, the male and his female" (Genesis 7:2). So all the way before a Jew, before the father of the Jews, God made a distinction with the animals. The clean were eatable while the unclean were not. It is not some arbitrary identification either. God specifically made certain creatures to eat, digest, and turn the garbage of the earth into poison to be retained in the body instead of released back into the earth. They were to be God's garbage cleaners. Vultures are a good example of such in which they are part of the early crew that shows up to pull the flesh off of a corpse. Pigs devour everything. And in the sea, God has His crabs, lobsters, squids, and other such creatures to keep the waters clean. What these large creatures do not finish, the insects take care of, otherwise, this planet would have become inhabitable in a short period of time.

So how can we tell what is clean and unclean? What is eatable and not eatable? Well, let us start with the land animals. "Speak unto the children of Israel, saying, These [are] the beasts which ye shall eat among all the beasts that [are] on the earth. Whatsoever parteth the hoof, and is clovenfooted, [and] cheweth the cud, among the beasts, that shall ye eat. Nevertheless these shall ye not eat of them that chew the cud, or of them that divide the hoof: [as] the camel, because he cheweth the cud, but divideth not the hoof; he [is] unclean unto you. And the coney, because he cheweth the cud, but divideth not the hoof; he [is] unclean unto you. And the hare, because he cheweth the cud, but divideth not the hoof; he [is] unclean unto you. And the swine, though he divide the hoof, and be clovenfooted, yet he cheweth not the cud; he [is] unclean to you. Of their flesh shall ye not eat, and their carcase shall ye not touch; they [are] unclean to you" (Leviticus 11:2-8).

Now no doubt someone will say that a pig and a cow will eat the same things, even a goat is known to have eaten a tin can or two. The difference is not in what they eat as in how it is processed. A cow can eat a candy bar with a wrapper on it still, digest the candy bar, and poop out the wrapper fully intact. A pig's digestive system will actually digest the wrapper, which goes into the blood stream and poisons the meat, yet people eat the creature from its tail to its snout.

Yet others may begin to wonder how this is part of being sober, being vigilant. Well, it is a proven true science fact that those that abstain from these unclean meats have a better quality of life and longer life at that. Sure, there are exceptions to the rule, but in general, it is true. And for those that say that they do not care if they live to fifty or a hundred, they just want to enjoy life, then God has a message for them. "Love not the world, neither the things [that are] in the world. If any man love the world, the love of the Father is not in him" (1 John 2:15). So go to church, give to the church, do all the wonderful things for the church, but realize this, because the attitude is enjoying the meats offered by the world, it will all be for naught. On top of that, our duty is to "Go ye therefore, and teach all nations, baptizing them in the name of the Father, and of the Son, and of the Holy Ghost" (Matthew 28:19). This commission is not for the pastor or church officials alone. This is for every born again Christian. And we cannot obey Jesus' command to share the gospel if we are dead. God did not make us in such a way to have a short life, and that life is to be sharing the gospel. Further study also reveals that eating unclean meats, in fact meat in general, slows down the thought processes. We are to have clarity of mind. So it is sinful to not be in reasonable health. Remember, "your body is the temple of the Holy Ghost [which is] in you, which ye have of God, and ye are not your own" (1 Corinthians 6:19).

So now let us see what God says about sea creatures. "These shall ye eat of all that [are] in the waters: whatsoever hath fins and scales in the waters, in the seas, and in the rivers, them shall ye eat. And all that have not fins and scales in the seas, and in the rivers, of all that move in the waters, and of any living thing which [is] in the waters, they [shall be] an abomination unto you: They shall be even an abomination unto you; ye shall not eat of their flesh, but ye shall have their carcases in abomination. Whatsoever hath no fins nor scales in the waters, that [shall be] an abomination unto you" (Leviticus 11:9-12). That means the popular shell fish ought not to be eaten, and that is not just an option, please note that it is an abomination in the eyes of God to eat them.

Even the air creatures have a list. "And these [are they which] ye shall have in abomination among the fowls; they shall not be eaten, they [are] an abomination: the eagle, and the ossifrage, and the ospray, And the vulture, and the kite after his kind; Every raven after his kind; And the owl, and the night hawk, and the cuckow, and the hawk after his kind, And the little owl, and the cormorant, and the great owl, And the swan, and the pelican, and the gier eagle, And the stork, the heron after her kind, and the lapwing, and the bat. All fowls that creep, going upon [all] four, [shall be] an abomination unto you" (Leviticus 11:13-20).

And let us not leave out the bugs. "Yet these may ye eat of every flying creeping thing that goeth upon [all] four, which have legs above their feet, to leap withal upon the earth; [Even] these of them ye may eat; the locust after his kind, and the bald locust after his kind, and the beetle after his kind, and the grasshopper after his kind. But all [other] flying creeping things, which have four feet, [shall be] an abomination unto you" (Leviticus 11:21-23).

Also, rodents are on God's list as well. "These also [shall be] unclean unto you among the creeping things that creep upon the earth; the weasel, and the mouse, and the tortoise after his kind, And the ferret, and the chameleon, and the lizard, and the snail, and the mole. These [are] unclean to you among all that creep: whosoever doth touch them, when they be dead, shall be unclean until the even. And upon whatsoever [any] of them, when they are dead, doth fall, it shall be unclean; whether [it be] any vessel of wood, or raiment, or skin, or sack, whatsoever vessel [it be], wherein [any] work is done, it must be put into water, and it shall be unclean until the even; so it shall be cleansed" (Leviticus 11:29-32).

Now the Antichrist and the "Spirit of Antichrist" would have people believe that all such things were old Jewish rules and all were of a spiritual matter, however, unlike the declaration of the person being unclean, like in Leviticus 11:28, where it says, "And he that beareth the carcase of them shall wash his clothes, and be unclean until the even: they [are] unclean unto you", eating these creatures is a state of the creature. The word "unclean" in the Bible is unfortunately used two different ways, and Antichrist and the "Spirit of Antichrist" try to confuse them. There is the state of spiritual uncleanness and there is the forbiddance of an object. When it comes to eating creatures, it is forbiddance just like a doctor would tell a patient not to drink rat poison. Why? Because the patient will die. Now God in His mercy does not allow instant death from eating these abominations. In fact, not everyone gets the same reaction. But these creatures are very unhealthy causing illness, disease, and premature death in most cases overall. Uncleanness of an animal is about how the animal was created. Does it retain the poisons in the body or not? It is not what they eat as opposed to what is extracted out the other end.

Now the Antichrist and the "Spirit of Antichrist" mix up the spiritual and the status use of the word "unclean" so much so that they will try to convince people that Jesus cleaned up all of this nonsense and we are free to eat whatever we want. "Are ye so without understanding also? Do ye not perceive, that whatsoever thing from without entereth into the man, [it] cannot defile him; Because it entereth not into his heart, but into the belly, and goeth out into the draught, purging all meats? And he said, That which cometh out of the man, that defileth the man. For from within, out of the heart of men, proceed evil thoughts, adulteries, fornications, murders, Thefts, covetousness, wickedness, deceit, lasciviousness, an evil eye, blasphemy, pride, foolishness: All these evil things come from within, and defile the man" (Mark 7:18-23). Interestingly, this has nothing to do with being allowed to eat bacon, pork chops, or having a pig roast. It has nothing to do with going to a lobster house or eating cats and dogs.

First, realize that in Israel at this time, no one was eating anything unclean in regards to the meat object, however, in addition to the unclean rules as in regards to the status of the creature, the Pharisees made up additional rules. Jesus' words were spoken in that context for if one backs up to the beginning of the chapter, the Bible says, "Then came together unto him the Pharisees, and certain of the scribes, which came from Jerusalem. And when they saw some of his disciples eat bread with defiled, that is to say, with unwashen, hands, they found fault. For the Pharisees, and all the Jews, except they wash [their] hands oft, eat not, holding the tradition of the elders. And [when they come] from the market, except they wash, they eat not. And many other things there be, which they have received to hold, [as] the washing of cups, and pots, brasen vessels, and of tables. Then the Pharisees and scribes asked him, Why walk not thy disciples according to the tradition of the elders, but eat bread with unwashen hands? " (Mark 7:1-5) In fact, this same exchange of words is found in the book of Matthew, and watch carefully what Jesus actually says. "Do not ye yet understand, that whatsoever entereth in at the mouth goeth into the belly, and is cast out into the draught? But those things which proceed out of the mouth come forth from the heart; and they defile the man. For out of the heart proceed evil thoughts, murders, adulteries, fornications, thefts, false witness, blasphemies: These are [the things] which defile a man: but to eat with unwashen hands defileth not a man" (Matthew 15:17-20). So no, Jesus was not doing away with clean and unclean animals. He was stripping away the additional traditions that the Pharisees attached.

As proof that this was true, let us address some other twisting that the Antichrist and the "Spirit of Antichrist" enjoy. "On the morrow, as they went on their journey, and drew nigh unto the city, Peter went up upon the housetop to pray about the sixth hour: And he became very hungry, and would have eaten: but while they made ready, he fell into a trance, And saw heaven opened, and a certain vessel descending unto him, as it had been a great sheet knit at the four corners, and let down to the earth: Wherein were all manner of fourfooted beasts of the earth, and wild beasts, and creeping things, and fowls of the air. And there came a voice to him, Rise, Peter; kill, and eat. But Peter said, Not so, Lord; for I have never eaten any thing that is common or unclean. And the voice [spake] unto him again the second time, What God hath cleansed, [that] call not thou common. This was done thrice: and the vessel was received up again into heaven. Now while Peter doubted in himself what this vision which he had seen should mean, behold, the men which were sent from Cornelius had made enquiry for Simon's house, and stood before the gate, And called, and asked whether Simon, which was surnamed Peter, were lodged there. While Peter thought on the vision, the Spirit said unto him, Behold, three men seek thee" (Acts 10:9-19). It is the famous sheet that now commands that everyone can eat any creature!

Taking note that Peter did not eat anything off of the sheet and even stated, "Not so, Lord; for I have never eaten any thing that is common or unclean" (Acts 10:14) proves that back when Jesus was walking the earth physically and rebuking the clean and unclean practice, it was about the ceremonial washing of hands, instruments, and furniture, not the animals themselves, otherwise, Peter would have had pork chops by the time the vision was given.

Now let us address this situation in which true Christians recognize that this is a vision being given. The vision is symbolic. Further, it is not by coincidence that the sheet comes down three times and there are three Gentiles that show up. Gentiles or non-Jews were considered unclean people. And if one would just read the rest of the chapter, the vision in which even Peter doubted of what it meant, knowing it could not have meant to eat unclean animals (Acts 10:17), we get the answer. "And he said unto them, Ye know how that it is an unlawful thing for a man that is a Jew to keep company, or come unto one of another nation; but God hath shewed me that I should not call any man common or unclean" (Acts 10:28). So it has nothing to do with the physical consumption of the forbidden creatures.

With both the popular Jesus miracle, which never happened, and the sheet addressed in the Book of Acts, there is one more verse stretched by the Antichrist and the "Spirit of Antichrist" that would have people believe in the miracle of every prayer over a meal instead of the prayer just being a thankfulness to God. "For every creature of God [is] good, and nothing to be refused, if it be received with thanksgiving" (1 Timothy 4:4). The clarification is found in the next verse. "For it is sanctified by the word of God and prayer" (1 Timothy 4:5). Please note that food is considered holy only by both the Word and prayer, and not just by praying over. Before digging into a bacon cheeseburger, if one prays, the bacon does not all of a sudden get less poisonous. And what does the Word say about foods? Pigs are unclean! Lobster is unclean! Crabs are unclean! And many other delicacies of today are unclean! Therefore, a simple prayer over pork tenderloin does not make it holy to be eaten.

Since Christ wants people in the fittest condition possible to be used of Him to spread the gospel, why is it that so many people listen to the Antichrist or the "Spirit of Antichrist" feasting on these forbidden creatures wondering why they have all kinds of arthritic symptoms, stomach problems, and much of today's cancers? The answer is that they put Antichrist above Jesus Christ even if they do not believe in God. Satan, "the thief cometh not, but for to steal, and to kill, and to destroy", but Jesus said, "I am come that they might have life, and that they might have [it] more abundantly" (John 10:10). Lives are being destroyed mostly by what people eat. They are unable to concentrate on God with all the aches and pains suggested by old age, old injuries, the weather, inheritance, and many other excuses, when in reality, it is the food. They are unable to be focusing upon God as they are distracted from the medications affecting the mind including drowsiness for who can read the Bible when such things put people to sleep? They are unable to be used of God while laid up after surgery and are on restrictions, sometimes for the rest of their lives. There are many ways for Satan to destroy people's lives through the consumption of food, however, Jesus not only offers eternal life but in this life, we can have it more abundantly than the average person, but all of it is not for selfish purposes.

How Does History Repeat Itself?

The Bible says, "Now all these things happened unto them for ensamples: and they are written for our admonition, upon whom the ends of the world are come" (1 Corinthians 10:11). So right off the start, Antichrist and the "Spirit of Antichrist" would not have people study the things written. This is why tradition supersedes the Bible in most denominations. But what examples were written? "Moreover, brethren, I would not that ye should be ignorant, how that all our fathers were under the cloud, and all passed through the sea; And were all baptized unto Moses in the cloud and in the sea; And did all eat the same spiritual meat; And did all drink the same spiritual drink: for they drank of that spiritual Rock that followed them: and that Rock was Christ" (1 Corinthians 10:1-4). The Antichrist and the "Spirit of Antichrist" would have people believe the Old Testament is a dead historical reference and make fun of those that apply the physical happenings into a spiritual application for those living at the end of time. Both of which are wrong.

Seeing Christ was actually that rock that Moses struck for water makes Jesus words take on a whole new meaning, for He had said, "Search the scriptures; for in them ye think ye have eternal life: and they are they which testify of me" (John 5:39). Although there are hundreds of verses in the Old Testament that directly prophesy of Jesus, when He spoke those words, He meant to do serious scripture study to see how it all relates. Sure, the Bible foretells, "Therefore the Lord himself shall give you a sign; Behold, a virgin shall conceive, and bear a son, and shall call his name Immanuel" (Isaiah 7:14), but as we saw, Jesus is also in all that transpired in the Old Testament. In fact, it is safe to say that those who do not spend significant time in the Old Testament will not understand the New Testament and, as Jesus said, it is only through that understanding that we shall have eternal life.

Do realize that many Christians are uncomfortable and even have animosity towards spiritualizing these Bible stories, but as you see so far, that is exactly the intent of the Bible. The Old Testament is not a dead letter. Antichrist and the "Spirit of Antichrist" would have people think that the contents are for background information while the New Testament is where we are today. Interestingly, much of the New Testament is actually an explanation of the Old, and in the form we are about to walk through.

Keep in mind, we do not have time to reveal all references in the Old Testament to Jesus, but we are going to go through some very significant events that parallel not only Jesus, but even paint a picture of end time events.

To start off with, do realize that Adam and Eve lost access to the Tree of Life, which was "in the midst of the garden" (Genesis 2:9), by breaking the Ten Commandments, but "Blessed [are] they that do his commandments, that they may have right to the tree of life, and may enter in through the gates into the city" (Revelation 22:14). So the notion that we can enter Heaven by grace of forgiveness alone is but a falsehood. There is the grace that empowers obedience too.

But let us look at other stories in more detail with Jesus and the backdrop of the second coming in perspective.

How Does Cain and Abel Reveal the Last Days?

Looking at things more as the physical representing the spiritual, we have Cain and Abel. Abel represents those, as in a church or God's people, that live in obedience depending upon the shed blood of the Lamb of God (Genesis 4:4), while Cain claimed to be worshipping the true God but not according to God's ways, but by his own way, or what we call tradition of men today (Genesis 4:5). So we have two groups of Christians today represented by these two people, just as both are known to be having "One Mind". Is that "One Mind" in Christ or Antichrist?

Cain did not live in a repentant mindset but in a celebration thought process by only offering "the fruit of the ground", which is only a thankfulness attitude and not a repentant one, much like today's Christians claiming to be filled with the Spirit through a positive only message and song instead of reflection and deep sorrow for having sinned for it is too uncomfortable at church if people feel guilt of their sins.

Like Cain, there was not a feeling to worry about sinning because, well, he was saved. Realize though that "the LORD set a mark upon Cain" (Genesis 4:15) just as deceived Christians will receive the Mark of the Beast eventually. As Cain persecuted Abel for no other reason but he being righteous, likewise the so called Christians that want to believe we are saved the easy way will get fed up with the constant reminder that "strait [is] the gate, and narrow [is] the way, which leadeth unto life" (Matthew 7:14) and shall "cause that as many as would not worship the image of the beast should be killed" (Revelation 13:15), where the image is forced compliance to the greater good.

How Does Noah Point to the Last Days?

Jesus said, "As it was in the days of Noe, so shall it be also in the days of the Son of man" (Luke 17:26). The truth was in a specific boat or church. No other boat saved people. Although today God has people in all different denominations and not even in denominations, there is but one correct collection of truth that saves and soon there will be global invitation spoken very loudly, "Come out of her, my people, that ye be not partakers of her sins, and that ye receive not of her plagues" (Revelation 18:4), where "her" refers to the false main church along with her daughters.

Just as Noah was the correct preacher of the day despite others who preached against Noah, today the denominations are lining themselves up by loudly speaking against the truth, convincing honest and sincere people not to investigate, to lull people into trusting that they are saved without obedience, without serious study of God's Word, without discipline, without sacrifice. Throwing around terms like "legalist", "Pharisee", "Judadizer", "cult", and other names does not help matters much. But Jesus said, "For there shall arise false Christs, and false prophets, and shall shew great signs and wonders; insomuch that, if [it were] possible, they shall deceive the very elect" (Matthew 24:24), where the very elect know their Bibles, not just aware of popular content.

Just as Noah preached for "an hundred and twenty years" (Genesis 6:3), there should be no surprise that the warning of the imminent return of Christ has been preached almost two hundred years, which is since the Great Awakening of the mid 1800's, especially since "The Lord is not slack concerning his promise, as some men count slackness; but is longsuffering to us-ward, not willing that any should perish, but that all should come to repentance" (2 Peter 3:9).

And just as Noah was told that probation had closed, meaning that the opportunity to respond to the message of salvation had closed, yet destruction was not "For yet seven days" (Genesis 7:4), likewise, the earth's probation before Jesus returns will also close. The message of salvation will cease before the second coming. When the seven last plagues begin, as the Bible writer John saw, "The temple was filled with smoke from the glory of God, and from his power; and no man was able to enter into the temple, till the seven plagues of the seven angels were fulfilled" (Revelation 15:8). Did you catch that? Noah had seven days to wait for the flood while God has seven last plagues. In any case, it is during the sixth plague that Jesus shows up for "Behold, I come as a thief. Blessed [is] he that watcheth, and keepeth his garments, lest he walk naked, and they see his shame" (Revelation 16:15). So the notion that there is a pre-tribulation rapture of the church is but a lie that people will not realize until it is too late. All those people who waited to see what was going to happen during those seven days realized the reality of things too late.

Instead of being protected in a boat, God's people will be kept away in the mountains (Matthew 24:16-20). And please take note that Noah was still left on the earth during the flood. Although protected in the ark, nevertheless, he was still on the earth. The equality of being in the boat is not symbolic of protection through a secret rapture but is where God's people will be: in the mountains (Matthew 24:16). And we know that being left behind is better than being taken because it was the rest of the people that are described as "For as in the days that were before the flood they were eating and drinking, marrying and giving in marriage, until the day that Noe entered into the ark, And knew not until the flood came, and took them all away" (Matthew 24:38-39). The ones taken are those outside of the ark. The ones left behind are those in the ark. This is just as Jesus describes. "The Son of man shall send forth his angels, and they shall gather out of his kingdom all things that offend, and them which do iniquity; And shall cast them into a furnace of fire: there shall be wailing and gnashing of teeth. Then shall the righteous shine forth as the sun in the kingdom of their Father. Who hath ears to hear, let him hear" (Matthew 13:41-43). Notice the sequence. The lost are gathered first or taken away and the left behind are the righteous.

There are probably many more parallels with Noah but this do know that when it was all over, it was Noah who stepped upon a cleansed earth. It was cleansed by water, but the next time a righteous person steps on a clean earth, it will be by fire. "Looking for and hasting unto the coming of the day of God, wherein the heavens being on fire shall be dissolved, and the elements shall melt with fervent heat? Nevertheless we, according to his promise, look for new heavens and a new earth, wherein dwelleth righteousness" (2 Peter 3:12-13).

How Does What Happened At the Tower of Babel Apply To the Last Days?

Looking briefly at the tower of Babel, we see deeper into the fact that God said that He would not destroy the entire world by a flood again (Genesis 9:11-17) but the people did not take God at His Word and said, "Go to, let us build us a city and a tower, whose top [may reach] unto heaven; and let us make us a name, lest we be scattered abroad upon the face of the whole earth" (Genesis 11:4). Interestingly, "The whole earth was of one language, and of one speech", much like English and even the Internet automatic translators are helping to bring it back to one again.

On top of that, in the day of Babel "the people [is] one, and they have all one language" (Genesis 11:6), just as the world seems to be unifying on some very serious issues in which just since the 1960's great progress has been made to become one in more than language. Unheard of before but today it seems we all serve the same god, well, it is not the true God though. But to bring in non-believers into this global final scene, there is something grander. It has multiple names but encompassing every nation, even those that fight against each other, is this thing called Global Warming, Climate Change, or whatever other name they want to use. Under this supposed concern, global regulations are being developed, penalties instituted for non-compliance, individual rights being trampled upon, and much more. And the moral spokes person that is now leading the charge is none other than the pope.

How Does Abraham Reveal the Last Days?

Now with Abraham, there are so many parallels that one could write a book on Abraham alone. The most famous story is where humans are represented by Isaac while Abraham is playing the role of God the Father, in which death is the only payment for sin. The substitute sacrifice of the animal caught in the bush was truly the sacrifice of Jesus for us humans.

But beyond that for our sake today, we have Abraham, known as Abram at the time, being called to a separated life from the world he knew to go to a land that was promised. We too are called, "Come out from among them, and be ye separate, saith the Lord" (2 Corinthians 6:17) and not only to be separate from the world creating a distinction between Christian and non-Christian, but "Come out of her, my people, that ye be not partakers of her sins, and that ye receive not of her plagues" (Revelation 18:4) in which we leave the false doctrines of "Antichrist" and the "Spirit of Antichrist" joining God's church, "which keep the commandments of God, and have the testimony of Jesus Christ" (Revelation 12:17).

How Does Lot Parallel With the Last Days?

Skipping ahead, Jesus said, "Likewise also as it was in the days of Lot; they did eat, they drank, they bought, they sold, they planted, they builded; But the same day that Lot went out of Sodom it rained fire and brimstone from heaven, and destroyed [them] all. Even thus shall it be in the day when the Son of man is revealed"

(Luke 17:28-30). Here, we see many parallels to spiritual applications. First, we have Lot. God was not to "take them out of the world, but that thou shouldest keep them from the evil" (John 17:15), however, instead of remaining separate, by simply having "pitched [his] tent toward Sodom" (Genesis 13:12), he ended up in the city or world. Basically, as the church tries to fit in with the world, it can only spell disaster for the church family. Today, Christian pretty much are very worldly, despite the Bible saying, "Love not the world, neither the things [that are] in the world. If any man love the world, the love of the Father is not in him" (1 John 2:15).

The second parallel drawn is the immorality that was practiced. "Sodom and Gomorrha, and the cities about them in like manner, giving themselves over to fornication, and going after strange flesh" (Jude 1:7). The primary sin of Sodom and Gomorrah was mostly sex related, and being oversexed, even strange flesh, as defined by Romans chapter 1 is none other than "men, leaving the natural use of the woman, burned in their lust one toward another; men with men working that which is unseemly" (Romans 1:27). It is not by coincidence that we live in a day and age that sex is so flaunted in the face of God than ever before, and homosexuality is very much out of the closet.

The third parallel is the use of messengers before the destruction. Originally, "three men" (Genesis 18:2), which were heavenly messengers, were on their way to Sodom. The one, being God, stayed with Abraham while the other two proceeded onward (Genesis 18:22). It is not by coincidence that before God destroys this planet at the second coming, three angels are sent as messengers (Revelation 14:6, 8, 9). There is a principle that God binds Himself by in which, "the Lord GOD will do nothing, but he revealeth his secret unto his servants the prophets" (Amos 3:7). That is because "The Lord is not slack concerning his promise, as some men count slackness; but is longsuffering to us-ward, not willing that any should perish, but that all should come to repentance" (2 Peter 3:9).

The fourth parallel is represented by the woman, Lot's wife. Even Jesus said, "Remember Lot's wife" (Luke 17:32). As a woman represents a church, we see the reason why Antichrist refuses to become more biblical in doctrines. We also see why the "Spirit of Antichrist" is so much into downgrading sin and the Ten Commandments. The heart is still in the world. The notion of removing the world from the heart of people is so foreign. Tell a Christian that television, movies, unclean foods, much of today's clothing styles, a lot of today's music are all to be discarded, along with needing to pay tithe, share the gospel, study the Bible on a daily basis, and more are all things to do, and hardly a person would want to sign up. That is because they love the world.

The fifth parallel is where Lot and his daughters were to flee to. "Escape to the mountain, lest thou be consumed" (Genesis 19:17). Not by coincidence, Jesus speaking about end time events said, "Then let them which be in Judaea flee into the mountains" (Matthew 24:16).

The sixth parallel is quoted from Jude, in which it is written, "Sodom and Gomorrha, and the cities about them in like manner, giving themselves over to fornication, and going after strange flesh, are set forth for an example, suffering the vengeance of eternal fire" (Jude 1:7). Is Sodom and Gomorrah still burning? No. Is God ever going to change His mind about Sodom and Gomorrah by restoring those cities and the original inhabitants? No, never. Eternally will God ever change His mind? No. Therefore, hell is not a place of burning now, as Sodom is set as an example to be executed later. And hell will not burn throughout eternity either. Jesus clearly taught that, "So shall it be at the end of the world: the angels shall come forth, and sever the wicked from among the just, And shall cast them into the furnace of fire: there shall be wailing and gnashing of teeth" (Matthew 13:49-50). And in that day it will be said, "Fire came down from God out of heaven, and devoured them" (Revelation 20:9), "And ye shall tread down the wicked; for they shall be ashes under the soles of your feet in the day that I shall do [this], saith the LORD of hosts" (Malachi 4:3). There is no purpose for hell to burn throughout eternity but the fire that is known as hell fire will be eternal. There will be no undoing it. It shall stand forever.

How Do the Events of the Exodus Prepare Us for the Last Days?

Skipping even further in the series of examples is the most serious of parallels, the Exodus. We start with the fact that Pharaoh said, "Who [is] the LORD, that I should obey his voice?" (Exodus 5:2) This is symbolically uttered by atheists today who question the existence of God, but is also applicable to all Christians who symbolically say, "Who is this Lord that commands obedience to His Bible and those Ten Commandments?" And both of these sentiments are very much strongly influencing Christians into merging evolution and creation along with having people live without regards to obedience.

The specific message that was being spoken was the command to rest (Exodus 5:5). It is not by coincidence, as predicted, God will send a generation of people with the same message. "Thou shalt raise up the foundations of many generations; and thou shalt be called, The repairer of the breach, The restorer of paths to dwell in. If thou turn away thy foot from the sabbath, [from] doing thy pleasure on my holy day; and call the sabbath a delight, the holy of the LORD, honourable; and shalt honour him, not doing thine own ways, nor finding thine own pleasure, nor speaking [thine own] words: Then shalt thou delight thyself in the LORD; and I will cause thee to ride upon the high places of the earth, and feed thee with the heritage of Jacob thy father: for the mouth of the LORD hath spoken [it]" (Isaiah 58:12-14). In fact, it is one of the last day messages symbolized by, an "angel fly in the midst of heaven, having the everlasting gospel to preach unto them that dwell on the earth, and to every nation, and kindred, and tongue, and people, Saying with a loud voice, Fear God, and give glory to him; for the hour of his judgment is come: and worship him that made heaven, and earth, and the sea, and the fountains of waters" (Revelation 14:6-7). Tracing the words "made heaven, and earth, and the sea", one ends up on the fourth commandment, which says, "Remember the sabbath day, to keep it holy. Six days shalt thou labour, and do all thy work: But the seventh day [is] the sabbath of the LORD thy God: [in it] thou shalt not do any work, thou, nor thy son, nor thy daughter, thy manservant, nor thy maidservant, nor thy cattle, nor thy stranger that [is] within thy gates: For [in] six days the LORD made heaven and earth, the sea, and all that in them [is], and rested the seventh day: wherefore the LORD blessed the sabbath day, and hallowed it" (Exodus 20:8-11).

As a result of a call to rest, Pharaoh commanded, "Let there more work be laid upon the men, that they may labour therein; and let them not regard vain words" (Exodus 5:9). It was an attempt to make sure there was no time left to keep such an observance. Likewise, those in the last days who choose to "keep the commandments of God, and the faith of Jesus" (Revelation 14:12), including the Sabbath rest, will be forced, coerced, and even threatened with death to go against such and to keep the pagan day instead because there will be a "one mind" movement to "cause that as many as would not worship the image of the beast should be killed" (Revelation 13:15).

Now when one goes up against Christ, they lose, but people are so stubborn. God's next step was, "I will at this time send all my plagues upon thine heart, and upon thy servants, and upon thy people; that thou mayest know that [there is] none like me in all the earth" (Exodus 9:14). And so it was that ten plagues fell and all the while "the heart of Pharaoh was hardened, neither would he let the children of Israel go" (Exodus 9:35). Likewise, at the end of time, God will send "seven angels having the seven last plagues; for in them is filled up the wrath of God" (Revelation 15:1). Interestingly, during the outpouring of the plagues in Egypt, eventually the plagues were no longer affecting the people of Israel. "I will sever in that day the land of Goshen, in which my people dwell, that no swarms [of flies] shall be there" (Exodus 8:22). In the beginning, the Israelites were being corrected for their rebellion towards God through the mistrust in Moses. In the end though, there is going to be a difference set between those in the group with the wrong "one mind" as opposed to those having Christ's "one mind". "And the first went, and poured out his vial upon the earth; and there fell a noisome and grievous sore upon the men which had the mark of the beast, and [upon] them which worshipped his image" (Revelation 16:2). Those that have the Seal of God will not receive the plagues. But do notice that during the plagues, like Pharaoh, when "the fourth angel poured out his vial upon the sun; and power was given unto him to scorch men with fire. And men were scorched with great heat, and blasphemed the name of God, which hath power over these plagues: and they repented not to give him glory" (Revelation 16:8-9). "And blasphemed the God of heaven because of their pains and their sores, and repented not of their deeds" (Revelation 16:11). That is some serious stubbornness.

Finally, just as Israel was present during the tribulation of their time and during the plagues, they were delivered when it was over. Actually, it was during the seriously but deadly plague that they were delivered for Pharaoh "called for Moses and Aaron by night, and said, Rise up, [and] get you forth from among my people, both ye and the children of Israel; and go, serve the LORD, as ye have said" (Exodus 12:31). Likewise, there is no pre-tribulation, but there is God's protection through the final events. And right before the deadliest of all plagues is poured out, the second coming event occurs. "Behold, I come as a thief. Blessed [is] he that watcheth, and keepeth his garments, lest he walk naked, and they see his shame. And he gathered them together into a place called in the Hebrew tongue Armageddon" (Revelation 16:15-16). Why is it not during the deadliest plague? The last plague states, "And every island fled away, and the mountains were not found" (Revelation 16:20). It will be very difficult to still be on islands and in the mountains waiting upon Jesus to show up during that time.

Now let us pause for a moment and seriously see the flaw that the Jesuit Ribera of the papacy proposed and much of the Protestant world accepts. How many times have we heard that that Antichrist will mass together armies in a valley called Megiddo? That is a large part of the false theory about a future Antichrist. Please look at those verses in Revelation 16 again. The Bible says, "Behold, I come as a thief. Blessed [is] he that watcheth, and keepeth his garments, lest he walk naked, and they see his shame. And he gathered them together into a place called in the Hebrew tongue Armageddon" (Revelation 16:15-16). The question is, who does the gathering? It says, "He gathered them". So who is the "He". Well, in the context, it appears to be the one that says, "I come as a thief". Who is coming as a thief? "Watch therefore: for ye know not what hour your Lord doth come. But know this, that if the goodman of the house had known in what watch the thief would come, he would have watched, and would not have suffered his house to be broken up. Therefore be ye also ready: for in such an hour as ye think not the Son of man cometh" (Matthew 24:42-44). It is Jesus. So Jesus is the one that gathers the people of God, the saved, and not the Antichrist. This is a major, major flaw in believing in the future Antichrist. Besides, the word "Armageddon" does not refer to the valley that these false teachers would have one believe. Please note that the word "Armageddon" is written in Greek because that is what the New Testament was written in, but John specifically states that we need to look it up in the Hebrew tongue. Even *Wikipedia* defines Armageddon as meaning the word "mount". Not by coincidence, there is a bigger battle than a little area on earth call Megiddo, and it is bigger than all of the armies of the world. It is the battle to see who shall rule all beings in the universe. Satan says, "I will ascend into heaven, I will exalt my throne above the stars of God: I will sit also upon the mount of the congregation, in the sides of the north: I will ascend above the heights of the clouds; I will be like the most High" (Isaiah 14:13-14). Did you catch it? Armageddon is not about the valley of Megiddo but Jesus is going to gather His people into the "mount of congregation", which in Hebrew, is God's appointed place. Basically, it is Heaven. And by doing so, Jesus declares He is the victor, and to Satan, He "shalt be brought down to hell, to the sides of the pit" (Isaiah 14:15). This even fits the overall plan, for Jesus said, "I go and prepare a place for you, I will come again, and receive you unto myself; that where I am, [there] ye may be also" (John 14:3). And "the Lord himself shall descend from heaven with a shout, with the voice of the archangel, and with the trump of God: and the dead in Christ shall rise first: Then we which are alive [and] remain shall be caught up together with them in the clouds, to meet the Lord in the air: and so shall we ever be with the Lord" (1 Thessalonians 4:16-17).

Now if everything would have gone as planned, the final piece would have been a perfect example of end time events. From the call to keep a time of rest, to the persecution of God's people, to the seven last plagues, to the deliverance, to the entrance into the Promised Land. As many of God's examples of events to be fulfilled spiritually, humans have messed it up. But Joshua and Caleb had it right. "Caleb stilled the people before Moses, and said, Let us go up at once, and possess it; for we are well able to overcome it" (Numbers 13:30). God was to drive out all of the inhabitants and give the Israelites the Promised Land. Now one may say, "Wait! There's no enemies in Heaven to remove first. This doesn't match the possession of the Promised Land." Oh, but it does.

Heaven is not our Promised Land; the earth is. "His seed shall inherit the earth" (Psalms 25:13). "Those that wait upon the LORD, they shall inherit the earth" (Psalms 37:9). "The meek shall inherit the earth" (Psalms 37:11). "For [such as be] blessed of him shall inherit the earth" (Psalms 37:22). "Blessed [are] the meek: for they shall inherit the earth" (Matthew 5:5). But we cannot just inherit the earth. When Jesus shows up and takes to Heaven those that have been sleeping in Christ and those that are alive at the time of the event (1 Thessalonians 4:16-17), that leaves those that are sleeping without Christ still in the graves and the lost at the time of the second coming crying out, "Mountains and rocks, Fall on us, and hide us from the face of him that sitteth on the throne, and from the wrath of the Lamb" (Revelation 6:16). "And then shall that Wicked be revealed, whom the Lord shall consume with the spirit of his mouth, and shall destroy with the brightness of his coming" (2 Thessalonians 2:8). Basically, "the rest of the dead lived not again until the thousand years were finished" (Revelation 20:5). After the thousand years of the saints being in Heaven experiencing the time "that the saints shall judge the world" (1 Corinthians 6:2) and "that we shall judge angels" (1 Corinthians 6:3), a relocation from Heaven back to this earth as our final promised destination then occurs for "John saw the holy city, new Jerusalem, coming down from God out of heaven, prepared as a bride adorned for her husband" (Revelation 21:2). But while that is happening, "they that have done evil, unto the resurrection of damnation" come alive (John 5:29). "They went up on the breadth of the earth, and compassed the camp of the saints about, and the beloved city" (Revelation 20:9). They are our enemies in the Promised Land. And as God promised the Israelites that He would drive out the enemies if they just had faith in Him, so likewise, "fire came down from God out of heaven, and devoured them" (Revelation 20:9). "Their flesh shall consume away while they stand upon their feet, and their eyes shall consume away in their holes, and their tongue shall consume away in their mouth" (Zechariah 14:12). And it "shall burn as an oven; and all the proud, yea, and all that do wickedly, shall be stubble: and the day that cometh shall burn them up, saith the LORD of hosts, that it shall leave them neither root nor branch" (Malachi 4:1). We then begin eternity with Heaven relocated upon earth. "And they shall build houses, and inhabit [them]; and they shall plant vineyards, and eat the fruit of them" (Isaiah 65:21).

Now many experiences of the Israelites in the desert continue to set examples for those living in the last days. Of those experiences, one is specifically identified to be avoided. The reason we are spiritualizing these stories is because Paul said to, but couched in his reference is a specific item to at least consider. Here is the full passage from Paul: "Moreover, brethren, I would not that ye should be ignorant, how that all our fathers were under the cloud, and all passed through the sea; And were all baptized unto Moses in the cloud and in the sea; And did all eat the same spiritual meat; And did all drink the same spiritual drink: for they drank of that spiritual Rock that followed them: and that Rock was Christ. But with many of them God was not well pleased: for they were overthrown in the wilderness. Now these things were our examples, to the intent we should not lust after evil things, as they also lusted. Neither be ye idolaters, as [were] some of them; as it is written, The people sat down to eat and drink, and rose up to play. Neither let us commit fornication, as some of them committed, and fell in one day three and twenty thousand. Neither let us tempt Christ, as some of them also tempted, and were destroyed of serpents. Neither murmur ye, as some of them also murmured, and were destroyed of the destroyer. Now all these things happened unto them for ensamples: and they are written for our admonition, upon whom the ends of the world are come" (1 Corinthians 10:1-11). There are many things that are listed in those verses, and we think of all the experiences in the desert beyond the list given, why did Paul pick these specific items? By the inspiration of God, Could Paul have seen through a vision our day and what we would struggle with that matched those of the Israelites? And if we think everything is acceptable to God when it is not, would not God have the same reaction? "But with many of them God was not well pleased: for they were overthrown in the wilderness" (1 Corinthians 10:5).

What did they do that God slaughtered them in the desert? They all claimed to be God's people, in fact, Jude also makes reference to these things. "I will therefore put you in remembrance, though ye once knew this, how that the Lord, having saved the people out of the land of Egypt, afterward destroyed them that believed not" (Jude 1:5). It was not simply that they did not believe God existed. It did not take much faith to believe "the LORD went before them by day in a pillar of a cloud, to lead them the way; and by night in a pillar of fire, to give them light; to go by day and night" (Exodus 13:21). Therefore, believe must be their actions based upon what they think. As a reminder, we too understand and accept that all we have to do is "Believe on the Lord Jesus Christ, and thou shalt be saved" (Acts 16:31), but that belief comes with action. If I believe the building I am in is on fire because someone warned me, my action of leaving the building shows the belief. Likewise, if I believe on the Lord Jesus Christ, my belief compels me to live in obedience to His Ten Commandments and the Word of God, just as Revelation 12:17 tells us, for such people "keep the commandments of God, and have the testimony of Jesus Christ."

One particular reference of unbelief even while believing on God is described in the Book of Hebrews. Regarding the Sabbath discussion and comparing the fact that the Sabbath still exists while pointing out how the Israelites reacted, it is said, "Seeing therefore it remaineth that some must enter therein, and they to whom it was first preached entered not in because of unbelief" (Hebrews 4:6). No doubt that this describes the event that angered God. God just got done saying, "Six days ye shall gather it; but on the seventh day, [which is] the sabbath, in it there shall be none" (Exodus 16:26), yet "it came to pass, [that] there went out [some] of the people on the seventh day for to gather, and they found none" (Exodus 16:27), so "the LORD said unto Moses, How long refuse ye to keep my commandments and my laws?" (Exodus 16:28) So again, just because we believe we are saved does not make it so. If we are doing things against what God stands for, we can believe all we want in His existence but "in works they deny [him], being abominable, and disobedient, and unto every good work reprobate" (Titus 1:16).

Therefore, let us realize that what we are about to study is not a list of things to do to be saved, but understand that these are a list of things that need addressed once we receive the gift of eternal life for we still have the free will to throw it away.

Take the Ten Commandments for instance. A lot of people think the Israelites tried to keep them to be saved. That is not so. The Ten Commandments actually begin with "I [am] the LORD thy God, which have brought thee out of the land of Egypt, out of the house of bondage" (Exodus 20:2). God saved them and then He expected them to keep the commandments, not the other way around.

So, the first item on the list is in 1 Corinthians 10:6, which says, "Now these things were our examples, to the intent we should not lust after evil things, as they also lusted." Now according to Isaiah 28:9-10, we ought to do a Bible study and look in the books of Exodus, Leviticus, Numbers, and Deuteronomy for specific verses containing the word "lust" or a form thereof to find out if it is a generic reference about all different types of things or was there a specific thing they lusted for that we ought not to lust for either lest we face the same consequence. This time the consequence would be hell instead of dying in the desert. Now we limit our search to the desert because that is where Paul directed us to, however, reading it elsewhere in other Books in which make reference to the desert experience, such as here in Corinthians, ought to also be considered. Just the generic reference of "lust of the flesh, and the lust of the eyes" (1 John 2:16) is not to be considered for it does not apply to the desert experience specifically. So with that in mind, let us see what we find. And remember, in those books, we are looking at it from the perspective of the Israelites.

And right away we come across the verse that says, "And the mixt multitude that [was] among them fell a lusting: and the children of Israel also wept again, and said, Who shall give us flesh to eat?" (Numbers 11:4) So eating flesh is what they lusted after. Do keep in mind, we have the mixed multitude, who were Egyptians, probably encouraging the lusting. Being formally pagan, this may be a reference to animals with blood as well as the forbidden list, as discussed earlier, like pigs and shell fish. So we move on in our search to see if there is something more specific, and there is. "And he called the name of that place Kibrothhattaavah: because there they buried the people that lusted" (Numbers 11:34). In fact, this matches the experience from the reference in Corinthians. The Israelites were overthrown or died in the wilderness for their lusting.

So the next logical step is to back up through the verses and read the specifics, but one should also notice that it is the same chapter that the original mix multitude verse was in. Now in the verse about the lusting after flesh, the next verse says, "We remember the fish, which we did eat in Egypt freely." So fish is one of those flesh items, but wait! Is not fish, especially with fins and scales, clean or eatable? Yes it is, yet God is not well pleased with them for wanting fish. Well, let us read on. "But now our soul [is] dried away: [there is] nothing at all, beside this manna, [before] our eyes" (Numbers 11:6). From this verse it looks like all that the Israelites had to eat was manna. There was manna bread, manna soup, manna slices, manna cereal, manna this, manna that. What we have is that God was trying to bring them back to the original diet of "every herb bearing seed, which [is] upon the face of all the earth, and every tree, in the which [is] the fruit of a tree yielding seed; to you it shall be for meat" (Genesis 1:29). In other words, God was trying to make the Israelites Vegetarians, even Vegans in the desert, which they would have none of it. In fact, that same spirit is among many humans today. Mention being Vegetarian and people get all crazy. "Got to have protein!" "Got to have meat for health!" That is interesting. Daniel and his friends chose "pulse to eat, and water to drink" (Daniel 1:12) all the days of captivity and "their countenances appeared fairer and fatter in flesh than all the children which did eat the portion of the king's meat" (Daniel 1:15). In fact, they were found "ten times better than all the magicians [and] astrologers that [were] in all his realm" (Daniel 1:20). So do not tell Daniel, if you could, that a Vegetarian diet is unhealthy.

But continuing on with the Israelites being overthrown in the desert, we see that they were relentless. Moses even talked to God about the matter. "Whence should I have flesh to give unto all this people? for they weep unto me, saying, Give us flesh, that we may eat" (Numbers 11:13). God's response is basically, paraphrasing, "You want to eat meat? I will give so much, you won't be able to handle it." In actual words, He said that He would give "a whole month, until it come out at your nostrils" (Numbers 11:20). "And there went forth a wind from the LORD, and brought quails from the sea, and let [them] fall by the camp, as it were a day's journey on this side, and as it were a day's journey on the other side, round about the camp, and as it were two cubits [high] upon the face of the earth. And the people stood up all that day, and all [that] night, and all the next day, and they gathered the quails: he that gathered least gathered ten homers: and they spread [them] all abroad for themselves round about the camp. And while the flesh [was] yet between their teeth, ere it was chewed, the wrath of the LORD was kindled against the people, and the LORD smote the people with a very great plague. And he called the name of that place Kibrothhattaavah: because there they buried the people that lusted" (Numbers 11:31-34). Quails, can you believe it? Quails, which are clean or eatable birds.

That means that these people died, not because they craved pork chops, pork tender loin, lobsters, crabs, but just flesh. They rejected the Vegetarian diet. And what does God say about the last days? "Now all these things happened unto them for ensamples: and they are written for our admonition, upon whom the ends of the world are come" (1 Corinthians 10:11). Now the reason for such a drastic call in the last days is because of what example Daniel was. When it comes to understanding scripture, there is no doubt that Vegetarians are a people who can see the scriptures clearer than non-Vegetarians, especially those that are continuing to eat meat with blood in it still, which is forbidden not only from the Old Testament but the New as well (Acts 15:20, 15:29, 21:25). Vegetarians, in general, are not taking as many medications, which affects the mind, to deal with all the self inflicted diseases and cancers through meat eating. Please note that this is in general. Sure Vegetarians can contract these health issues, but non-bias research reveals that Vegetarians live longer, have less health problems, and even retain their thought processes longer as opposed to those consuming meat.

Now that is just the lust item that Paul referenced. The next item is described in 1 Corinthians 10:7, which says, "Neither be ye idolaters, as [were] some of them; as it is written, The people sat down to eat and drink, and rose up to play." Tracing this is easy. Just look up the words "rose up to play" and one finds themselves in the context where "Aaron said unto them, Break off the golden earrings, which [are] in the ears of your wives, of your sons, and of your daughters, and bring [them] unto me. And all the people brake off the golden earrings which [were] in their ears, and brought [them] unto Aaron. And he received [them] at their hand, and fashioned it with a graving tool, after he had made it a molten calf: and they said, These [be] thy gods, O Israel, which brought thee up out of the land of Egypt. And when Aaron saw [it], he built an altar before it; and Aaron made proclamation, and said, To morrow [is] a feast to the LORD. And they rose up early on the morrow, and offered burnt offerings, and brought peace offerings; and the people sat down to eat and to drink, and rose up to play" (Exodus 32:2-6).

So none of us probably would build our own idol and call it God and worship it, however, the gold that was used to make the calf was in the form of jewelry. Although, God commanded, "Speak now in the ears of the people, and let every man borrow of his neighbour, and every woman of her neighbour, jewels of silver, and jewels of gold" (Exodus 11:2), it was not a means to flatter oneself. It was meant to be used as payment for their slave years, as well as to be used in a future use, like lining the sanctuary and making sanctuary vessels with melted down gold, even the silver (Exodus 35). Nowhere in Exodus 11 or 12 does it state that God commanded the Israelites to put it on. They were to collect it. So at some point, self gratification took over and by the time the golden calf incident happened, they had put it on. Even if putting it on was what they did, they should have put it on for the simplest mode of carrying it out of Egypt since crates of the stuff would have been very weighty, but then again, to travel with so much around one's neck and hanging from their ears and writs would have been uncomfortable also.

Therefore, this warrants another mini study. What does God think of jewelry? Going directly to God's attitude towards jewelry, we read in Genesis 35:1-2, "And God said unto Jacob, Arise, go up to Bethel, and dwell there: and make there an altar unto God, that appeared unto thee when thou fleddest from the face of Esau thy brother. Then Jacob said unto his household, and to all that [were] with him, Put away the strange gods that [are] among you, and be clean, and change your garments." Jacob was going to make an atonement for sin, but God would not accept His service until these strange gods were removed. Were these people worshipping a different gods? What were these strange gods that are to be put away? Genesis 35:3 4 answers it. "And let us arise, and go up to Bethel; and I will make there an altar unto God, who answered me in the day of my distress, and was with me in the way which I went. And they gave unto Jacob all the strange gods which [were] in their hand, and [all their] earrings which [were] in their ears; and Jacob hid them under the oak which [was] by Shechem." God considers rings and bracelets in people's hands and earrings as strange gods, and God commands "Thou shalt have no other gods before me" (Exodus 20:3). Now that word "before" does not mean order either; it means in addition to.

Now some people reason that because we are going to receive a crown, which is jewelry, that God is not so displeased with ornamentation, but let us look closer at that reference. Revelation 4:9-11 says, "And when those beasts give glory and honour and thanks to him that sat on the throne, who liveth for ever and ever, The four and twenty elders fall down before him that sat on the throne, and worship him that liveth for ever and ever, and cast their crowns before the throne, saying, Thou art worthy, O Lord, to receive glory and honour and power: for thou hast created all things, and for thy pleasure they are and were created." Note that these cannot stand wearing the crown in the physical presence of God and cast it off. If they cannot stand jewelry that God placed on their heads, do you think we should take pleasure in decorating ourselves now?

Let us examine a few more verses. Exodus 33:4-6 says, "And when the people heard these evil tidings, they mourned: and no man did put on him his ornaments. For the LORD had said unto Moses, Say unto the children of Israel, Ye [are] a stiffnecked people: I will come up into the midst of thee in a moment, and consume thee: therefore now put off thy ornaments from thee, that I may know what to do unto thee. And the children of Israel stripped themselves of their ornaments by the mount Horeb." Here, God's people are about to enter the Promise Land and they were wearing the ornaments. This displeased God greatly, and He referred to them as "stiffnecked people." We are about to enter the heavenly Promised Land and therefore should we not also remove the jewelry. This further confirms that the original command to take the jewelry from the Egyptians before leaving Egypt was not for the purpose of selfish adorning. It was simply to be taken.

Besides, what is jewelry associated with? Hosea 2:13 says, "And I will visit upon her the days of Baalim, wherein she burned incense to them, and she decked herself with her earrings and her jewels, and she went after her lovers, and forgat me, saith the LORD." Jewelry is associated with idol worship throughout the Bible. Why? Because the purpose of it draws people to the outward appearance of the body instead of the inner, and it appeals to the selfish tendencies we all have. When we allow such prideful acts to occur in our lives, we begin to forget God of whom should receive all the glory.

While we are on the subject of outward appearance, let us read 1 Timothy 2:9-10, in which it says, "In like manner also, that women adorn themselves in modest apparel, with shamefacedness and sobriety; not with broided hair, or gold, or pearls, or costly array; But (which becometh women professing godliness) with good works." What is meant by "Modest apparel"? Well, according to Webster's New World Dictionary: Clothing, garments, attire; to clothe, dress. So why do many businesswomen wear short, short skirts, when they are forever pulling down on the skirt? They must know too much is being revealed, right? And, how about men at the pools and beaches in those near nothing swim suits? You think God is pleased with this? Or how about a Christian that is not kept? And while we are on this subject, do you think there should be a difference in clothing for specific occasions? Would you wear gardening clothes to a wedding? Would you wear pool clothing to a funeral? Then, should we wear everyday clothes to church? It is true that God looks upon the heart, but does that mean God is pleased when we put no difference between the clean and the unclean, the common and the uncommon regarding His church service. The manner of dress directly shows the respect we have for God and His Sabbath. Now there is a balance here. God does not expect people to spend an unaffordable amount on church clothing, but all of that is a side note to the topic in which we are directly commanded to not be putting on gold, pearls, or any costly appearance, even if it is not all that costly and only appears that way.

And while we are also on the subject of clothing for a moment, God wants no confusion between genders? Deuteronomy 22:5 says, "The woman shall not wear that which pertaineth unto a man, neither shall a man put on a woman's garment: for all that do so [are] abomination unto the LORD thy God." There is to be a distinctive difference between men and women clothing, but today there is a great push for couples to dress as if they were twins, dress in a manner that leaves people wondering if that is a guy or a girl, and much more, all of which is wrong.

In addition to the clothing topic and jewelry, 1 Timothy 2:9-10, also refers to "shamefacedness." What does this refer to? Plainly speaking, it is makeup. God made all women beautiful. Covering the face with makeup is saying to God, "Thanks God, but let me fix your flaws."

Also notice what type of people makeup is associated with in the Bible. 2 Kings 9:30 says, "And when Jehu was come to Jezreel, Jezebel heard [of it]; and she painted her face, and tired her head, and looked out at a window." This is where we get the phrase, "That girl looks like a little Jezebel."

In addition to the New Testament reference of 1 Timothy 2:9-10 referring to jewelry, 1 Peter 3:3-4 also says, "Whose adorning let it not be that outward [adorning] of plaiting the hair, and of wearing of gold, or of putting on of apparel; But [let it be] the hidden man of the heart, in that which is not corruptible, [even the ornament] of a meek and quiet spirit, which is in the sight of God of great price." Adornment should not be on the outside, rather it is to be on the inside, in other words, Satan's counterfeit has been revealed. You see, the devil has it all mixed up. He has people thinking that outside decorations is what makes the person when in fact it is what is on the inside that counts. God made us in His image. Can any of us improve on that?

Basically, what is happening is that all through history, the majority of people were practical people. They did not spend on dime on anything needless. Now in the past century and a half, equivalent to when God declared the end of time period was, the devil has made it easier and easier to get money and in turn has made it easier and easier to believe that a waste here and a waste there is no big deal. And if we are going to waste it, why not make our bodies attractive, attention getting? In short, the devil is buying everyone's souls by rewarding them with jewelry, dress, and simply flaunting of the body. Up through the 1800's both men and women were very modest. Over time, the closer we get to the present time, less and less skin is covered and more and more is being revealed. Pretty soon we will all be attending office meetings, going to school, buying groceries completely naked. Clothing will be optional if time lasts much longer.

And do not take my word for it. All of this was preached in the churches even up through a few decades ago pointing to the fact that God did not change, people did. "I exhort you to wear no gold, no pearls, or precious stones. I do not advise women to wear rings, earrings, or necklaces. It is true that these things are little, very little things, therefore they are not worth defending. Therefore give them up, let 'em drop, throw them away without another word else a little needle may cause much pain in the flesh, a little self indulgence much hurt to your soul. Alas, to what a fearful extent is that friendship of the world that is enmity with God, now cherished among the professed followers of Christ! How widely have the popular churches throughout Christendom departed from the Bible standard of humility, self-denial, simplicity, and godliness. Do not waste any part of so precious a talent, merely in gratifying the desire of the eye, by superfluous or expensive apparel, or by needless ornaments. Waste no part of it in curiously adorning your houses; in superfluous or expensive furniture; in costly pictures, painting, gilding.... Lay out nothing to gratify the pride of life, to gain the admiration of praise of men.... 'So long as thou doest well unto thyself, men will speak good of thee.' So long as thou are 'clothed in purple and fine linen,' and farest 'sumptuously every day,' no doubt many will applaud thy elegance of taste, thy generosity and hospitality. But do not buy their applause so dear. Rather be content with the honor that cometh from God." - John Wesley, Works, Sermon 50, The Use of Money.

Also notice how the two classes of people are dressed. One group is lost while the other is saved. Revelation 17:3-5 says, "So he carried me away in the spirit into the wilderness: and I saw a woman sit upon a scarlet coloured beast, full of names of blasphemy, having seven heads and ten horns. And the woman was arrayed in purple and scarlet colour, and decked with gold and precious stones and pearls, having a golden cup in her hand full of abominations and filthiness of her fornication: And upon her forehead [was] a name written, MYSTERY, BABYLON THE GREAT, THE MOTHER OF HARLOTS AND ABOMINATIONS OF THE EARTH." The corrupt, fallen system is the one that is decked out in precious jewels. Now notice the saved group, where Revelation 12:1-2 says, "And there appeared a great wonder in heaven; a woman clothed with the sun, and the moon under her feet, and upon her head a crown of twelve stars: And she being with child cried, travailing in birth, and pained to be delivered." God's people are represented by pure natural beauty and not wearing jewelry, makeup, or immodest clothing. Which group do you want to be associated with?

But how about wearing of the Christian cross? Again, what makes a Christian according to the Bible? That which is one inwardly. Besides, the cross is actually not a Christian symbol. Some versions of the crosses are pagan. "The ankh (crux [where we get crucifix from] ansata) was an ancient Egyptian T-shaped cross surmounted with a loop. It symbolized the creative energies of the male and female and the essence of life. The simple T-shaped cross is named for the Greek letter tau." 1996 Grolier Multimedia Encyclopedia.

And what did God prophesy would happen in the church? Ezekiel 8:14 says, "Then he brought me to the door of the gate of the LORD'S house which [was] toward the north; and, behold, there sat women weeping for Tammuz." The "T" in Tammuz is where the cross came from. It was in reverence to Tammuz. If Jesus were sacrificed by a bullet or gun, would you wear that? In fact, if Martin Luther were alive today, I believe that he would nail the 95 thesis on every denomination's door. Additionally, all we have to do is look at Jesus. What jewelry did He wear? None.

And when we reference jewelry, take note what John Henry Cardinal Newman (1801-1890) wrote an essay on The Development of Christian Doctrine published in 1920 by Longmans, Green and Company. It said, "Incense, holy water, holy days and seasons, processions, the ring in marriage are all of pagan origin and sanctified by their adoption into the church."

And one final word from the Lord on this subject is found in Isaiah 3:16-24, which says, "Moreover the LORD saith, Because the daughters of Zion are haughty, and walk with stretched forth necks and wanton eyes, walking and mincing [as] they go, and making a tinkling with their feet: Therefore the Lord will smite with a scab the crown of the head of the daughters of Zion, and the LORD will discover their secret parts. In that day the Lord will take away the bravery of [their] tinkling ornaments [about their feet], and [their] cauls, and [their] round tires like the moon, The chains, and the bracelets, and the mufflers, The bonnets, and the ornaments of the legs, and the headbands, and the tablets, and the earrings, The rings, and nose jewels, The changeable suits of apparel, and the mantles, and the wimples, and the crisping pins, The glasses, and the fine linen, and the hoods, and the vails. And it shall come to pass, [that] instead of sweet smell there shall be stink; and instead of a girdle a rent; and instead of well set hair baldness; and instead of a stomacher a girding of sackcloth; [and] burning instead of beauty."

So when there is reference made to the Israelites making a golden calf, that is not just us avoiding making statues to worship, but it is every aspect of that situation including the fact we are to avoid the use of jewelry, especially that which is not practical. It is practical to wear a watch, but even in such, be careful of the investment. There are watches and there is jewelry that tells time. There is a difference.

Now let us address the obscure reference of, "rose up and play" (Exodus 32:6, 1 Corinthians 10:7). One of the universal definitions is to play is to be in sports competition. The spirit of needing to show one's superiority over another in some type of show of sportsmanship is what God is addressing. And interestingly, this seems to occur more and more often while the challenges of life decreases. Increase the challenges and society could not care any less about sports. Despite all of the positive purposes to be part of a sports program, at any level, the bottom line is that it is not well pleasing to God. Again, the attitude of playing to be better than another person or group is not the spirit of a Christian. Christians are to seek out those that are falling behind and encourage them along the way for we are all in the same race, and we all can be winners. Overall, sports is a waste of time, especially watching game after game on television. The time that could be spent in studying God's Word, sharing the gospel with others, even becoming better educated in the necessities of life that people do not seem to have time for, and also time that could be spent tending to those things that need attending, like housework, helping others, and more, all of it is wasted away in watching the game. Those that participate in the game seek nothing more than the trophy that will eventually burn up when the earth is set aflame (2 Peter 3:7). On top of that, again for those that participate in the sporting activity spend countless hours personally as well as collectively, called practice, trying to become the best player they can be while their Christian characters suffers. And then there are the unfortunate ones that are seriously injured, some crippled for life, and others suffering death. All for what? A shot of people's applause? Look at the number of sports figures that suffer from memory loss. Having memory loss means a loss of religious memory as well. So, sports is not something that God would have us be involved with. Now picking up a bat and ball and tossing it about is not an issue as that can be considered one of those touted benefits. Those promoting sports always point to the healthful exercise. Well, one can get the same without it being a competition as well. But it is that fever of competition that makes people insanely reject all of what has been said claiming there is nothing wrong with sports. God says that there is.

And while we are on the subject, the word "play" also refers to something else that is a universally accepted definition. It is called "dance". After "the people sat down to eat and to drink, and rose up to play" (Exodus 32:6), it appears that things got a bit out of hand for by the time Moses returned, "It came to pass, as soon as he came nigh unto the camp, that he saw the calf, and the dancing" (Exodus 32:19). This was not a good situation for "Moses' anger waxed hot, and he cast the tables out of his hands, and brake them beneath the mount" (Exodus 32:19). On top of that, "Moses saw that the people [were] naked" (Exodus 32:25). Now that "naked" reference does not mean that breasts and privates were exposed, but it sure does mean that they were not in "modest apparel" (1 Timothy 2:9). All dancing is not condemned for "David danced before the LORD" (2 Samuel 6:14), but the pairing of unmarried couples, touching in ways that God intended to be touched only between husband and wife, is what is condemned. Showing up to dances with clothing that indeed reveals the "goods" is very common today and condemned of God as nothing more than participating in whoredom. Watching dance shows on television in which they dance provocatively and dress sexually is in God's eyes considered pornography, but society is desensitized to it all and thinks that this whole discussion is a throwback to the 1800's. Even such a comment should wake people up to the realization that something is wrong. If God's people did not do these things for thousands of years, what makes the last hundred or so years any different? Did God change or did humans? It also shows how we are living in the last days as we shall see in a moment.

So do realize, that both sports and dancing are covered in this little word called "play", and it is being completely ignored, as expected, by the people of the world, but it should not be among Christians and yet it is. There are Christian into sports and following sports more so than many non-Christians. There are Christians who will be so excited about dance that nothing else matters. All of it is but a distraction from our high and holy calling.

Now returning back to the Book of Corinthians, Paul would not have us miss this next interesting fact and warning. "Neither let us commit fornication, as some of them committed, and fell in one day three and twenty thousand" (1 Corinthians 10:8). No doubt that this is referring to the incident right before entering the Promised Land. "And Israel abode in Shittim, and the people began to commit whoredom with the daughters of Moab. And they called the people unto the sacrifices of their gods: and the people did eat, and bowed down to their gods. And Israel joined himself unto Baalpeor: and the anger of the LORD was kindled against Israel" (Numbers 25:1-3). "And, behold, one of the children of Israel came and brought unto his brethren a Midianitish woman in the sight of Moses, and in the sight of all the congregation of the children of Israel, who [were] weeping [before] the door of the tabernacle of the congregation" (Numbers 25:6).

Sex is a distraction, and Satan knows it. He has used it throughout history to deter holy men away from God's purpose. Sometimes he is successful, "And it came to pass in an eveningtide, that David arose from off his bed, and walked upon the roof of the king's house: and from the roof he saw a woman washing herself; and the woman [was] very beautiful to look upon" (2 Samuel 11:2), and "when Solomon was old, [that] his wives turned away his heart after other gods: and his heart was not perfect with the LORD his God" (1 Kings 11:4). Sometimes he is not so successful, "And it came to pass after these things, that his master's wife cast her eyes upon Joseph; and she said, Lie with me. But he refused, and said unto his master's wife, Behold, my master wotteth not what [is] with me in the house, and he hath committed all that he hath to my hand; [There is] none greater in this house than I; neither hath he kept back any thing from me but thee, because thou [art] his wife: how then can I do this great wickedness, and sin against God? And it came to pass, as she spake to Joseph day by day, that he hearkened not unto her, to lie by her, [or] to be with her. And it came to pass about this time, that [Joseph] went into the house to do his business; and [there was] none of the men of the house there within. And she caught him by his garment, saying, Lie with me: and he left his garment in her hand, and fled, and got him out" (Genesis 39:7-12). Overall, Satan is very successful, so when the armies of Israel just could not be overpowered by any of the enemies of earth, Satan pulled out his last trick, sex. And as the account states, well over twenty thousand mighty men fell to Satan's ploy.

As this book demonstrates, we are on the verge of entering into the heavenly Promised Land. There is a very good possibility that it is going to happen in our lifetime, "But of that day and hour knoweth no [man], no, not the angels of heaven, but my Father only" (Matthew 24:36), yet, "When ye shall see all these things, know that it is near, [even] at the doors" (Matthew 24:33). So what does that mean? It means that all along, Satan has tried to upend God's messengers in various ways. He tried persecution, argument, even being ignored, but without complete success. So, in these last days, does anyone really think it is a coincidence that not only has the gay agenda come out of the closet, but it seems that we, as a society, have left much of our clothing in the closet flaunting our nakedness.

That is not a coincidence either, where the people back then did those things "in the sight of Moses, and in the sight of all the congregation of the children of Israel" (Numbers 25:6). That matches our day perfectly. Not only is sex running rampant, it is running blatantly, as if there are no consequences. All of these movements are not good, in which society has moved from showing on television, married couples in separate beds to full on soft porn during the day. We have moved from wholesome families being hinted at the ones to only have intimacy to mostly, if not always, showing unmarried couples. Singers wear less and less and try to make their music covers more and more provocative. We always have known that sex sells, but it seems that it has been incorporated in everything from selling fast food to even selling toothpaste. Exposure to sex begins at the children level where the "adult" innuendos are not so implied anymore but are embedded in the cartoons. If one is eighteen and not actively having sex, they are very much pressured to give up their virginity. In fact, such is no longer prized to have but something to throw away at adulthood, if not earlier. Even on the Internet with all the flashing sidebar ads, there's bound to be something sexual eventually if not frequently. The more society yells, "Don't treat us women as sex objects", the more they are losing. How hypocritical for young ladies to claim they are not a sex object when they are dressing like sex objects! Revealing butt cheeks and breasts are going to draw the attention. God calls it nakedness, even while fully clothed by societal standards. And speaking of which, the pool and the beaches are places where Christians ought not be attending. They call it eye candy; God calls it lusting (Matthew 5:28)!

Is it a coincidence that for the most part, society up through the 1800's were dressed without showing cleavage, without revealing the body's form, without revealing the goods, but since then as we are approaching the second coming, anything and everything is permitted. Also interestingly, the devil seems to be flaunting it at a staggering pace that society's reaction is just getting mauled. People were all upset with the breast exposure during the Super Bowl by Janet Jackson, yet, everyone seems to be into twirking, which is worse. And what is even worse, is that twirking is old news. We have moved on to stronger sexual content, but accepted by society. If we were to take some of the imagery of today and go back just ten years, people then would never guess that society would degrade to the level of accepting of it.

It all points to one thing. Satan "knoweth that he hath but a short time" (Revelation 12:12), and a very short time in fact. The question is, "When will Christians see through these things and choose to stand with Moses?"

Next on Paul's list to avoid repeating is the reference in 1 Corinthians 10:9, which says, "Neither let us tempt Christ, as some of them also tempted, and were destroyed of serpents." In the full context, the Bible says, "And the people spake against God, and against Moses, Wherefore have ye brought us up out of Egypt to die in the wilderness? for [there is] no bread, neither [is there any] water; and our soul loatheth this light bread. And the LORD sent fiery serpents among the people, and they bit the people; and much people of Israel died. Therefore the people came to Moses, and said, We have sinned, for we have spoken against the LORD, and against thee; pray unto the LORD, that he take away the serpents from us. And Moses prayed for the people. And the LORD said unto Moses, Make thee a fiery serpent, and set it upon a pole: and it shall come to pass, that every one that is bitten, when he looketh upon it, shall live. And Moses made a serpent of brass, and put it upon a pole, and it came to pass, that if a serpent had bitten any man, when he beheld the serpent of brass, he lived" (Numbers 21:5-9).

First, notice the rebellious heart, especially regarding all of those Vegetarian diet plans. They not only disagreed with the diet, they "loathed" it. One would think they would have learned their lessons from the whole quail incident, but remember, "it [is] a stiffnecked people" (Exodus 32:9). Now when the Bible says, "The LORD sent fiery serpents among the people" (Numbers 21:6), it is more of an allowance for up until this point, God had been working many miracles, one of which was to keep the poisonous snakes and even scorpions away from the people (Deuteronomy 8:15). Besides, why would God purposely send the snakes and turn around to offer a solution? So God, in His act of revealing what people took for granted, simply removed His hand of protection. This is much like what we do with God today. Many take God for granted, especially those that do not acknowledge Him. When He says, "Wherefore turn [yourselves], and live" (Ezekiel 18:32), that is not a threat like, "Obey me or I'm going to send a bolt of lightning." Rather, God is simply stating that He will one day remove all of His blessings, which includes providing "the breath of all mankind" (Job 12:10). Hell fire's purpose is not really for torture as it is to remove the corpses. When it is time, God will only provide His free gift of breath to His beings, the heavenly angels and the saved of this planet. Sure, people will be alive at the time, but that is the punishment part for even a parent should "withhold not correction from the child" (Proverbs 23:13). Even so, sin is really what is cleansed away with the fire of hell. It just so happens that people are attached to sin and will burn with it, experiencing "weeping and gnashing of teeth" (Matthew 8:12), for if the purpose of hell fire was not to eradicate sin, why is it that the "heavens and the earth" will burn (2 Peter 3:7)? Fire purifies, and since "those that wait upon the LORD, they shall inherit the earth" (Psalms 37:9), no one wants to inherit a sin ravaged planet. Fire will cleanse it then, and "God shall wipe away all tears from their eyes; and there shall be no more death, neither sorrow, nor crying, neither shall there be any more pain: for the former things are passed away. And he that sat upon the throne said, Behold, I make all things new" (Revelation 21:4-5), including the fact that He will "create new heavens and a new earth" (Isaiah 65:17).

Now speaking of the solution for the fiery serpents, some mistaken the creation of the snake on a pole as the allowance for the use of idols in worship of God, but not so fast. If this were the case, then destroying the object many years later when people were worshipping with it would not have happened. "Hezekiah the son of Ahaz king of Judah" (2 Kings 18:1) "removed the high places, and brake the images, and cut down the groves, and brake in pieces the brasen serpent that Moses had made: for unto those days the children of Israel did burn incense to it: and he called it Nehushtan" (2 Kings 18:4). Besides, God is the one that called for the object to be made, unlike many today who fashion statues on their own initiation.

So the bottom line to this reference is to "be content with such things as ye have" (Hebrews 13:5). We ought not be complaining about our lifestyle by saying things like, "Look at all the other people at this gathering. They get to get all that great smelling food." "My unmarried friends get to enjoy sex." "Look at all the people enjoying the movies." "Look at all the people enjoying all kinds of music." "All we have is this clean food diet, maybe even Vegetarian diet." "All I have is a few choices, if any, of these boring television programs." "All I have to listen to are these old hymns. Can't even listen to much of the Christian music of the day." All of this is wrong, leading into our next Bible reference that Paul uses in his list of things not to repeat.

The Bible says, "Neither murmur ye, as some of them also murmured, and were destroyed of the destroyer" (1 Corinthians 10:10). Even Jude wrote, "These are murmurers, complainers, walking after their own lusts; and their mouth speaketh great swelling [words], having men's persons in admiration because of advantage" (Jude 1:16). In fact, we are to "Do all things without murmurings and disputings" (Philippians 2:14). These are the legalists. These are the people trying to earn Heaven. These are the people going through the motions because the Bible says so. In fact, one can keep the Ten Commandments, but if it is with the attitude described earlier, "can't do this" and "have to do that", then live like the world and forget God because the end result is the same. Those that go to Heaven are those that "delight to do thy will, O my God: yea, thy law [is] within my heart" (Psalms 40:8). Sure, they live obeying the rules, just like the complaining group, but the motivation is different. If a person is truly saved, they will delightfully live in obedience. Those that obey because they have to will be lost. And those that they think the problem is the obeying part instead of the attitude and live in disobedience to the Ten Commandments, well, they too will be sadly lost.

Christians ought not to be depressants. "Blessed [are] the poor in spirit: for theirs is the kingdom of heaven. Blessed [are] they that mourn: for they shall be comforted. Blessed [are] the meek: for they shall inherit the earth. Blessed [are] they which do hunger and thirst after righteousness: for they shall be filled. Blessed [are] the merciful: for they shall obtain mercy. Blessed [are] the pure in heart: for they shall see God. Blessed [are] the peacemakers: for they shall be called the children of God. Blessed [are] they which are persecuted for righteousness' sake: for theirs is the kingdom of heaven. Blessed are ye, when [men] shall revile you, and persecute [you], and shall say all manner of evil against you falsely, for my sake" (Matthew 5:3-11).

How Do the Feast Days Reveal the Activities of History and Especially the Second Coming?

The ultimate spiritual relationship between the physical Old Testament and the spiritual New Testament are the feast days. Many think that God had the Jews perform all kinds of tasks and rituals just to prove and acknowledge that God is, well, God. They then think that Jesus shows up, and since the people did not understand through all of those rituals, they were replaced. This is not true. The Bible teaches, "Thy way, O God, [is] in the sanctuary" (Psalms 77:13). On top of that, God has a principle that he operates by in which it is said, "Surely the Lord GOD will do nothing, but he revealeth his secret unto his servants the prophets" (Amos 3:7). Basically, the whole plan of salvation that cuts through quite a bit of the misunderstandings in doctrines is all laid out in the sanctuary feast days. So, it would be greatly beneficial to study the physical aspects of the feasts days to see how they apply spiritually.

PASSOVER:

Let us begin with Passover. It is found in Leviticus 23:4-5, where it says, "These [are] the feasts of the LORD, [even] holy convocations, which ye shall proclaim in their seasons. In the fourteenth [day] of the first month at even [is] the LORD'S passover."

What was the purpose of Passover? According to Exodus 12:11-13, the Bible says, "And thus shall ye eat it; [with] your loins girded, your shoes on your feet, and your staff in your hand; and ye shall eat it in haste: it [is] the LORD'S passover. For I will pass through the land of Egypt this night, and will smite all the firstborn in the land of Egypt, both man and beast; and against all the gods of Egypt I will execute judgment: I [am] the LORD. And the blood shall be to you for a token upon the houses where ye [are]: and when I see the blood, I will pass over you, and the plague shall not be upon you to destroy [you], when I smite the land of Egypt." This feast recalled when the Israelites were in Egypt and an Angel of the Lord passed over each house that sacrificed a lamb and spread the blood on their doorposts. This was in preparation of the journey to the Promised Land. The angel was sent in connection to the tenth plague that came upon Egypt.

So how does this point spiritually, more specifically, how does it point to Jesus, as all of the feasts do? In Matthew 26:2, we read "Ye know that after two days is [the feast of] the passover, and the Son of man is betrayed to be crucified." Jesus knew exactly what day and hour He was to die; He was to die in place of the Passover lamb. And thanks to the God inspired Daniel, He also knew the year He would die – 31 A.D.

How did Jesus know that 31 A.D. was the year? As reminder, Daniel 9:24 tells of a seventy week prophecy that actually tells Daniel what would happen over the next four hundred and ninety years. It includes anointing the most Holy, which pinpointed the baptism of Jesus to be 27 A.D. and not sooner, so that is one reason why Jesus waited so long before beginning His ministry. It identified that righteousness, as in Christ's righteousness, would be ushered in as well as defeating sin and transgressions (Daniel 9:24). All this begins when the command is sent to rebuild Jerusalem, including the temple (Daniel 9:25). Even the statement directly of the name Messiah is used in that verse and pinpoints that at four hundred and eighty three years into the prophecy, He would show up. That happened at Jesus' baptism in 27 A.D.

Now, those that hold onto the theory that Daniel 9:27 is thrown into the future for the last seven years, we ask, have you really considered the significance? First, the sacrificial system would then still be an obligation, and besides, there is not a hint that the seventy week prophecy is to be broken up. And again, reminding everyone that verse 27 reference is incorrectly being applied to Antichrist when it is about Jesus Christ, for in the middle of that final week, specifically in 31 A.D., Jesus defeated sin and Satan by the cross, defeated death by rising again, and ushered in His righteousness. Although Christ righteousness has always existed, it was only revealed at the cross. But if people insist on throwing the event into the future, not only are they implying a separation of time, but they are also making the fulfillment of the entire prophecy to be broken. The cross, which ended the sacrifices, as prophesied, can only be fulfilled if the final week of the prophecy stays with all of the events ending in 34 A.D., which is exactly what we are proposing. So that is how Jesus knew when to be baptized starting His public ministry and when He would die. In fact, Stephen was even stoned on time causing the church to not concentrate in Israel any longer but to take it to other lands, as Jesus said, "Ye shall be witnesses unto me both in Jerusalem, and in all Judaea, and in Samaria, and unto the uttermost part of the earth" (Acts 1:8). The prophecy states "Seventy weeks are determined upon thy people," which in mathematical terms, comes out to four hundred and ninety prophetic days or literal years. It is one chop ("determined") off of the larger time prophecy found in Daniel 8:14, known as the two thousand and three hundred year prophecy. It is not four hundred and eighty-three days are cut off for Daniel's people and then another seven cut off at another time. It is four hundred and ninety are cut off. And during that four hundred and ninety year time frame, sixty-nine weeks or four hundred and eighty-three prophetic days lead up to the arrival of the Messiah (verse 25). After His arrival, He will be cut off (verse 26). And verse 27 goes into detail of exactly when Jesus would be cut off or crucified and the significance thereof.

Besides, it does not make sense that God would have made a covenant with Israel, then make a new covenant for the Christian period, and then return to the prior covenant for the last seven years or even come up with a third one. Instead, four hundred and ninety years were for the Jews, which ended in 34 A.D. and until the second coming, we are under the new covenant. It was predicted to happen. "Behold, the days come, saith the LORD, that I will make a new covenant with the house of Israel, and with the house of Judah" (Jeremiah 31:31). It did happen for "Jesus the mediator of the new covenant" (Hebrews 12:24). And "this [is] the covenant that I will make with the house of Israel after those days, saith the Lord; I will put my laws into their mind, and write them in their hearts: and I will be to them a God, and they shall be to me a people" (Hebrews 8:10).

Now, did any one substantiate the claim that the Passover lamb pointed to Jesus? In the two verses of John 1:29, 36, the Bible says, "The next day John seeth Jesus coming unto him, and saith, Behold the Lamb of God, which taketh away the sin of the world. And looking upon Jesus as he walked, he saith, Behold the Lamb of God!" So the answer is yes; John the Baptists also saw the feast day of Passover about to be fulfilled by specifically stating the reference to the Passover Lamb and pointing to Jesus being the Lamb of God. He knew it was not just some annual feast day. He knew the deeper significance of the blood of the Lamb. Passover was not just a literal remembrance of the last plague in Egypt and the blood on the door post protecting from death of the first born, but rather it was the spiritual significance of Jesus being that Lamb. The blood on the door posts that prevented death in the home and causing the angel of death to pass over the home was spiritually pointing to all being able to lay claim to the blood of Christ that prevents our death "for the wages of sin [is] death" (Romans 6:23). But why will we not die? Because of the blood of Jesus.

In addition to all of that, did you know that the Passover lamb was not to have a broken bone? This is according to Numbers 9:10-12. "Speak unto the children of Israel, saying, If any man of you or of your posterity shall be unclean by reason of a dead body, or [be] in a journey afar off, yet he shall keep the passover unto the LORD. The fourteenth day of the second month at even they shall keep it, [and] eat it with unleavened bread and bitter [herbs]. They shall leave none of it unto the morning, nor break any bone of it: according to all the ordinances of the passover they shall keep it." Jesus fulfilled this point as well. "For these things were done, that the scripture should be fulfilled, A bone of him shall not be broken" (John 19:36).

And just as the blood on the doorposts saved the souls inside, specifically the first born from death, Jesus' blood saves us from eternal death. 1 Peter 1:18-19 states, "Forasmuch as ye know that ye were not redeemed with corruptible things, [as] silver and gold, from your vain conversation [received] by tradition from your fathers; But with the precious blood of Christ, as of a lamb without blemish and without spot."

How sure are we that Jesus fulfilled the Passover requirements? Matthew 27:50-54 says, "Jesus, when he had cried again with a loud voice, yielded up the ghost. And, behold, the veil of the temple was rent in twain from the top to the bottom; and the earth did quake, and the rocks rent; And the graves were opened; and many bodies of the saints which slept arose, And came out of the graves after his resurrection, and went into the holy city, and appeared unto many. Now when the centurion, and they that were with him, watching Jesus, saw the earthquake, and those things that were done, they feared greatly, saying, Truly this was the Son of God." Why else would God tear the curtain while the Passover lamb was about to be sacrificed by the high priest that day? This tearing of the curtain symbolized the end of the sacrificial system.

Here is another parallel. The plague that people were being saved from was not only a death plague, it was specific. "And all the firstborn in the land of Egypt shall die, from the firstborn of Pharaoh that sitteth upon his throne, even unto the firstborn of the maidservant that [is] behind the mill; and all the firstborn of beasts" (Exodus 11:5). Interestingly, our substitute taking on the penalty of sin, which is death (Romans 6:23), happened to be known as the "Firstborn" (Romans 8:29).

UNLEAVEND BREAD:

Now let us take a look at the feast called Unleavened Bread, since we now have the forgiving sacrifice or gift of eternal life. Leviticus 23:6-8 says, "And on the fifteenth day of the same month [is] the feast of unleavened bread unto the LORD: seven days ye must eat unleavened bread. In the first day ye shall have an holy convocation: ye shall do no servile work therein. But ye shall offer an offering made by fire unto the LORD seven days: in the seventh day [is] an holy convocation: ye shall do no servile work [therein]." This was a time to purge out the leaven, which was symbolic of sin.

Can anyone else confirm that Jesus fulfilled this feast? Paul writes in 1 Corinthians 5:7-8 says, "Purge out therefore the old leaven, that ye may be a new lump, as ye are unleavened. For even Christ our passover is sacrificed for us. Therefore let us keep the feast, not with old leaven, neither with the leaven of malice and wickedness; but with the unleavened [bread] of sincerity and truth." Just as Jesus physically fulfilled the feast of Passover through the cross, the physical manifestation of fulfilling the feast of unleavened bread is revealed by a changed character in the recipient of God's grace.

These two feast combined addresses the false doctrine of cheap grace. Those that claim that all one needs to do is "just believe" are only living in the Feast of Passover. As a true Christian, we need to be living in all seven feasts. So once we have been given the gift of eternal life through the spiritual Feast of Passover, to show our belief and acceptance, we are, by the grace of God, to also purge from our lives all things that are sinful. This supports the understanding of salvation in that one who receives the gift of eternal life then will go on into obedience, especially to the Ten Commandments, "for sin is the transgression of the law" (1 John 3:4). In other words, once saved one then keeps the Ten Commandments. Notice the order. Jesus dies shedding His blood providing forgiveness or grace, and then the next feast is removing sin from our life, which means that we are living by the power of His grace to be obeying God's commandments. The feast of Unleavened Bread did not precede Passover. Passover comes first. So does the gift of salvation, but once one has the gift, then sin is removed.

As the Bible stated, God's way is in the sanctuary (Psalms 77:13). The whole plan of salvation is there. If we would only bring our doctrines to the sanctuary or feast days, only the truth would be revealed. So, thus far salvation by justification only without actual sanctification, making people holy, is wrong. Once saved, always saved is wrong. "Just believe" is wrong. And when we say wrong, it is in the invitation type where we want all to be saved so we invite everyone to the correct understanding of faith and works. We invite everyone to live in both the Feast of Passover and Unleavened Bread.

FIRST FRUITS:

The third feast was known as First Fruits. It is found in Leviticus 23:9-14, which says, "And the LORD spake unto Moses, saying, Speak unto the children of Israel, and say unto them, When ye be come into the land which I give unto you, and shall reap the harvest thereof, then ye shall bring a sheaf of the firstfruits of your harvest unto the priest: And he shall wave the sheaf before the LORD, to be accepted for you: on the morrow after the sabbath the priest shall wave it. And ye shall offer that day when ye wave the sheaf an he lamb without blemish of the first year for a burnt offering unto the LORD. And the meat offering thereof [shall be] two tenth deals of fine flour mingled with oil, an offering made by fire unto the LORD [for] a sweet savour: and the drink offering thereof [shall be] of wine, the fourth [part] of an hin. And ye shall eat neither bread, nor parched corn, nor green ears, until the selfsame day that ye have brought an offering unto your God: [it shall be] a statute for ever throughout your generations in all your dwellings." The Wave Sheaf or First Fruits was the gathering of the first fruits of the field and offering them to the Lord thanking Him for such a bountiful harvest that is to come. It was understood that the Lord who provided the first fruits would also provide for a grand harvest. These items were also to be the best of the field.

Now, how does this apply to Jesus and us? According to 1 Corinthians 15:20-23, the Bible says, "But now is Christ risen from the dead, [and] become the firstfruits of them that slept. For since by man [came] death, by man [came] also the resurrection of the dead. For as in Adam all die, even so in Christ shall all be made alive. But every man in his own order: Christ the firstfruits; afterward they that are Christ's at his coming." Jesus is the best and first fruits for the understanding of the resurrection pointing to a blessed hope for all, and that there will be a great harvest or resurrection of the dead in our near future.

With that understood, this addresses many topics of the Bible, especially the understanding of death. What this means is that up through the time of Jesus, when a person died, they basically did what God said, "In the sweat of thy face shalt thou eat bread, till thou return unto the ground;

for out of it wast thou taken: for dust thou [art], and unto dust shalt thou return" (Genesis 3:19). There is no mention of a spirit floating away, a soul escaping a shell of a body, reincarnation. We simply cease to exist and are dead, or as the Bible says, "sleep". Sure, Enoch and Elijah were taken alive and at some point Moses was resurrected (Jude 1:9), but the real reason that Jesus' resurrection was so significant is that people did not do such on a regular basis. When people died, they were dead. It became such an understanding that people simply sleep until the resurrection that "the Sadducees say that there is no resurrection, neither angel, nor spirit" (Acts 23:8). God said in the beginning that "thou shalt surely die" (Genesis 2:17), while it is the devil who says "Ye shall not surely die" (Genesis 3:4). In today's language, God says that we will completely die, while the devil teaches that we do not completely die, in that, there is some entity of us that still lives on.

On top of that, the believers specifically "taught the people, and preached through Jesus the resurrection from the dead" (Acts 4:2). This was not just a different belief; this was an entirely new concept. The only encounter with the dead that people were aware of was the Satanic personating of the prophet Samuel. King Saul was cut off from God for "the LORD answered him not, neither by dreams, nor by Urim, nor by prophets" (1 Samuel 28:6), so he asked "his servants, Seek me a woman that hath a familiar spirit, that I may go to her" (1 Samuel 28:7). Already that is a forbidden act. Then when the witch was successful in pulling off her act of calling up a spirit, not calling down from Heaven where Samuel would have gone upon death, "Saul perceived that it [was] Samuel" (1 Samuel 28:14) but did not know it was Samuel for he only "perceived" it. Well, we ought to know it was not Samuel because "the dead know not any thing" (Ecclesiastes 9:5). So to use this satanic incident to prove that we have spirits that escape at death is nothing short of believing in spiritualism, of which the Bible says, "In the latter times some shall depart from the faith, giving heed to seducing spirits, and doctrines of devils" (1 Timothy 4:1). And it is not by coincidence that there is such an explosion of movies and television programs that promote such.

Many will claim to have had a dead relative talk with them, but unfortunately "they are the spirits of devils, working miracles" (Revelation 16:14). This is because each of us are assigned angels, at least one good and one bad. The angel knows us better than our own parents know us, even spouses. So appearing in a spirit form, able to relate to all kinds of experiences, is an easy task for evil angels to pull off. Do keep in mind, even the evil angels have perfect memory, so whole conversations can easily be repeated. Just because humans have trouble recalling things from a few hours ago, both good and bad angels can recall every detail of anyone's life with ease. Basically, never judge an angel based upon human restrictions.

But the bottom line is, the feast of first fruits, representing a sample of the grand resurrection is what this feast is celebrating. The last feast is the great harvest when everyone else will be resurrected, but more on that latter. So even the doctrine about death needs to be sent through the feast days to see if it stands. There is no room to believe in any immediate afterlife scenario.

Now this action of Jesus being the first fruit, helps put other verses in perspective, otherwise, they make no sense. When Paul was called into court, his defense was, "I am a Pharisee, the son of a Pharisee: of the hope and resurrection of the dead I am called in question" (Acts 23:6). He did not say, "I am a Pharisee, the son of a Pharisee: of the hope of my spirit going to Heaven after death." In fact, Paul specifically wrote elsewhere, "Henceforth there is laid up for me a crown of righteousness, which the Lord, the righteous judge, shall give me at that day: and not to me only, but unto all them also that love his appearing" (2 Timothy 4:8). Paul looked forward to everyone experiencing eternal life together, not one at a time at death.

Luke wrote, "And have hope toward God, which they themselves also allow, that there shall be a resurrection of the dead, both of the just and unjust" (Acts 24:15), where it says that there is a "resurrection of the dead" and not the "resurrection of the bodies". Please note that when there is a resurrection, these bodies are not coming up out of the grave. We get new incorruptible bodies "For this corruptible must put on incorruption, and this mortal [must] put on immortality" (1 Corinthians 15:53). We do not have immortality right now, but we will when Jesus returns. To have a spirit floating off to Heaven would be immortality. In fact, it continues on by saying, "So when this corruptible shall have put on incorruption, and this mortal shall have put on immortality, then shall be brought to pass the saying that is written, Death is swallowed up in victory. O death, where [is] thy sting? O grave, where [is] thy victory?" (1 Corinthians 15:54-55) Now if our spirits went somewhere at death, could we not say at that time that death has nothing on us? Of course we could. There would be no sting of death. It would be a great release into something better, but instead, who we are is what will be resurrected on that day. Additionally, Paul wrote, "To them who by patient continuance in well doing seek for glory and honour and immortality, eternal life" (Romans 2:7). Now if he knew at death he would be in Heaven in spirit form then eternal life and being immortal would already have begun. Instead,

Paul said that we seek for it or look forward to that future date, such as the second coming, in which we receive it.

So now, we have Jesus fulfilling these feasts by His death taking care of Passover, His perfect life being completed by purging out sin, and now His resurrection being an example for the future harvest. For us, the Passover of Jesus is the free gift that will allow us to pass over into eternal life at that day; the Unleavened Bread is the power of Jesus to purge us of our sins; and the First Fruits gives us hope in the reality that there will be a resurrection for we have a sample of such with Jesus, and probably those that came out of the graves at the time of Jesus resurrection. The Bible says, "And the graves were opened; and many bodies of the saints which slept arose, and came out of the graves after his resurrection, and went into the holy city, and appeared unto many" (Matthew 27:52-53). So that too should be proof that we are asleep until the resurrection, otherwise, would they not have just come down from Heaven instead, if they were already up there. No, they came up out of the graves.

And for those that say, "No. Everyone went to hell before the cross and Jesus went and rescued the righteous ones", all we have to say is that such is satanic, even though it is a teaching of the Antichrist. That means Daniel, who we see no recorded sin, would have been suffering the flames of fire for no good reason. Besides, the Bible said that they came from the graves, not from the place of torment.

PENTECOST:

Now let us see what Pentecost reveals. It is found in Leviticus 23:15-22, which says, "And ye shall count unto you from the morrow after the sabbath, from the day that ye brought the sheaf of the wave offering; seven sabbaths shall be complete: Even unto the morrow after the seventh sabbath shall ye number fifty days; and ye shall offer a new meat offering unto the LORD. Ye shall bring out of your habitations two wave loaves of two tenth deals: they shall be of fine flour; they shall be baken with leaven; [they are] the firstfruits unto the LORD. And ye shall offer with the bread seven lambs without blemish of the first year, and one young bullock, and two rams: they shall be [for] a burnt offering unto the LORD, with their meat offering, and their drink offerings, [even] an offering made by fire, of sweet savour unto the LORD. Then ye shall sacrifice one kid of the goats for a sin offering, and two lambs of the first year for a sacrifice of peace offerings. And the priest shall wave them with the bread of the firstfruits [for] a wave offering before the LORD, with the two lambs: they shall be holy to the LORD for the priest. And ye shall proclaim on the selfsame day, [that] it may be an holy convocation unto you: ye shall do no servile work [therein: it shall be] a statute for ever in all your dwellings throughout your generations. And when ye reap the harvest of your land, thou shalt not make clean riddance of the corners of thy field when thou reapest, neither shalt thou gather any gleaning of thy harvest: thou shalt leave them unto the poor, and to the stranger: I [am] the LORD your God." A special day appearing fifty days after the feast of First Fruits is what the Bible calls "Pentecost" (Acts 2:1) in the New Testament and Feast of Weeks (Exodus 34:22, Deuteronomy 16:10, 16:16, 2 Chronicles 8:13) in the Old Testament.

When Jesus was on earth, He made a promise, "Nevertheless I tell you the truth; It is expedient for you that I go away: for if I go not away, the Comforter will not come unto you; but if I depart, I will send him unto you" (John 16:7). When did the comforter come? The answer is in Acts 2:1-4, which says, "And when the day of Pentecost was fully come, they were all with one accord in one place. And suddenly there came a sound from heaven as of a rushing mighty wind, and it filled all the house where they were sitting. And there appeared unto them cloven tongues like as of fire, and it sat upon each of them. And they were all filled with the Holy Ghost, and began to speak with other tongues, as the Spirit gave them utterance." Now Pentecost is not a Christian day, but rather it was a feast day that the Jews practiced in which Jesus fulfilled by marking the sending forth of the new church organization for Jesus had said, "I will build my church; and the gates of hell shall not prevail against it" (Matthew 16:18).

Now let us look at the feast day in regards it being applicable to Christians. Although we are involving the waving of the fruits and even the reference to first fruits is being mentioned, the focus ought to be upon the use of leaven. This feast is not referring to yet another type of resurrection; this first fruits is an acknowledgement of empowering the first fruits of the early church. One could say that this is the official start of the Christian Church seeing for fifty days since the death and resurrection of Jesus, they did nothing but spend time with Jesus physically and then in prayer. "He shewed himself alive after his passion by many infallible proofs, being seen of them forty days, and speaking of the things pertaining to the kingdom of God" (Acts 1:3), and then the last ten days, "All continued with one accord in prayer and supplication" (Acts 1:14). But what they did not do is try to preach the gospel to anyone yet. That did not come until the fiftieth day.

"And suddenly there came a sound from heaven as of a rushing mighty wind, and it filled all the house where they were sitting. And there appeared unto them cloven tongues like as of fire, and it sat upon each of them. And they were all filled with the Holy Ghost, and began to speak with other tongues, as the Spirit gave them utterance. And there were dwelling at Jerusalem Jews, devout men, out of every nation under heaven. Now when this was noised abroad, the multitude came together, and were confounded, because that every man heard them speak in his own language" (Acts 2:2-6). And what was the result? "Then they that gladly received his word were baptized: and the same day there were added [unto them] about three thousand souls" (Acts 2:41). This was the official public ministry of the Christian church.

Therefore, instead of more people being resurrected, it is actually a celebration of being empowered by the Holy Spirit to go forth with the gospel. And that same power exists today, in fact, it is the motivation of all new converts. And if one is not compelled to share the gospel with others upon conversion, then one probably should rethink if they have been converted.

So where leaven normally represents sin, in this case it does not. This is the only feast that leaven is used instead of purposely removing the leaven. The removal of leaven is the removing of sin while using leaven is being filled with the Holy Spirit for "A little leaven leaveneth the whole lump" (Galatians 5:9).

Even Jesus used leaven in a parable, "The kingdom of heaven is like unto leaven, which a woman took, and hid in three measures of meal, till the whole was leavened" (Matthew 13:33). Here, the woman, representative of God's church, took the power of the kingdom of heaven and leavened the whole lump. That empowerment, not by coincidence, came in three measures, representative of God the Father, God the Son, and the Holy Spirit. So there is good leaven and bad leaven.

Now speaking of Pentecost and the gift of the Holy Spirit but specifically in the form of the use of tongues, let us investigate a bit deeper into the controversial topic. What used to be reserved for Pentecostal churches is now prevalent in just about all denominations. It is the speaking in tongues. Some denominations go so far to declare that if one does not speak in tongues, that person is not saved. And that is just not right.

First question that should come to mind is that if the speaking in tongues confirms a person to be saved, would they then not be part of a new single denomination? The reason they should be part of a single denomination instead of staying where they are at is because not all members of these denominations seem to practice such experiences. There are but small pockets in each denomination, some larger than others, that speak in tongues. One would think that such people would gravitate towards each other instead of keeping people separate, and as a result, form another denomination.

Second question is, how can confirmation of being saved with the sign of the gift of tongues be so when each person believes something differently? The Bible teaches that when one is filled with the Holy Spirit, it means that "he will guide you into all truth" (John 16:13). And that is not just some of the truth but all of the truth. Again, if two spirit filled Christians speaking in tongues from different denominations are indeed filled with the spirit, logical sense convicts such people to draw together with being likeminded, especially when non-practicing members are actually having animosity towards tongue speaking Christians.

But let us investigate closer the gift of tongues, which we do believe in. To start with, please note the use of tongues in this event known as Pentecost. The tongues were actually used to convey a real language, in this case, many real languages. Here is more information on the day of Pentecost. "And how hear we every man in our own tongue, wherein we were born? Parthians, and Medes, and Elamites, and the dwellers in Mesopotamia, and in Judaea, and Cappadocia, in Pontus, and Asia, Phrygia, and Pamphylia, in Egypt, and in the parts of Libya about Cyrene, and strangers of Rome, Jews and proselytes, Cretes and Arabians, we do hear them speak in our tongues the wonderful works of God. And they were all amazed, and were in doubt, saying one to another, What meaneth this?" (Acts 2:8-12) There was no need to list out the languages if speaking in tongues was just a bunch of babbling, but so that we understood that tongue speaking is a real language instead of a bunch of babbling past off as some heavenly language that only the tongue speaker and Heaven understand, the list was provided. It also reveals the purpose of tongue speaking and that is for the preaching of the gospel across language barriers.

Looking at another incident of speaking in tongues, please take note that "There was a certain man in Caesarea called Cornelius" (Acts 10:1). And it is purposely stated that "Ye know how that it is an unlawful thing for a man that is a Jew to keep company, or come unto one of another nation; but God hath shewed me that I should not call any man common or unclean" (Acts 10:28). The point is, we have two different nations, two different languages, and who knows what other nations were representative in the room, but in either case, a special event occurred. "While Peter yet spake these words, the Holy Ghost fell on all them which heard the word. And they of the circumcision which believed were astonished, as many as came with Peter, because that on the Gentiles also was poured out the gift of the Holy Ghost. For they heard them speak with tongues, and magnify God. Then answered Peter, Can any man forbid water, that these should not be baptized, which have received the Holy Ghost as well as we?" (Acts 10:44-47) Now the key here is that Peter understood what Cornelius said and answered directly unlike earlier when "Peter opened [his] mouth, and said, Of a truth I perceive that God is no respecter of persons" (Acts 10:34). So more than likely there was a bit of interpretation going on but when the Spirit entered the gentiles, Peter understood what he heard directly in his own native language. That is because Cornelius was not babbling but speaking in Peter's language.

Another incident recorded in the Book of Acts is, "And it came to pass, that, while Apollos was at Corinth, Paul having passed through the upper coasts came to Ephesus: and finding certain disciples, He said unto them, Have ye received the Holy Ghost since ye believed? And they said unto him, We have not so much as heard whether there be any Holy Ghost. And he said unto them, Unto what then were ye baptized? And they said, Unto John's baptism. Then said Paul, John verily baptized with the baptism of repentance, saying unto the people, that they should believe on him which should come after him, that is, on Christ Jesus. When they heard [this], they were baptized in the name of the Lord Jesus. And when Paul had laid [his] hands upon them, the Holy Ghost came on them; and they spake with tongues, and prophesied" (Acts 19:1-6). Again we have different nationalities involved here. Paul was not from Ephesus. Now it is a good possibility that these disciples did indeed speak the same language as Paul, but possibly not the rest of the group. And so when they were blessed with the Holy Spirit they could speak natively and to Paul because that is how tongues work. It is the ability to speak once in one's own language and everyone in their own language hears things as if it were spoken in the hearer's native language. There is no hint of babbling but there is a strong implication of real languages involved here because the Bible makes it a point to make known where these people were from.

"Now there are diversities of gifts, but the same Spirit. And there are differences of administrations, but the same Lord. And there are diversities of operations, but it is the same God which worketh all in all. But the manifestation of the Spirit is given to every man to profit withal. For to one is given by the Spirit the word of wisdom; to another the word of knowledge by the same Spirit; To another faith by the same Spirit; to another the gifts of healing by the same Spirit; To another the working of miracles; to another prophecy; to another discerning of spirits; to another [divers] kinds of tongues; to another the interpretation of tongues: But all these worketh that one and the selfsame Spirit, dividing to every man severally as he will" (1 Corinthians 12:4-11). First of all, notice who hands out the gifts. It is the Holy Spirit. We do not just pray for the ability to speak in tongues and it magically happens. On Pentecost, those gathered together did not even hint at such a request. It happened as the Holy Spirit deemed it necessary. Second, the purpose of all of the gifts is for the diversity that is necessary to conduct the operation of the church. What is the operation? "Go ye therefore, and teach all nations, baptizing them in the name of the Father, and of the Son, and of the Holy Ghost: Teaching them to observe all things whatsoever I have commanded you: and, lo, I am with you alway, [even] unto the end of the world" (Matthew 28:19-20). So which type of tongues helps with this operation? Does babbling some unknown tongue in the congregation accomplish the gospel commission, or does visiting a foreign country and the Holy Spirit acting as an interpreter between languages? Obviously it is the latter.

Besides, if one were to visit a church that practices speaking in tongues, it surely comes across as it being the most important item when it is the least according to God. The Bible says, "And God hath set some in the church, first apostles, secondarily prophets, thirdly teachers, after that miracles, then gifts of healings, helps, governments, diversities of tongues" (1 Corinthians 12:28). Please note that the most important gift is that of apostles or missionaries. Second most important thing is to have are prophets, which interestingly, are usually condemned in most denominations today because they do not believe in modern day prophets. Third most important thing is to have are teachers. Then take note the use of the phrase "after that" meaning, far down the list and used in rare cases. If any of them had significant practice, then we would not see such wording. "After that" is along the lines of saying, "And then there is this other stuff." The gifts after those words are not even numbered, so that is how far down the list they are. Now if a church has missionaries, prophets, and teachers, do not think then that they can have permission to practice weekly tongue séances. The remaining gifts are only used when necessary. We do not mean they are insignificant, but they are not to be in the position that many practice today. If everyone speaks the same language, there is no need to confuse the congregation with some foreign, even God only understood language. Even churches that center around miracles and healings are wrong.

No matter how much today's Christians want to distance themselves from Israel and the Jews, in reality, we need to keep in mind that "Jesus Christ the same yesterday, and to day, and for ever" (Hebrews 13:8). "For I

[am] the LORD, I change not" (Malachi 3:6). The summary of it all is this, Adam and Eve were tested and failed. Sin cut God the Father off and so Jesus was promised to be the Lamb of God. In the meantime, God uses humans to teach humans and not angels or even Himself, outside of little moments in time. In so doing, we have a period of a strong leader to teach the truth of God, followed by a nation, and followed by a spiritual nation. Adam and Eve received the promise (Genesis 3:15) that they passed on to every succeeding generation that lived afterwards. Abel was killed (Genesis 4:8) and the lineage of Seth began (Genesis 4:25, Genesis chapter 5), however, most people, even today, choose to sin and be selfish rather than live in obedience (Genesis 6:5) and eventually such became the norm back then that it threatened all mention of God if Noah were simply to have dropped dead (Genesis 6:8). So a flood was sent (Genesis 6:17). God tried again with Abraham (Genesis 12:1), Isaac (Genesis 17:19), and Jacob (Genesis 32:26) until we get to the point that it is time to spread the message wider by using a nation. So Moses and the Israelites step in (Deuteronomy 7:7), which eventually dissolved into ten kingdoms being dispersed (Ezekiel 12:15) leaving Benjamin and Judah to be the kingdom of Judah occupying the nation of Israel (Jeremiah 17:26) and introducing the term "Jews" (Ezra 6:14). From there, Jesus was to show up, be accepted, and empower the nation to go forth to teach the world (Daniel 9:24-27) only they had rejected Him (Mark 15:13), crucified Him (Mark 15:25), and did everything they could to work against Him (John 11:48). Therefore, Jesus said, "Upon this rock I will build my church; and the gates of hell shall not prevail against it" (Matthew 16:18). Unfortunately, in the spirit of compromising to increase the numbers in the church, the visible church took on pagan traditions causing true worshippers to go into hiding (Revelation 12:6). When it was time for the truth to come forth, people like Hus and Martin Luther and many other reformers tried calling the main church away from their compromised ways, but they refused, hence the persecutions took place at the hand of the church (Revelation 17:6). Unfortunately, many Protestants are compromisers at heart and driven by such a spirit, we have tens of thousands of different Christian denominations and sects doing no differently than the Vatican, which is that they are not to solidly forming doctrine by the Bible and the Bible alone. Yet, God still has a people that adhere to such for they "keep the commandments of God, and have the testimony of Jesus Christ" (Revelation 12:17), as well as, "keep the commandments of God, and the faith of Jesus" (Revelation 14:12). They also have the "patience of the saints" (Revelation 14:12). It is the same theme from Adam and Eve until the end of time: Turn people to God and be saved! That never changed, only the methodology. So in reality, there is no difference between Jew and Christian, between Israel and the Patriarchs, yet Christians today try to make it a point of contention. How sad, but this explains why Christians believe in gifts only since Pentecost, Israel was under the law but Christians are under grace, Israel was all about the physical objects but Christians go by faith, and on and on we could go.

Continuing with tongues, we come across the popularly quoted Corinthian chapter. It begins with the words, "Though I speak with the tongues of men and of angels" (1 Corinthians 13:1), many separate tongues into two lines. One is the languages found on the planet (men), while there is another language that only angels understand. First off, this is a mere comparison. This is not establishing that such is the case, but if it were so, if a person "have not charity," then they would be able to say, "I am become [as] sounding brass, or a tinkling cymbal" (1 Corinthians 13:1). The second thing is that if we had the ability to speak the language of angels, what purpose would that serve? It is not like angels answer back. In fact, just like any foreign language, sometimes the accent is off, and one can tell that something was not conveyed properly by the look on the recipient's face. This is not possible seeing that we do not get to see such faces. So all we may know is that we are butchering the language when we practice such babblings. And thirdly, would that then mean us impure humans are dictating, having one way conversation, into a pure environment? How dare we think we can barge into that atmosphere while so many still practice sin! Worship from mankind should be, well, from mankind. So to justify speaking babble as a special gift of tongues based upon this verse is one of those thoughts of building a house upon sand. Besides, when Jesus shows up, it is declared in the same chapter, "Whether [there be] tongues, they shall cease" (1 Corinthians 13:8). That sounds contradictory to the thought that if we are speaking a heavenly language that angels understand, now that we would be in their presence, ought we not speak their language the more instead of ceasing? The truth of the matter is that in the beginning, "the whole earth was of one language" (Genesis 11:1), but then there was an incident. "So the LORD scattered them abroad from thence upon the face of all the earth: and they left off to build the city. Therefore is the name of it called Babel; because the LORD did there confound the language of all the earth: and from thence did the LORD scatter them abroad upon the face of all the earth" (Genesis 11:8). When Jesus returns and gathers us for Heaven, we will more than likely all be endowed with God's initial language, whatever that was.

And then moving on in sequence to chapter 14, what is used to justify tongue speaking is actually a condemnation of the babblings promoted in most churches. It begins with, "Follow after charity, and desire spiritual [gifts], but rather that ye may prophesy" (1 Corinthians 14:1). So if there is any gift to be desired, it is that of prophesy, but interestingly, it is the most rejected of all gifts. Many Christians do not believe in modern day prophets. Many Christians consider all prophets today and in the most recent centuries as false. And the world laughs at such things since they are reduced to tabloid newspapers, 1-900 numbers, and comical on television as well as in the movies. But instead of desiring prophesying, tongues seems to be the most desired by Christians who believe in the modern false form.

The next verse combined with the third verse reveals the truth in what is about to be further addressed. "For he that speaketh in an [unknown] tongue speaketh not unto men, but unto God: for no man understandeth [him]; howbeit in the spirit he speaketh mysteries. But he that prophesieth speaketh unto men [to] edification, and exhortation, and comfort" (1 Corinthians 14:2-3). If one were to just focus on the first sentence, it really comes across as a positive practice and desire to speak in tongues. It comes across as, "Sure, people only hear babbling because they are unconverted, but that is alright, I am speaking to God!" They also think that they have a special insight into the mysteries of God, when in fact the meaning is more along the lines, "Who knows what such tongue speaking people are saying? What a mystery! There is something not right in their minds to do this." How do we know these are the intentions? The use of the word "but" to start the next sentence tells us that a contrast is being conveyed. It also fits in with the first verse. The edification, the exhortation, the comfort is being brought to the church when prophets of God speak. This is the gift, as the first verse states, that we ought to desire. And sandwiched in between is this contrary verse that pushes the importance of speaking in a non understandable tongue down, as if to say, "Do not give in to that impression of the devil to start speaking babbly words."

This is further clarified by the fourth verse, "He that speaketh in an [unknown] tongue edifieth himself; but he that prophesieth edifieth the church" (1 Corinthians 14:4). Are we to edify ourselves? Of course not. Our goal always is to edify the church. So the beginning of this chapter is nothing short of condemning churches for the practice of this false gift that is used to brag about their Christianity instead of promoting the gospel commission.

So after strongly putting tongues in the position it is supposed to be, Paul turns around, and says, "I would that ye all spake with tongues, but rather that ye prophesied: for greater [is] he that prophesieth than he that speaketh with tongues, except he interpret, that the church may receive edifying" (1 Corinthians 14:5). Did Paul really now elevate tongues to the point that he wants everyone speaking in tongues? Did he just make an allowance for people to speak in tongues as long as someone can tell people what it means? As Peter states regarding Paul's writings, "they that are unlearned and unstable wrest, as [they do] also the other scriptures, unto their own destruction" (2 Peter 3:16). The unstable in this case are those that insist that babbling is the gift of tongues. The unlearned are those that do not take in the whole Bible and understand the deeper meaning of things. These are the people who think church is about having a good time. Nowhere in these verses so far is there any reference to babbling being a positive thing. The reason why it would be great that everyone spoke in tongues is because if everyone knew Italian, German, Spanish, etc. that means we would be able to understand each other easily, but if we cannot speak, we surely cannot understand it, so unless there is an interpreter to tell the meaning, the church does not get edified. Ever have someone or a group from a foreign country come to church and express the wonderful workings of God in their native language? What good is it if no one can interpret? Does the church get edified? Except for some exciting gestures, the person or people speaking are just wasting their breath on the congregation. Additionally, Paul did not just undo the first four verses with, "I would that ye all spake with tongues" for he immediately stayed consistent by saying, "BUT rather that ye prophesied." So verse 5 is not a contradiction to the first four verses, but poor words used out of contextual meaning.

Besides, what I just shared is exactly what verse 6 is all about. "Now, brethren, if I come unto you speaking with tongues, what shall I profit you, except I shall speak to you either by revelation, or by knowledge, or by prophesying, or by doctrine?" What use is it if an Italian visited a congregation and there was no one that understood Italian? But if that same Italian spoke in the congregation's language providing revelation, knowledge, prophesy, or doctrine, now we have a blessed congregation. So this too is a verse in lowering the importance of babbling in church passing it off as tongues.

So Paul continues to admonish the case against "unknown tongues" by saying, "And even things without life giving sound, whether pipe or harp, except they give a distinction in the sounds, how shall it be known what is piped or harped? For if the trumpet give an uncertain sound, who shall prepare himself to the battle? So likewise ye, except ye utter by the tongue words easy to be understood, how shall it be known what is spoken? for ye shall speak into the air" (1 Corinthians 14:7-9).

But most significantly is Paul's reference to the different voices or languages in the world. "There are, it may be, so many kinds of voices in the world, and none of them [is] without signification" (1 Corinthians 14:10). No language is without signification. The smallest group of people speaking in a certain dialect is just as important as billions of people speaking English. The point is, 1 Corinthians 14 is not about promoting an unknown tongue as a gift but rather is identifying real languages of this planet called earth. "Therefore if I know not the meaning of the voice, I shall be unto him that speaketh a barbarian, and he that speaketh [shall be] a barbarian unto me" (1 Corinthians 14:11).

And as a reminder, when we evaluate the gifts of the Spirit, we have to make sure we are not being influenced by the more populous presence on earth, the devil and his angels imitating the gift. "Even so ye, forasmuch as ye are zealous of spiritual [gifts], seek that ye may excel to the edifying of the church" (1 Corinthians 14:12). If the church is not edified, it is false. A healer being chauffeured, living in a mansion, wearing all that glitters, is not edifying the church but himself.

"Wherefore", those that visit a church from a foreign country, "let him that speaketh in an [unknown] tongue pray that he may interpret" (1 Corinthians 14:13). Hopefully these people will be able to pick up the language of the congregation.

Now even in one's personal life, praying in an unknown tongue is not beneficial "For if I pray in an [unknown] tongue, my spirit prayeth, but my understanding is unfruitful" (1 Corinthians 14:14). "What is it then? I will pray with the spirit, and I will pray with the understanding also: I will sing with the spirit, and I will sing with the understanding also" (1 Corinthians 14:15). In other words, being moved by the Spirit to pray, I'm certainly going to use my understandable language.

Even during public prayer, if one were to show forth the ability to speak in an "unknown tongue" what benefit is there to the congregation? "Else when thou shalt bless with the spirit, how shall he that occupieth the room of the unlearned say Amen at thy giving of thanks, seeing he understandeth not what thou sayest?" (1 Corinthians 14:16). But if one persists anyways, "For thou verily givest thanks well, but the other is not edified" (1 Corinthians 14:17). In other words, the person praying is getting the attention but the church is not edified, and that is wrong. "Yet in the church I had rather speak five words with my understanding, that [by my voice] I might teach others also, than ten thousand words in an [unknown] tongue" (1 Corinthians 14:19). This is definitely not a positive reference for "unknown tongues". And then Paul gets a little sarcastic towards those that persist in this babbling and showing off. "Brethren, be not children in understanding: howbeit in malice be ye children, but in understanding be men" (1 Corinthians 14:20).

Then Paul draws upon the Old Testament example, by saying, "In the law it is written, With [men of] other tongues and other lips will I speak unto this people; and yet for all that will they not hear me, saith the Lord" (1 Corinthians 14:21). In looking up in the Old Testament words from this verse, we find a similar reference in Isaiah 28:11, "For with stammering lips and another tongue will he speak to this people." This is interesting because right before it, the Bible says, "Whom shall he teach knowledge? and whom shall he make to understand doctrine? [them that are] weaned from the milk, [and] drawn from the breasts. For precept [must be] upon precept, precept upon precept; line upon line, line upon line; here a little, [and] there a little" (Isaiah 28:9-10). It is almost as if God is saying, "The topic of tongues is a controversial topic, so to understand the proper meaning, do a Bible search with precepts, whole verses, even parts of verses that apply. Further, immediately after Isaiah 28:11, the following appears: "To whom he said, This [is] the rest [wherewith] ye may cause the weary to rest; and this [is] the refreshing: yet they would not hear" (Isaiah 28:12). When we see the word rest, the Sabbath ought to come to mind, especially after reading all of Hebrews 4, yet, people do not want to hear about the Sabbath. In fact, those that practice in the church the use of speaking in "unknown tongue" use this gift of the devil to feel confirmed in rejecting the Sabbath, just as stated: "yet they would not hear". So Paul, in 1 Corinthians 14:21, is even drawing the Sabbath subject into the discussion, but people will not hear.

And the Paul gets very specific. "Wherefore tongues are for a sign, not to them that believe, but to them that believe not: but prophesying [serveth] not for them that believe not, but for them which believe" (1 Corinthians 14:22). This verse alone tells us that any church that practices speaking in tongues during a church service is absolutely wrong. Tongues are not for the believer's purposes; it is for missionary work or those that do not believe. And prophesy is not for the tabloids, 1-900 numbers, or any other public purpose but is for the church. And if a church were in the middle of such a service and a prospective person enters in, "If therefore the whole church be come together into one place, and all speak with tongues, and there come in [those that are] unlearned, or unbelievers, will they not say that ye are mad? But if all prophesy, and there come in one that believeth not, or [one] unlearned, he is convinced of all, he is judged of all: And thus are the secrets of his heart made manifest; and so falling down on [his] face he will worship God, and report that God is in you of a truth" (1 Corinthians 14:23-25).

Now here is a question. "How is it then, brethren? when ye come together, every one of you hath a psalm, hath a doctrine, hath a tongue, hath a revelation, hath an interpretation. Let all things be done unto edifying" (1 Corinthians 14:26). Is it not amazing that when tongues are spoken, in many cases the whole congregations get involved in babbling. Paul brings such practices into question.

And again, in the next verse, Paul is not actually encouraging speaking in tongues, but is addressing when there is a multicultural gathering, let us do everything orderly. "If any man speak in an [unknown] tongue, [let it be] by two, or at the most [by] three, and [that] by course; and let one interpret. But if there be no interpreter, let him keep silence in the church; and let him speak to himself, and to God" (1 Corinthians 14:27-28).

Even prophesying has to be done orderly. "Let the prophets speak two or three, and let the other judge. If [any thing] be revealed to another that sitteth by, let the first hold his peace. For ye may all prophesy one by one, that all may learn, and all may be comforted. And the spirits of the prophets are subject to the prophets" (1 Corinthians 14:29-32). Please note that prophets will never contradict prior prophets. In other words, modern prophets are subject to the Bible. So if a person declares to be a prophet and says that God has changed the Sabbath, that is not right, for that prophet would be contradicting quite a few Bible writers, who were all prophets, from Moses through Paul, even John and Peter. The reason modern prophets are subject to the Bible is "For God is not [the author] of confusion, but of peace, as in all churches of the saints" (1 Corinthians 14:33).

In summary of the tongues, here is the bottom line. "Wherefore, brethren, covet to prophesy, and forbid not to speak with tongues. Let all things be done decently and in order" (1 Corinthians 14:39-40). And we are not forbidding speaking in tongues; we are just providing insight to the proper and orderly conduct of speaking in a foreign language.

Now since the subject of prophets has come up, we would do a disservice if we did not set it to proper biblical practice as well. Evidently from the chapter we just reviewed verse by verse, prophets are expected and encouraged. Jesus Himself said, "Beware of false prophets" (Matthew 7:15); He did not say, "Beware of prophets." Therefore, there must be true ones, but as usual, the devil counterfeits what God has and does so by the multitude of options. Elijah was the true prophet of the day, yet Satan had not just one or two, but it was said, "Then said Elijah unto the people, I, [even] I only, remain a prophet of the LORD; but Baal's prophets [are] four hundred and fifty men" (1 Kings 18:22). Jeremiah was the true prophet of his day, and Satan had "The prophets prophesy falsely, and the priests bear rule by their means" (Jeremiah 5:31). Do you really think Noah was the only one making predictions? Satan had his prophets of the day as well. And it is not a coincidence that the end of time is marked by the dethroning of the Antichrist in 1798 and an explosion of prophets have come on the scene since then. Besides, the Bible clearly teaches, "Despise not prophesyings. Prove all things; hold fast that which is good" (1 Thessalonians 5:20-21). On top of that, Joel 2:28-29 states, "And it shall come to pass afterward, [that] I will pour out my spirit upon all flesh; and your sons and your daughters shall prophesy, your old men shall dream dreams, your young men shall see visions: And also upon the servants and upon the handmaids in those days will I pour out my spirit."

So, how does one prove a true prophet from a false one?

1. Numbers 12:6 states, "And he said, Hear now my words: If there be a prophet among you, [I] the LORD will make myself known unto him in a vision, [and] will speak unto him in a dream." The first test is that a prophet receives messages from God through visions and dreams. Receiving them out of staring at "water or the flame every night" causing self hypnosis is not how God works.

2. Deuteronomy 18:22 states, "When a prophet speaketh in the name of the LORD, if the thing follow not, nor come to pass, that [is] the thing which the LORD hath not spoken, [but] the prophet hath spoken it presumptuously: thou shalt not be afraid of him." A prophet must be 100% accurate when he or she says, "The Lord has revealed..." If there is an error, that person is not of God because God is never wrong, right?

3. Deuteronomy 13:1-4 states, "If there arise among you a prophet, or a dreamer of dreams, and giveth thee a sign or a wonder, And the sign or the wonder come to pass, whereof he spake unto thee, saying, Let us go after other gods, which

thou hast not known, and let us serve them; Thou shalt not hearken unto the words of that prophet, or that dreamer of dreams: for the LORD your God proveth you, to know whether ye love the LORD your God with all your heart and with all your soul. Ye shall walk after the LORD your God, and fear him, and keep his commandments, and obey his voice, and ye shall serve him, and cleave unto him." God says that He will allow false prophets to be 100% accurate in regards to signs, but test what they say. If they speak contrary to the Word of God or His commandments, God wants to know who you will follow Him or the false prophet. And many do follow after false prophets especially those who speak against the law. This is reiterated in Isaiah 8:20, "To the law and to the testimony: if they speak not according to this word, [it is] because [there is] no light in them."

4. 2 Kings 5:15-16 states, "And he returned to the man of God, he and all his company, and came, and stood before him: and he said, Behold, now I know that [there is] no God in all the earth, but in Israel: now therefore, I pray thee, take a blessing of thy servant. But he said, [As] the LORD liveth, before whom I stand, I will receive none. And he urged him to take [it]; but he refused." Naaman was trying to buy off or give a reward unto Elisha who refused to accept it. From this illustration, a prophet does not charge a fee.

5. 2 Peter 1:20 states, "Knowing this first, that no prophecy of the scripture is of any private interpretation." A prophet does not reinterpret another prophet's visions and dreams; rather, they speak in harmony with those interpretations.

6. 2 Peter 1:21 states, "For the prophecy came not in old time by the will of man: but holy men of God spake [as they were] moved by the Holy Ghost." All credit is given to God and never taken upon themselves. Remember who we are to edify.

7. Isaiah 58:1 states, "Cry aloud, spare not, lift up thy voice like a trumpet, and shew my people their transgression, and the house of Jacob their sins." Prophets are not for enjoyment but rather for revealing the sins of the people and to call them to repentance. And it is not an easy job. People do not like to hear that they have to change their ways. No wonder prophets have been killed and stoned.

8. Isaiah 24:21 states, "And it shall come to pass in that day, [that] the LORD shall punish the host of the high ones [that are] on high, and the kings of the earth upon the earth." Prophets always reveal God's judgment that is coming upon the earth and upon those who choose not to repent.

9. 1 Corinthians 14:4 states, "He that speaketh in an [unknown] tongue edifieth himself; but he that prophesieth edifieth the church." If the prophet begins to call people to follow him or her, that is not God's prophet. God's prophet will lift up the church and draw people to be more active in the church.

10. Daniel 10:17 states, "For how can the servant of this my lord talk with this my lord? for as for me, straightway there remained no strength in me, neither is there breath left in me." A prophet will not breathe during a vision and will lose all consciousness.

11. Matthew 7:16-20 states, "Ye shall know them by their fruits. Do men gather grapes of thorns, or figs of thistles? Even so every good tree bringeth forth good fruit; but a corrupt tree bringeth forth evil fruit. A good tree cannot bring forth evil fruit, neither [can] a corrupt tree bring forth good fruit. Every tree that bringeth not forth good fruit is hewn down, and cast into the fire. Wherefore by their fruits ye shall know them." Now be careful. Let us not judge the skin of the fruit. The fruit may look good but be rotten on the inside. Their entire character has to be put under a magnifying glass. Now we are not judging the person as going to heaven or hell, for the Bible condemns such, however, we are told to judge the actions if they be right or wrong. So if a prophet preaches one message and lives another type of lifestyle, that is not a prophet of God.

That is eleven tests with the addition that all tests must be 100% satisfied. Additionally, God has a pattern that He works with. He predicts the event well before it occurs with one or more prophets, and when the event is to occur, another prophet or prophets issue the final warnings. Let us look at a few examples.

1. Who predicted well in advance that the flood was coming? Enoch by naming his son Methuselah, which means, "At his death, it shall come." Which prophet was used to warn the people when the time of the flood was to be fulfilled? Noah.

2. Who predicted the captivity of the Israelites in Egypt? Abraham (Genesis 15:13). Which prophet brought them out of Egypt? Moses.

3. Who predicted the Babylonian captivity? Jeremiah (Jeremiah 25:11-12). Which prophet was around during that time? Daniel.

4. Who predicted the first coming of Jesus? Just about all the Old Testament prophets. Which prophet ushered in the first coming of Jesus? John the Baptist.

So what is the purpose of the prophets? Ephesians 4:11-13 tells us, "And he gave some, apostles; and some, prophets; and some, evangelists; and some, pastors and teachers; For the perfecting of the saints, for the work of the ministry, for the edifying of the body of Christ: Till we all come in the unity of the faith, and of the knowledge of the Son of God, unto a perfect man, unto the measure of the stature of the fulness of Christ." Are the saints perfect? Do we have a unified faith? No of course not. Christianity is the most broken faith compared to any other. Then Apostles, Prophets, Evangelists, Pastors, and Teachers all have a role to play in guiding the body of Christ.

And what protection is there when following the prophets? According to Ephesians 4:14-16, we are told, "That we [henceforth] be no more children, tossed to and fro, and carried about with every wind of doctrine, by the sleight of men, [and] cunning craftiness, whereby they lie in wait to deceive; But speaking the truth in love, may grow up into him in all things, which is the head, [even] Christ: From whom the whole body fitly joined together and compacted by that which every joint supplieth, according to the effectual working in the measure of every part, maketh increase of the body unto the edifying of itself in love."

So, why Did prophesying seem to disappear? Jeremiah 26:4-6 reveals to us, "And thou shalt say unto them, Thus saith the LORD; If ye will not hearken to me, to walk in my law, which I have set before you, To hearken to the words of my servants the prophets, whom I sent unto you, both rising up early, and sending [them], but ye have not hearkened; Then will I make this house like Shiloh, and will make this city a curse to all the nations of the earth."

God tells us that when the people fall away from the Word of the Lord and His Law, He will not pour out His Spirit. It would be made like Shiloh. And the greatest period of falling away was that of the dark ages. This is reiterated in Lamentations 2:9, which says, "Her gates are sunk into the ground; he hath destroyed and broken her bars: her king and her princes [are] among the Gentiles: the law [is] no [more]; her prophets also find no vision from the LORD." Clearly, when the law is dismissed, the prophets will not receive messages from God.

In returning to the main topic of feast days, so far we have taken care of four of the major feasts days out of the seven listed. Again, we have Jesus fulfilling Passover with His death, fulfilling Unleavened Bread with His perfect life purging out sin, fulfilling First Fruits with His resurrection, and at Pentecost with sending the Holy Spirit. Likewise, we have eternal life because of Jesus being our Passover; we have victory over sing because Jesus being the Unleavened Bread and not influenced by sin in the slightest; we have hope in the grand resurrection that all who die in Christ will enjoy together because of Jesus being the first fruits of those that sleep; and we have the empowerment to go forth to make converts thanks to Jesus' Pentecostal power of the Holy Spirit. Now since Jesus perfectly fulfilled these first four feasts, of which all pertain to the first coming of Christ, then there should be no doubt that the three remaining feasts, which all pertain to the second coming, will also be fulfilled.

Now the first coming feast days were all fulfilled basically instantaneously, however, the feasts regarding the second coming are drawn out. That is because if they are all fulfilled instantaneously, basically Jesus will show up unannounced and catch many off guard and even more people would be lost. That is just not how God operates for "the Lord is not slack concerning his promise, as some men count slackness; but is longsuffering to us-ward, not willing that any should perish, but that all should come to repentance" (2 Peter 3:9).

TRUMPETS:

Even the first of the remaining feast days reveals the character of God's patience and love towards the human race. It is called the Feast of Trumpets, which in short means, it is a warning towards an event so that none may be lost. This is found in Leviticus 23:23-25, which says, "And the LORD spake unto Moses, saying, Speak unto the children of Israel, saying, In the seventh month, in the first [day] of the month, shall ye have a sabbath, a memorial of blowing of trumpets, an holy convocation. Ye shall do no servile work [therein]: but ye shall offer an offering made by fire unto the LORD."

It is not by coincidence that God had the first four feasts in the spring offering life and power while the last three feasts occur in the autumn as the cycle is dying, hinting towards the end of the world. It is also not a coincidence that in between is the long hot summer, which many associate with drought and during the dark ages under Antichrist reign. "Behold, the days come, saith the Lord GOD, that I will send a famine in the land, not a famine of bread, nor a thirst for water, but of hearing the words of the LORD: And they shall wander from sea to sea, and from the north even to the east, they shall run to and fro to seek the word of the LORD, and shall not find [it]" (Amos 8:11-12). And then all of a sudden, a Bible explosion occurred in the 1800's. Bible societies sprung up; preachers were preaching gospel grace; the world was exploding with beautiful messages as well as very concerning messages, one of which is outlined in the Book of Revelation.

The feast of trumpets is fulfilled by Jesus awakening His people. The Bible says, "And I saw another mighty angel come down from heaven, clothed with a cloud: and a rainbow [was] upon his head, and his face [was] as it were the sun, and his feet as pillars of fire: And he had in his hand a little book open: and he set his right foot upon the sea, and [his] left [foot] on the earth" (Revelation 10:1-2). Now how many angels conduct Bible studies with humans? None. God Himself does not go door to door looking for potential people to study with or talk to. So since Revelation is built upon "signifying" objects, even angels represent things.

According to Psalms 104:4, questions are asked and synonyms are used. "Who maketh his angels spirits; his ministers a flaming fire." From this verse, we see angels represent the activity of ministering. That is even their purpose, as in Matthew 4:11 states, "Then the devil leaveth him, and, behold, angels came and ministered unto him." So the act of ministering is represented with the angel keeping in mind that a book is in use and therefore, to minister with a book, specifically the scriptures, is to be ministering with the gospel. But as a reminder, God did not commission angels to go and preach the gospel, He told humans, "Go ye into all the world, and preach the gospel to every creature" (Mark 16:15). So the angel is representing all who take the gospel to the world.

Now "The waters which thou sawest," as a reminder, "are peoples, and multitudes, and nations, and tongues" (Revelation 17:15). That would mean the land would be the opposite, which is the sparsely populated. Therefore the messengers are to go to the populated and unpopulated areas of the world. The angel having his foot on land and in the sea is representative of a global message, which is pretty much how God works, for Jesus said, "This gospel of the kingdom shall be preached in all the world" (Matthew 24:14).

So continuing in Revelation 10, the Bible says, "And cried with a loud voice, as [when] a lion roareth: and when he had cried, seven thunders uttered their voices. And when the seven thunders had uttered their voices, I was about to write: and I heard a voice from heaven saying unto me, Seal up those things which the seven thunders uttered, and write them not" (Revelation 10:3-4). What the seven thunders uttered, God only knows, but what we do know is that a loud voice is used. Interestingly, other angels do the same thing (Revelation 14:7, 9, 15, and 18), all of which are warnings. That means the world should stop in their tracks and seriously contemplate these things, but the devil has the world chasing after objects, desiring the things of the world, and overall, too busy to stop and think.

"And the angel which I saw stand upon the sea and upon the earth lifted up his hand to heaven, And sware by him that liveth for ever and ever, who created heaven, and the things that therein are, and the earth, and the things that therein are, and the sea, and the things which are therein, that there should be time no longer: But in the days of the voice of the seventh angel, when he shall begin to sound, the mystery of God should be finished, as he hath declared to his servants the prophets." (Revelation 10:5-7). Again, God's creatorship is being acknowledged here. To the Christian, that should be an obvious statement. God indeed created all things. What is the seriousness of having to pause and make such a statement? Well, placing this chapter some time shortly after 1798, which is the time the deadly wound struck the Antichrist, it is not by coincidence that the world was calling into question the existence of God and God's title of being Creator. Charles Darwin was beginning to offer an alternative understanding of how things came into existence.

And not by coincidence, around the same time, there should be a message about "time no longer". In relationship with the gospel, "time no longer" could imply a message about the second coming. And was there such a message after 1798 and around the time of Charles Darwin? There sure was. According to *Wikipedia*, an event known as the "Great Disappointment" occurred. This is where a Baptist minister, William Miller, along with many others independently around the world, predicted the coming of Jesus in 1844. Fortunately for us, he and the others were wrong about the event, although the other items preached upon were not so much in error, and we ought to be careful to dismiss all of his studies simply because Jesus did not show up.

The timing of their message was right on time. The rising of God's prophet or prophets was right on time. The message content was even predicted to be in error and was right on time. Up until then, people did not consider the nearness of the second coming all that much, but since then, that seems to be on many people's minds.

"And the voice which I heard from heaven spake unto me again, and said, Go [and] take the little book which is open in the hand of the angel which standeth upon the sea and upon the earth" (Revelation 10:8). Now the fact that a little book is now open implies that it first was closed or sealed. Searching through the Bible, there is only one little book that was ever sealed and predicted to be opened at a later date. Not by coincidence that later date seems to fit the 1800's, in which the Book of Daniel was unsealed. "But thou, O Daniel, shut up the words, and seal the book, [even] to the time of the end: many shall run to and fro, and knowledge shall be increased" (Daniel 12:4). "And he said, Go thy way, Daniel: for the words [are] closed up and sealed till the time of the end" (Daniel 12:9). The timing of opening the book would be when people could run to and fro as well as having their knowledge increased. And the 1800's certainly saw that both physically and spiritually. Transportation modes increased beginning in the 1800's while concordances made Bible running to and for easier. In both cases, knowledge has greatly increased since the 1800's and continues to explode today.

"And I went unto the angel, and said unto him, Give me the little book. And he said unto me, Take [it], and eat it up; and it shall make thy belly bitter, but it shall be in thy mouth sweet as honey. And I took the little book out of the angel's hand, and ate it up; and it was in my mouth sweet as honey: and as soon as I had eaten it, my belly was bitter" (Revelation 10:9-10). The sweet taste of the gospel predicting Jesus' soon return indeed seemed so sweet at the time, but when Jesus did not show up in 1844, a great disappointing feeling set in.

But there is good news. "And he said unto me, Thou must prophesy again before many peoples, and nations, and tongues, and kings" (Revelation 10:11). There is still a second coming message to be preached to the entire world including to kings! But it is the corrected message that is to go forth. So though the group around the world in 1844 got the message of the event wrong, the fact that Jesus woke up the world to the imminent thought that the second coming is very soon has happened right on time. We indeed are living in the last days, not as some people think restricting it to a mere twenty or so years, but rather since 1798, God has been trying to get the message around the world about the true meaning of being prepared. Unfortunately, Satan has his "man" to "deceive you" (Matthew 24:4) called Antichrist.

"And many false prophets shall rise, and shall deceive many" (Matthew 24:11), even while preaching about the second coming being soon, "For there shall arise false Christs, and false prophets, and shall shew great signs and wonders; insomuch that, if [it were] possible, they shall deceive the very elect" (Matthew 24:24). And look at the 1800's regarding prophets. Many famous ones arose right on time. Some are God's but the majority are Satan's. To dismiss all as Satan's would contradict prophecy.

So now, we begin with Jesus fulfilling the Feast of Trumpets with the 1800's Advent message of which we get to participate in by adhering to the trumpet or warning message as well when going forth with the proper message announcing the next feast, the Feast of Atonement, which is a feast regarding judgment. Interestingly, before Jesus shows up (Revelation 14), there are warning messages provided as well. One of those messages states, "Fear God, and give glory to him; for the hour of his judgment is come" (Revelation 14:7). What this tells us is that this message was not to be preached by the apostles. It was not even to be preached by those living up through the Dark Ages. It is a message for those living at the end of time, in which is again, not the last five, ten, even twenty years of earth but a period of time spanning over a hundred year period, like in the days of Noah. That means that this message and the others connected with it should have been declared beginning in the 1800's and continuing to the present day and even into the future until Jesus comes, well, at least pretty close to that event.

ATONEMENT:

The Feast of Atonement is found in Leviticus 23:26-32, which says, "And the LORD spake unto Moses, saying, Also on the tenth [day] of this seventh month [there shall be] a day of atonement: it shall be an holy convocation unto you; and ye shall afflict your souls, and offer an offering made by fire unto the LORD. And ye shall do no work in that same day: for it [is] a day of atonement, to make an atonement for you before the LORD your God. For whatsoever soul [it be] that shall not be afflicted in that same day, he shall be cut off from among his people. And whatsoever soul [it be] that doeth any work in that same day, the same soul will I destroy from among his people. Ye shall do no manner of work: [it shall be] a statute for ever throughout your generations in all your dwellings. It [shall be] unto you a sabbath of rest, and ye shall afflict your souls: in the ninth [day] of the month at even, from even unto even, shall ye celebrate your sabbath."

Please notice the seriousness of this period. This is a period of time that we are to afflict our souls and make an offering with fire, and if we do not, despite claiming to be saved, we will be lost. Again, the notion that we cannot be lost once we are "saved" goes completely against the expression of this feast day. We are to make sure we are ready to meet a holy God. We are to especially be walking in all of the light, "blameless". "Wherefore, beloved, seeing that ye look for such things, be diligent that ye may be found of him in peace, without spot, and blameless" (2 Peter 3:14). The reason is because before Jesus, our "one mediator between God and men" (1 Timothy 2:5), shows up the second time, He will cease mediating for a period of time. But hardly a Christian is afflicting their souls. In fact, most Christians seem to embrace what they are to be afflicting over. Exposing oneself to the filth of television and movies, hearing of evils through music, all of it ought to be removed from our lives yet so many do not as if it is just normal life. It is normal life, for those going to hell.

The Bible says, "And he saw that [there was] no man, and wondered that [there was] no intercessor: therefore his arm brought salvation unto him; and his righteousness, it sustained him" (Isaiah 59:16). Similar wording appears in Revelation 15:8, "And the temple was filled with smoke from the glory of God, and from his power; and no man was able to enter into the temple, till the seven plagues of the seven angels were fulfilled." Putting the two together, when we sin, "we confess our sins, he is faithful and just to forgive us [our] sins, and to cleanse us from all unrighteousness" (1 John 1:9). That is for us who "come boldly unto the throne of grace, that we may obtain mercy, and find grace to help in time of need" (Hebrews 4:16). Now for Jesus to return, He needs to change clothes "For he put on righteousness as a breastplate, and an helmet of salvation upon his head; and he put on the garments of vengeance [for] clothing, and was clad with zeal as a cloke" (Isaiah 59:17), and then He will address the people of earth "According to [their] deeds, accordingly he will repay, fury to his adversaries, recompence to his enemies; to the islands he will repay recompence" (Isaiah 59:18), which is exactly what is predicted in Revelation 22:12, which says, "behold, I come quickly; and my reward [is] with me, to give every man according as his work shall be" (Revelation 22:12). But here is the point. Right before Jesus comes again with His reward, there is a declaration made in Heaven. "He that is unjust, let him be unjust still: and he which is filthy, let him be filthy still: and he that is righteous, let him be righteous still: and he that is holy, let him be holy still" (Revelation 22:11). Once that declaration is made, Jesus changes clothing getting ready to return. From that period of time until Jesus shows up, there will be no switching sides. And if we commit a sin during that time, there will be no way of confessing that sin since the Mediator we confess to will be gone, hence we will have that sin when Jesus returns, and be lost for "the Redeemer shall come to Zion, and unto them that turn from transgression in Jacob, saith the LORD" (Isaiah 59:20). Notice our Redeemer is showing up for only those that have made a complete turn from their transgressions. All those who continue in dismissing the commandments and obedience and are careless about even the little sins now, are going to be in for sad surprise then. "To day if ye will hear his voice, harden not your hearts" (Hebrews 3:15).

And I am not sure if everyone caught a key word in this feast as well as the others. The phrase is "it shall be an holy convocation unto you". That is a gathering together. It is being unified. It is not a time to be splitting into further denominations. It is not a time to be allowing people to believe what they want to believe all believing differently from one another. It is a time for unity. Satan knows this. That is why he is working on unifying all denominations and all religions underneath the pope all the while God is unifying His people in the Word. In other words, we are either having the "one mind" on the side of the devil or the "one mind" of Christ.

Now I would like to pause here and reveal something else that is very, very serious. The first four feasts were all fulfilled in Jesus from the cross to Pentecost. All during that time, the Sabbath of Friday sundown to Saturday sundown was practiced by the people of the time. Even right before Pentecost, regarding journeying, it is said, "Then returned they unto Jerusalem from the mount called Olivet, which is from Jerusalem a sabbath day's journey" (Acts 1:12). So there was no need to discuss the Sabbath subject. But if you read all of Leviticus 23, the first four feasts make no reference to the keeping the feast as a Sabbath. Sure, for Pentecost there was counting from the Sabbath days, seven to be exact, but even Pentecost has no mention of keeping it as a Sabbath. Then we get to the fifth, sixth, and even the seventh feast days and here is what they say:

- For the Feast of Trumpets, "In the seventh month, in the first [day] of the month, shall ye have a sabbath, a memorial of blowing of trumpets" (Leviticus 23:24).

- For the Feast of Atonement, "It [shall be] unto you a sabbath of rest, and ye shall afflict your souls: in the ninth [day] of the month at even, from even unto even, shall ye celebrate your sabbath" (Leviticus 23:32).

- For the Feast of Harvest, "Also in the fifteenth day of the seventh month, when ye have gathered in the fruit of the land, ye shall keep a feast unto the LORD seven days: on the first day [shall be] a sabbath, and on the eighth day [shall be] a sabbath" (Leviticus 23:39).

Now here are some facts and not moments considered coincidences. After Pentecost and before the 1800's, the Antichrist went through the motions to "think to change times and laws" (Daniel 7:25) by removing the second commandment against statues, splitting the last commandment so we have two coveting commandments, and did a double change on keeping the times regarding the Sabbath day. The Antichrist changed the day of reckoning from God's sunsets (Genesis 1:14) into the midnight to midnight schedule and then moved the Sabbath from the seventh day of the week over to the first day of the week. Now keep in mind, the Antichrist only thinks they have done so, while in Heaven, it is not so. The Ten Commandments stand unchanged, and the Sabbath is still sunset Friday to sunset Saturday on the seventh day of the week.

So with the Sabbath pretty much having been replaced by Sunday at the hands of humans, when it is time for the last three feasts to be fulfilled in reality and not symbolically as they were practiced in the Old Testament, God has to address one of the major issues of the time, for "Verily my sabbaths ye shall keep: for it [is] a sign between me and you throughout your generations; that [ye] may know that I [am] the LORD that doth sanctify you" (Exodus 31:13). How can we afflict our souls, which is a sanctifying process, while transgressing majorly on the one commandment that is above all other nine? We cannot. It is above the others because it is the only one of the Ten that serve as the connecting sign between us and God. So, when the Feast of Trumpets is being sounded in the 1800's, an awareness of the true Sabbath is also coming about. Even as early as 1650, the Seventh Day Baptists were developing into a denomination that brought attention to the true Sabbath. Then after the disappointment in the mid 1800's, when Jesus did not show up, we entered into the period known as the atonement, in which the Sabbath attention had grown in prominence. According to the Bible, after the second coming, referring to the last feast known as the Feast of Harvest, it says, "It shall come to pass, [that] from one new moon to another, and from one sabbath to another, shall all flesh come to worship before me, saith the LORD" (Isaiah 66:23). No wonder the commandment begins with the word "Remember" (Exodus 20:8) because God knew the Israelites would forget the Sabbath during their captivity in Egypt, and God knew Christians would forget the Sabbath during their captivity of darkness under Antichrist. It is not a coincidence that only the last three feasts make mention of the Sabbath, so for those that think, "What's the big deal?", please look at it from God's perspective.

Now under the Feast of Trumpets, we have the Sabbath being called upon to be kept. This is especially true when one looks at the warning messages before Jesus returns. "Fear God, and give glory to him; for the hour of his judgment is come: and worship him that made heaven, and earth, and the sea, and the fountains of waters" (Revelation 14:7). The words "made heaven and earth, the sea" are directly quoted out of the Sabbath commandment.

Also under the Feast of Trumpets is the call to afflict our souls readying to be judged and this too is in Revelation 14:7, which says, "for the hour of his judgment is come." Please note the present tense. Contrary to popular belief we are not going to all line up before the great white throne after the second coming. Judgment is happening now.

As for us humans, "it is appointed unto men once to die, but after this the judgment" (Hebrews 9:27). That means that when Jesus shows up declaring, "my reward [is] with me", He knows who is coming in "the resurrection of life" as opposed to "the resurrection of damnation" (John 5:29). That also means that when John "saw the dead, small and great, stand before God; and the books were opened: and another book was opened, which is [the book] of life: and the dead were judged out of those things which were written in the books, according to their works" (Revelation 20:12), does not mean they get to physically stand before God's throne to be judged. First, that means everyone gets to go to Heaven, including Hitler, Saddam, and even Judas among many others only to then be kicked down to hell. It does not make sense to parade the multitude like that through Heaven only to be sent to hell. But what does make sense and fits the scenario is that to stand means for it to be done by our record. Our record will be reviewed no matter how great or small. Interestingly, that also fits the fact that if one is dead, how can they be physically standing? Are the propped up? The verse says that "the dead" are judged. It does not say the "spirit of the dead", "the souls of the dead", or even "the resurrected dead". So if one is dead, only one's record is what stands.

Now, before we go any further, we need to be under the same understanding about matters regarding verses in the Bible. Just like the word "law" applies to the Ten Commandments, the ceremonial laws, laws in general and depending upon the context, which sometimes is hard, only then can we know which one or ones are being referenced. Likewise, the word judgment or the form thereof may refer to different parts of the judgment all classed as judgment. For instance, we know that when Jesus shows up, He is going to "execute judgment upon all" (Jude 1:15), and the Father has given Jesus "authority to execute judgment also, because he is the Son of man" (John 5:27). As the verses state, this would be the carrying out or enforcement of decisions. That is just one phase of God's judgment. We do not serve a god that arbitrarily zaps people; there is a reason behind His actions. Jesus is not just going to say, "Enough is enough! Times up!", and then return taking some arbitrarily to Heaven and casting the rest to Hell. So there must be other parts to the umbrella term of "judgment".

As we also have read, books are used in the judgment. Anyone reviewing something but not executing an action, we would call that part of the judgment phase the investigation. And with that said, we can begin to see the phases are matching any court case, in which, there is an investigation, a verdict, and an execution. As for the verdict, the Bible says, "He that is unjust, let him be unjust still: and he which is filthy, let him be filthy still: and he that is righteous, let him be righteous still: and he that is holy, let him be holy still" (Revelation 22:11). That pretty much looks like every verdict has been handed out, in fact, once that is done, then it is time for Jesus to return.

Now when we suggest such a methodology to God's way of conducting the judgment, people are quick to say, "God is God and He can wrap up the judgment in a blink of an eye. What are we waiting for?" Well, that is not exactly how God works. Remember, the whole universe is watching things play out. None of this is for the benefit of God. It is all for the benefit of the observers. Is Satan right that we do not need a set of laws, known as the Ten Commandments? Is Satan right that God is a selfish, unloving being? So God places Himself under operating restrictions. He is not going to pick a moment in time and snap His fingers, though He could do that. Although He operates outside of our time frame, He has chosen to work with us in our time frame. Therefore, it is only upon death at this point that the investigation and verdict is declared, but at some point such investigation will switch to the living and evidently by the time the first plague is poured out in that all cases will have been decided for "no man was able to enter into the temple, till the seven plagues of the seven angels were fulfilled" (Revelation 15:8).

So, with that stage set, let us take a look at a few verses regarding the judgment. First of all, as a reminder, the period leading up to the second coming is covered by the statement, "the hour of his judgment is come" (Revelation 14:7). It is here and well under way, otherwise if judgment did not happen until after the second coming, this verse would make no sense. And the only way it makes sense even in the present tense is by knowing that we are being investigated only. The verdict and execution is later. And by the way, everyone will be executed. One group will literally be executed in hell fire while the others will be experiencing their record being executed.

What do we mean that our records, assuming we are the saved ones, will be executed? Well, "every idle word that men shall speak, they shall give account thereof in the day of judgment" (Matthew 12:36). Couple that with the fact that John saw people "were judged every man according to their works" (Revelation 20:13). And if we think it is only that which we speak and do, think again. "In the day when God shall judge the secrets of men by Jesus Christ according to my gospel" (Romans 2:16). Jesus will investigate (judge) the secrets that are locked in one's mind. Those words, those works or actions are all recorded and have to be explained. Either we have honestly confessed our sins, therefore they are blotted out or executed out of the record, or we did not, and so our name is blotted out instead and we will be executed.

Now let us make sure such a system exits. The Bible says, "Then they that feared the LORD spake often one to another: and the LORD hearkened, and heard [it], and a book of remembrance was written before him for them that feared the LORD, and that thought upon his name. And they shall be mine, saith the LORD of hosts, in that day when I make up my jewels; and I will spare them, as a man spareth his own son that serveth him. Then shall ye return, and discern between the righteous and the wicked, between him that serveth God and him that serveth him not" (Malachi 3:16-18). So there is a Book of Remembrance, remembering every idle word, every action, every thought. And notice the description of who is considered God's and who is considered Satan's. All of our deeds, do they serve God or self and Satan? The latter is the ones that "serve Him not".

Our purpose on earth is not to get the most out of life despite what we are told. There are only two main purposes for living. Learn and love who God is by making a commitment to be a true Christian is the first, and the second is to love our neighbors as ourselves and share the gospel to hopefully save as many as possible. Outside of that though, we do have to survive this planet with getting a job and providing for the family, but it should not supersede God's two primary jobs we have already been assigned. Too many people get wrapped up in "the cares of this world, and the deceitfulness of riches, and the lusts of other things entering in, choke the word, and it becometh unfruitful" (Mark 4:19). It does not even need to be bad things either. It could simply be waking up, punching the clock, coming home, tending to the family and the house, day after day without significant amount of time with God or any effort to share with others. And significant time is more than meal prayers and crawling into bed prayers.

Another significant description is the multiple references to the fact that the saved "feared the Lord". Interestingly, the vast majority of people and especially Christians do not do this. That is why that is part of the last day message, "Fear God, and give glory to him" (Revelation 14:7). And "Let us hear the conclusion of the whole matter: Fear God, and keep his commandments: for this [is] the whole [duty] of man" (Ecclesiastes 12:13). So only Ten Commandment keeping people get their sins wiped off the books.

Now that takes care of one of the books used in the judgment, but there is another book that is most worthy of mentioning. You see, during the judgment, "another book was opened, which is [the book] of life" (Revelation 20:12), "And whosoever was not found written in the book of life was cast into the lake of fire" (Revelation 20:15). That is a very serious book.

We are either asking God, "Hide thy face from my sins, and blot out all mine iniquities" (Psalms 51:9), or "the LORD shall blot out his name from under heaven" (Deuteronomy 29:20). Ideally, "He that overcometh, the same shall be clothed in white raiment; and I will not blot out his name out of the book of life, but I will confess his name before my Father, and before his angels" (Revelation 3:5). So it is our duty to confess every known sin and by our actions to put into practice what we confessed them as in forsaking them. In other words, confessing to God on Monday about the sinful party weekend knowing full well that there are party plans for the following weekend is not a good confession. "Be not deceived; God is not mocked: for whatsoever a man soweth, that shall he also reap" (Galatians 6:7).

And by the way, believe in God or not, "we must all appear before the judgment seat of Christ; that every one may receive the things [done] in [his] body, according to that he hath done, whether [it be] good or bad" (2 Corinthians 5:10). Basically, using earthly courtroom terms, our docket must pass before Christ and no one is exempt.

And speaking of non-believers, can someone be a good person but just not get involved in all of this witnessing stuff? The Bible says, "He that is not with me is against me: and he that gathereth not with me scattereth" (Luke 11:23), so the answer is no. We are either committed to the whole package or we are counted as against Jesus.

However, there is still room for the honest at heart atheist. God takes everything into consideration. There will be people in Heaven that never knew Jesus for they are described as "[one] shall say unto him, What [are] these wounds in thine hands? Then he shall answer, [Those] with which I was wounded [in] the house of my friends" (Zechariah 13:6). Notice how this person never heard the story of Jesus, but Jesus does not hesitate to tell the story. This is a scene after the second coming and during eternal life.

And since we referenced it, did you know that the wounds in Jesus' hands and feet will be the only constant reminder of sin throughout eternity? Our God will bear the marks of what sin had caused. More importantly, those marks will forever reveal the love of God towards the human race, so much love that He was willing to die for us. No wonder it is said, "The transgression thereof shall be heavy upon it; and it shall fall, and not rise again" (Isaiah 24:20). But how is it so that only the marks will last throughout eternity? God says, "Their sins and iniquities will I remember no more" (Hebrews 10:17). Of course God knows all things, so He simply will never remind us. Besides, at some point our minds are wiped from ever having committed a sin. When we are finally declared to be holy still, there will be no remembrance of our sin. Right now when we confess our sins, we still remember. Even during all of those ancient sacrifices, "in those [sacrifices there is] a remembrance again [made] of sins every year" (Hebrews 10:3). Jesus' sacrifice, once completely applied to us, will cause us to forget those sins.

In contrast with the earthly sacrificial system, it is said, "For then would they not have ceased to be offered? because that the worshippers once purged should have had no more conscience of sins. But in those [sacrifices there is] a remembrance again [made] of sins every year. For [it is] not possible that the blood of bulls and of goats should take away sins" (Hebrews 10:2-4). What is being contrasted is Jesus' sacrifice to the sacrifices offered during the feast of atonement. The way it was to operate was that once the sin was confessed upon the sacrifice, the animal was then sacrificed, people were to have forgotten that they committed the sin, however that is not how it actually worked. They continued to remember it. But when Jesus judges us, which is to set the verdict of "he that is righteous, let him be righteous still: and he that is holy, let him be holy still" (Revelation 22:11) we will then have those sins purged from our minds. That means the dead in Christ shall arise without an awareness of sins. That also means the last generation living is going into the seven last plagues unable to recall a single sin since the mediator will stop mediating, as discussed earlier.

That should be more than fantastic news. Could you imagine entering into the time "that [there was] no intercessor" (Isaiah 59:16) and able to recall past sins still, even though they have already been confessed? I do not know how your mind works, but most of my temptations are usually caused by Satan pushing the right trigger buttons to recall from memory certain things to come to the forefront. "Don't you remember how that was? Don't you remember how that made you feel? Wouldn't you like that sensation again?" Besides, "God shall wipe away all tears from their eyes; and there shall be no more death, neither sorrow, nor crying, neither shall there be any more pain: for the former things are passed away" (Revelation 21:4). If I am to experience eternity with people knowing my sins and I am recalling those events, I am going to have tears, pain, and sorrow. How could I ever face a person that I cheated something out of? Sure there is powerful and true forgiveness but there is also being uncomfortable. Besides, what would happen if two people who plotted the murder of someone were all reunited in Heaven because they later all came to salvation? Just how would that turn out? And even though "in the resurrection they neither marry, nor are given in marriage, but are as the angels of God" (Matthew 22:30), what would happen if two people who had multiple sex partners saw each other? Would it be appropriate to discuss the illicit affair? Would they not mention it, yet knowing full well that each time they meet up in eternity those thoughts come to mind? Remembering our sins just does not serve a good purpose, but rather, it could start the whole issue all over again at some point.

Sin was never to exist, but by freewill, it came about. Caught off guard, angels believed lies of Lucifer because they did not know what a lie was. And Adam and Eve were never to know sin either, but they did. So since sin is the result of Satan, why would God permit that mark on every being throughout eternity? He would not.

Now for those that turn to the sheep and goats parable to undo this understanding of the judgment, please be careful. The Bible does say, "When the Son of man shall come in his glory, and all the holy angels with him, then shall he sit upon the throne of his glory: And before him shall be gathered all nations: and he shall separate them one from another, as a shepherd divideth [his] sheep from the goats: And he shall set the sheep on his right hand, but the goats on the left" (Matthew 25:31-33). First of all, the story is a parable. Literal goats and sheep are not going to line up, but even so, all it states is that the God shall separate the people, and that fits perfectly well. When Jesus returns with His reward, "The Son of man shall send forth his angels, and they shall gather out of his kingdom all things that offend, and them which do iniquity; And shall cast them into a furnace of fire: there shall be wailing and gnashing of teeth" (Matthew 13:41-42). To the righteous, "the dead in Christ shall rise first: Then we which are alive [and] remain shall be caught up together with them in the clouds, to meet the Lord in the air: and so shall we ever be with the Lord" (1 Thessalonians 4:16-17). So there is no contradiction. All cases will have been settled. When Jesus shows up, it is just execution time.

So as we have learned, in the investigative part of the judgment, that when we "confess our sins", not only is Jesus "faithful and just to forgive us [our] sins, and to cleanse us from all unrighteousness" (1 John 1:9), but He will "blot out all mine iniquities" (Psalms 51:9) from the Book of Remembrance. However, if we do not confess and forsake our sins, He will "blot out his name out of the book of life" (Revelation 3:5). So it is important to be in a state of repentance, watching and "hating even the garment spotted by the flesh" (Jude 1:23) because we are to be living in a state of atonement, a time people "shall afflict your souls" (Leviticus 23:27) for "whatsoever soul [it be] that shall not be afflicted in that same day, he shall be cut off from among his people" (Leviticus 23:29). That garment is Christ's righteousness that Jesus freely gives us, but just like a real garment of white, one would not go and play some tackling sport or adventure into a coal mind with it on lest it would get dirty. In this case, the dirt is sin. Therefore, let us look at a few verses on the Book of Life.

When God was well upset with the Israelites and said to Moses, "Let me alone, that I may destroy them, and blot out their name from under heaven" (Deuteronomy 9:14), that name was not the name Israel. That name was individual names from the Book of Life. And what that means regarding Heaven is that "there shall in no wise enter into it any thing that defileth, neither [whatsoever] worketh abomination, or [maketh] a lie: but they which are written in the Lamb's book of life" (Revelation 21:27). "And whosoever was not found written in the book of life was cast into the lake of fire" (Revelation 20:15).

Unfortunately we are not able to see this book and no, it is not the same as the church records. But this do know, when it comes to the Antichrist, "all that dwell upon the earth shall worship him, whose names are not written in the book of life of the Lamb slain from the foundation of the world" (Revelation 13:8). And for those that defend the Antichrist, here is a stark warning, "if any man shall take away from the words of the book of this prophecy, God shall take away his part out of the book of life, and out of the holy city, and [from] the things which are written in this book" (Revelation 22:19). That means that all who at the Vatican accepted Ribera's futuristic Antichrist theory as something to teach to the world, all those that were embracing such a theory among Protestants around the early 1900's developing into the "Left Behind" concept, and all of the faithful followers of the theory, which takes away the application of most of Revelation past chapter 3 from being applicable to Christians are very much in danger of having their names permanently removed from the Book of Life.

Now although we cannot see this book nor is there a sign that reveals to us the status of things, we can tell a little by our reaction to salvation if our names are in the Book of Life or not. As in the days of the apostle Paul, it was said, "And I intreat thee also, true yokefellow, help those women which laboured with me in the gospel, with Clement also, and [with] other my fellowlabourers, whose names [are] in the book of life" (Philippians 4:3), which means if a person's name is in the Book of Life, they but cannot help themselves in sharing the gospel. Although not all those that share the gospel are going to be saved, especially those that share the false gospels, one should realize that if they have no desire to help save others, then more than likely their name is not in the Book of Life.

Another way to know if the name may be in the Book of Life is to do a quick self-examination and then get our eyes back on Jesus. If we are continuing in sin, especially without repentance, then we know our name is not in the Book of Life for "He that overcometh, the same shall be clothed in white raiment; and I will not blot out his name out of the book of life, but I will confess his name before my Father, and before his angels" (Revelation 3:5). And for those that think all we have to do is believe, well, we need to believe correctly, "For whatsoever is born of God overcometh the world: and this is the victory that overcometh the world, [even] our faith. Who is he that overcometh the world, but he that believeth that Jesus is the Son of God" (1 John 5:4-5). The other choice is that if "a man is overcome, of the same is he brought in bondage" (2 Peter 2:19), and we know if we are in bondage to sin, then we are not free to Jesus (John 8:31-34).

So we see that our names in the Book of Life is the most important thing, therefore, it should receive the most amount of our attention. It is only they that do so that get to look forward to the next feast.

TABERNACLES OR INGATHERING:

The Feast of Tabernacles or Ingathering is celebrated in recognition of a great harvest feast. It appears in Leviticus 23:33-44, which says, "And the LORD spake unto Moses, saying, Speak unto the children of Israel, saying, The fifteenth day of this seventh month [shall be] the feast of tabernacles [for] seven days unto the LORD. On the first day [shall be] an holy convocation: ye shall do no servile work [therein]. Seven days ye shall offer an offering made by fire unto the LORD: on the eighth day shall be an holy convocation unto you; and ye shall offer an offering made by fire unto the LORD: it [is] a solemn assembly; [and] ye shall do no servile work [therein]. These [are] the feasts of the LORD, which ye shall proclaim [to be] holy convocations, to offer an offering made by fire unto the LORD, a burnt offering, and a meat offering, a sacrifice, and drink offerings, every thing upon his day: Beside the sabbaths of the LORD, and beside your gifts, and beside all your vows, and beside all your freewill offerings, which ye give unto the LORD. Also in the fifteenth day of the seventh month, when ye have gathered in the fruit of the land, ye shall keep a feast unto the LORD seven days: on the first day [shall be] a sabbath, and on the eighth day [shall be] a sabbath. And ye shall take you on the first day the boughs of goodly trees, branches of palm trees, and the boughs of thick trees, and willows of the brook; and ye shall rejoice before the LORD your God seven days. And ye shall keep it a feast unto the LORD seven days in the year. [It shall be] a statute for ever in your generations: ye shall celebrate it in the seventh month. Ye shall dwell in booths seven days; all that are Israelites born shall dwell in booths: That your generations may know that I made the children of Israel to dwell in booths, when I brought them out of the land of Egypt: I [am] the LORD your God. And Moses declared unto the children of Israel the feasts of the LORD."

As the name Ingathering implies, this is a collection of all the fruit of the land. This is truly the great harvest and is depicted in Mark 13:26-27. "And then shall they see the Son of man coming in the clouds with great power and glory. And then shall he send his angels, and shall gather together his elect from the four winds, from the uttermost part of the earth to the uttermost part of heaven." Also, Revelation 14:14-16 brings a vivid picture for. "behold a white cloud, and upon the cloud [one] sat like unto the Son of man, having on his head a golden crown, and in his hand a sharp sickle. And another angel came out of the temple, crying with a loud voice to him that sat on the cloud, Thrust in thy sickle, and reap: for the time is come for thee to reap; for the harvest of the earth is ripe. And he that sat on the cloud thrust in his sickle on the earth; and the earth was reaped." Jesus will soon return to gather the fruit of the land, which are you and I if we remain faithful. So the fulfillment of this feast will be at the second coming.

The time of rejoicing before the Lord is pictured in Revelation 7:9-10, which says, "After this I beheld, and, lo, a great multitude, which no man could number, of all nations, and kindreds, and people, and tongues, stood before the throne, and before the Lamb, clothed with white robes, and palms in their hands; And cried with a loud voice, saying, Salvation to our God which sitteth upon the throne, and unto the Lamb."

And recalling from Leviticus, notice that in addition to the weekly Sabbath (Leviticus 23:38), these feast days were also to be Sabbaths (Leviticus 23:7, 23:21, 23:24-25, 23:30-32, 23:35-36) carrying the same rest requirements as the weekly Sabbath. Notice also that they floated through the days of the week being on specific days of the month (Leviticus 23:5-6, 23:11, 23:15 16, 23:24, 23:27, 23:32, 23:34, 23:39).

Now, did you also notice that the judgment and second coming are two separate events (feasts). How can that be? That is because all cases have to be decided before Jesus returns.

Interestingly, these feasts were given to Moses in exact order of fulfillment. That was not by chance. It began with Jesus being sacrificed as our Passover Lamb and chronologically moved forward to when Jesus will gather in the elect – saints!

We are a people who need the Passover blood that washes away our sins in forgiveness, who need the power to purge out all the leaven of sins from our existence, who trust in the fact that Jesus proves there is life after death being an example of the first fruits, who need the power of the Holy Spirit that Jesus sends, so as to go forth warning people of the coming event, while we make a final check to make sure we can stand during the time without an Intercessor, hoping to be part of the great harvest.

How Does Building An Ancient Temple Parallel the Last Day Events?

In the reign of Solomon, God's house was constructed (1 Kings 6:2), known as Solomon's temple. While constructing it, "the house, when it was in building, was built of stone made ready before it was brought thither: so that there was neither hammer nor axe [nor] any tool of iron heard in the house, while it was in building" (1 Kings 6:7).

The apostle Paul makes this comparison, "Now therefore ye are no more strangers and foreigners, but fellow citizens with the saints, and of the household of God; And are built upon the foundation of the apostles and prophets, Jesus Christ himself being the chief corner [stone]; In whom all the building fitly framed together groweth unto an holy temple in the Lord: In whom ye also are builded together for an habitation of God through the Spirit" (Ephesians 2:19-22).

There was a quarry in which stones were hewn, shaped, and then brought to Jerusalem to be fitted perfectly into place without the use of instruments. What a challenge that was, but it was the command of God "For whatsoever things were written aforetime were written for our learning, that we through patience and comfort of the scriptures might have hope" (Romans 15:4).

A lot of ministers use the story to preach on reverence in the sanctuary of a church, although today, most churches seem to have completely, and on purpose, lost all such respect. Anyways, another application is that of Jerusalem being a type of Heaven while the quarry being this planet. All the workings of the stones was done at the quarry so that the stones were prepared to live together by just placing them together. That means our characters are being formed on earth now. The work to make us perfect is being done now. There will be no magical transformation at the second coming. There definitely will not be any work performed in Heaven. The work is now. The removal of sin is happening now.

How Does the Time of Elijah Reveal Last Day Events?

Highlighting only a few things, we see a direct parallel between the events with Elijah and mostly those of the Dark Ages and specifically the Antichrist.

First, we have the whore, Jezebel (2 Kings 9:22), who painted her face (2 Kings 9:30), which matches "THE MOTHER OF HARLOTS AND ABOMINATIONS OF THE EARTH" (Revelation 17:5), who "was arrayed in purple and scarlet colour, and decked with gold and precious stones and pearls, having a golden cup in her hand full of abominations and filthiness of her fornication" (Revelation 17:4). We also have Ahab , who "did evil in the sight of the LORD above all that [were] before him" (1 Kings 16:30), matching that activities of "a scarlet coloured beast, full of names of blasphemy" (Revelation 17:3). Basically, this is a story of when the church (woman) and the state (king) marry and try to rule the subjects, just like Antichrist.

The full story is found in 1 Kings 16 and runs through 2 Kings 9. The symbolism involved does not by chance find representation in Antichrist, in fact, one begins to wonder if John, who wrote the Book of Revelation, was not trying to draw the parallel himself, like he does with many other stories. To have the second beast of Revelation 13, sometimes referred to as "the false prophet" (Revelation 16:13), "doeth great wonders, so that he maketh fire come down from heaven on the earth in the sight of men" (Revelation 13:13). And you have a fire showdown to prove between the false gods under Jezebel and the true God of Heaven (1 Kings 18:24).

So we pick up the story with "Ahab the son of Omri did evil in the sight of the LORD above all that [were] before him" (1 Kings 16:30) just as pagan Rome also did evil by physically crucifying Jesus and then persecuting Christians for many years, but seeing that no matter how much pagan Rome persecuted Christians to exterminate them, Christianity seemed to flourish. So a new tactic was implemented. "He took to wife Jezebel" (1 Kings 16:31), which under Constantine, pagan Rome married Papal Rome.

Now Ahab "reared up an altar for Baal in the house of Baal" (1 Kings 16:32). That was considered paganism. Well, again, that is what the Antichrist is built upon with pagan statues renamed to Christian people, pagan symbols throughout including sundials and obelisks, pagan rituals, like lent, and holidays like Easter and Christmas instead of resurrection day and the birth of Christ, though it is passed off as a reference to them. And of course the presence of sun worship, especially using Sunday as the day of worship in contrast to God's Sabbath day.

So God sends a prophet, Elijah, who states, "there shall not be dew nor rain these years" (1 Kings 17:1). Now when he said three years, that was more like a minimum. For James wrote, "Elias was a man subject to like passions as we are, and he prayed earnestly that it might not rain: and it rained not on the earth by the space of three years and six months" (James 5:17). But it is not by coincidence that the period of the Antichrist reign of past, where the Holy Spirit was pretty much squashed in the church, is referred to "a time and times and the dividing of time" (Daniel 7:25) that Antichrist "shall wear out the saints of the most High" (Daniel 7:25). It is not by coincidence that there would be "a time, times, and an half; and when he shall have accomplished to scatter the power of the holy people" (Daniel 12:7). And during that time, "to the woman were given two wings of a great eagle, that she might fly into the wilderness, into her place, where she is nourished for a time, and times, and half a time, from the face of the serpent" (Revelation 12:14). Basically, Elijah's lack of rain for three and a half literal years matches up with Antichrist's prophetic three and a half years reign, or the prophetic forty-two months, or the prophetic one thousand two hundred and sixty days, all of which equate to three and a half years.

Now during the drought, God told Elijah, "hide thyself by the brook Cherith, that [is] before Jordan" (1 Kings 17:3), however, eventually Elijah's food and water source dried up, literally. "And it came to pass after a while, that the brook dried up, because there had been no rain in the land" (1 Kings 17:7). So God said, "Arise, get thee to Zarephath, which [belongeth] to Zidon, and dwell there: behold, I have commanded a widow woman there to sustain thee" (1 Kings 17:9).

Remember, a woman is symbolic of the church (compare Jeremiah 6:2 to Isaiah 51:16). And where is she located? Is she among the populous of Israel? No. Neither was the woman of Revelation 12:6, which says, "The woman fled into the wilderness, where she hath a place prepared of God, that they should feed her there a thousand two hundred [and] threescore days." Although, in our case, we have Elijah fleeing, still he comes across a woman. And what does the woman have? "I have not a cake, but an handful of meal in a barrel, and a little oil in a cruse: and, behold, I [am] gathering two sticks, that I may go in and dress it for me and my son, that we may eat it, and die" (1 Kings 17:12). However, "Elijah said unto her, Fear not; go [and] do as thou hast said: but make me thereof a little cake first, and bring [it] unto me, and after make for thee and for thy son. For thus saith the LORD God of Israel, The barrel of meal shall not waste, neither shall the cruse of oil fail, until the day [that] the LORD sendeth rain upon the earth" (1 Kings 17:13-14).

Now here is the point. What does the flour and the oil represent? Well, Jesus said, "Man shall not live by bread alone, but by every word that proceedeth out of the mouth of God" (Matthew 4:4), and flour is surely used in making bread. The oil on the other hand, which was very useful in fuel in lamps, is depicted in Revelation 4:5 as, "seven lamps of fire burning before the throne, which are the seven Spirits of God." So between the bread or Word of God and God's Spirits or Holy Spirit, the church in the wilderness is the one true church while the main visible church was not, much like the situation even today, where the Antichrist comes off as the world's religious leader claiming even to have authority over the Word of God and empowered by the Holy Spirit but in reality, the people with the true Spirit and the true understanding of the Word of God are those described as, "the remnant of her seed, which keep the commandments of God, and have the testimony of Jesus Christ" (Revelation 12:17). So how true it is from the words of Elijah. In God's true church, the Word of God shall not cease, and the Holy Spirit will not dry up.

Now during this time "Jezebel cut off the prophets of the LORD" but "Obadiah took an hundred prophets, and hid them by fifty in a cave, and fed them with bread and water" (1 Kings 18:4), which matches the slaughter of many Protestant leaders of the dark ages as predicted, where John "saw the woman drunken with the blood of the saints, and with the blood of the martyrs of Jesus: and when I saw her, I wondered with great admiration" (Revelation 17:6). Of course God hid His people as well, like the Waldensians. Not by coincidence, God says, "He shall dwell on high: his place of defence [shall be] the munitions of rocks: bread shall be given him; his waters [shall be] sure" (Isaiah 33:16).

"And it came to pass, when Ahab saw Elijah, that Ahab said unto him, [Art] thou he that troubleth Israel?" (1 Kings 18:17) The same will be said of those refusing to go along with the image of the beast and mark of the beast, so much so that he will "cause that as many as would not worship the image of the beast should be killed" (Revelation 13:15).

"And he answered, I have not troubled Israel; but thou, and thy father's house, in that ye have forsaken the commandments of the LORD, and thou hast followed Baalim" (1 Kings 18:18). And the same is true of Antichrist, where he "think to change times and laws" (Daniel 7:25), which is a forsaking of the Lord's commandments, and being described as "a leopard, and his feet were as [the feet] of a bear, and his mouth as the mouth of a lion: and the dragon gave him his power, and his seat, and great authority" (Revelation 13:2) is inherited paganism from Greece, Medo-Persia, Babylon, and especially pagan Rome of which is what being led by Baalim is (Judges 2:11-12).

"Now therefore send, [and] gather to me all Israel unto mount Carmel, and the prophets of Baal four hundred and fifty, and the prophets of the groves four hundred, which eat at Jezebel's table" (1 Kings 18:19). In comparison, Mount Carmel was a place of showdown, and a significant showdown with the Antichrist happened when Martin Luther faced many, many bishops and cardinals.

"And Elijah came unto all the people, and said, How long halt ye between two opinions? if the LORD [be] God, follow him: but if Baal, [then] follow him. And the people answered him not a word" (1 Kings 18:21). In Martin Luther's day, the two opinions were traditions and the Bible. Today, among the group having the wrong one mind, it is trying to put on Christianity while enjoying the world. Elijah's voice tells us to stop trying to do this and choose. Either give up Christianity and enjoy the worldly ways or be a Christian and forsake the world.

"Then said Elijah unto the people, I, [even] I only, remain a prophet of the LORD; but Baal's prophets [are] four hundred and fifty men" (1 Kings 18:22). And such remains the case today. For every preacher that is truly of God having the "one mind" of Christ there are at least four hundred and fifty preachers that are not of God and have the "one mind" supporting Antichrist and the spirit thereof. Despite their sincere love of God, they are not of God. Disobedience is never of God.

While the prophets of Baal "leaped upon the altar which was made" (1 Kings 18:26) "and they cried aloud, and cut themselves after their manner with knives and lancets, till the blood gushed out upon them" (1 Kings 18:28), Elijah offered a simple prayer, "Hear me, O LORD, hear me, that this people may know that thou [art] the LORD God, and [that] thou hast turned their heart back again" (1 Kings 18:37). Today, in the Spirit of Antichrist, lots of noise is made with the Christian rock music and speaking in tongues while the true believer daily and calmly enter into study and prayer. The rejection of the old hymns for the new modern music is no different than the Baal worshippers. In fact, to do so is not a matter of making exciting music instead of singing those boring hymns, even the messages conveyed are wrong. Bible phrases yanked out of context and thrown into songs with a really good beat is a distortion and even a brainwashing away from God's meaning. We have songs that encourage overcoming depression while God wants us to overcome sin (1 John 5:4-5). That roaring lion within is not Jesus for "the devil" is "as a roaring lion, walketh about, seeking whom he may devour" (1 Peter 5:8). For the most part, gone is the conviction from hymns towards ridding oneself of sin, being under God's judgment, and living holy lives, and in is the music that simply claims to be a child of God while living in sin.

"Then the fire of the LORD fell, and consumed the burnt sacrifice, and the wood, and the stones, and the dust, and licked up the water that [was] in the trench. And when all the people saw [it], they fell on their faces: and they said, The LORD, he [is] the God; the LORD, he [is] the God" (1 Kings 18:38-39) only in our day, the opposite shall be true. "And he doeth great wonders, so that he maketh fire come down from heaven on the earth in the sight of men, and deceiveth them that dwell on the earth by [the means of] those miracles which he had power to do in the sight of the beast; saying to them that dwell on the earth, that they should make an image to the beast, which had the wound by a sword, and did live" (Revelation 13:13-14).

"And Elijah said unto them, Take the prophets of Baal; let not one of them escape. And they took them: and Elijah brought them down to the brook Kishon, and slew them there" (1 Kings 18:40), and God will do so with the Antichrist and the false prophet. "And the beast was taken, and with him the false prophet that wrought miracles before him, with which he deceived them that had received the mark of the beast, and them that worshipped his image.

These both were cast alive into a lake of fire burning with brimstone" (Revelation 19:20).

With this portion of the story of Elijah being the high point in the parallels in time, we encourage that the rest of the chapters be personally studied for additional parallels and lessons.

How Does Daniel and King Nebuchadnezzar Parallel the Last Day Events?

The fact that John makes reference to Babylon in more than one verse in Revelation (Revelation 14:8, 16:19, 17:5, 18:2, 18:10, 18:21) tells us that there is definitely a connection between then and the last days.

When to "Judah came Nebuchadnezzar king of Babylon unto Jerusalem, and besieged it" (Daniel 1:1), the same is happening on a mental basis. All the Bible beliefs have been besieged. First, between documentaries, so called experts, and sitcoms on television alone, society has been inundated with the thought that the Bible is inaccurate, full of errors, an ancient book, missing facts, having contradictory content, suggesting that there was a conspiracy or agenda in assembling the Bible, and much more. If that were not sufficient to doom Christians, society turns around and declares what is forbidden by the Bible as the norm. It is the norm to sleep together after three dates. Homosexuality is the norm. It is the norm to throw the child into day care and public school while chasing the mighty dollar. It is the norm to know that the Bible contains fables and that evolution is fact, instead of just a theory. It is the norm to marry, divorce for no good reason, and remarry. And the countless movies and television programming that puts people in Heaven right away is not only the norm but fully brainwashed.

And with "part of the vessels of the house of God" (Daniel 1:2) being carried off is very much like the doctrines once taught by the first century Christians but altered over time especially by the Antichrist and continued on with the "Spirit of Antichrist". These include casting down the Sabbath, changing or discarding the Ten Commandments, bringing in various forms of baptism and including baby baptism, placing people in mostly Heaven but also Hell immediately after death instead of sleeping, proposing God is a tyrant that gets His jollies by burning people throughout eternity, and much more.

The fact that Babylon thought to take the promising youth and "teach the learning and the tongue of the Chaldeans" (Daniel 1:4), which is re-education, is no different than what is happening with youth in public schools, where God and prayer are out, but in is evolution, sex education, encouragement for greed, sports bragging rights, and more. By the time a young Christian graduates elementary school, including high school, the desire for God and godly things has been so squashed that it is very unlikely the youth ever have a strong relationship with God, if any at all.

Now "Daniel purposed in his heart that he would not defile himself with the portion of the king's meat, nor with the wine which he drank: therefore he requested of the prince of the eunuchs that he might not defile himself" (Daniel 1:8), in fact, it was requested, "Prove thy servants, I beseech thee, ten days; and let them give us pulse to eat, and water to drink" (Daniel 1:12). This turns out to be a Vegetarian diet. Although the Bible does make allowance for meat, in the very last days, which we are in, a clear mind and clean body internally is the recommendation. This is achieved in a Vegetarian diet, even a Vegan one.

"And in the second year of the reign of Nebuchadnezzar Nebuchadnezzar dreamed dreams, wherewith his spirit was troubled, and his sleep brake from him. Then the king commanded to call the magicians, and the astrologers, and the sorcerers, and the Chaldeans, for to shew the king his dreams. So they came and stood before the king" (Daniel 2:1-2). Now is that not typical? The world has a crisis, in this case, a nightmare, and worldly solutions are sought after instead of turning to the true God. Even today, people still count on astrology, are amazed by magicians, and especially given over to sorcerers and worldly education. In the last days, the world is quite influenced, "for thy merchants were the great men of the earth; for by thy sorceries were all nations deceived" (Revelation 18:23), "But the fearful, and unbelieving, and the abominable, and murderers, and whoremongers, and sorcerers, and idolaters, and all liars, shall have their part in the lake which burneth with fire and brimstone" (Revelation 21:8). So sorcerers play an influential role along with the merchants of the world. Interestingly, the Greek word for sorcerers is "pharmakeia" and is defined as "the use or the administering of drugs", according to the Bible Lexicon. That is where we get the word "pharmacy" from, and not by coincidence, pharmacists are definitely influencing the world, along with seeking an education. In the United States, it is the expectation that beyond college, one become educated with achieving a degree. Having an Associate's Degree used to be something special. Today, it is treated as common as a high school degree. Therefore, Bachelor degrees are sought after, and even then that does not seem sufficient to stand out. So a Master's Degree is highly encouraged.

As stated, nothing from nearly twenty five hundred years ago seems to have changed, yet as back then and is true today, it is nothing but "lying and corrupt words" (Daniel 2:9). "For this cause the king was angry and very furious, and commanded to destroy all the wise [men] of Babylon. And the decree went forth that the wise [men] should be slain; and they sought Daniel and his fellows to be slain" (Daniel 2:12-13). Here we have a death decree followed by an intervention of God after Daniel and his friends sought the "mercies of the God of heaven" (Daniel 2:18). This is much like the decrees of Europe during the Dark Ages, which was open slaughter of Protestants. Such only ceased thanks to the fact that "the earth helped the woman, and the earth opened her mouth, and swallowed up the flood which the dragon cast out of his mouth" (Revelation 12:16), which is symbolic of what we studied earlier. The rise of a nation in an unpopular area of the earth around the late 1700's is none other than the United States, which stopped the flood or "peoples, and multitudes, and nations, and tongues" (Revelation 17:15) from being "drunken with the blood of the saints, and with the blood of the martyrs of Jesus" (Revelation 17:6).

But later, after the hype of Daniel interpreting the dream died down, "Nebuchadnezzar the king made an image of gold, whose height [was] threescore cubits, [and] the breadth thereof six cubits" (Daniel 3:1). Now instead of a physical object, the second beast or country of Revelation 13, the United States, "should make an image to the beast, which had the wound by a sword, and did live" (Revelation 13:14), which is to turn our country into the reflection of that first beast, the Vatican. "And he had power to give life unto the image of the beast, that the image of the beast should both speak, and cause that as many as would not worship the image of the beast should be killed" (Revelation 13:15), which a country speaks through its laws. So expect laws that are more dragon like than lamb like. In fact, it is already happening. Please note that Nebuchadnezzar 's image involved the number 666, while the Bible says, "Here is wisdom. Let him that hath understanding count the number of the beast: for it is the number of a man; and his number [is] Six hundred threescore [and] six" (Revelation 13:18).

"Then an herald cried aloud, To you it is commanded, O people, nations, and languages, [That] at what time ye hear the sound of the cornet, flute, harp, sackbut, psaltery, dulcimer, and all kinds of musick, ye fall down and worship the golden image that Nebuchadnezzar the king hath set up: And whoso falleth not down and worshippeth shall the same hour be cast into the midst of a burning fiery furnace" (Daniel 3:4-6). Notice there is death decree as well, but also notice that music is involved. Interestingly, when the new style music replaced the traditional hymns, all of a sudden, Protestants have a chummier relationship with the Vatican, so much so that in 2017, Evangelicals and Catholics are set to sign an agreement that ends the animosity or protest. This is to take place on the date of the five hundredth anniversary of what is considered the official beginning of the Protestant Reformation, the nailing of Martin Luther's ninety-five thesis. Has the Vatican fixed the ninety five points listed? Of course not. That means the Protestants have rejected the points themselves.

"Wherefore at that time certain Chaldeans came near, and accused the Jews" (Daniel 3:8). "There are certain Jews whom thou hast set over the affairs of the province of Babylon, Shadrach, Meshach, and Abednego; these men, O king, have not regarded thee: they serve not thy gods, nor worship the golden image which thou hast set up" (Daniel 3:12). Now remember, these Jews, Daniels three friends of "Shadrach, Meshach, and Abednego" (Daniel 3:14) were to be taught "the learning and the tongue of the Chaldeans" (Daniel 1:4), so in essence, their own family turned them in. Well, during the tribulation ahead, "For I am come to set a man at variance against his father, and the daughter against her mother, and the daughter in law against her mother in law. And a man's foes [shall be] they of his own household" (Matthew 10:35-36). And as a reminder, we had studied earlier every reference to the tribulation and it ends up being a fact that we will be living through the time of tribulation and not be raptured before hand. This will also be a time where "they shall put you out of the synagogues: yea, the time cometh, that whosoever killeth you will think that he doeth God service" (John 16:2).

"Shadrach, Meshach, and Abednego, answered and said to the king, O Nebuchadnezzar, we [are] not careful to answer thee in this matter. If it be [so], our God whom we serve is able to deliver us from the burning fiery furnace, and he will deliver [us] out of thine hand, O king. But if not, be it known unto thee, O king, that we will not serve thy gods, nor worship the golden image which thou hast set up" (Daniel 3:16-18). Basically, "they overcame him by the blood of the Lamb, and by the word of their testimony; and they loved not their lives unto the death" (Revelation 12:11), much like during the Dark Ages as well as in the future.

"And he commanded the most mighty men that [were] in his army to bind Shadrach, Meshach, and Abednego, [and] to cast [them] into the burning fiery furnace" (Daniel 3:20), but "Then Nebuchadnezzar the king was astonied, and rose up in haste, [and] spake, and said unto his counsellors, Did not we cast three men bound into the midst of the fire? They answered and said unto the king, True, O king. He answered and said, Lo, I see four men loose, walking in the midst of the fire, and they have no hurt; and the form of the fourth is like the Son of God" (Daniel 3:24-25). This will be no different than the survivors of the final death decree, which states, "Here is the patience of the saints: here [are] they that keep the commandments of God, and the faith of Jesus" (Revelation 14:12). Jesus saw the Hebrew boys through their tribulation as they chose to obey God, and the faith of Jesus with obedience to His commandments will see us through too. In fact, once those plagues begin to fall, it is doubtful that any saved person will have hurt come upon them. It would only serve Satan's purpose at that point to have true Christians die seeing there will be no switching sides, as studied earlier. "He that is unjust, let him be unjust still: and he which is filthy, let him be filthy still: and he that is righteous, let him be righteous still: and he that is holy, let him be holy still" (Revelation 22:11).

"[Then] Nebuchadnezzar spake, and said, Blessed [be] the God of Shadrach, Meshach, and Abednego" (Daniel 3:28), which matches the fact that all the lost will eventually "every knee shall bow to me, and every tongue shall confess to God" (Romans 14:11). And "That at the name of Jesus every knee should bow, of [things] in heaven, and [things] in earth, and [things] under the earth; And [that] every tongue should confess that Jesus Christ [is] Lord, to the glory of God the Father" (Philippians 2:10-11).

How Does Daniel and Belshazzar Parallel the Last Day Events?

"Belshazzar the king made a great feast to a thousand of his lords, and drank wine before the thousand. Belshazzar, whiles he tasted the wine, commanded to bring the golden and silver vessels which his father Nebuchadnezzar had taken out of the temple which [was] in Jerusalem; that the king, and his princes, his wives, and his concubines, might drink therein. Then they brought the golden vessels that were taken out of the temple of the house of God which [was] at Jerusalem; and the king, and his princes, his wives, and his concubines, drank in them. They drank wine, and praised the gods of gold, and of silver, of brass, of iron, of wood, and of stone. In the same hour came forth fingers of a man's hand, and wrote over against the candlestick upon the plaister of the wall of the king's palace: and the king saw the part of the hand that wrote. Then the king's countenance was changed, and his thoughts troubled him, so that the joints of his loins were loosed, and his knees smote one against another" (Daniel 5:1-6).

This is much like today's society, which is a form of Babylon still. It is called confusion and specifically paralleling blatant sin. The raunchy content that is passed off as entertainment, the blatant sinning among Christians thinking obedience has nothing to do with salvation, the fact that sinful lives get more respect that the pure lives, all of it is just blatant in God's face. Eventually God is going to reveal Himself and then there will be a whole lot of knees knocking. Unfortunately, it will be too late.

"The king cried aloud to bring in the astrologers, the Chaldeans, and the soothsayers. [And] the king spake, and said to the wise [men] of Babylon, Whosoever shall read this writing, and shew me the interpretation thereof, shall be clothed with scarlet, and [have] a chain of gold about his neck, and shall be the third ruler in the kingdom" (Daniel 5:7). And as usual, society turns to worldly solutions. In fact, horoscopes are a serious business today.

"Then was Daniel brought in before the king. [And] the king spake and said unto Daniel, [Art] thou that Daniel, which [art] of the children of the captivity of Judah, whom the king my father brought out of Jewry? I have even heard of thee, that the spirit of the gods [is] in thee, and [that] light and understanding and excellent wisdom is found in thee" (Daniel 5:13-14). Now in the future, the world will eventually turn to religion for "I saw three unclean spirits like frogs [come] out of the mouth of the dragon, and out of the mouth of the beast, and out of the mouth of the false prophet. For they are the spirits of devils, working miracles, [which] go forth unto the kings of the earth and of the whole world, to gather them to the battle of that great day of God Almighty" (Revelation 16:13-14).

"And this [is] the writing that was written, MENE, MENE, TEKEL, UPHARSIN. This [is] the interpretation of the thing: MENE; God hath numbered thy kingdom, and finished it. TEKEL; Thou art weighed in the balances, and art found wanting. PERES; Thy kingdom is divided, and given to the Medes and Persians. Then commanded Belshazzar, and they clothed Daniel with scarlet, and [put] a chain of gold about his neck, and made a proclamation concerning him, that he should be the third ruler in the kingdom. In that night was Belshazzar the king of the Chaldeans slain. And Darius the Median took the kingdom, [being] about threescore and two years old" (Daniel 5:25-31).

So eventually, Babylon saw its doom, much like spiritual Babylon will see its doom. "And the sixth angel poured out his vial upon the great river Euphrates; and the water thereof was dried up, that the way of the kings of the east might be prepared" (Revelation 16:12). John is drawing on the fall of Babylon as a parallel because the ultimate fall of Babylon, which is the Antichrist and the "Spirit of Antichrist" with all of their followers, is at the time of the second coming.

The reference of the kings of the east, parallels the fact that Jesus tells us from what direction He will be returning from. "For as the lightning cometh out of the east, and shineth even unto the west; so shall also the coming of the Son of man be" (Matthew 24:27). And the plurality of kings to refer to Jesus as "King of Kings" (Revelation 19:16). "And I saw heaven opened, and behold a white horse; and he that sat upon him [was] called Faithful and True, and in righteousness he doth judge and make war. His eyes [were] as a flame of fire, and on his head [were] many crowns; and he had a name written, that no man knew, but he himself. And he [was] clothed with a vesture dipped in blood: and his name is called The Word of God. And the armies [which were] in heaven followed him upon white horses, clothed in fine linen, white and clean. And out of his mouth goeth a sharp sword, that with it he should smite the nations: and he shall rule them with a rod of iron: and he treadeth the winepress of the fierceness and wrath of Almighty God. And he hath on [his] vesture and on his thigh a name written, KING OF KINGS, AND LORD OF LORDS. And I saw an angel standing in the sun; and he cried with a loud voice, saying to all the fowls that fly in the midst of heaven, Come and gather yourselves together unto the supper of the great God; That ye may eat the flesh of kings, and the flesh of captains, and the flesh of mighty men, and the flesh of horses, and of them that sit on them, and the flesh of all [men, both] free and bond, both small and great. And I saw the beast, and the kings of the earth, and their armies, gathered together to make war against him that sat on the horse, and against his army. And the beast was taken, and with him the false prophet that wrought miracles before him, with which he deceived them that had received the mark of the beast, and them that worshipped his image. These both were cast alive into a lake of fire burning with brimstone. And the remnant were slain with the sword of him that sat upon the horse, which [sword] proceeded out of his mouth: and all the fowls were filled with their flesh" (Revelation 19:11-21).

Now let us address one more aspect in this parallel, and that is how Babylon was conquered that night without much effort. On top of that, about one hundred and fifty years before Cyrus was born, Isaiah wrote, "Thus saith the LORD, thy redeemer, and he that formed thee from the womb, I [am] the LORD that maketh all [things]; that stretcheth forth the heavens alone; that spreadeth abroad the earth by myself; That frustrateth the tokens of the liars, and maketh diviners mad; that turneth wise [men] backward, and maketh their knowledge foolish; That confirmeth the word of his servant, and performeth the counsel of his messengers; that saith to Jerusalem, Thou shalt be inhabited; and to the cities of Judah, Ye shall be built, and I will raise up the decayed places thereof: That saith to the deep, Be dry, and I will dry up thy rivers: That saith of Cyrus, [He is] my shepherd, and shall perform all my pleasure: even saying to Jerusalem, Thou shalt be built; and to the temple, Thy foundation shall be laid. Thus saith the LORD to his anointed, to Cyrus, whose right hand I have holden, to subdue nations before him; and I will loose the loins of kings, to open before him the two leaved gates; and the gates shall not be shut; I will go before thee, and make the crooked places straight: I will break in pieces the gates of brass, and cut in sunder the bars of iron: And I will give thee the treasures of darkness, and hidden riches of secret places, that thou mayest know that I, the LORD, which call [thee] by thy name, [am] the God of Israel. For Jacob my servant's sake, and Israel mine elect, I have even called thee by thy name: I have surnamed thee, though thou hast not known me" (Isaiah 44:24-45:4).

Many miracles come from those verses. We have a reference to needing a redeemer for the nation. That means before the captivity happened, God predicted that it would happened about eighty years ahead of time. God, in showing Isaiah the future, names the redeeming person by the name Cyrus. On top of that, God told Isaiah that before it all happened that the nation of Israel would be split into two kingdoms. You may be asking how this is so. Well, in the north, we had the ten tribes known as Israel. In the south, we have the two tribes known as Judah. This prophecy clearly states that Judah would be carried off, so was Israel, but only Judah is commanded to return and rebuild. And not only that, but explicitly Cyrus is the one that will eventually start the three decree command to go and execute what Daniel wrote in prophecy years later. "Know therefore and understand, [that] from the going forth of the commandment to restore and to build Jerusalem unto the Messiah the Prince [shall be] seven weeks, and threescore and two weeks: the street shall be built again, and the wall, even in troublous times" (Daniel 9:25). Such a command is found in the book of Ezra. "But in the first year of Cyrus the king of Babylon [the same] king Cyrus made a decree to build this house of God" (Ezra 5:13).

Now here is the real interesting part. All of this was prophesied before these events happened including how Cyrus would bring down Babylon. It would involve drying up the rivers and taking advantage of the river gates being left open. And this will be repeated spiritually, hence why we are studying it. So, physical Babylon was this huge city that positioned itself over the river Euphrates. It was an impregnable city that chariot races were held on the top of these walls. The only vulnerability would be by boat coming down the river or swimming as the walls of Babylon only crossed over the waters. So, Babylon constructed gates or leaved gates that went down into the river to the floor. These gates were not solid as it allowed the river water to flow through, but it was sturdy and strong with openings that were not large enough for anybody to pass through. However, the gates would be opened and closed from time to time for whatever reason. Maybe if the gates were constantly closed, debris would collect. In either case, on the night of Cyrus' attack, "Belshazzar the king made a great feast to a thousand of his lords, and drank wine before the thousand" (Daniel 5:1). In other words, much drunken carelessness was happening. At the same time, this caused the guards to not be so watchful and not close the gates for the night nor watch the activity of the river. And we say activity because up a ways along the river, Cyrus had a huge project under way. He was creating a new pathway for the river, and on this night they made the final break through. The Euphrates was diverted away from Babylon; the river dried up; the armies of Cyrus marched down the riverbed; and when they got to where the gates were, Cyrus found them open; so he marched right into the center of the city, and "In that night was Belshazzar the king of the Chaldeans slain" (Daniel 5:30).

Now according to Revelation 16:12, the Bible says, "the sixth angel poured out his vial upon the great river Euphrates; and the water thereof was dried up, that the way of the kings of the east might be prepared." Remembering that this is signified or symbolic language, the river being made up of water "are peoples, and multitudes, and nations, and tongues" (Revelation 17:15). So that means the Antichrist's support among their followers will finally cease. They will realize their lost condition. The "Spirit of Antichrist" will have lost its influence as well. Just as the combined kings of the Medes and Persians, the ultimate "KING OF KINGS, AND LORD OF LORDS" (Revelation 19:16) will show up "and the beast was taken, and with him the false prophet that wrought miracles before him, with which he deceived them that had received the mark of the beast, and them that worshipped his image. These both were cast alive into a lake of fire burning with brimstone. And the remnant were slain with the sword of him that sat upon the horse, which [sword] proceeded out of his mouth: and all the fowls were filled with their flesh" (Revelation 19:20-21).

How Does Daniel and the Medes And Persians Parallel the Last Day Events?

"It pleased Darius to set over the kingdom an hundred and twenty princes, which should be over the whole kingdom; And over these three presidents; of whom Daniel [was] first: that the princes might give accounts unto them, and the king should have no damage" (Daniel 6:1-2). Daniel in this case represents the freedom to exercise our religion as we see, in fact, it is protected by the constitution. Darius then, would represent the government. Many people think that it is impossible to bring in a worship law into this country of the United States to "worship the first beast" (Revelation 13:12) and to "worship the image of the beast" (Revelation 13:15) along with getting "a mark in their right hand, or in their foreheads" (Revelation 13:16), which is another worship item, but Bible prophecy says that it will happen.

"All the presidents of the kingdom, the governors, and the princes, the counsellors, and the captains, have consulted together to establish a royal statute, and to make a firm decree, that whosoever shall ask a petition of any God or man for thirty days, save of thee, O king, he shall be cast into the den of lions. Now, O king, establish the decree, and sign the writing, that it be not changed, according to the law of the Medes and Persians, which altereth not. Wherefore king Darius signed the writing and the decree" (Daniel 6:7-9). Now the law, especially of the Mark of the Beast, is not going to come from the government down to the people. It will come from the people up through the government. The citizens of the United States are going to demand the Sunday legislation and even atheists will be on board. And if we think that our constitution would prevent such, look at our past:

- Japanese United States citizens are locked up during World War II for the sole reason that they were Japanese. According to quoting National Park Service, "The internment of Japanese Americans in the United States was the forced relocation and incarceration during World War II of between 110,000 and 120,000 people of Japanese ancestry who lived on the Pacific coast in camps in the interior of the country. Sixty-two percent of the internees were United States citizens. The U.S. government ordered the removal of Japanese Americans in 1942, shortly after Imperial Japan's attack on Pearl Harbor."

- William Clinton is impeached but the people demanded that he stay in office being a popular president, a violation of the constitution. "The United States Constitution states in Article II, Section 4: "The President, Vice President and all civil Officers of the United States, shall be removed from Office on Impeachment" (The History Place).

- "The Supreme Court has held that Sunday closing laws do not violate the separation of church and state" (Freedom From Religion Foundation).

"Now when Daniel knew that the writing was signed, he went into his house; and his windows being open in his chamber toward Jerusalem, he kneeled upon his knees three times a day, and prayed, and gave thanks before his God, as he did aforetime" (Daniel 6:10). It is important to note that despite all other laws in which we are told, a Christian ought "to be subject to principalities and powers, to obey magistrates, to be ready to every good work" (Titus 3:1), but when it comes to violation between obeying God, "We ought to obey God rather than men" (Acts 5:29).

"Then these men assembled, and found Daniel praying and making supplication before his God. Then they came near, and spake before the king concerning the king's decree; Hast thou not signed a decree, that every man that shall ask [a petition] of any God or man within thirty days, save of thee, O king, shall be cast into the den of lions? The king answered and said, The thing [is] true, according to the law of the Medes and Persians, which altereth not. Then answered they and said before the king, That Daniel, which [is] of the children of the captivity of Judah, regardeth not thee, O king, nor the decree that thou hast signed, but maketh his petition three times a day" (Daniel 6:11-13). Unfortunately the future law for the Mark of the Beast is not a matter of hiding from the government. There is something, like natural disasters, that are going to cause the citizens to be willing to hand over to the government those that will be in violation of the law, hence why Jesus said, "When ye therefore shall see the abomination of desolation, spoken of by Daniel the prophet, stand in the holy place, (whoso readeth, let him understand:) Then let them which be in Judaea flee into the mountains: Let him which is on the housetop not come down to take any thing out of his house: Neither let him which is in the field return back to take his clothes. And woe unto them that are with child, and to them that give suck in those days! But pray ye that your flight be not in the winter, neither on the sabbath day: For then shall be great tribulation, such as was not since the beginning of the world to this time, no, nor ever shall be" (Matthew 24:15-21).

"Then the king commanded, and they brought Daniel, and cast [him] into the den of lions" (Daniel 6:16). This parallels, "cause that as many as would not worship the image of the beast should be killed" (Revelation 13:15).

But Daniel was able to say, "My God hath sent his angel, and hath shut the lions' mouths, that they have not hurt me: forasmuch as before him innocency was found in me; and also before thee, O king, have I done no hurt" (Daniel 6:22). And so it will be as well for those in the last days. There will be survivors for if those that have "one mind" on the side of the Mark of the Beast were successful in eradicating those having "one mind" of Christ, then how could it be said, "Then we which are alive [and] remain shall be caught up together with them in the clouds, to meet the Lord in the air: and so shall we ever be with the Lord" (1 Thessalonians 4:17). We would all be dead. So we too shall have God's protection, but it will be very stressful, just as sleeping with the lions would be. The events of the very last days among the protected will be, "He that walketh righteously, and speaketh uprightly; he that despiseth the gain of oppressions, that shaketh his hands from holding of bribes, that stoppeth his ears from hearing of blood, and shutteth his eyes from seeing evil; He shall dwell on high: his place of defence [shall be] the munitions of rocks: bread shall be given him; his waters [shall be] sure. Thine eyes shall see the king in his beauty: they shall behold the land that is very far off" (Isaiah 33:15-17) and then "It shall be said in that day, Lo, this [is] our God; we have waited for him, and he will save us: this [is] the LORD; we have waited for him, we will be glad and rejoice in his salvation" (Isaiah 25:9). But notice that this is only for those that walk righteously and speak uprightly despising getting gain by oppressing, despising the taking of bribes, that stops their ears from hearing bloodshed and shutting their eyes from seeing evil.

To walk righteously is to be living in obedience to the Ten Commandments for "the righteousness of the law might be fulfilled in us, who walk not after the flesh, but after the Spirit" (Romans 8:4). As we see, we need to cease from all the flesh attractions and be seeking constantly the Spirit. In other words, anyone living to enjoy life instead of spending time in God's Word by the hours and not minutes, spending time with God in prayer "without ceasing" (1 Thessalonians 5:17), to be basically a religious person to the point of even being called a "religious fanatic" is a person that is nothing more than a fake Christian. People that are really into watching and cheering for sports teams all summer, or all winter, or whenever their favorite team is on, are part of the deceived ones. Those that follow television programs and celebrities, surfing the Internet trying to get the inside scoop, are all deceived. Those that like to party, even when not using drugs or alcohol, are being deceived. They are all being deceived into spending time with the world and not becoming a righteous person.

To speak uprightly means we are ceasing from the jabbing, jesting, joking that involves hurting people, lying, or any other sin. It also means that we cease from the trivial conversations like the constant sports and celebrity and television conversations.

To despise getting gain by oppression includes being honest in all transactions, including selling a house, a car, or any other object. It involves putting in an honest day's work. It is avoiding all gains that is actually classed as stealing as well as taking advantage of someone.

To despise taking of bribes is pretty much just that, but it also includes that we ought not be appreciative of lobbyists, as in the ones that are out for greed. Even if we agree with certain legislation, to pay off politicians in any form should be despised. All these backroom deals should make us sick. The notion of a politician voting for a law that normally they would be against in exchange for a highway to nowhere only to create jobs somewhere else is bribery and disgusting. Even for ourselves, being in favor of an outcome only because it benefits ourselves is a form of bribery. If the result benefits the majority, in the eyes of God, we ought to be for such even if it disadvantages ourselves.

To stop our ears from hearing bloodshed, to stop our eyes from seeing evil today, is basically a call to turn off the television. Even in the criminal shows where we are on the side of the good guys, bloodshed and evil is displayed very vividly. Those into shows containing any evil is wrong, which pretty much describes them all because if it is not murder, it is demonstrating physical altercations, or verbal abuse. If that is not the sin in the show, then there is implied illicit sexual content, meaning, an encouragement of activity that God would not approve, even if never shown nor even physically implied. Just the verbal exchange is sufficient. And again, maybe the show is not about violence or any form of sex, there are many other evils well portrayed that we dismiss for the sake of entertainment. Although it may not be sinful, the promise is that those that do turn the television off and stop going to the movies, they are the ones that will find protection in the mountains, be provided food, and eventually see Jesus breaking through the clouds. To lead a Christian life while still indulging in worldly television is to risk making it.

"And the king commanded, and they brought those men which had accused Daniel, and they cast [them] into the den of lions, them, their children, and their wives; and the lions had the mastery of them, and brake all their bones in pieces or ever they came at the bottom of the den" (Daniel 6:24). And in the end "And I saw heaven opened, and behold a white horse; and he that sat upon him [was] called Faithful and True, and in righteousness he doth judge and make war. And the remnant were slain with the sword of him that sat upon the horse, which [sword] proceeded out of his mouth: and all the fowls were filled with their flesh" (Revelation 19:11, 21).

How Does John the Baptist Parallel the Last Day Events?

"In those days came John the Baptist, preaching in the wilderness of Judaea, and saying, Repent ye: for the kingdom of heaven is at hand. For this is he that was spoken of by the prophet Esaias, saying, The voice of one crying in the wilderness, Prepare ye the way of the Lord, make his paths straight" (Matthew 3:1-3). So before the second coming, the same is true. First, for John to be preaching from the wilderness means that He was not part of the acceptable religions of the day. He rejected the teachings of the Pharisees and Sadducees. He did not agree with the scribes and the lawyers. Today, we say that the truth lies not with the acceptable denominations, in fact, they are pretty much compromised. They are either the Antichrist or the "Spirit of Antichrist" where we reject the popular theologians, the hierarchy, even the lawyers involved in religious matters. We also reject the modern versions of the Bible that today's scribes have published. The primary reason for such a rejection is because the so called Greek manuscripts have the influence of the Vatican written on them, known as the Latin transcripts. Only the King James Version and maybe the Geneva Bible escape that influence. And yes, that includes the rejection of the popular New International Version.

Let us face it, any church accepting Sunday as the Christian Sabbath is compromised and influenced by the "Spirit of Antichrist". Any denomination accepting life immediately after death has been influenced by the "Spirit of Antichrist". Any denomination that does not care about what their flock eats or drinks is influenced by the "Spirit of Antichrist". That pretty much eliminates all but two, three, or maybe four denominations.

Now the fact that John had a specific message, according to Isaiah, "The voice of him that crieth in the wilderness, Prepare ye the way of the LORD, make straight in the desert a highway for our God" (Isaiah 40:3), those in the last days to be used of God like John the Baptist will also have a specific message. It is found in Revelation 14:6-12, "And

I saw another angel fly in the midst of heaven, having the everlasting gospel to preach unto them that dwell on the earth, and to every nation, and kindred, and tongue, and people, Saying with a loud voice, Fear God, and give glory to him; for the hour of his judgment is come: and worship him that made heaven, and earth, and the sea, and the fountains of waters. And there followed another angel, saying, Babylon is fallen, is fallen, that great city, because she made all nations drink of the wine of the wrath of her fornication. And the third angel followed them, saying with a loud voice, If any man worship the beast and his image, and receive [his] mark in his forehead, or in his hand, The same shall drink of the wine of the wrath of God, which is poured out without mixture into the cup of his indignation; and he shall be tormented with fire and brimstone in the presence of the holy angels, and in the presence of the Lamb: And the smoke of their torment ascendeth up for ever and ever: and they have no rest day nor night, who worship the beast and his image, and whosoever receiveth the mark of his name. Here is the patience of the saints: here [are] they that keep the commandments of God, and the faith of Jesus."

But in addition to that, John came rebuking their dress and gluttony by "wearing his raiment of camel's hair, and a leathern girdle about his loins; and his meat was locusts and wild honey" (Matthew 3:4). Likewise, those living in the last days will not be given into such things either. The dress shall be in "modest apparel, with shamefacedness and sobriety; not with broided hair, or gold, or pearls, or costly array" (1 Timothy 2:9). The food shall not contain blood, as noted three times in the book of acts, and will also do as Peter says, "I have never eaten any thing that is common or unclean" (Acts 10:14).

"But when he saw many of the Pharisees and Sadducees come to his baptism, he said unto them, O generation of vipers, who hath warned you to flee from the wrath to come?" (Matthew 3:7) So John was very direct and pointed, in fact, today it seem such people that know what is going on have turned up the directness. In fact, time is running out to be just so careful. And the call in general is "Bring forth therefore fruits meet for repentance" (Matthew 3:8). Today, we call people to a more specific fruit: complete obedience to the Ten Commandments.

"And think not to say within yourselves, We have Abraham to [our] father: for I say unto you, that God is able of these stones to raise up children unto Abraham" (Matthew 3:9), and today, we would say, "And think not to say within yourselves, We are saved: for I say unto you, that God is able of these stones to raise up children that are Christian."

"I indeed baptize you with water unto repentance: but he that cometh after me is mightier than I, whose shoes I am not worthy to bear: he shall baptize you with the Holy Ghost, and [with] fire" (Matthew 3:11). And the same is true today, but it is not the Holy Spirit that makes people crawl on the floor, sing spiritual songs, and speak in incomprehensible words. Rather, the Holy Spirit "will reprove the world of sin, and of righteousness, and of judgment" (John 16:8), and "He will guide you into all truth" (John 16:13). So if people claim to be filled with the Spirit while sinning, they are not filled with the Holy One. If they are rejecting any truth, they may be filled with the Spirit but it is not the wholly one.

How Does Jesus' First Coming Parallel the Last Day Events?

We begin the parallel with a date. The time of the Messiah was given to Daniel, in which it is stated, "Seventy weeks are determined upon thy people and upon thy holy city, to finish the transgression, and to make an end of sins, and to make reconciliation for iniquity, and to bring in everlasting righteousness, and to seal up the vision and prophecy, and to anoint the most Holy" (Daniel 9:24). From a larger time prophecy of days representing years (Numbers 14:34, Ezekiel 4:6), seventy weeks of days or years or four hundred and ninety days of years are cut off for Daniel's people, the Jews. There is much to accomplish in that time frame including welcoming "the most Holy". All we need is a starting point.

"Know therefore and understand, [that] from the going forth of the commandment to restore and to build Jerusalem unto the Messiah the Prince [shall be] seven weeks, and threescore and two weeks: the street shall be built again, and the wall, even in troublous times" (Daniel 9:25). So when the command to rebuild Jerusalem happens and the people begin building, that is when we can begin counting towards the arrival of the Messiah, the Prince.

When was the command to rebuild Jerusalem uttered? Well, as predicted from earlier, Cyrus would be involved. "Now in the first year of Cyrus king of Persia, that the word of the LORD by the mouth of Jeremiah might be fulfilled, the LORD stirred up the spirit of Cyrus king of Persia, that he made a proclamation throughout all his kingdom, and [put it] also in writing, saying, Thus saith Cyrus king of Persia, The LORD God of heaven hath given me all the kingdoms of the earth; and he hath charged me to build him an house at Jerusalem, which [is] in Judah" (Ezra 1:1-2). However, looking at the command, we see that it is not a command to rebuild Jerusalem as it was command to focus on the temple. That is not what the prophecy of Daniel said. It said, "From the going forth of the commandment to restore and to build Jerusalem" (Daniel 9:25). This command stated, "Build him an house at Jerusalem" (Daniel 9:25). And think not that it is implied. The land of Jerusalem was still known as Jerusalem, but the walls that defined it as a city was still broken down; the merchant buildings were still broken down; so the clock had not yet started for the Messiah to come. Therefore, 536 B.C. is not the starting point.

Then along comes Darius in 520 B.C., in which he also made a decree. "In the first year of Cyrus the king [the same] Cyrus the king made a decree [concerning] the house of God at Jerusalem, Let the house be builded, the place where they offered sacrifices, and let the foundations thereof be strongly laid" (Ezra 6:3). It too focused upon the house "where they offered sacrifices", but not involving Jerusalem once again. So still the clock did not begin.

Finally, in 457 B.C., "Artaxerxes king of Persia" (Ezra 7:1) towards "This Ezra" who "went up from Babylon; and he [was] a ready scribe in the law of Moses, which the LORD God of Israel had given: and the king granted him all his request, according to the hand of the LORD his God upon him" (Ezra 7:6). "And whatsoever more shall be needful for the house of thy God, which thou shalt have occasion to bestow, bestow [it] out of the king's treasure house. And I, [even] I Artaxerxes the king, do make a decree to all the treasurers which [are] beyond the river, that whatsoever Ezra the priest, the scribe of the law of the God of heaven, shall require of you, it be done speedily" (Ezra 7:20-21). And as we see, not only is the house of God to be rebuilt but it is to be financed by the king under Ezra's direction. But someone is going to say, "Hold on! This is still the house of God and not Jerusalem." And looking at the Book of Ezra alone, one would be correct. But turning to the simultaneous time frame of the Book of Nehemiah, "in the twentieth year of Artaxerxes the king" (Nehemiah 2:1), these questions and answers are recorded. "Wherefore the king said unto me, Why [is] thy countenance sad, seeing thou [art] not sick? this [is] nothing [else] but sorrow of heart. Then I was very sore afraid, And said unto the king, Let the king live for ever: why should not my countenance be sad, when the city, the place of my fathers' sepulchres, [lieth] waste, and the gates thereof are consumed with fire? Then the king said unto me, For what dost thou make request? So I prayed to the God of heaven. And I said unto the king, If it please the king, and if thy servant have found favour in thy sight, that thou wouldest send me unto Judah, unto the city of my fathers' sepulchres, that I may build it. And the king said unto me, (the queen also sitting by him,) For how long shall thy journey be? and when wilt thou return? So it pleased the king to send me; and I set him a time. Moreover I said unto the king, If it please the king, let letters be given me to the governors beyond the river, that they may convey me over till I come into Judah; And a letter unto Asaph the keeper of the king's forest, that he may give me timber to make beams for the gates of the palace which [appertained] to the house, and for the wall of the city, and for the house that I shall enter into. And the king granted me, according to the good hand of my God upon me" (Nehemiah 2:2-8).

So now with the beginning of the long decree of King Artaxerxes beginning in 457 B.C., we follow the 483 years for each day of the prophecy. We are leaving the final week off for now because that applies to something other than the arrival of the Messiah. Keeping in mind that there is no zero year, we end up in 27 A.D. The event that was to take place, according to Daniel, was to "anoint the most Holy" (Daniel 9:24). So what is recorded regarding an anointing in 27 A.D., especially involving the Messiah? "Now in the fifteenth year of the reign of Tiberius Caesar, Pontius Pilate being governor of Judaea, and Herod being tetrarch of Galilee, and his brother Philip tetrarch of Ituraea and of the region of Trachonitis, and Lysanias the tetrarch of Abilene, Annas and Caiaphas being the high priests, the word of God came unto John the son of Zacharias in the wilderness" (Luke 3:1-2). As one may know, dates are not in the Bible, but a list of who is who serves just as well. If one were to figure out all the overlapping reigns in each of these positions, the time would be 27 A.D. when John the Baptist was well recognized as being quite active in his ministry and would perform a very important task. "Now when all the people were baptized, it came to pass, that Jesus also being baptized, and praying, the heaven was opened, And the Holy Ghost descended in a bodily shape like a dove upon him, and a voice came from heaven, which said, Thou art my beloved Son; in thee I am well pleased" (Luke 3:21-22). That is one heavenly anointing.

Now in addition to being baptized right on time, the prophecy states that "in the midst of the week he shall cause the sacrifice and the oblation to cease" (Daniel 9:27). Seven days being a week of time, we must ask what event happened three and a half years after Jesus' baptism, remembering that each day represents a year. Did Jesus do anything that caused the sacrifices to be of insignificance? And the answer is, Yes! "Jesus, when he had cried again with a loud voice, yielded up the ghost. And, behold, the veil of the temple was rent in twain from the top to the bottom; and the earth did quake, and the rocks rent" (Matthew 27:50-51). The sacrificial system was made no longer necessary since the real Lamb was sacrificed that day.

The only thing that remains then is the fact that the Jews were given specifically four hundred and ninety years, being cut off from a longer time prophecy, for it states, "Seventy weeks are determined upon thy people", which is the four hundred and ninety days, which are prophetic of years. So, did anything mark the closing event? And again, the answer is, Yes! "And they stoned Stephen, calling upon [God], and saying, Lord Jesus, receive my spirit. And he kneeled down, and cried with a loud voice, Lord, lay not this sin to their charge. And when he had said this, he fell asleep" (Acts 7:59-60). "And Saul was consenting unto his death. And at that time there was a great persecution against the church which was at Jerusalem; and they were all scattered abroad throughout the regions of Judaea and Samaria, except the apostles" (Acts 8:1). Basically, the all out slaughter of Christians in Israel forced the gospel to go to all the world, marking the closing of the timeframe. It is not a coincidence that God said at the end of the four hundred and ninety prophetic days that the Jews would be cut off and the gospel was now being scattered beyond the borders of Israel. It is also not a coincidence that when asked, "Lord, how oft shall my brother sin against me, and I forgive him? till seven times?" (Matthew 18:21) that the answer by Jesus was "I say not unto thee, Until seven times: but, Until seventy times seven" (Matthew 18:22). What is seventy times seven? Four hundred and ninety. Please note that Jesus left it open ended. He did not say the word "times" because it was not "times", but Jesus could not say years because they were not ready for it. But Jesus treated the time prophecy not as two pieces in which seven years is yet future. He was counting side that last seven years already. The four hundred and ninety was running out.

Jesus knew the time was running out. He also was able to say in His first year of His ministry, His second, and even part of His third, "My time is not yet come" (John 7:6). He knew that from the baptism in the fall of 27 A.D., He would not face death on the cross until the spring of 31 A.D. Nowhere else is the time of the crucifixion stated. Jesus did not have a feeling of "my time is not yet come". Jesus had a date from Daniel 9:27 confirming that in the last week of time, seven literal years, it was to remain intact with the prior four hundred and eighty three years.

So how does this apply to the second coming? An implied date is given to us in Daniel 12:4 and 9, which says, "But thou, O Daniel, shut up the words, and seal the book, [even] to the time of the end: many shall run to and fro, and knowledge shall be increased", and "Go thy way, Daniel: for the words [are] closed up and sealed till the time of the end." The implied date is when people can move freely about with easy and knowledge increases, which we have arrived twice, as mentioned before. That physical ability to move about on this planet started in the 1800's. Our knowledge explosion all so began in the 1800's. From a spiritual sense, with concordances and now technology, running through the Book of Daniel and the whole Bible has been made much easier, again starting in the 1800's. Knowledge of the prophetic books as well as the rest of the Bible skyrocketed with the birth of Bible societies and focused preachers, again since the 1800's. On top of that, the four hundred and ninety day or year prophecy that was "determined upon" or cut off for Daniel's "people", the Jews (Daniel 9:24), comes from the longer time prophecy.

Looking closer at Daniel 9:24 to Daniel 9:27, it seems an angel shows up to provide an explanation of time. This is found in Daniel 9:23, "At the beginning of thy supplications the commandment came forth, and I am come to shew [thee]; for thou [art] greatly beloved: therefore understand the matter, and consider the vision" (Daniel 9:23). Why now? Daniel said, "I set my face unto the Lord God, to seek by prayer and supplications, with fasting, and sackcloth, and ashes" (Daniel 9:3). And from Daniel 9:4 until the angel arrives is that prayer. So now we back up in Daniel 8, and find out that this angel was explaining an overwhelming prophecy, so overwhelming that in the middle of the explanation, "I Daniel fainted, and was sick [certain] days; afterward I rose up, and did the king's business; and I was astonished at the vision, but none understood [it]" (Daniel 8:27). What made him sick? "The vision of the evening and the morning which was told [is] true: wherefore shut thou up the vision; for it [shall be] for many days" (Daniel 8:26). Now how many days is that? "And he said unto me, Unto two thousand and three hundred days; then shall the sanctuary be cleansed" (Daniel 8:14).

So let us put this in perspective. In Daniel 8, there is a prophecy that involves a lot of detail. The period of time that is covered is twenty-three hundred days. The angel explains all of the details except about the time. Dwelling on the time, Daniel became very ill because he was hoping that life on this planet, as we know it, would be over shortly and paradise would begin, but not only is that unlikely in the near future from Daniel's perspective, but even a couple thousand more years are to be experienced. Every good Jew looked forward to the first coming of Christ, but with the potential of Jesus not showing up for more than two thousand years seemed oh so overwhelming. That is the part that Daniel did not realize was actually sooner than later, but as the angel was going to reveal when the Messiah was to show up, he fainted. After asking his friends what this vision could mean and continuing to do his assigned work, the answer came in a smaller chunk. Of the twenty-three hundred day prophecy, the first four hundred and ninety days are for the Jews to do many things including welcoming the Messiah for the first time. There is only one cutting off or amount of time that is "determined". That means the four hundred and ninety days are one lump sum, unlike many who try to take the final seven days and throw them into the future as if there is a future seven year tribulation period, as proposed by the Jesuit, Ribera. If that were so, then the angel would have said, "There are sixty-nine weeks determined upon thy people and later another seven." The angel did not say that. There is only one "determined" or "cut off".

Now that Jesus confirmed in 27 A.D. by His baptism that 457 B.C. is the starting point of the four hundred and ninety prophetic days or literal years and then further confirmed by causing the "the sacrifice and the oblation to cease" (Daniel 9:27) in 31 A.D. and the Jews finally rejecting as a nation God's divine plan in 34 A.D. sending the gospel to the Gentiles, that means the final date of the twenty-three hundred prophetic days or literal years is three times confirmed. Using the math of twenty-three hundred days minus four hundred and ninety of them for the Jews, that leaves from 34 A.D. an additional eighteen hundred and ten days left, representing literal years. That brings us to the middle of the 1800's, specifically to 1844, the year of the Great Awakening time period, which is also symbolized in sequence of feast days as the Feast of Trumpets. On top of that, the Revelation chapter 10 prophecy fits so well here also, in which during the years leading up to 1844, a worldwide proclamation was being uttered, which as predicted, would end up in a great disappointment (Revelation 10:1-10). And shortly after that, the correct understanding of the event of 1844 would be understood and told to the whole world (Revelation 10:11).

So both Jesus and the events of the second coming parallel in that they are both given specific dates and both predicted by the prophet Daniel, in fact, even with the same prophecy of time.

A third parallel between Jesus and the events of the second coming is found in location. According to Genesis 49:10, the Bible says, "The sceptre shall not depart from Judah, nor a lawgiver from between his feet, until Shiloh come; and unto him [shall] the gathering of the people [be]." So Jesus should be born in the land of Judah, but more specifically, Micah 5:2 says, "But thou, Bethlehem Ephratah, [though] thou be little among the thousands of Judah, [yet] out of thee shall he come forth unto me [that is] to be ruler in Israel; whose goings forth [have been] from of old, from everlasting."

The location that brings forth the last day message is also revealed. As studied earlier, Revelation 12 tells us that the true church is persecuted and goes into hiding (Revelation 12:13-14), which was fulfilled during the dark ages; multitudes from every nation would seek her harm (Revelation 12:15); but an unpopulated country would rise to power around the end of the 1700's (Revelation 12:16), as fulfilled by the United States; of which all of the European born denominations would compromise, but this one group would not. They are identified as keeping all of God's Ten Commandments and having "the testimony of Jesus Christ" (Revelation 12:17). So the United States is the focus point for the events to begin regarding the last days.

A fourth parallel is in the work, as being defined ahead of time. Some think Jesus walked the earth as a kind person who was sinless, and died for us. Although that is the general aspect of things, Jesus actually had a specific plan given to Him. "Then the eyes of the blind shall be opened, and the ears of the deaf shall be unstopped. Then shall the lame [man] leap as an hart, and the tongue of the dumb sing" (Isaiah 35:5-6).

Likewise, it is not the duty of the church in the last days to just preach the gospel, but to have a specific message that goes with the gospel. "And I saw another angel fly in the midst of heaven, having the everlasting gospel to preach unto them that dwell on the earth, and to every nation, and kindred, and tongue, and people, Saying with a loud voice, Fear God, and give glory to him; for the hour of his judgment is come: and worship him that made heaven, and earth, and the sea, and the fountains of waters. And there followed another angel, saying, Babylon is fallen, is fallen, that great city, because she made all nations drink of the wine of the wrath of her fornication. And the third angel followed them, saying with a loud voice, If any man worship the beast and his image, and receive [his] mark in his forehead, or in his hand, The same shall drink of the wine of the wrath of God, which is poured out without mixture into the cup of his indignation; and he shall be tormented with fire and brimstone in the presence of the holy angels, and in the presence of the Lamb: And the smoke of their torment ascendeth up for ever and ever: and they have no rest day nor night, who worship the beast and his image, and whosoever receiveth the mark of his name" (Revelation 14:6-11).

The fifth parallel is that both Jesus and those that have the "One Mind" of Christ, kept the Sabbath. Regarding Jesus, it was said, "As his custom was, he went into the synagogue on the sabbath day, and stood up for to read" (Luke 4:16), while the group that has the specific last day message preaches, "Worship him that made heaven, and earth, and the sea, and the fountains of waters" (Revelation 14:7), which is a direct quote from the fourth commandment, "Remember the sabbath day, to keep it holy" (Exodus 20:8).

The sixth parallel is the activity of restoring the Sabbath to its original position. Hidden by mounds of legalism, Jesus "said unto them, The sabbath was made for man, and not man for the sabbath: Therefore the Son of man is Lord also of the sabbath" (Mark 2:27-28), while the last day group, it is described as "And [they that shall be] of thee shall build the old waste places: thou shalt raise up the foundations of many generations; and thou shalt be called, The repairer of the breach, The restorer of paths to dwell in. If thou turn away thy foot from the sabbath, [from] doing thy pleasure on my holy day; and call the sabbath a delight, the holy of the LORD, honourable; and shalt honour him, not doing thine own ways, nor finding thine own pleasure, nor speaking [thine own] words: Then shalt thou delight thyself in the LORD; and I will cause thee to ride upon the high places of the earth, and feed thee with the heritage of Jacob thy father: for the mouth of the LORD hath spoken [it]" (Isaiah 58:12-14).

The seventh parallel is that "Jesus went about all Galilee, teaching in their synagogues, and preaching the gospel of the kingdom, and healing all manner of sickness and all manner of disease among the people" (Matthew 4:23). Not only was the gospel preached then, but those with the specific message also preach the gospel for they go about "having the everlasting gospel to preach unto them that dwell on the earth, and to every nation, and kindred, and tongue, and people" (Revelation 14:6). Now this is typically the confusing part. People think that the gospel is all that is necessary to be saved. It is not. The gospel message is about salvation, but it also includes specific, timely messages for that period of which if not obeyed is equally condemning as not accepting the gospel.

For instance, believe it or not, Noah had the gospel and called people into the ark. If people said, "I believe in God but I'm not getting in the boat", no matter if they had the correct understanding or not, they are considered lost. Today, that message is not applicable but the gospel still is. Likewise, Moses had the gospel and told people that it was time to get out of Egypt. All those that would have said, "I accept God's grace and I believe in God" would have been lost if they remained. Well, the gospel may be the same, but the activity of leaving Egypt is not. John the Baptist had the gospel and the message about Jesus' first coming. The gospel is not different but the arrival of Jesus is definitely different because He is coming a second time.

Now, for those that question who had and did not have the gospel be careful in doing a word search. According to the Bible, the first use of the word gospel is in the Book of Matthew. In fact, all explicit uses of the word "gospel" is reserved for the New Testament, as to imply that the gospel is New Testament and the Law is Old Testament. Even though that is all that there is, it is nothing more than an implication to think that way. Jesus said, "The time is fulfilled, and the kingdom of God is at hand: repent ye, and believe the gospel" (Mark 1:15). When one hears the gospel, true belief comes with true repentance. Such is not reserved for the New Testament but is found in the Old as well. Besides, in the New Testament, the Bible says, "Foreseeing that God would justify the heathen through faith, preached before the gospel unto Abraham, [saying], In thee shall all nations be blessed" (Galatians 3:8). So the gospel was in Abraham's day. According to Romans 10:16, the gospel was around in Isaiah's day. That is Old Testament times.

And the gospel involves obedience for the Bible says, "For the time [is come] that judgment must begin at the house of God: and if [it] first [begin] at us, what shall the end [be] of them that obey not the gospel of God?" (1 Peter 4:17) "In flaming fire taking vengeance on them that know not God, and that obey not the gospel of our Lord Jesus Christ" (2 Thessalonians 1:8). So if someone thinks that the gospel is just about "Jesus saves", think again. The gospel is the declaration that God exists. It is the declaration that God is love. It is the declaration that humans have sinned. It is the declaration that God saves us from the penalty of our sins. It is the declaration that God sent His Son, named Jesus, to accomplish this. It is the declaration that to all that believe the gospel may now have power to be sons and daughters of God to be able to live holy lives. It is the declaration that in the end, we may experience eternal life. These declarations are what are conveyed to humans, and "the devils also believe, and tremble" (James 2:19), but to the true Christian, we believe, they are to obey. What do we obey? Well, Jesus said, "Teaching them to observe all things whatsoever I have commanded you" (Matthew 28:20). So if we believe that we are saved from our sins, we will observe things like not lusting after the opposite gender (Matthew 5:28) or get unnecessarily angry with people (Matthew 5:22), among many other things.

So in the last days, the gospel message is combined with the last day messages being very involved in Bible prophecy. That means, true Christians will not be careless with their knowledge. They will not be careless with prophecy. Going to church, dropping money in the collection plate, and singing nicely is not the description of a true Christian. A true Christian will "Study to shew thyself approved unto God, a workman that needeth not to be ashamed, rightly dividing the word of truth" (2 Timothy 2:15). They will not fear prophecy but embrace the understanding of the Antichrist, the image of the beast, the mark of the beast, and much more. Overall, the ones with the true gospel are the most knowledgeable in the area of prophecy.

Further, we bring this parallel of the gospel to light because many, many Christians see a book like this being very much not gospel oriented. In fact, they even accuse such authors as promoting unkindness and hate, traits very much not of Jesus. On the contrary, we have done nothing but uplift Jesus so much so that we hate to see His doctrines trampled upon; we hate to see sincere Christians being deceived out of eternal life; we hate seeing the devil win at encouraging people to sin; in other words, we may not be completely kind, but we are full of love. And no one said that kindness outweighs love. In fact, kindness can be the unloving thing to do. A young man willing to help an old lady across the street only to snatch the purse does a kind deed but did not do a loving thing. A person kindly buying cigarettes for another does not love that person because such a person would not help them have a short life. Somewhere along the years, kindness has became the evaluation of all actions, when Jesus declared, "If ye love me, keep my commandments" (John 14:15). It is love that is most important. And out of love, we are trying to "teach all nations" (Matthew 28:19) and trying to do it by "speaking the truth in love" (Ephesians 4:15). And love hurts some times. As a child reaches up to pull a boiling pot of water upon themselves, if one is across the room and cannot get there in time, yelling NO in a very audible manner is necessary even if it is going to cause the child to cry.

So this is the gospel message coupled with today's warnings, and those not aware of the situation, are not caring about the situation are going to feel the unkindness, but it is done because we have this love for everyone to be in Heaven, and it is our hope that no one fulfills the verse that states, "with all deceivableness of unrighteousness in them that perish; because they received not the love of the truth, that they might be saved" (2 Thessalonians 2:10).

In the eighth parallel, we see the love from both Jesus and the last day messengers. Jesus in tears uttered, "O Jerusalem, Jerusalem, [thou] that killest the prophets, and stonest them which are sent unto thee, how often would I have gathered thy children together, even as a hen gathereth her chickens under [her] wings, and ye would not! Behold, your house is left unto you desolate" (Matthew 23:37-38). The messengers of the last days will not be a group of people using the Bible to prove people to hell, but will be pleading with people to join the truth, so much so that we see them "weep between the porch and the altar, and let them say, Spare thy people, O LORD, and give not thine heritage to reproach, that the heathen should rule over them: wherefore should they say among the people, Where [is] their God?" (Joel 2:17) So many prove that God is with them because they can speak in tongues, do marvelous works like feeding thousands, and point to other signs and wonders, but in the end, "Many will say to me in that day, Lord, Lord, have we not prophesied in thy name? and in thy name have cast out devils? and in thy name done many wonderful works? And then will I profess unto them, I never knew you: depart from me, ye that work iniquity" (Matthew 7:22-23).

In the ninth parallel, we see a very serious and sad situation. "In that same hour said Jesus to the multitudes, Are ye come out as against a thief with swords and staves for to take me? I sat daily with you teaching in the temple, and ye laid no hold on me. But all this was done, that the scriptures of the prophets might be fulfilled. Then all the disciples forsook him, and fled" (Matthew 26:55-56). During a time of crisis, real Christianity is revealed hence why those that believe in pre-tribulation rapture are missing the point in "that we must through much tribulation enter into the kingdom of God" (Acts 14:22). "There shall be a time of trouble, such as never was since there was a nation [even] to that same time: and at that time thy people shall be delivered, every one that shall be found written in the book" (Daniel 12:1), at which time, "They shall put you out of the synagogues: yea, the time cometh, that whosoever killeth you will think that he doeth God service" (John 16:2) all the while the true Christians are "the remnant of her seed, which keep the commandments of God, and have the testimony of Jesus Christ" (Revelation 12:17). In both cases we see a mass exodus of Jesus' followers.

The tenth parallel involves the organized churches. In Jesus' day, "Then gathered the chief priests and the Pharisees a council, and said, What do we? for this man doeth many miracles. If we let him thus alone, all [men] will believe on him: and the Romans shall come and take away both our place and nation. And one of them, [named] Caiaphas, being the high priest that same year, said unto them, Ye know nothing at all, Nor consider that it is expedient for us, that one man should die for the people, and that the whole nation perish not" (John 11:47-50). In the last days, "But beware of men: for they will deliver you up to the councils, and they will scourge you in their synagogues; And ye shall be brought before governors and kings for my sake, for a testimony against them and the Gentiles" (Matthew 10:17-18). In fact, the parallel is so precise that even the church of the time "bound Jesus, and carried [him] away, and delivered [him] to Pilate" (Mark 15:1), of which Pilate was known as "Pontius Pilate the governor" (Matthew 27:2).

The eleventh parallel is in knowing the future persecution and embracing it. "Ye know that after two days is [the feast of] the passover, and the Son of man is betrayed to be crucified" (Matthew 26:2). "The Son of man shall be betrayed into the hands of men: And they shall kill him, and the third day he shall be raised again. And they were exceeding sorry" (Matthew 17:22-23). In the last days, instead of believing in pre-tribulation, we know the future, which is, "And he had power to give life unto the image of the beast, that the image of the beast should both speak, and cause that as many as would not worship the image of the beast should be killed" (Revelation 13:15), but we do not fear man. "If it be [so], our God whom we serve is able to deliver us from the burning fiery furnace, and he will deliver [us] out of thine hand, O king. But if not, be it known unto thee, O king, that we will not serve thy gods, nor worship the golden image which thou hast set up" (Daniel 3:17-18). And get this, instead of taking every precaution to avoid capture in the last days, true Christians will take "this gospel of the kingdom shall be preached in all the world for a witness unto all nations; and then shall the end come" (Matthew 24:14). That is not any gospel, but the specific true gospel, and that shall be taught right up until the end. Sure, one may knock on the wrong door and enter into a trap, but "they loved not their lives unto the death" (Revelation 12:11). If we have a choice between saving our own lives physically, or take the risk that who we share the saving message may actually be working for the wrong "one mind", we choose the risk!

The twelfth parallel again points to the large, formal, organized churches. Do not get us wrong. We believe in organized religion as God is organized, but when the majority of people believe something, it is probably wrong. For instance, in Jesus' day, "Jesus said unto them, Take heed and beware of the leaven of the Pharisees and of the Sadducees" (Matthew 16:6), and "Then understood they how that he bade [them] not beware of the leaven of bread, but of the doctrine of the Pharisees and of the Sadducees" (Matthew 16:12). The doctrines of the mainline bodies were off, yet anyone not in compliance was looked upon as a heretic. Much like today. If one is not part of the Catholic Church or mainline Protestant denominations, then one is mildly consider off-base or even lumped in as a cult follower.

Well, there is one major problem with most Protestant or Evangelical churches today. They are lead by "ungodly men, turning the grace of our God into lasciviousness, and denying the only Lord God, and our Lord Jesus Christ" (Jude 1:4). Now do not think we do not believe many are sincere. And in no way are we saying that such people are taking orders knowingly from the devil. What we are saying is that being motivated by fitting into the world, not living a disciplined life, and not believing in the miracle of God to help people cease from sinning, they have taken the grace message and turned it into something lasciviousness or wanting as in being in need of something. Well, the something they are missing is all the verses on sanctification or holy living. They are missing the call to be blameless (2 Peter 3:14), which is the inability to have some worldly person point out our hypocrisy of being Christian yet living in sin. They go so far as to deny that "God sending his own Son in the likeness of sinful flesh, and for sin, condemned sin in the flesh" (Romans 8:3). They deny that Jesus "took not on [him the nature of] angels; but he took on [him] the seed of Abraham" (Hebrews 2:16). They deny that we can "walk, even as he walked" (1 John 2:6), which means to live in obedience to God. In other words, they preach that Jesus came like Adam before sin entered the world, an example that we can never match. In realty, Jesus came in the same susceptibilities, propensities, temptations, towards sin as we experience every day, yet He had no evil in Him. There was no evil propensity. And from the moment of conversion, it is possible to live the life of Christ if we truly believe we have been given the "power to become the sons of God" (John 1:12) and being "partakers of the divine nature, having escaped the corruption that is in the world through lust" (2 Peter 1:4).

In the thirteenth parallel, Jesus disappoints His true believers by not showing up when expected. "Then said Martha unto Jesus, Lord, if thou hadst been here, my brother had not died' (John 11:21). In the last days, many shall expect Jesus, and He too will not show. In fact, many will say, "My lord delayeth his coming" (Matthew 24:48). More specifically, in a worldwide proclamation, Jesus was expected in 1844. And according to the Bible, the result of that teaching, "was in my mouth sweet as honey: and as soon as I had eaten it, my belly was bitter" (Revelation 10:10). It would be exciting only it ended in bitter disappointment.

How Does Stephen Parallel the Last Day Events?

"And they stoned Stephen, calling upon [God], and saying, Lord Jesus, receive my spirit. And he kneeled down, and cried with a loud voice, Lord, lay not this sin to their charge. And when he had said this, he fell asleep" (Acts 7:59-60), but before they killed him, he had said, "Ye stiffnecked and uncircumcised in heart and ears, ye do always resist the Holy Ghost: as your fathers [did], so [do] ye" (Acts 7:51). Today, many are stiffnecked as well in believing that to be filled with the Spirit means to babble, crawl around on the floor, shout out in a disrupting manner, and do all kinds of unbiblical or barely implied biblical things. The Holy Spirit is resisted because "when he is come, he will reprove the world of sin, and of righteousness, and of judgment" (John 16:8). On top of that, "he will guide you into all truth" (John 16:13). And we know this to be the case because hardly a Christian wants to hear the truth. As stated even moments ago, "with all deceivableness of unrighteousness in them that perish; because they received not the love of the truth, that they might be saved" (2 Thessalonians 2:10). So we make the same appeal: Cease from being stiffnecked!

Stephen went on to say, "Who have received the law by the disposition of angels, and have not kept [it]" (Acts 7:53). Even the Catholic church holds up a set of Ten Commandments, but not in most Protestant denominations. In fact, many who support the Ten Commandments only support nine for they try to help people forget the one that starts with the word "remember", as in, "Remember the sabbath day, to keep it holy. Six days shalt thou labour, and do all thy work: But the seventh day [is] the sabbath of the LORD thy God: [in it] thou shalt not do any work, thou, nor thy son, nor thy daughter, thy manservant, nor thy maidservant, nor thy cattle, nor thy stranger that [is] within thy gates: For [in] six days the LORD made heaven and earth, the sea, and all that in them [is], and rested the seventh day: wherefore the LORD blessed the sabbath day, and hallowed it" (Exodus 20:8-11). This and the other nine are not arbitrary commands. These are universal commands. These are the commands that existed before earth was made, in fact, even before the start of creation. These are the same commandments that shall guide us in the future eternal life for John wrote, "The temple of God was opened in heaven, and there was seen in his temple the ark of his testament" (Revelation 11:19). And what do you think is in the ark? Well, Hebrews 8:5 says, "Who serve unto the example and shadow of heavenly things, as Moses was admonished of God when he was about to make the tabernacle: for, See, saith he, [that] thou make all things according to the pattern shewed to thee in the mount." So since Moses made a duplicate of that which is in Heaven, then what Moses puts into the ark is the same as that which is in the ark in Heaven. "At that time the LORD said unto me, Hew thee two tables of stone like unto the first, and come up unto me into the mount, and make thee an ark of wood. And I will write on the tables the words that were in the first tables which thou brakest, and thou shalt put them in the ark" (Deuteronomy 10:1-2). In short, it is the Ten Commandments. Even the Sabbath is going to continue throughout eternity for "one sabbath to another, shall all flesh come to worship before me, saith the LORD" (Isaiah 66:23).

How Do Many More Parallels Reveal the Last Days?

We could spend many more pages on the subject for there are many more examples in the Bible relating to the second coming. We had to choose, but in our choices, we hope one realizes that these stories are not for historical record, some fable, old and unimportant content, or any such thing that would cause one to dismiss there studies.

We could have compared Joseph's life in prison to the dark ages and him rising to rule from a throne just like the saved in the end. "And I saw thrones, and they sat upon them, and judgment was given unto them" (Revelation 20:4).

Samson, though a poor example overall, shows the power of the woman (church), causing the true church to become persecuted as Samson was, only to one day have all their enemies defeated, not by his strength but by the power of the "Lord GOD" to have, as he prayed, "strengthen me" (Judges 16:28).

There are so many more characters worth studying that cuts through all of the wrong doctrines. Even David's life as well as Solomon's parallel for the last days. And who could forget Esther? The death decree to be sent forth to slaughter all of God's people, including Esther, a woman, the church, who makes an appeal to the king, as like our King, and is delivered.

We hope these thoughts have wetted your appetite to study more on your own.

What Is the Sequence of Final Events?

We know we are in the final events because when it comes to the Antichrist, "his deadly wound was healed: and all the world wondered after the beast" (Revelation 13:3). Basically, we are awaiting for "when they shall say, Peace and safety; then sudden destruction cometh upon them, as travail upon a woman with child; and they shall not escape" (1 Thessalonians 5:3).

Now we do not know if there has to be a formal declaration of the "peace and safety" existing, but in a general sense, we are there. We are not expecting a cessation of wars for Jesus Himself stated, "ye shall hear of wars and rumours of wars" (Matthew 24:6) and "Nation shall rise against nation, and kingdom against kingdom" (Matthew 24:7). In fact, since Jesus said, "As the days of Noe [were], so shall also the coming of the Son of man be" (Matthew 24:37), "the earth was filled with violence" (Genesis 6:11). So it is not a physical peace and safety among nations, let alone among people.

Seeing that peace mentioned in the Bible is more spiritual than physical, we propose the "one mind" religious movement bringing all the denominations and religions under the Antichrist umbrella is the fulfillment thereof. However, we also see that there is not enough support to declare "all the world", so we see a bit of assistance instigated by Satan through destruction. Nothing unifies people more than a crisis. Even weird laws are quickly enacted that would not have had a chance any other time.

In fact, John "saw another angel ascending from the east, having the seal of the living God: and he cried with a loud voice to the four angels, to whom it was given to hurt the earth and the sea, Saying, Hurt not the earth, neither the sea, nor the trees, till we have sealed the servants of our God in their foreheads" (Revelation 7:2-3). This is the primary reason why it has not happened yet. God's people have yet to be sealed. And as we studied in prior chapters that there is a logical progression. First, we have truth being sealed in us (Ephesians 1:13). Specifically, we have the Ten Commandments, being that the law is truth (Psalms 119:142), being sealed in us. And as a sign or seal (Romans 4:11), the specific commandment that contains God's name, title, and territory is none other than the Sabbath (Exodus 20:8-11), which are the components of a seal, however, people still dabble in sin. But at some point, they will cease from sin so that they can stand with "no intercessor" (Isaiah 59:16).

People often flock to religion during a great world crisis. Look how churches were exploding with people in September 2001 after the World Trade Towers were brought down. Now this event coming will actually have to be larger than a single event. An earthquake is not going to be the driving force because if we look at all the big earthquakes we have had, religion was not made a priority. So a multi-facet event is more than likely on the near horizon and when it happens, who do you think the world will flock towards for moral guidance? The Antichrist of course.

In addition to the Antichrist wound being well healed, the second beast that would form an image or act like the first beast or Antichrist also is well established. After being built upon Christian principles, laws now are existing with dragon-like wording since that is how a country speaks. With laws removing freedoms instead of establishing them and protecting them, the second beast is not only in existence but is the lone super power and has transitioned into the way of the dragon.

Now under the crisis, "all the world wondered after the beast" (Revelation 13:3), "who opposeth and exalteth himself above all that is called God, or that is worshipped; so that he as God sitteth in the temple of God, shewing himself that he is God" (2 Thessalonians 2:4), will suggest appeasing God by returning to worshipping God properly, though it will be the wrong day. In fact, those sentiments are already in place. Many evangelical leaders have been calling for Sunday to be practiced as it once had in this country pointing out that God is not well pleased. So whatever coming combination of disasters that Satan is preparing, when it hits, the answer of "Why" is already being provided.

Upon continual affects from the disasters, be it from nature, economics, health, or combination thereof, there will also be a stronger and stronger call to enforce by law the Mark of the Beast. And we do think it will be combination of things. When we said that Jesus listed the events of "nation shall rise against nation, and kingdom against kingdom: and there shall be famines, and pestilences, and earthquakes, in divers places" (Matthew 24:7), take note the we have wars, natural disasters or famines and earthquakes, along with health issues of pestilences. It will get to a point where, regarding the second beast, "he causeth all, both small and great, rich and poor, free and bond, to receive a mark in their right hand, or in their foreheads: And that no man might buy or sell, save he that had the mark, or the name of the beast, or the number of his name" (Revelation 13:16-17).

Things will start out innocently, but as anything, it will be considered the norm. The media will continuously identify those that are not complying as those that are troubling the peace, and like today, those that are wanting to defend the freedom of choice will be looked upon with hatred.

Being blamed for the world's problems, "they will deliver you up to the councils, and they will scourge you in their synagogues" (Matthew 10:17), "ye shall be brought before governors and kings for my sake, for a testimony against them and the Gentiles" (Matthew 10:18), with "a man's foes [shall be] they of his own household" (Matthew 10:36).

"Alas! for that day [is] great, so that none [is] like it: it [is] even the time of Jacob's trouble; but he shall be saved out of it" (Jeremiah 30:7). "Many shall be purified, and made white, and tried; but the wicked shall do wickedly: and none of the wicked shall understand; but the wise shall understand" (Daniel 12:10). So during the coming crisis, we have people becoming holy, which is, a "church, not having spot, or wrinkle, or any such thing; but that it should be holy and without blemish" (Ephesians 5:27). So God's people around the world will actually be ceasing from sin because there will be no blemish, not a spot of sin, not a wrinkle of problems, unlike what exists with Christians today where there are a whole lot of blemishes, spots, and wrinkles.

But then eventually judgment switches from judging the dead only unto the living. "For the time [is come] that judgment must begin at the house of God: and if [it] first [begin] at us, what shall the end [be] of them that obey not the gospel of God?" (1 Peter 4:17) And once the world is judged, it will eventually be declared, "He that is unjust, let him be unjust still: and he which is filthy, let him be filthy still: and he that is righteous, let him be righteous still: and he that is holy, let him be holy still" (Revelation 22:11). And once every case is decided, then "the temple" in Heaven will be "filled with smoke from the glory of God, and from his power; and no man was able to enter into the temple, till the seven plagues of the seven angels were fulfilled" (Revelation 15:8). This is called the close of probation, which happens before the seven last plagues and is a permanent decision. We will not be able to enter into the temple through prayer because at that time, it will be said, "[there was] no intercessor" (Isaiah 59:16). Jesus will cease hearing confessions, and He will "put on righteousness as a breastplate, and an helmet of salvation upon his head; and he put on the garments of vengeance [for] clothing, and was clad with zeal as a cloke" (Isaiah 59:17).

And then shall be released, "seven angels having the seven last plagues; for in them is filled up the wrath of God" (Revelation 15:1). "And I heard a great voice out of the temple saying to the seven angels, Go your ways, and pour out the vials of the wrath of God upon the earth" (Revelation 16:1).

THE FIRST PLAGUE:

Revelation 16:2 states, "And the first went, and poured out his vial upon the earth; and there fell a noisome and grievous sore upon the men which had the mark of the beast, and [upon] them which worshipped his image."

The primary focus of the first plague is to reveal the false miracle workers. People are flocking to signs and wonders and not following a "Thus Saith the Lord." Now there are true miracles, but we must be careful. According to Revelation 13:13-14, it says, "And he doeth great wonders, so that he maketh fire come down from heaven on the earth in the sight of men, And deceiveth them that dwell on the earth by [the means of] those miracles which he had power to do in the sight of the beast; saying to them that dwell on the earth, that they should make an image to the beast, which had the wound by a sword, and did live." "And the beast was taken, and with him the false prophet that wrought miracles before him, with which he deceived them that had received the mark of the beast, and them that worshipped his image. These both were cast alive into a lake of fire burning with brimstone" (Revelation 19:20).

God does not like it when evangelists profess to heal people in the name of God all to rake in the money. God reveals the false healers with the first plague. When the first plague occurs, all the people who trusted in these shysters will flock to them, and they will be powerless. Of course the people will then lose their trust in them, but it will be too late.

THE SECOND AND THIRD PLAGUES:

Revelation 16:3-7 states, "And the second angel poured out his vial upon the sea; and it became as the blood of a dead [man]: and every living soul died in the sea. And the third angel poured out his vial upon the rivers and fountains of waters; and they became blood. And I heard the angel of the waters say, Thou art righteous, O Lord, which art, and wast, and shalt be, because thou hast judged thus. For they have shed the blood of saints and prophets, and thou hast given them blood to drink; for they are worthy. And I heard another out of the altar say, Even so, Lord God Almighty, true and righteous [are] thy judgments."

Why the plague of blood? The answer is in the verses. People willfully chose not to accept the blood of Jesus and then killed His saints throughout the centuries especially during the Dark Ages. This plague will stop the shipping industry in its tracks as well as the fresh water supply. Do not worry though because to the faithful, God promises, "He shall dwell on high: his place of defence [shall be] the munitions of rocks: bread shall be given him; his waters [shall be] sure" (Isaiah 33:16). Just as God provided manna and water in the wilderness, it will also be provided to the faithful at the end of time.

THE FOURTH PLAGUE:

Revelation 16:8-9 states, "And the fourth angel poured out his vial upon the sun; and power was given unto him to scorch men with fire. And men were scorched with great heat, and blasphemed the name of God, which hath power over these plagues: and they repented not to give him glory."

Why the sun? All through the ages, man has worshipped the creation instead of the creator (Romans 1:25). Satan has picked the object of the sun to be worshipped and man has gone right along with it. The pagan empires of Babylon, Medo-Persia, Greece, and Rome were blatant about it. Papal Rome Christianized it and passed it on to the whole world.

God created the Sabbath day and yet man is determined to disobey this commandment by throwing them all away or by keeping only nine. God punishes willful disobedience by allowing the object of worship to burn the people. Remember, He warned them ahead of time. The warning appears in Revelation 14:7 "Saying with a loud voice, Fear God, and give glory to him; for the hour of his judgment is come: and worship him that made heaven, and earth, and the sea, and the fountains of waters." This is a direct quote from the fourth commandment.

And since people not only have broken the Sabbath commandment, they actually trusted in it to save them from the calamities in the form of the Mark of the Beast, God provides more than they can handle as a plague.

Further, is it a coincidence that God created the sun on the fourth day and that God's commandment regarding the Sabbath is the fourth one and that the fourth angel pours out this fourth plague? Remember that devout Christians do not believe in coincidences. Amen?

THE FIFTH PLAGUE:

Revelation 16:10-11 states, "And the fifth angel poured out his vial upon the seat of the beast; and his kingdom was full of darkness; and they gnawed their tongues for pain, And blasphemed the God of heaven because of their pains and their sores, and repented not of their deeds."

Why darkness? John 3:19 answers it by saying, "And this is the condemnation, that light is come into the world, and men loved darkness rather than light, because their deeds were evil."

THE SIXTH PLAGUE:

Revelation 16:12-16 says, "And the sixth angel poured out his vial upon the great river Euphrates; and the water thereof was dried up, that the way of the kings of the east might be prepared. And I saw three unclean spirits like frogs [come] out of the mouth of the dragon, and out of the mouth of the beast, and out of the mouth of the false prophet. For they are the spirits of devils, working miracles, [which] go forth unto the kings of the earth and of the whole world, to gather them to the battle of that great day of God Almighty. Behold, I come as a thief. Blessed [is] he that watcheth, and keepeth his garments, lest he walk naked, and they see his shame. And he gathered them together into a place called in the Hebrew tongue Armageddon."

Now we have a lot to cover. This is loaded with symbolism. To help understand these verses, let us visit literal Israel of ancient times and compare the similarities to the symbolic spiritual Israel or Christians.

1. Both Israels are persecuted by Babylon: Literal Israel in Jeremiah 50:33-34, "Thus saith the LORD of hosts; The children of Israel and the children of Judah [were] oppressed together: and all that took them captives held them fast; they refused to let them go. Their Redeemer [is] strong; the LORD of hosts [is] his name: he shall throughly plead their cause, that he may give rest to the land, and disquiet the inhabitants of Babylon." Spiritual Israel in Revelation 17:5-6, "And upon her forehead [was] a name written, MYSTERY, BABYLON THE GREAT, THE MOTHER OF HARLOTS AND ABOMINATIONS OF THE EARTH. And I saw the woman drunken with the blood of the saints, and with the blood of the martyrs of Jesus: and when I saw her, I wondered with great admiration."

2. Both Israels are forced to worship an image: Literal Israel in Daniel 3:14-15 "Nebuchadnezzar spake and said unto them, [Is it] true, O Shadrach, Meshach, and Abednego, do not ye serve my gods, nor worship the golden image which I have set up? Now if ye be ready that at what time ye hear the sound of the cornet, flute, harp, sackbut, psaltery, and dulcimer, and all kinds of musick, ye fall down and worship the image which I have made; [well]: but if ye worship not, ye shall be cast the same hour into the midst of a burning fiery furnace; and who [is] that God that shall deliver you out of my hands?" Spiritual Israel in Revelation 13:15 "And he had power to give life unto the image of the beast, that the image of the beast should both speak, and cause that as many as would not worship the image of the beast should be killed."

3. Both Israels refer to their persecutor as Babylon the Great: Literal Israel in Daniel 4:30 "The king spake, and said, Is not this great Babylon, that I have built for the house of the kingdom by the might of my power, and for the honour of my majesty?" Spiritual Israel in Revelation 17:5 "And upon her forehead [was] a name written, MYSTERY, BABYLON THE GREAT, THE MOTHER OF HARLOTS AND ABOMINATIONS OF THE EARTH."

4. Both Israels experience Babylon sitting on many waters: Literal Israel in Jeremiah 51:12-13 "Set up the standard upon the walls of Babylon, make the watch strong, set up the watchmen, prepare the ambushes: for the LORD hath both devised and done that which he spake against the inhabitants of Babylon. O thou that dwellest upon many waters, abundant in treasures, thine end is come, [and] the measure of thy covetousness." Spiritual Israel in Revelation 17:1 "And there came one of the seven angels which had the seven vials, and talked with me, saying unto me, Come hither; I will shew unto thee the judgment of the great whore that sitteth upon many waters."

5. Both Israels experience the river Euphrates drying up: Literal Israel in Isaiah 44:27-28 "That saith to the deep, Be dry, and I will dry up thy rivers: That saith of Cyrus, [He is] my shepherd, and shall perform all my pleasure: even saying to Jerusalem, Thou shalt be built; and to the temple, Thy foundation shall be laid." Spiritual Israel in Revelation 16:12 "And the sixth angel poured out his vial upon the great river Euphrates; and the water thereof was dried up, that the way of the kings of the east might be prepared."

6. Both Israels experience a call to come out of Babylon: Literal Israel in Jeremiah 51:6-8 "Flee out of the midst of Babylon, and deliver every man his soul: be not cut off in her iniquity; for

this [is] the time of the LORD'S vengeance; he will render unto her a recompence. Babylon [hath been] a golden cup in the LORD'S hand, that made all the earth drunken: the nations have drunken of her wine; therefore the nations are mad. Babylon is suddenly fallen and destroyed: howl for her; take balm for her pain, if so be she may be healed." Unfortunately, not all of literal Israel adhered to the call to come out of literal Babylon where they perished. They could not see how they were being poisoned. They enjoyed their lives, i.e., they were comfortable. Spiritual Israel in Revelation 18:4 "And I heard another voice from heaven, saying, Come out of her, my people, that ye be not partakers of her sins, and that ye receive not of her plagues." Will you come out of Babylon? Or will you enjoy the comforts of where you are? Will you be unable to see the poisons around you?

7. Both rescuers come from the "east": Literal Israel in Isaiah 41:2 "Who raised up the righteous [man] from the east, called him to his foot, gave the nations before him, and made [him] rule over kings? he gave [them] as the dust to his sword, [and] as driven stubble to his bow." Spiritual Israel in Matthew 24:27 "For as the lightning cometh out of the east, and shineth even unto the west; so shall also the coming of the Son of man be."

Now with that in mind, let us begin addressing the sixth plague more directly. How many people are involved in the battle? According to Revelation 16:14, it says, "For they are the spirits of devils, working miracles, [which] go forth unto the kings of the earth and of the whole world, to gather them to the battle of that great day of God Almighty."

So how is the whole world, billions upon billions, going to be affected if Armageddon is a literal battle somewhere on this earth in which the whole world cannot fit into? Further, is God really interested in who will win World War III? According to John 18:36, the Bible says, "Jesus answered, My kingdom is not of this world: if my kingdom were of this world, then would my servants fight, that I should not be delivered to the Jews: but now is my kingdom not from hence." So the answer is "No" because God's kingdom is not on this planet.

Besides, where is the real battle? Revelation 12:7 says, "And there was war in heaven: Michael and his angels fought against the dragon; and the dragon fought and his angels." And besides, we need to keep in perspective that the issue is not only human involvement but "the dragon gave him his power, and his seat, and great authority" (Revelation 13:2). That means that Satan is involved. Satan already has the majority of people on this planet in his hands. What interest would he have in a valley, or even a world war? None. But, in Satan's mind, the stakes are even higher than this planet "for thou hast said in thine heart, I will ascend into heaven, I will exalt my throne above the stars of God: I will sit also upon the mount of the congregation, in the sides of the north: I will ascend above the heights of the clouds; I will be like the most High" (Isaiah 14:13-14). And right there we see in the Hebrew tongue the word "Armageddon". It is the "mount of the congregation". It is all of the beings in the universe.

And as a reminder that completely destroys the theory of the 1500's when there were no nuclear weapons and no war rooms, the gathering of people is not by Satan or Antichrist. The context of Armageddon is in these verses: "Behold, I come as a thief. Blessed [is] he that watcheth, and keepeth his garments, lest he walk naked, and they see his shame. And he gathered them together into a place called in the Hebrew tongue Armageddon" (Revelation 16:15-16). So Jesus comes surprisingly like the arrival of a thief, unannounced. People are blessed if they have been watching and keeping their garments of righteousness spotless through a sanctified life. They are blessed with being gathered by Jesus into Armageddon, the mount of the congregation that we call Heaven. This is the second coming event where Jesus "shall send his angels with a great sound of a trumpet, and they shall gather together his elect from the four winds, from one end of heaven to the other" (Matthew 24:31). "For the Lord himself shall descend from heaven with a shout, with the voice of the archangel, and with the trump of God: and the dead in Christ shall rise first: Then we which are alive [and] remain shall be caught up together with them in the clouds, to meet the Lord in the air: and so shall we ever be with the Lord" (1 Thessalonians 4:16-17).

And the end result regarding Satan is that he "shalt be brought down to hell, to the sides of the pit" (Isaiah 14:15). "And he laid hold on the dragon, that old serpent, which is the Devil, and Satan, and bound him a thousand years, And cast him into the bottomless pit, and shut him up, and set a seal upon him, that he should deceive the nations no more, till the thousand years should be fulfilled" (Revelation 20:2-3).

Now, what does drying up of the river Euphrates mean? Revelation 16:12 says, "And the sixth angel poured out his vial upon the great river Euphrates; and the water thereof was dried up, that the way of the kings of the east might be prepared." Drying up some river in the Middle

East is not going to have a major affect on anything. With nuclear warheads and technology for water supplies, the Euphrates is considered peanuts in this great battle. And remember, everything is symbolic using historical literal situations.

In the time of literal Israel, the Euphrates River was the lifeline to Babylon. Symbolically, "the waters which thou sawest, … are peoples, and multitudes, and nations, and tongues" (Revelation 17:15). That means spiritual Babylon (false teachings) loses the support of its lifeline – the people.

So, who are the unclean spirits? "And I saw three unclean spirits like frogs [come] out of the mouth of the dragon, and out of the mouth of the beast, and out of the mouth of the false prophet" (Revelation 16:13). Well, it is none other than the counterfeit godhead, of which people use the word "trinity". The real godhead contains God the Father as the head, Jesus Christ the Son, and the Holy Spirit. The counterfeit has Satan as the head (dragon), the Antichrist as the Son (beast), and the False Prophet (image of the beast). And by the way, this is just one of the reasons a three-figure Godhead exits: If the counterfeit exists, then the original must exist.

Now, we can understand the difference between the Father and Satan as well as the difference between Jesus Christ and the Antichrist. But what about the Holy Spirit and the False Prophet? Well the purpose of the Holy Spirit is to "guide you into all truth: for he shall not speak of himself; but whatsoever he shall hear, [that] shall he speak: and he will shew you things to come" (John 16:13). "And when he is come, he will reprove the world of sin, and of righteousness, and of judgment" (John 16:8). The Holy Spirit will lead us back to the truth, which is found in the Word, Jesus, and the Law as stated before. The False prophet will try to do away with the Word by replacing it with fables, the theory of evolution, etc.; do away with the teachings of Jesus by substituting the teachings of man's traditions; and do away with the law by promoting that they can be changed and even done away with. Further, the Holy Spirit reproves us of sin, righteousness, and judgment. And what is sin? "Whosoever committeth sin transgresseth also the law: for sin is the transgression of the law" (1 John 3:4).

Why righteousness? "If ye know that he is righteous, ye know that every one that doeth righteousness is born of him" (1 John 2:29). So, the Holy Spirit will lead us to do what is right, that is to obey the Word of God in all points, keep His commandments, and keep those things that Jesus said we are to observe (Matthew 28:20).

Why judgment? Well, how are we judged? "So speak ye, and so do, as they that shall be judged by the law of liberty" (James 2:12). By the law, which liberates us from sin and Satan.

A lot of people do not like to think of the Holy Spirit this way. They like to have a good time with the Spirit. That is actually the False Prophet working.

So who are the Kings of the East? The Bible says, "And the sixth angel poured out his vial upon the great river Euphrates; and the water thereof was dried up, that the way of the kings of the east might be prepared" (Revelation 16:12). Again, to understand this, let us examine literal Israel. "That saith to the deep, Be dry, and I will dry up thy rivers: That saith of Cyrus, [He is] my shepherd, and shall perform all my pleasure: even saying to Jerusalem, Thou shalt be built; and to the temple, Thy foundation shall be laid" (Isaiah 44:27-28). First, there is Cyrus who is one of the two kings that joined together to conquer Babylon. It took the joint effort of the Medes and the Persians. According to Isaiah 45:1, it says, "Thus saith the LORD to his anointed, to Cyrus, whose right hand I have holden, to subdue nations before him; and I will loose the loins of kings, to open before him the two leaved gates; and the gates shall not be shut." Cyrus diverted the river Euphrates away from Babylon, and the two leaved gates inside Babylon, which were used to keep intruders from attacking using the river, were left open during a big party (Daniel 5). This allowed Cyrus to march right in and take over without much resistance. By the way, notice the verse describing the victory. It almost reads word for word out of Revelation. "And, behold, here cometh a chariot of men, [with] a couple of horsemen. And he answered and said, Babylon is fallen, is fallen; and all the graven images of her gods he hath broken unto the ground" (Isaiah 21:9).

Now, where does Jesus come from? "For as the lightning cometh out of the east, and shineth even unto the west; so shall also the coming of the Son of man be" (Matthew 24:27). Jesus is represented by the Kings of the east. This is confirmed by Ezekiel 43:2, "And, behold, the glory of the God of Israel came from the way of the east: and his voice [was] like a noise of many waters: and the earth shined with his glory." You may still be taken back by the fact that there is an "s" on the end of the word "kings". This is addressed by Revelation 19:11-21, which depicts the second coming in the context of a battle. "And I saw heaven opened, and behold a white horse; and he that sat upon him [was] called Faithful and True, and in righteousness he doth judge and make war. His eyes [were] as a flame of fire, and on his head [were] many crowns; and he had a name written, that no man knew, but he himself. And he [was] clothed with a vesture dipped in blood: and his name is called The Word of God. And the armies [which were] in heaven followed him upon white horses, clothed in fine linen, white and clean. And out of his mouth goeth a sharp sword, that with it he should smite the nations: and he shall rule them with a rod of iron: and he treadeth the winepress of the fierceness and wrath of Almighty God. And he hath on [his] vesture and on his thigh a name written, KING OF KINGS, AND LORD OF LORDS. And I saw an angel standing in the sun; and he cried with a loud voice, saying to all the fowls that fly in the midst of heaven, Come and gather yourselves together unto the supper of the great God; That ye may eat the flesh of kings, and the flesh of captains, and the flesh of mighty men, and the flesh of horses, and of them that sit on them, and the flesh of all [men, both] free and bond, both small and great. And I saw the beast, and the kings of the earth, and their armies, gathered together to make war against him that sat on the horse, and against his army. And the beast was taken, and with him the false prophet that wrought miracles before him, with which he deceived them that had received the mark of the beast, and them that worshipped his image. These both were cast alive into a lake of fire burning with brimstone. And the remnant were slain with the sword of him that sat upon the horse, which [sword] proceeded out of his mouth: and all the fowls were filled with their flesh." And here Jesus is referred to as the "King of Kings." There is the "s".

THE SEVENTH PLAGUE:

Revelation 16:17-21 states, "And the seventh angel poured out his vial into the air; and there came a great voice out of the temple of heaven, from the throne, saying, It is done. And there were voices, and thunders, and lightnings; and there was a great earthquake, such as was not since men were upon the earth, so mighty an earthquake, [and] so great. And the great city was divided into three parts, and the cities of the nations fell: and great Babylon came in remembrance before God, to give unto her the cup of the wine of the fierceness of his wrath. And every island fled away, and the mountains were not found. And there fell upon men a great hail out of heaven, [every stone] about the weight of a talent: and men blasphemed God because of the plague of the hail; for the plague thereof was exceeding great." With islands sinking and mountains crumbling, it will not be fit for man or beast. Keep in mind while this earth is falling apart, the saints will be on their way up (1 Thessalonians 4:17).

In regards to the hail, did you know that God has it already prepared? "Hast thou entered into the treasures of the snow? or hast thou seen the treasures of the hail, Which I have reserved against the time of trouble, against the day of battle and war?" (Job 38:22-23)

So now that the seven last plagues appear to be in the sequence of events and in the middle of the sixth one Jesus shows up, let us look at the details once again of the event. First, Jesus ends His ministry in Heaven as our High Priest (Hebrews 4:14), and "he put on righteousness as a breastplate, and an helmet of salvation upon his head; and he put on the garments of vengeance [for] clothing, and was clad with zeal as a cloke" (Isaiah 59:17). Upon showing up, "every eye shall see him, and they [also] which pierced him" (Revelation 1:7). That means the lost and the save get to see the event and is not a secret thing, but also take notice that those that crucified Jesus will also see Him.

Despite being dead right now with the fact that the "dead know not any thing" (Ecclesiastes 9:5), meaning, they are not in hell right now but are unconscious, they will be raised up specifically for this event. That is because Jesus is keeping His word. He said to those that were involved in His crucifixion, "Nevertheless I say unto you, Hereafter shall ye see the Son of man sitting on the right hand of power, and coming in the clouds of heaven" (Matthew 26:64).

So as Jesus is appearing, "the Lord himself shall descend from heaven with a shout, with the voice of the archangel, and with the trump of God: and the dead in Christ shall rise first" (1 Thessalonians 4:16). "All that are in the graves shall hear his voice, And shall come forth; they that have done good, unto the resurrection of life" (John 5:28-29). Now as they are coming up out of the grave, "Behold, I shew you a mystery; We shall not all sleep, but we shall all be changed, In a moment, in the twinkling of an eye, at the last trump: for the trumpet shall sound, and the dead shall be raised incorruptible, and we shall be changed. For this corruptible must put on incorruption, and this mortal [must] put on immortality. So when this corruptible shall have put on incorruption, and this mortal shall have put on immortality, then shall be brought to pass the saying that is written, Death is swallowed up in victory. O death, where [is] thy sting? O grave, where [is] thy victory? " (1 Corinthians 15:51-55). "To bring back his soul from the pit, to be enlightened with the light of the living" (Job 33:30), and "His flesh shall be fresher than a child's: he shall return to the days of his youth" (Job 33:25). "And it shall be said in that day, Lo, this [is] our God; we have waited for him, and he will save us: this [is] the LORD; we have waited for him, we will be glad and rejoice in his salvation" (Isaiah 25:9).

Now those that are lost but living at the time will say "to the mountains and rocks, Fall on us, and hide us from the face of him that sitteth on the throne, and from the wrath of the Lamb: For the great day of his wrath is come; and who shall be able to stand?" (Revelation 6:16-17).

"The Son of man shall send forth his angels, and they shall gather out of his kingdom all things that offend, and them which do iniquity; And shall cast them into a furnace of fire: there shall be wailing and gnashing of teeth" (Matthew 13:41-42). "I tell you, in that night there shall be two [men] in one bed; the one shall be taken, and the other shall be left. Two [women] shall be grinding together; the one shall be taken, and the other left. Two [men] shall be in the field; the one shall be taken, and the other left" (Luke 17:34-36). Now listen to the question and answer, "And they answered and said unto him, Where, Lord? And he said unto them, Wheresoever the body [is], thither will the eagles be gathered together" (Luke 17:37). "For as the lightning cometh out of the east, and shineth even unto the west; so shall also the coming of the Son of man be. For wheresoever the carcase is, there will the eagles be gathered together" (Matthew 24:27-28). "And then shall that Wicked be revealed, whom the Lord shall consume with the spirit of his mouth, and shall destroy with the brightness of his coming" (2 Thessalonians 2:8). It will be at that time that "Their flesh shall consume away while they stand upon their feet, and their eyes shall consume away in their holes, and their tongue shall consume away in their mouth" (Zechariah 14:12). "Then we which are alive [and] remain shall be caught up together with them in the clouds, to meet the Lord in the air: and so shall we ever be with the Lord" (1 Thessalonians 4:17). Please note that these are the ones left behind.

So the second coming event is when Jesus "will come again, and receive you unto myself; that where I am, [there] ye may be also" (John 14:3). We are gathered in Armageddon, the mount of the congregation, better known as Heaven. And with the saved living and dead, now raised to life, both in Heaven, and the lost that were living at the time ending up being destroyed, realize that the fourth group, the lost who are already in the grave, it is said, "the rest of the dead lived not again" (Revelation 20:5).

There is not a live human on this planet for if you remember those eagles, well, "I saw an angel standing in the sun; and he cried with a loud voice, saying to all the fowls that fly in the midst of heaven, Come and gather yourselves together unto the supper of the great God; That ye may eat the flesh of kings, and the flesh of captains, and the flesh of mighty men, and the flesh of horses, and of them that sit on them, and the flesh of all [men, both] free and bond, both small and great. And I saw the beast, and the kings of the earth, and their armies, gathered together to make war against him that sat on the horse, and against his army. And the beast was taken, and with him the false prophet that wrought miracles before him, with which he deceived them that had received the mark of the beast, and them that worshipped his image. These both were cast alive into a lake of fire burning with brimstone. And the remnant were slain with the sword of him that sat upon the horse, which [sword] proceeded out of his mouth: and all the fowls were filled with their flesh" (Revelation 19:17-21).

We already read several times about the islands sinking and mountains laying low, but did you know that this planet, covered in sin, cannot withstand the glorious return of Christ. "I beheld the earth, and, lo, [it was] without form, and void; and the heavens, and they [had] no light. I beheld the mountains, and, lo, they trembled, and all the hills moved lightly. I beheld, and, lo, [there was] no man, and all the birds of the heavens were fled. I beheld, and, lo, the fruitful place [was] a wilderness, and all the cities thereof were broken down at the presence of the LORD, [and] by his fierce anger. For thus hath the LORD said, The whole land shall be desolate; yet will I not make a full end. For this shall the earth mourn, and the heavens above be black: because I have spoken [it], I have purposed [it], and will not repent, neither will I turn back from it" (Jeremiah 4:23-28). And that is not creation flashback but is what will happen during the second coming.

Now with all humans left behind being dead and this planet becoming turned inside out, it basically becomes a pit to the devil for a thousand years. "All the kings of the nations, [even] all of them, lie in glory, every one in his own house. But thou art cast out of thy grave like an abominable branch, [and as] the raiment of those that are slain, thrust through with a sword, that go down to the stones of the pit; as a carcase trodden under feet. Thou shalt not be joined with them in burial, because thou hast destroyed thy land, [and] slain thy people: the seed of evildoers shall never be renowned" (Isaiah 14:18-20). And that is not a stretch of a theory as opposed to some place in the universe known as the pit. Clearly the Bible teaches that this planet turns into the pit for Satan. In other words, Satan gets to roam the earth with all the dead on it for "the pit be digged for the wicked" (Psalms 94:13), actually not literally the word "dug" but as it were the meaning of "prepared".

"The earth is utterly broken down, the earth is clean dissolved, the earth is moved exceedingly. The earth shall reel to and fro like a drunkard, and shall be removed like a cottage; and the transgression thereof shall be heavy upon it; and it shall fall, and not rise again. And it shall come to pass in that day, [that] the LORD shall punish the host of the high ones [that are] on high, and the kings of the earth upon the earth. And they shall be gathered together, [as] prisoners are gathered in the pit, and shall be shut up in the prison, and after many days shall they be visited"

(Isaiah 24:19-22). Remember, during the second coming, Revelation 19 describes the kings being feasted upon by the fowl. They are going to be left on this planet unburied. And all of it is described as the pit. So, to Lucifer, "Yet thou shalt be brought down to hell, to the sides of the pit" (Isaiah 14:15). This earth, known as the pit, is actually going to be hell.

Taking note that Satan will not be visited for "many days", we see in the Bible how long many days is exactly. "And he laid hold on the dragon, that old serpent, which is the Devil, and Satan, and bound him a thousand years, And cast him into the bottomless pit, and shut him up, and set a seal upon him, that he should deceive the nations no more, till the thousand years" (Revelation 20:2-3).

Even the atonement feast day depicts this understanding. During the cleansing of the sanctuary, there was a certain process to follow. "And he shall take the two goats, and present them before the LORD [at] the door of the tabernacle of the congregation. And Aaron shall cast lots upon the two goats; one lot for the LORD, and the other lot for the scapegoat. And Aaron shall bring the goat upon which the LORD'S lot fell, and offer him [for] a sin offering. But the goat, on which the lot fell to be the scapegoat, shall be presented alive before the LORD, to make an atonement with him, [and] to let him go for a scapegoat into the wilderness" (Leviticus 16:7-10). Notice that Satan, represented by the live goat, is lead to the wilderness, which is what this earth will be during the Millennium. Does this feast confirm that no human beings will be dead or alive on the earth? According to Leviticus 16:20-22, it does confirm this. "And when he hath made an end of reconciling the holy [place], and the tabernacle of the congregation, and the altar, he shall bring the live goat: And Aaron shall lay both his hands upon the head of the live goat, and confess over him all the iniquities of the children of Israel, and all their transgressions in all their sins, putting them upon the head of the goat, and shall send [him] away by the hand of a fit man into the wilderness: And the goat shall bear upon him all their iniquities unto a land not inhabited: and he shall let go the goat in the wilderness." With no one to tempt because everybody is either in heaven or dead, Satan has no power.

So with the righteous caught up to be with Jesus, the lost all dead, and the devil with his angels bound to this inside out earth, we have some time on our hands. How much time? Try a thousand years.

To further confirm that Satan is bound to the confines of earth and that earth is known as the pit, take note of the wording from Job regarding death, specifically the use of the word "pit". "They shall go down to the bars of the pit, when [our] rest together [is] in the dust" (Job 17:16). "He keepeth back his soul from the pit, and his life from perishing by the sword" (Job 33:18). Even David uses the same wording. "O LORD my rock; be not silent to me: lest, [if] thou be silent to me, I become like them that go down into the pit" (Psalms 28:1). "O LORD, thou hast brought up my soul from the grave: thou hast kept me alive, that I should not go down to the pit" (Psalms 30:3). "What profit [is there] in my blood, when I go down to the pit? Shall the dust praise thee? shall it declare thy truth?" (Psalms 30:9) "For my soul is full of troubles: and my life draweth nigh unto the grave. I am counted with them that go down into the pit: I am as a man [that hath] no strength" (Psalms 88:3-4). "O LORD: my spirit faileth: hide not thy face from me, lest I be like unto them that go down into the pit" (Psalms 143:7). Evidently Solomon, David's son, was taught the same understanding, for he wrote, "Let us swallow them up alive as the grave; and whole, as those that go down into the pit" (Proverbs 1:12). And to think, people say the Bible is inconsistent; not when it comes to the pit being on the earth. Isaiah wrote, "Fear, and the pit, and the snare, [are] upon thee, O inhabitant of the earth" (Isaiah 24:17). It is even synonymous with the grave, "For the grave cannot praise thee, death can [not] celebrate thee: they that go down into the pit cannot hope for thy truth" (Isaiah 38:18), keeping in mind that the last generation will not be placed in physical graves but the surface of the earth shall be their grave. Ezekiel continues the subject consistency by writing, "for they are all delivered unto death, to the nether parts of the earth, in the midst of the children of men, with them that go down to the pit" (Ezekiel 31:14), and asks rhetorically, "Whose graves are set in the sides of the pit" (Ezekiel 32:23).

So what happens during this time? Revelation 20:4 says, "And I saw thrones, and they sat upon them, and judgment was given unto them: and [I saw] the souls of them that were beheaded for the witness of Jesus, and for the word of God, and which had not worshipped the beast, neither his image, neither had received [his] mark upon their foreheads, or in their hands; and they lived and reigned with Christ a thousand years." The Saints will be with Christ, but notice that they will be on thrones judging. Judging what? 1 Corinthians 6:2 answers that question with, "Do ye not know that the saints shall judge the world? and if the world shall be judged by you, are ye unworthy to judge the smallest matters?" Well, that may be a surprise. Not only will the saints judge the world, but notice who else they will judge: "Know ye not that we shall judge angels? how much more things that pertain to this life?" (1 Corinthians 6:3). Which angels? 2 Peter 2:4 says, "For if God spared not the angels that sinned, but cast [them] down to hell, and delivered [them] into chains of darkness, to be reserved unto judgment." They will judge the fallen angels. By the way, those chains of darkness are the same chains that bind Satan to this earth.

Now Does anybody else substantiate this whole concept of Satan, pit, righteous taken to Heaven, earth being empty of live humans, and especially the judging part? Malachi 3:17-18 says, "And they shall be mine, saith the LORD of hosts, in that day when I make up my jewels; and I will spare them, as a man spareth his own son that serveth him. Then shall ye return, and discern between the righteous and the wicked, between him that serveth God and him that serveth him not."

Basically it is like this. Let us say that we make it to heaven. We will experience three great surprises. The first is that we are there. Praise the Lord! The second is that a whole bunch of people we thought would be there are not. The third is that a whole bunch of people we thought would not make it, they are there. Now suppose a loved one is missing and we went to Jesus and inquired of the reason, He would probably reply, "Sorry, they chose not to be here." You may doubt Jesus through all eternity. And do not think for a moment that all the saved will just accept Jesus at His Word. If that were true, then all of Christianity would be unified today. Instead, people twist His words, knowingly and unknowingly, but when it is black and white, well, one cannot argue one way or the other. So this is more of a show all the evidence. The purpose of this judgment is not to overrule the decisions that were made, but rather it is so we will know full well why a person is not there. In other words, Jesus knows best and knows exactly all of the things that need to be exercised before eternity can be set in motion preventing any rebellion from happening again.

We will see from the evidence that God was just. We will see that people had the wrong attitude when it comes to a relationship with Jesus. We will see that the real question was over obedience to God or rebellion towards God, and it is evidenced in His law. Therefore, "whosoever shall do and teach [them], the same shall be called great in the kingdom of heaven" (Matthew 5:19). Now on the other hand, all those that teach a different set of rules or that even teach that the rules no longer apply, well, Jesus says, "Whosoever therefore shall break one of these least commandments, and shall teach men so, he shall be called the least in the kingdom of heaven" (Matthew 5:19).

A second reason why Jesus permits the saints to judge is that for the whole history of the earth, God has been getting a bum rap. Every bad thing that occurs is known as "An Act of God". We will see that Satan was behind death, disaster, and problem.

A third reason is that time heals all wounds. We will not see sin for a thousand years. When we see it again, we will plead with God to put it out of the way permanently. Look at our choices today. We have become accustom, as a people, to walk around fights, on the street rapes, blatant muggings right in broad daylight, ignoring people bleeding to death pleading for someone to simply call 911, etc. We have become accustom to expect our entertainment, such as TV and the movies, to show various forms of nudity, use of foul language, and plenty of violence be it in the form of one person inflicting it on another or self inflicting, like walking in front of a moving vehicle. Other forms of sin are also found to be acceptable and still called entertainment as well. That includes the push of paganism, breaking the Sabbath, disobeying parents, lying, cheating, and stealing. And interestingly, we not only accept it as entertainment, but we tolerate it in our relationships. But after a thousand years of seeing sin not being tolerated at all, no acts of selfishness at all, no little lies or big lies at all, no paganism, no teasing, no dishonoring, no sinning at all for a thousand years, any hint of such remaining in our thought process will be removed. Then when it is time to deal with the punishment phase of the wicked, we will not hesitate to have God remove such filth from the face of the earth.

Now once the thousand years are completed, there is a third coming of Jesus to the earth. "And his feet shall stand in that day upon the mount of Olives, which [is] before Jerusalem on the east, and the mount of Olives shall cleave in the midst thereof toward the east and toward the west, [and there shall be] a very great valley; and half of the mountain shall remove toward the north, and half of it toward the south" (Zechariah 14:4). "All the land shall be turned as a plain from Geba to Rimmon south of Jerusalem" (Zechariah 14:10). That is because "I John saw the holy city, new Jerusalem, coming down from God out of heaven, prepared as a bride adorned for her husband" (Revelation 21:2).

"But the rest of the dead lived not again until the thousand years were finished" (Revelation 20:5). So now that we are after the thousand years, the wicked are resurrected. Not only that, "When the thousand years are expired, Satan shall be loosed out of his prison, And shall go out to deceive the nations which are in the four quarters of the earth, Gog and Magog, to gather them together to battle: the number of whom [is] as the sand of the sea. And they went up on the breadth of the earth, and compassed the camp of the saints about, and the beloved city" (Revelation 20:7-9).

So the city, New Jerusalem will be completely surrounded by the wicked, but they shall not prevail. They shall be stopped in their tracks, as it were, frozen in place. After whatever amount of time God allows in addressing the wicked, then "Fire came down from God out of heaven, and devoured them" (Revelation 20:9). "And death and hell were cast into the lake of fire. This is the second death" (Revelation 20:14). "But the fearful, and unbelieving, and the abominable, and murderers, and whoremongers, and sorcerers, and idolaters, and all liars, shall have their part in the lake which burneth with fire and brimstone: which is the second death" (Revelation 21:8). And from Satan, "Thou hast defiled thy sanctuaries by the multitude of thine iniquities, by the iniquity of thy traffick; therefore will I bring forth a fire from the midst of thee, it shall devour thee, and I will bring thee to ashes upon the earth in the sight of all them that behold thee" (Ezekiel 28:18). And when it is all done, "They shall be ashes under the soles of your feet in the day that I shall do [this], saith the LORD of hosts" (Malachi 4:3), "For, behold, the day cometh, that shall burn as an oven; and all the proud, yea, and all that do wickedly, shall be stubble: and the day that cometh shall burn them up, saith the LORD of hosts, that it shall leave them neither root nor branch" (Malachi 4:1).

Now in regards to the burning up of the lost, Satan, and the rest of the fallen angels, do realize that it is a permanent thing. Take for instance Sodom and Gomorrah. Did you know they suffered the vengeance of eternal fire? "Sodom and Gomorrha, and the cities about them in like manner, giving themselves over to fornication, and going after strange flesh, are set forth for an example, suffering the vengeance of eternal fire" (Jude 1:7). But you may ask how that can be. Sodom and Gomorrah are not still burning! That fire went out long ago. That is because the fire itself is not eternal; the use thereof is. In other words, Sodom and Gomorrah will never be reconstructed. Now the reason that this understanding is important is because that the same fire will be used in "the judgment of the great day" (Jude 1:6). That means hell will not burn for all eternity. A burning hell is not eternal. What will be eternal is the finality. There will never be a time where someone will be resurrected from hell. Once it is done, it is done for eternity.

No doubt someone will quote Jesus' words as a counterpoint. "Wherefore if thy hand or thy foot offend thee, cut them off, and cast [them] from thee: it is better for thee to enter into life halt or maimed, rather than having two hands or two feet to be cast into everlasting fire" (Matthew 18:8). The same holds true. The fire will go out, but the result will be everlastingly. Billions of years into eternity and all that were made ashes will remain dead.

Of course the statement, "And these shall go away into everlasting punishment: but the righteous into life eternal" (Matthew 25:46) may be confusing but looking at it, the words explain themselves. Jesus did not say that there would be everlasting punishing. He said it would be an everlasting punishment. Once He hands out His punishment, it will be done and over, but the results will remain everlastingly.

And then others might bring up the reference to "unquenchable fire". The verse states, "Whose fan [is] in his hand, and he will throughly purge his floor, and will gather the wheat into his garner; but the chaff he will burn with fire unquenchable" (Luke 3:17). And again, we do not disagree. We absolutely believe that once hell fire begins, there is no amount of water that will be able to be poured upon it to quench it, however, once everything is consumed, it will go out. Besides, God has already used unquenchable fire, and it is not burning still. "For [it is] the day of the LORD'S vengeance, [and] the year of recompences for the controversy of Zion. And the streams thereof shall be turned into pitch, and the dust thereof into brimstone, and the land thereof shall become burning pitch. It shall not be quenched night nor day; the smoke thereof shall go up for ever: from generation to generation it shall lie waste; none shall pass through it for ever and ever" (Isaiah 34:8-10). Is Zion still burning today? Of course not.

Even Peter states, "And turning the cities of Sodom and Gomorrha into ashes condemned [them] with an overthrow, making [them] an ensample unto those that after should live ungodly" (2 Peter 2:6). Please note that God reduced those cities to ashes and they serve as an example of God's action regarding hell. And we already read that they are indeed reduced to ashes.

Besides, a number of times the Bible says things like, "I will early destroy all the wicked of the land; that I may cut off all wicked doers from the city of the LORD" (Psalms 101:8), and "The LORD preserveth all them that love him: but all the wicked will he destroy" (Psalms 145:20). How can God destroy the wicked if they would be burning forever? He could not is the answer. They have to have a final demise for God to be able to say that they are destroyed.

As a reminder, there are only two choices: eternal life or no eternal life. It is written in many forms:

- John 3:15 says, "That whosoever believeth in him should not perish, but have eternal life." Note that it does not say "eternal perishing" but "perish", which is a final state.

- Romans 6:23 says, "The wages of sin [is] death; but the gift of God [is] eternal life through Jesus Christ our Lord." This death is referring to what the Bible calls, the second death. We all know what happens at the first death. We cease to exist on this planet. Well, why would we redefine the second death away from ceasing to exist into "eternal separation but still living"? Death is death especially when the other choice is eternal life once again. If death was allowing to live separate from God, do they not have eternal life then? Sure they would. And how do those that have the gift of eternal life get to live? By the power of Jesus Christ is how.

- Revelation 2:11 says, "He that overcometh shall not be hurt of the second death." Not hurt by the second death means to have the gift, that of eternal life. That means the second death is to cease to exist again, but this time it is eternal ceasing as if they never were.

- Revelation 20:6 says, "Blessed and holy [is] he that hath part in the first resurrection: on such the second death hath no power." And the first resurrection has a nickname, which Jesus said, "resurrection of life" (John 5:29), which is eternal life. So again, the first resurrection is for eternal life of which the second death has no power and that means the second death must have a power the opposite of life, which is death.

- John 5:29 says, "And shall come forth; they that have done good, unto the resurrection of life; and they that have done evil, unto the resurrection of damnation." Since we brought up the subject, do notice that there are two resurrections. One is for eternal life, mentioned just as "life", and the other is for damnation, as in, to suffer the second death. The second is not for "damning" but for "damnation", meaning, finality.

- Psalms 37:9 says, "For evildoers shall be cut off: but those that wait upon the LORD, they shall inherit the earth." God's people are going to inherit the earth. This earth will be redone and we get to claim it as our home. The evildoers are not relocated. They are cut off, as in, to cease from living. In fact, just in case we miss it, the Bible says in the very next verse, "For yet a little while, and the wicked [shall] not [be]: yea, thou shalt diligently consider his place, and it [shall] not [be]" (Psalms 37:10), and in the following verse to that, it explains those that get to live by saying, "But the meek shall inherit the earth; and shall delight themselves in the abundance of peace" (Psalms 37:11). Clearly when God says the wicked shall not be, that means anywhere, otherwise the verse would state, "the wicked shall not be on the earth" but it does not. It just states that they will not be.

- Psalms 37:22 says, "For [such as be] blessed of him shall inherit the earth; and [they that be] cursed of him shall be cut off." This is basically repeating the statement above, but it is worth noting, in that when God speaks, we ought to listen. When God speaks it twice, we ought to really listen.

- Proverbs 10:28 says, "The hope of the righteous [shall be] gladness: but the expectation of the wicked shall perish." Why do the expectations of the wicked perish? Because the wicked themselves also perish, as referenced by the other verses.

- Deuteronomy says, 30:15 "See, I have set before thee this day life and good, and death and evil." Seeing that both the good and the evil die the first death, this must be a contrast between eternal life and the second death, which it is. Besides, a few verses later, reference to Heaven and the implied relocation to earth, the clarification is, "I call heaven and earth to record this day against you, [that] I have set before you life and death, blessing and cursing: therefore choose life, that both thou and thy seed may live" (Deuteronomy 30:19).

- Proverbs 12:28 says, "In the way of righteousness [is] life; and [in] the pathway [thereof there is] no death." There is no second death to those that have life for surely all die the natural death, into the grave.

- Proverbs 13:14 says, "The law of the wise [is] a fountain of life, to depart from the snares of death." Keeping the commandments reveals a saved life that will have eternal life, while escaping the snares of the second death. And again, it is either life or death.

- Proverbs 14:27 says, "The fear of the LORD [is] a fountain of life, to depart from the snares of death." This is but similar to Proverbs 13:14.

- Jeremiah 21:8 says, "And unto this people thou shalt say, Thus saith the LORD; Behold, I set before you the way of life, and the way of death." This is similar to Joshua's call. Again, eternal life or second death are our only choices. It does not say "eternal life in Heaven" and "eternal death away from Heaven".

- Romans 5:21 says, "That as sin hath reigned unto death, even so might grace reign through righteousness unto eternal life by Jesus Christ our Lord." So sin and die the second death or live in righteousness and have eternal life.

- Romans 6:23 says, "For the wages of sin [is] death; but the gift of God [is] eternal life through Jesus Christ our Lord." Again, the gift is not Heaven; it is not clarified as just being with Jesus. It is eternal life or not having it, called death.

- Psalms 34:16 says, "The face of the LORD [is] against them that do evil, to cut off the remembrance of them from the earth." And that makes sense since the righteous will inherit the earth, but that means that everyone that knew wicked people will have to have their minds wiped of those memories. Yes, that means if we are missing a spouse, a parent, or child, it will be to us as if they never existed. That might sound heartless, but at the same time, it is choice. We chose to be there. Why should we feel sad for the people that we loved on earth that chose not to be there? We could never enjoy eternity with remembering them. So now if the wicked are totally wiped from our minds, what purpose does it serve to have the wicked burning somewhere else in the universe through eternity? What would happen if in our travels we came near enough to hell to hear people wailing? What purpose would that serve? If we do not remember anyone in hell, and we hear people crying and gnashing their teeth, would we not suspect that God is hiding some deep dark secret? Would that not start the rebellion all over again? So, the only solution is that hell ceases to burn once all of the lost humans and angels are consumed.

- Psalms 37:28 says, "For the LORD loveth judgment, and forsaketh not his saints; they are preserved for ever: but the seed of the wicked shall be cut off." So only the saints are preserved forever while the wicked are cut off. They do not have forever. To be preserved is to live throughout eternity. To be cut off in this contrast is to not live throughout eternity.

- Psalms 37:34 says, "Wait on the LORD, and keep his way, and he shall exalt thee to inherit the land: when the wicked are cut off, thou shalt see [it]." Those keeping God's way get to inherit the land, earth, while the wicked do not because they are cut off, destroyed, gone.

- Psalms 37:38 summarizes the last point by blatantly stating the fact. "But the transgressors shall be destroyed together: the end of the wicked shall be cut off." To be destroyed is to not exist. If a car is destroyed, it is no longer a car. If a person is destroyed, they are no longer a person. And just in case one misses that verse, Psalms 101:8 says the same thing. "I will early destroy all the wicked of the land; that I may cut off all wicked doers from the city of the LORD." There is no mistaking it. To be "cut off" is to be destroyed.

- Psalms 75:10 says, "All the horns of the wicked also will I cut off; [but] the horns of the righteous shall be exalted." And the way the righteous will be exalted is that they get to live forever, while the wicked get burned up.

- Proverbs 2:22 says, "But the wicked shall be cut off from the earth, and the transgressors shall be rooted out of it." To be rooted out of something is to lose all connection. A tree that has the roots removed and dug up ends up getting rid of it completely.

- Zephaniah 1:2-3 says, "I will utterly consume all [things] from off the land, saith the LORD. I will consume man and beast; I will consume the fowls of the heaven, and the fishes of the sea, and the stumblingblocks with the wicked; and I will cut off man from off the land, saith the LORD." That is very explicit. In fact, that sounds a lot like Zechariah 14:12, which says, "And this shall be the plague wherewith the LORD will smite all the people that have fought against Jerusalem; Their flesh shall consume away while they stand upon their feet, and their eyes shall consume away in their holes, and their tongue shall consume away in their mouth."

Now before anyone argues from the perspective of having been brainwashed by the Antichrist into believing God is some being that seeks an eternity of vengeance upon the lost just because they did not obey all of the rules, do keep in mind that we have not supplied just a verse or two but over twenty verses that tell us that we serve a loving God even during the worst possible moment that God will ever face. It is the moment that He removes from existence beings that He had created. That is billions upon billions of beings including the fallen angels. It is even hard for one to argue the context of the verses being anything but what we have concluded. So, those that believe in an everlasting hell that continues to burn without ever stopping, they have to explain all of these verses away, which are but a sample of the many others that we did not share. Now do not get us wrong. We also believe in an everlasting hell. It is just that we believe in a hell that will not be undone nor is it going to continuously burn. In other words, the hell of the Bible is a lot hotter than many believe. And for those that still insist on believing in such a hell that burns and burns and keeps burning but cannot explain these verses away, well then, that is some poor Bible studying going on.

We have successfully addressed all the verses that imply a continuous fire noting that they were mostly misunderstood verses, especially in the tense of the words used. So as a requirement of God, those that stick to the popular view now have the responsibility of explaining all of these verses away without leaving a doubt in our minds otherwise they are teaching that the Bible contradicts itself, which it does not.

And finally ask yourself, "What is the end result when eternal life begins?" Nahum 1:9 states, "What do ye imagine against the LORD? he will make an utter end: affliction shall not rise up the second time." One cannot make an utter end if the wicked get to roast and toast throughout eternity.

So now with the wicked all burned up, we see "a new heaven and a new earth: for the first heaven and the first earth were passed away; and there was no more sea. And I John saw the holy city, new Jerusalem, coming down from God out of heaven, prepared as a bride adorned for her husband. And I heard a great voice out of heaven saying, Behold, the tabernacle of God [is] with men, and he will dwell with them, and they shall be his people, and God himself shall be with them, [and be] their God. And God shall wipe away all tears from their eyes; and there shall be no more death, neither sorrow, nor crying, neither shall there be any more pain: for the former things are passed away. And he that sat upon the throne said, Behold, I make all things new. And he said unto me, Write: for these words are true and faithful" (Revelation 21:1-5). When God wipes away our tears, that is when our memory of those that were consumed will be gone as well. We will cease from crying over our loved ones at that time.

And that fire of hell makes the earth into material in which God will create a new heaven and earth. The new city is that of the New Jerusalem. God will, throughout all eternity, dwell on earth with man. And all the problems that sin had caused will have been put away for all eternity. And God adds, "these words are true and faithful." Praise the Lord. I am looking forward to this time, how about you?

This is reiterated in Isaiah 65:17-19, which says, "For, behold, I create new heavens and a new earth: and the former shall not be remembered, nor come into mind. But be ye glad and rejoice for ever [in that] which I create: for, behold, I create Jerusalem a rejoicing, and her people a joy. And I will rejoice in Jerusalem, and joy in my people: and the voice of weeping shall be no more heard in her, nor the voice of crying." Satan has tried to make heaven sound boring saying that every day, all day, we will be strumming harps and praising God or cleaning clouds. When God says there is joy that means that the saints will enjoy heaven beyond their greatest dreams.

"And they shall build houses, and inhabit [them]; and they shall plant vineyards, and eat the fruit of them. They shall not build, and another inhabit; they shall not plant, and another eat: for as the days of a tree [are] the days of my people, and mine elect shall long enjoy the work of their hands. They shall not labour in vain, nor bring forth for trouble; for they [are] the seed of the blessed of the LORD, and their offspring with them. And it shall come to pass, that before they call, I will answer; and while they are yet speaking, I will hear. The wolf and the lamb shall feed together, and the lion shall eat straw like the bullock: and dust [shall be] the serpent's meat. They shall not hurt nor destroy in all my holy mountain, saith the LORD" (Isaiah 65:21-25). Sure they will praise God and worship Him, but there is more. In addition to the mansion that Jesus and the Father are preparing for them, they will be able to build their own country estate and plant all types of things in the most perfect garden. Now it will take awhile until they perfect such skills, but they have all eternity to learn how to build and plant. Additionally, there will be no fear in petting a lion, a bear, or any other creature for that matter.

"For as the new heavens and the new earth, which I will make, shall remain before me, saith the LORD, so shall your seed and your name remain. And it shall come to pass, [that] from one new moon to another, and from one sabbath to another, shall all flesh come to worship before me, saith the LORD" (Isaiah 66:22-23). They will listen to the greatest preacher of all time on the Sabbath.

What Is the Last Opportunity?

So we have been made aware that "Surely the Lord GOD will do nothing, but he revealeth his secret unto his servants the prophets" (Amos 3:7). And this is what the prophets tell us:

- John wrote the words that Jesus stated, which are, "I will come again" (John 14:3).

- Isaiah wrote, "For, behold, the LORD will come with fire, and with his chariots like a whirlwind, to render his anger with fury, and his rebuke with flames of fire" (Isaiah 66:15).

- Malachi wrote, "Then shall ye return, and discern between the righteous and the wicked, between him that serveth God and him that serveth him not" (Malachi 3:18).

- Daniel wrote, "And in the days of these kings shall the God of heaven set up a kingdom, which shall never be destroyed" (Daniel 2:44).

- David wrote, "The righteous shall rejoice when he seeth the vengeance: he shall wash his feet in the blood of the wicked" (Psalms 58:10).

- Matthew wrote, "For as the lightning cometh out of the east, and shineth even unto the west; so shall also the coming of the Son of man be" (Matthew 24:27).

- Mark wrote, "And then shall they see the Son of man coming in the clouds with great power and glory" (Mark 13:26).

- Luke wrote, "Watch ye therefore, and pray always, that ye may be accounted worthy to escape all these things that shall come to pass, and to stand before the Son of man" (Luke 21:36).

- Paul wrote, "For the Lord himself shall descend from heaven with a shout, with the voice of the archangel, and with the trump of God: and the dead in Christ shall rise first" (1 Thessalonians 4:16).

- Peter wrote, "But the day of the Lord will come as a thief in the night; in the which the heavens shall pass away with a great noise, and the elements shall melt with fervent heat, the earth also and the works that are therein shall be burned up" (2 Peter 3:10).

- Jude wrote, "Behold, the Lord cometh with ten thousands of his saints" (Jude 1:14).

Now there are many more verses we could share on the subject as well as many more writers, but these should serve as a good sampling for the event that is going to come do this planet. That event is none other than the second coming, in which is not all that pleasant leading up to the event, as we have seen.

Now God has another pattern that we studied, and it is the fact that God uses a prophet or prophets to predict an event as well as another prophet or prophets to confirm the event. Methuselah's name predicted the flood coming while Noah was the prophet to confirm the event. Abraham was used to predict the captivity and eventual release of the Israelites in Egypt while Moses, Aaron, Miriam and others were used as prophets and a prophetess to confirm the event. Moses was used to predict entering into the Promised Land, Joshua was the prophet to confirm that event. Jeremiah was used to predict the Babylonian captivity while Daniel was the primary prophet to see it through. Almost all of the writers of the Old Testament were used to predict the first coming of Jesus, while John the Baptist, Simeon, Anna, and even Pilot's wife were used to confirm the event. Several prophets were used to predict that the nation of Israel or the Jews would eventually be cut off while Stephen was the prophet to confirm it. And as noted, there are many prophets that were used to predict the second coming. We ought to expect a prophet or prophets of this day. On top of that, being the most urgent message to be preached, God specifically states, "It shall come to pass afterward, [that] I will pour out my spirit upon all flesh; and your sons and your daughters shall prophesy, your old men shall dream dreams, your young men shall see visions" (Joel 2:28), and "Thou must prophesy again before many peoples, and nations, and tongues, and kings" (Revelation 10:11), referring to creating a movement of people with a specific message contained in Revelation 10.

On top of all of this, God, without the use of Bible type prophets, has a last day message or messages that needs to go to the world. In fact, when these are given, know full well it is the last opportunity to be saved. And when the last seconds of time are ticking away, God will re-enforce the final messages, so when you hear them, as the Bible says, "harden not your hearts" (Hebrews 3:8, 3:15, 4:7).

The urgency of these messages is coupled with the symbolic description of the second coming. "And I looked, and behold a white cloud, and upon the cloud [one] sat like unto the Son of man, having on his head a golden crown, and in his hand a sharp sickle. And another angel came out of the temple, crying with a loud voice to him that sat on the cloud, Thrust in thy sickle, and reap: for the time is come for thee to reap; for the harvest of the earth is ripe. And he that sat on the cloud thrust in his sickle on the earth; and the earth was reaped" (Revelation 14:14-16). No doubt are we to make a connection with the term harvest and the feast days in which the last feast day is the harvest symbolizing the second coming.

What this confirms is that the call to make an atonement, the prior feast in the serious of seven found in Leviticus 23, is applicable today rebuking all those who are being deceived into a party like, celebration in Christianity. It is not time to celebrate. It is a time to repent! Of course this rebukes the concept of "once saved, always saved" as such believers do not believe that being in a continued mode of repentance is for a Christian. According to the feast, it is required.

And then prior to the call for repentance was the feast of trumpets, a wakeup call. As already studied, many dates and events center around the mid 1800's. That puts the feast day fulfillment of warning sometime in the earlier part of the 1800's of which we ought not easily dismiss the event called the Great Second Coming Awakening. Also, we ought not dismiss the fact that the devil was so active with false prophets during the middle 1800's, implying, God must have been busy too. So to reject all the professed prophets of the time would be unwise.

But now, as we studied quite well and in depth, there are so many signs that are just pinpointing the fact that those born in the 1960's and after may actually get to see the event known as the second coming. Although we shall not make an absolute prediction with dates, it is not by coincidence that the most morally rebellious activities started in the 1960's along with other religious ones.

Accepting the pope on United States soil for the first time in 1965 is not a coincidence. Sexual perversions being thrown into everyone's face, including the start of coming out of the closet for homosexuals, is not by coincidence. The fact that school prayer and other forms of religion was yanked from public schools during that time is not a coincidence either. The fact that a world religious ecumenical movement, the working together between religions so as to unify, started in the 1960's is not a coincidence. The fact that the country declared Sunday legislature not a conflict between church and state during the 1960's is also not a coincidence. The fact that shortly thereafter, this country started upending the Christian principles it was founded upon and replaced them with immoral laws like abortion on demand all the way up to now redefining marriage, all of which is not by coincidence.

Now as mentioned, the greatest event of all time, including greater than the first coming, is not something God wants the inhabitants of earth to be taken by surprise for "The Lord is not slack concerning his promise, as some men count slackness; but is longsuffering to us-ward, not willing that any should perish, but that all should come to repentance" (2 Peter 3:9). And "when they shall say, Peace and safety; then sudden destruction cometh upon them, as travail upon a woman with child; and they shall not escape. But ye, brethren, are not in darkness, that that day should overtake you as a thief" (1 Thessalonians 5:3-4). So we ought to expect an end time prophet or prophets, however, we are not going to take the time to evaluate before your eyes anybody particular or people for that matter.

All along we have presented collection upon collection of Bible verses without the influence of quotes from prophets. One of the reasons is because a true Christian is to "Despise not prophesyings. Prove all things; hold fast that which is good" (1 Thessalonians 5:20-21). So if we actually tried to prove how a particular person was a true prophet, no longer are you proving it one way or the other but we are doing it. Such activity is between God and that person. You alone must do the proving.

But as mentioned just a moment ago, there are specific messages that are to be proclaimed before Jesus returns. In using the Bible, let us back up in Revelation and see those specific messages that each of us ought to be paying attention to.

"And I saw another angel fly in the midst of heaven, having the everlasting gospel to preach unto them that dwell on the earth, and to every nation, and kindred, and tongue, and people, Saying with a loud voice, Fear God, and give glory to him; for the hour of his judgment is come: and worship him that made heaven, and earth, and the sea, and the fountains of waters. And there followed another angel, saying, Babylon is fallen, is fallen, that great city, because she made all nations drink of the wine of the wrath of her fornication. And the third angel followed them, saying with a loud voice, If any man worship the beast and his image, and receive [his] mark in his forehead, or in his hand, The same shall drink of the wine of the wrath of God, which is poured out without mixture into the cup of his indignation; and he shall be tormented with fire and brimstone in the presence of the holy angels, and in the presence of the Lamb: And the smoke of their torment ascendeth up for ever and ever: and they have no rest day nor night, who worship the beast and his image, and whosoever receiveth the mark of his name. Here is the patience of the saints: here [are] they that keep the commandments of God, and the faith of Jesus. And I heard a voice from heaven saying unto me, Write, Blessed [are] the dead which die in the Lord from henceforth: Yea, saith the Spirit, that they may rest from their labours; and their works do follow them" (Revelation 14:6-13).

For the most part, all these topics that are contained in those verses are very much unknown in meaning or at least unknown in application in most denominations. If Jesus is showing up soon, should we not fully understand what these messages mean so as to be able to present them to the people so they too can be saved? Do we really think that God would have us in darkness leading up to the second coming until moments beforehand to finally figure out these details? If we wait until the beast and the image of the beast are fully revealed, it is going to be too late. That is like warning a person of the danger as it is happening; it does not serve much purpose. But if we are aware of the details ahead of time, then we truly can "Take heed that no man deceive you" (Matthew 24:4). We truly can avoid all the preachers that say "I am Christ" or Christian that "shall deceive many" (Matthew 24:5). We truly can avoid the "many false prophets shall rise, and shall deceive many" (Matthew 24:11). And we can truly avoid the "great signs and wonders" that "if [it were] possible, they shall deceive the very elect" (Matthew 24:24).

So let us examine piece by piece each phrase keeping in mind most of the material has been covered in one form or another in this book. You can pretty much say that this chapter is the summary of the book, however, just as those that think they understand an entire novel just based upon shorten notes, what gets lost is all the supportive reasons behind it. In other words, I can state that 2 times 3 is 6, but that does not explain the details of why, hence why it was necessary to learn counting prior to learning adding of numbers together, and then once we have those two basic things understood, multiplication was not all that hard. Likewise, to blatantly state who the beast is, that will do a disservice to the over 50 identifying marks of who the beast is as contained inside. So please, judge not the summary as being simply an opinion, but judge it as the need to go inside and see why. See the over 60 verses on the state of the dead. See why the last week of time in Daniel 9 is wrongly thrown into the future. See why Armageddon is not what popular Christianity thinks. See why the secret rapture has so many flaws to its theory.

Now, starting in Revelation 14:6 taking one part at a time, we read through to verse 13 and also Revelation 18:1-5:

AND I SAW ANOTHER ANGEL FLY IN THE MIDST OF HEAVEN (14:6)

So, how many warning messages have been given by angels? If there were any messages delivered by an angel, it typically was a communication between a human being or a hand full of human beings, not a worldwide proclamation. For instance, Daniel spoke to an angel (Daniel 9:21), so did Lot and his wife (Genesis 19:15), and shepherds (Luke 2:8-15), as well as others. And contrary to popular belief, how is the saving gospel delivered? It is delivered by the hands of human beings. It is not even delivered by simple conviction of God, which seems to be so popular today and believed by so many that the "Don't judge me" people get irked in the slightest mention of, "Did you know…?" Although conversion is between God and humans, the instrument to deliver the messages falls upon humans.

And keep in mind that we are dealing with symbolism for there will not be a literal beast as found in Revelation 13, therefore, the angel represents a message as opposed to the being that is delivering it. Besides, after looking at Revelation 10, we see an angel handing off a message to humans to preach. Jesus tells us, "Go ye into all the world, and preach the gospel to every creature" (Mark 16:15).

So the angel here as well as the ones we see are not going to be literal angels coming down with the gospel, but rather are symbolic of the messengers that have the message for the time at hand.

HAVING THE EVERLASTING GOSPEL (14:6)

There is no mistaking it. All of the subjects that we are about to encounter with these messages are gospel based. Those that think if people are heavy into Bible prophecy that somehow they have left Jesus out of the equation, well, think again! These messages are gospel based.

What we have is actually the gospel plus the message for the hour, meaning, for the current time, for instance, Noah had the gospel and preached to get into the ark. Moses had the gospel and preached to leave Egypt. Joshua had the gospel and preached to clear the land of the enemies of God and occupy the Promised Land. Jeremiah had the gospel and preached that there would be captivity. John the Baptist had the gospel and preached about the first coming. The apostles had the gospel and preached Christ, a risen Savior.

Many think the gospel is something Jesus taught and only told the apostles to teach, and that is not true. Naming four books as the gospel does not help matters. The Bible specifically says that the gospel was preached in the day of Abraham (Galatians 3:8) for instance.

Basically the gospel is the saving message. Joshua said it this way, "And if it seem evil unto you to serve the LORD, choose you this day whom ye will serve; whether the gods which your fathers served that [were] on the other side of the flood, or the gods of the Amorites, in whose land ye dwell: but as for me and my house, we will serve the LORD" (Joshua 24:15).

And all who did not obey the "belief" part perished. In other words, it was not good enough to believe in Jesus and not get in the ark. All those that said that they were fine on their own worshipping God, even correctly, who did not get into the ark ended up drowned. All those that would not have left Egypt would have been killed. All those that fought for Israel thinking they could beat the Babylonian army ended up dying. Jesus said, "He that is not with me is against me" (Matthew 12:30). So it is the same at the end of time. All those that believe in Sabbath keeping, salvation including sanctification, faith shown through works, etc. are going to join the movement of true Christians having these messages on their tongues.

One may have the gospel and still be lost is the bottom line, but make no mistake, the requirement to take action along with accepting the gospel is not denying the gospel; it is not earning the benefits of the gospel; it simply is the result of believing the gospel.

If one is truly saved, they "shalt love thy neighbour as thyself" (Leviticus 19:18). They shall try to save others for "he that hateth his brother is in darkness, and walketh in darkness, and knoweth not whither he goeth, because that darkness hath blinded his eyes" (1 John 2:11). And if one thinks that allowing someone to remain in ignorance is not "hating" their brother, think again. That is exactly what indifference is.

Now here is one more important aspect. If this is the saving message, which is the gospel along with specific end time saving words, when Jesus said, "And this gospel of the kingdom shall be preached in all the world for a witness unto all nations; and then shall the end come" (Matthew 24:14), that must mean we are looking at what the end time gospel is. That also means, by the use of the word "this" that Jesus knew that there would be multiple gospels where only one would be true, otherwise, He would have said "these".

So unfortunately to many sincere Christians, being part of a congregation that may have a gospel does not mean they will be saved. Please note at the same time that just joining the group that appears to have this message as part of their church does not automatically save them either. God has His people everywhere, and we shall see His plans in a little while later in this book.

TO PREACH UNTO THEM THAT DWELL ON THE EARTH (14:6)

Jesus said, "Go ye into all the world, and preach the gospel to every creature" (Mark 16:15). He also said, "Go ye therefore, and teach all nations, baptizing them in the name of the Father, and of the Son, and of the Holy Ghost: Teaching them to observe all things whatsoever I have commanded you: and, lo, I am with you alway, [even] unto the end of the world" (Matthew 28:19-20).

This is in contrast to the modern preaching and teaching, where preachers just tell people about justification and hope they pick up the sanctification on their own, or worse, the preachers teach sanctification comes at the second coming. In other words, today's preaching is all about how Jesus saves and nothing about the fact that now that you are in His saving grace, there are certain rules to obey. Such Christians will stop eating God's unhealthy garbage disposals known as unclean animals; they will stop watching and listening to content that is sinful; they will start paying tithe. In other words, it is the stop doing the bad and start doing the good.

We need to understand that there are three pieces to salvation. They are justification, sanctification, and glorification. Justification, the forgiveness of our sins (Romans 4:25, Romans 5:16). Sanctification, the holy living (1 Thessalonians 5:23). Glorification, changed into the in corruptible bodies to live throughout eternity (Romans 8:17). It is not Justification and sanctification/glorification. It is justification, sanctification, and glorification. Besides, 1 Thessalonians 5:23 tells us that sanctification happens before the second coming. "And the very God of peace sanctify you wholly; and [I pray God] your whole spirit and soul and body be preserved blameless unto the coming of our Lord Jesus Christ."

AND TO EVERY NATION, AND KINDRED, AND TONGUE, AND PEOPLE (14:6)

Jesus said, "And this gospel of the kingdom shall be preached in all the world for a witness unto all nations; and then shall the end come" (Matthew 24:14). So Revelation 14:6 is just a clarification that not only is every nation to receive the gospel, but every person must be witnessed to, and not only in the English language, but in the various tongues, so that no one can blame misunderstandings upon God.

Not by coincidence, Revelation 10:11 says, "And he said unto me, Thou must prophesy again before many peoples, and nations, and tongues, and kings." This is the last verse to the study we had much earlier on this angel that appears symbolically having small book that used to be closed but is now open, that contains a message about time running out, that would be misunderstood originally, like Jesus returning in the 1800's, but now after the fact that the people get the corrected message and are to go forth with it instead. And that message centers around Daniel 8:14, which says, "And he said unto me, Unto two thousand and three hundred days; then shall the sanctuary be cleansed."

This is the message because there was only one book that was sealed closed and later opened and that referred to time running out, and that is Daniel. Daniel 12:4 says, "But thou, O Daniel, shut up the words, and seal the book, [even] to the time of the end: many shall run to and fro, and knowledge shall be increased." Daniel 12:9, says, "And he said, Go thy way, Daniel: for the words [are] closed up and sealed till the time of the end." Daniel 8:17 says, "So he came near where I stood: and when he came, I was afraid, and fell upon my face: but he said unto me, Understand, O son of man: for at the time of the end [shall be] the vision." Daniel 8:19 says, "And he said, Behold, I will make thee know what shall be in the last end of the indignation: for at the time appointed the end [shall be]."

By using phrases like, "seal the book, even to the time of the end", "closed up and sealed till the time of the end", "at the time of the end", and "at the time appointed the end shall be" all point to Daniel dealing with time running out.

So in addition to having the gospel, in addition to having a specific message that is outlined in Revelation 14:6-13, there is also another specific message that is unique to the body of believers. It is called the sanctuary message. All of which help identify the true preaching from the false. It also identifies the fact that God is organized and does not have a message that is just by happenstance. Although people connected with giving the message can be like the Jews of old, where they thought simply being in the nation of Israel was a guarantee for salvation (John 8:33) all the while being hypocrites (Matthew 6:2), that does not diminish from the fact that God has a movement, not just another denomination.

SAYING WITH A LOUD VOICE (14:7)

A loud voice means that these people will be heard. They may be considered insignificant but they will get the world's attention.

And what will help with saying these things with a loud voice is the fact that they all live the message in addition to preaching it. Nothing distracts more from a Bible message than someone preaching the truth while living a lie. These people do not make excuses for sin in their life. These do not pick and choose what they will obey. The will have the character of Christ.

This is what set Jesus' message off from the Pharisees. It was said, "Never man spake like this man" (John 7:46). Jesus "taught them as [one] having authority, and not as the scribes" (Matthew 7:29). "And they were astonished at his doctrine: for he taught them as one that had authority, and not as the scribes" (Mark 1:22). Even Jesus said, "The scribes and the Pharisees sit in Moses' seat: All therefore whatsoever they bid you observe, [that] observe and do; but do not ye after their works: for they say, and do not" (Matthew 23:2-3).

This is much like many Christians today. The Bible says, "Thou shalt not commit adultery" (Exodus 20:14), yet they are as sexually active inappropriately as any other non-Christian. They excuse themselves because they are not saved by keeping the commandments. Although that is true, they will be lost for breaking them.

As the phrase goes, actions speak louder than words, so what the last day true Christian will do is speak the truth but also live it. That is what makes it loud.

FEAR GOD (14:7)

As stated before, people think they know God; they think they have a relationship with Him; they think they are right with God, when in fact, they have no fear or respect.

And as Solomon once wrote, "Let us hear the conclusion of the whole matter: Fear God, and keep his commandments: for this [is] the whole [duty] of man" (Ecclesiastes 12:13). So part of fearing God is obeying all of God's Ten of God's Commandments, and it is by this measurement that we can tell that the vast majority of Christians do not fear God since they are not keeping His commandments.

To fear God is not the type in which we are scared of Him, but there should be a realization that "Thus saith the LORD; Behold, I set before you the way of life, and the way of death" (Jeremiah 21:8). He alone offers life, while the other choice is death. So, "choose you this day whom ye will serve" (Joshua 24:15). In fact, "Fear him, which after he hath killed hath power to cast into hell; yea, I say unto you, Fear him" (Luke 12:5).

But it is not all about obedience and respect towards God when we "Fear Him". "For as the heaven is high above the earth, [so] great is his mercy toward them that fear him" (Psalms 103:11). "Surely his salvation [is] nigh them that fear him" (Psalms 85:9). It is a matter of receiving salvation and mercy, but again, only to those living in obedience to Him because the respect or fear of God.

Think of it this way generally speaking. Throughout the education system, there were teachers to be feared and teachers that were basically a joke when it came to keeping the classroom under control. The teachers that were feared, they enforced the rules and had organized classrooms. The teachers that did not enforce the rules, chaos was the rule of the room. Those students that appreciated the rules had no problems in actually being friends with the strict teacher. Those that did not want to have the rules made the teacher out to be a tyrant. So in the last days, "because sentence against an evil work is not executed speedily, therefore the heart of the sons of men is fully set in them to do evil" (Ecclesiastes 8:11), Christianity has basically become a group of people that do not fear God and live in disobedience. They treat God like the teacher that does not enforce the rules anymore and chaos reigns in the denominations today, let alone in the world. We have made Jesus too much our friend instead of our Father.

And that is the poison with today's psychology. For years parents were encouraged to be their children's friend. Nonsense! We are parents. We have rules. Rules are because we love our children and are trying to train them correctly. By being their friend and jointly breaking the rules simply causes a break down the structure. It is psychologist's way to "spoil you through philosophy and vain deceit, after the tradition of men, after the rudiments of the world, and not after Christ" (Colossians 2:8).

So for those that think the Commandments have been done away with, think again! To respond positively to fearing God is to live in obedience. "What then? shall we sin, because we are not under the law, but under grace? God forbid" (Romans 6:15). "Do we then make void the law through faith? God forbid: yea, we establish the law" (Romans 3:31). "For not the hearers of the law [are] just before God, but the doers of the law shall be justified" (Romans 2:13).

AND GIVE GLORY TO HIM (14:7)

In this generation, it is pretty hard to give God the glory. With sports figures bragging about being the best, businesses pushing to be the best, having a generation known as the "me" generation, and much more, it seems that all the glory is going to people. Even psychology encourages centering on one's own needs by saying,

"You can't love others if you don't love yourself". We are bombarded constantly with selfishness, when, according to the Bible, we are to live to serve God. "Then said Jesus unto his disciples, If any [man] will come after me, let him deny himself, and take up his cross, and follow me" (Matthew 16:24).

Specifically, we give glory to God with our bodies "For ye are bought with a price: therefore glorify God in your body, and in your spirit, which are God's" (1 Corinthians 6:20). That means what we do with our bodies either gives glory to God or Satan. And Satan is in the form of not being saved. What we do with our bodies is not enough to avoid sin, but we need to do the good. As Jesus said, "He that is not with me is against me" (Matthew 12:30). Neutrality is not an option.

Too many Christians think that as long as they are right with God, they can avoid sin but enjoy the world. They can avoid evil, but fit in with the crowd, but they may not necessarily do holy things either. They do not want to be a fanatic or draw attention to the fact they are a Christian, but Jesus condemns that attitude.

And so, God addresses the food, as we studied earlier, where Leviticus 11 is not just a Jewish restriction that Jesus lifted off when he said, "There is nothing from without a man, that entering into him can defile him: but the things which come out of him, those are they that defile the man" (Mark 7:15). The crowd He was addressing were a people that did not eat pork, lobster, and other unclean foods. What Jesus was addressing was "to eat with unwashen hands defileth not a man" (Matthew 15:20). A person could eat the right food, but the extra rules the Pharisees placed on the food preparation made it ceremonially unclean. As for the animals, there is nothing ceremonial about being clean and unclean as even Noah knew the difference (Genesis 7:2). And food is an issue, especially with regard to unclean foods, for at the second coming, "behold, the LORD will come with fire, and with his chariots like a whirlwind, to render his anger with fury, and his rebuke with flames of fire. For by fire and by his sword will the LORD plead with all flesh: and the slain of the LORD shall be many. They that sanctify themselves, and purify themselves in the gardens behind one [tree] in the midst, eating swine's flesh, and the abomination, and the mouse, shall be consumed together, saith the LORD" (Isaiah 66:15-17).

God also addresses the alcohol, where, "Wine [is] a mocker, strong drink [is] raging: and whosoever is deceived thereby is not wise" (Proverbs 20:1).

On top of that, there is the entertainment, where what we read, what we watch, what we listen too ought to be filtered through Philippians 4:8, which says, "Finally, brethren, whatsoever things are true, whatsoever things [are] honest, whatsoever things [are] just, whatsoever things [are] pure, whatsoever things [are] lovely, whatsoever things [are] of good report; if [there be] any virtue, and if [there be] any praise, think on these things." That does not leave much.

Further, we ought to dress "in modest apparel, with shamefacedness and sobriety; not with broided hair, or gold, or pearls, or costly array" (1 Timothy 2:9). We should also be careful of the logos, sayings, and other representation that our clothing states.

And God "hath called you is holy, so be ye holy in all manner of conversation" (1 Peter 1:15).

FOR THE HOUR OF HIS JUDGMENT IS COME (14:7)

The present tense of this verse indicates that people living right before the second coming will be judged beforehand instead of at the moment that "it is appointed unto men once to die, but after this the judgment" (Hebrews 9:27), but eventually the living need to be judged for Heaven or Hell for "Behold, I shew you a mystery; We shall not all sleep, but we shall all be changed" (1 Corinthians 15:51). That is not a change spiritually. That is a change physically. "In a moment, in the twinkling of an eye, at the last trump: for the trumpet shall sound, and the dead shall be raised incorruptible, and we shall be changed. For this corruptible must put on incorruption, and this mortal [must] put on immortality. So when this corruptible shall have put on incorruption, and this mortal shall have put on immortality, then shall be brought to pass the saying that is written, Death is swallowed up in victory" (1 Corinthians 15:52-54). Our change is into the bodies we will have for eternity, but not everyone gets new bodies, only those whose cases have been decided ahead of time to be accounted as receiving such. The Bible identifies such an event as from Heaven for it will be declared, "He that is unjust, let him be unjust still: and he which is filthy, let him be filthy still: and he that is righteous, let him be righteous still: and he that is holy, let him be holy still" (Revelation 22:11). And once all of the cases are decided, there is a period that there will be "no intercessor" (Isaiah 59:16). Through prayer, "no man was able to enter into the temple" (Revelation 15:8). That is because when Jesus shows up, He is able to say, "My reward [is] with me, to give every man according as his work shall be" (Revelation 22:12).

The concept of being judged ahead of the second coming is brought out in the feast days, where atonement, the sixth feast, is that of the judgment feast. The second coming is represented by the harvest feast, the seventh one.

During the judgment, although our works cannot save us, our works will give evidence of the heart. "Know ye not, that to whom ye yield yourselves servants to obey, his servants ye are to whom ye obey; whether of sin unto death, or of obedience unto righteousness?" (Romans 6:16)

We "shall be judged by the law of liberty" (James 2:12), and "every idle word that men shall speak, they shall give account thereof in the day of judgment" (Matthew 12:36).

All of this will happen before Jesus returns.

AND WORSHIP HIM THAT MADE HEAVEN, AND EARTH, AND THE SEA, AND THE FOUNTAINS OF WATERS (14:7)

Tracing these words through the Bible, such wording is found in Exodus 20:11, which is inside the fuller context of Exodus 20:8-11. "Remember the sabbath day, to keep it holy. Six days shalt thou labour, and do all thy work: But the seventh day [is] the sabbath of the LORD thy God: [in it] thou shalt not do any work, thou, nor thy son, nor thy daughter, thy manservant, nor thy maidservant, nor thy cattle, nor thy stranger that [is] within thy gates: For [in] six days the LORD made heaven and earth, the sea, and all that in them [is], and rested the seventh day: wherefore the LORD blessed the sabbath day, and hallowed it."

The reason there is a call back to the seventh day Sabbath is because the one commandment that starts with the word "remember" is the one that has been forgotten, thanks primarily to the Antichrist who "think to change times and laws" (Daniel 7:25) and then perpetrated by the "Spirit of Antichrist". Antichrist changed one time being the way we track days. God never intended midnight to midnight but rather sunset to sunset (Genesis 1:14). A second time change that has been implemented was to the day chosen as the Sabbath, now being the first day of the week, all built on assumptions.

With fire and smoke and audible sounds, the Ten Commandments were copied from the original that sits "in his temple the ark of his testament" (Revelation 11:19). "Moses was admonished of God when he was about to make the tabernacle: for, See, saith he, [that] thou make all things according to the pattern shewed to thee in the mount" (Hebrews 8:5). There, the Sabbath was written out. Today, preachers simply say, "Jesus rose on a Sunday, and the Holy Spirit came on a Sunday therefore we now have a new Sabbath." There is no command of God. There was no grand event that drew attention to the change. It is just based on an implication.

That is like the parents going away leaving the older children to fend for themselves at home. As one of the rules are being broken by one child, another child may speak up and say, "You know mom and dad don't allow that." The first child may reply, "Oh, it's Okay. They implied that I can do this." The second child would be a fool to go along with just an implication, yet Christianity does it with God every week believing upon implication that the Sabbath has been changed from sunset Friday and Saturday into Sunday from midnight to midnight.

The concept of the forgotten Sabbath day is also brought out in the feast days where the first four feast days, all fulfilled in Jesus around 31 AD, makes no mention of the Sabbath in Leviticus 23. But the last three feast days each make mention of it where, not by coincidence, between the fourth feast day (Pentecost) and the fifth (Trumpets) was a period of empty time containing no feasts. Symbolically, from Pentecost to the Great Awakening, this is known as the Dark Ages in which the Sabbath was changed to Sunday by the Antichrist, who brags to the world being her Mark of her Authority.

During the Great Awakening, small groups of Sabbath keepers sprung up, including the Seventh Day Baptists and others. After the Great Disappointment, we entered into the feast of Atonement, of which the Sabbath then became more and more pronounced with groups like Assemblies of Yahweh, Church of God Seventh Day, House of Yahweh Seventh Day, Logos Apostolic Church of God, Church of God Sabbatarian, Sabbath Rest Advent Church, Seventh-Day Adventist, Seventh-day Remnant home-churches, and Worldwide Church of God. And in the Harvest feast, representing the second coming, the Sabbath is mentioned again because "from one sabbath to another, shall all flesh come to worship before me, saith the LORD" (Isaiah 66:23), and that is throughout eternity.

Besides, "Blessed [are] they that do his commandments, that they may have right to the tree of life, and may enter in through the gates into the city" (Revelation 22:14). It does not say that Sabbath breakers or commandment breakers get to experience this. And when it says that they do His commandments, that is all ten, not just nine or an alternative version.

AND THERE FOLLOWED ANOTHER ANGEL, SAYING, BABYLON IS FALLEN, IS FALLEN (14:8)

Addressing the reference to Babylon, John is using a symbolic comparison. Yes, there is a great city in which the

Antichrist rules from, but no, it is not literal Babylon resurrected. In fact, God made a prediction, and despite attempts to rebuild Babylon, it remains in ruins. "And Babylon, the glory of kingdoms, the beauty of the Chaldees' excellency, shall be as when God overthrew Sodom and Gomorrah. It shall never be inhabited, neither shall it be dwelt in from generation to generation: neither shall the Arabian pitch tent there; neither shall the shepherds make their fold there" (Isaiah 13:19-20).

So Babylon is a symbol, as Revelation 1:1 states, of that reality regarding much of the Book of Revelation. It represents something more than a geographical location. First, the word Babylon comes from another word, Babel, of which "is the name of it called Babel; because the LORD did there confound the language of all the earth: and from thence did the LORD scatter them abroad upon the face of all the earth" (Genesis 11:9).

Now look around, where on earth is there a great city that primarily sends forth confusion and even scatters people abroad? No, we are not referring to driving on the wrong side of the road, although that is confusing. We are not talking about road signs that are confusing either. Whenever we read the Bible, the descriptions are spiritual or godly in nature. So what great city is confusing the people on God's doctrines? The Bible says, "For many deceivers are entered into the world, who confess not that Jesus Christ is come in the flesh. This is a deceiver and an Antichrist. Look to yourselves, that we lose not those things which we have wrought, but that we receive a full reward. Whosoever transgresseth, and abideth not in the doctrine of Christ, hath not God. He that abideth in the doctrine of Christ, he hath both the Father and the Son" (2 John 1:7-9). It is none other than the Antichrist, who, in past history definitely sent true Christians scattered abroad. Just ask the Waldensians, who found homes in caves and remote areas.

But Babylon is known for other things beyond confusion and scattering. The Bible says that Babylon conquered Jerusalem, "And the king spake unto Ashpenaz the master of his eunuchs, that he should bring [certain] of the children of Israel, and of the king's seed, and of the princes; Children in whom [was] no blemish, but well favoured, and skilful in all wisdom, and cunning in knowledge, and understanding science, and such as [had] ability in them to stand in the king's palace, and whom they might teach the learning and the tongue of the Chaldeans" (Daniel 1:3-4). Basically, there was a reeducation process, much like Antichrist presents today.

Does one really think evolution is an atheist thing? Think again! "Pope says evolution, Big Bang are real", according to USA Today, October 28, 2014. In the article, it states, "Pope Francis has waded into the controversial debate over the origins of human life, saying the big bang theory did not contradict the role of a divine creator, but even required it." May we ask how evolution, and especially the Bing Bang Theory, does not contradict the role of Creator? Are we saying that God did one zap to start the big bang and all else fell into place? That is like playing a game of pool where on the first shot all of the balls go into all the right pockets in exact sequence by the number on the ball, and all of us know that such is not possible. Besides, the odds of all of this happening is far greater than a pool game.

And interestingly, there indeed was a new tongue that only the privileged knew. Since the 1960's, it has pretty much been done away with, but church services (or the mass) was done in Latin and not the common language. So if someone wanted to follow along and understand the words, they had to learn Latin.

Now there is a reference to the fact that Babylon is fallen twice. Although we can look at the falling in more than one manner, please realize that both are acceptable and also fulfilled, or at least will be. Some see the double "fallen" reference as marking the death blow in 1798 being the first physical fall and then of course at the end of time when it will be fulfilled, "the beast was taken, and with him the false prophet that wrought miracles before him, with which he deceived them that had received the mark of the beast, and them that worshipped his image. These both were cast alive into a lake of fire burning with brimstone" (Revelation 19:20).

Another way of looking at the reference of the word "fallen" is to place one of the "fallen" times as again in 1798, when the pope was dethroned and the land confiscated. But the other reference to "fallen" is more spiritual when it fell away from the Word of God for its doctrines. This is supported in 2 Thessalonians 2:3-4 which says, "Let no man deceive you by any means: for [that day shall not come], except there come a falling away first, and that man of sin be revealed, the son of perdition; Who opposeth and exalteth himself above all that is called God, or that is worshipped; so that he as God sitteth in the temple of God, shewing himself that he is God."

In either case, symbolic Babylon has already fallen and is spreading confusion among Christians, scattering those that oppose the wrong teachings, teaching false science, and re-educating people.

THAT GREAT CITY (14:8)

The phrase "that great city" appears in the Bible ten times, seven of which are in Revelation. Referring to just "great city", we still have but seventeen verses. It apparently is connected with being a world influencer or capital, for instance, where in Jonah 1:2 it says, "Arise, go to Nineveh, that great city, and cry against it; for their wickedness is come up before me." The greatest world influencer is in Revelation 21:10, "And he carried me away in the spirit to a great and high mountain, and shewed me that great city, the holy Jerusalem, descending out of heaven from God."

At the time John wrote these words, the greatest city in his day was Rome. So therefore, beware of Rome, for out of Rome shall come doctrines of confusion, re-education to human traditions being above the Bible, and a scattering of those standing for the truth.

BECAUSE SHE MADE ALL NATIONS DRINK OF THE WINE OF THE WRATH OF HER FORNICATION (14:8)

Remember, the definition of the word "wine" or the purpose of referencing it here. The Bible says, "[It is] not for kings, O Lemuel, [it is] not for kings to drink wine; nor for princes strong drink: Lest they drink, and forget the law, and pervert the judgment of any of the afflicted" (Proverbs 31:4-5). So Babylon, that great city, Rome, will cause people to forget the Ten Commandments and pervert God's judgment, as in, teaching something different.

Not only has she taught the world to forget the Ten Commandments, she has an altered set to make sure that those that want to keep God's laws will still end up not keeping them. And as predicted, she even will "think to change times and laws" (Daniel 7:25), specifically changing the Sabbath not once but twice for it is on a different cycle of time and also on a different day, hence the plurality to the word "times". This of course is the opposite of the first message where people are being called to keep the Sabbath properly for a day beginning sunset Friday and ending sunset Saturday.

Of course in changing the law, where the idols are allowed and coveting is made into two commands, this transcends into the creation of other laws, like the requirement of holidays or else it is a sin, like disregarding God's health laws, like implementing a pagan ritual called Lent, like making it mandatory to go to a priest twice a year minimally to confess one's sins, and other things.

Now this wine is so poisonous that some of these things are rejected among Protestants but they go too far. The wine has caused many to toss out completely the Ten Commandments.

As for judgment, we could spend a ton of pages on the subject. This is inclusive of not only the standard that should be used to know if "Whose soever sins ye remit, they are remitted unto them; [and] whose soever [sins] ye retain, they are retained" (John 20:23). That standard is the Word of God, not counsels or a dictation of commands, nor even church fathers. Judgment has gotten so perverted by this wine that the world thinks if one criticizes an action that somehow people are judging other people.

The Bible teaches two types of judgment where judging actions is never being judgmental while judging people's destination is. Warning people if they continue sinning they will go to hell is actually a loving thing to do. Telling a person who is trying to clean up their life that they have no hope since they had a shady past is wrong.

Having the power to judge if a person ought to be a saint or not, is inclusive of the false judgment passed upon the world, where even secular media outlets report the proclamation of such sainthood activities. Having the power to grant annulments despite the definition of divorce given by Jesus, which is not allowed in the eyes of Rome, is sitting as judge and jury of such matters. Making up rules and holding people up as heretics for not complying is a form of judging.

But understand this view point. The wine is "the wrath of her fornication". Fornication is basically sex, in this case, spiritual sex. The Bible says, "Ye adulterers and adulteresses, know ye not that the friendship of the world is enmity with God? whosoever therefore will be a friend of the world is the enemy of God" (James 4:4). So making policies that helps the Antichrist machine to fit in with the world, yet appear religious is what is meant by spiritual sex.

Now there is a small difference in wording that we ought not to miss. One word is "adulterers" or "adulteresses" while the comparison is to the word "fornication". Adultery is when a married person has an illicit sexual encounter. Fornication is when a non-married person engages in illicit sexual activity. Please note that James is addressing Christians. "Know ye not Christians?" is basically what he wrote. A Christian is one who is married or espoused "to one husband, that I may present [you as] a chaste virgin to Christ" (2 Corinthians 11:2). So if such a person then turns and enjoys the things of the world after being married to Christ, then they are committing adultery. Babylon, that great city, on the other hand is technically not married to Christ as "the dragon gave him his power, and his seat, and great authority" (Revelation 13:2). Despite claiming to be the bride of Christ, Rome is actually still single. Therefore, as she indulges in the world, she is only committing fornication, not that it is a lesser thing, but she is not committing adultery for she is not truly married to Christ.

If she were married to Christ, then she would be more like Christ. She would not be "arrayed in purple and scarlet colour, and decked with gold and precious stones and pearls, having a golden cup in her hand full of abominations and filthiness of her fornication" (Revelation 17:4). She would not exalt a person as compared to the method Jesus appeared as, for "behold, thy King cometh unto thee, meek, and sitting upon an ass, and a colt the foal of an ass" (Matthew 21:5). She would not put to death those that disagree with her, for when Jesus was rejected by the Samaritans, "when his disciples James and John saw [this], they said, Lord, wilt thou that we command fire to come down from heaven, and consume them, even as Elias did? But he turned, and rebuked them, and said, Ye know not what manner of spirit ye are of. For the Son of man is not come to destroy men's lives, but to save [them]" (Luke 9:54-56).

And that brings us to the word "wrath". The wrath should be reserved to God. As for ourselves, we are told "whosoever shall not receive you, nor hear your words, when ye depart out of that house or city, shake off the dust of your feet" (Matthew 10:14), and "That ye resist not evil: but whosoever shall smite thee on thy right cheek, turn to him the other also" (Matthew 5:39), yet, many martyrs have become such at the hands of "that great city".

AND THE THIRD ANGEL FOLLOWED THEM, SAYING WITH A LOUD VOICE, IF ANY MAN WORSHIP THE BEAST (14:9)

Now the word "worship" does not necessarily mean bowing to the ground and praying in that person's name or to them. It does include assigning God's titles to the beast such as:

- Asking if the Pope is Jesus, the title of the article is, Pope Jesus?! Watters Asks New Yorkers About the Holy Father's Visit, Fox News, September 24, 2015.

- As the selected Vicar of Christ, Pope Francis comes to us in a moment of tremendous need — and not just spiritual, Fox News, March 20, 2013

- In announcing the policy shift Obama thanked His Holiness and said the Pope's "moral example shows us the importance of pursuing the world as it should be, rather than simply settling for the world as it is.", CNN, March 27, 2015.

And that is just a small sampling of secular news outlets that were tripping over each other to report on the pope, referring in all kinds of names and titles that are attributed to God. And by the way, the word "vicar", according to Dictionary.com, means "a person who acts in place of another; substitute."

But even if people do not attribute titles to the pope, even if one is very much against the pope, another form of worshipping the beast is to be obeying the beast. In other words, "Howbeit in vain do they worship me, teaching [for] doctrines the commandments of men" (Mark 7:7). By obeying the commands of the beast, they are worshipping the beast. Specifically, history, without any reasonable doubt points to the fact that pagan Rome encouraged early Christians to adopt Sunday instead of the Sabbath as the new day of worship of which the Catholic Church agreed to doing. So all those that adhere to still keeping Sunday are indirectly worshipping the beast even if not connected with the beast directly. Therefore, this is a call to stop it. Stop worshipping as commanded by the beast!

AND HIS IMAGE (14:9)

Of course this reference to the word "image" is referring to Revelation 13:14-15, "And deceiveth them that dwell on the earth by [the means of] those miracles which he had power to do in the sight of the beast; saying to them that dwell on the earth, that they should make an image to the beast, which had the wound by a sword, and did live. And he had power to give life unto the image of the beast, that the image of the beast should both speak, and cause that as many as would not worship the image of the beast should be killed."

In this day and age, a physical image like that of ancient Babylon is not going to deceive anyone. Besides, with the whole world once again involved, just how can the world come to a single location and worship the image? Will it be an annual required pilgrimage? Is everyone going to have to buy miniature versions of the statue? Of course not.

Ever hear the phrase "spitting image"? It means, according to Dictionary.com, "a close resemblance". So with beasts representing countries (Daniel 7:23), to erect an image to the first beast, being the Antichrist nation, that means the second beast would be a close resemblance. And a nation speaks through its laws. Therefore, laws will be made very similar to those of the first beast, where all was done by force with the first, so the second would do the same.

Now, we already studied the more than fifty points identifying the first beast to be located in Europe as a small country coming off as both religious and political having such rules that permit the blasphemous acts of claiming to be God and also having the power to forgive sins. And at this very point it is none other than the Vatican who uses a religious body known as the Catholic Church that according to historical references, slaughtered those with a dissenting view by the millions. Well to be an image, one would have to have such rules too. And it is prophesied that such will be. And so around the world, what power started out lamb like but seems to be a world influencer in a more dictatorial manner working with the Vatican in promoting its position in the world, like assisting them to take down the USSR? None other than the United States.

So, was this nation not found on freedoms? Of course it was. Many of them still exist today. But is this nation appearing less and less Christian and more and more dragon-like (forceful)? Of course it is. Recent articles include:

- Christian Pastor In Vermont Sentenced To One Year In Prison After Refusing To Marry Gay Couple, July 11, 2015.
- If you don't have health insurance: How much you'll pay, HealthCare.gov.
- Texas Minister Faces Jail Time After Refusing To Marry Gay Cousins, July 6th, 2015
- California Legislature passes mandatory vaccination bill, June 29, 2015

Again, obedience is a form of worship. So when laws are enacted contradicting the Bible, then we must reject the law and obey God (Acts 5:29). Just because a government enacts a law making something required does not mean we as citizens of the heavenly kingdom are to obey it. This disobedience is only in regards to contradictory commands, for at any other time, we are "to be subject to principalities and powers, to obey magistrates, to be ready to every good work" (Titus 3:1).

AND RECEIVE [HIS] MARK (14:9)

So just ask the beast what their mark is and then avoid it. Like we have stated numerous times, deny all one wants to on some of the points we shared regarding who the Antichrist is, but even if half of the points are inaccurate, that still leaves an overwhelming number of items still undebatable. People think that given a list of over fifty points that if they can disprove several of them that somehow that takes the heat off of who the finger of God points to. They do not factor in the point that if Antichrist fulfills all the others, maybe it them that cannot see the point correctly.

It has been about two thousand years since these things were written, and in that time, none other nation comes even close to fulfilling the items identified, not even close. For another religious power in Rome to appear slaughtering the saints and do what she has done and what she is doing today and announcing what she shall do soon is unlikely to be fulfilled in any other country. And all of these few points (being religious, located in Rome, slaughtering the saints) are three unarguable points.

Think of the questionable points like a self evaluation of one's own character. Who we want to be and who we really are can be two different things, especially if one goes down point by point. If one were to say, "I am patient, kind, helpful, considerate, intelligent, careful, aware of other's needs, etc.", and then someone was asked to describe that person, they may say, "They are patient, kind, helpful, considerate, not so smart, accident prone, aware of other's needs, etc." That does not negate that the second person is wrong about the self examined person who thought themselves differently.

For instance, trying to change the number 666 referenced in the Bible into the number 616 claiming interpretation error is not going to negate the rest of the list and that does not really mean they are correct. Pointing to other locations around the world that have seven mountains does not negate the fact that the seven mountains are to be in Europe. Pointing to all the Protestants who persecuted Catholic does not negate the fact that at the hands of the Vatican, millions were put to death for simply not complying with her demands. So try as they may to disqualify several points, there still remains the rest of the list. And besides, who knows a person better than ourselves? God. God is the one that generated the list. So God knows what the Antichrist really is, even better than the Antichrist herself.

And the beast does not hide the fact that it has a mark. In fact, it brags about it. Once again, from The Catholic Record of London, Ontario, Canada, September 1, 1923: "Sunday is our MARK of authority...the church is above the Bible, and this transference of Sabbath observance is proof of that fact."

But even without such a quote, just look at the evidence of what the Mark of the Beast is. First, of all, the Antichrist attacks the truth for "it cast down the truth to the ground; and it practised, and prospered" (Daniel 8:12). It happens to "think to change times and laws" (Daniel 7:25). "They worshipped the beast" (Revelation 13:4), of which replacing the Sabbath day of worshipping God with Sunday is a direct fulfillment.

On top of that, Daniel and Revelation are so paralleled. Daniel 7 states that Antichrist has "a mouth speaking great things" while Revelation 13:5 says, "a mouth speaking great things and blasphemies." Daniel 7:21 states that the Antichrist "made war with the saints, and prevailed against them" (Daniel 7:21) while Revelation 13:7 says that it would "make war with the saints, and to overcome them" (Revelation 13:7). Daniel 7:25 states that the Antichrist would have a reign described as "a time and times and the dividing of time" (Daniel 7:25) while Revelation 13:5 says it is "forty [and] two months". Daniel 7:25 says that Antichrist would "think to change times and laws" (Daniel 7:25) but Revelation 13:17 says it has "the mark." Nowhere in Revelation is there a reference to the law of God or the times in the law being changed, however, Daniel does not mention a mark. We conclude therefore and admitted by the Vatican that the Mark and the changing of the Sabbath into Sunday are one in the same.

And yet another way of discovering what the Mark of the Beast is happens to be by considering the Seal of God (Revelation 7:2). The Mark of the Beast would be the opposite of the Seal of God. Using Romans 4:11 to establish a word synonym between "seal" and "sign", we then can search the Bible very easily for the Sign of God. And the Bible says, "Verily my sabbaths ye shall keep: for it [is] a sign between me and you" (Exodus 31:13); "I gave them my sabbaths, to be a sign between me and them, that they might know that I [am] the LORD that sanctify them" (Ezekiel 20:12); and "hallow my sabbaths; and they shall be a sign between me and you, that ye may know that I [am] the LORD your God" (Ezekiel 20:20). That means Sunday must be a sign of loyalty to the Vatican, who Christianized the pagan day and has influenced the entire world with the supposed change in the times of the Sabbath as well as the commandment itself.

On top of that, do not forget the fact that the first angel is pleading that we worship God on the day He established during creation. "And on the seventh day God ended his work which he had made; and he rested on the seventh day from all his work which he had made. And God blessed the seventh day, and sanctified it: because that in it he had rested from all his work which God created and made" (Genesis 2:2-3). Now here in the third angel's message, God is sending a warning not to worship the false way. That includes rejecting the worship of the Beast who declares the new commandments, that includes rejecting any and all legislation of the United States and United Nations that goes against God's Ten Commandments, and it includes the rejection of the Mark. If both the Vatican and the United States are going to be influential with Sunday legislation, it makes one then have to conclude that the Mark is Sunday law.

So that is a number of ways at resolving what the Mark of the Beast happens to be and they all point to the same answer, not by coincidence.

IN HIS FOREHEAD OR IN HIS HAND (14:9)

Being a symbolic book and making comparison with the fact that we either have the Mark of the Beast in our forehead (Revelation 13:16) or the Seal of God there (Revelation 7:3), we realize that since the Seal is not a literal and visible engraving on our forehead, the word "forehead" must not be literally on the surface nor for the Mark either. The same goes for the hand. It is not a literal surface mark nor is it an under the skin object.

The phrase regarding the hand and forehead is not new in Revelation, for such has been stated before:

- Exodus 13:16 And it shall be for a token upon thine hand, and for frontlets between thine eyes: for by strength of hand the LORD brought us forth out of Egypt.

- Deuteronomy 6:8 And thou shalt bind them for a sign upon thine hand, and they shall be as frontlets between thine eyes.

- Deuteronomy 11:18 Therefore shall ye lay up these my words in your heart and in your soul, and bind them for a sign upon your hand, that they may be as frontlets between your eyes.

The hand is our actions, as stated in Ecclesiastes 9:10, which says, "Whatsoever thy hand findeth to do, do [it] with thy might; for [there is] no work, nor device, nor knowledge, nor wisdom, in the grave, whither thou goest." The forehead is the mind for God said, "For this [is] the covenant that I will make with the house of Israel after those days, saith the Lord; I will put my laws into their mind, and write them in their hearts: and I will be to them a God, and they shall be to me a people" (Hebrews 8:10). That means the Antichrist wants us in action and/or thought to go along with his laws instead.

THE SAME SHALL DRINK OF THE WINE OF THE WRATH OF GOD (14:10)

What is this wrath? Look no further than Revelation 15:1, which says, "And I saw another sign in heaven, great and marvellous, seven angels having the seven last plagues; for in them is filled up the wrath of God."

WHICH IS POURED OUT WITHOUT MIXTURE INTO THE CUP OF HIS INDIGNATION (14:10)

Right now, God mingles His mercy with His corrective actions. That is because God uses such actions in hopes to draw people unto Himself. But when the seven last plagues hit, it is with His full wrath. There is no holding back. The reason for such is because "[there was] no intercessor" (Isaiah 59:16). Christ's ministry in the heavenly temple will have ceased and as humans using prayer, "no man was able to enter into the temple" (Revelation 15:8). The buffer between God the Father and humans will have been removed prior to the seven last plagues.

AND HE SHALL BE TORMENTED WITH FIRE AND BRIMSTONE (14:10)

Now this is not an immediate activity during the seven last plagues or immediately following. This clearly is a reference to hell fire. All this verse is stating is that those who receive the seven last plagues get to suffer the fire and brimstone at some point then.

It is written, "And they went up on the breadth of the earth, and compassed the camp of the saints about, and the beloved city: and fire came down from God out of heaven, and devoured them" (Revelation 20:9). At that time, "there shall be wailing and gnashing of teeth" (Matthew 13:42).

IN THE PRESENCE OF THE HOLY ANGELS (14:10)

The reason the wicked shall be tormented before the presence of the angels is because "The Son of man shall send forth his angels, and they shall gather out of his kingdom all things that offend, and them which do iniquity; And shall cast them into a furnace of fire: there shall be wailing and gnashing of teeth" (Matthew 13:41-42). So if the angels are going to cast the lost into the furnace of fire, it makes sense that the lost will be burned before them.

AND IN THE PRESENCE OF THE LAMB (14:10)

"The next day John seeth Jesus coming unto him, and saith, Behold the Lamb of God, which taketh away the sin of the world" (John 1:29). So, referring to Jesus as the Lamb, if "fire came down from God out of heaven, and devoured them" (Revelation 20:9), it is expected that Jesus would oversee the burning of the wicked.

And for those that say that it is God the Father, be careful. The Bible says, "For the Father judgeth no man, but hath committed all judgment unto the Son" (John 5:22). That includes the investigation, verdict, and the punishment. And the Bible also refers to Jesus as our Father as well "For unto us a child is born, unto us a son is given: and the government shall be upon his shoulder: and his name shall be called Wonderful, Counsellor, The mighty God, The everlasting Father, The Prince of Peace" (Isaiah 9:6).

AND THE SMOKE OF THEIR TORMENT ASCENDETH UP FOR EVER AND EVER (14:11)

Some see this phrase as meaning the ceaseless ages of eternity. If that is so, that would contradict Revelation 20:9, which says, "fire came down from God out of heaven, and devoured them" (Revelation 20:9). One cannot burn throughout eternity when devoured. And just in case it was not caught, the word devoured means that we "shall tread down the wicked; for they shall be ashes under the soles of your feet in the day that I shall do [this], saith the LORD of hosts" (Malachi 4:3). Explicitly, "the day cometh, that shall burn as an oven; and all the proud, yea, and all that do wickedly, shall be stubble: and the day that cometh shall burn them up, saith the LORD of hosts, that it shall leave them neither root nor branch" (Malachi 4:1). And to the devil, "Thou hast defiled thy sanctuaries by the multitude of thine iniquities, by the iniquity of thy traffick; therefore will I bring forth a fire from the midst of thee, it shall devour thee, and I will bring thee to ashes upon the earth in the sight of all them that behold thee" (Ezekiel 28:18).

The words "forever and ever" is a relative term and does not mean throughout eternity. This is demonstrated in the Bible in several places. One place is when Hannah dedicated the prophet Samuel to be a temple worker. "But Hannah went not up; for she said unto her husband, [I will not go up] until the child be weaned, and [then] I will bring him, that he may appear before the LORD, and there abide for ever" (1 Samuel 1:22). But how long did Samuel serve in the temple? The Bible says, "Therefore also I have lent him to the LORD; as long as he liveth he shall be lent to the LORD. And he worshipped the LORD there" (1 Samuel 1:28). So it was only a life time, which is much like the wicked that will be burned. Forever will be as long as they resist bowing the knee to Jesus and finally be reduced to ashes.

Another example is with Jonah. How long was Jonah in the belly of the fish? These are the words of Jonah, "I went down to the bottoms of the mountains; the earth with her bars [was] about me for ever: yet hast thou brought up my life from corruption, O LORD my God" (Jonah 2:6). In reality, how long was Jonah's "forever" experience? The Bible says, "Now the LORD had prepared a great fish to swallow up Jonah. And Jonah was in the belly of the fish three days and three nights" (Jonah 1:17). So only three days was Jonah experiencing this most awful imprisonment in the fish. Who knows how many days it will take to reduce all of the wicked to ashes, but it will seem like forever.

AND THEY HAVE NO REST DAY NOR NIGHT (14:11)

When the fire begins, there will not be a period of rest. It will burn until the last wicked being is consumed, being the Devil the last to burn up. That is because once the fires begin, "Their worm dieth not, and the fire is not quenched" (Mark 9:44, 46, 48). That does not mean the fire will not go out; it just never stops until it is done for even Sodom and Gomorrah stands as examples of unquenchable or eternal fire being used yet it went out. "Even as Sodom and Gomorrha, and the cities about them in like manner, giving themselves over to fornication, and going after strange flesh, are set forth for an example, suffering the vengeance of eternal fire" (Jude 1:7). When the fire and brimstone came upon Sodom and Gomorrah, there was no way to quench it until it burned up everything, and so it will be with hell fire.

WHO WORSHIP THE BEAST AND HIS IMAGE, AND WHOSOEVER RECEIVETH THE MARK OF HIS NAME (14:11)

Remember worship takes on a important meaning when obedience is declared to be a type of worship. Shall we listen to the commands of the beast over the Bible? Shall we submit to the law of the land that the image of the beast dictates? Will we accept the authoritative sign of the beast over the sign of God? The details of all of these questions are addressed above and will not be repeated here.

HERE IS THE PATIENCE (14:12)

Do you get excited over major earthquakes, one after the other happening? Do you get excited seeing political moves happening? How about when wars and rumor of wars start escalating? All of that is natural, of course only if your heart reaches out to the families that go through such experiences. To be indifferent to death is to be lacking Christ in the heart.

My point is that it is also natural to just say, "Come on Jesus. How about today?" Well, there is only one thing that helps speed up the events. And yes, we do have an influence. "Looking for and hasting unto the coming of the day of God, wherein the heavens being on fire shall be dissolved, and the elements shall melt with fervent heat? " (2 Peter 3:12). We are also told that "this gospel of the kingdom shall be preached in all the world for a witness unto all nations; and then shall the end come" (Matthew 24:14).

Please take note that Jesus said, "this gospel" and not "a gospel". You see, there is only one gospel, and it is not simply saying, "Jesus saves." That is only part of the gospel. In fact, Jesus said, "Go ye therefore, and teach all nations, baptizing them in the name of the Father, and of the Son, and of the Holy Ghost: Teaching them to observe all things whatsoever I have commanded you: and, lo, I am with you alway, [even] unto the end of the world" (Matthew 28:19-20). So by not teaching "to observe all things" is not the true gospel, and that alone just eliminated a whole lot of denominations that say, "Doctrines don't matter!"

In fact, one of the early recognitions that so many false gospels are being taught is that one of the first things people are to do before accepting salvation is what John the Baptist and Jesus both initially preached on. "In those days came John the Baptist, preaching in the wilderness of Judaea, and saying, Repent ye: for the kingdom of heaven is at hand" (Matthew 3:1-2). "Jesus began to preach, and to say, Repent: for the kingdom of heaven is at hand" (Matthew 4:17). The key is the word "repent", which means, at the very least, a willingness to have the sinning stop "For if there be first a willing mind, [it is] accepted according to that a man hath, [and] not according to that he hath not" (2 Corinthians 8:12). That is because Jesus "shall save his people from their sins" (Matthew 1:21) and not in our sins. So any gospel that does not let people know that God is pleading, "My little children, these things write I unto you, that ye sin not" (1 John 2:1) is not the true gospel. Any gospel that does not teach to "born again Christians" the message "Whosoever is born of God doth not commit sin" (1 John 3:9) is not the true gospel.

So, being on board with the true gospel, which is the intent of this book, and going forth teaching others the same is how we hasten the day. But with that in mind, the actual point being made is that we must do it patiently. We are to go forth "in all [things] approving ourselves as the ministers of God, in much patience" (2 Corinthians 6:4). We are to go forth and "warn them that are unruly, comfort the feebleminded, support the weak, be patient toward all [men]" (1 Thessalonians 5:14). "And the servant of the Lord must not strive; but be gentle unto all [men], apt to teach, patient" (2 Timothy 2:24).

Our goal is not to just make sure everyone hears the gospel by doing it in an impatient manner, just so the end could happen. We are to share the gospel in a manner that is inviting when the people we want to share it with are open. Saying, "Don't you know you're going to go to hell!" is not patiently working with people. That does not mean we never say such words for even Jesus got very pointed using words like "Satan" (Matthew 16:23), hypocrites (Matthew 23:13), and others towards the stubborn and stiff necked.

But we are also to be "patient waiting for Christ" (2 Thessalonians 3:5). That is because the faster the second coming happens, the final decisions for souls will occur. Ask yourself, "Are my relatives, my friends, my neighbors ready for the second coming?" If the answer is no, then you can see why we need to be patient for the event because "The Lord is not slack concerning his promise, as some men count slackness; but is longsuffering to us-ward, not willing that any should perish, but that all should come to repentance" (2 Peter 3:9). Of course there is going to come a time that such people will never come to a decision to be saved, and God shall cut time off.

OF THE SAINTS (14:12)

Here is a popular misunderstanding. Saints are not people of high rank in Heaven. Saints are living breathing people on earth. Even in the Old Testament, it is declared:

- "O love the LORD, all ye his saints: [for] the LORD preserveth the faithful, and plentifully rewardeth the proud doer" (Psalms 31:23).

- "O fear the LORD, ye his saints: for [there is] no want to them that fear him" (Psalms 34:9). Interestingly, Revelation 14:7 calls upon all to "fear God", as if today's Christians do not, which, in reality, they do not for the most part.

- "God is greatly to be feared in the assembly of the saints, and to be had in reverence of all [them that are] about him" (Psalms 89:7). Now there is part of the reason for the lack of "fear"; it is because there is a lack of reverence.

- "Ye that love the LORD, hate evil: he preserveth the souls of his saints; he delivereth them out of the hand of the wicked" (Psalms 97:10). And here we see the prerequisite to being a saint. We have to love the Lord and hate the evil. And Jesus said, "If ye love me, keep my commandments" (John 14:15).

But we continue on into the New Testament showing that saints are real people and the insight of what it means to be a saint.

- "To them that are sanctified in Christ Jesus, called [to be] saints" (1 Corinthians 1:2). Please note that this is not a verse that says "will be sanctified" but "are sanctified". Saints are holy people. They practice holiness, all of the time.

- "Do ye not know that the saints shall judge the world? and if the world shall be judged by you, are ye unworthy to judge the smallest matters? Know ye not that we shall judge angels? how much more things that pertain to this life? " (1 Corinthians 6:2-3) Here we see the saints are able to be judges. If we can judge even the angels, we ought, as it states, be able to judge right from wrong. And those doing the wrong ought to be judged as being on the wrong path and offer help to pull them on to the right path.

- "And he gave some, apostles; and some, prophets; and some, evangelists; and some, pastors and teachers; For the perfecting of the saints, for the work of the ministry, for the edifying of the body of Christ" (Ephesians 4:11-12). Saints seek for perfection and spend significant time with material from apostles, prophets, evangelists, pastors, and teachers beyond the once a week attendance at church. But that is what church is for: perfecting. It is not for evangelism.

- "And walk in love, as Christ also hath loved us, and hath given himself for us an offering and a sacrifice to God for a sweetsmelling savour. But fornication, and all uncleanness, or covetousness, let it not be once named among you, as becometh saints" (Ephesians 5:2-3). As we see, saints "ought himself also so to walk, even as he walked" (1 John 2:6), referring to Jesus, avoiding fornication, unleanness, and covetousness. And fornication is not just about having sex. It includes the sexual innuendos that ought to be avoided in conversation, exposing oneself to sexual content both visually and audibly, and not be enterainted by such. Uncleannes covers basically all sinning for sin is the ultimate unclean act. And coveting is specifically mentioned because it leads to many other sins including being sinful itself. None of that is part of the saints.

- "To the end he may stablish your hearts unblameable in holiness before God, even our Father, at the coming of our Lord Jesus Christ with all his saints" (1 Thessalonians 3:13). To be part of the saints at the second coming, we are to be established in our hearts to the point of not being blamable in the area of holiness, in other words, having holy thoughts all of the time and not once allowing evil into the heart.

HERE [ARE] THEY THAT KEEP THE COMMANDMENTS OF GOD (14:12)

Now already addressed with the saints in a separate verse, here we have confirmation that we indeed are to be keeping the commandments. We just finished six verses of warnings, statements, and even calls to be reading this verse as if to say, "Do you want to avoid the beast, the image, and the mark? Do you want to avoid the seven last plagues, which is the wrath of God? Do you want to fear God and worship Him properly? Do you want to be a saint? Then keep God's commandments as they read." Here is the survival guide:

- Exodus 20:2-3: "I [am] the LORD thy God, which have brought thee out of the land of Egypt, out of the house of bondage. Thou shalt have no other gods before me." No other beings are to be considered God or even be considered a god. And to whom we obey we attribute them as a god of our lives, including living for ourselves. But take note, God is the one that delivers us from the worldly ways of Egypt and delivers us from bondage, which Jesus said, "Verily, verily, I say unto you, Whosoever committeth sin is the servant of sin" (John 8:34). That was in response to the Pharisee's statement, "We be Abraham's seed, and were never in bondage to any man" (John 8:33). Even Jesus "shall save his people from their sins" (Matthew 1:21) and not "in our sins". Therefore, since God saves us from the world, from sinning, we ought to obey Him as God and not the world, not even ourselves. And by all means, we out to cease from our sins for "whosoever sinneth hath not seen him, neither known him" (1 John 3:6).

- Exodus 20:4-6: "Thou shalt not make unto thee any graven image, or any likeness [of any thing] that [is] in heaven above, or that [is] in the earth beneath, or that [is] in the water under the earth: Thou shalt not bow down thyself to them, nor serve them: for I the LORD thy God [am] a jealous God, visiting the iniquity of the fathers upon the children unto the third and fourth [generation] of them that hate me; And shewing mercy unto thousands of them that love me, and keep my commandments." No object should control our lives. People who rather watch television instead of attending church treat television as their god. Those that do not want to be involved in Bible studies, sharing the gospel with others because they work hard all day and when they get home it is relaxing time before bed are treating relaxing time as their god. Those that choose not to pay tithe and give offerings because they have things they want to buy, bills to pay, and other uses for their money are treating those other monetary distributions as their god.

- Exodus 20:7: "Thou shalt not take the name of the LORD thy God in vain; for the LORD will not hold him guiltless that taketh his name in vain." Anyone that claims to be a Christian and are carelessly sinning are taking His name in vain even worse than the person that thinks "Jesus" makes a good swear word.

- Exodus 20:8-11: "Remember the sabbath day, to keep it holy. Six days shalt thou labour, and do all thy work: But the seventh day [is] the sabbath of the LORD thy God: [in it] thou shalt not do any work, thou, nor thy son, nor thy daughter, thy manservant, nor thy maidservant, nor thy cattle, nor thy stranger that [is] within thy gates: For [in] six days the LORD made heaven and earth, the sea, and all that in them [is], and rested the seventh day: wherefore the LORD blessed the sabbath day, and hallowed it." In short, anyone that is not keeping the seventh day Sabbath from sundown Friday until sundown Saturday are setting themselves up to receive the Mark of the Beast, which is the opposite of the Seal of God. The seal or sign of God is defined as:

- "Verily my sabbaths ye shall keep: for it [is] a sign between me and you throughout your generations; that [ye] may know that I [am] the LORD that doth sanctify you" (Exodus 31:13).

- "I gave them my sabbaths, to be a sign between me and them, that they might know that I [am] the LORD that sanctify them" (Ezekiel 20:12).

- "Hallow my sabbaths; and they shall be a sign between me and you, that ye may know that I [am] the LORD your God" (Ezekiel 20:20).

The opposite of keeping the Sabbath is keeping a different day, such as Sunday or no day which acknowledges either the beast, who set Sunday worship up in the first place, or yourself as God. God simply says, "If thou turn away thy foot from the sabbath, [from] doing thy pleasure on my holy day; and call the sabbath a delight, the holy of the LORD, honourable; and shalt honour him, not doing thine own ways, nor finding thine own pleasure, nor speaking [thine own] words: Then shalt thou delight thyself in the LORD; and I will cause thee to ride upon the high places of the earth, and feed thee with the heritage of Jacob thy father: for the mouth of the LORD hath spoken [it]" (Isaiah 58:13-24).

- Exodus 20:12: "Honour thy father and thy mother: that thy days may be long upon the land which the LORD thy God giveth thee." And this includes authority of any sort, where we ought to "be subject to principalities and powers, to obey magistrates, to be ready to every good work" (Titus 3:1) but also keep in mind "We ought to obey God rather than men" (Acts 5:29) when they are in conflict.

- Exodus 20:13: "Thou shalt not kill." For [it is] impossible for those who were once enlightened, and have tasted of the heavenly gift, and were made partakers of the Holy Ghost, And have tasted the good word of God, and the powers of the world to come, If they shall fall away, to renew them again unto repentance; seeing they crucify to themselves the Son of God afresh, and put [him] to an open shame" (Hebrews 6:4-6). Do you really want to put those nails back into Jesus' hands. But the ultimate killing is to kill one's self, which is suicide. And it is the most deadliest activity on this planet for to not respond to God's calling is suicide. "Turn ye, turn ye from your evil ways; for why will ye die" (Ezekiel 33:11).

- Exodus 20:14: "Thou shalt not commit adultery." God says, "Ye adulterers and adulteresses, know ye not that the friendship of the world is enmity with God? whosoever therefore will be a friend of the world is the enemy of God" (James 4:4). So sex is not the only way to commit adultery. Simply pretending to be a Christian and living like the world is being guilty enough.

- Exodus 20:15: "Thou shalt not steal." "What? know ye not that your body is the temple of the Holy Ghost [which is] in you, which ye have of God, and ye are not your own? For ye are bought with a price: therefore glorify God in your body, and in your spirit, which are God's" (1 Corinthians 6:19-20). So mistreating these bodies by putting in God's garbage disposals, called unclean meats; by putting in alcohol, tobacco, even pumping up on caffeine; by listening and watching the filth; all of it is stealing away from God's possession, our bodies. And of course, "Will a man rob God? Yet ye have robbed me. But ye say, Wherein have we robbed thee? In tithes and offerings" (Malachi 3:8).

- Exodus 20:16: "Thou shalt not bear false witness against thy neighbour." So by being a Christian and acting like the world and when called upon it, then providing an unbiblical excuse is a false witness. Not living up to the Christian standard of what makes a disciplined disciple of Christ is how we bear false witness. By declaring that one is saved by grace and declaring that sin is irrelevant is not only a false witness but "turning the grace of our God into lasciviousness, and denying the only Lord God, and our Lord Jesus Christ" (Jude 1:4) for "in works they deny [him], being abominable, and disobedient, and unto every good work reprobate" (Titus 1:16).

- Exodus 20:17: "Thou shalt not covet thy neighbour's house, thou shalt not covet thy neighbour's wife, nor his manservant, nor his maidservant, nor his ox, nor his ass, nor any thing that [is] thy neighbour's." And the simple wish that one could participate in worldly things, almost wishing that God would have waited a while longer to call you from the world so you could have enjoyed it longer, is a form of coveting. Looking over the history of one's life of all the things one has given up and wish that they could experience it one last time is coveting.

AND THE FAITH OF JESUS (14:12)

This declaration that there are people with the faith of Jesus answers His own question that He proposed while walking the earth in human form, "Nevertheless when the Son of man cometh, shall he find faith on the earth?" (Luke 18:8) The answer is, "Yes!" They are the ones that have so much faith in the power of God that they believe He is able to keep them in obedience to the Ten Commandments. They are so saved by faith that they can say, "I will shew thee my faith by my works" (James 2:18) not to be saved but because He has saved. That includes keeping the seventh day Sabbath for they believe the Sabbath is not to be works of salvation but they take God at His word in which He said, "I gave them my sabbaths, to be a sign between me and them, that they might know that I [am] the LORD that sanctify them" (Ezekiel 20:12). God does the sanctifying, the ability to live in complete obedience!

Although "by grace are ye saved through faith; and that not of yourselves: [it is] the gift of God" (Ephesians 2:8), but "do we then make void the law through faith? God forbid: yea, we establish the law" (Romans 3:31).

So keeping the Ten Commandments does not discredit faith nor even grace "for sin shall not have dominion over you: for ye are not under the law, but under grace. What then? shall we sin, because we are not under the law, but under grace? God forbid" (Romans 6:14-15).

AND I HEARD A VOICE FROM HEAVEN SAYING UNTO ME, WRITE, BLESSED [ARE] THE DEAD WHICH DIE IN THE LORD FROM HENCEFORTH: YEA, SAITH THE SPIRIT, THAT THEY MAY REST FROM THEIR LABOURS; AND THEIR WORKS DO FOLLOW THEM (14:13)

So this smacks against a fallacy in which, when one dies, prayers and offerings can change a deceased person's location of Heaven, Hell, or purgatory. "It is appointed unto men once to die, but after this the judgment" (Hebrews 9:27). No amount of prayers from the living, no amount of payment, called indulgences, is going to speed up the release of a soul to Heaven or even change the destination. When a person dies in the Lord, they are Heaven bound "and shall come forth; they that have done good, unto the resurrection of life" (John 5:29). However, if one dies not in the Lord, then "they that have done evil, unto the resurrection of damnation" (John 5:29).

Now also notice that the dead are blessed if they died in the Lord. It does not say, "Blessed are those walking the streets of gold in Heaven." When a person dies, there are certain words of comfort and none other. "But I would not have you to be ignorant, brethren, concerning them which are asleep, that ye sorrow not, even as others which have no hope. For if we believe that Jesus died and rose again, even so them also which sleep in Jesus will God bring with him. For this we say unto you by the word of the Lord, that we which are alive [and] remain unto the coming of the Lord shall not prevent them which are asleep. For the Lord himself shall descend from heaven with a shout, with the voice of the archangel, and with the trump of God: and the dead in Christ shall rise first: Then we which are alive [and] remain shall be caught up together with them in the clouds, to meet the Lord in the air: and so shall we ever be with the Lord. Wherefore comfort one another with these words" (1 Thessalonians 4:13-18). Do not try to comfort people with thoughts that a departed one is in Heaven, is reincarnated, is anywhere but sleeping in Jesus.

AND AFTER THESE THINGS I SAW ANOTHER ANGEL COME DOWN FROM HEAVEN (18:1)

This is known as the fourth angel. He, or the messengers, do not show up until Revelation 17 is well underway. It is under the future supreme reign of the Antichrist, exceeding the reign they enjoyed during the one thousand two hundred and sixty years before receiving the "deadly wound" (Revelation 13:3). In the same verse, the wound is healed. Revelation 17:8 describes the wound and healing as, "The beast that thou sawest was, and is not; and shall ascend out of the bottomless pit, and go into perdition: and they that dwell on the earth shall wonder, whose names were not written in the book of life from the foundation of the world, when they behold the beast that was, and is not, and yet is."

On top of that, we get a further timeframe regarding the arrival of the fourth angel from Revelation 17:10-11, which says, "And there are seven kings: five are fallen, and one is, [and] the other is not yet come; and when he cometh, he must continue a short space. And the beast that was, and is not, even he is the eighth, and is of the seven, and goeth into perdition." So we have seven beasts in which one is wounded and then comes back as the eighth beast. In trying to figure out which of the seven is being referred to, it would not be the seventh beast because then it would just be the seventh beast having a healed wound. Rather it is one of the prior six.

With beasts representing kingdoms (Daniel 7:23, Revelation 16:10), we see five kingdoms having been fallen, one ruling, and another not yet on the scene. By the way, it is not by chance that the Bible makes mention of seven beasts representing seven kingdoms. There is the lion (Daniel 7:4) representing Babylon, the Bear (Daniel 7:5) representing the Medes and Persian, the leopard (Daniel 7:6) representing Greece, and an ugly beast with horns (Daniel 7:7) representing Rome. It is during the fourth beast in which John, Jesus, and the rest of the apostles lived.

Now the fifth beast that is referenced is the one in Revelation 13:1-2, which represents the Antichrist, which receives the deadly wound. That is the beast that will come back and be the eighth beast, as we have been saying all along. But there are still two more beasts. One of them is in Revelation 13:11 being the United States, starting out in 1778 or so with lamb like horn principles but ending as a forceful dragon-like beast. The dragon, representative of Satan (Revelation 12:9), which simply means that the same characteristics Satan posses will be prevalent and are.

Force is never God's ways yet, vaccines are being forced upon people; we are forced to marry homosexuals or face prison time; we are forced to make wedding cakes with gay couples symbolized on top or lose the business; we are forced to accept abortion practices; we are forced to pay for unethical procedures; we are forced to carry health care; and the list goes on, all of which our founding fathers avoided and yet has become prevalent in these past forty years or so. These things were unheard of while practicing full freedom of religion and full freedom of being a republic.

But is the United States the sixth or the seventh beast? We answer that with the study of Revelation 11, where it states, "The beast that ascendeth out of the bottomless pit shall make war against them, and shall overcome them, and kill them" (Revelation 11:7).

What context is the beast in? Reading Revelation 11:1-2, it says, "And there was given me a reed like unto a rod: and the angel stood, saying, Rise, and measure the temple of God, and the altar, and them that worship therein. But the court which is without the temple leave out, and measure it not; for it is given unto the Gentiles: and the holy city shall they tread under foot forty [and] two months."

When John is given a reed to measure, God is not looking for dimensions, rather a head count. Those inside the temple are saved. Those outside in the court are lost. This theme is repeated in Zechariah 2:1-4, "I lifted up mine eyes again, and looked, and behold a man with a measuring line in his hand. Then said I, Whither goest thou? And he said unto me, To measure Jerusalem, to see what [is] the breadth thereof, and what [is] the length thereof. And, behold, the angel that talked with me went forth, and another angel went out to meet him, And said unto him, Run, speak to this young man, saying, Jerusalem shall be inhabited [as] towns without walls for the multitude of men and cattle therein."

Now, John is not counting only literal Jews. The symbols of Revelation signify the real (Revelation 1:1). Those inside the temple, the body of Christ are identified in Romans 2:28-29, which says, "For he is not a Jew, which is one outwardly; neither [is that] circumcision, which is outward in the flesh: But he [is] a Jew, which is one inwardly; and circumcision [is that] of the heart, in the spirit, [and] not in the letter; whose praise [is] not of men, but of God."

What is a Gentile? Malachi 1:11 tells us, "For from the rising of the sun even unto the going down of the same my name [shall be] great among the Gentiles; and in every place incense [shall be] offered unto my name, and a pure offering: for my name [shall be] great among the heathen, saith the LORD of hosts."

What is a Heathen? Ezekiel 39:7 sheds light on this by saying, "So will I make my holy name known in the midst of my people Israel; and I will not [let them] pollute my holy name any more: and the heathen shall know that I [am] the LORD, the Holy One in Israel." Heathens are those that pollute God's holy name especially when they say, "Thus Saith the Lord" when the Lord did not say thus. How do they do that? They take only a verse or two and build a whole teaching on it or pass off what looks religious without any Bible reference whatsoever. That is why we need to have plenty of verses to support our beliefs. This why we also do not just use general definitions either.

To ask what a Gentile is, would have gotten the response of, "A non-Jew." And we would have missed any further study. On top of that, when we asked what a heathen was, again, if we did not get the Bible definition, we would have missed the specific point of God's name being polluted since most of us would have answered that a heathen is some ungodly person, even a person that lives in sin or does not know God. Although that is a correct definition, it was not the definition we needed to unlock the mystery.

Now continuing in Revelation 11:2 notice that the same time period is again identified, of that being forty-two months, which calculates to one thousand two hundred and sixty days remembering a day is symbolic of a year (Numbers 14:34 and Ezekiel 4:6).

What happens during those years? Revelation 11:3 says, "And I will give [power] unto my two witnesses, and they shall prophesy a thousand two hundred [and] threescore days, clothed in sackcloth."

What is meant by sackcloth? Genesis 37:32-34 tells us, "And they sent the coat of [many] colours, and they brought [it] to their father; and said, This have we found: know now whether it [be] thy son's coat or no. And he knew it, and said, [It is] my son's coat; an evil beast hath devoured him; Joseph is without doubt rent in pieces. And Jacob rent his clothes, and put sackcloth upon his loins, and mourned for his son many days." It is a time of mourning. That means the two witnesses are witnessing during a time of great sadness, which today is known as the Dark Ages. This is the period of time when anyone caught with a Bible verse would have been burned at the stake. Unfortunately, people today do not appreciate the Word of God. They do not have time for the Word of God. They are not willing to stand up for the truth. It must break God's heart when people utter those words and act in those ways because during the Dark Ages, people went to their deaths over the Word of God.

Now, here is an important question. Do you know anybody one thousand two hundred and sixty years old? No, of course not. That eliminates human beings as the two witnesses.

So what are the two witnesses then? Revelation 11:4 say, "These are the two olive trees, and the two candlesticks standing before the God of the earth." Well that does not help much.

What does that mean? Zechariah 4:1-6 "And the angel that talked with me came again, and waked me, as a man that is wakened out of his sleep, And said unto me, What seest thou? And I said, I have looked, and behold a candlestick all [of] gold, with a bowl upon the top of it, and his seven lamps thereon, and seven pipes to the seven lamps, which [are] upon the top thereof: And two olive trees by it, one upon the right [side] of the bowl, and the other upon the left [side] thereof. So I answered and spake to the angel that talked with me, saying, What [are] these, my lord? Then the angel that talked with me answered and said unto me, Knowest thou not what these be? And I said, No, my lord. Then he answered and spake unto me, saying, This [is] the word of the LORD unto Zerubbabel, saying, Not by might, nor by power, but by my spirit, saith the LORD of hosts." They represent the Spirit of God. And what did the Spirit do? 2 Peter 1:21 tells us, "For the prophecy came not in old time by the will of man: but holy men of God spake [as they were] moved by the Holy Ghost."

That would refer to the Bible as being the witnesses. What does the Bible say about that in the context of "the two candlesticks" (Revelation 11:4)? Psalms 119:105 says, "Thy word [is] a lamp unto my feet, and a light unto my path."

And what are the two olive trees? Zechariah 4:11-14 "Then answered I, and said unto him, What [are] these two olive trees upon the right [side] of the candlestick and upon the left [side] thereof? And I answered again, and said unto him, What [be these] two olive branches which through the two golden pipes empty the golden [oil] out of themselves? And he answered me and said, Knowest thou not what these [be]? And I said, No, my lord. Then said he, These [are] the two anointed ones, that stand by the Lord of the whole earth." And focusing on the word "anointed", note the experience of Christ where Luke 4:18-21 tells us, "The Spirit of the Lord [is] upon me, because he hath anointed me to preach the gospel to the poor; he hath sent me to heal the brokenhearted, to preach deliverance to the captives, and recovering of sight to the blind, to set at liberty them that are bruised, To preach the acceptable year of the Lord. And he closed the book, and he gave [it] again to the minister, and sat down. And the eyes of all them that were in the synagogue were fastened on him. And he began to say unto them, This day is this scripture fulfilled in your ears." And what is Jesus described as? John 1:1-2, 14 says, "In the beginning was the Word, and the Word was with God, and the Word was God. The same was in the beginning with God. And the Word was made flesh, and dwelt among us, (and we beheld his glory, the glory as of the only begotten of the Father,) full of grace and truth." In the beginning of the whole earth was the word and will continue to the end.

The two witnesses are symbolic of the Word of God or the Bible, specifically, the Old and New Testament. Now you may ask how that is possible. Well, first we realize that the two witnesses are witnessing against a false system. The book of Daniel in the Old Testament clearly points out the false system while the book of Revelation in the New Testament also identifies the false system.

But many say the two witnesses are Elijah and Moses come back to life. How is that explained? In reading Revelation 11:5-6, the Bible does say, "And if any man will hurt them, fire proceedeth out of their mouth, and devoureth their enemies: and if any man will hurt them, he must in this manner be killed. These have power to shut heaven, that it rain not in the days of their prophecy: and have power over waters to turn them to blood, and to smite the earth with all plagues, as often as they will." It is true that under Elijah, the heavens were shut up and did not rain. Also true is that under Moses, many plagues including that of blood were poured out. But where is the source of these things? God and not man. They were just servants. How did Elijah know to warn the people that it would not rain? He was proclaiming a "Thus Saith the Lord" (2 Chronicles 21:12). And Moses did the same thing. Many times he told pharaoh, "Thus saith the LORD God of Israel, Let my people go" (Exodus 5:1). And the greatest opportunity that we have today is to hold a book full of verses containing "Thus Saith the Lord." All we have to do is submit to His will instead of our own. And the teachings of the New Testament are well supported by the Old, and the teachings of the Old Testament are well supported by the New. They are inseparable.

If that is not sufficient, think of it another way. Moses represents the law while Elijah represents the prophets being one of the greatest prophets to live. And that phrase is found throughout the Bible. To reject the law and the prophets brought great calamity. Being of the way of the Gentiles, it is said, "among the Gentiles: the law [is] no [more]; her prophets also find no vision from the LORD" (Lamentations 2:9). "Yea, they made their hearts [as] an adamant stone, lest they should hear the law, and the words which the LORD of hosts hath sent in his spirit by the former prophets: therefore came a great wrath from the LORD of hosts" (Zechariah 7:12). Even Jesus said, "Think not that I am come to destroy the law, or the prophets: I am not come to destroy, but to fulfil" (Matthew 5:17). Even the apostle Paul was on board with the law and the prophets. "And when they had appointed him a day, there came many to him into [his] lodging; to whom he expounded and testified the kingdom of God, persuading them concerning Jesus, both out of the law of Moses, and [out of] the prophets, from morning till evening" (Acts 28:23).

And who appeared with Jesus when He was transfigured? "There appeared unto them Moses and Elias talking with him" (Matthew 17:3). That is because Jesus had said, "These [are] the words which I spake unto you, while I was yet with you, that all things must be fulfilled, which were written in the law of Moses, and [in] the prophets, and [in] the psalms, concerning me" (Luke 24:44).

Further, did you know that according to 2 Samuel 1:17, Jasher was given power to shut up the heavens and it rained not? According to Amos 4:7, Amos also received the same power. Haggai 1:10-11 and Jeremiah 14:1-4 also state that Haggai and Jeremiah prophesied during a time it was prophesied not to rain. And many of the prophets saw plagues under their time of prophesying including Zechariah who saw both plagues and lack of rain (Zechariah 14:17-18).

To settle the issue that Elijah is not expected to show up physically, let us ask Jesus how He understood this? Matthew 17:11-13 tells us, "And Jesus answered and said unto them, Elias truly shall first come, and restore all things. But I say unto you, That Elias is come already, and they knew him not, but have done unto him whatsoever they listed. Likewise shall also the Son of man suffer of them. Then the disciples understood that he spake unto them of John the Baptist." So Jesus conveyed that it is not literal but spiritual. This is further confirmed in Luke 1:17, which states, "And he shall go before him in the spirit and power of Elias, to turn the hearts of the fathers to the children, and the disobedient to the wisdom of the just; to make ready a people prepared for the Lord." How did they know Elijah was to come? Malachi 4:5-6 says, "Behold, I will send you Elijah the prophet before the coming of the great and dreadful day of the LORD: And he shall turn the heart of the fathers to the children, and the heart of the children to their fathers, lest I come and smite the earth with a curse."

So after they have witnessed, what happens next? Revelation 11:7 says, "And when they shall have finished their testimony, the beast that ascendeth out of the bottomless pit shall make war against them, and shall overcome them, and kill them." A beast tries to kill them. How does one try to kill the Word of God? By physical destruction as well as making it seem like a book that cannot be trusted. Take for instance what was happening at the close of the

1700's in France. Napoleon denied the existence of God. He tried to exterminate the Bible and its teachings. He even set up a ten day week because a seven day week acknowledges the existence of God. Eventually, the ten day week would be forgotten. This same Napoleon is the one that sends his general into the Vatican to dethrone the pope for the pope was supposedly the representative of God and therefore to dethrone the pope was to complete the attack on God.

Now regarding the rejection of the seven day creation week, think about it for a moment. We have a scientific reason for a year right? That is how long it takes for the earth to go around the sun. We also know why there are thirty days in a month. It takes that long for the moon to go around the earth. We also know why there is a 24-hour day. It takes that long for the earth to rotate one cycle on its axis. But why do we have a week consisting of seven days? There is no scientific reason. If man had created a week, he would have picked something divisible into a month such as 6 days, 5 days, 3 days, or even 10 days, but not 7.

Also at this time, to try to make the Bible less trustworthy Satan used various scholars to write content against it. "Paine wrote the first part of Age of Reason (1794), a deistic statement of his religious views. All Paine's works reflect his belief in natural reason and natural rights, political equality, tolerance, civil liberties, and the dignity of man", 1996 Grolier Multimedia Encyclopedia. This led to putting reason above God. When it infiltrated the Christian world, it had a devastating effect. Christians were reasoning things of the Bible away such as creation week, the flood, and much more.

Is there any record of trying to kill the Bible physically? "But did France make war on the Bible? She did! And on November 26, 1793 a decree passed the French Assembly preventing the Bible. And under that decree the Bible was gathered and burned and every possible mark of contempt was heaped upon them. And all the institutions of the Bible were abolished. Baptism and Communion were abolished, the being of God was denied, and death pronounced as being an eternal sleep. The goddess of reason was set up in the person of a vile woman and publicly worshipped." Journal of Paris, 1793, No. 318. [Quoted in Buchez-Roux, Collection of Parliamentary History, volume 30, pages 200, 201.]

Now, how is the location of the prophecy identified? Revelation 11:8 tells us by saying, "And their dead bodies [shall lie] in the street of the great city, which spiritually is called Sodom and Egypt, where also our Lord was crucified." The location is identified as Sodom, Egypt, and Jerusalem, which is where our Lord was crucified, right? Wrong. A key word is required to unlock the single location and that word is "spiritually". This place is identified as having a spirit like that of Sodom, a spirit like that in Egypt, and a spirit that was present at the crucifixion of Jesus.

So, what was Sodom known for? Jude 1:7 explicitly tells us, "Even as Sodom and Gomorrha, and the cities about them in like manner, giving themselves over to fornication, and going after strange flesh, are set forth for an example, suffering the vengeance of eternal fire." Therefore, I would like to ask this as kind as possible, but what country is well known for its illicit sexual acts? Here is a hint. During World War I and II, it was one of the most preferred countries by GI soldiers. France is the answer.

What was Egypt known for? Exodus 5:2 tells us, "And Pharaoh said, Who [is] the LORD, that I should obey his voice to let Israel go? I know not the LORD, neither will I let Israel go." Under Napoleon, France denied the existence of God and still has its affects today. Though they claim to be a religious country, less than ten percent go to church.

What is meant by "where our Lord was crucified?" Spiritually, this refers to the killing of everything that had a religious connotation to it. Every priest, nun, minister, or anybody associated with religion was executed during these times. In studying the beheading of the king and queen of France during the peasant uprisings, most of the religious world was very corrupt especially in France including both Protestants and Catholics. The peasants finally had enough and revolted.

Before we continue onto the next verse, there was another reference to who the two witnesses are. Notice that "their dead bodies [shall lie] in the street." Does the Bible and the Bible alone identify what lies in the street? Isaiah 59:14 answers with saying, "And judgment is turned away backward, and justice standeth afar off: for truth is fallen in the street, and equity cannot enter." It is the truth that lies in the streets. Remember, truth is found in three locations: "Thy law [is] the truth" (Psalm 119:142), "Jesus saith unto him, I am the way, the truth, and the life" (John 14:6), and "Thy word is truth" (John 17:17). Of all three locations, only the Word is most applicable and also affirming.

How long will the Word remain dead in the streets? Revelation 11:9-10 says, "And they of the people and kindreds and tongues and nations shall see their dead bodies three days and an half, and shall not suffer their dead bodies to be put in graves. And they that dwell upon the earth shall rejoice over them, and make merry, and shall send gifts one to another; because these two prophets tormented them that dwelt on the earth." Now applying God's year for a day principle, a three and a half-year period would pass. And on November 26, 1793, France voted the Bible and religion out. After three years of anarchy, France reconsidered. It was brought up during the assembly in January 1797. Now that would only be three years. God said it would be three and a half years. So for some mysterious reason, the subject was tabled until June 7, 1797, which is the fulfillment of the prophecy.

What happened to the two witnesses after this period of time? Revelation 11:11-13 says, "And after three days and an half the Spirit of life from God entered into them, and they stood upon their feet; and great fear fell upon them which saw them. And they heard a great voice from heaven saying unto them, Come up hither. And they ascended up to heaven in a cloud; and their enemies beheld them. And the same hour was there a great earthquake, and the tenth part of the city fell, and in the earthquake were slain of men seven thousand: and the remnant were affrighted, and gave glory to the God of heaven." The Bible would be well appreciated. Notice the following quote: "Beginning in 1795 and expanding tremendously through the 1840s, a new revival known as the Second Great Awakening appeared. Evangelists such as Charles G. Finney emphasized free will, divine forgiveness for all, and the need of each person to freely accept or reject salvation" The 1995 Grolier Multimedia Encyclopedia. An American born movement, by the early 1800's, the Second Great Awakening stormed Europe.

"The model for most Bible societies, the British and Foreign Bible Society, was founded in 1804" The 1995 Grolier Multimedia Encyclopedia. Ever since this movement, there has never been a repressing of the Word to the same degree. In fact, the movement of taking the Word around the world finds its roots during this period of time.

One final word on the two witnesses. In regards to Elijah, the Bible says, "And it came to pass, as they still went on, and talked, that, behold, [there appeared] a chariot of fire, and horses of fire, and parted them both asunder; and Elijah went up by a whirlwind into heaven" (2 Kings 2:11). And as for Moses, "And Moses [was] an hundred and twenty years old when he died" (Deuteronomy 34:7), "Yet Michael the archangel, when contending with the devil he disputed about the body of Moses, durst not bring against him a railing accusation, but said, The Lord rebuke thee" (Jude 1:9). So Elijah never saw death and Moses saw death and was resurrected. Although everyone ought to do as God asks without question, do we really think that after appearing with Jesus on the mount, living in Heaven both beforehand as well as since then that God would say, "Elijah and Moses, I need you to go down and be witnesses, but there is a catch. You are going to die and lay dead in the streets for a while, but don't worry, you will be resurrected again and people will be in awe"? Do we really think God is going to reward Elijah and Moses with such? The answer is no. We have to remember that Revelation is a "signified" book. It is full of symbols representing other meanings.

So, which kingdom is the beast that was released? According to Revelation 11:7, the beast is released during the time that the Bible was cast down and belief in God was thrown out. We ask, what one word means "No belief in God"? Atheism. And what country gave birth to atheism? France in the late 1700's? George Hegel, born 1770 and died 1831, mixed atheism with the Bible. He reduced the Bible to simple stories and fables. Charles Darwin (1809-1882) took those writings and formulated the theory of evolution and in 1859 released the theory on the Origin of Species, which directly goes against the true origin. If there is no God, we need to answer the question: Where did we come from? Sigmund Freud (1865-1939) instituted sexual permissiveness. If there is no God, there is no consequence for our pleasures. Karl Marx (1818-1883) introduced Communism. Note that Hegel's theories were born during the atheistic period and influenced Karl Marx whose theories developed into a country's beliefs and ways. This is substantiated by the following quote: "[The] Germanic philosophical influence, that eventually contributed to statism and economic cartels in both countries, colored the political philosophy of American reformers of the period. People like John Dewey and Charles Beard were influenced early be George Hegel and Karl Marx. Hebert Croly was influenced by the French Positivist, Auguste Comte, who had some similarity to Hegel." (Chambelain, John, Farewell to Retorm, Pages 202, 203 and 230; Peter Smith, Gloucester, Ma., 1958).

All of them have greatly influenced our world that even today there is no way, short of the second coming, to right all the wrongs.

Now, what is the significance of Karl Marx? His writings lead to the most atheistic country known as Russia and its system known as Marxism or Communism. This system seemed unstoppable. There was the red threat of the 1940's and 1950's. The 1960's brought the system to our back door during the missile crisis. It seemed that there was no way to stop it. But God said it would not last and it came to an end so abruptly in 1991 that historians are still baffled. So one could say that France is the sixth head or connect it with Russia, of which the ideology was born around 1797 and lasted until 1991.

That means the United States is the seventh head and correctly so. What country is considered the lone super power, the world's police, the world's influencer? The United States is the answer. But get this, Revelation 17:10 says, "And there are seven kings: five are fallen, and one is, [and] the other is not yet come; and when he cometh, he must continue a short space." All other kingdoms are normal ruling kingdoms, but the United States will not rule supremely for a long period of time. It will be shorter than France/Russia, Vatican, Rome, Greece, Medo-Persians, and even Babylon, which ruled only sixty-nine years. That means the United States will lose its supreme power within sixty-nine years. And understand this, the clock has been ticking since January 1, 1992, but do realize this also, and that is if the United States was to be the lone superpower for sixty-eight years, would that be a significant time-frame to declare that "he must continue a short space"? We suggest not. We would suggest a number far shorter than sixty-nine years to be considered short. Is sixty years warranted of such a "short time" title? God only knows. Is it fifty? Is it forty? Is it half, like thirty-five, or even thirty? Again, only God knows.

But as of 2016, we have already entered into twenty-four of those years. At this point, can we look around and see any signs of crumbling? Oh yes we do, especially financially.

- "Major Economic Concerns Still Facing the United States", November 8, 2015.

- "United States Is Like 'Greece On Steroids'", June 30, 2015.

- "Greece-Like Crisis 'Could Happen To The United States' In 10 Years", June 30, 2015.

- "Can the global gloom sink the U.S. economy?", August 29, 2015.

Now someone more than likely is going to say, "Wait! John said in his day, five beasts were fallen. In his day, only three were fallen, and he was living in the fourth being Rome!" Although it is true that John penned, "And there are seven kings: five are fallen, and one is, [and] the other is not yet come; and when he cometh, he must continue a short space" (Revelation 17:10), we must read the entire chapter in context. According to, Revelation 17:3, the Bible says, "So he carried me away in the spirit into the wilderness" (Revelation 17:3).

What timeframe is known as the wilderness? According to Revelation 12:14, we are told, "And to the woman were given two wings of a great eagle, that she might fly into the wilderness, into her place, where she is nourished for a time, and times, and half a time, from the face of the serpent." The wilderness time is when the church was in hiding. It is the one thousand two hundred and sixty year period ending in 1798. In other words, John's perspective changed because in vision he was transported in time to witness the fall of the fifth beast, papal Rome, which means the fourth one was also fallen, being pagan Rome. The period of time discussed regarding France happened at the close of the wilderness time and so John could state that "one is", being atheism born in France and propagated by Russia.

So the timeframe of the fourth angel's appearance ought to be getting ready for when the United States does suffer the collapse, but still exist as a nation, the eighth beast comes onto the scene to finish out the time remaining in the world. It is during that time that the fourth angel gives the loudest of all cries, joining with the other three angels, all of which represents the last day people that have the true gospel going forth with the saving messages.

HAVING GREAT POWER (18:1)

Now this fourth angel, representing people that have the correct gospel as outlined in Revelation 14, have great power. The unconverted will think military, political, maybe even economical, but all of those would be incorrect. And no, these people do not become super humans either.

There is but one power that God grants to people. It is "According as his divine power hath given unto us all things that [pertain] unto life and godliness, through the knowledge of him that hath called us to glory and virtue: Whereby are given unto us exceeding great and precious promises: that by these ye might be partakers of the divine nature, having escaped the corruption that is in the world through lust" (2 Peter 1:3-4). God grants divine power to be used so as to overcome every single sin, every single temptation, every single distraction that this world has to offer.

So that means that the last generation on earth will not only be able to preach the victorious gospel but as a group be able to proclaim it. Let us face it, today, every denomination is full of mixed people, like the days of the Israelites. They were called the "mixed multitude" (Exodus 12:38). You could say that these are the ones that see the way of God, obey as much as they can of the way of God, but are not converted in the heart to the way of God. So when things get difficult, these are the first ones to complain and encouraged to return to their old life. "And the mixt multitude that [was] among them fell a lusting: and the children of Israel also wept again, and said, Who shall give us flesh to eat? We remember the fish, which we did eat in Egypt freely; the cucumbers, and the melons, and the leeks, and the onions, and the garlick: But now our soul [is] dried away: [there is] nothing at all, beside this manna, [before] our eyes" (Numbers 11:4-6).

In the church, there are true people of God who are serious about the standards and are trying, by the grace of God, to live by those standards, and no, they are not legalists. They are people who simply are doing what Jesus said to do. "If ye love me, keep my commandments" (John 14:15).

Then there are those that agree with the message, but do not see how anyone can have complete victory, and so they just make sure they do not do the really big sins while excusing what they class as little sins as being not so important. Unfortunately there is not a scripture that points to God says, "Do not kill but it is Okay to be angry." In fact, Jesus said quite the opposite. "Ye have heard that it was said by them of old time, Thou shalt not kill; and whosoever shall kill shall be in danger of the judgment: But I say unto you, That whosoever is angry with his brother without a cause shall be in danger of the judgment" (Matthew 5:21-22).

Then we have those that join because it sounds good, or their friends attend there, or family members are there, or it is an expectation by somebody. They just go through the motions, putting in their obligation, but never making a commitment. Do not ask these people to get involved because they will probably not.

And there are probably other groups in the church, but these are the main ones, yet God says, "Christ also loved the church, and gave himself for it; That he might sanctify and cleanse it with the washing of water by the word, That he might present it to himself a glorious church, not having spot, or wrinkle, or any such thing; but that it should be holy and without blemish" (Ephesians 5:25-27). Now that is not a second coming clean up; that is a prior to the second coming clean up, just as Revelation 18:1 is stating. And it is God's desire "That ye might walk worthy of the Lord unto all pleasing, being fruitful in every good work, and increasing in the knowledge of God; Strengthened with all might, according to his glorious power, unto all patience and long-suffering with joyfulness" (Colossians 1:10-11). And it is no credit to ourselves to be in this holy condition for "unto him that is able to do exceeding abundantly above all that we ask or think, according to the power that worketh in us, Unto him [be] glory in the church by Christ Jesus throughout all ages, world without end" (Ephesians 3:20-21). And it is "according to the gift of the grace of God given unto me by the effectual working of his power" (Ephesians 3:7).

Daniel even foresaw this event when he wrote, "Many shall be purified, and made white, and tried; but the wicked shall do wickedly: and none of the wicked shall understand; but the wise shall understand" (Daniel 12:10). To be made purified and white will happen while the wicked are still doing wicked things. So that is not the second coming. That is prior.

But here is the very sad part. The wicked are not the murderers, adulterers, liars, and thieves. People are being prepared today as Christians to be part of the wicked. That is because so many Christians are "Having a form of godliness, but denying the power thereof" (2 Timothy 3:5). And while they are denying the power, despite claiming to be full of the Holy Spirit, they are not, "For our gospel came not unto you in word only, but also in power, and in the Holy Ghost" (1 Thessalonians 1:5). These need to realize that "the kingdom of God [is] not in word, but in power" (1 Corinthians 4:20).

Now this is why the group has power. It will eventually be a group of people that have no hypocrites among them, no practicing sinners, no uncommitted Christians. This will be in stark contrast to all the other Christians who have no power or victory over sin, who excuse sin, who call any effort to gaining the upper hand upon sin as works of salvation thinking that it is all about faith and grace without works. God says, "Your faith should not stand in the wisdom of men, but in the power of God" (1 Corinthians 2:5).

To those that say, "Impossible!" Not only is all things possible with God, Christ "is able to keep you from falling, and to present [you] faultless before the presence of his glory with exceeding joy, To the only wise God our Saviour, [be] glory and majesty, dominion and power, both now and ever" (Jude 1:24-25). These are the ones "who are kept by the power of God through faith unto salvation ready to be revealed in the last time" (1 Peter 1:5). You see, it is all about the "gospel according to the power of God" (2 Timothy 1:8), "For the preaching of the cross is to them that perish foolishness; but unto us which are saved it is the power of God" (1 Corinthians 1:18).

And to all that say, "Just believe", well, "Ye do err, not knowing the scriptures, nor the power of God" (Matthew 22:29). God says, "For I am not ashamed of the gospel of Christ: for it is the power of God unto salvation to every one that believeth" (Romans 1:16-). There is real power in a Christian; not this weak undisciplined fake stuff for Jesus gave "as many as received him, to them gave he power to become the sons of God, [even] to them that believe on his name" (John 1:12).

Now while God is giving those with "one mind" of Christ the super natural power to live holy, sanctified lives, the world is providing human power to the Antichrist and they too have "one mind". "These have one mind, and shall give their power and strength unto the beast" (Revelation 17:13). That is because "none of the wicked shall understand; but the wise shall understand" (Daniel 12:10). They do not understand the power of God.

They do not understand the difference between obedience required of God to demonstrate a saved life as opposed to what they see as working one's way to Heaven. They do not understand how going along with the government because they are the government instead of where conflicts are, choosing the way of God. They do not understand how acts of kindness can be wrong. They do not understand how their preachers and teachers could be wrong and why they have to know the Word of God for themselves when their pastor has a degree from a religious school.

"God of Israel [is] he that giveth strength and power unto [his] people" (Psalms 68:35). Even Jesus said, "Ye shall receive power, after that the Holy Ghost is come upon you: and ye shall be witnesses unto me both in Jerusalem, and in all Judaea, and in Samaria, and unto the uttermost part of the earth" (Acts 1:8). What type of witnesses are we if we are still sinning and blatantly too! "Finally, my brethren, be strong in the Lord, and in the power of his might" (Ephesians 6:10).

Basically, there is nothing that speaks more powerfully than an obedient, commandment keeping Christian.

AND THE EARTH WAS LIGHTENED WITH HIS GLORY (18:1)

When it comes to God's glory, there is the physical presence of God and there is the representation of God. Seeing that the physical manifestation of God's glory does not happen until the second coming, this part of the verse must then refer to the representation because we are "Looking for that blessed hope, and the glorious appearing of the great God and our Saviour Jesus Christ" (Titus 2:13). That is because if God were to physically show His glory ahead of time that would take away from the event of the second coming in its glory. Besides, Jesus said, "Hereafter shall ye see the Son of man sitting on the right hand of power, and coming in the clouds of heaven" (Matthew 26:64), meaning in the context, the next time Jesus will appear is at the second coming, not sooner.

Representation means that God's people give recognized glory to God. This may be in the obvious form of singing, praying, and even in use of His Word as "the centurion saw what was done, he glorified God, saying, Certainly this was a righteous man" (Luke 23:47), referring to Jesus, but as Jesus said, "Ye are the light of the world" (Matthew 5:14), God's people give glory to Him by living lives representing His holy life.

The unconverted, especially those that have "one mind" on the side of Antichrist or the "Spirit of Antichrist" in the end "repented not to give him glory" (Revelation 16:9). So the opposite of those not giving glory to Him is that God does have a people on earth that give Him the glory, and this is what lightens the earth. In other words, the gospel going around the world for the end to come (Matthew 24:14) is not only a matter of preaching it but living it. There will be a number of people that believe the gospel power to deliver from all sins, not just permit entrance into Heaven for "unto the glory of God by us" (2 Corinthians 1:20). God's glory is revealed by us. We have an active role showing what God has done. When we sin, we show God to be weak. When we live in obedience, we glorify God's power in our lives. Now do not get me wrong, "all have sinned, and come short of the glory of God" (Romans 3:23), and it is sad that we have all done that. So now, "whether therefore ye eat, or drink, or whatsoever ye do, do all to the glory of God" (1 Corinthians 10:31). And remember, "ye are bought with a price: therefore glorify God in your body, and in your spirit, which are God's" (1 Corinthians 6:20).

Besides, what was the call of the first angel? "Fear God, and give glory to him" (Revelation 14:7). Evidently by the time the fourth angel shows up, symbolic of the very last day people of God who will see translation and not see death, have responded positively to the message and chose to reverence Him and live in complete obedience. Through these messages, God "hath called us to glory and virtue" (2 Peter 1:3), represent Him without a moments representation of Satan in our lives. Even the Bible says, "Having your conversation honest among the Gentiles: that, whereas they speak against you as evildoers, they may by [your] good works, which they shall behold, glorify God in the day of visitation" (1 Peter 2:12). So there will be people who positively respond to the messages.

In fact, that is the purpose of the gospel for the Bible confirms our understanding by saying, "Whereunto he called you by our gospel, to the obtaining of the glory of our Lord Jesus Christ" (2 Thessalonians 2:14). It also says, "That the name of our Lord Jesus Christ may be glorified in you, and ye in him, according to the grace of our God and the Lord Jesus Christ" (2 Thessalonians 1:12). So God's glory is revealed as we respond to the calling of the gospel , which calls us to live holy lives for by "ministering the gospel of God, that the offering up of the Gentiles might be acceptable, being sanctified by the Holy Ghost" (Romans 15:16). The gospel leads to a sanctified or holy life here and now.

We also glorify God through handling difficult situation with hope in God for "if [any man suffer] as a Christian, let him not be ashamed; but let him glorify God on this behalf" (1 Peter 4:16). So yes, there will be a decree ordering obedience to the Mark of the Beast versus the Seal of God, and yes that those who have "one mind" against Christ will "cause that as many as would not worship the image of the beast should be killed" (Revelation 13:15), but it will be through those situations that true Christians will shine the brightest. Instead of kicking and screaming and being uncooperative, they will be like Stephen who said, "I see the heavens opened, and the Son of man standing on the right hand of God" (Acts 7:56). "And they stoned Stephen, calling upon [God], and saying, Lord Jesus, receive my spirit. And he kneeled down, and cried with a loud voice, Lord, lay not this sin to their charge. And when he had said this, he fell asleep" (Acts 7:59-60). Even the early Christians, "they loved not their lives unto the death" (Revelation 12:11). "For what glory [is it], if, when ye be buffeted for your faults, ye shall take it patiently? but if, when ye do well, and suffer [for it], ye take it patiently, this [is] acceptable with God" (1 Peter 2:20). And the reason for this suffering is "That the trial of your faith, being much more precious than of gold that perisheth, though it be tried with fire, might be found unto praise and honour and glory at the appearing of Jesus Christ" (1 Peter 1:7).

AND HE CRIED MIGHTILY WITH A STRONG VOICE (18:2)

Notice this symbolic angel cries both mightily and strongly. The other angels were just loud. According to Psalms 68:33, the Bible says that God "doth send out his voice, [and that] a mighty voice" (Psalms 68:33). So God is specially backing this group as opposed to any group prior.

Today, there does not seem to be any might with what Christians teach. The evidence is found in the fact that atheism is growing; church attendance is dwindling; and what appears to be Christian is not what Christ taught. There is hardly conviction today. That is because Christians are too distracted with all that is around, both good and bad. Yes, Christians have to provide a living. Yes, Christians have to take care of the home. Yes, Christians have to tend to children or even elderly parents. Yes, there are bills to pay, places to go, and demands all around. Those are all the acceptable things.

The unacceptable is when God impresses the feeling, "I have a Bible study I want you to attend" and the reply is, "Any night but my TV night God!" God may impress the need to be going to church on Sabbath but instead, one chooses to sleep in. Television, news outlets, music all are distractions that are not in a good way, and in many cases, even unacceptable. Christians are so distracted by standing up against gun control, against abortion on demand, against invading another country, against political candidates, against the homosexual movement, against the aggressive version of women's liberation, against government mandated health care, and many other political positions. But all, both the good and the bad, distractions are not going to matter in the very last days.

First off, we will be dealing with "the time of Jacob's trouble" (Jeremiah 30:7). At the same time and even earlier, we will be endowed by God to go forth as the fourth angel through the power of the "latter rain" (James 5:7), which will be the modern version of Pentecost. We are to "Ask ye of the LORD rain in the time of the latter rain" (Zechariah 10:1). "Rejoice in the LORD your God: for he hath given you the former rain" (which was the Pentecostal outpouring of the Holy Spirit in the day of the apostles) "moderately, and he will cause to come down for you the rain, the former rain, and the latter rain" (Joel 2:23) during the last days. God, through the Holy Spirit, "shall come unto us as the rain, as the latter [and] former rain unto the earth" (Hosea 6:3).

So, "let us now fear the LORD our God, that giveth rain, both the former and the latter, in his season: he reserveth unto us the appointed weeks of the harvest" (Jeremiah 5:24). Please note that only those that "fear the Lord" will receive the rain of the Holy Spirit. Interestingly, once again, Revelation 14:7 calls us to do just that, "fear God". That is not by coincidence.

And take note as well the timing of the latter rain being for the time of the harvest. That is the last feast day, according to Leviticus 23, which ushers in the second coming. So before Jesus returns, not only do we have people actually keeping the commandments without blemish but they go forth with the latter rain of the Holy Spirit in such a mighty and strong manner speaking louder by example as well as in preaching than any sermon alone could ever provide.

SAYING, BABYLON THE GREAT IS FALLEN, IS FALLEN (18:2)

With this specific message being repeated from the second angel implies several things. One, when God repeats Himself, it is serious. So the notion of dismissing any of this as people just making mistakes, like seeing verses just a bit differently, is not the attitude we ought to be having. We should be getting out from underneath the Antichrist and the Spirit of Antichrist as quickly as possible as if our lives depended upon it. In fact, they do, as the rest of the verses reveal.

The second implication is that at this point it should be obvious that the points already covered in identifying the

Antichrist becomes unarguable that the people will have to be willing to ignore those points to show allegiance to the Antichrist, which unfortunately many will. A person could have a nasty, mean, obnoxious relative that no one likes to be around but be not a relative and say anything to the family about how nasty, mean, and obnoxious that person is and they all of a sudden come out defending that person. The same is true with the Antichrist. What some people see as a saving message, others see as attacks. Although the statements are true, the thought is, "How dare you pick on such a nice, helpful group of people!"

AND IS BECOME THE HABITATION OF DEVILS (18:2)

Now that is not literal devils. No one is calling the Vatican or its staff devils. In fact, many may be sincere, God fearing, God loving Christians at heart, however the Bible is clear that "the Spirit speaketh expressly, that in the latter times some shall depart from the faith, giving heed to seducing spirits, and doctrines of devils; Speaking lies in hypocrisy; having their conscience seared with a hot iron; Forbidding to marry, [and commanding] to abstain from meats, which God hath created to be received with thanksgiving of them which believe and know the truth" (1 Timothy 4:1-3).

Is the great spiritual city of Babylon full of doctrines of the devil? From the list provided, the answer is yes, but they are so convinced that God has granted them the ability to alter the commandments, reinterpret scripture, and a whole lot more, in that they do forbid marrying among priests and nuns, as well as commanding the forbiddance of meats during Lent. But it continues with doctrines on the state of the dead being possibly in hell, which does not exist right now; limbo, which recently was given up but that is what drove the taking advantage of the peasants in the day of the Dark Ages to exact funds from them; purgatory, where they roast and toast for thousands of years over a seventy or eighty year life of sins here and there; or they are in Heaven, which is usually granted only to saints. Speaking of saints, the unbiblical practice of humans determining a special level of people in Heaven is unfounded. Taking on God's titles is blaspheme. Of course changing the Ten Commandments by getting rid of the second or at least downplaying allowing for use of idols, splitting the last commandment on coveting into two, and of course completely upending the Sabbath day to a different day and different cycle of time are also fulfillment of devilish doctrines. There is also the allowance of unclean meats for consumption, doing away with the tithe requirement, confessing sins to a priest, all of which is devil instigated.

AND THE HOLD OF EVERY FOUL SPIRIT (18:2)

"For if he that cometh preacheth another Jesus, whom we have not preached, or [if] ye receive another spirit, which ye have not received, or another gospel, which ye have not accepted, ye might well bear with [him]" (2 Corinthians 11:4). "Beloved, believe not every spirit, but try the spirits whether they are of God: because many false prophets are gone out into the world. Hereby know ye the Spirit of God: Every spirit that confesseth that Jesus Christ is come in the flesh is of God: And every spirit that confesseth not that Jesus Christ is come in the flesh is not of God: and this is that [spirit] of Antichrist, whereof ye have heard that it should come; and even now already is it in the world" (1 John 4:1-3).

Any teaching that does not teach that Jesus "took not on [him the nature of] angels; but he took on [him] the seed of Abraham" (Hebrews 2:16) is in error. Taking on the seed of Abraham means that "we have not an high priest which cannot be touched with the feeling of our infirmities; but was in all points tempted like as [we are, yet] without sin" (Hebrews 4:15). In short, Jesus took on humanity like Adam after the fall so that we can become converted and do as Jesus said, "sin no more, lest a worse thing come unto thee" (John 5:14) and "go, and sin no more" (John 8:11),

Basically we have all kinds of doctrine that are acceptable, and it seems lately that more and more beliefs are starting to find their way to making a home at the Vatican. Evolution already found a home, not inspired by the Holy Spirit but rather one of the foul spirits.

AND A CAGE OF EVERY UNCLEAN AND HATEFUL BIRD (18:2)

"Your iniquities have turned away these [things], and your sins have withholden good [things] from you. For among my people are found wicked [men]: they lay wait, as he that setteth snares; they set a trap, they catch men. As a cage is full of birds, so [are] their houses full of deceit: therefore they are become great, and waxen rich. They are waxen fat, they shine: yea, they overpass the deeds of the wicked: they judge not the cause, the cause of the fatherless, yet they prosper; and the right of the needy do they not judge. Shall I not visit for these [things]? saith the LORD: shall not my soul be avenged on such a nation as this? A wonderful and horrible thing is committed in the land; The prophets prophesy falsely, and the priests bear rule by their means; and my people love [to have it] so: and what will ye do in the end thereof?" (Jeremiah 5:25-31) And this verse is very much appropriate as the time of Jeremiah was when they were headed into Babylonian captivity. And so much can be said about these verses realizing that the prophets or preachers or ministers prophesy falsely. The biggest lie is that of the "Left Behind" concept born in the 1500's but picked up by Protestants only since the turn of the twentieth century.

Now we ought to pray that "Our soul is escaped as a bird out of the snare of the fowlers" (Psalms 124:7), but that is only accomplished when "Thy word have I hid in mine heart, that I might not sin against thee" (Psalms 119:11). Otherwise, we are left open to the dictates of those in charge, those that are influential, even societal controls.

The Bible says, "For man also knoweth not his time: as the fishes that are taken in an evil net, and as the birds that are caught in the snare; so [are] the sons of men snared in an evil time, when it falleth suddenly upon them" (Ecclesiastes 9:12). "My people are destroyed for lack of knowledge: because thou hast rejected knowledge, I will also reject thee, that thou shalt be no priest to me: seeing thou hast forgotten the law of thy God, I will also forget thy children. As they were increased, so they sinned against me: [therefore] will I change their glory into shame. They eat up the sin of my people, and they set their heart on their iniquity" (Hosea 4:6-8).

People may even think they are doing the right thing when it is all a matter of controlling the masses, getting people to believe what they want them to believe, and even act in a similar manner.

So, "Hear the word of the LORD, ye children of Israel: for the LORD hath a controversy with the inhabitants of the land, because [there is] no truth, nor mercy, nor knowledge of God in the land. By swearing, and lying, and killing, and stealing, and committing adultery, they break out, and blood toucheth blood. Therefore shall the land mourn, and every one that dwelleth therein shall languish, with the beasts of the field, and with the fowls of heaven; yea, the fishes of the sea also shall be taken away" (Hosea 4:1-3).

FOR ALL NATIONS HAVE DRUNK OF THE WINE OF THE WRATH OF HER FORNICATION (18:3)

There is not a nation in which the church the beast has commandeered that it has not touched, and in so doing, recall the Bible saying, "[It is] not for kings, O Lemuel, [it is] not for kings to drink wine; nor for princes strong drink: Lest they drink, and forget the law, and pervert the judgment of any of the afflicted" (Proverbs 31:4-5). So the doctrines coming forth from that great city, Babylon, are poor judgments, altered commandments, and worldliness as specified by the use of the word "fornication". That would be spiritual fornication.

AND THE KINGS OF THE EARTH HAVE COMMITTED FORNICATION WITH HER (18:3)

Evidently the nations will have gone along with the policies of the beast, all for worldly gain because there is the word "fornication" mention of once again.

AND THE MERCHANTS OF THE EARTH ARE WAXED RICH THROUGH THE ABUNDANCE OF HER DELICACIES (18:3)

Now remember, God sees things we do not see. When He says the merchants of the earth have gotten rich with a relationship with the Antichrist, well, God knows more than we do, and being obvious fulfillment in other areas, why would we doubt that this is going on behind the scenes?

AND I HEARD ANOTHER VOICE FROM HEAVEN, SAYING, COME OUT OF HER, MY PEOPLE (18:4)

This is the obvious motivation for the reason this book was created, and other authors that believe these things to be true have written their appeals, and why so many with this message continue to look for ways to get the truth out there. True love for our neighbors, as Jesus said, "Thou shalt love thy neighbour as thyself"

(Mark 12:31), means that we are not indifferent toward people's eternal decisions. We will do everything including suffering persecution. "It is enough for the disciple that he be as his master, and the servant as his lord. If they have called the master of the house Beelzebub, how much more [shall they call] them of his household?" (Matthew 10:25).

Now coming out means that people cannot stay in their unbiblical beliefs. They cannot even stay in their current denominations. As we get closer and closer to Jesus' appearing, the deceptions are getting more and more intense. Why would anyone intentionally allow themselves to be subject to false sermon after false sermon on the wrong day to worship? And for those that think they have a keen mind and will not be influenced, then they must know better than God for He tells us more than one way not to be associated with such error. Israel was kept separate from other nations. Abraham and Isaac practiced not going back to their old land.

This is also an appeal to come out of all the false theories. Some people think, "Oh, I see the paganism in that now, but since I know better, I still can practice it." What!!! God tells us to stop doing that stuff. "And the times of this ignorance God winked at; but now commandeth all men every where to repent: Because he hath appointed a day, in the which he will judge the world in righteousness by [that] man whom he hath ordained; [whereof] he hath given assurance unto all [men], in that he hath raised him from the dead" (Acts 17:30-31). To repent is to cease from doing it.

THAT YE BE NOT PARTAKERS OF HER SINS (18:4)

Some call this guilt by association, and in essence, that is exactly what it is. If people insist on continuing in an observation mode in their old ways, God accounts such people as being guilty of doing it. Now, "the LORD [is] longsuffering, and of great mercy, forgiving iniquity and transgression, and by no means clearing [the guilty], visiting the iniquity of the fathers upon the children unto the third and fourth [generation]" (Numbers 14:18). Did you catch that? Although God is forgiving, He will not clear the guilty.

And a half-hearted effort is not going to be agreeable with Jesus, for He said, "He that is not with me is against me" (Matthew 12:30). That is not just in general but a wholehearted effort.

That means, all who say, "I will wait until I really see these signs coming true before making a commitment" have already made a commitment. They have chosen the world. We cannot enjoy the world all our lives and then switch to obedience at the end because we see things happening. It proves the heart was never into obeying God and proves the lack of faith.

AND THAT YE RECEIVE NOT OF HER PLAGUES (18:4)

And this is what we are hoping people would avoid: receiving the seven last plagues. Only through making a full and utter cut in all ties to the Antichrist and the Spirit of Antichrist will such be able to survive.

FOR HER SINS HAVE REACHED UNTO HEAVEN, AND GOD HATH REMEMBERED HER INIQUITIES (18:5)

Punishment is coming. It is called the fifth plague of darkness; sixth plague of losing support; and the seventh one when hail comes crashing down. She will be held accountable for every error ever taught "for this [is] the day of the Lord GOD of hosts, a day of vengeance, that he may avenge him of his adversaries: and the sword shall devour, and it shall be satiate and made drunk with their blood: for the Lord GOD of hosts hath a sacrifice in the north country by the river Euphrates" (Jeremiah 46:10).

So, "the Spirit and the bride say, Come. And let him that heareth say, Come. And let him that is athirst come. And whosoever will, let him take the water of life freely" (Revelation 22:17). What is your response?

God is not looking for people who say, "I believe these things but I'll wait until I really start seeing the signs." God wants us now and wants to use us now. What is your response to His calling?

Biography

Jerry O'Donnell was personally challenged to read the Bible for himself, so when the Lord opened an opportunity to do so, he took advantage of it by reading the entire Bible in one month. At the end, he saw so many contradictions practiced by so many Christians of which contradicted themselves, and asked himself how such confusion could be pleasing to God. At the same time, many questions were being raised in his mind that required answers, so a diligent study was underway.

Following the pattern set forth in Isaiah 28:9-10, the journey began. The verses starts off with "Whom shall he teach knowledge? and whom shall he make to understand doctrine?" That is exactly what was desired to be learned and understood. Now reading on to find out how to get that, Isaiah wrote, "[them that are] weaned from the milk, [and] drawn from the breasts." So the first step was to get off of the surface stories, the milk, and get into some serious studying, which verse ten tells specifically how to proceed. "For precept [must be] upon precept, precept upon precept; line upon line, line upon line; here a little, [and] there a little." So every precept or lesson is to be taken into consideration, every line or verse is to be gathered, and even the verses that contain a number of thoughts are to be include eliminating the other thoughts and focusing upon the little that is associated with the subject of investigation. Nothing is to be just discarded that touches on the topic being researched.

But that was not the only pattern followed. The Bible also says, "God is not [the author] of confusion" (1 Corinthians 14:33). That means that the verse have to be understood in a manner that there is no contradiction, which is confusion. God would not condemn an action in one place and then permit it in another. God would not uses verses to undo others.

As a result of years of studying, he set forth to share his findings. Starting out in conducting numerous Bible studies, moving on to holding seminars, and now sensing the nearness of time, the most up to date information at hand is presented in this book.

It is the author's desire that all would give as much diligence to making one's "calling and election sure" (2 Peter 1:10).

We invite you to view the complete
selection of titles we publish at:

www.AspectBooks.com

Scan with your mobile
device to go directly
to our website.

Please write or email us your praises, reactions, or
thoughts about this or any other book we publish at:

info@AspectBooks.com

Aspect Books titles may be purchased in bulk for
educational, business, fund-raising, or promotional use.
For more information, please e-mail:

BulkSales@AspectBooks.com

Finally, if you are interested in seeing
your own book in print, please contact us at

publishing@AspectBooks.com

We would be happy to review your manuscript for free.

www.ingramcontent.com/pod-product-compliance
Lightning Source LLC
Chambersburg PA
CBHW081347230426

43667CB00017B/2749